Communications
in Computer and Information Science 1522

More information about this series at https://link.springer.com/bookseries/7899

Barbara Wasson · Szilvia Zörgő (Eds.)

Advances in Quantitative Ethnography

Third International Conference, ICQE 2021
Virtual Event, November 6–11, 2021
Proceedings

 Springer

wide variety of aspects of society including insurance, healthcare, politics, COVID-19, social security, and community growth. The poster submissions, symposium descriptions, doctoral consortium papers, and keynote abstracts can be found in the ICQE21 Conference Proceedings Supplement.

The program chairs would like to thank the National Science Foundation (NSF) for their support for the conference which contributed to registration scholarships that reduced costs for returning attendees and fully covered registration for first-time attendees, students, and post-doctoral researchers. We would also like to thank the reviewers, committee members, and the fantastic ICQE support team.

November 2021   Barbara Wasson
                                                                Szilvia Zörgő

Organization

Program Committee Chairs

Barbara Wasson   University of Bergen, Norway
Szilvia Zörgő   Semmelweis University, Hungary

Program Committee

Andrew Ruis	University of Wisconsin-Madison, USA
Seung Lee	Pepperdine University, USA
Kamila Misiejuk	University of Bergen, Norway
Marta Jackowska	Aarhus University, Denmark
Rogers Kaliisa	University of Oslo, Norway
Marcia Moraes	Colorado State University, USA
Amanda Barany	Drexel University, USA
Mamta Shah	Elsevier, USA
Aneesha Bakharia	University of Queensland, Australia
Sarah Jung	University of Wisconsin-Madison, USA
Zach Swiecki	Monash University, Australia
Ayano Ohsaki	Advanced Institute of Industrial Technology, Japan
Denise Bressler	East Carolina University, USA
Ryan Baker	University of Pennsylvania, USA
Bian Wu	East China Normal University, China
Mike Phillips	Monash University, Australia
Srecko Joksimovic	University of South Australia, Australia
Roberto Martinez-Maldonado	Monash University, Australia
Guadalupe Carmona-Dominguez	University of Texas at San Antonio, USA

Conference Committee

Eric Hamilton (Co-chair)	Pepperdine University, USA
Danielle Espino (Co-chair)	Pepperdine University, USA
Brendan Eagan	University of Wisconsin-Madison, USA
Delaney Egan	University of Wisconsin-Madison, USA
Alice Jokodola	Pepperdine University, USA
Julia Lackey	University of Wisconsin-Madison, USA
Seung Lee	Pepperdine University, USA
Clare Porter	University of Wisconsin-Madison, USA
Dana Schneck	University of Wisconsin-Madison, USA
Szilvia Zörgő	Semmelweis University, Hungary

Contents

Case Studies

Theory and Methodology

Constructing Interpretations with Participants Through Epistemic Network Analysis: Towards Participatory Approaches in Quantitative Ethnography

Hazel Vega(✉) and Golnaz Arastoopour Irgens

Clemson University, Clemson, SC, USA
hvegaqu@clemson.edu

Abstract. As societal changes have brought forward issues of equity and social justice that challenge powered dynamics, participatory research approaches have gained traction. In quantitative ethnography (QE), recent calls have highlighted the potential of this approach to expand existing methods and imagine new tools for more collaborative ends. To address this new direction in QE, the purpose of this study was to describe how we used epistemic network analysis (ENA) discourse networks in interviews with pre-service teachers to build interpretations of qualitative data with them. We argue that ENA is a promising methodological tool for researchers and participants to co-construct deep data interpretations. Our findings suggest that discussions of ENA discourse networks provide a space for researcher-participant collaboration to co-construct interpretations of data by modifying codes, adding connections, and reacting to codes. Based on our findings, we contend that a participatory quantitative ethnography (PQE) approach that includes participants in data analysis requires a reconceptualization of QE tools specifically designed for co-interpretation.

Keywords: Participatory research · Researcher-participant collaboration · Teacher education

1 Introduction

As wide societal changes have brought forward issues of equity and social justice that challenge powered dynamics [1], participatory research approaches have gained traction [2–4]. The underlying principle of participatory research methods is that participants and researchers both engage in co-construction of knowledge throughout the research process [4–6]. While traditional research designs position the researcher as playing a central role in generating and shaping research, participatory methods recognize and value the expertise of participants, actively engaging them across research activities working side-by-side with researchers [7]. Such work requires acknowledging and addressing power hierarchies in research by keeping a critical look towards who researches, for what ends, and for whom. Addressing power issues supports research outcomes that respond to the needs of communities and individuals [1, 2].

© Springer Nature Switzerland AG 2022
B. Wasson and S. Zörgő (Eds.): ICQE 2021, CCIS 1522, pp. 3–16, 2022.
https://doi.org/10.1007/978-3-030-93859-8_1

In ethnography, this democratic form of inquiry suggests co-constructions and co-interpretations of cultures that offer thick descriptions created by both ethnographers and participants [5, 8, 9]. This joint process is particularly important in educational research in which practitioner-researcher partnerships and action research involving students are increasingly used to solve pressing problems in teaching and learning [2, 10, 11]. Participatory methods in ethnography, and more broadly, can contribute to (a) addressing long-standing issues of incomplete or thin representation of participants [12], (b) closing the gap between theory and practice [2, 13], and (c) generating solutions to problems that involve local cultural points of view [1, 14]. However, these affordances can only be realized if research practices, roles, and tools are reimagined to cultivate and sustain multiple perspectives [2].

An equitable researcher-participant relationship in the co-construction of knowledge recognizes the need for expanding methods that support heterogeneity of epistemologies and respond to the tensions embedded in the process [3, 10, 14]. Nonetheless, considerably less attention has been paid to the specific methods and tools required for such collaborative practices. In quantitative ethnography (QE), recent calls [15–17] have highlighted the potential of this approach to expand existing methods and imagine new tools for more collaborative ends. In this paper, we claim that one of the seminal tools of QE, Epistemic Network Analysis (ENA), can be used and expanded to facilitate researcher-participant collaboration. ENA creates weighted discourse networks from qualitatively coded data to visualize relationships across codes. In extant research in QE, the discourse networks generated by ENA have been predominantly used by the researcher in the data analysis phase. Thus, traditionally, although forms of participant validation have been included in QE, ENA has not been widely used with participants to capture their interpretations of the phenomenon under study. To address this gap, in this paper, we describe how we used ENA discourse networks to build interpretations of qualitative data with participants and argue that ENA is a promising methodological tool for researchers and participants to co-construct deep data interpretations.

2   Theory

Several approaches such as participatory action research and participatory design research have emerged from participatory methods. The commonality across these derived approaches is the premise that all individuals construct social meanings and have the capability of research and analysis [14]. This overarching principle is further explained by the following criteria (a) people should be active agents in their own lives, (b) research should respect research participants' own words, ideas, and understandings, (c) researchers and participants are equal, (d) research methods should be flexible, exploratory, and inventive, (e) both the researchers and research participants should enjoy the research [14, p. 192]. These ideas seek to blur the lines between the researcher and the researched, creating new opportunities for different roles. For instance, the role of the researcher shifts to that of a facilitator that establishes trust, practices listening, and shares control of the research with participants [18]. On the participants' side, participation should be seen as a continuum, from minimal involvement to sharing a role as co-researchers [3]. This continuum implies creating shared spaces offering varying levels of participation in stages of the research process and providing ways for participants and researchers to leverage their methods and expertise.

In ethnography, participation may seem redundant because ethnographic research is understood as participatory to the extent that ethnographers are participant observers in their participants' everyday activity [9]. However, an explicit focus on participation highlights how participants can be involved beyond data collection. The term participatory or collaborative ethnography has been used to describe the researcher-participant dialogical relationship to produce "multi-vocal" interpretations [18, p. 10]. This collaborative sensemaking "represents a deliberate way to structure participant-research relationships around mutuality and reciprocity" [10, p. 1]. One way to build these relationships is to focus on the knowledge generation process, and particularly whose voices are being heard and how [11, 20]. Of similar importance is to express empathy with participants, which means valuing their wisdom as legitimate ways of knowing from which research has yet a lot to learn from [11, 20]. Attention to process and empathy in collaboration may contribute to creating a shared ground where the emic (participants' perspectives and words) and the etic (researchers' and/or theoretical perspectives) meet to address research problems.

Previous participatory ethnographic research has underscored the role of the voices of participants in design processes, ethnographic writing, debriefing of interviews and observations, and member checks [7, 21, 22]. These voices not only provide increased validity to the research results, but they can also motivate participants to pursue their own interests and goals related to the phenomenon studied [10, 11]. This literature has also discussed that tensions are inherent to collaboration; however, these could be negotiated over time during knowledge building opportunities and with trusting relationships [e.g., 10].

Regarding the strategies or tools for researcher-participant collaboration, privilege has been given to strategies intended to maximize the efficiency of the time dedicated to fieldwork. Among these strategies are member checks, interviewing methods, participatory representations of space and activity, and joint revision of documents and artifacts [23]. However, methods are not inherently participatory [14, 23]. The extent to which they become more or less participatory depends on how mutuality and responsibility are shared and constructed by participants and researchers.

2.1   New Opportunities for Participatory Research in QE

Prominent scholars in the QE field have urged for new directions towards participatory approaches. Arastoopour Irgens' [16] keynote address during the first International Conference of Quantitative Ethnography emphasized the advantages of QE to include stakeholders in research. As an inclusive methodology, QE can make assumptions and data interpretations transparent for the research community and participants [16]. According to Arastoopour Irgens, through computational methods and human interpretations, QE can confront biases that may be problematic in data interpretation.

Inclusivity in QE can also amplify the multiplicity of voices involved in doing consequential research. Arastoopour Irgens urged for the development of new tools that are sensible to issues of equity and power, preserve ethnographic meanings, and improve thick descriptions.

Following Arastoopour Irgens' remarks, Buckingham Shum's keynote [15] during the second International Conference of Quantitative Ethnography raised awareness about the potential of tools within QE to support collaborative approaches in this field. According to Buckingham Shum, ENA affords processing that includes "continuous internal/external cognition interplay and shared focus of visual attention, and accessible shared language for joint sensemaking". In this sense, the power of ENA resides in its capability to scaffold joint cognition and interpretation with others in research. These reflections push our thinking to consider the ways in which data visualizations could shape the etic and emic perspectives and how they can influence each other in researcher-participant collaborations. However, as acknowledged by Buckingham Shum, further development of existing tools is needed to accommodate the interactivity and malleability required for on-the-fly co-interpretations of data.

An example of how ENA representations have been used with participants is Phillips et al.'s pilot study [17]. They explored professional decision-making of six teachers in the subjects of math, science and technology in a secondary school in Australia. They created discourse networks using ENA with coded data from the teachers' lesson plans, and subsequently conducted interviews with participants. In these discussions, some teachers validated the researcher's analysis acknowledging that they captured their tacit understandings of their teaching practices. Other teachers were surprised to see that their networks did not represent all the areas in their decision-making. Having the opportunity to examine the networks with the researcher allowed them to identify that the cause of this difference was that they worked with lesson plans that were not as detailed as those of other teachers, which limited the connections across codes in the networks. This finding suggests that taking back ENA representations to participants may provide a fuller picture of the phenomenon studied. Additionally, this practice demonstrated the interaction between the etic perspective embedded in the networks and emic understandings of practice among teachers.

As QE continues to grow and take new directions, participatory approaches need to address pressing issues of power and equity in research. One area that may contribute to that end is the expansion of tools towards collaborative interactions between researchers and participants. Hence, the purpose of this paper is to explore how ENA can be used by both researchers and participants to co-construct data interpretations.

3 Methods

This study drew from a larger project exploring the identity development of English as a foreign language (EFL) pre-service teachers in Costa Rica [24, 25]. In this larger study, we used interview data to elucidate how the participants grappled with self and socially assigned expectations and identities, following Seidman's [24] three-interview framework for phenomenological studies. This framework includes a first interview for describing experiences relevant to the topic of interest, a second one for further exploring details of experiences, and a third one for reflecting on the meanings of those experiences. This method underscores participants' active role, allowing them to describe and interpret their context-bound experiences [24]. For this paper, we focus on the third interview, which was when we elicited reflection on experiences using ENA discourse networks.

3.1 Context and Participants

The larger study is set in a foreign language in a four-year teacher education program in a public university in Costa Rica. As in the rest of Latin America, in Costa Rica, English plays a fundamental role for socioeconomic development, thus there is a high demand for highly qualified English teachers. In a suburban campus, this education program prepares English teachers to teach at secondary or adult education level to meet the demands for English education in the country. Coursework in this program includes a combination of English language learning and language learning pedagogies. Also, pre-service teachers have several classroom experiences through observations and practicum opportunities to develop their skills. They tend to draw from these experiences when reflecting about their identities.

The participants in the larger research were four Spanish-English bilingual pre-service teachers enrolled in this program. For the purposes of this study, we chose two focal participants, who engaged in a thorough reflection process during the interviews, and particularly in the last one. Moreover, the selection of these two participants affords the provision of a detailed account of their interaction with ENA during the interview process. At the time of the interviews, Nancy and Isabel (pseudonyms) had finished their coursework and were expecting to enter the teaching context soon. They voluntarily participated in the study after an open call for recruitment sent to the students of the program.

3.2 Data Collection and Analysis

As mentioned previously, we focused on the third interview because it was when we used the ENA discourse networks with the participants. This interview aimed at reflecting on the experiences described in previous interviews. Each interview was about 90 min, and they were transcribed using a combination of automated and manual transcription. The ENA discourse networks shared with participants were created using coded discourse data from previous interviews from each participant. These networks showed the connections across the codes of adoption, rejection, and tensions in identity negotiation in relation to the idealized figure of the native English speaker.

Prior to the interview, to share the ENA discourse networks with the participants, we developed a script to ensure accessible language for the discussion of the networks. In this script, we included (a) a simple description of the elements of networks such as the nodes and the lines, (b) the meanings of the codes; for example, the script included the following: *"This is a network that represents the main topics discussed in your first interview and how they are connected to each other. For instance, the 3 main topics were adoption, tension, and rejection. Those circles or nodes are the main topics you discussed. The links or lines between them show that you connected those topics or talked about them together at some point. Let's look at the topics first. Adoption was when you talked about things/practices you liked from the program and you would like to incorporate in your teaching, for example you talked about...* Let's look at the lines, see that some are thick, and others are thin. A thick line says that you made many connections between those 2 topics. A thin line means that you made fewer connections between 2 topics. No line means that you did not make any connections." We also included (c) specific examples of their own utterances for some of the codes, and (d) pauses and spaces for questions or clarification. Also, the researcher prepared questions to elicit reflection and scaffold the discussion about ENA discourse networks.

During the interview, the researcher led with the premise that the networks were open to interpretation, acknowledging that they were still in construction, and they were created out of a snapshot of the participants' thinking as recorded in an interview setting. Thus, any addition, change, deletion, question, or further interpretation was valuable to understand their reflections on their identities and construct robust analyses together with the researcher. For instance, in the script, we stated: *"This network is just an interpretation of what you said in the interview. There might be many possible interpretations. There's no right or wrong answer. I would like to know how* **you** *see it."* The researcher showed the ENA discourse networks to the participants using a tablet and annotated the networks including participants' proposed edits. When annotations were made, the researcher confirmed the accuracy of the annotations with the participant. As the discussion of the ENA discourse networks unfolded, participants required additional examples of utterances and clarifications, which were provided when needed.

To conduct the analysis of the data for this study, the researchers first gained a preliminary understanding of the participants' interactions with the ENA discourse networks. Then, they focused on the instances where participants added or changed interpretations of the networks. Once these instances were identified, open coding was conducted resulting in categories related to the types of interactions with ENA discourse networks, for example modifying a code. Using these categories, analytic memos were written for each participant. Then, these memos were used to select the focal participants and guide the remaining coding process. In a second round of coding, the categories were expanded and refined.

4   Results

In previous studies [25, 26], we have discussed how EFL pre-service teachers negotiated their identities adopting or rejecting practices from their teaching education program. The participants in our study were native Spanish speakers getting prepared to teach English at the secondary level. Our findings suggested that participants faced tension around the dominant discourse of an idealized native English-speaking teacher. This tension in identity negotiations led to feelings of frustration and self-doubt when participants contrasted themselves with a superior native speaker figure with default expertise for language learning and teaching. To provide context for the results in this paper, Table 1 shows a summary of the codes used in the ENA discourse networks we shared with our participants.

Table 1. Summary of codes included in the ENA discourse networks.

Code	Definition
Adoption	Taking on an established practice from the community of practice (CoP), applying it in teaching and/or language learning
Rejection	Rejecting an established practice from the CoP by showing disagreement or full dissatisfaction with the CoP
Tension	Demonstrating tension when an established practice from the CoP poses a conflict for identity negotiation. This is demonstrated by not showing full satisfaction with the practices of the CoP, mixed negative and positive comments about them, and/or strong/negative emotions
The native speaker as the standard	Expressing perspectives about an established practice related to the idealized native speaker, who represents the target language norms against which the non-native speaker measures proficiency
Reflections on accents	Expressing perspectives about an established practice related to ideas about accent that suggest judgements of legitimacy of accents in relation to a standard language variety
NNS less legitimate practices	Expressing perspectives about an established practice related to personal linguistic practices perceived as less legitimate than those of an imagined native speaker

In this section, we describe participants' reactions and interpretations of ENA discourse networks. Three main categories were identified: (1) modifying codes, (3) adding connections across codes, and (3) reacting to a code.

4.1 Modifying Codes

As it can be observed in the ENA discourse network (Fig. 1), Nancy's network shows that she predominantly adopted discourses that positioned the native English speaker as the standard to follow. In previous interviews, she explained that she intends to incorporate as much as possible interactions with native English speakers in her classes because students would benefit from that kind of input. However, when looking at the network, she decided to modify the code, questioning the term "native speaker" and explained what adoption of that ideology means for her. She asserted,

"I want to clarify, *native speakers. What are they? Right? Who are they?* So that's what confuses me and creates a little bit of a gray area [...] But what if we could get people like me? With a C1 [advanced English level] who would agree to come or even especially now with the Zoom meetings and everything. What if I can get someone here in Costa Rica to talk with students? [...] So, *my adoption would be anyone who can have a great English level like a C1.* That to me would be an adoption. So yeah, more advanced because that could be a very useful resource. [...] You know, so that's something to consider what a native speaker is."

When revisiting her ideas through the ENA discourse network, Nancy had an opportunity to challenge the term *native speaker* used by the researcher saying that it is broad, and it needs to be more contextualized. For example, English native speakers from Canada or from the US are very different. And even within those contexts, there is a wide variety of accents and dialects, thus it is necessary to have a more nuanced understanding of who this native speaker figure is if she is to adopt this ideology. In a further questioning of the term, she explained that English native speakers might not have the contextual knowledge to interact successfully with students, and it would be difficult to have access to them. In that case, other nonnative speakers, even from Costa Rica would not only be willing to visit her class, but they would also know more about the culture and the language learning process of their students than English native speakers from a completely different setting.

Having made this reflection, Nancy modified the term explaining that a *more advanced speaker* is an option because students need a more knowledgeable other but not necessarily a native speaker. A person with a C1 level (advanced) is also likely to provide comprehensible input to students and meaningful interaction for English language learning. This way, Nancy described that to an extent, she was adopting that discourse. However, through the ENA discourse network discussion, she explained that she was more interested in the quality of guidance that more advanced speakers could bring to her class, regardless of their native speaker status. In this discussion, the researcher pointed to other instances in which she had expressed similar ideas about how central it was for her to provide such guidance to students. This researcher-participant co-interpretation of a code through ENA representations allowed the participant and the researcher to arrive at a more contextualized definition of a code by tying it back to previous data and expanding their understanding of this code.

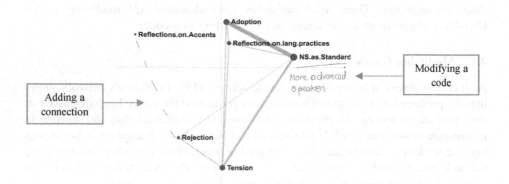

Fig. 1. Nancy's annotated ENA discourse network.

4.2   Adding Connections

We found that when discussing ENA discourse networks, participants added absent connections or reinforced those already existing. In Nancy's case, when the researcher asked if she would change anything about the connections across codes, she added a connection between the rejection and reflections on accents (Fig. 1). The code rejection referred to practices or discourses from their community of practice that they did not intend to take in their teaching. The code reflections on accents referred to perspectives about accents suggesting judgements of legitimacy of accents in relation to a standard language variety. The connection between these two codes meant that the participant did not agree with judging accents that did not approximate standard forms. Nancy explained that in previous interviews, she had not referred to accents explicitly, but looking at the ENA discourse network, she thought that based on her experience, she should pay more attention to accents in her teaching. To explain why that connection was necessary, Nancy referred to her experience with accents having been born in Costa Rica, moving to the US at the age of seven, and going back to Costa Rica as a teenager.

> "*I can see it in Spanish*, when I arrived here [Costa Rica]. I thought I spoke Spanish because, you know, in the US, I was a little bit *self-conscious of my accent as a learner*, but not so much. But when I arrived here and I start speaking Spanish and my friends would say like, Oh, you speak funny. I'm like, but I'm speaking Spanish. But then, so I realized, *oh there's accents in every language* and there's no right or wrong."

Nancy decided to add this connection because by reflecting to her own language learning experiences, she realized that accents may have a crucial role for learners. By saying *I can see it in Spanish* and acknowledging that she once was *self-conscious about her acce*nt, she is becoming aware that judging accents against rigid standard forms is a reality for language learners. In her case, she received judgement in the US because of her Spanish accent, and back in Costa Rica, she was judged because her Spanish had an English accent. Seeing that no connections had been made to reflections on accents made her look into her own experiences to uncover that *accents in every language* may influence how one and others perceive ways of speaking. Thus, although at the time, she did not mention this experience, further exploration on this matter allowed her to bring back her thinking about accents and how they may affect language learners.

In Isabel's case, she made an already existing line thicker between the codes of rejection and reflections on language practices (Fig. 2). The relationship between these two codes indicates that the participant expressed perspectives rejecting ideas characterizing their linguistic practices as bilinguals as less legitimate than those of a monolingual native speaker. An example of this would be code-switching between English and Spanish. Like Nancy, Isabel connected back to her experience to say that she actually rejected practices that did not support the use of Spanish in English classes. She recalled an experience in her teaching education program, in student presentations when students have a low level of English, and teachers expect them to not resort to Spanish. She narrated the following.

> "*I would still make it thicker*. Because I have seen it many times. Not really with myself, but with other classmates, that made me feel really *uncomfortable* and even fear the teacher because of their reaction. I have an example. […] This person [the professor] would make some difficult questions about politics and religion [during student presentations], and because they [presenters] couldn't understand, they answered Spanish, this person [professor] would get mad […] *I don't think that's right*."

To elicit this reflection, the researcher provided several possible examples of bilinguals' language practices. It took Isabel a few minutes to realize that she actually had observed the situation described multiple times, and every time, she had felt *uncomfortable*. Even though she had not been in her classmates' position, she thought that it *was not right* to completely deny students the possibility to use Spanish when needed. Since the line between rejection and reflections on language practices was very thin in her ENA discourse network, she decided that a slightly thicker line would better reflect how she thought about the role of the first language for bilingual learners. She said that that line should be as thick as the line between reflections on language practices and reflections on accents.

As observed in these two examples, the discussion of ENA representations with participants resulted in adding connections, whether it was to make stronger connections between codes (Isabel) or to include a new one (Nancy). This addition of connections allowed participants to link their experiences to the codes established by the researcher providing additional context and understanding of the nature of the connections between codes.

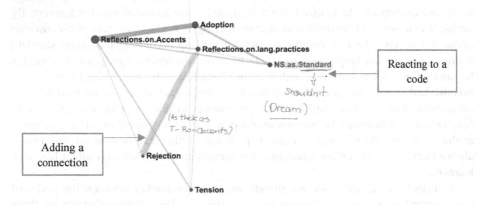

Fig. 2. Isabel's annotated ENA discourse network.

4.3   Reacting to a Code

Isabel's annotated ENA discourse networks shows her reaction to the code of the native speaker as a standard. Different from Nancy, she thought the code was an accurate description of her thoughts; however, she acknowledged that it needed to change. During previous interviews, Isabel had expressed that she was frustrated because despite spending much energy and time to perfect her pronunciation, she had a marked accent that made her sound nonnative in English. The following quote describes her reaction to the code of the native speaker as a standard after looking at some of her utterances coded for it.

> "I haven't said that very explicitly. That is true. So, you understood me correctly. But I know it's not, *it shouldn't be*. Not yet, but I guess that in the future, when I read your research, maybe I'm going to think I was being too harsh on myself [...] Maybe *I'm going to come with a closure of not being the best, not being native*. I guess that is going to change at some point in the future. And with experience because right now I've just had my practicum, and that's it.

Maybe in the future. Those lines will get thicker or maybe, I don't know, *some of the words that you wrote there maybe are going to change into others.*"

As observed in Isabel's quote, she agrees with the code and the interpretation for it. Nevertheless, when looking at this explicit relationship in the ENA, it became clear for her that it *should not* be the way to perceive her linguistic performance. She is being harsh judging herself using the *native speaker* as a benchmark. These are her present self-perceptions, but these views are subject to change as she gains more teaching experience. She is opening the possibility of *changing* this code in the future, hoping that when she begins to teach, she can give credit to her multiple strengths without paying excessive attention to her pronunciation.

This participant-researcher discussion of ENA representations resulted in participant's reaction to a code. This means that although the code was not modified, the participant took the interpretation of the code to reflect about her own views and imagine how she could change, and in turn how the network itself could possibly change.

5   Discussion and Conclusion

Our findings suggest that discussions of ENA discourse networks provide a space for researcher-participant collaboration to co-construct interpretations of data by modifying codes, adding connections, and reacting to codes. In this research, participatory ENA discussions made visible the voices of participants for joint data interpretation. For example, when modifying a code, the participant brought her contextualized understanding of the code *the native speaker as a standard* to expand the definition created by the researcher. By reconceptualizing this code, both the participant and the researcher recognized that a standard for language learning can go beyond a native speaker and also include a more advanced speaker, who is capable of providing modeling and guidance to the language learner. This expansion of the code involved the inclusion of multiple perspectives in data interpretation that required the researcher to listen and the participant to actively work with the researcher to interpret the data. This sort of co-interpretation may allow the researcher and participant to step into more symmetrical roles that challenge traditional power hierarchies in research, which ultimately may support outcomes that better respond to the needs of communities and individuals [1, 2].

In addition to welcoming participants' perspectives, participatory ENA discussions construct results that show a fuller picture of the phenomenon being studied. In this study, when adding connections to ENA representations, participants showed more nuanced understandings of their experiences as they reflected on the configuration of the codes. This reflection contributed to a more solid understanding of these teachers' identity formation compared to previous interviews. For instance, one of the participants introduced her experiences with accents to explain how they rejected normative ideologies from their teacher education program about native English speakers. By including such new revelations from participants during co-interpretation sessions, QE studies can provide richer, thick descriptions that provide another layer where etic and emic perspectives come together. While we acknowledge that this study is limited to a small sample of interview data, we recognize that the findings evidence the potential of creating participatory discussions using ENA representations. These discussions should not only serve as member-checking [27] or as a point to departure for reflections with participants. They should be a collaborative ground, where the emic and etic perspectives from both the researcher and the participants dynamically interact and feed each other.

Looking specifically at the affordances of ENA in this researcher-participant collaborative space, we highlight Buckingham Shum's [15] assertions about ENA's "continuous internal/external cognition interplay and shared focus of visual attention." In our discussions with participants, the ENA discourse networks provided a tangible representation of teacher's self-conceptualization of their identity development through connections among the codes of tension, rejection, acceptance, and the cultural components of the teacher education program. The discussions were not only about the codes, but also how they were related to each other. The node links elicited a cognitive response from participants that facilitated reflection on their identities and the relationships between identity components. This interaction with the outputs of the ENA tool scaffolded a form of joint cognition that dynamically facilitated the (re)-construction of etic and emic perspectives. Importantly, these participatory practices in QE allows for a shared space for researchers and participants to experiment and start a process of co-design of tools.

Although this study suggests that ENA discourse network representations provided a foundation for joint cognition and interpretation, there is still a need to expand QE tools to support collaborative spaces for researchers and participants to tell multi-vocal stories [15, 16, 28]. A participatory quantitative ethnography (PQE) approach that includes participants in data analysis requires a reconceptualization of QE tools specifically designed for co-interpretation. Tools must be designed such that researchers and participants have access and abilities to co-create thick descriptions together in moment-to-moment interactions. Affordances and features of the tools need to be carefully considered, including annotation, discussion, and how to visualize the co-constructed knowledge. Such design choices will affect the roles, responsibilities, and power dynamics between researcher and participant and in turn, will affect the interpretation of the data and how the story is ultimately told.

Although this preliminary study introduced a PQE approach using ENA discourse network with teachers to explore their identity development, this study has also raised many questions for pursuing a new line of PQE research in the QE community. Particularly, in collaboration during data analysis, we think it is important to think about the following questions: how can data interpretation be open and accessible to participants? What complications may arise from such process? How should we leverage researchers and participants' expertise to arrive at deeper understandings of research phenomena in ways that benefit all stakeholders? How can we resolve tensions, disagreements, and issues of confirmation bias when co-constructing data interpretations? As QE researchers explore these questions and develop new PQE tools, the field will develop more equitable research practices in collaboration with our participants as partners and in turn, richer thick descriptions of cultural phenomena.

References

1. Zavala, M.: What do we mean by decolonizing research strategies? Lessons from decolonizing, Indigenous research projects in New Zealand and Latin America. Decolonization: Indigeneity. Educ. Soc. **2**, 55–71 (2013)
2. Bang, M., Vossoughi, S.: Participatory design research and educational justice: studying learning and relations within social change making. Cogn. Instr. **34**, 173–193 (2016). https://doi.org/10.1080/07370008.2016.1181879
3. Brown, N.: Scope and continuum of participatory research. Int. J. Res. Method Educ. 1–12 (2021). https://doi.org/10.1080/1743727X.2021.1902980
4. Philip, T.M., Bang, M., Jackson, K.: Articulating the "How", the "For What", the "For Whom", and the "With Whom" in concert: a call to broaden the benchmarks of our scholarship. Cogn. Instr. **36**, 83–88 (2018). https://doi.org/10.1080/07370008.2018.1413530
5. Campbell, E., Lassiter, L.E.: From collaborative ethnography to collaborative pedagogy: reflections on the other side of middletown project and community-university research partnerships: from collaborative ethnography to collaborative pedagogy. Anthropol. Educ. Q. **41**, 370–385 (2010). https://doi.org/10.1111/j.1548-1492.2010.01098.x
6. Hacker, K.: Community-Based Participatory Research. SAGE Publications, Inc., London (2013)
7. Erickson, F.: Studying side by side: collaborative action ethnography in educational research. In: Spindler, G., Hammond, L.A. (eds.) Innovations in Educational Ethnography: Theory, Methods, and Results, pp. 235–257. L. Erlbaum Associates, Mahwah (2006)
8. Geertz, C.: The Interpretation of Cultures: Selected Essays. Basic Books, New York (2017)
9. Heath, S.B., Street, B.V.: On Ethnography: Approaches to Language and Literacy Research. Teachers College Press [u.a.], New York (2008)
10. Plummer, E.C., et al.: Participatory Ethnography: Developing a High School Writing Center in Partnership. N Penn GSE Perspect. Urban Education (2019)
11. Stapleton, S.R.: Teacher participatory action research (TPAR): a methodological framework for political teacher research. Action Res. **19**, 161–178 (2021). https://doi.org/10.1177/1476750317751033
12. Jackson, J.L.: Thin Description: Ethnography and the African Hebrew Israelites of Jerusalem. Harvard University Press, Cambridge (2013)
13. Gutiérrez, K.D., Vossoughi, S.: Lifting off the ground to return anew: mediated praxis, transformative learning, and social design experiments. J. Teach. Educ. **61**, 100–117 (2010). https://doi.org/10.1177/0022487109347877
14. Beazley, H., Ennew, J.: Participatory methods and approaches: tackling the two tyrannies. In: Desai, V., Potter, R.B. (eds.) Doing Development Research, pp. 189–199. SAGE, London (2006)
15. Buckingham Shum, S.: Quantitative ethnography visualizations as tools for thinking. In: 2nd International Conference of Quantitative Ethnography (ICQE) (2021)
16. Arastoopour Irgens, G.: Quantitative ethnography across domains: where we are and where we are going. In: 1st International Conference of Quantitative Ethnography (ICQE). University of Wisconsin (2018)
17. Phillips, M., Siebert-Evenstone, A., Kessler, A., Gasevic, D., Shaffer, D.W.: Professional decision making: reframing teachers' work using epistemic frame theory. In: Ruis, A.R., Lee, S.B. (eds.) ICQE 2021. CCIS, vol. 1312, pp. 265–276. Springer, Cham (2021). https://doi.org/10.1007/978-3-030-67788-6_18
18. Chambers, R.: The origins and practice of participatory rural appraisal. World Dev. **22**, 953–969 (1994). https://doi.org/10.1016/0305-750X(94)90141-4

19. Lassiter, L.E.: The Power of Kiowa Song: A Collaborative Ethnography. University of Arizona Press, Tucson (1998)
20. Fals Borda, O.: Kinsey Dialogue Series #1: the origins and challenges of participatory action research. Particip. Res. Pract. **10** (1999)
21. Darrouzet, C., Wild, H., Wilkinson, S.: Participatory ethnography at work practicing the puzzle palaces of a large, complex healthcare organization. In: Cefkin, M. (ed.) Ethnography and the Corporate Encounter: Reflections on Research in and of Corporations, pp. 61–94. Bergham Books, US (2009)
22. Hockey, J., Forsey, M.: Ethnography is not participant observation: Reflections on the interview as participa-tory qualitative research. In: Skinner, J. (ed.) The Interview an Ethnographic Approach, pp. 69–87. Routledge (2012)
23. Campbell, J.: A critical appraisal of participatory methods in development research. Int. J. Soc. Res. Methodol. **5**, 19–29 (2002). https://doi.org/10.1080/13645570110098046
24. Seidman, I.: Interviewing as Qualitative Research: a Guide for Researchers in Education and the Social Sciences. Teachers College Press, New York (2019)
25. Vega, H., Arastoopour Irgens, G.: Identity negotiation of pre-service teachers of English as a Foreign language. In: 14th International Conference of the Learning Sciences, pp. 1190–1197. International Society of the Learning Sciences (2020)
26. Vega, H., Irgens, G.A., Bailey, C.: Negotiating tensions: a study of pre-service English as Foreign language teachers' sense of identity within their community of practice. In: Ruis, A. R., Lee, S.B. (eds.) ICQE 2021. CCIS, vol. 1312, pp. 277–291. Springer, Cham (2021). https://doi.org/10.1007/978-3-030-67788-6_19
27. Birt, L., Scott, S., Cavers, D., Campbell, C., Walter, F.: Member checking: a tool to enhance trustworthiness or merely a nod to validation? Qual. Health Res. **26**, 1802–1811 (2016). https://doi.org/10.1177/1049732316654870
28. Arastoopour Irgens, G.: Using quantitative ethnography to tell stories that have not been told before. In: International Society for Quantitative Ethnography Webinar Series (2020)

Deliberation as an Epistemic Network: A Method for Analyzing Discussion

Peter Levine[1]([⊠]) [iD], Brendan Eagan[2] [iD], and David Williamson Shaffer[2] [iD]

[1] Tufts University, Medford, USA
Peter.Levine@tufts.edu
[2] University of Wisconsin-Madison, Madison, USA

Abstract. Deliberations are discussions about what an institution, community, or nation should do, and are essential for maintaining a robust democracy. This study examined whether Epistemic Network Analysis (ENA) can complement existing methods for assessing deliberations, none of which fully account for the dynamic interplay among specific speech acts and speakers that unfolds over the course of a conversation. In this pilot study, students at two universities deliberated about the same issue online. ENA models of discussions at each university with the content of speech acts as nodes showed differences between discussions at the two universities that were consistent with a qualitative analysis of the transcripts, but also revealed patterns that were not initially apparent in the qualitative account. This suggests that ENA is a valuable tool for modeling deliberations.

Keywords: Deliberation · Epistemic Network Analysis · ENA · Habermas · Democracy · Deliberative democracy

1 Introduction

Deliberations are discussions about what an institution, community, or nation should do. Deliberation is important in a democracy. It allows individuals to influence public opinion and official decisions and may convert opinions and desires into more reflective judgments. Deliberation is a subset of conversation that meets certain normative criteria, such as reasonableness and equity, although these criteria are debated.

Analyzing deliberations can yield insights that inform efforts to change the format and structure of conversations or to educate people (participants and moderators) to play their roles better. It can also inform people who need to decide whether a given discussion met a standard for being a deliberation. Although judgments of quality ultimately depend on normative principles, rigorous mathematical methods for analyzing and representing deliberations can provide the material for debating such principles and applying them to specific cases.

One general approach to analyzing a deliberation is to treat the ideas that individuals convey as network nodes, and the connections they cite or imply between their own ideas as links. Then it is possible to model each participant's statements during a deliberation as an epistemic network (a network of ideas), and the discussion as a

© Springer Nature Switzerland AG 2022
B. Wasson and S. Zörgő (Eds.): ICQE 2021, CCIS 1522, pp. 17–32, 2022.
https://doi.org/10.1007/978-3-030-93859-8_2

whole as one amalgamated network for the group. This method benefits from the special affordances of Epistemic Network Analysis (ENA), which produces a network visualization where the positions of nodes are meaningful and comparable across separate discussions.

In this study, two demographically different groups of students at different universities discussed the same topic (the social determinants of health) in online fora. They answered survey questions about their impressions of the discussion, e.g., how diverse they considered the opinions they heard expressed. The text of their discussions was analyzed using ENA. Ideas were coded, and ideas that were expressed in close proximity were considered linked by the speaker. Graphs were generated for the separate discussions and were compared. The resulting models of the two discussions confirmed the authors' impressions but also provided clear and quantified representations that would be useful for assessment.

2 Theory

Deliberation is a means to improve opinions by giving citizens the benefit of other people's perspectives. President Woodrow Wilson said that "The whole purpose of democracy is that we may hold counsel with one another" [44]; and some contemporary political theorists share that view [1].

According to the influential theory of Jürgen Habermas, deliberating citizens exchange reasons for why their claims about public issues are: (1) true, (2) just or fair, and (3) sincere [18, 19]. A *valid communication* is one that would persuade other people of its truth, justice, and sincerity in the absence of coercion and other barriers, such as lack of time and attention. A *valid claim* would attain consensus in what Habermas envisions as an "ideal speech situation" in which "no force except that of the better argument is exercised" [17]. For instance, a speaker's popularity or status would not matter; only her ideas would. The benefits of seeking consensus include better public understanding of what is right and good and richer and more defensible inner thoughts [18].

Habermas has contributed to the theory of *deliberative democracy*, in which citizens' voluntary conversations about current, controversial issues in the public sphere play a politically essential role [9]. Many others have enriched the theory or sought to apply it by designing deliberative fora or reforming laws and policies to encourage deliberation. Deliberating about current, controversial, public issues is also a valuable educational experience, enhancing students' knowledge of the issues under consideration, grasp of alternative perspectives, skills for interacting with other people, and motivations to participate in civic life [23, 39].

In real life, conversations can go well or badly. Habermas is fully aware that the "*ideal* speech situation" is a heuristic; actual discussions never meet the ideal. For example, discussions of contested political issues in the United States frequently display such flaws as *motivated reasoning* (selecting evidence to confirm a pre-existing view), *balkanization* into like-minded groups, *incivility* that discourages people from participating, and the *dominance of ideology* over evidence [16, 25].

Thus, the problem of assessing *deliberative quality* arises. The raw material for assessment may be a transcript of an actual conversation. On its face, it shows a whole series of utterances attributed to various people that can be coded in various ways, e.g., as right or wrong, civil or uncivil, a question or a claim. Deliberation, however, is more than just a temporal series of statements, because (in Habermas' terms) deciding whether a given turn of talk is a valid communication or valid claim can only be determined by the larger context in which it sits. Characterizing the quality of a deliberative discussion thus requires accounting both for the individual statements of participants *and* the way in which they relate to the statements of others in the conversation. Only with such a contextual model could we characterize statements as being *deliberatively virtuous*, and therefore only with such a model could we apply normative judgements about the degree to which deliberative ideals were met in a discussion.

We argue that creating such a model would be an important step in both the study and practice of deliberation because being able to make such assessments should yield insights into how to improve actual discussions in educational settings and civil society alike. Specifically, we advocate the application of ENA to the assessment of deliberation. ENA is a well-developed and widely employed method, but it has not previously been applied to deliberations of public issues. We show that it can address limitations in existing methods for assessing deliberative quality and improving deliberations.

2.1 Current Approaches to Evaluating Deliberation

Many efforts to assess deliberations rely on coding transcripts for evidence of deliberative virtues, such as hearing another person's arguments, or vices, such as expressing disrespect [14, 41]. Other approaches survey participants and/or independent observers for their general impressions of the quality of an observed deliberation [27].

To address the subjectivity of evaluations by human observers, many studies use rubrics or scoring guides. Multiple raters apply the same rubric to the text of a deliberation and resolve disagreements. A prominent example is the Deliberative Quality Index (DQI) [41]. An alternative approach, meant to address concerns about raters' subjectiveness, is to count specific deliberative "moves" and then compare the frequency of such moves across multiple discussions [3, 20, 22, 28, 31, 43, 46].

Such methods have produced insights about where and when deliberation occurs and who participates. However, we see limitations that can be addressed by new methods that employ network analysis—and specifically, ENA.

Any method that asks human raters to assess speech must direct their attention to some specific, concrete material. For example, raters can be asked to evaluate a whole deliberation according to a rubric or to assess each individual's participation. In DQI, "The unit of analysis... is a speech, that is, the public discourse by a particular individual delivered at a particular point in a debate. Thus, the entire discourse is broken down into smaller speech units" [41].

Choosing a focus for assessment is challenging because a deliberation consists of many utterances by at least several people, unfolding over time and relating to each other. For instance, a given speech may be a response to something someone else said. Bächtiger and Parkinson advocate paying attention to the "interpersonal dynamics"

[5] in deliberation. But it is unlikely that human raters can rigorously assess the relationships among all the "smaller speech units" and all the speakers and listeners in a conversation, because these are very numerous. One approach to constructing more contextual models has been to use *network models* that account for the relationships between people and ideas in a discussion. For example, Black and colleagues [4] use network analysis in which the nodes of a network are people and the links between them are different forms of discourse, such as agreements, disagreements, or questions. They argue that a network visualization enables the "discovery of patterns and relationships in data that would otherwise be obscured."

In this paper, we build on this network analytic approach. Like Black and colleagues, we propose that network analysis will reveal features of a discussion that have face validity and normative or evaluative significance and that would otherwise be overlooked.

2.2   Networks in Deliberation

People who discuss a social or political issue can be understood as members of a *social* network, in which the nodes are individual human beings, and each link represents one person influencing another. Social networks can be modeled by looking at actual patterns of interaction between individuals. For example, if Participant 2 (P2) in a discussion is consistently replying to or referencing the comments of Participant 1 (P1), but P1 rarely refers to P2, then we might assert that P2's thinking is influenced by P1 more than P1's thinking is influenced by P2. Social network analysis is not a focus of this paper.

Each individual's views on the issue under discussion can also be conceptualized as an *epistemic* network: a set of linked ideas, where the nodes are ideas being discussed and each link represents an individual's belief that the ideas are related to one another. As individuals discuss a topic, they disclose some of their own ideas and connections, and these in turn connect with others' points. For example, if Participant 1 (P1) in a discussion of climate change argues that we should *limit carbon emissions* because *human activity contributes to climate change*, then they are making a claim that two ideas (carbon emissions and the contribution of human activity to climate change) are related to one another. If Participant 2 (P2) replies by arguing that any actions we take towards *mitigating climate change* need to be *equitable to populations with fewer resources*, then they are also linking two ideas (mitigation and equity). However, by making this statement in response to P1, P2 is also linking both mitigation and equity to carbon emissions and to human activity as a driver of climate change [37].

These accumulating statements can be modeled as an epistemic network for the group, or as a set of epistemic networks for each individual, and these networks can be visualized either as evolving structures or as a representation of the discussion as a whole. Diagramming discussions as epistemic networks reveals areas of focus (what is being connected to what) and degrees and types of complexity (how many connections there are and how strong are they).

As the epistemic network of the group grows and changes, both individuals' opinions and their locations in the social network may change. Both the social network and the epistemic network can be characterized holistically, not just as the aggregate of distinct utterances.

2.3 Epistemic Network

Epistemic networks can be modeled using *epistemic network analysis* (ENA). ENA models the structure of connections between ideas (referred to here as nodes or Codes) both within and between individuals.

ENA assumes: (1) that it is possible to systematically identify a set of meaningful features in the data (Codes); (2) that the data has local structure (conversations); and (3) that an important feature of the data is the way that Codes are connected to one another within conversations [37, 38]. For example, the Codes in a deliberation about climate change would be the key ideas or issues of climate change. That is, a main theoretical assumption of ENA is that repeated co-occurrences of two or more Codes in the same portion of a discourse can reveal epistemic networks which characterize an underlying Discourse, or pattern of talk within some cultural context [15, 37]. ENA models the connections between Codes by quantifying the co-occurrence of Codes within conversations, producing a weighted network of co-occurrences [29].

In the discussion of climate change described above, the hypothetical speaker P1 could link two ideas with a logical connector—for example, "*Because* human beings are causing global warming, we had better limit carbon." However, ENA does not rely on such explicit connections. It is based on theories of discourse (more specifically *discourse analysis* and *epistemic frame theory*) in which temporal proximity entails semantic linkage. That is, because of the nature of human interaction in typical settings (including but not limited to deliberative discussions), people (a) make internally coherent contributions—or at any rate contributions that reflect the structure of their ideas—and (b) respond to the context in which their utterances are made. Thus, temporal proximity of concepts implies meaningful relationships. There are, of course, specific instances where one or the other of these assumptions might be violated, and any mathematical analysis is only a model of some phenomenon in the world. However, our detailed examination did not suggest any reason to believe that these assumptions were violated either frequently or systematically in the data used for this study. It is true that the version of ENA used here does not model the valence or causal claims being made between ideas, and this is a topic we return to in the discussion. For more on these issues in general, see [37].

In ENA network visualizations, the positions of nodes are fixed using a deterministic algorithm (a linear regression) that is (a) performed on the entire set of networks and (b) is co-registered with the ENA metrics that characterize the networks. When integrating a graph produced by ENA, one can attribute *meaning* to the *position* of nodes.

The co-registration of summary statistics and visualizations is made possible by the fact that, in any given ENA space, all networks have the same node locations but differ in their strength of connections, or edge weights. Nodes are positioned such that the centroid of each network (determined by the edge weights) corresponds with the network metric(s) for that network. This co-registration of network visualizations and metrics creates a method for interpreting the dimensions of the ENA metric space.

Networks that score *higher* on a dimension in the network space are those that have stronger connections among and to the *nodes* that are positioned towards the *positive* end of the dimension. Contrariwise, networks that score *lower* on a dimension in the network space are those that have stronger connections among and to the nodes that are positioned towards the *negative* end of the dimension.

As a result, researchers can use ENA to statistically analyze the content (rather than just the structure) of a set of networks, interpret the meaning of those statistics in terms of the content of the networks, and perform visual comparisons of networks. Of particular use in comparing networks is the ability to compare two network models by subtracting their connections weights from each other to create a *difference network graph*. The resulting difference network graph shows which connections are stronger in one network compared to another and is particularly useful for comparing groups of networks (for example, the discussions from two different classrooms) by constructing the mean network for each group and comparing them statistically and visually.

2.4   Research Purpose - Use of Networks in This Study

In this study, online discussions of the same topic in two different contexts were modeled as epistemic networks. Specifically, we use ENA and a Quantitative Ethnographic approach more broadly to address the following research questions:

RQ1: Can ENA be used to measure different deliberative discourse patterns in online forum discussions in similar course from two different universities?

RQ2: If so, what might lead to these differences and what implications could they have on assessing deliberation and developing norms for teaching deliberation?

This method produced substantive findings. For instance, one conversation was more complex (as a whole) than the other, although the less complex one was more consistent with scientific consensus. In general, by applying Epistemic Network Analytics to these deliberations, we clarified and quantified aspects of the conversations that can then be normatively assessed and compared. More generally, in this study we aim to demonstrate how ENA can be used to assess deliberation and inform the development of normative principles for, and principled assessment of deliberative discussions.

3   Methods

3.1   Sample and Settings

Students were recruited from an undergraduate course at Tufts University, a private liberal arts institution in Massachusetts (n = 30), and Kansas State University (KSU), a public institution in Kansas (n = 48).

Tufts students are generally seen as liberal, with few explicit conservatives. KSU is more ideologically diverse. We did not ask participating students about their own ideologies or partisan identities. However, the precinct where Kansas State University is located split 51%-39% for Hilary Clinton over Donald Trump in 2016, and Trump won the neighboring precinct to the west, which contains many apartment buildings catering to KSU students. All the precincts around Tufts University favored Clinton by margins of at least three-to-one, and the nearest precinct that Trump won was a 17-min drive away [6]. Although students can come to either institution from anywhere in the world, these statistics about the two communities offer a meaningful contrast: Tufts is considerably more progressive than KSU.

The Tufts group was racially, ethnically, and culturally diverse (7 students of color and 12 white students; 80% female). However, all of the Tufts students reported that their mothers had completed college, an indicator of relatively high social class. The KSU group was less racially heterogeneous (80% white), and 89% had mothers with college degrees.

Each group conducted three deliberations in online forums, separately from each other. We posit that the epistemic networks of these deliberations changed over time, but on different timescales. Each new discussion has its own epistemic network, which changed every time a student posted a comment. The slate was then cleared for the next discussion. To illustrate an epistemic network, we focus on one specific discussion, regarding the social determinants of health. This discussion was the first of three at KSU and the second of three at Tufts.

In both cases, the instructors (who are not authors of this paper) agreed to ask their students to participate in online discussions, for the purpose of this research study. At Tufts, the course was devoted to science policy. The Tufts students were assigned a substantial reading about the racial and class determinants of health outcomes [8]. They also experienced a class visit by an expert on that topic who emphasized the injustice of health disparities. At KSU, the course was concerned with communication studies. The students received much less direct instruction on the social determinants of health before they discussed that topic online: just a link to a short online document that did not emphasize race or class [33]. Thus, any differences in the discussions might result from the students' demographics, contexts, and prior beliefs or from the way the topic had been presented. We do not purport to explain the differences in terms of causal or contextual factors, but simply to elucidate them.

We also collected social network data by asking students before and after each deliberation to name the other students who influenced them. We interpreted each such response as a social network connection (an edge) from the influencer to the influenced. Counting the number of such connections indicated substantial changes in individuals' network centrality over time that seemed plausibly related to the roles they played in each discussion. However, for reasons of space and because the social network data were simple and preliminary, we do not report those results here.

To measure students' opinions of the topic and their assessment of the deliberation, they were asked before each discussion to write a very short essay describing their opinion of the topic and to answer survey items about their interest in it. After each discussion, they were asked a battery of questions, drawn from [27] about their opinions of the discussion, the issue, and deliberation in general. (Since not all students who participated in this discussion answered all the survey questions, the numbers of respondents vary somewhat in each analysis.)

They conducted their discussions online using a simple threaded comment platform provided for courses at Tufts. At Tufts, the discussions were for credit and graded, and students had the option of a different short writing assignment if they did not want to be part of the research study. At KSU, the discussions were for extra credit, and there was an option of an alternative extra-credit writing assignment for students who did not want to participate in the research. Students who completed all the surveys received $10 gift certificates.

All the text was captured, the speakers were matched with the survey questions, and the dataset was anonymized for analysis.

Two human coders reviewed the text and coded it for the following concepts: Personal Choice, Prejudice, Opportunity, Hard Work, Upbringing, Class, and Race (see Table 1). These codes emerged from a grounded analysis as the main topics of discussion. Coding was validated using social moderation, where two or more raters code the data independently and then resolve any differences to reach consensus on all coding for the entire dataset [21, 37].

Epistemic Network Analysis was then used to analyze the text. Figure 2 shows the results.

We utilized the ENA 1.7.0 Web Tool (version 1.7.0) [29], with individual students as the units of analysis nested within each school. We analyzed each discussion post independently, constructing a network model for each post where a connection between two codes is defined by whether or not they both appear in the post being modeled. The resulting networks were aggregated for posts for each student in the model. In sum, the ENA model was defined as Units: School, Student; Conversation: Post (whole conversation model); Codes: see codebook above.

The ENA model normalized the networks for all students before they were subjected to a dimensional reduction, which accounts for the fact that students had different numbers of posts in the discussions. For the dimensional reduction, we used a *means rotation* followed by a singular value decomposition (SVD). The means rotation produces a first dimension that passes between the mean values of two groups (in this case, KSU and Tufts), and can be read as the dimension which shows the greatest differences between the two groups. The SVD produces a second dimension orthogonal to the first that accounts for the most remaining variance in the data after removing the first (means rotated) dimension. See [37, 42].

Networks were visualized using network graphs where nodes correspond to the codes, and edges reflect the normalized frequency of co-occurrence, or connection, between two codes. The result is two coordinated representations for each unit of analysis: (1) a plotted point, which represents the location of that unit's network in the low-dimensional projected space, and (2) a weighted network graph. The positions of the network graph nodes are fixed, and those positions are determined by an optimization routine that minimizes the difference between each plotted point and the corresponding centroid of its weighted network graph. Because of this *co-registration* of network graphs and projected space, the positions of the network graph nodes—and the connections they define—can be used to interpret the dimensions of the projected space and explain the positions of plotted points in the space. Our model had co-registration correlations of 0.86 (Pearson) and 0.86 (Spearman) for the first dimension and co-registration correlations of 0.81 (Pearson) and 0.79 (Spearman) for the second, suggesting that positions of nodes for the network graphs provide a reliable interpretation of the differences captured on each dimension.

Table 1. Codebook.

Code	Definition	Example
Upbringing	Discussion of raising children including personal experience	Because of how I was raised, I could not truly relate to what my teacher was trying to convey to us
Prejudice/Discrimination	Discussion of judgement or unfair treatment directed against someone or a group of people based on factors including: age, sex, skin color, speech, income, education, sexual orientation, disability, religion and politics	I agree with you... that all races should be treated equally, however this is not the reality of our society. **Discrimination and prejudice** is still very much alive and it definitely affects peoples' well-being
Opportunity	Discussion of situations or occasions which make it possible to have good or bad health outcomes	For some of us, going to college is a thing that we knew is going to happen in our lives and we never question if we might go or no. But for some people they do not have this **opportunity** to afford college...
Class	Discussion of economic/social class (socioeconomic status)	I do believe that race, **class**, and social factors can have an effect on a human being's health and well-being
Race/Ethnicity	Discussion of categories of people who identify with each other based on similarities such as common ancestral, language, social, cultural or national experiences. Discussion of race or ethnicity	For some of us, going to college is a thing that we knew is going to happen in our lives and we never question if we might go or no. But for some people they do not have this **opportunity** to afford college...
Daily decisions	Discussion of making day to day personal choice about how one lives their life	Before I came here, I used to not drink at all, but alter coming here the fact that I was not drinking made me feel like I don't fit into the group. ... So again, our friends can influence us in taking **decisions** that could affect our health
Hard work	Discussion or overcoming the odds or difficult circumstances with hard work (classic bootstrap narrative)	Because In my personal experience my mother worked very hard to get where she is today... She worked hard and I 100% believe she has earned and deserves all that she has today

In addition to modeling the deliberations with ENA, we read the deliberations to validate that the network models represented meaningful connections made by students and to identify illustrative qualitative examples.

4   Results

Figure 1 shows the mean discourse network for the social determinants of health deliberation at Tufts (on the left in blue) and the mean discourse network for KSU (on the right in red). Subtracting one network from the other produces the difference network is in the middle.

The graphs on the left (Tufts) and right (KSU) show the mean of students' discourse from each group as a single graph. The nodes are ideas, and they are in the same locations on all three graphs, which allows comparison. As described above in the method section, their locations are determined by a dimensional reduction followed by a linear regression, and as a result, the location of the notes can be used to interpret the axes of the metric space. The links between nodes indicate the relative frequency with which students referred to pairs of ideas in the same post.

The axes can be interpreted by examining the labels of the nodes that are closer to them (similar to principal component analysis). In this case, the positions of the nodes suggest that the left-right axis of the space can be characterized by the contrast between concepts related to personal beliefs (daily decisions and prejudice/discrimination) and concepts related to upbringing, with *personal beliefs to the left* and *upbringing to the right*.[1]

While personal beliefs can be understood as broadly determined by one's upbringing, in the case of this study they have been defined and are expressed differently in the data. Specifically, the code upbringing relates to *direct explicit discussion of raising children or personal childhood experiences of how someone was raised* while, in contrast, the codes daily decisions and prejudice and discrimination refer to *making day to day personal choice about how one lives their life* and *judgement, or unfair treatment directed against someone or a group of people* respectively. In addition these codes cooccur relatively infrequently in the data and are not defining features of the mean discourse network for KSU or Tufts or the differences between them.

The most prominent connection of concepts made by students at Tufts was between class and race/ethnicity. (An example is a Tufts student's statement: "When talking about the Flint, Michigan water crisis, it was shocking to hear that companies … are often built where the majority of the community is minority and low income)." In contrast, the students at KSU made the most connections between class and upbringing,

---

[1] It is also possible, of course, to interpret the up-down axis; however, we are not making use of that information in this analysis. Because of the dimension reduction technique used, differences between the two groups are projected to the first axis of the metric space, as we will show below.

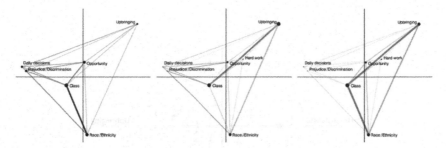

Fig. 1. Mean discourse networks for Tufts (left, blue), KSU (right, red), and a difference network graph (center). X-axis MR1 (16.8%), Y-axis SVD2 (16.9%). (Color figure online)

followed closely by connections between class and race/ethnicity and between upbringing and race/ethnicity. Many of the Tufts student emphasized the ways that race and class work together to reinforce inequity (what some would call "intersectionality"). The KSU students were more focused on what they perceived as the different behaviors of people from higher and lower socioeconomic background, and they disagreed about the reasons for those differences.

In the difference network we can see a noticeable red triangle of connections between upbringing, class, and race/ethnicity were more prominent in the discussion at KSU compared to Tufts. This is the case in spite of the fact that the strongest connections in the Tufts network is between class and race/ethnicity. The only connections that were more prominent in the Tufts network contain prejudice/discrimination or daily decisions.

Fourteen of the twenty-one (66%) possible connections among the concepts were stronger in the KSU network graph. This is reflected in fourteen lines being red and seven being blue in the difference network. These results align with our overall observation that the KSU discussion contained more diverse views. This network analysis and preceding qualitative account of student deliberation allow us to interpret the following statistical results.

Figure 2 shows the plotted points which correspond to individual student discourse networks from the social determinants of health deliberation. The points for students from Tufts are in blue and the points for students from KSU are in red. (Some points in the graph are overlapping, so the total number of visible points is less than the total number of data points.) The squares are the means of the points and the boxes around the squares are 95% confidence intervals on both dimensions.

There was a statistically significant difference between the mean of the plotted points for Tufts students compared to KSU students along the x dimension, which, as above, represents *personal beliefs versus upbringing*. A two-sample t test assuming unequal variance showed Tufts (mean = −0.384, SD = 0.124, N = 13 was statistically significantly different from KSU (mean = 0.143, SD = 0.197, N = 35; p < 0.001).

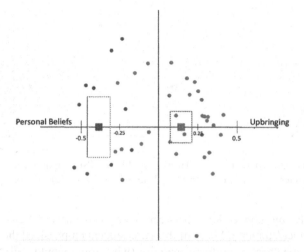

Fig. 2. Plotted points – Tufts in Blue and KSU in Red. (Color figure online)

5   Discussion and Next Directions

The differences revealed by the ENA have face-validity in the sense that they are consistent with our reading of the interview transcripts and our understanding of differences between the two courses, particularly the greater ideological diversity at KSU and the more extensive treatment of social determinants of health at Tufts. In brief, KSU students debated whether or not people are responsible for their own health because of bad behavior and problematic upbringings. Some credited good health to personal characteristics, such as hard work. Tufts students did not air those explanations but shared the view that public health is a function of social circumstances.

What should we make of the differences between the two groups' conversations? We could turn to the students for assessments, but we would find only small differences. In both groups, students reported after the discussion that the topic was important, that they had carefully considered others' views and understood what other people said, and that others had understood them. In both groups, students reported that the discussion had helped them to understand the topic, although mean responses to that question were somewhat stronger at Tufts than at KSU. Tufts students felt more strongly than KSU students that our democracy would be stronger if more people experienced this kind of discussion. Tufts students were less likely to observe a lot of disagreement within their group than KSU students were. KSU students were more likely to say that the topic of social determinants of health is important.

A great deal of evidence from the social sciences supports the consensus view in the Tufts classroom, that race and class do affect health outcomes [8, 26]. Thus, one could argue that the difference in the two discussions was a greater degree of sophistication or awareness among the Tufts students. However, this focus might not have been due to students' educations, backgrounds, or institutions. The Tufts course was more focused on health equity. Or, one might conclude that the Tufts conversation was better because it began with a factual premise: students explored nuances and applications of this premise while also increasing the cohesiveness of their group.

On the other hand, as measured by ENA, the Tufts students did not make as many connections across as many topics or ideas as the students at KSU did. Tufts students did not grapple with, or even experience, a set of opinions that came up at KSU and were incorporated into a more complex epistemic network for the class as a whole. (Because ENA compares means for the groups, the differences in the number of participants and number of comments would not matter.)

One implication for instructors may thus be that existing disagreements within a class can serve as "deliberative asset[s]" [23]. Topics on which the students happen to disagree provide better practice for deliberation. From this perspective, a drawback of the Tufts conversation was the relative homogeneity of opinion. When a group is focused on a relatively small number of issues, it may be worth choosing readings and other prompts that expand the range of ideas that the students can incorporate into their arguments.

On the other hand, some ideas are inconsistent with current academic consensus. The KSU students were not taught about social determinants of health, but if they had been, they might have restricted the topics they discussed. That suggests a possible tradeoff between scholarly expertise–learning to think like a specialist–and deliberative complexity.

In the end, judgments as to quality of deliberation require normative principles; however, our analysis here shows that these network analyses accomplish two important steps toward the ultimate goal of evaluating deliberative discussions. First, the analyses reveal aspects of the conversation that pose normative issues, and thus could lead to the development of principled assessments. Moreover, the network analyses provide quantitative metrics that could be used to implement such assessments. This paper provides just one potential analytical approach in this arena and suggests a few logical next steps.

First, ENA (as presently developed) treats all codes alike. That assumption underlines the mathematics of the method. ENA yields insights into complexity and connectedness but may overlook the fact that certain ideas are logically related in various ways. For example, to believe in the impact of race on health is the *opposite* of disbelieving in it. At Tufts, everyone who invoked race did so to emphasize racial injustice. At KSU, some commented in favor and others against this idea. Current applications of ENA do not consider relationships such as oppositeness, which would be a useful next step.

Another next step would be to use ENA as a way to model how students are influencing each other through the interactions of their discourse networks. These steps would advance the method of ENA itself and could prove valuable in the study of political deliberations more broadly.

As noted earlier, we collected simple social network metrics from the students. Integrating social network analysis with ENA would be another step.

Finally, such methods must be tested on larger samples and not merely with US undergraduates discussing issues for academic credit.

Acknowledgements. This work was funded in part by the National Science Foundation (DRL-1661036, DRL-1713110, DRL-2100320), the Wisconsin Alumni Research Foundation, and the Office of the Vice Chancellor for Research and Graduate Education at the University of Wisconsin-Madison. The opinions, findings, and conclusions do not reflect the views of the funding agencies, cooperating institutions, or other individuals.

References

1. Allen, D.: Talking to Strangers: Anxieties of Citizenship since Brown v. Board of Education. University of Chicago Press, Chicago (2004)
3. Andrist, S., Collier, W., Gleicher, M., Mutlu, B., Shaffer, D.W.: Look together: analyzing gaze coordination with epistemic network analysis. Front. Psychol. **6**, 1016 (2015)
4. Black, L.W., Welser, H.T., Cosley, D., DeGroot, J.M.: Self-governance through group discussion in Wikipedia: measuring deliberation in online groups. Small Group Res. **42**(5), 595–611 (2011)
5. Bächtiger, A., Parkinson. J.: Mapping and Measuring Deliberation: Towards a New Deliberative Quality. Oxford University Press, Oxford (2019)
6. Bächtiger, A., Niemeyer, S., Neblo, M., Steenbergen, M.R., Steiner, J.: Toward more realistic models of deliberative democracy disentangling diversity in deliberative democracy: competing theories, their blind spots and complementarities. J. Polit. Philos. **18**(1), 32–63 (2010)
7. Bloch, M., Buchanan, L., Katz, J., Quealy, K.: An extremely detailed map of the 2016 Election. https://www.nytimes.com/interactive/2018/upshot/election-2016-voting-precinct-maps.html
8. Bordes, A., Usunier, N., Garcia-Duran, A., Weston, J., Yakhnenko, O.: Translating embeddings for modeling multi-relational data. In: Burges, C.J.C., Bottou, L., Welling, M., Ghahramani, Z. (eds.) 26th International Conference on Neural Information Processing Systems, pp. 2787–2795. Curran Associates, Red Hook (2013)
9. Braveman, P., Egerter, S., Williams, D.R.: The social determinants of health: coming of age. Annu. Rev. Public Health **32**, 381–398 (2011)
10. Calhoun, C.: Habermas and the Public Sphere. MIT Press, Cambridge (1994)
11. Cress, U., Hesse, F.W.: Quantitative Methods for Studying Small Groups. The International Handbook of Collaborative Learning, pp. 93–111 (2013)
12. Csanadi, A., Eagan, B., Shaffer, D.W., Kollar, I., Fischer, F.: Collaborative and individual scientific reasoning of pre-service teachers: new insights through epistemic network analysis (ENA). In: Smith, B.K., Borge, M., Mercier, E., Lim, K.Y. (eds.) 12th International Conference on Computer-Supported Collaborative Learning 2017, CSCL, vol. 1, pp. 215–222. International Society of the Learning Sciences, Singapore (2017)
13. Drieger, P.: Semantic network analysis as a method for visual text analytics. Procedia Soc. Behav. Sci. **79**, 4–17 (2013)
14. DiSessa, A.A.: Constructivism in the Computer Age. Erlbaum, Hillsdale (1988)
15. Gastil, J., Black, L., Moscovitz, K.: Ideology, attitude change, and deliberation in small face-to-face groups. Polit. Commun. **25**(1), 23–46 (2008)
16. Gee, J.P.: An Introduction to Discourse Analysis: Theory and Practice. Routledge, London & New York (1999)
17. Glaeser, E.L., Sunstein, C.R.: Does more speech correct falsehoods? J. Leg. Stud. **43**, 65–93 (2014)
18. Habermas, J.: Legitimation Crisis. Heinemann, Portsmouth (1976)

19. Habermas, J.: The Theory of Communicative Action, Lifeworld and System: A Critique of Functionalist Reason, vol. 2. Beacon Press, Boston (1987)
20. Habermas, J.: Between Facts and Norms: Contributions to a Discourse Theory of Law and Democracy. MIT Press, Cambridge (1996)
21. Han, S-H., Schenck-Hamlin, W., Schenck-Hamlin, D.: Inclusion, equality, and discourse quality in citizen deliberations on broadband. J. Public Deliberation 11(1), Article no. 3 (2015)
22. Herrenkohl, L.R., Cornelius, L.: Investigating elementary students' scientific and historical argumentation. J. Learn. Sci. 22(3), 413–461 (2013)
23. Hess, D.: Controversy in the Classroom: The Democratic Power of Discussion. Taylor & Francis, Milton (2009)
24. Hess, D., McAvoy, P.: The Political Classroom: Evidence and Ethics in Democratic Education. Routledge, London (2014)
25. Hutchins, E.: Cognition in the Wild. MIT Press, Cambridge (1995)
26. Kahan, D.: Ideology, motivated reasoning, and cognitive reflection: an experimental study. Judgm. Decis. Mak. 8, 407–424 (2013)
27. Kawachi, I., Daniels, N., Robinson, D.E.: Health disparities by race and class: why both matter. Health Aff. 24(2), 343–352 (2005)
28. Knobloch, K.R., Gastil, J.: Civic (Re)socialisation: the educative effects of deliberative participation. Politics 35, 183–200 (2015)
29. Leighter, J.L., Black, L.: "I'm Just Raising the Question": terms for talk and practical metadiscursive argument in public meetings. West. J. Commun. 74, 547–568 (2010)
30. Marquart, C.L., Hinojosa, C., Swiecki, Z., Eagan, B., Shaffer, D.W.: Epistemic Network Analysis (2018)
31. Morrell, M.E.: Empathy and Democracy: Feeling, Thinking, and Deliberation. Penn State Press, University Park (2010)
32. Murray, T., Stephens, L., Woolf, B.P., Wing, L., Xu, X., Shrikant, N.: Supporting social deliberative skills online: the effects of reflective scaffolding tools. In: Ozok, A.A., Zaphiris, P. (eds.) OCSC 2013. LNCS, vol. 8029, pp. 313–322. Springer, Heidelberg (2013). https://doi.org/10.1007/978-3-642-39371-6_36
33. Murray, T., Woolf, B.P., Xu, X., Shipe, S., Howard, S., Wing, L.: Towards supporting social deliberative skills in online classroom dialogues and beyond. In: International Conference on Intelligent Tutoring Systems 2012, ITS, pp. 666–668 (2012)
34. ODPHP, Social Determinants of Health. https://www.healthypeople.gov/2020/topics-objectives/topic/social-determinants-of-health/. Accessed 4 June 2021
36. Quardokus Fisher, K., Hirshfield, L., Siebert-Evenstone, A.L., Arastoopour, G., Koretsky, M.: Network analysis of interactions between students and an instructor during design meetings. In: Proceedings of the American Society for Engineering Education (2016)
37. Ruis, A.R., Rosser, A.A., Quandt-Walle, C., Nathwani, J.N., Shaffer, D.W., Pugh, C.M.: The hands and head of a surgeon: modeling operative competency with multimodal epistemic network analysis. Am. J. Surg. 216(5), 835–840 (2018)
38. Sanders, L.M.: Against deliberation. Political Theory 25(3), 347–376 (1997)
39. Shaffer, D.W.: Quantitative Ethnography. Cathcart Press, Madison (2017)
40. Shaffer, D.W., Collier, W., Ruis, A.R.: A tutorial on epistemic network analysis: analyzing the structure of connections in cognitive, social, and interaction data. J. Learn. Anal. 3(3), 9–45 (2016)
41. Shaffer, D.W., Ruis, A.R.: Handbook of learning analytics. In: Lang, C., Siemens, G., Wise, A.F., Gasevic, G. (eds.) Society for Learning Analytics Research, Alberta (2017)

42. Shaffer, T.J., Longo, N.V., Manosevitch, I., Thomas, M.S.: Deliberative Pedagogy: Teaching and Learning for Democratic Engagement. Michigan State University Press, East Lansing (2017)
43. Steenbergen, M.R., Bächtiger, A., Spörndli, M., Steiner, J.: measuring political deliberation: a discourse quality index. Comparative European Politics 1, 21–48 (2003)
44. Sullivan, S.A., et al.: Using epistemic network analysis to identify targets for educational interventions in trauma team communication. Surgery Comparative European Politics 163, 938–943 (2017)
45. Trénel, M.: Measuring the Deliberativeness of Online Discussions (2004)
46. Wilson, W.: The New Freedom: A Call for the Emancipation of the Generous Energies of a People. New York (1912)
47. Wooldridge, A.R., Carayon, P., Eagan, B.R., Shaffer, D.W.: Quantifying the qualitative with epistemic network analysis: a human factors case study of task-allocation communication in a primary care team. IIE Trans. Healthcare Syst. Eng. 8, 1–72 (2018)
48. Woolf, B., Murray, T., Osterweil, L., Katsch, E., Clark, L., Wing, L.: SoCS: The Fourth Party: Improving Computer- Mediated: Deliberation Through Cognitive, Social and Emotional Support. NSF Annual Report (2012)
49. Young, I.M.: Activist challenges to deliberative democracy. Political Theory 29(5), 670–690 (2001)

Approaching Structured Debate with Quantitative Ethnography in Mind

Jennifer Scianna[1]([✉]) (iD), Rogers Kaliisa[2] (iD), Jamie J. Boisvenue[3] (iD),
and Szilvia Zörgő[4] (iD)

[1] University of Wisconsin-Madison, Madison, WI, USA
jscianna@wisc.edu
[2] University of Oslo, Oslo, Norway
[3] University of Alberta, Edmonton, AB, Canada
[4] Semmelweis University, Budapest, Hungary

Abstract. Structured Debate (SD) is a constrained discourse style that is popular in many different forums. The expansion of SD to online platforms leaves many questions about addressing this type of data during analysis. Quantitative Ethnography (QE) may provide a framework for the considerations that need to be made when analyzing SD datasets. In this paper, we review the ways in which QE methods are compatible with SD and the challenges associated with applying this approach. Using data from an online SD forum, we present a narrative of decision-making throughout the analysis process. We found that QE allows for a myriad of insights to be gained from this form of data depending on the approach one takes, including insights into structures, content, and participation. This work intends to serve as a model for researchers hoping to utilize QE on SD and, more broadly, for approaching novel datasets.

Keywords: Structured Debate · Quantitative Ethnography · Data preparation

1 Introduction

1.1 Classroom and Online Structured Debates

Structured Debate (SD) is a form of discourse that occurs in various settings including politics, economics, law, and business [1], as well as education [2]. SD is unique in that participant contributions are heavily structured and are arranged in a dichotomous "pro"/"con" configuration, that is, arguments for or against an initial claim [2]. As a pedagogical tool, SD promotes critical and rational thinking; students are required to organize and convey their thoughts in a logical and structured manner and need to be able to scrutinize and respond to claims made by the opposing side. During classroom SDs students are usually divided into two teams, one group argues for and one against an initial claim, such as: "Information production on social media should be uncensored". Arguments are disclosed in a structured manner, for example, a series of affirmative and opposing arguments are presented alternately, which is followed by a recess, and then rebuttals for the arguments. The teacher may impose strict time limits for each section and may set requirements for logical and rhetorical devices students

© Springer Nature Switzerland AG 2022
B. Wasson and S. Zörgő (Eds.): ICQE 2021, CCIS 1522, pp. 33–48, 2022.
https://doi.org/10.1007/978-3-030-93859-8_3

should employ. This is an established way of practicing critical thinking, building rational arguments, learning about logical fallacies, and exercising emotional self-regulation [3]. Online platforms are also beginning to offer a forum for such debating [4]; for example, DebateMap[1], eDeb8[2], and Kialo[3] provide an interface for participants to join a discussion on a certain topic. Several of these online platforms have been intentionally designed for pedagogical usage [5], while others have been retrofitted to serve the needs of educators [6]. Each participant can add an argument by designating it as a pro or a con to the initial claim, or they may choose to comment on any subsequent pro/con claim also by designating their argument as pro/con. In any given debate, there is much to be gained by analyzing pro/con arguments in relation to each other and to the initial claim. Furthermore, the content of each claim can be examined individually, and quantifying these aspects of the data presents an opportunity for identifying patterns in the entire corpus.

At first glance, SD may seem like an ideal candidate for quantification: its highly structured nature offers opportunities for segmenting, coding, and modelling such a dataset, but several issues may arise precisely in these realms; these can be addressed with Quantitative Ethnography (QE). QE is a unified, quantitative – qualitative methodology that provides tools and techniques for quantifying discourse data and representing it together with other types of data in a unified dataset [7]. Although SD is a common form of discourse and denotes a valuable repository for examining several aspects of education and development, such as critical thinking and collaboration, and albeit QE is a methodology suited for curating and analyzing such data, literature is scarce in this area.

Quantitative Ethnography researchers are yet to endeavor into the domain of SD. Thus far, the conversation surrounding debate has labelled it as a feature of more varied discourse. Barany et al. [8] analyzed student discussions and included "debate" as a type of interaction, but the authors were not specifically centered on investigating ways in which students formally engage in debate, nor did they explicitly deal with the structure of debate in general. Similarly, Nachtigall and Sung [9] utilize debate as a code to describe student interactions during collaboration, but do not delve into the components of that debate. Hamilton & Hobbs [10] considered political debates which would tend to be included as SD, but their analysis strayed from the pro/con focus and towards a more epistemic view of arguments and positions. We were interested in utilizing QE methodology to map the structure of SDs, identify challenges and affordances of debate discourse, and explore some ways to model such data. In this paper, we consider the nuances of analyzing SD using quantitative ethnographic methods.

1.2   Key Facets of Structured Debate

Structured Debate, also referred to as constraint-based argumentation [11], is a specific form of discourse where participants support position statements with evidence to

---

[1] https://debatemap.app/.

[2] http://www.edeb8.com/.

[3] www.kialo.com.

expose the different sides of an issue. Katzenstein [1] proposed that SD included several features that should be considered when analyzing this style of discourse: argument structure, stimulus operationalization, subject training, sample, and debate method. While they were primarily concerned with SD in business settings, these considerations can help identify aspects of the discourse in alternative settings as well.

Argument structure is related primarily to the format of the debate. For example, in some SDs, participants may have clear roles that they perform throughout the event. Musselman [12] utilized roles to help engage all participants. Antagonists were responsible for arguing a set position, Questioners limited discussion once an argument had run its course, and Conciliators developed compromises between the extreme positions. In digital spaces, we see some of these same roles come to light; online forums often have different roles for those who are actively involved in the debate, those who are moderating, and those who are engaged from the sidelines. Participants in the debate practice evidence-based reasoning to construct arguments supporting their position and refuting their opponents. Participants in the audience may vote, deliberate, provide written feedback, or ask questions.

Other aspects of the formal structure include the number of team members, purpose of each participant's turn, and even the activities that occur outside of the debate [2]. While information about participant educational background or preparation is not readily available to researchers in many digital spaces, it may be critical to know whether participants in a debate accessed information on their own or if they were all given the same information prior to the debate. This relates to the concept of subject training because participants may not be familiar with the content of the debate or with the structure. Consideration should be given to whether the participants are experts or not when considering the data.

Finally, the pattern of discourse is variable between different forms of SD. Interactions typically occur in either rounds or branches. In rounds, participants commonly engage in three phases: introduction, refutation, and conclusion [2]. Conversely, a branching structure allows participants to add support or rebuttals at any stage of the debate. Virtual spaces that support branching debate, such as Kialo and DebateMap, do not limit participants to a certain number of rounds. There are also hybrid formats such as the Human Continuum where participants consider their stance towards a topic and position themselves along a continuum. They then debate with neighbors providing evidence for a set amount of time, move if they feel their position has changed, and then begin again [6].

1.3   Previous Approaches to Analyzing Structured Debate

Non-digital SD has typically been studied in terms of activity design [1], pedagogical practice [12], and impact on learning [2]. These studies primarily focus on the structure of the activity itself compared to the outcome, but they rarely focus on the intricacies of discourse happening within the debates themselves. QE could provide a toolkit for addressing this analysis gap in literature.

Research on digital SD platforms has been centered around natural language processing techniques. The ability to clarify a participant's overall stance has been of interest to language processing researchers [4]. For example, Bolton et al. used debate data from Kialo to train an AI agent that was capable of debating with a user [13].

Thus far, investigations into debate discourse have encountered common challenges. For example, understanding the stances expressed in these debates requires modeling both textual content and users' conversational interactions. Bolton et al. addressed this struggle by filtering down their data to a subset of the datasets where positions were predictable [13]. Currently, there is a gap in how researchers with a more computational or qualitative focus can model conversations which switch perspectives while still being interrelated. Challenges of determining the true meaning of sentiment or other discourse modelling strategies will likely also fail to deliver in this context. These issues can be addressed with QE, a unified methodology that enables the systematic coding and representation of discourse- and metadata (i.e., information characterizing or accompanying data). The following is a modular account and worked example of how the QE methodological framework can be employed for SD analyses, for data from online branching SD platforms. The materials produced during our process (e.g., operationalization, codebook, dataset) are openly available in our public repository: placeholder for blinding purposes.

2   A Quantitative Ethnographic Approach to Structured Debate: Challenges and Affordances

2.1   Identifying Potential Research Questions

General Considerations. As with all data, SDs are suitable for answering only certain types of research questions, which are based on the affordances and constraints of how the data was generated, its characteristics, content, and structure. Due to the aims and the nature of debate, collected data will lend itself well to comparing and contrasting two principal opinions, which are generally broken down into their respective supporting arguments. Thus, data is symbolically (or in the case of some virtual platforms, literally) colored according to this dichotomy. Apart from being inherently dichotomous, SD data can be considered threaded: each pro/con argument can be conceptualized as a parent claim, which can have one or more children, affirmative or negative claims of their own. Threading can take many forms in SD data based on the structure of the debate or any meaningful and relevant system designated by the researcher. Thus, SD data, among many other characteristics, exhibits two main qualities: it is usually both dichotomous and threaded. This provides an opportunity to gain an in-depth understanding of two opposing opinions, for example, examining its content, the kind of supporting evidence that was utilized, similarities between arguments on one or both sides of the debate, etc. It also enables analyses on the relationship among claims and the deeper structure of the entire corpus. Due to the ways in which participants interact in a SD, it would be more challenging to discern public opinion based on the resultant data. This is because participants may be participating in SD through the role of devil's advocate [1] or be assigned a viewpoint in conflict with their own [12].

Our Example. We used data from an online SD platform in the topic of COVID-19 and herd immunization; the initial claim was that "Herd immunization is achievable". We defined our research questions in three domains: 1) Content (RQ1: What is the content of the claims?), 2) Structure (RQ2: How are the claims related to each other and how can the structure of the corpus be described?), and 3) Positionality (RQ3: What does the pro/con stance entail in terms of relation and meaning?). As explained in greater detail below, codes were developed for each of these domains separately.

2.2 Data Collection

General Considerations. While synchronous classroom debates would generally be audio-recorded and then transcribed, collecting data from online platforms usually entails manual or automatic scraping [14]. When data is scraped automatically, it may come in many forms with different types of content. For example, for each claim, Kialo provides a unique identifier, positionality, and the text itself, e.g., "1.1.1.2.1. Con: Text goes here [with hyperlink words here] (and actual link here)." The identifier denotes the position of a claim in the "generations" (claims belonging to different parents but on the same level of debate structure) succeeding the initial claim; here it is the fourth generation or level. The position of the line is noted as a "Con". Furthermore, the use of brackets connotes areas of text that are hyperlinks with the address of the link designated by parentheses. DebateMap, another online SD forum, includes similar information (ID and positionality), but they disclose a list of parent claims and offspring, timestamp, author, and metadata that other participants vote on (truth, relevance, and impact). As a point of ethics and data protection, researchers need to be aware of who owns the data, even when it is public, and what kind of data they are processing and how [15].

Our Example. We manually scraped data from an online platform by modelling it in a text file, mimicking the process of automatically scraping the data with the built-in downloading feature. We did not scrape the content of claims, rather, we performed discourse coding by using the interface; in our mock-up, we designated a unique identifier for each claim, noted their autogenic positionality specified by the interface (pro/con), and made note of whether hyperlinks were added to the claim as supporting evidence. We opted for creating a mock-up instead of scraping the data in order to protect user identity and avoid any intellectual property concerns. The online platform we chose allows participants to add any number of children to the initial claim and to each subsequent claim; thus, it can be classified as a forum for branching debate. Our publicly available dataset contained one initial claim and 65 subsequent arguments on 6 levels.

2.3 Data Curation

General Considerations. In the QE framework, discourse is first segmented into "utterances", the smallest unit of analysis. Utterances are commonly operationalized as a sentence or a turn-of-talk from a participant. Each utterance receives a unique identifier.

For utterances to be associated with discourse codes and metadata, they are eventually represented in a dataset called a qualitative data table. Such a dataset contains the raw data (e.g., individual claims) in rows, while columns contain variables, such as who made the claim, what positionality it had, when the claim was made, and where it is in a claim structure; these can all be considered metadata and can be represented with categorical values. Raw data is also accompanied by discourse coding, codes developed for qualitative data describing any relevant aspects of the content, such as whether the claim contained a reference to a certain theme pertinent to the research question. This coding is represented in binary form, that is, every time a code is present in an utterance, it receives a 1, and if the code is not present, it is designated a zero. Metadata is used to group utterances, e.g., a team making a series of claims or a round in which a claim occurred, while discourse codes are employed to provide a quantified, more abstract version of the utterance's content. Apart from the raw data, discourse codes, and metadata, the qualitative data table may also contain information on segmentation, i.e., ways of dividing discourse into meaningful parts. Segmentation may be performed based on metadata or other ways of grouping discourse, such as threading or theme-oriented delineation. The qualitative data table signifies a dataset where both qualitative and quantitative data can co-exist, be integrated, and be further processed in analysis and modelling.

Our Example. We decided to use a QE tool, the Reproducible Open Coding Kit (ROCK) [16], to aid us in data curation and coding. The ROCK is a standard aimed at making qualitative and QE research more transparent and machine readable, and it is implemented in an R package that enables specifying metadata, aggregating information to create the qualitative data table, and performing various analyses. The ROCK is also implemented in a graphical user interface (iROCK) that eases manual coding of text files (see below). We placed scraped data into a plain text file; each line of data contained the following: UIDs indicating the location of the claim in the debate structure (e.g., 1.1.1.2.1.), its positionality (e.g., Con), and a label for any embedded hyperlinks. In the ROCK standard, data providers are called "cases"; in this instance we considered each utterance as belonging to a different data provider, even if a single participant could have added more than one claim. In other initiatives, where participants themselves are also units of analysis, each data provider could be given an ID and utterances could be assigned to these cases. Each utterance ended with a newline character; thus, every utterance was on a separate line. Our dataset contained 66 codable lines of data from 66 cases. See Sect. 2.7 for a schematic version of our qualitative data table.

2.4 Designating Metadata

General Considerations. There are several variables that can be considered as potential ways of grouping utterances in SD. Metadata for online SD data could potentially include timestamps, participant IDs, number of comments added to claims, number of edits made to claims, number of views a claim receives, number of children a claim has, its positionality, and any other type of value the online platform or the researcher assigns to specific claims or debates.

Positionality. Pro/con positions hold a different meaning depending on platform and debate structure. For round-based platforms (such as eDeb8), the position of each participant is assigned prior to the discussion. It is therefore reasonable to assume that the content of each utterance by the participant will be consistent with the assigned position. Conversely, in the case of online branching SD (such as Kialo or Debate-Map), a student may take on several viewpoints, may be against the initial claim, but support several child claims, or vice-versa. Thus, the positionality of a claim to both its parent and to the initial claim is crucial in understanding claims and stances of individual participants, diverging/converging viewpoints, and in mapping discourse structure on a grander scale. Positionality can be represented as metadata; in this case, each claim may receive a categorical value "pro" or "con" and this may be used to group utterances in the corpus. If both the relationship to the initial claim, as well as the relationship to the parent (in instances when these two differ) is of interest, these can constitute separate variables in metadata.

Our Example. In the ROCK standard, metadata that are characteristics of data providers are called attributes. We decided to designate the following attributes to each case: *case ID* (cid; label was almost identical to UID), claim's *relation to its parent* (PC; pro/con), claim's *relation to initial claim* (APC; pro/con), *alignment* of relation to parent and initial claim (align; "concordance" = if both pro or both con / "discordance" if mixed pro and con), number of *children* (child; claims directly stemming from claim), number of *descendants* (desc; all succeeding claims). Case IDs were placed into the discourse in their respective lines in a format that enabled the ROCK to process other attributes describing the same case. The chosen attributes were utilized to represent information relevant to our research questions: relation to parent and initial claim, as well as alignment all gave us information about positionality, whereas number of children and descendants supplied metadata on segmentation and threading (see Sect. 2.6 below).

2.5 Discourse Code Development and Coding

General Considerations. Discourse codes are typically used in qualitative research to capture elements of interest within discourse for later exploration and possible aggregation [17, 18]. Endless possibilities exist for defining discourse codes and they are ultimately determined by the research questions. Some codes may represent a more literal aspect of the data, such as the code "vaccine" in the case of a debate on herd immunization. In developing such codes (as with any kind of code), researchers should be mindful of the granularity they wish to represent. In SD, granularity may manifest in common themes associated with pro and con arguments; if these themes are captured in a label and definition that allows for coding regardless of positionality, it may act as a foundation upon which the two sides can be compared and contrasted regarding how a particular piece of content is being employed to make an argument. For example, instead of just indicating the general topic of "vaccine", one might develop a code e.g., "vaccine efficacy" which could traverse positionality and be employed in arguments that are both for and against the initial claim. Codes in isolation will rarely describe claim content accurately [17, 18]; code co-occurrences, on the other hand, offer a way to capture what distinguishes a pro and con claim. Other potential discourse codes include those that encapsulate ways in which an argument is made in terms of rhetorical devices (e.g., logos, pathos, ethos), type of reasoning (e.g., inductive or deductive), logical fallacies (e.g., circular argument, false dilemma, ad hominem), and so on. Additionally, forms of evidence brought to support a claim (e.g., empirical, testimonial, anecdotal, analogical) may be of interest regarding SD as well.

Relevance. In branching debates, where an initial claim can have any number of descendants, the content of claims may have different relationships to the initial claim, depending on which generation they belong to. The content of the initial claim will most likely be closest to its children and grandchildren; as one inspects generations farther from the initial claim, their content may be vastly different. Using the example above, first generation claims may be making arguments about vaccine efficacy, while later generations are formulating opinions on vitamins and nutrition. On many online platforms, debates are allowed to branch out organically into related topics. Depending on the research question and the code system, this may mean that other discourse codes need to be developed, or this "distance" to the initial claim needs to be represented in some other way.

Our Example. We developed codes that aimed to denote the literal content of claims (n = 3) and types of evidence brought to support an argument (n = 3). Content codes relied on the nature of the claim's discourse whereas evidence codes were more related to the presence of supporting sources being linked to the claim. These were developed in several phases: 1) four researchers inspected the dataset and performed free, inductive coding on the corpus; 2) these tentative codes were triangulated; and 3) a final coding scheme was created. The final version of these codes was applied to the corpus deductively via synchronous social moderation with the aid of iROCK. Another code was developed to express "distance" from the content of the initial claim; the code Relevance was expressed on a scale of 1 to 3, one being the most relevant (based on the debate's description available on the online platform and also based on the content of the initial claim), and 3 being the least relevant (content did not contain topics, themes expressed in the debate description and initial claim). This was a single code that could receive three different values, e.g.: [[Relevance||1]]. A full description of our codes can be found in our codebook available in our repository.

2.6 Discourse Segmentation

General Considerations. Segmentation entails dividing discourse into meaningful parts [7]; this process aids interpretability and performing various analyses. One such analysis involves "coding-and-counting", that is, looking at code frequencies in various segments of the data or the entire dataset, while other types of analyses may examine code co-occurrences (see below). In both these techniques, frequencies may be markedly affected by how the discourse is segmented. Segmentation delineates temporal context [19], which is defined based on several considerations. For example, in SD data, meaningful segments may be delineated by the parent – child relationship (one claim and all its children) or this may be further divided into a parent with its pro children in one segment and its con children in another. Yet another meaningful segment may be a parent claim and all its descendants, or all claims within a generation regardless of which parent they belong to. Again, positionality may play a crucial role in analysis, thus the latter two scenarios may only be meaningful if further subdivided according to positionality. Additionally, claims may retain content-based relationships with each other across parents and generations: claims are relational. A claim made further out on one branch may actually come temporally before - and inform - a claim added to a relatively shorter branch. However, since each claim is a direct response to their parent, this relationship may be more consistent and therefore significant in analyses. These differing temporal contexts can be indicated with various types of segmentation. Decisions in segmentation are highly dependent on debate structure and aims of research. Figure 1 contains different forms of segmentation for "round-based" debates, which may all be meaningful in the context of e.g., a classroom SD.

Any number of "rounds" can be added to the above structure, and that would have implications on segmentation as well. Although debate structure can differ significantly when taken to an online platform, decisions concerning segmentation are very similar in offline/online and round-based/branching debates. Figure 2 displays an example of a branching debate and some possible ways of creating meaningful segments, temporal relationships among claims. Red and green nodes represent claims that were categorized as con or pro claims, respectively – both were specified in relation to their parent.

The branching nature of many online SD platforms raises two important questions: how will positionality be represented and what will constitute a meaningful segment or thread? In a debate structure where any number of child claims can be added to any claim, positionality is affected by choices in segmentation. For example, when considered as belonging to segment A, claim 11 is a pro argument; it is a child of claim 12, which disagrees with its own parent. Yet, since claim 12 disagrees with claim 13, which disagrees with the initial claim, if we consider claim 11 as part of segment B, it becomes a con because of its relation to the initial claim. Meaningful segments can be delineated by immediate family (parent and child/children, e.g., claims 1, 2, and 3), multiple generations (e.g., claims 4–6 and 10–12), or span a generation respective of or irrespective of positionality (e.g., claims 3, 6, and 9).

Our Example. Threading was designated with the ROCK standard by prepending tildes (~) to claims; the number of tildes connoted the generation to which the claim belonged, thus indicating the parent of each claim. The initial claim received no tilde, its children were indicated with one tilde, its grandchildren with two, and so on. This information was processed by the ROCK and appeared as a variable in our qualitative data table: a column containing a number from 1 to 7 for each claim.

POSSIBLE SEGMENTATION	POSITIONALITY AND ACTIVITY	DETAILS
	Affirmative opening argument	Summary of pro arguments
	Opposing opening argument	
	Affirmative argument 1	Claim backed by evidence
	Opposing argument 1	
	Recess	Confer and discuss with team
	Opposing rebuttal	Defend own claim and rebut
	Affirmative rebuttal	opposing team's claim
	Opposing closing argument	Summarize debate and make
	Affirmative closing argument	final arguments

Fig. 1. Example of structured classroom debate.

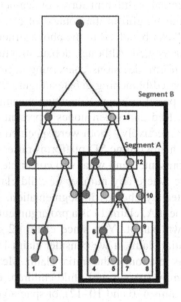

Fig. 2. Example of a simple branching debate where each parent bears only two children with opposing positions. To understand the position of Claim 9, its parent and grandparent claim must be considered. (Color figure online)

2.7   Analysis and Data Modelling

General Considerations. SD data can be analyzed and modelled in several ways. For example, approaches such as topic modelling can provide insights as to the main components of the arguments. Alternatively, research may be more interested in the ways in which participants contribute to the debate in what ways which may be best demonstrated with a social networking or integrated approach. The key affordance of QE methodology is that both qualitative and quantitative data can be represented in a unified dataset, and such a qualitative data table can be employed to perform various analyses, for example, Epistemic Network Analysis (ENA). ENA is commonly used for analyzing the structure of connections in coded data by quantifying and modeling the co-occurrence of codes as dynamic, weighted node-link networks. Such networks can be employed to compare discourse visually and statistically from individuals or groups [20]. This method has been used, for example, to analyze the development of learners' epistemic frames during play [21] and measure the co-occurrence of concepts within the conversations, topics, or activities that take place during learning [20], yet it has not been employed for SD. ENA offers insight into how codes interact in a single claim or a group of claims to produce meaning; code co-occurrences can be aggregated to scrutinize patterns in claim content or debate structure.

Aggregation. To employ ENA as an analytical tool, discourse codes, metadata, and segmentation need to be aggregated in a systematic manner. Each utterance (claim) receives its own row in this data table, while metadata appears in separate columns in categorical form. Segmentation is represented in one or more columns, as a number indicating temporal context or threading, which allows for utterances to be grouped together. Discourse codes are represented in binary form in separate columns; if a code manifests in a particular claim, it receives a 1, if it does not, it is designated a zero. We employed the ROCK R package to aggregate the above information as illustrated in Table 1.

Table 1. The schematic version of our Qualitative data table.

UID	CID	PC	APC	ALIGN	LEVEL	CHILD	DESC	DISCOURSE CODE 1	DISCOURSE CODE 2	DISCOURSE CODE 3
1.1	1_1	Pro	Pro	Concord	2	3	10	0	0	1
1.1.1	1_1_1	Con	Pro	Discord	3	2	4	1	1	0
1.1.1.1	1_1_1_1	Pro	Con	Discord	4	1	1	0	1	0

Model Parameterization. To produce networks with ENA, several parameters need to be specified, which depend on what the researcher intends to model and how. The parameter "unit" operationalizes who or what a network is produced for, e.g., individual or groups of data providers (cases). In our example, each claim originated from a separate case. However, if we had collected data from a classroom debate, for example, where data providers belong to distinct teams, several claims could originate from a single case. Alternatively, other forms of segmentation can be employed to model the interaction of discourse codes: a family (parent claim and its children) or a generation (level) in a debate structure can constitute a unit. Any form of segmentation or any piece of metadata can potentially be designated as a unit for which a network can be generated. Temporal context is operationalized by the model parameter "conversation"; this determines the segment(s) of discourse where code co-occurrences can take place, i.e., which lines of discourse are grouped together. Again, any form of segmentation or piece of metadata can constitute a conversation. Co-occurrences among discourse codes are accumulated in ENA by a "stanza window", which specifies how co-occurrences are computed. In our example, we utilized a "whole conversation" stanza window for our aggregation approach and applied it to individual levels; this aggregated code co-occurrences across all cases in each level (our conversations). We chose this because we were particularly interested in how the claims that were further from the central claim varied, not in their connection to their parent (which would lean more towards a threaded approach). If one was more interested in the development of discourse over time and believed that the conversation built on itself, an infinite or moving stanza might be more appropriate.

Model Generation. We created several models to visualize our data regarding our research questions on content, structure, and positionality. Figure 3 shows the interaction of discourse codes related to the literal content of claims and types of evidence brought to support an argument (n = 6). Levels of debate structure constituted our units as well as our conversations; co-occurrences were accumulated with a weighted whole conversation stanza window.

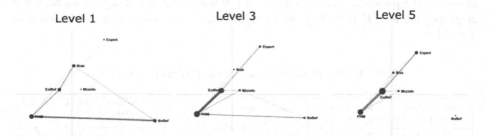

Fig. 3. ENA models of discourse across three labels of debate. Nodes reference codes whereas edges note the frequency of co-occurrence between the connected codes. Level 1 shows greater connections between the two bottommost codes whereas Level 5 shows codes concentrated to the leftmost x-axis and positive y-axis.

As depicted in these models, levels closer to the initial claim exhibited more connections among content codes, while later generations (more distant descendants of the initial claim) made less connections. Interestingly, the likelihood of a participant backing their claim with an external reference (as opposed to not employing such evidence) became higher in later generations.

We also modeled positionality on various levels of discourse. Figure 4 depicts how frequently autogenic pro and con claims aligned with their relation to the initial claim.

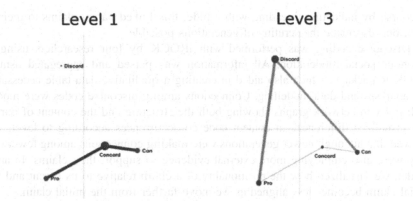

Fig. 4. A comparison of position and relationship to the initial claim on level 1 and level 3.

Figure 4 shows that on the first level (i.e., children of the initial claim), user designated pro and con claims aligned with their relation to the initial claim ("concord"), that is, claims which were e.g., against their parent, were also against the initial claim. By level three, more misalignment ("discord") can be observed, as positionality with respect to the initial claim changes because of con arguments in the second level "re-positioning" their child claims.

3   Discussion

We aimed to map the affordances and challenges of taking a quantitative ethnographic approach to scrutinizing SD discourse. We discussed general considerations and worked examples in the domain of formulating feasible research questions, collecting and curating SD data, designating metadata, performing coding and segmentation, as well as analyzing and modelling the data. Our process description suggests that research questions answerable with SD discourse are primarily those comparing two viewpoints regarding the same initial claim, although online platforms may provide a venue for organic debate branching into other subject areas as well. Our research questions included mapping the content, structure, and positionality of SD discourse on an online platform enabling branching debate.

To begin, we curated a dataset containing 66 claims, including the one initial claim dictated by the debate creators; these were considered as originating from 66 different data providers (cases). We considered each claim as our smallest unit of segmentation (utterance), each claim received a unique identifier and was appended a newline character in a text file. We designated the following metadata (attributes): case ID (cid), positionality relative to parent (PC), positionality relative to initial claim (APC), alignment of the latter two attributes (concord/discord), number of children, and number of descendants. We developed discourse codes to capture the literal content and type of argumentation used in a claim, as well as indicate the relevance of utterances relative to the debate description and content of the initial claim. We segmented discourse by indicating threading with a tilde; this linked parent claims to their children, but also made the scrutiny of generations possible.

Discourse coding was performed with iROCK by four researchers using synchronous social moderation. All information was parsed and aggregated using the ROCK R package, which also aided in creating a qualitative data table necessary for QE analyses and data modelling. Connections among discourse codes were modelled with ENA in network graphs showing both the structure and the content of our data. We visualized differences in content code co-occurrences according to level, which showed that although newer generations were making connections among fewer codes, they were also employing more external evidence to support their claims. In another model, we visualized how the positionality of a claim relative to its parent and to the initial claim becomes less aligned as we move farther from the initial claim.

Our process description aimed to highlight unique characteristics of SD discourse and how those can be addressed within a QE framework. Among these features are positionality, relevance, and threading. Positionality presents an issue analogous to sentiment analysis; in the latter technique, an algorithm tags pieces of content as "positive", "negative", or "neutral" [22]. Yet, in the case of branching SD on an online platform, a dataset can contain two manners of categorization: one pertaining to the claim's relation to its parent and one to the initial claim, and these two may not be aligned. Continuing with the analogy, it is like retaining two sets of sentiments for each utterance, and in many cases, the utterance may be labeled as e.g., both a "positive" and a "negative" sentiment. Which is true? They are both accurate categorizations of positionality, and either one's primacy will depend on how relational context is operationalized, which in turn is founded on the research question in focus.

Another consideration central to SD discourse is that of overall claim relevance. Although code development for most corpuses involves the same challenge - utilizing codes that capture discourse content well considering research aims - SD discourse does present a unique aspect. Since SD-related research questions will most likely involve comparing two key viewpoints on the same initial claim, branching debate structures where discussion can evolve organically into a plethora of topics poses a challenge for both inductive (bottom-up) and deductive (top-down) coding. It is difficult to develop a code structure that covers all pertinent components of branching SD discourse content, and most likely such code structures become large and unwieldy. Deductive coding (that is, using a limited, predetermined set of codes on the corpus) on the other hand, may lead to analyses that do not capture content to the desired extent.

Lastly, albeit SD is not the only source of threaded data, it does exhibit unique characteristics compared to e.g., more salient social media data (Twitter, Facebook, Reddit). Common to all these threaded data is the endeavor of determining temporal context, i.e., contextualizing an utterance: how far do we need to trace back in the data to understand an utterance and provide context for it? In Facebook data, for example, a comment can be contextualized within a thread (post and all comments), but a comment may have replies just pertaining to that comment, which may warrant a segmentation of its own. Yet branching SD data inspired the question of whether temporal context can span across a generation (children from multiple parents), which in Facebook data would mean contextualizing a comment-and-reply together with other comments-and-replies from under different posts. Thus, although segmentation frequently poses a challenge, and threaded data is quite common, debates, especially online branching debates, introduce new questions in this domain.

4 Concluding Remarks

QE is a growing community of researchers interested in bridging a methodological gap between quantitative, qualitative, and mixed-methods researchers. The ubiquity of SD to varied settings supports the notion that it is not a matter of *if* QE researchers will encounter such discourse, but rather *when*. In this paper, we aimed to provide a framework of considerations for researchers as they undertake analysis of this type of discourse.

While these decisions were sensical for the dataset we sought to explore, there are more potential aggregation and display methods yet to be explored in the QE community. Each new development allows for expanded analytical opportunities for researchers, and it is here that we are excited to see the community grow. New digital environments will continue to develop in response to business, educational, and social demands, especially in a post-Covid era trying to navigate new-found freedoms of distance working, learning, and collaboration. As we continue to push on our own methods with novel data formats and sources, we will continue to refine our processes.

Acknowledgements. We would like to acknowledge the International Society for Quantitative Ethnography for their work in building a community which brought the authors together for the 2nd COVID Data Challenge.

References

1. Katzenstein, G.: The debate on structured debate: toward a unified theory. Organ. Behav. Hum. Decis. Process. **66**, 316–332 (1996). https://doi.org/10.1006/obhd.1996.0059
2. Cariñanos-Ayala, S., Arrue, M., Zarandona, J., Labaka, A.: The use of structured debate as a teaching strategy among undergraduate nursing students: a systematic review Nurse Educ. Today **98**, 104766 (2021). https://doi.org/10.1016/j.nedt.2021.104766
3. Healey, R.L.: The power of debate: reflections on the potential of debates for engaging students in critical thinking about controversial geographical topics. J. Geogr. High. Educ. **36**, 239–257 (2012). https://doi.org/10.1080/03098265.2011.619522
4. Sridhar, D., Getoor, L., Walker, M.: Collective stance classification of posts in online debate forums. In: Proceedings of the Joint Workshop on Social Dynamics and Personal Attributes in Social Media, pp. 109–117. Association for Computational Linguistics, Baltimore, Maryland (2014). https://doi.org/10.3115/v1/W14-2715
5. McElfresh, J.: Spirited: A Web Application for Structured Debate. http://nrs.harvard.edu/urn-3:HUL.InstRepos:33797385
6. McGreevy, P.D., et al.: The use of a virtual online debating platform to facilitate student discussion of potentially polarising topics. Animals (Basel). **7**, 68 (2017). https://doi.org/10.3390/ani7090068
7. Williamson Shaffer, D.: Quantitative Ethnography. Cathcart Press, Madison (2017)

8. Barany, A., Shah, M., Foster, A.: Connecting curricular design and student identity change: an epistemic network analysis. In: Ruis, A.R., Lee, S.B. (eds.) ICQE 2021. CCIS, vol. 1312, pp. 155–169. Springer, Cham (2021). https://doi.org/10.1007/978-3-030-67788-6_11

9. Nachtigall, V., Sung, H.: Students' collaboration patterns in a productive failure setting: an epistemic network analysis of contrasting cases. In: Eagan, B., Misfeldt, M., Siebert-Evenstone, A. (eds.) ICQE 2019. CCIS, vol. 1112, pp. 165–176. Springer, Cham (2019). https://doi.org/10.1007/978-3-030-33232-7_14

10. Hamilton, E., Hobbs, W.: Epistemic frames and political discourse modeling. In: Ruis, A.R., Lee, S.B. (eds.) ICQE 2021. CCIS, vol. 1312, pp. 32–46. Springer, Cham (2021). https://doi.org/10.1007/978-3-030-67788-6_3

11. Cho, K.-L., Jonassen, D.H.: The effects of argumentation scaffolds on argumentation and problem solving. ETR&D. **50**, 5–22 (2002). https://doi.org/10.1007/BF02505022

12. Musselman, E.G.: Using structured debate to achieve autonomous student discussion. Hist. Teach. **37**, 335–349 (2004). https://doi.org/10.2307/1555673

13. Bolton, E., Calderwood, A., Christensen, N., Kafrouni, J., Drori, I.: High quality real-time structured debate generation. arXiv:2012.00209 [cs] (2020)

14. Mitchell, R.E.: Web scraping with Python: collecting data from the modern web (2018)

15. Krotov, V., Redd, L., Silva, L.: Legality and ethics of web scraping, Communications of the Association for Information Systems (forthcoming). Communications of the Association for Information Systems (2020)

16. Zörgő, S., Peters, G.-J.Y.: Epistemic Network Analysis for Semi-Structured Interviews and Other Continuous Narratives: Challenges and Insights, psyarxiv.com/j6n97

17. Saldaña, J.: The Coding Manual for Qualitative Researchers. SAGE, Los Angeles (2013)

18. Shaffer, D.W., Ruis, A.R.: How we code. In: Ruis, A.R., Lee, S.B. (eds.) ICQE 2021. CCIS, vol. 1312, pp. 62–77. Springer, Cham (2021). https://doi.org/10.1007/978-3-030-67788-6_5

19. Siebert-Evenstone, A.L., Arastoopour, G., Collier, W., Swiecki, Z., Ruis, A., Williamson Shaffer, D.: In search of conversational grain size: modelling semantic structure using moving Stanza windows. J. Learn. Anal. **4**, 123–139 (2017). https://doi.org/10.18608/jla.2017.43.7

20. Williamson Shaffer, D., Collier, W., Ruis, A.: A tutorial on epistemic network analysis: analyzing the structure of connections in cognitive, social, and interaction data. J. Learn. Anal. **3**, 9–45 (2016). https://doi.org/10.18608/jla.2016.33.3

21. Scianna, J., Gagnon, D., Knowles, B.: Counting the game: visualizing changes in play by incorporating game events. In: Ruis, A.R., Lee, S.B. (eds.) ICQE 2021. CCIS, vol. 1312, pp. 218–231. Springer, Cham (2021). https://doi.org/10.1007/978-3-030-67788-6_15

22. Misiejuk, K., Scianna, J., Kaliisa, R., Vachuska, K., Shaffer, D.W.: Incorporating sentiment analysis with epistemic network analysis to enhance discourse analysis of Twitter data. In: Ruis, A.R., Lee, S.B. (eds.) ICQE 2021. CCIS, vol. 1312, pp. 375–389. Springer, Cham (2021). https://doi.org/10.1007/978-3-030-67788-6_26

The Expected Value Test: A New Statistical Warrant for Theoretical Saturation

Zachari Swiecki(✉) ⓘ

Monash University, Melbourne, Australia
zach.swiecki@monash.edu

Abstract. The basic goal of quantitative ethnography (QE) is to use statistics to warrant theoretical saturation. In QE studies that use epistemic network analysis (ENA), statistical comparisons between two or more samples are often used as warrants. However, no standard quantitative techniques have been developed to provide warrants absent of differences between samples—e.g., for the data overall or for particular individuals in the data. In this paper, I introduce the expected value test (EVT), a technique for finding statistical warrants for single samples in the context of ENA-based QE analyses. Building on the concepts of agreement due to chance and randomization, the EVT generates a distribution of networks whose edge weights approximate the expected value of the edge weights due to chance. Using these distributions affords tests of statistical significance been observed networks and chance-based networks. These tests provide warrants that connections observed qualitatively and measured by ENA are theoretically saturated.

Keywords: Quantitative ethnographic methods · Epistemic network analysis · One-sample tests · Cohen's kappa · Randomization tests

1 Introduction

Quantitative ethnography (QE) is a system of reasoning that uses statistics to warrant claims about *theoretical saturation*—when qualitative observations constitute a meaningful pattern in some discourse [8]. These warrants are typically in reference to qualitative and quantitative differences between two or more samples, for example differences between the discourse patterns of control and treatment groups.

However, in many cases, researchers may not be able to, or do not wish to, compare samples. Instead, they can or want to say something about the data overall, one group, or one particular individual. For example, perhaps they only have qualitative data on one class of students with no meaningful subgroups. Or, they are more interested in *describing* the discourse patterns of individuals rather than using those patterns to *predict* whether individuals behave more like one group or another. Unfortunately, there are no standard quantitative techniques for warranting theoretical saturation in the context of QE for situations like these.

In this paper, I introduce a novel technique—the expected value test (EVT)—that addresses this limitation of QE. The technique works by generating data that simulates random connections in the discourse. Models produced from this simulated discourse

© Springer Nature Switzerland AG 2022
B. Wasson and S. Zörgő (Eds.): ICQE 2021, CCIS 1522, pp. 49–65, 2022.
https://doi.org/10.1007/978-3-030-93859-8_4

can then be compared to the model produced from the observed discourse. If the observed model is found to be statistically significantly different from the random models, there is evidence that the connections present in the discourse are not produced at random, but instead are a systematic property of the discourse. In turn, there is evidence that these connections are theoretically saturated. Here, I describe the EVT and use it to warrant that observed connections in the discourse of military teams are theoretically saturated.

2 Background

2.1 Saturation

The grounded theory perspective on qualitative analysis argues that theoretical saturation is the point at which researchers repeatedly find similar instances of the same phenomena of interest; it is the point at which further analysis would reveal nothing new [4]. As Shaffer describes, "the basic idea of Quantitative Ethnography is simple: Use statistics to warrant theoretical saturation in qualitative analyses," [8] (pg. 393). Statistics—specifically, significance tests—warrant theoretical saturation because they give evidence that a particular observation is not simply a random property of the sample we have, but a pattern in the larger population of data we could sample from—in other words, if we were to continue to sample data, we would see the same things over and over again. In QE, statistics typically come in two forms: significant interrater reliability measures, such as Cohen's kappa and Shaffer's rho, and significant parameters from epistemic network analysis (ENA), such as differences between ENA scores [8]. This paper is concerned with the later kind of statistics.

In a standard QE analysis using ENA, researchers develop qualitative interpretations about the connections that individuals or groups make in their discourse. They then analyze the discourse using ENA, which quantifies connections in a particular way. ENA produces parameters that can be tested using well-known statistical methods.[1] For example, this was the process that my colleagues and I used to analyze the discourse of military teams in training [11].

In that study, which compared individuals in treatment and control conditions, our qualitative analysis found that treatment individuals tended to respond to information with decisions, and control individuals tended to respond to information by seeking information—that is, asking questions. To statistically warrant these claims, we analyzed the data using ENA. The ENA dimension that accounted for the biggest difference between treatment and control individuals distinguished them in terms of connections to decisions versus connections to seeking information. Using the average ENA scores for individuals in each condition on this dimension, we conducted Mann-Whitney tests and found that treatment individuals made significantly more connections to decisions and control individuals made significantly more connections to seeking information. This result provided a statistical warrant for our original qualitative claims.

---

[1] Crucially, though less important to the arguments in this paper, researchers also *close the interpretive loop*—that is, they judge whether their qualitative interpretations align with the quantitative results.

2.2 Samples

As the example above highlights, our statistical warrant came in the form of a significant difference between two groups, or *samples*, of individuals. Such comparisons between samples are common statistical warrants in ENA-based QE analyses [1, 5, 10, 12]. However, in cases where researchers wish to say something about the connections that an individual or group made absent of the differences from others, the appropriate statistical test to use is less clear. Given some ENA-based parameter about one individual or one group of individuals or the ENA model overall, what statistical warrant should be used?

This question is not a new one in the field of statistics. Essentially, it is the difference between a one-sample and a two-sample test. Like the analysis of military teams, many ENA-based approaches to QE use two-sample tests to warrant qualitative claims. In their most basic form, the parameter difference between the samples (say the difference between mean ENA scores on a particular dimension) is calculated and that differences is compared to zero. One-sample tests work similarly, however, differences between samples cannot be calculated, so the difference between a parameter on the sample is compared to some other meaningful value. In many cases, this value is zero—if it is significantly different from zero, then some difference is actually there—but the meaning of zero may differ from test to test. Cohen's kappa provides one such example.

2.3 Chance

Cohen's kappa is a widely applied statistic for measuring inter-rater reliability—the extent to which two raters make similar categorizations of data [2]. In the learning sciences and other fields, kappa is used to measure the agreement between two process of assigning qualitative codes to data. Often, these processes are done by human raters, but in other cases they may be automated. Regardless of who or what codes the data, kappa measures how often the two raters agree.

Importantly, however, the kappa statistic differs from simply calculating the number of cases in which the raters agree divided by the total number of cases—percent agreement. It is possible that the two raters may agree simply due to chance—for example, if both raters randomly assigned codes to the data, we would likely find that their assignments agreed some of the time. To account for this, the kappa calculation incorporates the expected level of agreement due to chance. The outcome of this correction is a statistic whose zero value corresponds to the level of chance agreement. One way in which Cohen's kappa is meaningful, then, is the extent to which it measures a pattern that is different from what we would expect due to chance.[2]

---

[2] Another way in which Cohen's kappa is meaningful is the extent to which it generalizes, which is addressed by Shaffer's rho.

The expected value test (EVT) draws inspiration from Cohen's kappa in the sense that it suggests a meaningful value to which we can compare an ENA-based parameter for a single sample. Just as two-raters might agree on their ratings by chance—that is, their rating values may co-occur frequently—individuals may make connections between concepts at random. As a thought experiment, say we took a transcribed and coded conversation between two friends and shuffled the codes and order of talk—that is, we simulated a scenario where *when* a person talks and *what* they talk about is not based on their interaction with others. If we found that the connections we observed in the real conversation and the connections we observed in the simulated conversation were the same (or very similar) it would cast doubt on the claim that the two friends were meaningfully responding to one another. In statistical terms, our observations would be common under the null hypothesis of randomization. In other words, our claims about this conversation would be statistically unwarranted.

This example illustrates the basic idea of the EVT: compare an ENA parameter value for a sample to the value we would expect that parameter to take if the connections in the discourse were occurring due to chance alone.

2.4   Related Work

The randomization process of the EVT builds upon work done by Csanadi and colleagues [3]. In their study, they sought to test whether the temporal ordering of the discourse was meaningful. To do so, they compared an ENA model produced from an observed dataset to an ENA model produced from a dataset in which they randomized the order of the lines. The EVT extends this randomization process in two important ways.

First, Csanadi and colleagues only randomized the order of the lines. This is appropriate for testing whether the temporal nature of the data is important, but it is not sufficient for testing whether the connections in the discourse are theoretically saturated. In co-occurrence-based models like ENA, it matters where the discourse occurs because connections are identified within particular segments of discourse and may form between an individual's lines and the lines of others. However, connections may also form within single lines. Simply reordering the lines ignores the impact of within line connections.[3] So, even if the order of the lines are randomized, systematic patterns of connections may still be present. To achieve the effect of chance-based co-occurrences, we therefore need to randomize the presence or absence of the codes in the discourse as well as the order of the lines.

Second, to produce a model with which to investigate the importance of line order, Csanadi and colleagues randomized the dataset *once* and then compared the original ENA model to the model created from the randomized data. They did so by testing for

---

[3] In the coded data examined by Csanadi and colleagues, each line could be coded for only one code, therefore this issue did not apply to their data. However, in other contexts, multiple codes may be assigned to the same line.

statistical differences between the original and random networks in the low-dimensional space produced by ENA. While this method is adequate for demonstrative purposes, it has two important limitations. First, by randomizing only once, it ignores the variation that may be present between different random datasets. Second, by comparing the networks in the lowdimensional space, the method tests for differences between summaries of the networks and not their overall structure. This means that other potentially important differences (or similarities) between the observed and random networks might be missed. The EVT addresses both of these issues by creating a *distribution* of chance-based networks and making statistical comparisons between the *complete networks*, rather than their low-dimensional projections.

2.5 Research Questions

To demonstrate the EVT, I used it to address the research question: RQ1—Does the EVT suggest that the connections observed in the discourse of military teams are theoretically saturated? Furthermore, because any reliable test should identify situations where the test passes and where it fails, I also address the research question: RQ2—Can the EVT suggest when observed connections are theoretically saturated and when they are not? In other words, to provide statistical warrants for claims about theoretical saturation regarding single samples, I used the EVT to test whether the connections observed overall in these data were significantly different from chance. To examine the discriminatory power of the technique, I used it to test whether the connections observed for specific individuals were significantly different from chance.

The data used here have been analyzed multiple times from a QE perspective (e.g., see [11]). Each of these prior analyses suggested that the observed connections in the discourse were theoretically saturated. The warrants for these claims were in-depth qualitative analyses of the data, quantitative results that suggest that different groups of individuals made different patterns of connections, and alignment between the qualitative and quantitative results. However, no quantitative warrants have been provided for the connections observed in the data overall, or for particular individuals in these data. The EVT was designed to provide such warrants.

3 Methods

3.1 Data

Data from air defense warfare (ADW) teams was collected as part of the Tactical Decision Making Under Stress project [6]. 94 individuals in 16 teams participated in simulated scenarios to test the impact of a decision-support system (DSS) and teamwork training on team performance. During the scenarios, teams performed the *detect-to-engage sequence*, which entailed using computer-based tools to detect and identify ships and aircraft in the vicinity—referred to as *tracks*—assess whether they were threats and decide whether to respond with warnings or combat orders.

Each team consisted of six officers assigned to particular roles. Two officers held command roles and four held supporting roles. The command roles were the

Commanding Officer (CO) and the Tactical Action Officer (TAO). They were responsible for making tactical decisions, such as when to warn or engage tracks. Support roles were the Identification Supervisor (IDS), the Air Warfare Coordinator (ADWC), the Tactical Information Coordinator (TIC), and the Electronic Warfare Supervisor (EWS). They were responsible for reporting critical information to commanders, such as the detection of threats, their identification—for example, whether the threat was a jet, ship, or helicopter—and their behavior— for example, their speed and location relative to the warship.

During the training scenarios, team members communicated via an open-channel radio system. The dataset analyzed here consists of transcripts of team talk that were segmented for analysis by turn of talk for a total of 12,027 turns.

3.2   Coding

The transcripts were labelled for the presence or absence of the codes described in Table 1. These codes were developed, validated, and applied to the data as part of a prior analysis [11]. The coding scheme was validated using Cohen's kappa and Shaffer's rho as part of a process that compared the ratings of two human raters with automated classifiers. The automated classifiers were validated using the standard threshold for kappa (>.65) and a rho threshold of <0.05. All pairwise combinations of raters (humans and automated classifier) achieved kappa >0.83 and rho (0.65) <0.05.

Table 1. Codes, definitions, and examples.

Code	Definition	Example
Detection	Talk about radar detection of a track or the identification of a track, (e.g., vessel type)	IR/EW NEW BEARING, BEARING 078 APQ120 CORRELATES TRACK 7036 POSSIBLE F-4
Track behavior	Talk about kinematic data about a track or a track's location	AIR/IDS TRACK NUMBER 7021 DROP IN ALTITUDE TO 18 THOUSAND FEET
Assessment	Talk about whether a track is friendly or hostile, the threat level of a track, or indicating tracks of interest	TRACKS OF INTEREST 7013 LEVEL 5 7037 LEVEL 5 7007 LEVEL 4 TRACK 7020 LEVEL 5 AND 7036 LEVEL 5
Status updates	Talk about procedural information, e.g., track responses, or talk about tactical actions taken by the team	TAO ID, STILL NO RESPONSE FROM TRACK 37, POSSIBLE PUMA HELO
Seeking information	Asking questions regarding track behavior, identification, or status	TAO CO, WE'VE UPGRADED THEM TO LEVEL 7 RIGHT?

(*continued*)

Table 1. (*continued*)

Code	Definition	Example
Recommendation	Recommending or requesting tactical actions	AIR/TIC RECOMMEND LEVEL THREE ON TRACK 7016 7022
Deterrent orders	Giving orders meant to warn or deter tracks	TIC AIR, CONDUCT LEVEL 2 WARNING ON 7037
Defensive orders	Giving orders to prepare defenses or engage hostile tracks	TAO/CO COVER 7016 WITH BIRDS

3.3   Analysis

The EVT includes the following main steps, which are described in more detail below:

1. Generate a model from the observed data.
2. Generate a distribution of models from data in which the codes and lines have been repeatedly randomized—that is, a distribution of chance-based models.
3. Calculate the similarity of the observed model to the average, or *centroid*, of the chance-based models. Calculate the distribution of similarities of the chance-based models to the centroid. Compare the observed similarity to the distribution.

Observed Model. I modeled the observed data using the R implementation of ENA [7]. ENA uses a moving window to construct a network for each line in the data, here defined as each turn of talk. Edges in the network are defined as the co-occurrence between codes in the current line and codes within the window, operationalized as a specific number of prior lines. To create networks for individuals, ENA aggregates the networks associated with their lines and normalizes this aggregated network. ENA represents each individual's network visually as a weighted network graph in which the nodes correspond to codes, and the edges are the normalized rate of co-occurrence between the codes.[4] These networks can be plotted and subtracted from other networks to show the connections that are stronger in one network relative to the other.

Distribution of Chance-Based Models. To create a distribution of chance-based models, the EVT constructs multiple simulated datasets based on the frequency of talk for each individual in the data and the frequency of their code occurrences. Figure 1 provides an overview of this process. Given the observed data, for each conversation, the EVT algorithm splits the data by each unique unit of analysis. For each unit, the algorithm then shuffles their code values by code. Next, the data is recombined in the original order in which the lines of data occurred. Finally, the line order is randomized. The effect of this process is to simulate situations in which these units randomly

---

[4] Typically, ENA also performs a dimensional reduction on the collection of normalized and centered networks via singular value decomposition. However, the analysis presented here focused on the complete networks rather than their projections in a low dimensional space.

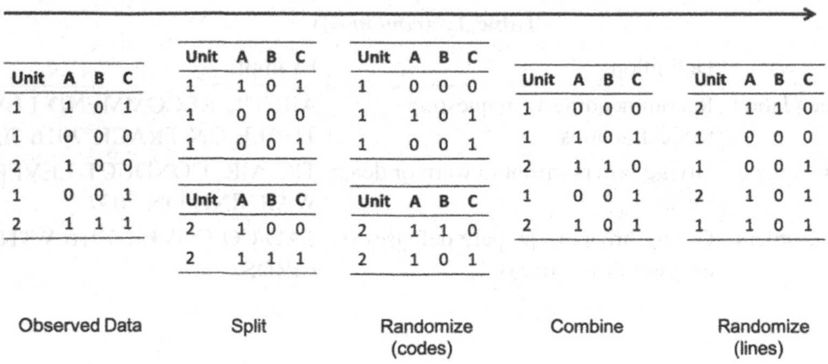

Observed Data			
Unit	A	B	C
1	1	0	1
1	0	0	0
2	1	0	0
1	0	0	1
2	1	1	1

Split

Unit	A	B	C
1	1	0	1
1	0	0	0
1	0	0	1

Unit	A	B	C
2	1	0	0
2	1	1	1

Randomize (codes)

Unit	A	B	C
1	0	0	0
1	1	0	1
1	0	0	1

Unit	A	B	C
2	1	1	0
2	1	0	1

Combine

Unit	A	B	C
1	0	0	0
1	1	0	1
2	1	1	0
1	0	0	1
2	1	0	1

Randomize (lines)

Unit	A	B	C
2	1	1	0
1	0	0	0
1	0	0	1
2	1	0	1
1	1	0	1

Fig. 1. Overview of the EVT randomization process.

produced coded discourse—for example, if they randomly chose when to speak and what to speak about given their overall talk and code frequencies in a given conversation. Due to the stochastic nature of the process, the simulation is repeated a large number of times—here, 1000 times. For each of the randomized datasets, an ENA model is created using the same specifications used for the observed model. This produces a distribution of chance-based ENA models.

Significance Testing. Constructing an ENA model from the observed data and a distribution of models from the randomized data affords a statistical comparison between the observed model and the chance-based models. Broadly, this comparison involves calculating the centroid (average) of the chance-based models. Next, the similarity of the observed model to the centroid is calculated. Additionally, the similarity of each chance-based model to the centroid is calculated. This last step yields a distribution of similarity metrics under the null hypothesis that the connections identified in the models were due to chance. In other words, if the connections were due to chance alone, this is the distribution of similarities between models we would see. If the similarity of the observed model to the centroid is greater than 95% of the values in this distribution, we reject the null. That is, with a type I error rate of 0.05, we conclude that the observed model is significantly different than chance.

In general, then, the EVT is simply an empirical hypothesis test. It empirically generates the null hypothesis distribution rather than assuming it has a particular form (as is done in parametric tests) and the p value is calculated as the number of observations in the null hypothesis distribution that are more extreme than the test statistic—here, the similarity between the observed model and the chance-based centroid.

More formally, let the normalized network for unit i using the observed data be $\mathbf{v}^i$ for $i = 1, \ldots, m$, where m is the number of units of analysis, and let the normalized network for unit i using randomized data j be $\mathbf{v}_j^{*i}$ for $j = 1, \ldots, n$, where n is the total number of randomized datasets. $\mathbf{v}^i$ and $\mathbf{v}_j^{*i}$ are both vectors where each element of the vector is the normalized co-occurrence rate for a given connection—that is, the edge weight of a given line typically represented in ENA visualizations. $\mathbf{v}^i$ is the observed model for the unit; $\mathbf{v}_j^{*i}$ is the chance-based model for the unit, given some randomized data.

Next, construct the centroid (i.e., average of the co-occurrence vectors) of the n chance-based models for a given unit: $\bar{\mathbf{v}}^{*i}$. The similarity of the observed model to this centroid is defined as the Euclidean distance between the two:

$$d^i = \left| \mathbf{v}^i - \bar{\mathbf{v}}^{*i} \right| \tag{1}$$

Likewise, the similarities of the chance-based models to the centroid for each randomized dataset j are:

$$d_j^{*i} = \left| \mathbf{v}_j^{*i} - \bar{\mathbf{v}}^{*i} \right| \tag{2}$$

Next, construct the distribution $D\left(d_1^{*i}, d_n^{*i}\right)$—that is, the distribution of distances between the chance-based models and their centroid for the ith unit. We can think of d^i, then, as the test statistic and $D\left(d_1^{*i}, d_n^{*i}\right)$ as the null hypothesis distribution. We can then calculate an empirical p value by counting the number of observations in $D\left(d_1^{*i}, d_n^{*i}\right)$ that are more extreme (greater than) d^i. If this value is less than α (here, 0.05), we conclude that the observed model is significantly different from chance.[5]

Equations (1) and (2) test whether a given *individual's* model is significantly different from their chance model. We can modify these equations to test whether the overall model (that is, the model on the entire dataset of all individuals) is significantly different from chance. To do so, we simply compute the average distance from the observed models to their centroids:

$$\bar{d} = \frac{\sum_{i=1}^m \left| \mathbf{v}^i - \bar{\mathbf{v}}^{*i} \right|}{m} \tag{3}$$

and the average distance between the chance-based models and their centroids:

$$\bar{d}_j^* = \frac{\sum_{i=1}^m \left| \mathbf{v}_j^{*i} - \bar{\mathbf{v}}^{*i} \right|}{m} \tag{4}$$

Finally, construct the distribution of average distances from the chance-based models to their centroids, $\bar{D}(\bar{d}_1^*, \bar{d}_n^*)$, and use this distribution and (3) to compute the empirical p value.

To address RQ1, I conducted a qualitative analysis of the overall ADW discourse informed by findings from my prior work [11]. I then sought a quantitative warrant for my observations using an EVT that compared the average distance of the observed models to the centroids of the chance-based models (Eq. 3) to the distribution of average distances of the chance-based models to their centroids (distribution of Eq. 4). To address RQ2, I conducted qualitative analyses of the discourse of two specific

---

[5] In this sense, the EVT is essentially an empirical version of Hoetelling's T test. However, for that test, the squared Mahalanobis distance is used in place of the Euclidean distance and a normal distribution is assumed.

individuals in the data—one whose observed model was highly *dissimilar* to chance and one whose observed model was highly *similar* to chance, as measured by Eq. 1. I conducted two separate EVTs for these individuals to determine whether their observed models differed significantly from chance. For both research questions, I compared observed and chance-based networks using network subtractions and coordinated these findings with qualitative interpretations of the data.

4   Results

4.1   RQ1

The results of the overall qualitative analysis suggested that many individuals had patterns of connections between Detection and Track Behavior and between Deterrent Orders and Detection. In the data, it was common to see individuals report information about the detection and behavior of tracks in the same line. For example, when an EWS announced to their team: "NEW TRACK AT BEARING 068 APQ120 CORRELATES TO 7036 POSSIBLE F-4," they are reporting the detection of a new track whose radar (APQ120) suggests it is a F-4 jet. Behavior information is passed as the track's location at bearing 068. Similarly, it was common in the data to see commanding officers make connections between Detection and Deterrent Orders. For example, when a TAO said: "TRACK 7036 WAS ID AS F-4. ISSUE LEVEL 2 WARNINGS TO TRACK 7036.", they passed information about the detection and identification of the track as an F-4 and immediately gave an order to issue warnings to the track. Here, warnings are deterrents that announce the presence of the warship and request that the track identify themselves and their intentions.

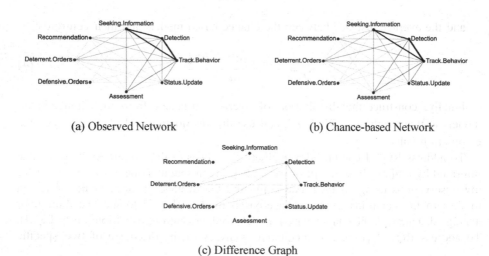

(a) Observed Network   (b) Chance-based Network

(c) Difference Graph

Fig. 2.   Network comparison for overall data.

Figure 2 shows the shows the network models for these data.[6] On the left is the observed mean network. On the right is the mean chance-based network— that is, the mean network representation of the chance-based centroids. Below is their difference graph. Here, connections in red occurred more frequently than chance and connections in blue occurred less frequently than chance. Both the observed and the chance-based networks suggest strong connections between Detection and Track Behavior and Detection and Deterrent Orders. However, the difference graph suggests that these connections (along with most others) occurred less frequently than chance.

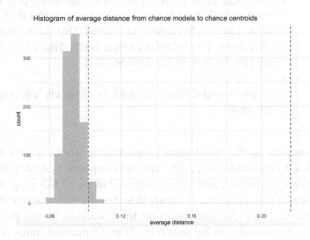

Fig. 3. Histogram of average distance from chance models to chance centroids.

The results of the EVT for the overall data are summarized in Fig. 3. The histogram shows the distribution of the average distances between the chance-based models and their centroids—that is, the null hypothesis distribution. The red dashed line marks the 95th percentile of the distribution. The black dashed line marks the value of the average distance of the observed models from the chance-based centroids (our test statistic). Because this distance is greater than 95% of the null hypothesis distribution, the EVT indicates that the observed models are significantly different from chance with an empirical p value of 0. The effect size of this difference, as measured by Cohen's d, is massive ($d = 25$). The results suggest that there is a strong pattern of connections in this discourse and the qualitative observations are theoretically saturated.

4.2   RQ2

The results of the qualitative analysis of the individual whose observed network was highly dissimilar to chance, a CO, suggests that they made systematic connections between information about potential threats and deterrent orders (see Table 2). Recall

---

[6] Because a dimensional reduction was not used to project the networks in a lowdimensional space, I have positioned the nodes of these networks in a circle to simplify their presentation.

that in ADW discourse, potentially hostile radar contacts are referred to as tracks and they are given identification numbers by the team. Also note that in these data, speakers often began their turns of talk by addressing the member(s) of the team for whom the message is intended followed by who was speaking. Thus, "CO/TAO" should be read as "CO, this is TAO."

Table 2. CO

Line	Speaker	Utterance
1	TAO	CO/TAO FOR TRACK 7002 THE LA COMBANTE DSS IS GIVING ORIGION AS EVIDINCE OF A THREAT HOWEVER IT IS COMING FROM OR-MANI UAE TERRITORIAL WATERS
2	CO	I DON'T FEEL TO COMFORTABLE WITH THAT LET ME SEE WHAT HIS RANGE IS TO THE SOUTH
3	TAO	14
4	CO	ONCE HE CLOSES INTO 10 LETS GO AHEAD AND GIVE HIM A LEVEL ONE

The excerpt begins as the TAO passes information about a new track (7002) identified as a La Combattante ship. The decision-support system (DSS) suggests classifying this track as threat based on its origin, but the TAO is questioning this classification. The CO responds (line 2) saying that they are not "comfortable" with the ship and proceeds to check the distance from their warship to the potential threat. The TAO provides the distance in the next line (3) as 14 nautical miles. Then, the CO gives a deterrent order, telling the TAO to send a "LEVEL ONE" warning to the track once the ship is within 10 nautical miles (line 4).

The excerpt illustrates that this CO made meaningful connections between their own discourse and the discourse of the team. In particular, it shows that they made tactical decisions ("GO AHEAD AND GIVE HIM A LEVEL ONE") based on information from another team member.

Figure 4 shows the network models for this individual. On the left is their observed network. On the right is their average chance-based network—that is, the network representation of their chance-based centroid. Below is their difference graph. Their observed network suggests that the CO made strong connections between Deterrent Orders and information such as Track Behavior, Assessment, and Detection. The difference graph suggests that these connections occurred more frequently than expected due to chance.

Figure 5 summarizes the results of the EVT for this individual. The black dashed line indicates that the distance between the observed model and the chance-based centroid is greater than 95% of the distances between the chance-based models and the centroid (red dashed line). Some values in the distribution do exceed the test statistic, hence the empirical p value for this test is 0.001, indicating that the observed model is significantly different from chance. The effect size of this difference is very large, $d = 6.5$. The results suggest that there is a strong pattern of connections in this individual's discourse and the qualitative observations are theoretically saturated.

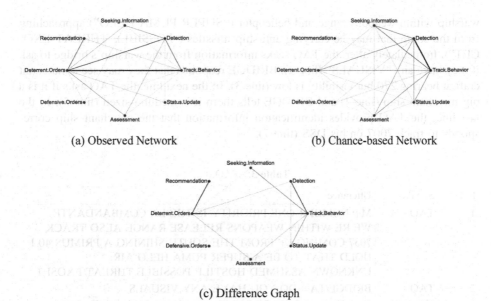

(a) Observed Network

(b) Chance-based Network

(c) Difference Graph

Fig. 4. Network comparison for CO.

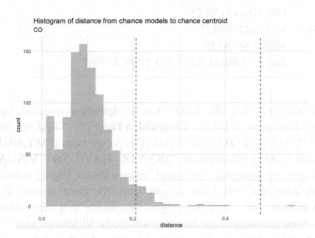

Fig. 5. Histogram of distances for CO (Color figure online).

The results of the qualitative analysis of the individual whose observed network was highly similar to chance, a TAO, suggests that they had densely connected talk (see Table 3). The excerpt begins as the TAO provides a large amount of information about their highest priority tracks: They call out a La Combattante ship that has the warship within weapons range and helicopter ("SUPER PUMA HELO") approaching from the south that may be carrying anti-ship missiles ("POSSIBLE THREAT EXO-CET"). Immediately after, the TAO seeks information from the warship's bridge to ask if they have any "VISUALS" (line 2). BRIDGE responds that they may see a merchant craft at bearing 270 but visibility is low (line 3). In the next line, the TAO asks if it is a big merchant ship (line 4) and BRIDGE tells them it is medium-sized (line 5). In the last line, the TAO provides identification information that the merchant ship corresponds to track 7007 on his DSS (line 7).

Table 3. TAO.

Line	Speaker	Utterance
1	TAO	MY NUMBER ONE PRIORITY IS THE LA COMBANDANTE WE'RE WITHIN WEAPONS RELEASE RANGE ALSO TRACK 7037 COMING UP FROM THE SOUTH SHINING A PRIMUS 40 I HOLD THAT TO BE A SUPER PUMA HELO AIR UNKNOWN ASSUMED HOSTILE POSSIBLE THREAT EXOSET
2	TAO	BRIDGE/TAO DO YOU HAVE ANY VISUALS
3	BRIDGE	TAO THIS IS BRIDGE I KIND OF MAKE OUT CONTACT BEARING 270 REAL HAZY HARD TO MAKE OUT LOOKS LIKE A POSSIBLE MERCHANT CRAFT
4	TAO	BIG MERCHANT?
5	BRIDGE	MEDIUM-SIZED
6	TAO	MEDIUM. AYE
7	TAO	THAT CORRELATES TO TRACK 7007

The excerpt illustrates that this TAO's talk is densely connected, including connections among Detection ("THAT CORRELATES TO TRACK 7007"), Track Behavior ("COMING UP FROM THE SOUTH"), Assessment ("MY NUMBER ONE PRIORITY"), and Seeking Information ("DO YOU HAVE ANY VISUALS").

Figure 6 shows the observed (left) and chance-based (right) networks for this individual. Both networks reflect the connections discussed above. The difference graph (bottom) includes only faint thin edges, suggesting that the connections in the two models occurred at similar rates. In other words, the difference graph suggests that the observed network is not very distinguishable from the chance-based network.

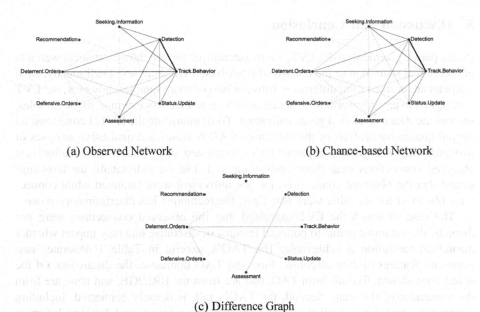

(a) Observed Network   (b) Chance-based Network

(c) Difference Graph

Fig. 6. Network comparison for TAO.

Figure 7 summarizes the results of the EVT for this TAO. The dashed lines indicate that the distance between the observed model and its chance-based centroid (black dashed line) is less than the 95% of the distances between the chance-based models and the centroid (red dashed line). In particular, the empirical p value for this test is 0.64. The EVT indicates that this individual's model is *not* significantly different from chance and suggests that the qualitative observations are not theoretically saturated.

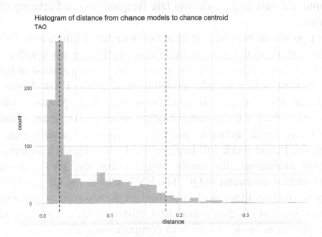

Fig. 7. Histogram of distances for TAO.

5 Discussion and Conclusion

In this paper, I introduced the EVT, a novel technique for providing statistical warrants of theoretical saturation in the context of ENA-based QE analyses. Traditionally, such warrants are derived from differences between two or more samples; however, the EVT is designed to provide warrants in situations where researchers examine single samples, such as the data overall or a given individual. To demonstrate the EVT, I conducted an overall qualitative analysis of the discourse of ADW teams and qualitative analyses of two particular individuals. Separate EVTs suggested that, overall, the qualitatively observed connections were theoretically saturated. For the individuals, the tests suggested that the observed connections for one individual were saturated while connections observed for the other were not. Thus, the technique has discriminatory power.

The case in which the EVT suggested that the observed connections were not theoretically saturated points to potential features of discourse that may impact whether theoretical saturation is achievable. The TAO's excerpt in Table 3 illustrates two important features of their discourse. First, the TAO dominates the discussion. Of the seven lines shown, five are from TAO, two are from the BRIDGE, and none are from the remainder of the team. Second, the TAO's talk is densely connected, including connections between Detection, Track Behavior, Assessment, and Seeking Information. To put these points in perspective, on average, the CO shown in Table 2 accounted for only 11% of the team's coded talk and 2% of the talk coded for two or more codes. In contrast, this TAO accounted for 36% of the team's coded talk and 20% of the talk coded for two or more codes—the highest percentages of any member of the team.

These measures suggest that highly active and densely connected individuals may be less likely to produce connections for which we can warrant theoretical saturation. In other words, individuals like this TAO may make connections that are statistically indistinguishable from random noise. This seems plausible—if an individual talks about everything all of the time, it is unlikely that they will make systematic patterns of connections. Future work will explore this hypothesis in more detail by varying features of the simulated data (e.g., code and talk frequencies) and relating those features to EVT outcomes.

The results I presented here have at least two important limitations. First, this study was based upon data collected from a single context. Future work will investigate the utility of the EVT in a variety of contexts. Second, the demonstration of the EVT relied on parameters derived from a specific modeling technique—ENA. However, the only constraint that the EVT places on models is that they produce vectors of co-occurrences. In turn, the EVT can accommodate other co-occurrence-based modeling techniques such as social network analysis, sequential pattern mining, and lag sequential analysis. Future work will explore the EVT with such techniques.

Despite these limitations, the results suggest that the EVT provides plausible warrants for theoretical saturation in QE. The EVT adds to the QE toolkit by providing a technique for warranting theoretical saturation in the absence of differences between samples. As such, it can strengthen quantitative ethnographic claims in situations where researchers are unable to or do not wish to compare samples.

References

1. Bressler, D.M., Bodzin, A.M., Eagan, B., Tabatabai, S.: Using epistemic networkanalysis to examine discourse and scientific practice during a collaborative game. J. Sci. Educ. Technol. **28**(5), 553–566 (2019)
2. Cohen, J.: A coefficient of agreement for nominal scales. Educ. Psychol. Meas. **20**, 37–46 (1960)
3. Csanadi, A., Eagan, B., Kollar, I., Shaffer, D.W., Fischer, F.: When coding-andcounting is not enough: using epistemic network analysis (ENA) to analyze verbal data in CSCL research. Int. J. Comput.-Support. Collab. Learn. **13**(4), 419–438 (2018)
4. Glaser, B., Strauss, A.: The Discovery of Grounded Theory. Aldine, Chicago (1967)
5. Hod, Y., Katz, S., Eagan, B.: Refining qualitative ethnographies using epistemic network analysis: a study of socioemotional learning dimensions in a humanistic knowledge building community. Comput. Educ. **156**, 103943 (2020)
6. Johnston, J.H., Poirier, J., Smith-Jentsch, K.A.: Decision making under stress: creating a research methodology. In: Cannon-Bowers, J.A., Salas, E. (eds.) Making Decisions Under Stress: Implications for Individual and Team Training, pp. 39–59. American Psychological Association, Washington D.C (1998)
7. Marquart, C., Swiecki, Z., Collier, W., Eagan, B., Woodward, R., Shaffer, D.W.: rENA: Epistemic Network Analysis (Version 0.2.1.2) (2018). https://cran.rstudio.com/web/packages/rENA/index.html
8. Shaffer, D.W.: Quantitative Ethnography. Cathcart Press, Madison (2017)
9. Shaffer, D.W., Collier, W., Ruis, A.R.: A tutorial on epistemic network analysis: analyzing the structure of connections in cognitive, social, and interaction data. J. Learn. Anal. **3**(3), 9–45 (2016)
10. Ruis, A.A., Rosser, A.A., Quandt-Walle, C., Nathwani, J.N., Shaffer, D.W., Pugh, C.M.: The hands and head of a surgeon: modeling operative competency with multimodal epistemic network analysis. Am. J. Surg. **216**(5), 835–840 (2018)
11. Swiecki, Z., Ruis, A.R., Farrell, C., Shaffer, D.W.: Assessing individual contributions to collaborative problem solving: a network analysis approach. Comput. Hum. Behav. **104**, 105876 (2020)
12. Wu, B., Hu, Y., Ruis, A.R., Wang, M.: Analysing computational thinking in collaborative programming: a quantitative ethnography approach. J. Comput. Assist. Learn. **35**, 421–434 (2019)

Zero Re-centered Projection: An Alternative Proposal for Modeling Empty Networks in ENA

David Williamson Shaffer[ID], Brendan Eagan[(⊠)][ID],
Mariah Knowles[ID], Clara Porter[ID], and Zhiqiang Cai[ID]

University of Wisconsin–Madison, Madison, WI 53711, USA
{beagan,zhiqiang.cai}@wisc.edu

Abstract. This paper examines the impact of having empty networks in an Epistemic Network Analysis model, that is, units whose networks contain no connections in a given model. These empty networks, also known as zero points, can negatively impact the interpretive validity of Epistemic Network Analysis spaces. In this study, we explore a change in the underlying mathematics and algorithm of Epistemic Network Analysis that we argue will make models easier to interpret accurately.

Keywords: Epistemic network analysis · ENA · Projections

1 Introduction

Many epistemic network analysis (ENA) models contain units (people, groups, or other items of interest) that have no connection between codes in the model. There is nothing particularly unusual or inherently problematic about having such *zero points*, or units in model that have no information on the variables of interest. However, in ENA models, empty networks can cause an interpretive problem in two ways: (1) the position of empty networks in an ENA model can be difficult to interpret, and as a result, (2) they can make interpretations of the overall model less reliable.

In this paper, we look at a change in the ENA mathematics and algorithm, and we argue that this change will make models easier to interpret accurately.

2 Background

2.1 Zero Values

In many analysis techniques, researchers can encounter units of analysis that have zero values for all of the variables in a model: for example, students who score a zero on a test—or perhaps a zero on every test—or an assembly line that has zero stoppages during the time of observation.

Depending on the statistical method being used, the nature of the question, and why points might have zero values in the first place, researchers deal with zero points in

B. Wasson and S. Zörgő (Eds.): ICQE 2021, CCIS 1522, pp. 66–79, 2022.
https://doi.org/10.1007/978-3-030-93859-8_5

different ways. For example, Fayaz explains that many statistical methods, including regression, involve dropping units that don't have any connections from the data if translations or transformations are not employed to handle the zero points [2]. Others approaches may actually introduce units with all zero values into their data to solve other problems. For example, attitude analyses sometimes purposely create a zero point provide reference or context for other points on the scale [3]. Scott [4] argues that in *social network analysis* (SNA), data points should be translated (that is, have a constant value added) such that units with no connections become outliers in a visualization. Some regression analyses place zero-valued units in the middle of the range of possible values for the variable or variables; others perform non-linear transformations (for example, log transforms) to account for zero values.

Because there are many possible ways of accounting for zero values, any analysis technique—and any analyses using that technique—has to provide a justification for the particular choice or choices made.

2.2   Zero Values in ENA

To date, the quantitative ethnography community—and users of ENA more widely— have not addressed this question (or provided such justifications) in detail.

To address this issue, we first ask: Do zero points actually present a problem for ENA analyses? After answering that question with a definitive *yes*, we then examine why, and provide a proposal for addressing the issue in a more theoretically sound way.

Wherefore Art Thou Romeo? Consider, for example, an analysis of two Shakespeare plays, *Romeo and Juliet* and *Hamlet* (taken from [1]).

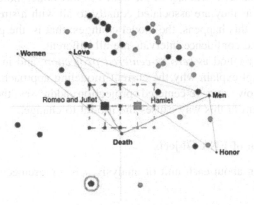

Fig. 1. ENA model comparing characters from *Hamlet* and *Romeo and Juliet*

In this example:

Data were the Lines of the plays
Conversations were each scene of each act of each play
Units of analysis were each character in each play
Codes were men, women, honor, love, and death

The stanza window was four lines [5], with a binary model. The data was normalized and the model used a means rotation [6] with Characters from *Hamlet* and Characters from *Romeo and Juliet* as the two groups.

The resulting model is shown in Fig. 1.

Perhaps not surprisingly, there are a number of characters in the plays who do not refer at any point to men, women, honor, love, or death (or, more specifically, do not make connections between these codes). The location of these characters in the ENA space is indicated by the pink circle.

This location of the zero points is difficult to interpret. In what sense are characters who say nothing (or nothing relevant to the model) more like characters in *Romeo and Juliet* than *Hamlet*? Moreover, an ordinary reading of the ENA space would indicate that these characters would be making more connections to death than to love—being low in the ENA space where death is rather than high in the space where love is. But this makes little sense, as by definition these characters make no connections between any codes!

Where Truth is Hid, Though it Were Hid, Indeed, /Within the Center. We thus propose that from an *interpretive* point of view, a more logical position for the zero points would be to place them at the origin of the graph, as shown in the right diagram of Fig. 2. Now these characters are neither more similar to *Romeo and Juliet* or *Hamlet*, and they are not associated with any of the codes in the model more than any others—which makes sense as they are associated equally to all with a strength of zero.

Notice that when this happens, the model changes: that is, the plotted points, node positions, means, and confidence intervals are all different.

We refer to this method as *zero re-centered projection*, and in the following sections, we will attempt explain why the current modeling approach leads to this interpretive problem, how zero re-centered projection addresses the issue, and why resolving the problem in this way causes the model to change.

2.3 Interpretation of ENA Objects

In ENA, information about each unit of analysis, i is represented in four distinct but coordinated ways:

1. as an *adjacency matrix*, A_i, showing the cumulative connections for each pair of codes for that unit;
2. as a (usually normalized) *adjacency vector*, v_i, that represents the location of the adjacency matrix, A_i in a high dimensional space, where each dimension represents the (normalized) connections between a pair of codes in the adjacency matrix;

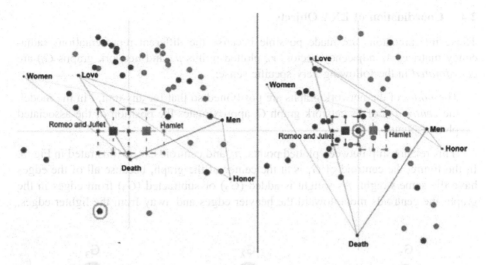

Fig. 2. Zero re-centered ENA model comparing characters from *Hamlet* and *Romeo and Juliet* (right) compared to the same model using the current ENA projection (left)

3. as a *plotted point*, p_i that represents the location of the adjacency vector v_i under a projection from the space of adjacency vectors; and
4. as a *network graph*, G_i, whose edges represent the values in the adjacency vector, A_i, and whose centroid approximates the location of the plotted point

A key feature of ENA is that the locations of a plotted point, p_i, can be *interpreted* in terms of its network graphs, G_i, in the following sense:

Points that are located up/down/right/left in the space, have *network graphs* that have strong connections in the up/down/right/left part of the space.

So, for example, the characters with red plotted points in Fig. 1 are more toward the right side of the diagrams because they have network graphs with strong connections between codes on the right side of the diagrams—which is what the red lines on the network graphs indicate. Characters with blue plotted points in Fig. 1 are more toward the left side of the diagrams because they have network graphs with strong connections between codes on the left side of the diagrams—which is what the blue lines on the network graphs indicate. Thus, we interpret the location of the points in terms of the kinds of connections that their networks contain. In Fig. 1, we can thus interpret the differences between the plays in the sense that both plays are about death, but characters in *Romeo and Juliet* make more connections between death, women, and love, whereas characters in *Hamlet* associate death more with themes of men and honor.

2.4   Coordination of ENA Objects

These interpretations are made possible because the different representations (adjacency matrices A_i, adjacency vectors v_i, plotted points p_i, and network graphs G_i) are *coordinated* in the following very specific sense:

> The *nodes* of the network graphs are positioned so that for any unit, i in the model, the *centroid* c_i of its network graph G_i approximates the position of the associated plotted point p_i.

This relationship between plotted points, p_i, and centroids, c_i, is illustrated in Fig. 3. In the figure, the centroid of G_1 is at the center of the graph, because all of the edges have the same weight. As weight is added (G_2) or subtracted (G_3) from edges in the graph, the centroids move toward the heavier edges and away from the lighter edges.

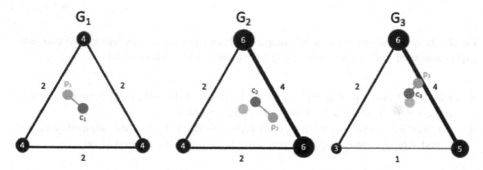

Fig. 3. Three network graphs, showing the relationship among node weights (white numbers in black circles), connection strength (numbers along graph edges), centroids ($c1$–$c3$ in red), and plotted points ($p1$–$p3$ in green). Distance between the plotted point and centroid for each graph is shown with a green line. Larger distances between centroids and plotted points make interpretations of plotted points in terms of network graphs less reliable. (Color figure online)

The centroid for a network graph is computed as follows. First, compute the total weight, w_j, for each node, N_j as the sum of the weights of the edges connected to it. (This is shown in Fig. 3) Then, for the x coordinate of c_i, X_{c_i} is computed as the weighted average of the x coordinates, x_j, of the nodes n_j:

$$X_{c_i} = \frac{x_j w_j}{w_j}$$

Y_{c_i} is computed similarly.

Thus, if the plotted point, p_i for some adjacency matrix, A_i, is close to its centroid, c_i, then the edge weights in its corresponding network graph, G_i, will allow us to interpret the position of its plotted point in terms of the connections between nodes.

In turn, if *in general* plotted points and centroids are aligned in this way, then the positions of the nodes make it possible to interpret the *dimensions* of the plotted points in terms of the *positions* of the nodes. This is referred to as the *co-registration* of plotted points, p_i, and network graphs, G_i, and it is a critical—indeed, crucial—step in interpreting ENA models.

2.5   More Mischance/On Plots and Errors Happen

Of course, plotted points and centroids are never completely coincident, as illustrated by the green lines in Fig. 3. This discrepancy can be quantified for each dimension by correlating the coordinates of the plotted points, p_i, and centroids, c_i. Thus, if X_c and X_p are vectors of the x coordinates of the centroids and plotted points respectively, we compute the Pearson correlation as:

$$\text{X axis goodness of fit} = r_x = \frac{\sum_k \frac{Xc_k - \overline{X}_c}{s_c} \frac{X_{p_k} - \overline{X}_p}{s_p}}{n-1}$$

where n is the total number of points and s_c and s_p are the standard errors of X_c and X_p respectively. Goodness of fit for the y axis is computed similarly. Other methods of correlation can be used as well, and ENA automatically computes both Pearson and Spearman correlations.

Correlation is an appropriate measure of goodness of fit because network graphs have no inherent scale relative to the values of plotted points. Thus, correlation provides a scale-invariant (or scaleless) measure of the degree of coregistration of a set of plotted points, p_i, and network graphs, G_i.

As a result, the goodness of fit quantifies *the degree to which the dimensions of the plotted points can be accurately interpreted by the network graphs*—and thus whether the interpretations of differences between plotted points are valid.

2.6   A Mote It is to Trouble the Mind's Eye

And this brings us to the heart of the matter. In general, it is important to have high correlations between plotted points and centroids to warrant reliable interpretations of the coordinates of the plotted points—and generally desirable to have correlations $r \geq 0.9$. However, has shown in Table 1 in the analysis of *Hamlet* and *Romeo and Juliet* above, the original correlations (using the usual ENA positioning of zero points) are below this desirable threshold, and well below it in the case of the y axis.

Table 1. Correlations between plotted points and network centroids.

Axis of interest	Original model correlation	Zero re-centered correlation
X	0.88	0.93
Y	0.75	0.94

On the other hand, Table 1 shows that if we position the zero points at the origin, as in the right diagram of Fig. 1, the goodness of fit measure for this data is higher, and more specifically above 0.9 on both dimensions.

Thus, the problem with positioning zero points in the usual manner is two-fold:

1. The location of zero points, or the points corresponding to empty networks, is difficult to interpret; and
2. The interpretation of the positions of *all of the other plotted points* in the model becomes less reliable

In fact, it was precisely the problem of understanding why some models had low goodness of fit (sometimes far worse than the example above) that led us to investigate the mathematical implications of zero points in ENA models.

We turn to that issue in the next section of the paper.

3 Zero's Fault

3.1 Projecting Zero

To understand this fault or flaw—that is, why empty networks can cause interpretive problems—recall that each adjacency matrix, A_i, in the model shows the cumulative connections for each pair of codes for that unit. Each adjacency matrix, A_i is represented as an adjacency vector, v_i, that represents the location of the adjacency matrix, A_i in a high dimensional space, where each dimension represents the (normalized) connections between a pair of codes in the adjacency matrix.

The set of adjacency vectors, v_i, is then projected into a 2-dimensional plane by centering the vectors on their mean, $\bar{v}$ and multiplying by a rotation matrix, R. Different projections (for example, means rotation or singular value decomposition) use different rotation matrices, but those differences are not important here.

Thus, we compute each p_i as:

$$p_i = R \times (v_i - \bar{v})$$

This is useful because it projects the mean of the vectors v_i to the origin of the ENA space:

$$R \times (\bar{v} - \bar{v}) = R \times 0 = 0$$

However, because all of the connections in an empty network, A_0, are zero, all of the values of v_0 will be zero. And as a result:

$$p_0 = R \times (0 - \bar{v})$$

That is, empty networks appear as the projection of $-\bar{v}$ in the original space.

Thus, empty networks are not projected to the origin of the ENA space unless the mean of the vectors is zero: that is, $\bar{v} = 0$. But that is essentially impossible, because all of the connection counts in the adjacency matrices A_i are either zero or positive. As a result, there are no negative values in any adjacency vector, v_i. So unless all $v_i = v_0$, $\bar{v} = 0$.

The empty networks will only be projected to the origin of the ENA space if all of the networks are empty!

3.2 Zero's Centroid

The fact that empty networks are not projected to the origin by itself creates the interpretive problem described above: how should we interpret the position of any plotted point, p_0, from an empty network. But, perhaps more important, it also causes the overall goodness of fit for the model to drop.

To see why, recall that we compute the centroid, c_i, of a network graph, G_i as:

$$X_{c_i} = \frac{x_j w_j}{w_j}$$

However, because in an empty network, A_0, all of the node weights, $w_j = 0$, the location of the centroid, c_0 will be:

$$X_{c_0} = \frac{x_j w_j}{w_j} = \frac{x_j \times 0}{w_j} = 0$$

That is, the centroid of an empty network will always be at the origin.

In other words, while the projected point, p_0, for an empty network will *never* be at the origin, its centroid, c_0 will *always* be at the origin.

As a result, using ENA's usual projection method:

1. The presence of a an empty network will always reduce the goodness of fit—that is, the interpretive reliability—of an ENA model; and, more to the point,
2. The presence of many empty networks in a data set has the potential to significantly reduce the goodness of fit of a model.

4 Zero Re-centering

The result of this unavoidable mathematical mismatch between p_0 and c_0—that is, the projected location of empty networks and the centroid of empty networks—is that the location of empty networks using ENA's current projection method will always be difficult to interpret, and models with many empty networks will be difficult interpret reliably overall.

In other words, we argue that ENA's projection method should be revised so as to deal with zero points in a way that will not compromise interpretive validity.

Given that the centroid of empty networks, c_0, will always be at the origin, it seems unavoidable that any solution to this problem would involve a projection where the projected point for empty networks, p_0, should also be at the origin. In this section of the paper, we examine two alternatives: un-centered projection and zero re-centered projection.

4.1   Un-centered Projection

Recall that ENA's current projection is of the form:

$$p_i = R \times (v_i - \bar{v})$$

That is, the set of adjacency vectors, v_i, is projected into a 2-dimensional plane by centering the vectors on their mean, $\bar{v}$ and multiplying by a rotation matrix, R.

If instead we compute:

$$p_i = R \times (v_i)$$

that is, we do not center the vectors on their mean, then instead of projecting the *mean* to the origin of the ENA space, the empty networks are placed at the origin, as shown in Fig. 4.

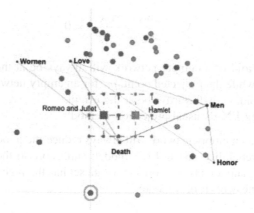

Fig. 4. ENA model of *Hamlet* and *Romeo and Juliet* using an un-centered projection

Because ENA uses a linear projection, this ENA model is essentially equivalent to the original (Fig. 1), but shifted so that the zero points are at the origin of the ENA space rather then the mean.

This approach addresses the problem that empty networks create for goodness of fit because using an un-centered projection, $p_0 = c_0 = 0$. However, the positions of the nodes now show that the y axis is capturing almost exclusively the difference between the characters with empty networks and all of the other characters: most of the plotted points are at the top of the graph (high y values), with many zero points at the origin and a few points in between.

This highlights a critical feature of many ENA models: namely, that this model uses *normalized adjacency vectors.*

The question of normalization arises because two units of analysis (characters in the ENA models here) can have the same *patterns* of discourse, but one might have more data than the others. To see why, imagine that two characters in a play had exactly the same coded lines, but one repeated those same coded lines 50 times each. Both adjacency vectors would go in the same direction from the origin in the space of adjacency vectors, v_i, but the character with 50 times as many lines would have a vector 50 times as long.

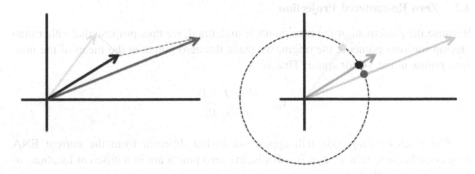

Fig. 5. Illustration of the process of normalizing ENA data

Figure 5 illustrates this idea. The black vector points in a similar direction to the blue vector, but is closer in length to the red vector. Without normalization (left image), the black vector appears more similar (closer) to the red vector than the blue. When the vectors are normalized to have the same length (right image), the black vector is more similar to the blue vector.

Thus, normalization accounts for differences in the total number of coded lines of data for each unit in a model.

The process of normalization has been described elsewhere [1], but briefly, normalization transforms the original adjacency vectors, v_i, into normalized vectors $v_i^* = \frac{v_i}{|v_i|}$, which are then used in the projection:

$$p_i = R \times (v_i^* - \bar{v}^*)$$

That is, each adjacency vector is divided by its length, such that all of the vectors have length $|v_i^*| = 1$. Or almost all the vectors. Because zero vectors have no length, their normalized value is:

$$v_0^* = \frac{v_0}{|v_0|} = \frac{0}{0}$$

which is undefined.

That is, zero points in a normalized plot have no inherent position in the normalized vector space. The current ENA projection (and thus an un-centered projection) place zero points at the origin of the space of normalized vectors, v_i^*. But that position—in an ENA model with normalized data—is, in fact, arbitrary.

4.2 Zero Re-centered Projection

Because the placement of the zero points is undefined, we thus propose that rather than placing the zero points at the origin, we place the zero points at the mean of the non-zero points in the vector space. That is:

$$v_0^* = \frac{v_i^* \forall v_i^* I = 0}{|v_i^* \forall v_i^* \ 0|}$$

The resulting projection will appear somewhat different from the current ENA projection because now $v* I_0 = 0$—that is, the zero points are in a different location, so the projection will change.

However, as shown in Fig. 2, this produces a model where the zero points are easy to interpret sensibly: they have no connections, and thus sit at the center of the ENA space. They are neither similar to nor different from either play in the model.

5 For 'tis a Question Left Us Yet to Prove

To test whether these alternative projections address questions of goodness of fit, we conducted a simulation study using the data from *Hamlet* and *Romeo and Juliet*.

We hyothesized that:

1. Models with the un-centered projection and the zero re-centered projection would both outperform the current ENA projection method in terms of goodness-of-fit; and
2. The difference in goodness of fit between the current ENA projection and the alternative methods would be larger as the number of zero points in the model rose.

The original data set had a total of 71 characters, 21 of whom had empty networks using the model described above. To conduct the simulation, we first chose a set of target numbers of empty networks, $k = \{0, 1, ..., 61\}$. We kept a minimum of 10 non-zero networks because if there are fewer non-zero points than codes, nodes cannot be reliably placed.

For each value of k, we randomly sampled the original data 1000 times. For each sample, we randomly chose (with replacement) 71-k characters with non-zero adjacency matrices. We then added k units with zero adjacency matrices to make a new set of 71 units.

For each of the 1000 data sets, we constructed six ENA models. We used *singular value decomposition* (SVD) and a *means rotation* (MR). Then, for each rotation method, we constructed three models: one using ENA's current projection method, one using un-centered projection, and one using zero re-centered projection.

For each model over the 1000 sampled data sets, we computed the goodness of fit on the x axis using a Pearson correlation coefficient, and found the mean correlation and standard error using the Fisher z-transformation.

Figure 6 shows the results, with the percentage of zero points $\left(\frac{100}{71}k\right)$ on the x axis and correlation on the y axis.

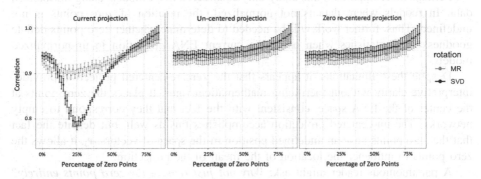

Fig. 6. Correlations for MR (red) and SVD (teal) for the current projection (left), un-centered projection (center), and zero re-centered projection (right). (Color figure online)

As expected, both the un-centered projection and the zero re-centered projection outperformed the current ENA projection. However, the simulation study suggests that the difference was only significant for the means rotation; SVD performed similarly for both models.

The results did not confirm our second hypothesis. The difference in performance did increase as the percentage of zero points went from 0% to 25%. However, the difference *decreased* as the percentage of zero points rose further, with differences becoming statistically insignificant after 50% of the points in the model were zero points.

This is likely because as the number of zero points increases, the mean of the vectors, $\bar{v}$, gets closer to zero, so the difference between plotted points and centroids for zero points decreases: that is, $p_0 - c_0 \rightarrow 0$. Thus, as the number of zero points increases past some point (25% of the data in this case), their impact on goodness of fit becomes smaller.

Further work will be required to determine why these effects were not seen in a model using SVD rather than a means rotation.

6 Discussion

This work has clear limitations, not least of which is that we only conducted an empirical study using one data set. Thus, although the mathematical argument may be sound, further research will be needed to determine what levels of zero points create poor goodness of fit for the current ENA projection relative to either alternative projection. Further work should also address the question of why models using SVD did not show the same differences as models using a means rotation—including a more thorough analysis of whether this finding holds in a wider range of data sets and models, and if so, whether the difference can be explained mathematically.

Perhaps more important, this study only considered ENA models using normalized data. In models where data is not normalized, the position of zero points is not undefined. Thus, further work will be needed to determine whether zero points deflate goodness of fit statistics when using the current ENA projection in un-normalized models.

Despite these limitations, it appears that the zero re-centered projection provides interpretive clarity without sacrificing mathematical rigor. It places the zero points at the center of the ENA space, consistent with the fact that they correspond to empty networks. The un-centered projection accomplishes this as well, but despite the fact that the zero points have an undefined position in the space of vectors, v_i, it allows the zero points to influence the location of the mean of the projection.

A parsimonious reader might ask: *Why not just remove the zero points entirely?* This would surely solve the problem they create for goodness of fit. However, it would also potentially lead to inflated Type I error rates: that is, it could lead a researcher to conclude that the differences between two groups are statistically significant when in fact they are not.

To see why, imagine any data set with a statistically significant difference between two groups. If we add one hundred million zero points to each group, the difference would almost certainly no longer be significant. Zero points impact statistical measures on the plotted points other than goodness-of-fit, so they cannot simply be removed to improve goodness-of-fit without potentially impacting other important model statistics.

Similarly, an empirically-minded reader might ask: *If this is such a big problem, why hasn't anyone said anything about it before?* Again a fair question, and one that we think is answered in two ways. First, although researchers always should be concerned with goodness-of-fit in models, that is not always the case, even in a community as concerned with interpretive validity as QE researchers. That is, people may just not have noticed that there was a problem with goodness-of-fit in their models. Second, as our experiment shows, these problems only arise when the number of zero points is in a particular range of proportions to the total number of data points—and the number of data sets for which this is the case may be small.

There may be situations in which a zero re-centered model is not the best choice when using normalized data, although what such reasons might be is not evident from the current study. In fact, we were not able to think of any such situations—although of course that doesn't mean that they don't exist.

We thus recommend that researchers use the zero re-centered model when working with normalized data unless they have specific reasons not to.

Acknowledgements. This work was funded in part by the National Science Foundation (DRL-1661036, DRL-1713110), the Wisconsin Alumni Research Foundation, and the Office of the Vice Chancellor for Research and Graduate Education at the University of Wisconsin–Madison. The opinions, findings, and conclusions do not reflect the views of the funding agencies, cooperating institutions, or other individuals.

References

1. Bowman, D., et al.: The mathematical foundations of epistemic network analysis. In: Ruis, A. R., Lee, S.B. (eds.) ICQE 2021. CCIS, vol. 1312, pp. 91–105. Springer, Cham (2021). https://doi.org/10.1007/978-3-030-67788-6_7
2. Fayaz, M.: Dealing with Missing Data. http://www.realstatistics.com/descriptive-statistics/missing-data/
3. Guttman, L., Suchman, E.A.: Intensity and a zero point for attitude analysis. Am. Sociol. Rev. **12**(1), 57 (1947). https://doi.org/10.2307/2086491
4. Scott, J.: Social Network Analysis. CPI Group (2017)
5. Siebert-Evenstone, A.L., Irgens, G.A., Collier, W., Swiecki, Z., Ruis, A.R., Shaffer, D.W.: In search of conversational grain size: modeling semantic structure using moving Stanza windows. J. Learn. Analyt. **4**(3), 123–139 (2017)
6. Zachari Swiecki, A.R., Ruis, C.F., Shaffer, D.W.: Assessing individual contributions to collaborative problem solving: a network analysis approach. Comput. Hum. Behav. **104**, 105876 (2020)

Choosing Units of Analysis in Temporal Discourse

Amanda Barany[1](✉) ⓘ, Michael Philips[2] ⓘ,
Anthony J. Taiki Kawakubo[3] ⓘ, and Jun Oshima[3] ⓘ

[1] Drexel University, Philadelphia, USA
amb595@drexel.edu
[2] Monash University, Melbourne, Australia
[3] Shizuoka University, Shizuoka, Japan

Abstract. Despite the promise of quantitative ethnographic approaches for visualizing the trajectories of change over time (temporal analysis) further work is needed to develop strategies for accurately representing phenomena. This holds especially true for identifying the relational context of discourse, which includes the creation of time units that group lines of data for the purpose of interpretation. While in-depth interpretive review of discourse may serve as the 'gold standard' for identification of thematic time units, this approach is tedious and may not be appropriate for larger datasets. Incremental approaches, such as creating a new unit for every ten lines of chronological data, are functional for larger datasets, but may lack nuance. This work introduces the Knowledge Building Discourse Explorer (KBDeX), which computationally identifies relational units using socio-semantic network analysis, allowing for the identification of time units based on characteristics of the discourse that can be systematically applied to larger datasets. To examine the utility of each approach, epistemic networks of COVID-19 press releases from seven countries were created with time units derived from the incremental and computational approaches, which were then compared to the interpretive approach. Results indicated that KBDeX and incremental network means were closer to the 'gold standard' interpretive approach in some instances. Two countries' trajectories are examined in greater depth to understand when each approach might be most appropriate. The work concludes with a discussion of the affordances and constraints of each approach, and contexts in which they may be useful.

Keywords: Temporal analysis · ENA trajectories · Epistemic Network Analysis (ENA) · Knowledge Building Discourse Explorer (KBDeX)

1 Introduction

As the data generated around phenomena have become exponentially ubiquitous, detailed, and digitally accessible, research across disciplines has increasingly focused less on the simple *outcome* of participation in an experience at a specific point in time, and more on characterizing the process, or *trajectory* of change as it manifests chronologically. Quantitative ethnographic techniques such as epistemic network analysis have shown promise for visualizing trajectories of phenomenon in fields such

© Springer Nature Switzerland AG 2022
B. Wasson and S. Zörgő (Eds.): ICQE 2021, CCIS 1522, pp. 80–94, 2022.
https://doi.org/10.1007/978-3-030-93859-8_6

as medicine [1], education [2] and political science [3] by allowing for the creation of comparative models that can illustrate relationships between themes or constructs from one time unit to the next [4]. Applying quantitative ethnographic techniques to temporal data is not without methodological challenges, however. Brohinsky and colleagues [4] stressed the importance of building temporal epistemic networks based on meaningful time units that can optimally demonstrate conceptual shifts over time. Zörgő and colleagues [5] described a similar need from the perspective of data segmentation: to establish relational context by grouping items into meaningful segments within or across which connections may or may not be measured and visualized. This work explores the application of three methods for identifying and visualizing meaningful units of analysis in temporal data: (1) the interpretive approach, in which researchers delimited the datasets based on qualitative thematic review of the discourse, (2) the incremental approach, in which researchers chunked discourse into uniform units (every ten lines of discourse), and (3) the computational approach, in which researchers leveraged the Knowledge Building Discourse Explorer (KBDeX) to identify meaningful relational units using socio-semantic network analysis [6].

2 Theory

Temporality has long been considered a crucial component researchers should consider when analyzing human behavior (e.g., [7]), and discourse data has been regularly used to illustrate temporal change given its potential to elucidate how social and cultural perspectives and identities are negotiated between individuals and groups through written and spoken language [8]. When conducting discourse analysis, researchers pay attention to how social interaction between participants is structured as sequences of a stanza: "sets of lines [conversation turns] devoted to a single topic" [9, p. 137]. By examining how participants co-construct their discourse as sequences of a stanza, researchers can interrogate the cultural practices behind the semiotics. Sequences of a stanza can also compare a single individual's discourse to herself at a prior point in time as she repeatedly mediates "an inner solidarity with a group's ideals and identity" [10, p. 109].

In the field of quantitative ethnography (QE), discourse data has been quantified to elucidate underlying qualitative patterns, with emerging research not only demonstrating how crucial temporality is as a consideration in discourse analysis [11], but also exploring techniques for visualizing and understanding the temporality of discourse data using QE approaches [5, 6, 12, 13]. Siebert-Evenstone and colleagues [13] proposed the sliding stanza-window method for appropriately capturing the temporality of the discourse data. First, they discussed the unit of analysis from the perspective of dialogism [14]. Each single conversation turn was conceptualized as a component that depended upon its previous and following conversational turn. In doing so, they proposed setting the stanza window size in Epistemic Network Analysis (ENA) based on the dependency of conversation turns, or how many conversation turns should be grouped into a unit of analysis. While fixing the window size may have the advantage of making a quick computational analysis possible, a disadvantage of rigidly setting the unit of analysis is that it ultimately may lead to errors when representing patterns in the discourse with variable temporal changes.

To solve this problem, Siebert-Evenstone and colleagues [13] developed an algorithm called the moving stanza window method by referring to existing work [15, 16]. When applying the sliding method, the algorithm can cover possible interdependency of conversation turns. Their comparative analysis of two different algorithms to analyze the same discourse dataset (i.e., aggregate conversation method versus the moving stanza window method) demonstrated that the moving stanza window method identified critically different epistemic frames of discourse.

Although the moving stanza window method goes beyond the traditional ENA concerns regarding the sensitivity to the temporality of discourse data, there are several problems still to overcome. First, it sets the size of the stanza window as fixed. The original idea of the stanza is a set of conversation turns or lines (if the dataset is the discourse transcript) devoted to a single topic [8], meaning that the size of the stanza may change over discourse. Some stanzas are short, while others are long, depending on the topics. Second, while the sliding method can cover possible interdependency of conversation turns, it might ultimately include sequences of turns that should not be grouped into the same stanzas, or units of analysis. Identifying the units of analysis that most appropriately represent the stanza groupings in a given discourse may ultimately alleviate some of these issues when the temporal data is later quantified using QE approaches. In existing quantitative ethnographic research, units of analysis in temporal data have been selected using different approaches.

2.1   Interpretive Approaches

Discourse analysis has traditionally been conducted qualitatively as a way to account for the nuance and complexity of socially situated change. Csanadi and colleagues [11] state that many traditional quantitative analyses of discourse utilize a 'coding-and-counting' based strategy. A limitation of such an approach is the lack of consideration of the temporal nature of discourse data. Their study revealed that analyses which consider temporal proximity, particularly the temporal co-occurrence of codes, provides greater insights than those that can be developed simply through coding-and-counting.

While approaches such as ENA, which consider temporal co-occurrences, provide greater insights into discourse data, there is still a substantial amount of time and labor that is required to prepare and code even moderately sized data sets prior to developing visualizations through ENA. An interpretive analysis of discourse data to identify units of analysis may exist as the 'gold standard' in that it allows qualitative researchers to immerse themselves in the nuance of the data's relational context to identify where a thematic stanza grouping begins and ends. The interpretive approach may not always be practical for the analysis of large or detailed datasets, however. Given the relatively small size of the dataset curated for this investigation, we would argue that interpretive approach is both feasible and valuable, but like every methodological decision, the use of interpretive approaches comes with both opportunities and limitations.

2.2 Incremental Approaches

When visualizing temporal phenomenon using epistemic network analysis, Brohinsky and colleagues [4] point out difficulties with making different time units legible for easy comparison. With legibility in mind, existing epistemic networks of temporal data often apply structural time units to the discourse data; examples of these structural units in QE studies include meetings [17], global meetups [18] and class periods [2]. Other trajectory studies have superimposed incremental numerical units, such as splitting the chronological dataset into two equal halves to gain an overall picture of change [19] or into more nuanced incremental units of ten lines of data [20]. While these approaches each carry value for visualizing patterns of change, these imposed structural or incremental units may not always support meaningful understanding of the phenomena, or in some cases may even obscure meaning by linking together thematically distinct units or bisecting meaningfully connected lines. While potentially limited in terms of accurately visualizing patterns in temporal phenomena, incremental time units may still prove useful in exploratory research, when datasets are too large to adopt an in-depth interpretive approach, or when other approaches are not possible.

2.3 The Knowledge Building Discourse Explorer (KBDeX)

Another approach to examining discourse data from the perspective of knowledge building involves the use of socio-semantic network analysis of the discourse, which has been developed based on temporal network analysis in computational social science [21]. The Knowledge Building Discourse Explorer (KBDeX) calculates and visualizes a temporal network of discourse based on the temporal change in the cooccurrences of vocabularies used in the discourse [6, 12, 22]. In their proposed analytics procedure, the authors [6] combined the moving stanza window method and the network lifetime. The network lifetime is the algorithm by which established connections between nodes based on the co-occurrences are canceled out if the same connections do not appear in the specific numbers of the following conversation turns. For example, the algorithm connects Word A and Word B because their co-occurrence appears in line number one in a transcript. The connection is canceled out if the same connection does not appear within the following three lines of the transcript. The threshold of the network lifetime in this case is three. By applying the combined algorithm in their socio-semantic network analysis, the authors demonstrated temporal trajectories of discourse topics over time.

In this way, the KBDeX computational approach builds on the structure of the discourse itself to identify meaningful time units in the data to visualize using epistemic network analysis. Unlike traditional interpretive approaches to identifying time units, KBDeX can also be applied to large datasets, while remaining more attuned to the relational context of the discourse than incremental approaches. In this work, we explore the utility of KBDeX by building epistemic networks of press release data using each of the three approaches to test whether the incremental units or computationally derived time units more closely replicate the 'gold standard' interpretive approach. Our research aim is to examine what differences manifest when the trajectories of thematic associations in international press releases are visualized in epistemic networks using time units of analysis derived from the interpretive (qualitative), incremental (units of 10 lines), and computational (KBDeX) approaches.

3 Study Design

This project began as part of the International Society for Quantitative Ethnography's data challenge held in April and May of 2020. This event saw international teams come together via web conferencing platforms to use quantitative ethnographic approaches and tools to explore large data sets related to the rapidly unfolding COVID-19 pandemic. The authors were members of a team who explored differences in discourse from government press releases in the United States and New Zealand. The project resulted in a video (https://www.epistemicanalytics.org/2021/01/08/press-conferences-on-covid-19-donald-trump-vs-jacinda-ardern/) which summarized findings from this work.

With a desire to expand our understanding of the ways other governments responded to the COVID-19 crisis in the early days of the pandemic, the authors worked together in the second QE data challenge in April of 2021. The team expanded their exploration to five additional countries including the United Kingdom, France, India, South Africa, and Japan. These countries were chosen for their geographic and cultural diversity. All countries had published open-source transcripts of their remarks that were either in English or that were in formats that could be translated into English by the authors.

3.1 Data Collection

To build the dataset, researchers downloaded transcripts of press releases or public addresses given by governmental leaders from seven countries from late February to late March of 2020 (see Table 1). Press release data was segmented by paragraph as it was structured in each transcript; most lines of data consisted of approximately 1–3 sentences with some variation by country. This timeframe was selected as most countries were releasing their first public statements that specifically referenced COVID policies and practices. Based on the accessibility of press releases, researchers selected 1–2 countries from five of the six populated continents. Two press releases in the sample (New Zealand and the United States) also included transcriptions of the question-and-answer sessions following their press releases, which were removed so that the style of discourse remained uniform across the dataset. Press releases included in the sample were translated into English upon collection or were obtained in translated form.

Table 1. Press releases by country.

Continent	Country	Date	Speaker	Lines
Africa	South Africa	March 23, 2020	Yoshihide Suga	123
Asia	India	March 19, 2020	Narendra Modi	50
	Japan	February 29, 2020	Cyril Ramaphosa	31
Australia/Zealandia	New Zealand	March 24, 2020	Jacinda Ardern, Grant Roberston	29
Europe	France	March 16, 2020	Emmanuel Macron	31
	United Kingdom	March 17, 2020	Boris Johnson, Patrick Vallance, Chris Whitty	39
North America	United States	March 27, 2020	Donald Trump	17

3.2 Coding

A priori themes were selected by the authors using an inductive thematic analysis [23], involving the identification and iterative development of topics that emerged based on open-ended review of the transcripts (see Table 2). Two researchers independently coded lines of data for the presence or absence of each sub-construct with an average agreement of 94.3%.

Table 2. A priori codes.

Continent	Sub-codes	Examples
Medical	Positive	Emergency workers; social distancing; adequate PPE and tests; decreased or low COVID-19 cases
	Negative	Lack of PPE; hospital overflow; lack of tests or testing
Economic	Positive	Commerce; trade; workplace
	Negative	Price gouging; debt; stock market crashes
Social/Community	Positive	Empathy; community; unity; education
	Negative	Nationalism; xenophobia; racism; lockdown; closed schools
Political	Positive	Supporting political leaders; affirming successes

4 Methods

Epistemic networks were generated using time units derived from the interpretive, incremental, and computational approaches, while all other aspects of model development were standardized. We defined the units of analysis as all lines of data associated with a single value of the variable Country.Comp (data for every country) subset by Segment.Comp (the type of time units applied to each country). As such, chronological lines of discourse for each country appeared in the dataset three times, with the units of analysis differing based on which approach was leveraged. The networks visualized the relationships between the positive and negative sub-codes for each of the four qualitative themes identified in the data (8 sub-codes total). The moving stanza window set to four in all cases based on a review of the transcripts and their conversation structure. Conversations were segmented by Country so that associations were not calculated across different press releases.

The overall model had co-registration correlations of 0.98 (Pearson) and 0.98 (Spearman) for the first dimension and co-registration correlations of 0.95 (Pearson) and 0.96 (Spearman) for the second. These measures indicate that there is a strong goodness of fit between the visualization and the original model.

4.1 Approach 1: Interpretive Time Units

In the qualitative interpretive approach, a researcher read through the press release transcripts and identified section breaks in the discourse at which the government leaders substantively shifted from one topic to another in their press releases. This approach required multiple readings of passages of discourse where leaders began to shift their focus. On occasions, the change was one small statement or a distinct utterance which was part of a larger segment of text and the reading and rereading revealed that while there may have been a slight, momentary change in the focus of the discourse, there was not a substantive shift which warranted a segmentation. For example, the South African Prime Minister, Cyril Ramaphosa made the following three statements in lines 28–30 of the press release analyzed:

(28) We must therefore do everything within our means to reduce the overall number of infections and to delay the spread of infection over a longer period – what is known as flattening the curve of infections. (medical positive)

(29) It is essential that every person in this country adheres strictly – and without exception – to the regulations that have already been put in place and to the measures that I am going to announce this evening. (social negative)

(30) Our analysis of the progress of the epidemic informs us that we need to urgently and dramatically escalate our response. (medical negative)

While it could be interpreted that the speaker's focus shifted from line 28 to line 29, the qualitative researcher decided that there was not a segmented break as lines 31 to 45 returned the focus of the statements predominantly to the 'medical' theme. This approach allows for researchers to acknowledge subtle changes in utterances and consider them in relation to the statements preceding and following the change in focus. This becomes particularly important when multiple themes may be coded to a series of utterances and the focus of the discourse requires considered, nuanced analysis of the utterances. In their analysis of thematic analysis such as this, Herzog, and colleagues [24] suggest that this "is an interpretative method in qualitative data analysis: classifications and interpretations occur through complex and largely informal considerations that cannot be fully expressed in replicable terms such as a complete algorithm" (p. 10), but recognize that this can be a labor intensive and can take long periods of time to complete if dealing with medium to larger data sets.

4.2   Approach 2: Incremental Time Units

The incremental approach to generating time units involved chunking the lines of data into groups of ten and numbering them chronologically. This resulted in chronologically numbered units of roughly the same discourse length applied uniformly across the press releases of different countries, with two temporal units for the United States (17 lines), three temporal units for New Zealand (29 lines), four temporal units for Japan (31 lines), France (32 lines) and the United Kingdom (39 lines), five units for India (50 lines), and 13 units for South Africa (123 lines).

4.3   Approach 3: Computational Time Units Using KBDeX

KBDeX was used to computationally identify time units of analysis for the data based on the algorithm of the network lifetime in the temporal network analysis of discourse. The algorithm detects sequences of lines (conversation turns) depending on the discourse topics computed by the co-occurrences of words representing speakers' ideas. First, based on the co-occurrences of words selected by researchers, the algorithm calculates the total value of the standardized degree-centralities of words in the discourse network whenever new conversation turns (lines in the transcript) are added to the analyzed discourse dataset. Second, the total value of degree centralities changes over time because the connections between words are dynamically changed by the network lifetime criteria. We set the network lifetime = 1 in this study as the most strict criteria for detecting stanzas. The visualization of the temporal change in the total value of degree centralities looks like a pulse of discourse. The algorithm can then identify the beginning and end of each time unit in the discourse (or sequences of conversation turns devoted to the same topics) by finding the cutting-off points with another threshold: two consecutive declines of the total value of degree centralities (see Fig. 1). For a detailed explanation of the KBDeX approach, please see publications by the author [6, 12, 22].

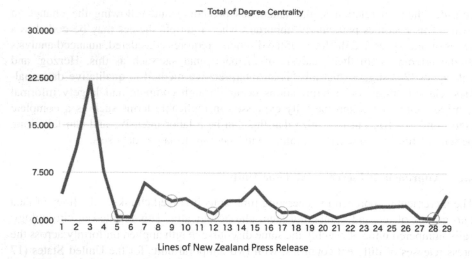

Fig. 1. The changes in degree centrality mapped for the New Zealand press release using the KBDeX approach. The points at which one time unit ends and another time unit begins are marked in red, which are points at which there are two consecutive declines of the total value of degree centralities. (Color figure online)

5   Results

Figure 2 shows the differences in network means for each country when units of analysis identified by each approach are applied. The network means for each country are clustered relatively near each other in the three-dimensional space in most cases (green, red, and blue means), suggesting some commensurability between the three approaches. Between network means for the same country, there were no statistically significant differences when tested using a nonparametric Mann-Whitney test, though the relatively small sample sizes for some of the press release datasets may have also contributed to this result.

The average distances between means for the incremental and computational approaches in relation to the 'gold standard' approach were calculated by subtracting the numerical X and Y coordinates for both incremental and computational approaches from the numerical X and Y coordinates of the interpretive means (see Table 3). For press release data from France, India and Japan, network means using time units derived from KBDeX were positioned closer to the 'gold standard' interpretive means. For press release data from New Zealand, South Africa, the United Kingdom, and the United States, network means using time units derived from the incremental approach were positioned closer to the interpretive network means. In most cases, the difference in distance from each mean to the interpretive means was small (.02–.15).

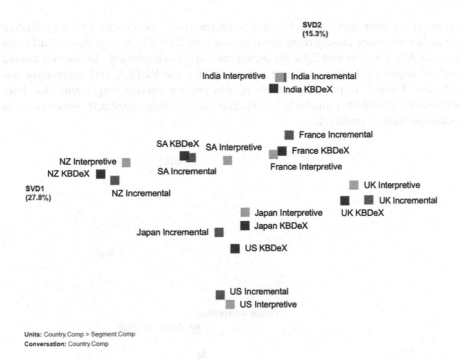

Fig. 2. Means for coded press releases with relational segmentation by interpretive, incremental, and the computational KBDeX approaches.

Table 3. Distance between incremental and KBDeX means and the interpretive means.

Country	Interpretive X	Interpretive Y	Avg. Distance KBDeX	Average distance incremental
France	0.07	−0.32	**0.05**	0.17
India	0.27	0.08	**0.05**	0.13
Japan	0.84	−0.13	**0.09**	0.11
New Zealand	−0.76	0.03	0.13	**0.10**
South Africa	−0.05	0.04	0.17	**0.14**
United Kingdom	0.32	0.62	0.06	**0.01**
United States	−0.04	−0.97	0.22	**0.07**
AVERAGE			0.11	0.10

A model of the trajectories for France (see Fig. 3) was created to show a country case in which the KBDeX approach more closely aligned with the interpretive approach. Figure 3 illustrates how dividing the units into increments of 10 lines in this case missed nuance in the discourse identified interpretively between units 1–3. Specifically, units 2–3 in the interpretive trajectory (green) involve initial discussions of negative medical outcomes the country was facing, followed by a shift toward some discussion of positive social/community (expressing solidarity) and negative political topics. This pattern that was highlighted as interpretively meaningful by the qualitative researcher was more closely represented in time unit 2 for KBDeX (pulled toward these themes) than it was in unit 2 for the incremental approach (already skewing up toward medical negative). In the final time unit means for the KBDeX and interpretive trajectories (4 and 6 respectively), there is also precise overlap, suggesting that both approaches identified a similarly meaningful unit of time (repeated associations to social/community positive).

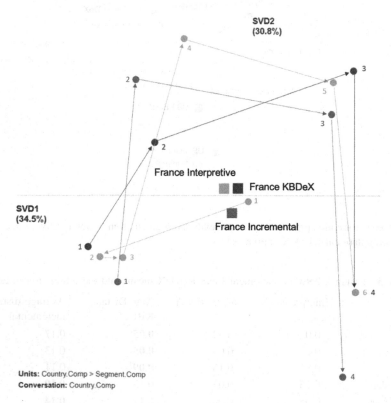

Fig. 3. Trajectories of change in associations between themes in the France press release using units derived from interpretive (green), incremental (red) and computational (blue) approaches. (Color figure online)

A model of the trajectories for the United States (see Fig. 4) was also selected as a case in which the *incremental* approach more closely aligned with the interpretive approach. In the 17 lines of US press release data, KBDeX only identified one instance in which there were two consecutive decreases in degree centrality (between line 14 and 15). Conversely, the interpretive approach resulted in three distinct temporal units across the leader's discourse that were spread more evenly throughout the speech. The difference in the KBDeX model likely stems from the fact that the lines in time unit 1 were computational identified as homogenous, which could stem from the more repetitive speech patterns that were noted in this leader. Time unit 2 also only consisted of three lines of data, suggesting that KBDeX may not be as appropriate for use with smaller datasets.

Ultimately, the incremental approach aligned more closely with the more evenly delineated interpretive time units. It should be noted, however, that the nuance of the shift toward politically negative topics in unit 2 of the interpretive approach is not as visible in the incremental approach, which essentially split the data in half.

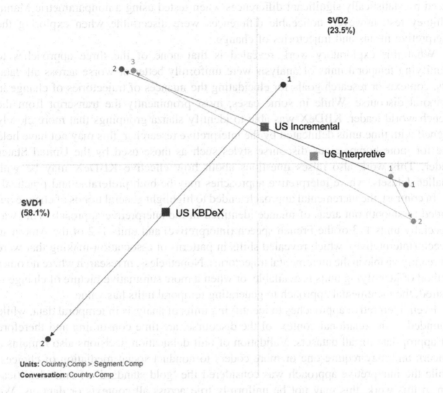

Units: Country.Comp > Segment.Comp
Conversation: Country.Comp

Fig. 4. Trajectories of change in associations between themes in the United States press release using units derived from interpretive (green), incremental (red) and computational (blue) approaches. (Color figure online)

6 Discussion and Conclusion

Analysis of discourse has long been a methodological approach to understand complex phenomena. Recently, developments in quantitative tools such as epistemic network analysis and KBDeX have provided researchers with innovative and practical opportunities to analyze discourse data, particularly those of larger sizes where traditional qualitative approaches may not always be possible. While these approaches build on traditional interpretive approaches, they also come with their own limitations. This study examined the differences that manifested when the trajectories of thematic associations in international press releases were visualized in epistemic networks using time units of analysis derived from the interpretive (qualitative), incremental (units of 10 lines), and computational (KBDeX) approaches.

Data in the form of transcripts of press releases or public addresses given by governmental leaders from seven countries impacted by the COVID-19 pandemic during late February to late March of 2020 were analyzed in relation to four main, a-priori themes together with positive and negative sub-themes. While the results from the interpretive, incremental and computational approaches applied to the data produced no statistically significant differences when tested using a nonparametric Mann-Whitney test; however, noticeable differences were discernible when exploring the interpretive means and trajectories of change.

What this exploratory work revealed is that none of the three approaches to identifying temporal units of analysis were uniformly better or worse across all datasets, contexts or research goals for elucidating the nuances of trajectories of change in temporal discourse. While in some cases, most prominently the transcript from the French world leader, KBDeX was able to identify stanza groupings that more closely aligned with time units delineated by the interpretive researcher, this may not have held true for more homogenous discourse styles such as those used by the United States leader. This work also raises questions about how effective KBDeX may be with smaller datasets, where interpretive approaches may be both preferable and practical.

In contrast, the incremental approach tended to highlight general trends of change but tended to smooth out areas of nuance identified in the interpretive approach. This was especially units 1–3 of the French speech (interpretive) and units 1–2 of the American speech (interpretive), which revealed shifts in patterns of association-making that were not readily visible in the incremental trajectories. Nonetheless, in research where no other method of identifying units is available, or when a more summative picture of change is desired, the incremental approach to generating temporal units has value.

Even interpretive approaches to identifying units of analysis in temporal data, while grounded in the relational context of the discourse, are time consuming and therefore not appropriate for all datasets. Validation of unit delineation decisions also remains a concern and may require one or more coders to conduct social mediation of choices. While the interpretive approach was considered the 'gold standard' of unit identification in this work, this may not be uniformly true across all contexts or datasets. We hope this work inspires QE researchers to critically examine which approaches they choose when preparing temporal data to visualize trajectories of change over time.

Important limitations of this exploratory work include the small sample sizes for press release data (17 to 123 lines per country), which may have skewed network means in some cases. The line segmentation of press release data was also not standardized or reduced to the smallest possible piece of information in some cases. Transcripts were segmented as they were structured in their transcripts, which resulted in instances where one or more sentences were coded as a single line. Segmenting the dataset by sentence in future work may also reveal more nuanced outcomes and shed light on the applications of KBDeX for identifying time units. Finally, trajectory data was limited to a short period of time for each country (the length of one speech). Supplementing the dataset with further press releases might reveal interesting insights into the trajectories of change in leader discourse over time.

Acknowledgements. Thank you to the organizers of the ICQE data challenges for connecting the team of authors on this project, and for facilitating our continued collaboration in this research.

References

1. D'Angelo, A.L.D., Ruis, A.R., Collier, W., Shaffer, D.W., Pugh, C.M.: Evaluating how residents talk and what it means for surgical performance in the simulation lab. Am. J. Surg. **220**(1), 37–43 (2020)
2. Barany, A., Shah, M., Foster, A.: Connecting curricular design and student identity change: an epistemic network analysis. In: Ruis, A.R., Lee, S.B. (eds.) ICQE 2021. CCIS, vol. 1312, pp. 155–169. Springer, Cham (2021). https://doi.org/10.1007/978-3-030-67788-6_11
3. Hamilton, E., Hobbs, W.: Epistemic frames and political discourse modeling. In: Ruis, A.R., Lee, S.B. (eds.) ICQE 2021. CCIS, vol. 1312, pp. 32–46. Springer, Cham (2021). https://doi.org/10.1007/978-3-030-67788-6_3
4. Brohinsky, J., Marquart, C., Wang, J., Ruis, A.R., Shaffer, D.W.: Trajectories in epistemic network analysis. In: Ruis, A.R., Lee, S.B. (eds.) ICQE 2021. CCIS, vol. 1312, pp. 106–121. Springer, Cham (2021). https://doi.org/10.1007/978-3-030-67788-6_8
5. Zörgő, S., Swiecki, Z., Ruis, A.R.: Exploring the effects of segmentation on semi-structured interview data with epistemic network analysis. In: Ruis, A.R., Lee, S.B. (eds.) ICQE 2021. CCIS, vol. 1312, pp. 78–90. Springer, Cham (2021). https://doi.org/10.1007/978-3-030-67788-6_6
6. Ohsaki, A., Oshima, J.: Socio-semantic network analysis of discourse using the network lifetime and the moving stanza window method. In: Eagan, B., Misfeldt, M., Siebert-Evenstone, A. (eds.) Advances in Quantitative Ethnography, Communications in Computer and Information Science, vol. 1112, pp. 326–333. Springer, Cham. (2019)
7. Li, A., Cornelius, S.P., Liu, Y.Y., Wang, L., Barabási, A.L.: The fundamental advantages of temporal networks. Science **358**(6366), 1042–1046 (2017)
8. Gee, J.P.: Situated language and learning: a critique of traditional schooling. Psychology Press (2004)
9. Gee, J.P.: An Introduction to Discourse Analysis: Theory and Method. 3rd edn. Routledge (2011)
10. Erikson, E.H.: Identity and the Life Cycle: Selected Papers. International Universities Press, New York (1959)
11. Csanadi, A., Eagan, B., Kollar, I., Shaffer, D.W., Fischer, F.: When coding-and-counting is not enough: Using epistemic network analysis (ENA) to analyze verbal data in CSCL research. Int. J. Comput.-Support. Collab. Learn. **13**(4), 419–438 (2018)
12. Ohsaki, A., Oshima, J.: Socio-semantic network analysis of knowledge-creation discourse on a real-time scale. In: Ruis, A.R., Lee, S.B. (eds.) ICQE 2021. CCIS, vol. 1312, pp. 170–184. Springer, Cham (2021). https://doi.org/10.1007/978-3-030-67788-6_12
13. Siebert-Evenstone, A.L., Irgens, G.A., Collier, W., Swiecki, Z., Ruis, A.R., Shaffer, D.W.: In search of conversational grain size: modelling semantic structure using moving stanza windows. J. Learn. Anal. **4**(3), 123–139 (2017)
14. Bakhtin, M.M.: The bildungsroman and its significance in the history of realism. In: Speech Genres and Other Late Essays. 2nd edn. University of Texas Press (1986)
15. Dyke, G., Kumar, R., Ai, H., Ros., C.P.: Challenging assumptions: using sliding window visualizations to reveal time-based irregularities in CSCL processes. In: van Aalst, J., Reiser, B. J., Hmelo-Silver, C., Thompson, K. (eds.) The Future of Learning: Proceedings of the 10th International Conference of the Learning Sciences (ICLS '12), vol. 1, pp. 363–370. International Society of the Leaning Sciences, Sydney, Australia (2012)

16. Suthers, D.D., Desiato, C.: Exposing chat features through analysis of uptake between contributions. In: Proceedings of the 45th Hawaii International Conference on System Sciences (HICSS-45), pp. 3368–3377. IEEE Computer Society, Maui, HI, USA (2012)
17. Nash, P., Shaffer, D.W.: Epistemic trajectories: mentoring in a game design practicum. Instr. Sci. **41**(4), 745–771 (2013)
18. Espino, D., Lee, S., Eagan, B., Hamilton, E.: An initial look at the developing culture of online global meet-ups in establishing a collaborative, STEM media-making community. In: Lund, K., Niccolai, G.P., Lavoué, E., Hmelo-Silver, C., Gweon, G., Baker, M. (eds.) A Wide Lens: Combining Embodied, Enactive, Extended, and Embedded Learning in Collaborative Settings: International Conference on Computer Supported Collaborative Learning (CSCL), vol. 2, pp. 608–611. International Society of the Learning Sciences, Lyon, France (2019)
19. Barany, A., Foster, A.: Examining identity exploration in a video game participatory culture. In: Eagan, B., Misfeldt, M., Siebert-Evenstone, A. (eds.) ICQE 2019. CCIS, vol. 1112, pp. 3–13. Springer, Cham (2019). https://doi.org/10.1007/978-3-030-33232-7_1
20. Shah, M., Barany, A., Siebert-Evenstone, A.: "What would happen if humans disappeared from earth?" tracing and visualizing change in a pre-school child's domain-related curiosities. In: Ruis, A.R., Lee, S.B. (eds.) ICQE 2021. CCIS, vol. 1312, pp. 232–247. Springer, Cham (2021). https://doi.org/10.1007/978-3-030-67788-6_16
21. Lazer, D., et al.: Computational social science. Science **323**(5915), 721–723 (2009)
22. Oshima, J., Oshima, R., Matsuzawa, Y.: Knowledge building discourse explorer: a social network analysis application for knowledge building discourse. Educ. Tech. Res. Dev. **60**(5), 903–921 (2012)
23. Creswell, J.W.: Educational Research: Planning, Conducting, and Evaluating Quantitative and Qualitative Research, vol. vol. 4. Pearson, Boston, MA (2015)
24. Herzog, C., Handke, C., Hitters, E.: Analyzing talk and text II: thematic analysis. In: Van den Bulck, H., Puppis, M., Donders, K., Van Audenhove, L. (eds.) The Palgrave handbook of methods for media policy research, pp. 385–401. Springer, Cham (2019). https://doi.org/10.1007/978-3-030-16065-4_22

A Qualitative Analysis of Connection-Making in the NGSS

Amanda L. Siebert-Evenstone(✉) iD

University of Wisconsin-Madison, Madison, USA
alevenstone@wisc.edu

Abstract. New models of science education have proposed a new way of conceptualizing science learning as interconnected and practice-based. This vision was operationalized in the Framework for K-12 Education and the Next Generation Science Standards (NGSS) as the principle of 3-dimensional learning, which unifies content and practices by connecting crosscutting concepts, disciplinary core ideas, and science and engineering practices. Subsequently, standards, curricula, and assessments of 3-dimensional learning must now account for these connections. One way to check for consistency across standards and curricula is through alignment studies which allow researchers to conduct a systematic analysis of the relationships between curricular components. However, assessing 3-dimensional learning necessarily means assessing the connections between the three dimensions, but it is not clear at what level connections matter. Therefore, in this study, I conduct a qualitative analysis of the NGSS to identify how connections are made between the three dimensions as a first step toward building mathematical models of 3-dimensional learning in the NGSS.

Keywords: Next generation science standards · Grounded analysis · Connections · Epistemic network analysis

1 Introduction

Standards-based reforms such as the Next Generation Science Standards (NGSS Lead States, 2013) have changed the landscape of education. These reforms have introduced new ways of conceptualizing what students should be able to do, changed teaching practices, and required changes in assessments. Instead of learning content and then applying it, the NGSS proposed an integrated and connected view of science education by introducing the principle of 3-dimensional learning. As such, the NGSS provide an important artifact of what scientists and science educators deem valuable and core to the pursuits of this discipline and how students could learn how to think like scientists. To explore what it means to make 3-dimensional connections, I used a grounded analysis to investigate what pattern of ideas emerges across the NGSS. In this study, I analyze how 3-dimenstional learning manifests as connections within the NGSS. The ultimate goal of this study is to identify and justify what counts as a connection for future modeling choices in epistemic network analysis (ENA).

B. Wasson and S. Zörgő (Eds.): ICQE 2021, CCIS 1522, pp. 95–113, 2022.
https://doi.org/10.1007/978-3-030-93859-8_7

2   Theory

With the goal of improving K-12 science education, the *Framework for K-12 Science Education* [1], or simply the *Framework,* was developed through a collaboration between the National Research Council, the National Science Teachers Association, the American Association for Advancement of Science, and Achieve, Inc. This project united science experts, researchers, and educators to create a new vision for science education and consequently a new set of K-12 education standards, the *Next Generation Science Standards* [2].

The *Framework* and the NGSS hoped to address these ambitious goals of a new vision for science by creating a set of standards that were interconnected, progressive, and coherent. Students would engage in the cultural practices of science in an environment where content and practices were inseparable through a new learning paradigm, called *3-dimensional learning,* which attempts to unify content and practices by outlining three interconnected educational components that represent habits of mind, content knowledge, and scientific themes. Importantly, each standard would include each of these three dimensions to ensure this inseparability. Further, each discipline would use a reduced set of content and then revisit this content with increasing sophistication as students progressed through the K-12 curricula. Using this 3-dimensional approach, curricula would have a sense of unity and coherence across disciplines and grades. Instead of learning content and then applying it, the *Framework* proposed an integrated and holistic view of science education that makes connections between knowledge and skills within inquiry activities. Building on this work and others, the NGSS attempts to address the history of fragmented and disconnected science learning [3] through *connected learning*: a view of learning based on the idea that complex thinking in a domain involves not only becoming proficient in basic skills and concepts, but also learning the systematic relationships between these core components [4–8].

Because the major underlying principle of the NGSS is connected learning, subsequent curriculum and assessments must consider how knowledge elements are interrelated. Importantly, instead of simply counting dimensions, curriculum and assessments must account for the connected nature of practices, content, and concepts when making claims about 3-dimensional learning.

2.1   The Three Dimensions of Learning

A critical feature of 3-dimensional learning are the three dimensions themselves. The *Framework* and resulting NGSS outlined a coherent system of K-12 education that explicitly links content and practice. These three dimensions were created to be interrelated, progress across grades, and provide coherence within and across disciplines.

1. *Science and engineering practices* (SEP), or simply practices, describe the processes inquiry and design in addition to providing a framework for talking about the tools, behaviors, and habits of mind that scientists and engineers use when engaging with investigations and design processes.

2. The second dimension of 3-dimensional learning includes the *Crosscutting concepts* (CCC), which describe broad and overarching themes that span across all domains of science. The goal of CCCs is to link ideas from a domain-specific activity to other activities, contexts, and disciplines as well as providing a common vocabulary for such connection-making. These themes help students better understand science ideas across contexts and disciplines.
3. The last dimension is the *disciplinary core ideas* (DCI) which outline the content knowledge that students should learn and revisit across their K-12 education. By limiting the number of DCI's to 12, students can revisit ideas over time, developing a deeper understanding of the most important disciplinary concepts[1].

In other words, the SEPs describe what students should know how to do, the DCIs describe what students should learn about, and the CCCs describe broad and overarching themes of science.

2.2 Unpacking the NGSS

In the process of creating a coherent, connected, progressive set of standards, the NGSS also became a complex and multilayered document [9, 10]. On the one hand, the NGSS is purposely complex to remedy issues of simplicity and fragmentation. But on the other hand, the NGSS, and all of its supporting documents, appendices, resources, and guides can be unwieldy to teachers, researchers, and policymakers. In order to understand three-dimensional learning in the NGSS, it is helpful to understand how the standards are organized.

The standards focus on four disciplines that organize what content areas are addressed. The three science disciplines include Physical Sciences (PS), Life Sciences (LS), and Earth and Space Sciences (ESS). New to these standards is the inclusion of a fourth discipline: Engineering, Technology, and Applications of Sciences (ETS; hereafter referred to simply as "Engineering"). Each of the disciplines is divided into DCIs, which are the fundamental content components that are important to understand within that domain. Mirroring the structure of the *Framework*, PS2 refers to the 2nd core idea from the Physical Sciences section of the *Framework* and addresses "Motion and Stability: Forces and Interactions." The DCIs are further subdivided into *sub-ideas*, which describe specific content expectations for that DCI. These DCIs and sub-ideas form one of the dimensions in 3-dimensional learning described above.

Within the NGSS, standards are separated into three semantically important groups —*grade bands*—or sets of school levels, which include elementary school (K-5), middle school (6–8), and high school (9–12).

While the disciplines and grade bands provide organizational structure, the actual standards are depicted differently. The standards use the phrase *core idea* to describe a DCI for a specific grade or grade band. These core ideas manifest as a *page* of the NGSS, where each page of the NGSS depicts a single core idea. Within each page, the

---

[1] A full list and description of each SEP, DCI, and CCC is available in the *Framework* or NGSS and is omitted in this article due to space constraints.

standards are separated into three main sections of information, where a single standard may have up to 14 pieces of information describing what students should learn.

The standards themselves, called *performance expectations* (PE), describe what students should be able to do using the SEPs, DCIs, and CCCs by the end of that grade band. Each PE provides a statement that summarizes all of the pieces that comprise that PE including the SEP, DCI, and/or CCC that are required to demonstrate that understanding. This statement is supplemented by the clarification statement and/or an assessment boundary, which provide more specific descriptions or qualifications.

Each PE is also assigned a code that tags the information and identifies the grade or grade band and core idea. For example, MS-PS4-3 is the code for Middle School – Physical Sciences: Waves and Their Applications in Technologies for Information Transfer – 3rd PE in this core idea set. These codes are used in the foundations' section to identify which aspect of 3-dimensional learning is associated with which PE. The codes also correspond to the order and tagging of ideas that were presented in the original *Framework*.

Underneath the performance expectations, the NGSS outline the specific expectations for each component of 3-dimensional learning. Here, each dimension lists the name of SEP, DCI, and CCC and includes a bullet point that provides a more specific description of what students should be able to do for that PE.

One way to evaluate whether a curriculum or assessment meets the objects of the NGSS—specifically, the underlying principle that calls for students to understand and make connections between the three dimensions—is to measure the relationship between standards and materials claiming to address those standards.

2.3   Alignment

One way to check the consistency between standards and new programs or measures is through the idea of *alignment*, that is, the degree of agreement between a set of standards and the materials or activities that intend to address those standards [11, 12]. In many cases, alignment studies compare standards and assessments [13, 14], however, alignment is also a useful frame to compare any combination of standards, texts, instruction, teacher training, tests, or other components of a curriculum [15].

Importantly, each of these curricular components are created and implemented by different people. For example, the *Framework* was written at the national level by groups of policymakers, researchers, teachers, and organizations. The NGSS was written by groups of similar experts from 26 states. The curriculum and materials were made by a different set of designers. Then, the curriculum is implemented by different teachers and districts. And in the case of standardized tests, again a different set of designers created those assessments.

Measuring alignment between curricular components can give researchers and educators more insights about each component. If the components align, then there is some degree of consistency in what should be taught, what is taught, and/or what is assessed. Similarly, inconsistencies in alignment can lead to unmet objectives. For example, if teachers create or use units that do not address important ideas from the standards, there is a possibility that students may do well in that unit but show poor achievement on standardized tests [16].

Thus, alignment studies allow researchers to conduct a systematic analysis of the relationships between curriculum components to provide information about the degree of agreement between planned, enacted, intended, and/or assessed curriculum [17]. The results of such studies can then inform changes in curricula and implementation.

2.4   Approaches to Measuring Alignment

Three common methods to measure alignment are (1) the Webb Alignment Tool [14], (2) Surveys of Enacted Curriculum [13], and (3) the Achieve Model [18].

The Webb Alignment Tool (WAT) analyzes alignment between standards and state assessments by analyzing the content and knowledge complexity to assess four relationships between standards and assessments. The goal of this method is to use content and depth of knowledge coding to provide qualitative information and statistics about the structure of alignment between standards and assessments.

The Surveys of Enacted Curriculum (SEC) analyzes alignment between standards, assessments, and classroom instruction for content and knowledge complexity to produce a summary measure of alignment. The goal of this method is to create a common content and cognitive demand rating that allows visual and mathematical comparisons across states.

The Achieve Methodology analyzes alignment between standards and assessments using content and performance to assess five alignment relationships. The goal of this method is to measure content and student performance to provide ratings, qualitative reports, and metrics that describe the structure of alignment between standards and assessments.

Each of the three methodologies employs expert review that includes trained evaluators—parents, teachers, educators, researchers, or subject matter experts—to compare alignment. These experts read materials and assign codes to the data to identify what content is being covered and how difficult that content is. In turn, these ratings are used to calculate metrics of alignment. Each of these methods uses a combination of qualitative and quantitative methodologies to arrive at their alignment conclusions.

In all three cases, the methods assume that alignment is less of a yes or no question, but rather a question of how the materials are related. Each of these methods quantifies qualitative ratings to conduct systematic comparisons. The goal of these methodologies is not to make assertions of more or less aligned, but rather to make comparisons about how specific content and difficulty are related. Importantly, all three of the methodologies provide a mathematical model of the structure of alignment which provides summative information about the ways in which specific components are aligned such as how much information is covered or how many standards are addressed by at least one assessment item.

In other words, all three methodologies use expert review to conduct mixed-methods evaluations in order to capture the structure of alignment.

2.5   Measuring Alignment for the NGSS

While these are well-known and employed alignment tools, none of them have been used to assess alignment for the NGSS. These methods are designed to isolate components and then assess alignment on an item-by-item basis because they were created in a time when standards were a "mile wide and an inch deep," which can be seen in how the methods try to capture the breadth and range of content across standards and assessments.

However, the introduction of 3-dimensional learning fundamentally changed the nature and goal of science assessment [9]. Whereas previous standards were "discrete, decontextualized knowledge, year-by-year, unconnected standards" (p. 3), the NGSS were designed to reflect the complexity and interrelated nature of modern science. These connected and three-dimensional standards introduce challenges for existing alignment methods at a time when curricula and assessments are undergoing radical changes and alignment studies could provide useful insights for developers of new materials.

To address these shortcomings, the creators of the Achieve Methodology, updated and adapted their technique for the NGSS into what is called the *EQuIP rubric* [19]. EQuIP, or Educators Evaluating the Quality of Instructional Products, was developed to measure the quality of science curricula and the alignment of curricula to the NGSS. Instead of focusing on content and difficulty, the members of a Science Peer Review Panel use the EQuIP rubric assesses all three dimensions of connected learning and checks for the integration of these dimensions.

Importantly, the EQuIP rubric assesses all three dimensions of connected learning and checks for the integration of these dimensions. Reviewers first document evidence and rate quality for a single dimension. Then, reviewers assess how the curriculum integrates the three dimensions. In the rubric, *integration* is defined as "Student sense-making of phenomena and/or designing of solutions requires student performances that integrate elements of the SEPs, CCCs, and DCIs" (EQuIP Rubric, 2016, p. 7). Therefore, integration addresses the connected nature of the three dimensions and provides an evaluation of these connections for a given curriculum. This provides both qualitative evidence of each criterion and a quantitative assessment of that evidence. After independently reviewing the materials using the EQuIP rubric, the panel writes a consensus report that details their assessment of the materials and provides feedback on how to improve the curriculum.

In other words, EQuIP uses expert review to conduct mixed-methods evaluations about the integration of 3-dimensional learning. At the same time, the EQuIP methodology provides a score about whether the overall unit is high quality or needs revisions, or about whether categories or category components show evidence of quality. However, the rubric provides no mathematical model of how any of these grain sizes meet the criteria only quantification of whether or not they meet criteria. This is not necessarily a problem when comparing one, two, or even three curricula with the standards because researchers and developers can look at the ratings and track those numbers back to the qualitative evidence behind them. But even the task of comparing two curricula using the qualitative reports becomes time-consuming and complicated. Comparing any more than three curricula would require quantitative support for those comparisons. The three methodologies above provide a mathematical model of how curricula aligned not just whether or not they are "E" an excellent or provide "adequate evidence." Mathematical models provide summative information about the nature of alignment.

In many ways, the EQuIP rubric uses similar processes as the three methods above. All four methods use expert review to conduct mixed-methods evaluations. However, there are two important differences between the methods. The EQuIP rubric can provide a score about whether the dimensions are integrated but no mathematical model of how they are integrated. On the other hand, all three methods above provide quantitative measures about the structure of alignment to facilitate comparisons between curricula and identifying issues, but none of these methods assess connections or integration between components.

Therefore, an alignment methodology for 3-dimensional learning would use expert review to conduct qualitative and quantitative evaluations that capture the structure of integration—the ways in which the three dimensions are connected within standards and curriculum. Therefore, the key to assessing 3-dimensionality is assessing the structure of integration between dimensions.

2.6 Modeling the Structure of Integration

To measure the structure of integration, I propose employing a quantitative ethnographic approach. As opposed to mixed-method research that often provides a quantitative measure of differences and then a set of qualitative examples that attempt to explain those differences, a *quantitative ethnography* [20, 21] works to identify qualitative stories and then provide statistical warrants that these stories generalize within that dataset and situations with a similar culture or context. Quantitative ethnography (QE) affords the ability to check that the local meaning-making is truly a pattern across that data set. By using statistics to compare data that is inseparably linked to ethnographic descriptions, QE employs a unified, rather than mixed, methods approach [23].

Once the key concepts are identified, the structure of connections between these concepts can be represented as a network of relationships. One tool for measuring and visualizing connections is epistemic network analysis [ENA; 22, 23]. When ENA models the structure of connections between concepts, this results in a visual representation of the pattern of relationships, a mathematical model of the structure, and a way to statistically compare the quantified version of the underlying qualitative data. In other words, quantitative ethnography can employ expert review to conduct unified methods evaluations to measure the structure of integration.

2.7 Current Study

Alignment studies allow researchers to conduct a systematic analysis of the relationships between curriculum components, but to assess 3-dimensionality alignment studies must be adapted to measure the structure of integration, which are the ways in which the three dimensions are connected within standards and curriculum.

While this study attempts to operationalize connection-making in 3-dimensional learning, one dimension plays a different role than the others. The DCIs act as both a structural element in the standards as well as one of the three dimensions of learning. One goal of the DCIs was to provide a way to revisit the same content with greater sophistication over time, however, because of this, the same DCIs exist in every grade band. If all grade-bands include all DCIs then the DCIs will always be represented. If this analysis is interested in the structure of connections and the same ideas appear in exactly the same place, there is no added information for including them. Every page includes a DCI, but not every page includes SEPs or CCCs. Therefore, I account for connectivity to the DCI at the page level and look for connections between SEPs and CCCs for a given DCI.

Another challenge in measuring the structure of integration is identifying the appropriate level at which connections should be measured. Connections could be measured by PE, groups of PEs, DCIs, pages, disciplines, grade bands, and combinations of those grain sizes. In typical alignment analyses, the unit of analysis is a single standard, in this case, a PE. Assessing 3-dimensional learning necessarily means assessing the connections between the three dimensions, but it is not necessarily clear at what level connections matter. Knowing the appropriate level for understand how ideas are related is fundamental to deciding appropriate conversations and segmentation structure in ENA. Therefore, in this study, I conduct a qualitative analysis of the NGSS to identify how connections are made between the three dimensions as a first step toward building mathematical models of the NGSS using ENA.

Therefore, this paper addresses the question: *What is an appropriate level to model the structure of integration?*

3   Methods

3.1   Data

The NGSS are a set of K-12 science content standards that set expectations for what students should be able to do that are (1) organized as 59 pages, where each page represents a discipline-specific topic, and (2) grouped into three grade levels (elementary, middle, and high school), where each level contains a grade level-specific version of that topic. At the elementary level, the NGSS break out pages by specific grade, so there are more pages in this level. Across the NGSS, there are 37 pages for elementary school, 12 for middle school, and 12 for high school (see Fig. 1 for a depiction of a single page).

Each page includes a set of performance expectations at the top of the page and the 3-dimensional learning components that specify how to achieve the PE at the bottom of the page.

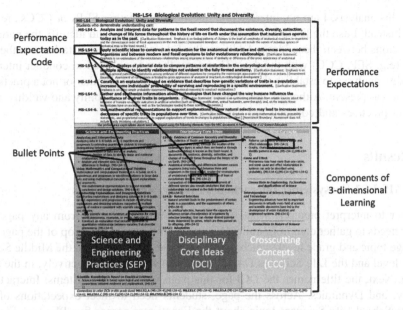

Fig. 1. Depiction of one page of the NGSS.

3.2 Qualitative Analysis

The three components of 3-dimensional learning are the SEPs, CCCs, and DCIs. However, the DCI serve a different role in 3-dimensionality than the other two dimensions as they are structural, occur on every page, but also are one of the dimensions. Therefore, I examine the ways in which SEPs and CCCs are connected within the context of the given DCI.

The NGSS defines, explains, and assigned 8 SEPs and 7 CCC across the document. Rather than creating codes from the text, this analysis uses these embedded 15 concepts as the codes (for more detail please see the NGSS itself). Therefore, this analysis does not code the data as the data is already coded. Instead, I conducted a grounded analysis of the NGSS to identify the ways in which SEPs and CCCs were connected in the context of the DCI [24].

I employed a snowball approach to analyzing the data. One PE was the smallest atomic unit that would include a connection between SEP and CCC. I started with a single PE from one page in the middle of the standards to start my analysis: MS-LS2-1. I then analyzed how the PE made connections between SEP and CCC and what other information I might need to understand that relationship. After analyzing that PE and the PEs on that page, I chose another page from the same DCI and grade band (i.e. MS-LS4) and again started by analyzing one PE on that page. After the second page, I looked at other pages in the grade band and across the standards to see if the properties of connection identified on the first two pages applied to other pages or if there was any new information. After finding that the three themes identified on a single page were universal properties of connection making, I stopped my snowball sampling after reaching this saturation.

In this analysis, I am not interested in questioning whether SEPs or CCCs are on a page. Instead, I use the listed SEPs and CCCs as a way to try and identify the nature of connections between these ideas. Additionally, I do not code the data I use embedded codes (e.g. SEP, CCC) with the data. Therefore, there is no need to conduct interrater reliability analyses to establish the validity and reliability of whether or not a practice or concept was present. Although, this is not to claim that the reliability and validity of the existing practices and concepts are perfect.

4   Results

4.1   MS-LS2 Ecosystems: Interactions, Energy, and Dynamics

In order to interpret precisely what students are supposed to do from any page, the reader needs to gather data from multiple sources on that page. The top of the page lists the page topic and grade level, which in this example, is a page from the Middle School Grade level and the Life Sciences Discipline (i.e. MS and LS, respectively, in the topic name). Next, the title names the DCI for this page which is Ecosystems: Interactions, Energy, and Dynamics. Across the page, students need to meet expectations of this Middle School Life Sciences topic about the Ecosystem across five PEs (see Fig. 2).

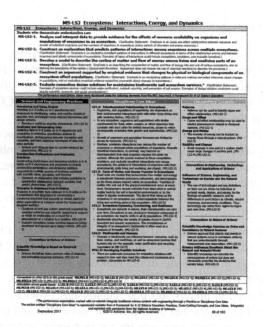

Fig. 2. Full page for MS-LS2.

During my grounded analysis, I found three ways that information is related on a page: semantically, typographically, and conceptually.

Semantic Connections. First, SEPs and CCCs are related semantically because the information they contain combine to make a PE. For example, in the first PE (MS-LS2-1) in the DCI for Ecosystems: Interactions, Energy, and Dynamics, students are asked to interpret relationships between organisms within ecosystems:

> Analyze and interpret data to provide evidence for the effects of resource availability on organisms and populations of organisms in an ecosystem.

Based on the information listed in the PE, we might think that students need to analyze resource availability data. However, to fully understand what students need to be able to know and do, we need to look below in the sections on 3-dimensional learning to see how students achieve this PE.

MS-LS2-1 addresses the interdependencies of organisms within an ecosystem. Each ecosystem has a limited amount of resources that support or fail to support organisms and to understand resource availability students can investigate how populations fluctuate based on both competition for resources and the effects on population size. One way to understand this relationship is by using a SEP to learn about a broader theme known as the CCC. This PE is comprised of ANALYZING AND INTERPRETING DATA [SEP bullet point 2] and CAUSE AND EFFECT [CCC bullet point 2]. For ecosystem interactions, students engage in "analyzing and interpreting data" specifically about how "cause and effect relationships may be used to predict phenomena in natural or designed systems." Analyzing the 3-dimensional components reveals that data analysis is about cause and effect relationships and that students need to use this interpreted information to make predictions.

So by design, PEs are comprised of an SEP and a CCC and the PE statement in the top white section summarizes the information in the bottom three boxes. In this way, each SEP and CCC are directly connected to the PE statement. At the same time, a PE's underlying SEP and CCC are also related to one another because the SEP describes what students should know how to do explicitly about the broad and overarching themes identified in the CCC. In other words, the PE, SEP, and CCC are all semantically related to one another because they are parts of one idea.

Typographical Connections. Next, components are connected typographically across the page because all information is tagged with a PE code. In the first example, the performance expectation is tagged with the PE code MS-LS2-1. This code identifies the PE by grade level, DCI, and number. This PE code is unique and only ever refers to this explicit standard and its semantically related components. For example, each piece of information that comprises MS-LS2-1 is tag with this code (see Fig. 3).

Fig. 3. MS-LS1 tagged with red boxes around each MS-LS2-1 PE code.

Moreover, if we search the NGSS for this PE code, it never appears on any other page. This means that PE codes only tag information for that PE and do not refer to other PEs. Even when there is overlap between 3-dimensional elements, such as how MS-LS2-4 and MS-LS2-5 refer to the same CCC (STABILITY AND CHANGE [CCC bullet point 4]), both PE codes are listed after the description. Therefore, connections between PE components are explicitly and typographically tagged with a code to maintain the references between parts of the page.

Conceptual Connections. Finally, components are conceptually connected within the page. For example, in the second performance expectation on this page (MS-LS2-2), students are asked to explain organisms in different ecosystems:

Construct an explanation that predicts patterns of interactions among organisms across multiple ecosystems.

In order to meet this expectation, students are expected to make connections between CONSTRUCTING EXPLANATIONS AND DESIGNING SOLUTIONS [SEP bullet 3] and PATTERNS [CCC bullet 1]. In this case, students meet the PE when they can "construct an explanation that includes qualitative or quantitative relationships between variables that predict phenomena" by learning how "patterns can be used to identify cause and effect relationships." Nevertheless, in order for students to find cause and effect patterns, we would need to look back to the first PE to see how the cause and effect relationships were made as well as use the qualitative or quantitative data that was analyzed and interpreted to meet the first expectation. In other words, the second PE relies on and is connected to the first PE.

Similarly, MS-LS2-4 also requires students to use "empirical evidence", which could be qualitative or quantitative like in MS-LS2-2, but in this case, students use evidence to "support or refute an explanation or a model" (ENGAGING IN ARGUMENT FROM EVIDENCE [SEP bullet 4]). So MS-LS2-4 requires data in a similar way as the second PE, and would be used to evaluate explanations, which the second PE constructs.

But for MS-LS2-4 this data may also be used to evaluate models. If we look across the page, there is another PE that addresses models. In the third PE (MS-LS2-3), students generate evidence about matter and energy within ecosystems (ENERGY AND MATTER [CCC bullet point 3]) by having students "develop a model to describe phenomena" (DEVELOPING AND USING MODELS [SEP bullet point 1]). Again, MS-LS2-4 depends on skill and knowledge gather by engaging with another PE (i.e. MS-LS2-3).

Therefore, in order to understand a PE, we also have to look at the relationships and dependencies that PE has with other PEs and subsequently their underlying SEPs and CCCs. In order to understand one PE, we need to understand the other PEs. Furthermore, everything on a page is by definition about a common disciplinary topic. All PEs on a page address different facets of what students should know and be able to about a topic, in this case about Ecosystems: Interactions, Energy, and Dynamics.

Taken together, we cannot understand a single component without understanding the whole page. In other words, the page is conceptually related. We are unable to make sense of ideas on a page at a level smaller than the page itself. In particular, though, it means that SEPs and CCC are systematically related to one another on a single page.

Connections Beyond a Page. While I argue that sensemaking occurs at the page level, there are certain times when one page references ideas outside of that page. For example, the fifth PE (MS-LS2-5) asks students to use principles from engineering design and biodiversity to evaluate solutions:

Evaluate competing design solutions for maintaining biodiversity and ecosystem services.

This final PE is built on engaging in argument from evidence [SEP bullet 5] and stability and change [CCC bullet 4]. But unlike the other PEs on this page, this PE draws content from another DCI in this discipline and a DCI from a different discipline. In this version of engaging in argument from evidence, students are specifically evaluating design solutions, which is based on principles from Engineering (ETS1.B developing possible solutions [DCI bullet 9]) and ideas about biological diversity from Life Sciences (LS4.D: biodiversity and humans [DCI bullet 8]). For example, the DCI about biodiversity and humans asks students to consider the ways the environment affects human access to resources:

Changes in biodiversity can influence humans' resources, such as food, energy, and medicines, as well as ecosystem services that humans rely on—for example, water purification and recycling. The text listed above is an excerpt from the following paragraph from the Framework addressing middle school expectations about the relationship between humans and biodiversity:

"By the end of grade 8. Biodiversity is the wide range of existing life forms that have adapted to the variety of conditions on Earth, from terrestrial to marine ecosystems. Biodiversity includes genetic variation within a species, in addition to species variation in different habitats and ecosystem types (e.g., forests, grasslands, wetlands). *Changes in biodiversity can influence humans' resources, such as food, energy, and medicines, as well as ecosystem services that humans rely on—for example, water purification and recycling.*" (p. 166, emphasis added)

The Framework describes all aspects of humans' relationship with biodiversity that students should know by the end of middle school. Across this grade level, students should learn how geological formations and earth conditions affect the range and variation of species, genetic variation, habitats, ecosystem types, and finally the interaction between humans and ecosystem services. Therefore, information from the Framework matters for understanding student expectations in this PE.

However, this PE and ultimately this page do not require students to understand earth conditions, or genetic variation, habitat types, or ecosystem types. This sub-idea, LS4.D, lists multiple content requirements, however, the only important component for this PE and therefore the page is the final sentence italicized above. This same text is listed on the page for MS-LS2. Across the page, students only need to understand how human behavior affects and is affected by ecosystem services. Importantly, the NGSS replicates only the important information from the Framework that is necessary for this topic and omits information that is unnecessary in this context.

Therefore, we do not need to use the Framework to interpret a given page. Instead, the most relevant information from those pages is embedded on the MS-LS2 page. In other words, all connections and all information needed to understand a page is written on that page. That is, a page is the smallest unit of analysis that represents the integration of 3-dimensional connections.

Connections Between Pages. So far, I have argued that the NGSS makes semantic, typographical, and conceptual connections within a page, and that when invoking information from other resources, the pertinent information from outside resources is embedded directly on the page, making it unnecessary to use the original source.

After identifying the three types of connection-making, I explore another page from the same grade level and discipline as the first example but that addresses a different DCI called Biological Evolution: Unity and Diversity. For this page, students engage with six PEs about this topic.

For biological evolution, the first PE (MS-LS4-1) asks students to analyze and interpret data, but in this topic, students are asked to interpret fossil records using graphs:

Analyze and interpret data for patterns in the fossil record that document the existence, diversity, extinction and change of life forms throughout the history of life on Earth under the assumption that natural laws operate today as in the past.

Specifically, to meeting expectations for this PE, students need to "analyze and interpret data to determine similarities and differences in findings" (ANALYZING AND INTERPRETING DATA [SEP bullet point 2]) by using "graphs, charts, and images... to identify patterns in data" PATTERNS [CCC bullet point 2]. We would not know that analyzing patterns would include using graphs unless we also looked at the SEP and CCC on the page that describe precisely students should know and do. Similar to the previous page, the PE, SEP, and CCC are all parts of the same idea and therefore are semantically related.

In the second PE (MS-LS4-2), students address a different set of concepts about evolution and are asked to explain patterns in anatomical development. Students address this PE when they can "construct an explanation that includes qualitative or quantitative relationships between variables that predict phenomena" (CONSTRUCTING EXPLANATIONS AND DESIGNING SOLUTIONS [SEP bullet point 4]) by learning how "patterns can be used to identify cause and effect relationships" (PATTERNS [CCC bullet point 1]). But, similar to the first page, in order for students to find cause and effect patterns, we would need to look back to the first PE or another PE on the page to identify appropriate qualitative or quantitative data that was analyzed and interpreted to meet the first expectation. That is, the second page also shows that PEs are conceptually related to one another across a page.

Unlike the first page, this page makes no references to other disciplines or DCIs. And, of course, each of these examples is tagged with a PE code that identifies all important information relevant to that PE. As a result, this page also shows the semantic, conceptual, and typographic connections between information.

Importantly, though, MS-LS4-2 makes the same SEP to CCC relationship that was included in MS-LS2-2. Even though there is overlap between these two PE, this page incorporates this relationship in a different way than the other page. In order to understand the relationship between CONSTRUCTING EXPLANATIONS AND DESIGNING SOLUTIONS and PATTERNS, we must look at the rest of the page. For example, both MS-LS2-2 and MS-LS4-2 build on the first PE—and presumably other PEs—from their respective pages. For the previous page, the first PE linked ANALYZING AND INTERPRETING DATA and CAUSE AND EFFECT, whereas the first PE on this page linked ANALYZING AND INTERPRETING DATA and PATTERNS.

In this way, it is impossible to understand the overlap between pages without looking at all of the connected ideas on either page. Thus, when there is the same combination of SEP and CCC on two pages, they are used in different ways because they are connected to different things on each page. In this case, the first page expects students to learn about Ecosystems while the second page expects students to learn about Biological Evolution. In other words, the page remains the correct level when analyzing the connections between SEP and CCC.

Representing Relationships and Dependencies from one Page. One way we can compare the ideas on a page is to visualize the relationships between practices and concepts as connections (see Fig. 4).

Fig. 4. Connections between practices and concepts for MS-LS2.

In this figure, the practices and concepts are represented as circles, and connections are represented as green lines. This visualization connects all practices and concepts to one another to represent all of the possible relationships and dependencies between the ideas on a page. Not everything on a page may be directly related, however, enough of the page is connected to see how each idea builds on one another. In MS-LS2 all eight practices and concepts are shown as connected to one another in this manner.

In comparison, MS-LS4 would be represented as (see Fig. 5):

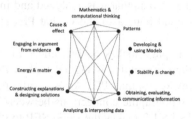

Fig. 5. Connections between practices and concepts for MS-LS4.

From these visualizations, there are a few features that stand out for each page. If we look at the original page depiction, MS-LS4 addresses four practices and two concepts. On the other hand, MS-LS2 addresses four practices and four concepts. Because of how practices and concepts were addressed, MS-LS2 included more of each, and therefore also had a larger amount of connections than in MS-LS4 At the same time, merely counting the number of practices and concepts strips away the relationships and dependencies that were evident in the examples above.

For this representation, I argue that it does not make sense to count repeated concepts or practices more than once. A *weighted network* would preserve each time an idea is included while a *binary network* only includes that ideas were included and not how many times they are included. MS-LS4 includes both PATTERNS and CAUSE AND EFFECT three times each, but that does not necessarily mean that students need to understand those concepts three times as well. Therefore, I argue that a binary model is sufficient to capture connections.

Importantly, though, these visualizations can capture the similarities and differences between the two pages. Both pages have students CONSTRUCTING EXPLANATIONS AND DESIGNING SOLUTIONS about PATTERNS. At the same time, both examples showed that the practices and concepts on a given page are related to and dependent on other practices and concepts on that page. While there may be common connections between practices and concepts, there are also other relationships and dependencies to others.

In the end, MS-LS2 is about Ecosystems while MS-LS4 is about Evolution. We might expect that both pages discuss some common content, however, we would not expect everything to be the same, nor that the content is taught or learned in the same way. For example, we can use the networks to easily notice two key differences across the pages. On the one hand, MS-LS4 explicitly calls for students to USE MATHEMATICS

AND COMPUTATIONAL THINKING as well as OBTAINING, EVALUATING, AND COMMUNICATING INFORMATION while MS-LS2 does not include either of those practices. On the other hand, MS-LS2 expects students to learn about ENERGY AND MATTER, STABILITY AND CHANGE, ENGAGING IN ARGUMENT FROM EVIDENCE, and DEVELOPING AND USING MODELS, while MS-LS4 does not require any of these practices or concepts.

Therefore, I argue binary networks for each page represent the semantic, typographical, and conceptual connections for both that MS-LS2 and MS-LS4 and are able to show differences between the two pages.

5 Discussion

The goal of this analysis was to understand how connections are made between SEPs and CCCs in a given DCI. The first theme that emerged when analyzing a single PE. In this case, was that connections were made between a single SEP and CCC because each of these components combined to form the PE statement, and therefore connections are semantic because they comprise a single idea. The second theme that emerged was that the standards embedded PE codes to help users identify what on a page was related, and therefore connections are also typographical because they are tagged on the page. The final theme that emerged was that all PEs on a page addressed different aspect of the same grade-band specific DCI. The entire page is about a single DCI and by measuring questions across a page, connections between SEPs and CCCs account for information about the DCI. Therefore, connections are conceptual because everything on a page is systematically related.

By analyzing references to other pages and the similarities and differences between pages, this analysis also revealed that all connections and all information needed to understand a page is written on that page. That is, a page is the smallest unit of analysis that represents the integration of 3-dimensional connections.

Finally, this analysis represented these relationships within a page as a network model that included all possible connections between SEPs and CCCs for that grade band-specific DCI. These visualizations were able to retain the important information from the qualitative analyses. By using binary summation, all potential relationships and dependencies were modeled.

Based on this work, future epistemic network analyses will identify connections as being within a conversation if they are on the same page of the document. Additionally, these epistemic network analyses will sum connections using binary summation.

At the same time there are certain limitations to this analysis. First, binary summation is only one way that connections could be represented across a page. Other analyses could explore different ways to measure these relationships and dependencies including using a weighted accumulation. Additionally, in this analysis, I analyzed two of the 59 pages. Although I reached saturation, future analyses could include more pages or include a second evaluator to see if there is agreement about the ways in which practices and concepts are connected.

At the same time, this grounded analysis of connections revealed three important results. First, this study shows that practices and concepts are related in semantic, typographical, and conceptual ways. Second, analyzing connections at the page level can capture the three types of connections. Finally, the results show that connections can be represented using binary summation because the key differences between pages is connections and not the counts of practices and/or concepts. The results of this analysis can be used to parameterize the qualitative results into a quantitative model of integration and used to investigate differences between disciplines and grade bands from the NGSS.

References

1. National Research Council: A Framework for K-12 Science Education: Practices, Crosscutting Concepts, and Core Ideas. National Academies Press, Washington, DC, D.C. (2012). https://doi.org/10.17226/13165
2. NGSS Lead States: Next Generation Science Standards: For States, By States. National Academies Press, Washington, DC (2013). https://doi.org/10.17226/18290
3. Reiser, B.J., Mcgill, T.A.W.: Coherence from the Students ' Perspective: Why the Vision of the Framework for K-12 Science Requires More than Simply " Combining " Three Dimensions of Science Learning, vol. 1 (2017)
4. Bransford, J.D., Brown, A.L., Cocking, R.R.: How People Learn: Brain, Mind, Experience, and School. National Academies Press, Washington, DC (1999). https://doi.org/10.17226/9853
5. Jacobson, M.J., Wilensky, U.: Complex systems in education: scientific and educational importance and implications for the learning sciences. J. Learn. Sci. 15, 11–34 (2006). https://doi.org/10.1207/s15327809jls1501_4
6. Wilensky, U., Resnick, M.: Thinking in levels: a dynamic systems approach to making sense of the world. J. Sci. Educ. Technol. 8, 3–19 (1999). https://doi.org/10.1023/A:1009421303064
7. Chi, M.T.H., Feltovich, P.J., Glaser, R.: Categorization and representation of physics problems by experts and novices. Cogn. Sci. 5, 121–152 (1981). https://doi.org/10.1207/s15516709cog0502_2
8. Dreyfus, H.L., Dreyfus, S.E.: Peripheral vision expertise in real world contexts. Organ. Stud. 26, 779–792 (2005)
9. Gorin, J., Mislevy, R.J.: Inherent measurement challenges in the next generation science standards for both formative and summative assessment. Invitational Research Symposium onScience Assessment, Washington, DC (2013)
10. Feinstein, N.W., Kirchgasler, K.L.: Sustainability in science education? how the next generation science standards approach sustainability, and why it matters. Sci. Educ. 99, 121–144 (2015). https://doi.org/10.1002/sce.21137
11. Bhola, D.S., Impara, J.C., Buckendahl, C.W.: Aligning tests with states' content standards: methods and issues. Educ. Meas. Issues Pract. 22, 21–29 (2003). https://doi.org/10.1111/j.1745-3992.2003.tb00134.x
12. Fulmer, G.W., Tanas, J., Weiss, K.A.: The challenges of alignment for the next generation science standards. J. Res. Sci. Teach. 55, 1076–1100 (2018). https://doi.org/10.1002/tea.21481
13. Porter, A.C.: Measuring the content of instruction: uses in research and practice. Educ. Res. 31, 3–14 (2002)
14. Webb, N.L.: Issues related to judging the alignment of curriculum standards and assessments. Appl. Meas. Educ. 20, 7–25 (2007)

15. Kurz, A., Elliott, S.N., Wehby, J.H., Smithson, J.L.: Alignment of the intended, planned, and enacted curriculum in general and special education and its relation to student achievement. J. Spec. Educ. **44**, 131–145 (2010). https://doi.org/10.1177/0022466909341196
16. McGehee, J.J., Griffith, L.K.: Large-scale assessments combined with curriculum alignment: agents of change. Theory Pract. **40**, 137–144 (2001)
17. Martone, A., Sireci, S.G.: Evaluating alignment between curriculum, assessment, and instruction. Rev. Educ. Res. **79**, 1332–1361 (2009). https://doi.org/10.3102/0034654309341375
18. Rothman, R., Slattery, J.B., Vranek, J.L., Resnick, L.B.: Benchmarking and Alignment of Standards and Testing (CSE Technical Report No. CSE-TR-566), Los Angeles, CA (2002)
19. Achieve: EQuIP rubric for lessons & units: science (Version 3.0) (2016)
20. Shaffer, D.W.: Quantitative Ethnography. Cathcart Press, Madison, WI (2017)
21. Eagan, B., Misfeldt, M., Siebert-Evenstone, A. (eds.): ICQE 2019. CCIS, vol. 1112. Springer, Cham (2019). https://doi.org/10.1007/978-3-030-33232-7
22. Siebert-Evenstone, A.L., et al.: In search of conversational grain size: modelling semantic structure using moving stanza windows. J. Learn. Anal. **4**, 123–139 (2017). https://doi.org/10.18608/jla.2017.43.7
23. Shaffer, D.W., Collier, W., Ruis, A.R.: A tutorial on epistemic network analysis: analyzing the structure of connections in cognitive, social, and interaction data. J. Learn. Anal. **3**(3), 9–45 (2016). https://doi.org/10.18608/jla.2016.33.3
24. Corbin, J., Strauss, A.: Grounded theory research: procedures, canons, and evaluative criteria. Qual. Sociol. **13**, 3–21 (1990)

Telling Stories of Transitions: A Demonstration of Nonlinear Epistemic Network Analysis

Mariah A. Knowles[✉]

University of Wisconsin-Madison, Madison, USA
mariah.knowles@wisc.edu

Abstract. I demonstrate nonlinear modeling and clustering in extension to existing Quantitative Ethnography methods as an approach to telling stories of transitions. The Epistemic Network Analysis (ENA) algorithm is a three step process: it represents qualitative data as a high dimensional space that models the connections between qualitative codes; it uses multidimensional scaling to reduce the dimensionality of that space while highlighting features of interest; and it projects a network representation onto that scaled space as a way to illustrate the dynamics of those features. Existing multidimensional scaling algorithms used by ENA have been linear, which have limitations in elucidating major life transitions as they are experienced: Such stories are nonlinear, with ebbs, flows, and structural breaks. Therefore, to capture such dynamics, I introduce Nonlinear ENA, which deviates from traditional ENA by using a nonlinear multidimensional scaling algorithm, and I demonstrate how one might tell a temporal story with Nonlinear ENA by telling the story of my first year on feminizing hormones.

Keywords: Epistemic Network Analysis · Nonlinear ENA · Analytic autoethnography · Transitions · Transgender

1 Introduction

At the previous ICQE, I spoke with others who had interest in using Quantitative Ethnography (QE) to model stories that move over time. From my analytic autoethnographic work, I have such a story and a dataset, these pose interesting methodological concerns, and these have been central to my own coming to understand QE methodology.

In 2020, I began Hormone Replacement Therapy (HRT) [1]. I am transgender and a woman, and HRT was an important part of my gender and social transition. I kept extensive notes, which served three purposes. One, they allow changes to be seen that happen too gradually to notice otherwise. Two, they are a space for practicing and shaping conceptions of shifting identities. Three, they are analytic moments for developing theoretic sensitivity and perception of autoethnographic experiences under study [2].

B. Wasson and S. Zörgő (Eds.): ICQE 2021, CCIS 1522, pp. 114–128, 2022.
https://doi.org/10.1007/978-3-030-93859-8_8

These notes have provided me an interesting dataset for examination during my journey with QE: This data is temporal, it has a simple structure otherwise, it has no a priori groups or clusters, and I am deeply and intrinsically motivated towards "getting the story right."

With this data, I asked: How can QE be used to tell a temporal story? One might ask a similar question of non-temporal data that still "moves" over a continuous variable [3]. Either way, such story-telling might have two subtasks: use QE to provide evidence of saturation, and use QE to tell a rich qualitative story whose turns are guided by quantitative features.

Initial analysis using QE's existing linear modeling methods demonstrated two obstacles for this second subtask. One, there are parts of the story that it misses. Two, the story that it does tell is uninsightful to the point of being misleading. Incorporating nonlinear modeling into my analytical process resolved those issues.

In this paper, I demonstrate that extending existing QE methodology with a non-linear projection algorithm (in this case UMAP) and a clustering algorithm (in this case DBSCAN) provides several affordances when working with temporal data. First, it allowed me to make systematic decisions about how to relate units with similar units nearby in time when I had no a priori structure. Second, it identified which of many qualitatively meaningful moments actually incurred a structural break. Third, it neatly modeled nonlinear behavior, where early on in the year I repeatedly started and stopped HRT. Fourth, it visualized the effect of that structural break on that nonlinear behavior. Fifth, these results were reflectively surprising, which promoted clearer theoretical thinking. Finally, these results provided not only grounded and saturated content, but also grounded and saturated structure by which to organize my narrative. In this way, the nonlinear extension to existing QE methods allowed me to tell a richer, more informed story, without caricaturizing my transition experiences.

2 Relevant Theory

2.1 Analytic Autoethnography

Autoethnography allows examination of one's own experiences that would not other-wise be observable to other researchers [4, 5]. I am providing an account based on personal daily notes, which out of potential for embarrassment I would not be likely to share with another researcher, and I suspect there are other transwomen who feel the same given the current political climate in the United States around trans issues [6]. And in Analytic Autoethnography (AA), "authors seek to discover or better understand some aspect of their existence as communicable and applicable in abstracted form" [5], the purpose of which is to provide "structured analysis of one's own experiences with the intention of gaining broad social and cultural insights" [7]. Authors are free to choose a style of expression, such as evocative or analytical, as best suits their project needs. Given my aims of self-study and explicit analysis, AA is appropriate for this project.

To achieve self-study and explicit analysis, AA includes inter alia four tenets [5, 8]. One, the researcher must be a "complete member of the social world under study" [8]. I am a complete member researcher of the transwoman social world, and felicitously due to the COVID-19 pandemic, I have been able to connect remotely with other transwomen in ways I would not have been able to otherwise. Two, the researcher must be deeply aware of the reciprocal influence between themselves, the social world under study, and their analytical methods. I have been analytically reflexive as such, this project developing in tandem with my own learning of QE methods. Fleshing out the reciprocal influence between the two has been a powerful motivation this past year: I simultaneously sought deeper understanding into my own heavily politicized identity and to be able to back up that understanding with honest and flawless methods. Three, in AA works, the researcher must be a visible social actor, their own lived experiences incorporated into the story, and those experiences treated as data for analysis. I am the central social actor in the story told below, the only other actors relevant for this paper being occasional strangers and my doctor. Four, AA works must be committed to the agenda of "us[ing] empirical data to gain insight into some broader set of social phenomena" [8]. I am committed to the analytic agenda: "[O]urs is a collective and cumulative enterprise of knowledge" [5], so while I do not present this work as representative of all transwomen's experiences during their first years on HRT, nor do I present this work for the sake of theory-building about trans experiences, I do present it as a demonstration for how to work with temporal data in a way that does not caricaturize its participants, and I take seriously the task of "getting the story right" backed specifically by analytic methods.

2.2   Desire and Damage

In this work, I refuse to structure my story around gender dysphoria, trauma, or generally "damage." Research that starts from these positions is research that's "thinking of ourselves as broken" [9]. There is a long history of social-justice-oriented qualitative research that centers on "damage" done on the social worlds under study, underpinned by the theory of change that, by documenting loss, political gains can be obtained. However, this theory of change ignores the historical context and structural power struggles surrounding that ostensible damage: "After the research team leaves, after the town meeting, after the news cameras have gone away, all we are left with is the damage" [9].

I instead adopt a desire-based frame. Desire centers "complexity, contradiction, and the self-determination of lived lives," and it often flips scripts of blame and power [9]. This is not to say that desire-based frameworks are naively optimistic. They account for loss and despair just as well as they account for hope, vision, and communal wisdom. For example, my qualitative codes capture dysphoria and non-happiness just as well as longing, affirmation, coming out, and crying (these are happy tears), and in my analysis below, tensions between doubt and desire are front and center.

2.3   Transitions

Stories of transitions abound in healthcare and in life, such as becoming a parent, exiting sex work, and new jobs [10–12]. QE work has been done on transitions, but none whose models are grounded in a theory of transition as an *experience* [13, 14]. Transitions are marked by a number of essential properties, such as the following. First, subjects *engage with* transitions through information seeking, preparation, and so on; for example, my engagements included decisions about taking doses, reflections in daily notes, information seeking online and with my doctor, and this analytic autoethnographic project. Second, transitions result *from change* and result *in change*. Subjects may desire, confront, and have complex relationships with such changes. Third, transitions occur over *time spans*, and the bounds, stages, stability, continuity, ebb and flow, and linearity of a time span can be complex: "In evaluating transition experiences, it is important to consider the possibility of flux and variability over time" [10]; for example, the stages of my first year on HRT moved in jumps and spurts, some days dragging on, others flying by, and some caught in vicious cycles. Finally, transitions are pockmarked by *critical events* which can result in changes to stability, engagement, self-awareness, certainty, routines, and so on. Put another way, transitions contain "structural breaks," changes in qualitative central tendencies.

With these properties in mind, I will model time as a story composed of "types" of days, influenced in part by the march of time, and with no other *a priori* structure.

3   Methods

3.1   Context and Data Collection

On February 14th, 2020 I started feminizing hormone replacement therapy. This consisted of an initial consult with a doctor specializing in gender affirming care, daily doses of Spironolactone and Estradiol, occasional follow-ups with my doctor over Zoom, and occasional blood work to monitor my testosterone and estrogen levels. (As treatment plans are individualized, others' therapy may include other practices and/or medications [1].) In addition, over the year that followed, I kept notes in two forms, daily "checkboxes" of emerging themes and in-the-moment reflections in a notes app on my phone.

3.2   Qualitative Coding

On February 14th, 2021, a year after I started HRT, and in the days leading up to then, I re-read and inductively coded all daily notes using a grounded-theory inspired approach [15]. Some themes emerged in my notes during the year and were simplified to a checkbox. However, not all of these, in retrospect, were qualitatively insightful, and several were apparent only in the re-read. For example, an early code for "craving salt" provided no value, and I did not notice the salience of "spelling out recipes for makeup/etc." until the end. My goal during this inductive coding process was to model an honest and complete account of my experiences with HRT that first year. And as the sole coder, the logic is that I am providing a qualitative description that is inherently perspectival, not "objective," and so no inter-rater reliability checks were necessary [4, 16]. To limit implicit bias and expose inconsistencies during this coding process, data were triangulated with an assemblage of other media produced during and leading up to the year under study: text messages, selfies, old hand-written journals, browser histories, credit card transactions, and messages with my doctor [4, 17]. The resulting themes are defined in Table 1.

Table 1. Codebook

Label	N	Code	Example
DoseTracking	42	A journal entry tracking the exact time of an HRT does	"7:35a e."
Happy	136	A checkbox marking days in which I felt happy	18 Oct. 2020, when my partner and I were called "ladies" during a date downtown
NonHappy	120	A checkbox marking days in which I felt a non-happy emotion, such as anxiety, depression, etc	18 Oct. 2020, when my partner still called me "he" because I was not out to our friends yet
SkippedDose	95	A checkbox marking days on which I skipped my HRT dose	30 Jul.–16 Aug. 2020, when I had run low and would not be able to refill my prescriptions until the Fall semester
Sweets	130	A checkbox marking days on which I craved sweets, such as chocolate or caffeinated drinks	31 Aug. 2020, when I was too afraid to enter the make-up aisle at Target and bought and ate junk food instead
BODY	153	A checkbox or journal entry tracking changes to my body, feelings, or behaviors	A checkbox marking days on which my skin was oily, which estrogen has the effect of decreasing, or the entry, "Haven't felt [mental] fog in a while."
LEARN	56	A checkbox or journal entry tracking my efforts to self-teach about (trans)womanhood, such as through research or experimentation	Citing hormone treatment guidelines from Boston University or the entry, "Tried something new with my makeup."
REFLECT	137	A checkbox or journal entry tracking my reflections with my identity as situated within or connected to various domains, such as family and religion	"…looking at a photo of my grandma…" or "This is one of my favorite videos, [link], 'You have unconditional permission to be your ******* self'"
PROGRESS	88	A checkbox or journal entry tracking my progress towards my transition goals. (At my initial consult, I stated my goals as, "I value happiness, passing, and understanding," gesturing to suggest that understanding was the highest priority. After some experience, "passing" was redrawn as "safety.")	A checkbox marking days in which I passed in public, either by accident or on purpose, such as 18 Oct. 2020 when I passed downtown, or the entry, "Accepting myself as a woman makes sense."

3.3   Epistemic Network Analysis

Epistemic Network Analysis (ENA) was used to accumulate qualitative connections and construct an initial linear model of the year [18]. Units of analysis were defined as all events associated with a given day. The ENA algorithm typically uses a moving window to judge co-temporality when constructing a network model [19]. However, because each conversation in my data consists of a single line (the data associated with a given day), the size of the window used by the algorithm was moot.

In the initial linear model, the resulting networks were not aggregated, as the data lacked *a priori* groups. In the subsequent linear model informed by the clusters discussed below, the resulting networks were aggregated by cluster number.

The ENA model normalized the networks for all units before they were subjected to any dimension reductions. In the initial linear model, the reduction used singular value decomposition, which produces orthogonal dimensions that maximize the variance explained by each. In the nonlinear model discussed below, the reduction used uniform manifold approximation and projection, which aims to preserve local information over global information. And in the final linear model, another singular value decomposition was used, this time rotated to place the effect of **Day** on the x-axis and the highest remaining variance on the y-axis.

Networks were visualized using network graphs where nodes correspond to the qualitative codes and edges reflect the relative frequency of co-occurrence between two codes. In the final linear model, these networks were compared using network difference graphs that illustrate differences between pairs of clusters by subtracting the weight of each connection in one cluster from the corresponding connection of the other. To improve legibility and parsimony of the resulting difference plots, Pearson correlations were run between the grouping variable and each connection, and connections with correlations below 30% were omitted.

To further test for differences between pairs of clusters, I applied a Mann-Whitney test to the location of the points in the final projected ENA space for units in each cluster, with a Bonferroni correction.

3.4   Nonlinear ENA

The ENA algorithm is a three step process. First, ENA represents qualitative data as a high dimensional space that models the connections between qualitative codes [18]. Second, ENA uses multidimensional scaling to reduce the dimensionality of that space while highlighting features of interest [18]. And third, ENA projects a network representation onto that scaled space as a way to illustrate the dynamics of those features [18]. Existing multidimensional scaling algorithms used by ENA have been linear, such as Means Rotation and Principle Component Analysis [18]. Linear dimensional reduction retains global information and is useful for hypothesis testing [20]. However, linear dynamics lead to stories told structurally around two points: a control vs. a treatment, a before vs. an after, or so on. Such stories fail to model the richness of transitions as experienced, as discussed in the results below. Therefore, my departure from existing ENA is to use a nonlinear multidimensional scaling algorithm instead. Nonlinear dimension reduction retains local information and is useful for hypothesis generation [20], and nonlinear dynamics, as demonstrated in the results below, captured the local ebbs and flows of a transition as experienced.

Density-Based Spatial Clustering of Applications with Noise (DBSCAN) has been used in the context of ENA before, DBSCAN has been used with Uniform Manifold Approximation and Projection (UMAP) outside of QE for temporal data visualization, and empirically UMAP has seen success in retaining insightful global structures [21, 22]. Therefore, I select UMAP and DBSCAN as my nonlinear dimension reduction and clustering algorithms for this demonstration. UMAP was used to reduce the dimensionality of a matrix where each column corresponded to a single ENA unit, and each row corresponded to a different ENA connection, with one row added to represent the normalized **Day** number. This results in a model that can be used to project the high dimensional space to a 2-dimensional plane and project additional points into that plane. Density-based clusters of similar "types" of days within that plane were then detected and labeled using DBSCAN.

To visualize UMAP and DBSCAN results, units were initially visualized color-coded on a spectrum from red (early days) to green (middle days) to blue (later days), and then subsequently color-coded based on cluster number. Networks were then projected into the space drawing on the network projection algorithm already used by ENA: In existing ENA visualization techniques, network connections are drawn as straight lines, such that the "elbow" of the line occurs at its mid point, and units are as near as possible to the "center of mass" of their respective networks' elbows [18]. A consequence of this is, if a unit has only connections between two given codes, then one expects that unit to be positioned exactly on that connection's elbow, though in practice this is approximate. So in deciding how to visualize networks in the UMAP space, I retained that intuition. Hypothetical units were constructed for each pair of codes such that that "unit" has only connections between that pair of codes and a missing value for its **Day** number. These network "units" were then projected into the UMAP plane and used as positions for connection elbows. The consequence of this is that units are visualized in the "neighborhoods of the elbows" for which they are likely to have connections. Nodes were then positioned such that, were the lines straight, units would be as close as possible to their networks' centers of mass. This is the same method used in ENA, and it has three consequences. One, nodes tend to be positioned legibly. Two, nodes positioned towards the edges of the plot are those that one should expect most linearly discriminate the global structure modeled by the plot. Three, specific to the nonlinear context here, one should expect clusters positioned near a given node to have many, various connections to that node.

4   Results

4.1   Existing Methods

The initial ENA model (Fig. 1) had a co-registration Pearson correlation of 94% along the x-axis and 92% along the y-axis, indicating a strong goodness of fit between the visualization and the original model. The x-axis captures the difference between (left) days that made connections to **Happy** vs. (right) those that made connections to

SkippedDose. The y-axis captures the difference between (bottom) days that connected **Happy**, **NonHappy**, and **Sweets** vs. (top) those that connected **REFLECT**, **BODY**, and **LEARN**.

In other words, the x-axis appears to model time, as early in the HRT process I was feeling doubts and skipped doses some days, and later, once I began to stick with it, I was happier more often. And the y-axis appears to model a difference between intro-spective days vs. days on which I was anxious and consumed caffeine: An accident of being stuck in my house during the pandemic, I ran out of caffeinated drinks, at which point I realized I craved drinks like Red Bull (**Sweets**) when I was anxious (**Non-Happy**), which compounded the anxiety.

These results are affirming! It warms my heart to see **Happy** placed in systematic contrast to **SkippedDose**. However, there are three immediate qualitative problems. One, this does not tell a rich story: "Happiness," no matter how morally relevant, is a thin concept. Two, what story it does tell too readily supports deficit narratives: The story is reduced to two poles, an ostensible "before" and "after," around which one can read my transition as a movement out of "damage" without any indication of where my own hopes might factor into that story. Three, it gets the story wrong: Skipping doses did not happen at the beginning of the story, tracking doses did, and the event that most brought about a structural break in my networks is missing:

In the first few months on HRT, I repeatedly started and stopped taking my pre-scriptions, a vicious cycle between (a) dysphoria and desire prompting me to start and (b) doubt prompting me to stop. Then, I ran low on pills. I ran out of refills. My doctor retired. Because I had taken these breaks, I messed up the timing we had worked out at my initial consult, and I was unable to get my prescriptions filled by another university doctor until nearer the Fall semester when my student status would resume. When things picked up around July and August, I had doubts again. However, this time I had several months of daily notes to reflect on. Re-reading these, I noticed that each time I had doubts was in the days leading up to picking up refills from the pharmacy. In my anxious mind, I would have to "prove" to the pharmacist that I deserved my pre-scription. I would have to "prove" it to my family, my friends, co-workers, students. And so I would stop. I communicated this to my new doctor at our first meeting. She sent me an email shortly after with a simple solution: She would put me down for a three-month dose so I would have to go to the pharmacist less often. It was this event, more than any other, that allowed me to find stability in my transition and move towards the goals I set for myself on my very first day: "I value happiness, passing, and understanding."

The existing linear approaches to ENA fail to capture these tensions between doubt and desire. The proposed nonlinear extension, on the other hand, elucidates it.

4.2 Nonlinear ENA

In the nonlinear projection (Fig. 2), **Happy**, **DoseTracking**, and **SkippedDoses** are placed around the edges, and the remaining nodes towards the center. The dose-related codes appear in opposition to happiness, as though creating a Y-shaped plot. Visually, the red to blue shift suggests an "arrow" of time that moves from the bottom left, where I tracked the doses I was taking down to the minute (information that I did not need but felt the need to keep anyway); over to the bottom right where I skipped doses; then back to the left, now a bit further up; and eventually continuing up and left towards **Happy**.

DBSCAN detected six clusters, numbered in order from earliest first-occurring unit to latest first-occurring unit. For brevity, I omit clusters 3 and 4 from discussion here: they are small; they are qualitatively less insightful than the others; and a discussion of clusters 1, 2, 5, and 6 suffices to demonstrate the method.

Between February 14th, 2020 and August 23rd, 2020, clusters 1 and 2 co-occurred. During that period I alternated between "1-type" days and "2-type" days, with a longer 2-type period over the Summer. Then, until November 14th, 2020, cluster 1 and cluster 5 co-occurred, with 1-type days decreasing in frequency and 5-type days increasing. Then, until the end of the year under study, cluster 5 and cluster 6 similarly co-occurred, with 5-type decreasing and 6-type increasing.

Visually, cluster 1 is located in the neighborhood of connections to **DoseTracking**. Cluster 2 is similarly located near **SkippedDose** and cluster 5 near **Happy**. Cluster 6 is located in the neighborhood of the connection between **Happy** and **PROGRESS**. Notice too that cluster 1 has a "chunk" missing, corresponding to the Summer 2-type days when I was unable to refill my prescriptions.

4.3   Quantitative Results

All statistical tests reported below are adjusted with a Bonferroni correction of $\alpha/4$. Table 2 gives summary statistics of code counts within clusters 1, 2, 5, and 6. Using a χ^2 test, I reject the null hypothesis in favor of the alternative that there is some relationship between these clusters and the counted codes at the $\alpha = 0.05$ level ($\chi^2 = 349.482$, $p < 0.0001$).

Table 2. Code counts for clusters 1, 2, 5, and 6.

Cluster	BODY	Dose-Tracking	Happy	LEARN	Non-Happy	PROG-RESS	RE-FLECT	Skipped-Dose	Sweets
#1	37	39	3	18	28	5	27	0	22
#2	23	0	7	6	6	4	21	36	12
#5	37	1	60	20	26	40	39	0	32
#6	0	0	12	6	1	11	0	0	0

The final ENA model (Fig. 1) was limited to only units in clusters 1, 2, 5, and 6 and rotated to show the effect of the **Day** number along the x-axis. This model had a co-registration Pearson correlation of 98% along the x-axis and 91% along the y-axis, indicating a strong goodness of fit between the visualization and the original model. Along the y-axis, a Mann-Whitney test showed that cluster 1 (Md1 = 0.17, N1 = 53) was statistically different at the $\alpha = 0.05$ level from cluster 2 (Md2 = -0.19, N2 = 36, $p < 0.0001$, U = 1789). Similarly, along the x-axis cluster 1 (Md1 = -0.29) was statistically different from cluster 5 (Md5 = 0.19, N5 = 69, $p < 0.0001$, U = 3654), and

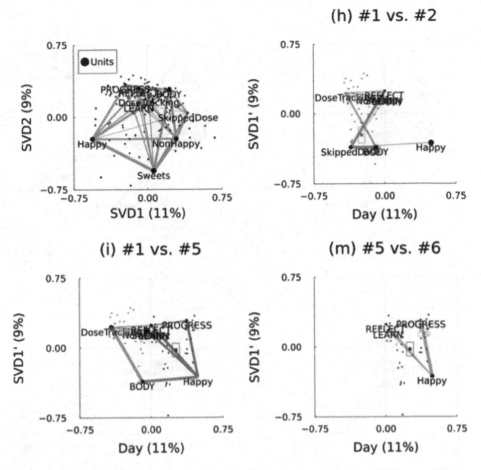

Fig. 1. Linear results (top left). ENA plot with SVD rotation. (remaining) Difference between group-wise networks in a linear projection showing the effect of **Day** along the x-axis. Group means and confidence intervals are shown by squares and the boxes around them. Also note that groups did not exist *a priori* and were detected through the non-linear process.

cluster 5 was statistically different from cluster 6 (Md6 = 0.44, N6 = 12, p < 0.012, U = 224).

Figure 2 shows the connections most prominent in each of those clusters. As was suggested by the placement of the nodes, cluster 1 was dominated by connections to **DoseTracking**, had connections to and between the introspective codes, and had few connections to **Happy** or **Progress**. Cluster 2 had connections between **SkippedDose**, **Reflect**, and **BODY**, with few other connections. Cluster 5 was dominated by connections to **Happy**, with many connections to and between the introspective codes, connections to **PROGRESS**, and almost no connections to **DoseTracking** or **SkippedDose**. Cluster 6 had almost only connections between **Happy** and **PROGRESS**.

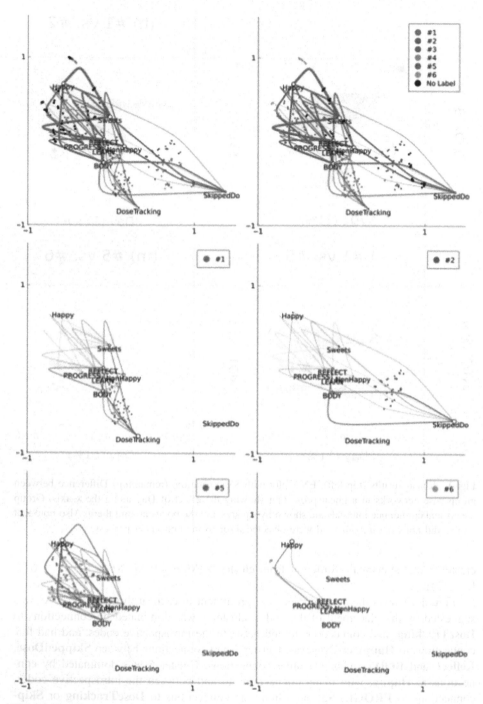

Fig. 2. Non-linear results (top left). Spectral color coding to show movement of time, from red to green to blue (top right). Cluster-wise color coding (remaining). Group-wise networks in the UMAP projection. (Color figure online)

Figure 1 shows the difference between these clusters in their time order: cluster 1 vs. cluster 2, cluster 1 vs. cluster 5, and cluster 5 vs. cluster 6. First, among other possible differences, cluster 1 had more connections to **DoseTracking** and cluster 2 had more connections to **SkippedDose**. Cluster 2 also had a few more connections between **SkippedDose** and **Happy**: giving up can bring about its own ostensible form of happiness. Second, and similarly, cluster 1 had more connections to **DoseTracking** and cluster 5 had more connections to **Happy**, most notably the connection with **PROGRESS**. Finally, among other possible differences, cluster 6 had relatively more connections between **Happy** and **PROGRESS** than cluster 5.

4.4 Qualitative Description

To better understand the difference between clusters 1, 2, 5, and 6, I focus my attention to **PROGRESS** in connection to the three dominating codes, **Happy**, **DoseTracking**, and **SkippedDose**.

The only occurrence of **PROGRESS** during the earlier half of cluster 1 was on April 27th, 2020. At this point, I had started and stopped HRT a few times. That day, I wrote:

> [1] 9:10p in my last note [this date], I was also thinking, from that dream, that I am tired of picking myself apart to get at the kinds of womanhood that are important to me. Can't I say, I want to be a woman, and that be enough?
> [2] e -s
> [3] 10p did i want to be shirley temple as a little kid?

In the first line, I am marking the time, to the minute, for this reflection, and on the second line I am marking that I took an Estradiol and not a Spironolactone at that time ("e -s"). On the final line, about 20 min after the Estradiol would have finished dissolving under my tongue and when I would have been getting ready for bed, I wrote a quick reflective question about my childhood: I recalled being into Shirley Temple when I was young and living at my grandmother's, and I wanted to note the memory so that I might reflect on it more later. But the most important part of this note was at the end of the first line: I was tired of all the ways I had been seeking "proof" during those first few months and so I, probably linguistically influenced by "ain't I a woman," wrote my first affirmation during the year under study, here as a rhetorical question.

Daily notes were rare during cluster 2. Most of the data I have for that period comes from my "checkbox" app, which was a quick and habitual end to my day after working out and before going to bed each night. But as the Fall semester was starting up, and when I had, once again, started and stopped HRT, I wrote:

> [1] when i stopped taking hrt both times and my breast development reduced it hurt it felt like coming home to realize your dog had died
> [2] i felt strong, powerful last night, doing yoga. like korra. lots of warrior 1 and 2

In the first line, I am trying to capture a specific kind of sadness, describing for the first time in my notes the relationship between concrete changes to my body and my sense of self. But this description of loss should be read with a tension of happiness to it: This was a clear, recent, and analytic moment that I could point to to abate my anxious mind. Holding onto that, I was able to let go of some worries, and I wrote an affirmation on the second line, relating myself to Korra, the queer and female protagonist of the cartoon series *The Legend of Korra*.

That act of affirmation was a rare bit of progress during this time period. It is easier to see my state of mind during cluster 2 by seeing the notes I wrote in cluster 1 right before a string of 2-type days. On May 4th, 2020, I logged that I had taken Estradiol without Spironolactone at 8:05am. At 3:40pm, I reflected on my relationship with gender and with cognitive behavior therapy. And at 5:15pm, I recounted the first time I had passed as a woman in public during the year under study: I was called "ma'am" while standing in line at Menards. But then weeks later, I wrote comments such as "thinking about stopping hrt" and "i am leaning towards stopping hormones."

Then September 15th, 2020, because I had talked with my doctor about how my doubts surfaced every time I was getting ready to visit the pharmacist, she sent me the message, "If you would be interested, I could put in 3-month supply worth of the medications for you to pick up at once. This would mean less trips to the pharmacy, which might be helpful for you." During the months that followed, I stopped tracking my doses. I simply took them. I passed more and more often in public as I gained the confidence to wear more female-coded clothes. And I wrote affirmations more often, such as "I'm not late onset I'm late opportunity," responding to an imagined critic that might criticize me for my later in life transition.

Throughout cluster 5, I had taken many steps towards building a stock of new clothing, new glasses, signing up for a make-up subscription service, and so on. The emotional and material capital I had gained during cluster 5 enabled me to start coming out to more friends, then co-workers, and eventually, in cluster 6, to my students and my hair stylist. All throughout my first year on HRT, it was these moments of incremental and concrete progress, enabled by repeat analytic reflection and support from my care providers, that allowed me to feel more comfortable as myself around other people and to write the following, towards the end of the year under study and days after the previous ICQE conference:

[1] got called maam on the phone when talking to [my dentist]
[2] ive been feeling really good about myself lately
[3] the haircut really helps [heart emoji]

5   Discussion

In this paper, I asked, *How can QE be used to tell a temporal story?*. To answer this, I have demonstrated Nonlinear ENA, an extension to existing QE methods that incorporates a nonlinear projection algorithm (in this example UMAP) and a clustering algorithm (in this example DBSCAN). This extension provides several affordances when working with temporal data. I illustrated this method using analytic autoethnographic data collected during my first year of feminizing hormone replacement therapy.

First, these techniques allowed me to make systematic decisions about how to relate units with similar units nearby in time when I had no *a priori* structure. Grouping the days into weeks or months would have imposed an artificial structure, one that would not have aligned with the time period as experienced in the day-to-day. Nor would grouping the days into equal-sized units have captured the ebb and flow and sometimes back and forth between multiple "types" of days.

Second, it identified which of many qualitatively meaningful moments actually incurred a structural break and provided a grounded and saturated structure by which to organize my narrative. Yes, I structured my account around the importance of an email from my doctor, but in my initial reflections before running the UMAP analysis, I was less informed about whether other personally important moments would have also incurred structural breaks: Coming out to my advisor, choosing a new name, quitting caffeine, and so on.

Third, it neatly modeled nonlinear behavior and visualized the effect of a structural break on that nonlinear behavior. I was only able to escape the vicious cycle of starting and stopping HRT once my doctor changed my dose to a three-month supply.

Finally, these results were reflectively surprising, which promoted clearer theoretical thinking. To me, "coming out" was the end of the story originally. And while that may be true in literal time order, its theoretical insight was limited by its infrequency: Once I came out to everyone in my day-to-day life, there was no one left to come out to, so **Out** was structurally different from other low-level codes. Even in earlier iterations of the UMAP projections where **Out** was a node, **Happy** retained its dominant position. It was reflecting on this that I realized: The insight I was drawn towards wasn't about coming out in itself, but about the different forms that progress took on when in connection to each of the time periods.

Altogether, these affordances allowed me to tell a rich, informed, and desire-based story that I was unable to tell using existing QE methods. In future work, I hope to refine this technique for data with multiple participants and for use with continuous variables other than time.

References

1. Deutsch, M.: Overview of feminizing hormone therapy. https://transcare.ucsf.edu/guidelines/feminizing-hormone-therapy. Accessed 15 Apr 2021
2. Antony, A.: Tacit knowledge and analytic autoethnography: methodological reflections on the sociological translation of self-experience. In: Revealing Tacit Knowledge: Embodiment and Explication. Transcript, Verlog. 139–167 (2015)
3. Knowles, M., Shaffer, D.W.: Hierarchical epistemic network analysis. In: Ruis A.R., Lee S. B. (eds.) Second International Conference on Quantitative Ethnography: Conference Proceedings Supplement. ICQE 2021. The International Society for Quantitative Ethnography (2021)
4. McDonald, N. et al.: Reliability and inter-rater reliability in qualitative research: norms and guidelines for CSCW and HCI Practice. In: Proceedings of the ACM on Human-Computer Interaction (2019)
5. Vryan, K.D.: Expanding analytic autoethnography and enhancing its potential. J. Contemp. Ethnogr. **35**(4), 405–409 (2006)
6. Astor, M.: Asa Hutchinson, G.O.P. Governor of Arkansas, Vetoes Anti-Transgender Bill. New York Times (2021)

7. Brown, N.M.: Methodological cyborg as black feminist technology: constructing the social self using computational digital autoethnography and social media. Cultural Studies & Critical Methodologies **19**(1), 55–67 (2019)
8. Anderson, L.A.: Analytic autoethnography. J. Contemp. Ethnogr. **35**(4), 373–395 (2006)
9. Tuck, E.: Suspending damage: a letter to communities. Harv. Educ. Rev. **79**(3), 409–428 (2009)
10. Meleis, A.I., et al.: Experiencing transitions: an emerging middle-range theory. Adv. Nurs. Sci. **23**(1), 12–28 (2000)
11. Levitt, H.M., Ippolito, M.R.: Being transgender: the experience of transgender identity development. J. Homosexual. **61**(12), 1727–1758 (2014). https://doi.org/10.1080/00918369. 2014.951262
12. Nehushtan, H.: Embodying normalcy: women exiting sex work and the boundaries of transformation. Qual. Sociol. **43**(4), 565–581 (2020)
13. Ohsaki, A., Oshima, J.: Socio-semantic network analysis of knowledge-creation discourse on a real-time scale. In: Ruis, A.R., Lee, S.B. (eds.) ICQE 2021. CCIS, vol. 1312, pp. 170–184. Springer, Cham (2021). https://doi.org/10.1007/978-3-030-67788-6_12
14. Wooldridge, A.R., Haefli, R.: Using epistemic network analysis to explore outcomes of care transitions. In: Eagan, B., Misfeldt, M., Siebert-Evenstone, A. (eds.) ICQE 2019. CCIS, vol. 1112, pp. 245–256. Springer, Cham (2019). https://doi.org/10.1007/978-3-030-33232-7_21
15. Emerson, R., et al.: Processing Fieldnotes: Coding and Memoing. Writing Ethnographic Fieldnotes, Chicago (2011)
16. Shaffer, D.W., Ruis, A.R.: How we code. In: Ruis, A.R., Lee, S.B. (eds.) ICQE 2021. CCIS, vol. 1312, pp. 62–77. Springer, Cham (2021). https://doi.org/10.1007/978-3-030-67788-6_5
17. Hughes, S.A, Pennington, J.L.: Autoethnography: Process, Product, and Possibility for Critical Social Research. SAGE Publications (2017)
18. Shaffer, D.W.: Quantitative Ethnography. Cathcart, Madison (2017)
19. Siebert-Evenstone, A., et al.: In search of conversational grain size: modelling semantic structure using moving stanza windows. J. Learn. Anal. **4**(3), 123–139 (2017)
20. Nguyen, L.H., Holmes, S.: Ten quick tips for effective dimensionality reduction. PLOS Computat. Biol. **15**(6), e1006907 (2019). https://doi.org/10.1371/journal.pcbi.1006907
21. Ali, M., Jones, M.W., Xie, X., Williams, M.: TimeCluster: dimension reduction applied to temporal data for visual analytics. Vis. Comput. **35**(6–8), 1013–1026 (2019). https://doi.org/10.1007/s00371-019-01673-y
22. Nguyen, H., et al.: Establishing trustworthiness through algorithmic approaches to qualitative research. In: Ruis, A.R., Lee, S.B. (eds.) ICQE 2021. CCIS, vol. 1312, pp. 47–61. Springer, Cham (2021). https://doi.org/10.1007/978-3-030-67788-6_4

Epistemic Network Analysis Visualization

Yuanru Tan[(⊠)] ⓘ, Cesar Hinojosa, Cody Marquart,
Andrew R. Ruis ⓘ, and David Williamson Shaffer ⓘ

Wisconsin Center for Education Research, University of Wisconsin–Madison,
Madison, WI, USA
yuanru.tan@wisc.edu

Abstract. Visualization plays an important role in Epistemic Network Analysis (ENA), not only in graphical representation but also to facilitate interpretation and communicate research findings. However, there is no published description of the design features behind ENA network graphs. This paper provides this description from a graphic design perspective, focusing on the design principles that make ENA network graphs aesthetically pleasing and intuitive to understand. By reviewing graphic design principles and examining other extant network visualizations, we show how the current ENA network graphs highlight the most important network characteristics and facilitate sense-making.

Keywords: Epistemic network analysis · Network graphs · Data visualization · Design principles

1 Introduction

The purpose of this paper is to explain the *network graph* visualization of Epistemic Network Analysis (ENA) from a graphic design perspective. ENA is a network analysis technique for quantifying and visualizing the connections among coded data by modeling the co-occurrence of codes [19]. Such connections are represented as weighted networks that can be interpreted both statistically and visually. Since its inception, ENA has become a dominant analytical technique used in Quantitative Ethnography (QE) studies [12]. QE is a growing field unifying rigorous computational methods and grounded ethnographic techniques to facilitate thick description at scale [18].

ENA's success is not only attributable to its analytical affordances, but also the *statistically* meaningful and *visually* interpretable network visualizations it produces. In previous work, Bowman et al. [3] discussed how the alignment between ENA network visualization and its summary statistics is achieved from a mathematical perspective. In this paper, we explore *how* ENA network graph visualizations facilitate interpretation of network models and communication of analytic findings. Thus, the intended contribution of this work is to explicate the graphic design principles manifested in ENA visualizations and to explore how ENA network graph visualizations can be used as "tools for thinking" [17].

In what it follows, we center the discussion around three guiding questions: (1) What are the graphic design principles that inform the design of ENA network

B. Wasson and S. Zörgő (Eds.): ICQE 2021, CCIS 1522, pp. 129–143, 2022.
https://doi.org/10.1007/978-3-030-93859-8_9

graph visualizations? (2) Why do ENA networks require custom visualizations rather than existing network visualization strategies? and (3) How were the aforementioned graphic design principles applied to design ENA network graph visualizations?

2 Theory: Graphic Design

2.1 Design Elements

Design elements, also known as *elements of design*, are the most fundamental graphic design units from which all visual artifacts are created [4, 16]. In the context of graphic design, the most commonly cited seven design elements include point, line, shape, color, texture, value, and space [4, 16]. Each type of design element can be described using various attributes. For example, lines can hold attributes such as being thick, thin, dashed, dotted, horizontal, vertical, and so on.

Design elements are usually used in combination to form complex items, or *artifacts*. For example, Node-Link diagrams, as shown in Fig. 1, are a type of network graph representing the relationships between objects: the objects are represented with points (nodes), and the relationships between objects are represented with lines (links).

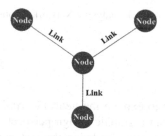

Fig. 1. A simplified representation of a Node-Link diagram.

To convey visual messages efficiently in the construction of artifacts, designers apply *design principles* to design elements in order to regulate the arrangement of and interaction among the elements [7]. Before we discuss the specifics of design principles, there are two fundamental attributes of the seven design elements that are often manipulated to apply various design principles, namely the *visual weight* and the *placement* of design elements.

Visual Weight of Design Elements. Every design element in a visualization exerts an attractive force that draws the eye of the viewer. The greater the force, the more the eye is drawn. This force is called *visual weight* [4]. For example, research shows that an object is visually heavy if it is dark or large [22, 23]. Therefore, the variance of visual weight is crucial in realizing effects of design principles that emphasize the creation of difference such as *contrast* and *visual hierarchy*, which are discussed in detail below.

Placement of Design Elements. While *visual weight* is usually applied to emphasize differences between individual elements, the *placement* of design elements is usually used to establish a visual connection among elements. For example, placement can be used to indicate relationships, such as similarity between objects. Research shows that viewers tend to interpret objects that are placed physically closer as being associated: the closer they are, the stronger the association is [4]. Placement can also be used to create flow by arranging elements with different visual weights in a certain pattern [4]. For example, when objects are placed in a way that larger or darker ones are in the foreground while smaller and lighter ones are in the background consistently, viewers tend to feel a sense of depth as larger and darker objects appear to be closer, even in a two-dimensional space. With such a sense of depth, even without explicit gestural signs such as arrows, a flow is present from near to far that guides viewers through the visualization along a particular path. These two major applications of placement manifest themselves respectively in two design principles called *proximity* and *perspective*, which are discussed in detail below.

2.2 Design Principles

Design principles are frameworks that define and regulate how design elements interact with one another, with their context, and with their viewers [7, 9]. Through the appropriate application of design principles, designers can optimize the arrangement of design elements to convey specific visual messages. While there are dozens of variations of design principles used in graphic design [4], the following four principles are most pertinent to our discussion of network visualizations specifically.

Design Principle 1: Contrast. *Contrast* refers to the use of differences in visual weight to signal differences in design elements [7]. Contrast can be formed when extra visual weight is given to one element relative to another. The greater the visual weight difference, the greater the contrast. Essentially, establishing contrast is dependent on the difference in attributes, such as shape and color.

For example, in Fig. 2 no contrast exists on the left example because visual weight is evenly distributed given the elements are identical in both shape and color. On the right, contrast is present because of the different visual weights created by differences in color and shape. For example, elements in red attracts more attention as they carry more visual weight again a white background. We can also observe that the contrast is enhanced when the two elements contrast in both shape and size.

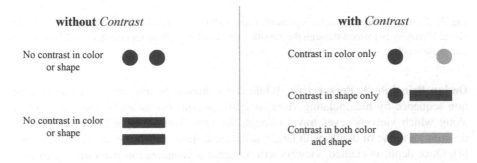

Fig. 2. Left: no contrast in shown due to equally distributed visual weight. Right: contrast is formed between elements with different shapes or colors.

Design Principle 2: Visual Hierarchy. After we understand that *Contrast* can be achieved through the uneven distribution of visual weight, it is important to consider how we can take advantage of the distribution of visual weight to manage the distribution and path of viewers' attention. In other words, designers want to control which information in the visualization is prioritized and in what order, a design principle called *visual hierarchy*.

Visual hierarchy is the arrangement of design elements in order of importance, or in order of the intended sequence that designers expect viewers to land their eye on [4]. Because elements with similar visual weight will naturally exhibit similarity, the proper use of visual weights is foundational in signaling visual hierarchy [4]. Size and color are two primary ways to establish visual hierarchy. Research shows that the eye is naturally drawn to larger parts of a design first [23]. In design terms, that means a larger object has more priority than a smaller object. Similar to size, objects that are darker hold higher priority as well and are more likely to be seen before objects that are lighter. Therefore, it is important to make sure that the most important element that you want viewers to pay attention to holds the heaviest visual weight.

Watzman [22] proposed the Squint Test to evaluate visual hierarchy. For example, to evaluate the visual hierarchy of the two examples in Fig. 3 below, simply squint your eyes at either example. As you look at it, is there a dominant element that attracts your eye first and the most? When the visual hierarchy is set up appropriately, the element you noticed first should be the one with the heaviest visual weight, such as the thickest and darkest lines.

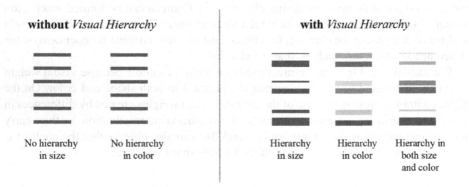

Fig. 3. Left: no visual hierarchy is present because all lines are in identical size and color. Right: visual hierarchy is formed through the variation of visual weight as represented by differences in size and/or color.

Design Principle 3: Perspective. While *visual hierarchy* triggers the intended attention sequence by manipulating visual weights, *perspective* is applied to create a flow along which viewers' eyes travel through the visualization. Specifically, *perspective* describes a sense of depth, with larger or darker objects appearing closer to the viewer [4]. Once depth is created, viewers will navigate a visualization from most proximate elements to most remote. There are many ways to create flow, such as shadows, gradient, size, and color. The two that are related to network visualization specifically are size and color given that points and lines are two major design elements used in networks.

In the three examples in Fig. 4, although nodes and lines are placed in similar arrangement, they differ in size and color. By placing larger and darker elements in the foreground in a consistent manner such as the example on the right, a sense of depth is present and viewers' eyes naturally flow from the foreground to background. Compared to the other two examples, although the middle one includes variance in size and color, a "see-through" effect is not present given that it does not have a consistent manner when it comes to the order of elements placement.

without *Perspective*   **without** *Perspective*   **with** *Perspective*

Fig. 4. Left: perspective is absent due to the absence of depth created by the unified node and line attributes. Middle: perspective is absent despite the presence of depth due to inconsistent placement of nodes and lines with different visual weight. Right: perspective is present because of the ordered variance in elements' visual weight and placement.

Design Principle 4: Proximity. *Proximity* refers to the use of relative distance between design elements to indicate relationship. When applying proximity, elements that are similar or related are placed into closer proximity to form a visual connection, while elements that are dissimilar or unrelated are place farther apart to disrupt or discourage visual connection [4].

For example, assuming that a set of 12 nodes can be divided into three categories based on their similarity, Fig. 5 below shows how proximity conveys such a message visually. On the right, more similar nodes are clustered, or placed physically closer to one another than they are to any other nodes. This makes it easy for the viewer to identify which nodes are related to one another and which are not.

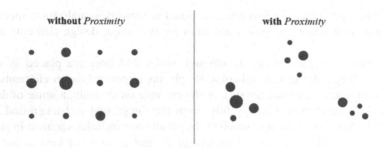

Fig. 5. Left: nodes are placed in equal distance without proximity variance, providing no information about which nodes are similar or dissimilar. Right: the distance between nodes is varied to indicate similarity and difference.

3   Background: Network Visualization

Before we explain how the aforementioned graphic design principles are applied in ENA visualizations, we briefly review other extant network graph visualizations and discuss why they are not suitable for visualizing ENA networks.

3.1   Graph Layout Algorithms

Over the past three decades, a wide range of graph layout algorithms have been developed to support visualization of network models [2, 10, 13]. Among two-dimensional layout methods that draw Node-Link diagrams, there are eight represen-tative layouts in five families based on groupings commonly used in the literature [20, 21]. Due to space limitations, we present one popularly used and publicly available layout, the *Fruchterman Reingold* (FR) layout [10], as an example to explain why ENA models require custom visualizations.

The Fruchterman Reingold (FR) layout belongs to the *force-directed* family, a class of algorithms that produces graphs by simulating interactions as a system of forces. The resulting layout is an "equilibrium state" of the system [10]. Since its inception in 1991, new FR variants are still introduced every year [21]. While each new FR variant might have its unique affordances, the resulting FR visualizations generally share the three characteristics below [6, 10, 11, 14]:

1. Node positions are not deterministic. Each time the FR algorithm is run, it will result a visualization with slightly different node layout. For example, graphs A and B in Fig. 6 represent the same network model drawn using the same FR algorithm, but they have different node positions.

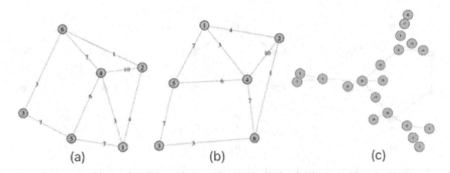

Fig. 6. Three graphs drawn in FR layout using igraph R package [5]. (a) and (b) represent the same six-node network with different node position. (c) represents a larger network of 20 nodes.

2. Edge crossing and node overlapping are minimized. Since node position is not deterministic, the algorithm places nodes and edges iteratively until it approaches or fully satisfies this aesthetic criterion. For example, in relatively sparse networks such as A, B, and C in Fig. 6, edge crossing and node overlapping are fully avoided.
3. Nodes that share more connections are closer to each other. As a force-directed algorithm, nodes in FR layout repulse each other when they get close and the edges act as springs that attract connected nodes together. As a result, a force balance is achieved in the graph, and nodes that are connected more strongly are placed closer. For example, in graph C, clusters are formed visually because the more connected nodes are placed closer together.

3.2 Challenges in Visualizing ENA Networks

As Bowman et al. [3] argued, a key feature that differentiates ENA from traditional network analytical approaches is that ENA produces *content-based* summary statistics that can be used to compare the *content* rather than the *structure* of networks. In other words, instead of comparing networks using structural summary statistics such as network density without reference to specific nodes, ENA compares networks in terms of which nodes are connected and how more or less strongly they are connected. Therefore, (1) enabling such content comparison visually and (2) representing the resulting differences visually become two core challenges that ENA network graph visualizations need to address.

To address the first challenge, ENA places its nodes in a network space through a process called *co-registration*, which results a single metric space with fixed node position for all networks in the same ENA model. With a set of fixed node position, multiple networks can be compared directly regarding connected nodes and connection strength. For example, in Fig. 7, since (a) and (b) share the same node position, it is visually clear that which pairs of nodes are strongly or weakly connected in one graph but not the other. However, although (b) and (c) visually look identical, they are very different networks in terms of *content*. That is, which nodes are connected and their connection strength.

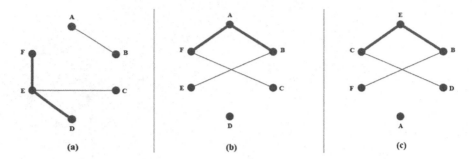

Fig. 7. Three weighted networks with same density but different patterns of connections. Specifically, (a) and (b) have identical node position but different connection pattern. (b) and (c) have different node position but appear to be but in fact not identical connection pattern.

The mathematical details of *co-registration* are beyond the scope of this paper and can be found in the work of Bowman et al. [3]. But in brief, *co-registration* is a process of producing network graph visualizations that meaningfully reflect the statistical properties of the network model. The fixed node position not only allows for meaningful comparison of the patterns of connections in multiple networks, also allows for interpretation of the metric space itself. Compared to the non-deterministic node position of FR layout (characteristics 1), ENA visualizes its network with a set of deterministic node position determined by *co-registration*. Furthermore, in ENA, the distance between nodes in the network space does not reflect connection strength as in FR layout, but represent similarity of the roles that different nodes have in network structure. The nodes that are closer to each other in an ENA space have more similar roles in the networks in which they appear. If an ENA network were visualized using *force-directed* algorithms such as FR layout, researchers would be unable to interpret the locations of networks in ENA space.

While *co-registration* addressed the first challenge in terms of enabling content comparison visually, the second challenge about how to visually represent the resulting differences between networks still remains. However, the second challenge in more of a graphic design challenge than an analytical challenge. As an analytical method, ENA is designed to model connections in weighted networks that usually have a small number of nodes but are densely connected [19]. Edge-crossings are mostly unavoidable in such networks. While edge-crossings can hinder readability and should be avoided in network visualizations [7, 15], it is hard to realize in ENA networks given its high density, fixed node position, and straight-lined edges. Although *force-directed* algorithms such as FR layout are optimized to avoid edge-crossing (characteristic 2), this affordance is not applicable to ENA visualization because of ENA's deterministic node position. Therefore, instead of removing edge-crossing, ENA visualizations need to represent connections in a readable and sensible way regardless of the potential edge-crossing challenges posed by its high network density. In the following section, we will elaborate on how the second challenge in addressed using graphic design principles.

4   Applying Design Principles in ENA Visualizations

In this section, we explain how the aforementioned four design principles—*contrast, visual hierarchy, perspective,* and *proximity*—are applied in the design of ENA visualizations. We use an undirected weighted network with density of 1.0 as a simplified example to demonstrate the transformation from a basic Node-Link diagram to an ENA visualization, step by step.

4.1   Use of Contrast to Emphasize Edges

Graph #1 in Fig. 7 represents a Node-Link diagram in a basic layout: nodes A, B, C, and D are connected using straight lines and connection weights are annotated using numbers next to each edge, varying from 0.2 to 1.0.

There are two noticeable problems in Graph #1. First, there is no clear focal point to draw viewers' attention. Since the structure of connections among codes are usually the primary research interest in ENA studies, we hope to attract viewers' eyes more to the edges in the network. To do so, we break the evenly distributed visual weight in Graph #1 by increasing the color contrast between nodes and edges to make edges stand out, as shown in Graph #2. With the increased color contrast, the connections between nodes represented by edges become more easily noticeable (Fig. 8).

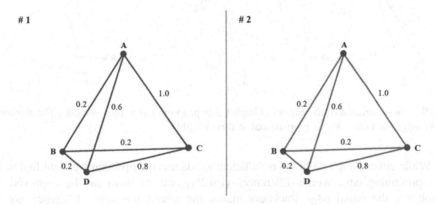

Fig. 8. Left: no color contrast between nodes and edges. Right: edges stand out because edges in red against white background creates stronger contrast

Second, in Graph #1, in order to understand differences in connection strength, viewers have to process the magnitude differences of the numbers next to each edge, which increases cognitive load. Also, in dense networks where edge-crossing is unavoidable, placing numerals next to already crossed edges adds additional ambiguity to the visualization. Therefore, the visual appearance of the edges not only needs to help viewers discriminate between edges base on their weights but also needs to keep the visualization as clean as possible. In next section, we explain how used the principle of visual hierarchy to emphasize stronger connections (edges with larger weights) and deemphasize weaker connections (edges with smaller weights).

4.2   Use of Visual Hierarchy to Differentiate Connection Weights

To help researchers identify the strongest connections between coded elements in ENA
network graphs, we assign the highest prominence to the edge with heaviest weight.
For example, in Graph #2, we want edge AC to be the edge that attracts the most
attention.

There are two ways to do this. One approach is to vary edge saturation (Graph #3),
the other is to vary edge thickness (Graph #4). To vary saturation, we first assign the
fully saturated color to edge AC, which has the largest weight, so that AC is the visually
heaviest element in the graph. Then, we make the level of saturation of all the other
edges proportional to their weights. For example, edge CD has a weight that is 80% of
the weight of edge AC, so the level of saturation in edge CD is 80% that of edge AC. The
end result of creating visual hierarchy through color saturation is shown in Graph #3. To
vary edge thickness, we use the same process. The edge with the largest weight is
assigned some maximum thickness, and the thicknesses of the remaining edges are
scaled proportionally. The end result is shown in Graph #4 (Fig. 9).

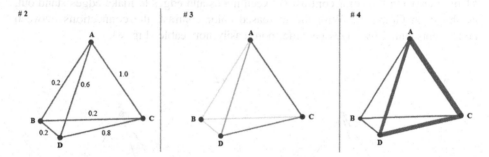

Fig. 9. The *saturation* of the edges in Graph # 3 is proportional to their weights. The *thickness*
of the edges in Graph # 4 is proportional to their weights.

While either Graph #3 or # 4 is sufficient to address the problem we identified in #2
by representing edge weigh differences visually, both of them can be improved. In
Graph #3, the equal edge thickness makes the visual hierarchy difference not as
noticeable as in Graph #4. In Graph #4, although the edge weight differences are
immediately clear, the edge-crossings appear to decrease readability due to all edges
being fully saturated. Therefore, we create the clearest visual hierarchy by using size
and color simultaneously as represented in Graph #5 (Fig. 10).

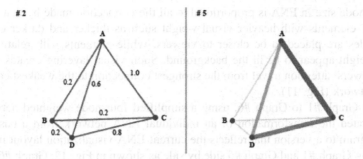

Fig. 10. Edges in Graph #5 are in different thickness and saturation to reflect actual edge weights. Heavier edges are thicker and more saturated than lighter edges.

In Graph #5, by proportionally scaling both thickness and saturation, viewers can easily estimate the differences in edge weights not only for any two edges but also across the network structure as a whole. In scientific visualizations, the degree of visual weight difference should mirror the intended analytic difference [1, 15], and the proportional scaling of saturation and thickness accomplishes this.

4.3 Use of Perspective to Guide Navigation

As of now, in terms of inspecting edge weight differences, the version presented by Graph #5 is readable. To further guide viewers navigate the visualization as a whole, we applied *perspective* to create a flow. As discussed before, by placing larger and darker elements in the foreground in a consistent manner, a sense of depth will present and viewers' eyes naturally flow from the foreground to background. To create such flow, on the basis of Graph #5, we adjust size of each node based on the connection made by that node. Since heavier edges are already placed on top of lighter edges and appear physically closer to viewers, large nodes automatically follow this pattern

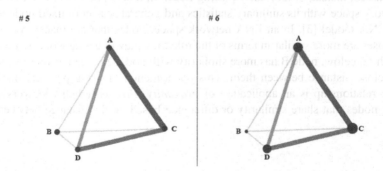

Fig. 11. Node sizes in Graph #6 are adjusted accordingly based on the connection weights.

because node size in ENA is proportional to all the connection made by that code. By doing so, elements with heavier visual weight such as thicker and darker edges and large nodes are placed to be closer to viewers, while elements with relative lighter visual weight appear to be in the background. Such visual layering creates a flow to guide viewers' attention travel from the strongest connection to the weakest connection in the network (Fig. 11).

From Graph #1 to Graph #6, using a simplified four-node weighted network, we demonstrated the transformation of an individual ENA network from a basic Node-Link diagram to a version that reflects the current ENA visualization layout in use. By comparing Graph #1 and Graph #6 side by side as shown in Fig. 12, Graph #6 presents viewers with a visualization that is not only visually self-explanatory, but also takes less time to identify the connection strength differences across the network, even without the numerals next to edges.

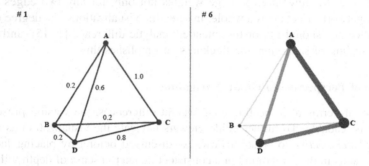

Fig. 12. Compare the initial Graph #1 with the finalized ENA visualization Graph #6.

4.4   Use of Proximity to Indicate Similarity and Difference

As discussed, instead of arbitrarily placing nodes in a network space, ENA co-register its network space with its summary statistics and generates a set of fixed node position for an ENA model [3]. In an ENA network space, nodes that are placed more physically closer are more similar in terms of the role they play in the network. For example, in Graph #6 below, node B has more similarity with node D in the network as indicated by the close distance between them. This phenomenon of using physical distance to indicate relationship is an application of *proximity*. *Proximity* helps viewers quickly identify nodes that share similarity or difference based on the distance between them.

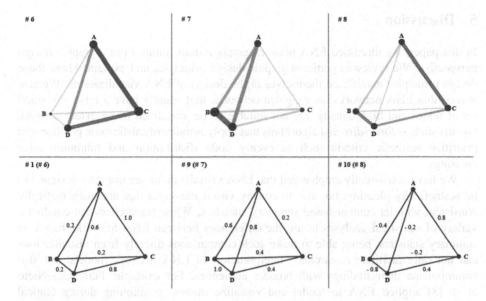

Fig. 13. In the top row, Graph #8 is the difference graph of Graph #6 and Graph #7. Edges in red in #8 represents the salient characteristics of #6, edges in blue in #8 represents the salient characteristics of # 7. Accordingly, in the bottom row, Graph #1, #9, and #10 are the basic Node-Link diagram version of Graph #6, #7, and #8.

Besides showing similarity and differences between nodes, the fixed node position is also an essential precondition to compare ENA networks visually. Because of the fixed node position, ENA can construct a subtracted network, which enables the identification of the most salient differences between two networks that belong to a same model. To do this, ENA subtracts the weight of each connection in one network from the corresponding weighted connection in another network, then visualize the connection strength difference. Similar as in individual networks, darker and thicker edges indicate larger differences in connection strength, and light and thinner edges indicate smaller differences in connection strength. Each edge is color-coded to indicate which of the two networks contains the stronger connection. For example, in Fig. 13, Graph #8 is a subtracted network of Graph #6 and #7. Based on the thickness and saturation of the color-coded edges, we can conclude that overall the subtracted network shows that relative to Graph #7, Graph #6 has the strongest connections in the upper right part of the space as presented by edge AC; although CD is also in red, the difference is not as strong as in AC because of the thinner and lighter edge of CD. Graph #7 has the strongest connections in the lower left part of the space as represented by BD relative to Graph #6.

5 Discussion

In this paper, we discussed ENA network graph visualizations from a graphic design perspective. We reviewed pertinent graphic design principles and explained how those design principles manifested themselves in the design of ENA visualizations. We also argued that ENA networks, as weighted networks that usually have a relatively small set of nodes and high density, are not suitable to be visualized using extant network layouts such as *force-directed* algorithms that apply nondeterministic node position and prioritize aesthetic criteria such as evenly node distribution and minimum edge crossings.

We have consistently emphasized that ENA visualizations are not only designed to be aesthetically pleasing, but also to convey visual messages that are mathematically consistent with its content-based summary statistics. While researchers can conduct a variety of statistical analyses to test the differences between ENA networks based on summary statistics, being able to make such comparisons directly from visualizations can not only facilitate researchers' interpretation of ENA network models, but also communicate their findings with broader audiences. For example, Fernandez-Nieto et al. [8] applied ENA to model and visualize nurses' positioning during clinical simulations and invited nurse teachers who did not have expertise in ENA to make sense of the ENA visualizations. Those teachers constructed consistent narratives about ENA network models and valued ENA visualizations as an accessible shared language for joint sense-making between researchers and practitioners.

Furthermore, we hope that this work provides a helpful perspective for visualization designers in reflecting on design choices in designing visualization for various purposes, but we recognize that designing is a versatile task and an iterative process that cannot be prescribed with fixed guidelines. Therefore, we look forward to being inspired by studies that use ENA visualizations in various contexts and disciplines.

Acknowledgements. This work was funded in part by the National Science Foundation (DRL-1661036, DRL-1713110), the Wisconsin Alumni Research Foundation, and the Office of the Vice Chancellor for Research and Graduate Education at the University of Wisconsin-Madison. The opinions, findings, and conclusions do not reflect the views of the funding agencies, cooperating institutions, or other individuals.

References

1. Allen, E.A., Erhardt, E.B.: Visualizing scientific data. In: Cacioppo, J.T., Tassinary, L.G., Berntson, G.G. (eds.) Cambridge Handbooks in Psychology. Handbook of Psychophysiology, pp. 679–697. Cambridge University Press, Cambridge (2017)
2. Battista, G.D., Eades, P., Tamassia, R., Tollis, I.G.: Graph Drawing: Algorithms for the Visualization of Graphs. Prentice Hall PTR, Hoboken (1998)
3. Bowman, D., et al.: The mathematical foundations of epistemic network analysis. In: Ruis, A.R., Lee, S.B. (eds.) ICQE 2021. CCIS, vol. 1312, pp. 91–105. Springer, Cham (2021). https://doi.org/10.1007/978-3-030-67788-6_7
4. Bradley, S.: Design Fundamentals: Elements, Attributes, and Principles. Vanseo Design, Colorado (2013)

5. Csardi, M.G.: Package 'igraph.' Netw. Anal. Vis. **3**(09), 2013 (2013)
6. Eades, P.: A heuristic for graph drawing. Congr. Numer. **42**, 149–160 (1984)
7. Evergreen, S., Metzner, C.: Design principles for data visualization in evaluation. New Dir. Eval. **2013**(140), 5–20 (2013)
8. Fernandez-Nieto, G.M., Martinez-Maldonado, R., Kitto, K., Shum, S.B.: Modelling spatial behaviours in clinical team simulations using epistemic network analysis: methodology and teacher evaluation. In: LAK21: 11th International Learning Analytics and Knowledge Conference (2021).https://doi.org/10.1145/3448139.3448176
9. Few, S., Edge, P.: Data Visualization: Past, Present, and Future. IBM Cognos Innovation Center (2007)
10. Fruchterman, T.M., Reingold, E.M.: Graph drawing by force-directed placement. Softw. Pract. Exp. **21**(11), 1129–1164 (1991)
11. Gibson, H., Faith, J., Vickers, P.: A survey of two-dimensional graph layout techniques for information visualisation. Inf. Vis. **12**(3–4), 324–357 (2013)
12. Kaliisa, R., Misiejuk, K., Irgens, G.A., Misfeldt, M.: Scoping the emerging field of quantitative ethnography: opportunities, challenges and future directions. In: Ruis, A.R., Lee, S.B. (eds.) ICQE 2021. CCIS, vol. 1312, pp. 3–17. Springer, Cham (2021). https://doi.org/10.1007/978-3-030-67788-6_1
13. Kobourov, S.G.: Force-directed drawing algorithms. In: Handbook of Graph Drawing and Visualization (2013)
14. Kwon, O.H., Crnovrsanin, T., Ma, K.L.: What would a graph look like in this layout? a machine learning approach to large graph visualization. IEEE Trans. Visual Comput. Graph. **24**(1), 478–488 (2017)
15. Lok, S., Feiner, S., Ngai, G.: Evaluation of visual balance for automated layout. In: Proceedings of the 9th International Conference on Intelligent User Interfaces, pp. 101–108 (2004)
16. Samara, T.: Design Elements: A Graphic Style Manual. Rockport Press, Beverly (2007)
17. Shum, S.B.: Quantitative ethnography visualizations as tools for thinking keynote. In: International Conference on Quantitative Ethnography (2021)
18. Shaffer, D.W.: Quantitative Ethnography. Cathcart Press, Madison (2017)
19. Shaffer, D., Ruis, A.: Epistemic network analysis: a worked example of theory-based learning analytics. Handbook of Learning Analytics (2017)
20. Tamassia, R. (ed.): Handbook of Graph Drawing and Visualization. CRC Press, Boca Raton (2013)
21. Von Landesberger, T., et al.: Visual analysis of large graphs: State-of-the-Art and future research challenges. Comput. Graph. Forum **30**(6), 1719–1749 (2011). Blackwell Publishing Ltd., Oxford
22. Watzman, S.: Visual design principles for usable interfaces. In: The Human-Computer Interaction Handbook: Fundamentals, Evolving Technologies and Emerging Applications, pp. 263–285 (2003)
23. Ware, C.: Information Visualization: Perception for Design. Morgan Kaufmann Publishers, Burlington (2000)

Methodology in the Mirror: A Living, Systematic Review of Works in Quantitative Ethnography

Szilvia Zörgő[1]([✉]) [iD], Gjalt-Jorn Ygram Peters[2] [iD], Clara Porter[3] [iD],
Marcia Moraes[4] [iD], Savannah Donegan[3], and Brendan Eagan[3] [iD]

[1] Care and Public Health Research Institute, Maastricht University, Maastricht,
The Netherlands
s.zorgo@maastrichtuniversity.nl
[2] Faculty of Psychology, Open University, Heerlen, The Netherlands
[3] University of Wisconsin-Madison, Madison, USA
[4] Colorado State University, Fort Collins, USA

Abstract. Quantitative Ethnography is a nascent field now formulating the specifics of its conceptual framework and terminology for a unified, quantitative – qualitative methodology. Our living, systematic review aims to shed light on decisions in research design that the community has made thus far in the domain of data collection, coding & segmentation, analysis, and how Quantitative Ethnography as a methodology is conceptualized. Our analysis intends to spur discussions on these issues within the community and help establish a lingua franca.

Keywords: Systematic review · Quantitative ethnography · Methodology

1 Introduction

Quantitative ethnography (QE) is a nascent field aiming to establish a unified, quantitative – qualitative research methodology. This endeavor entails the formulation of novel concepts, negotiation of terminology, and developing new techniques that serve a wide variety of research initiatives in multiple disciplines. There are some key hubs contributing to this process, but it is by and large a polycentric effort; currently circa 400 researchers from over 130 institutions in at least 30 countries engage with QE and the QE community to test and generate theories, implement theoretical constructs, and refine existing knowledge. Due to the interdisciplinary nature of QE, this conceptual framework needs to be traversable by researchers from a wide array of fields, and its terminology needs to be flexible enough to accommodate both novel forms of usage and some degree of standardization in order to shape a lingua franca.

QE research involves or is conducted on Discourse data [1, 2]; this may include data in the form of spoken or written speech (interview transcripts, log files, social media data, etc.), annotations on observations (field notes, structured observation, etc.), and visual data (video recordings, photovoice, etc.). Alongside discourse, other types of data may be collected as well. For example, when Shum et al. investigated teamwork in

B. Wasson and S. Zörgő (Eds.): ICQE 2021, CCIS 1522, pp. 144–159, 2022.
https://doi.org/10.1007/978-3-030-93859-8_10

nursing team simulations, apart from the discourse of participants, they also recorded heart rate, skin conductance, movement, and (co-)location [3]. Furthermore, different forms of metadata may be collected, e.g., Dowell et al. were interested in how individual-level roles and group compositions influence both student and group performance during collaborative interactions in online collaborative-learning environments. Aside from analyzing discourse, they collected metadata such as which dataset and which student group the data provider belonged to, as well as assigned a timestamp and a unique identifier for each of their contributions [4]. Metadata can be used to group data providers and their discourse, enabling a wide variety of analyses.

In order to represent various types of data in a single, unified dataset in a human and machine-readable format, qualitative data needs to be quantified. This is typically achieved through discourse segmentation and coding. Critically, discourse data needs to be transcribed, which involves a number of decisions, e.g., spoken words are transformed into sentences including punctuation and diarization – assigning spoken language to given speakers. Segmentation, or dividing discourse data into meaningful parts, may occur on several levels. The lowest level of segmentation is referred to as an *utterance*; in text data these are usually a sentence or a turn-of-talk [2]. Utterances may be grouped into "stanzas" and "conversations" to provide relational or temporal context. Content within discourse is represented by applying inductively (bottom-up, grounded) or deductively (top-down, a priori) developed discourse codes [5]. In the final dataset, each row of the "qualitative data table" [2] contains an utterance and each column represents a variable with values in categorical or binary form, which can be metadata or discourse codes. This unified dataset can then be employed for performing various analyses and modelling complex interactions.

Several tools and techniques have been developed under the auspices of QE, aiming to facilitate a part of the process described above or to enable various analyses using the generated dataset. For example, nCoder is a platform that can be utilized to develop, refine, validate, and implement automated coding schemes. One aspect of code validation is ensuring raters share a common understanding of each discourse code they employ; this is generally achieved through coder training and Inter-Rater Reliability (IRR) and tests of agreement, such as Cohen's Kappa. Aside from IRR testing, nCoder can be employed for automated coding based on classifiers, an algorithmic process that identifies whether a piece of data belongs to a certain category or class [5]. This is helpful when working with large corpora, for example. Another QE tool, the Reproducible Open Coding Kit (ROCK) is a standard for working with qualitative data, helping researchers organize data sources, designate characteristics of data providers, as well as code and segment discourse data. The ROCK is implemented in an R package and a graphical user interface that eases manual coding of data. [6].

Epistemic Network Analysis (ENA) has been the flagship tool within QE, enabling researchers to explore and model salient patterns in their data with network graphs. ENA depicts the structure of connections among codes in discourse by calculating the co-occurrence of each unique pair of codes within a designated segment of data, and aggregates this information in a cumulative adjacency matrix. ENA represents this matrix as a vector in high-dimensional space, which is then normalized to quantify relative frequencies of co-occurrence independent of discourse length or simple volume of talk. In this process, network connection strengths are transformed to fall between zero and one, and ENA then projects the networks as points into a low-dimensional space using singular value decomposition (SVD), which maximizes the variance explained. This analytical tool hence provides two, coordinated representations of the unified dataset: 1) network graphs, where the nodes in the model correspond to the codes in the discourse and the edges represent the relative strength of connection among codes, and 2) ENA scores, or the position of the plotted points on each dimension of the plotted points for units of each network in the low-dimensional space. ENA uses two parameters to operationalize relational context for each unit of analysis: conversation and stanza window. Conversations are groupings of utterances, which can be connected in a model, and stanza windows are an option for defining how connection structure is computed within conversations for a given unit of analysis. Network models are thus constructed based on researcher decisions made when creating the qualitative data table (e.g., operationalization of segmentation and coding) and decisions regarding network parameterization (e.g., designation of unit, conversation, stanza window) [7].

Due to the fact that decisions in research design, data collection, data transformation and representation all potentially affect results, and by virtue, conclusions drawn from those results, it is crucial to make conscious choices throughout the entire process. Well-informed decisions are founded on individuals' access to the cumulative knowledge that a field has generated. Such knowledge is in part conveyed via reporting on vital features of the research process within publications. In the case of QE, because it is still a developing methodology, reporting standards are yet to be solidified. Accumulated knowledge is also effectively conveyed through researchers taking advantage of Open Science (OS) practices, such as making their research process (codebook, analysis scripts, etc.) transparent via a public repository. OS principles and practices are gaining momentum in the scientific community, but primarily among initiatives involving quantitative methods. As a unified, quantitative – qualitative methodology, QE faces the challenges and affordances of both worlds regarding how OS principles may be implemented and what kind of practices may be developed.

As researchers aspiring to further refine QE methodology and to develop novel QE tools, we wanted to initiate a living (continuously ongoing) systematic review of the work that is being done in the QE community in order to see the choices we, as a community of scholars, have made in research design and operationalization. We were also interested in how QE scholars have conceptualized QE, how they have defined it for themselves and their audiences. We explored these topics in various QE works with the aim of 1) providing an overview of methodological decisions and potential choices one can make in a QE study, 2) shedding light on some challenges and opportunities of standardizing QE-related concepts and terminology, and 3) identifying areas where transparency may be beneficial for the community. We did not aim to reach final conclusions on methodological challenges or settle terminological debates; rather, we wanted to raise questions in these topics and explore some directions various QE authors have taken thus far. Furthermore, as we are performing a scoping review (i.e.: mapping out the literature without addressing substantive questions covered by the literature), we were not attempting a meta-analysis of any sort, nor a deep evaluation of any aspect of research design (e.g.: sampling, validation) as that is outside the focus of this review.

2   Methods

A more detailed description, including our decision-making processes, codebook, extraction template and other materials can be found in our public repository: https://osf.io/pa9jv/. This study was preregistered at Open Science Framework Registries.

2.1   Entity Specification

Our extraction process entailed coding for specific characteristics explicitly stated in the published works, from herein referred to as "entities". We developed a list of entities based on basic information constituting the citation and three guidelines: 1) Standards for reporting qualitative research: a synthesis of recommendations (SRQR; [8]) detailing general requirements for reporting in qualitative research, 2) The book Quantitative Ethnography [2] expounding fundamental aspects of QE-related research and specific features that can be considered and reported on in a QE study, and 3) Transparency standards covered by the Guidelines for Transparency and Openness Promotion in Journal Policies and Practices "The TOP Guidelines" [9]. A complete list of our entities, their sources, and justifications for employing them can be found here: https://osf.io/tvudx. Following this, we carried out a pilot study on the proceedings of the First Conference on Quantitative Ethnography, which included the phases of coding subsets of our data, triangulating our results, and refining our code system. Our complete process is available here: https://osf.io/46xtg. Subsequent to our pilot [10], the code system was finalized. Our final, complete codebook can be found here: https://osf.io/avkbn.

2.2   Search Strategy

Since QE developed from the discipline of learning sciences, and more generally social science, we considered databases with the most content regarding these (ERIC, JSTOR). We also considered databases with content related to healthcare and psychology (PubMed and PsycINFO), as many recent QE publications have been in this subject. This database search was complemented with the open Zotero database of QE hub University of Wisconsin-Madison. Our query string is identical with that used in the construction of the Zotero database, containing the term QE and the main tools developed in QE (ENA and nCoder). For the complete query including logical operators, see: https://osf.io/cb9ag. We did not attempt to obtain gray literature, only peer-reviewed publications were included.

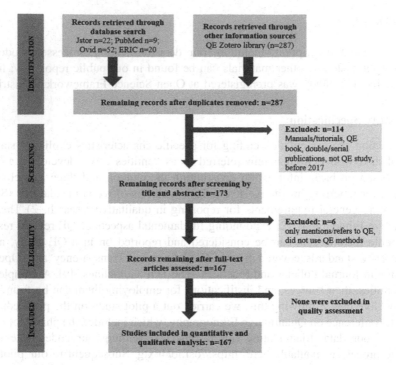

Fig. 1. PRISMA diagram depicting the screening and inclusion process of publications in Quantitative Ethnography following the year 2016. The present study contains 66 publications from the total.

2.3   Screening and Study Selection

The resulting hits were exported (2020/11/29) and screened by two independent screeners in one screening stage, which was followed by automatic duplication flagging. In the screening stage, we inspected titles, keywords, abstracts, and, if it was unclear whether to include or exclude a source based on that information, the full text was acquired and screened. We aimed to include all published works that report to have used QE methods in their initiative. Our query was highly inclusive, with very general terms and only limited to works in English language after 2016 and no specific geographical area. We excluded the book Quantitative Ethnography by Shaffer as we considered this as a methodological and temporal null point for QE-related publications; we wanted to see how the discipline has progressed since this seminal work, as conceptualized and operationalized by authors other than other than in this inaugural publication. Furthermore, we excluded duplicate and serial publications; all publications before the year 2017; and publications only mentioning or citing QE as a discipline or the tools nCoder and ENA (i.e. when these tools did not constitute the method of data collection or analysis). Figure 1 displays a PRISMA diagram of our screening process.

2.4 Data Extraction

Extraction in both our pilot and current phase was performed by humans and extraction was completed for entities only if the information was explicitly stated within the publication. Pairs of coders worked together on a single source, then triangulated their results and resolved any differences through social moderation. Extraction forms (source code files for R) were completed using Notepad++ by specifying variable values in a template file (available here: https://osf.io/ekxtj). All extraction forms (from the four individual raters and the final version the pair generated during triangulation) can be viewed in our repository. The four raters met regularly to discuss the coding process and update code definitions; two other researchers provided validation for coding and verified extraction formatting. All authors of included studies were invited via the International Society for Quantitative Ethnography (ISQE) newsletter to fill out a Qualtrics survey, which contained the items of our systematic review. Authors have continuous access to our results at our repository, and are welcome to contact us if they see errors in interpretation.

2.5 Statistical Analysis

All completed R source code files were processed by an R script ('metabefor' available at: https://gitlab.com/r-packages/metabefor), with which we could perform computations and generate overviews.

2.6 Thematic Analysis and Quantitative Content Analysis

The entity "QE conceptualization and use" was a string that yielded a large amount of qualitative data. To transform this data into a more abstract form, two researchers, working autonomously, employed different analytical approaches on the same data. One researcher used Thematic Analysis [11], the other utilized a word frequency count to identify words of potential interest and then employed a Key Word In Context Search (KWICS) to test for the consistency of usage of words [12]. After that, they worked together to reach a consensus regarding common themes and trends.

3 Results

3.1 Basic Information

At this point, we have processed 66 publications in our systematic review, following an alphabetical order in publication title. The list of included studies can be accessed here: https://osf.io/anmrq. This list also comprises the extractions from our pilot study, so several publications are from the year 2019 (n = 45). As we process more publications included into our living review, we will be able to report on them; now we focus on the 66 extractions performed thus far, which constitutes a fair sample as study title can be considered a random mode of sampling.

Authors were from a total of 22 countries, there were 19 international collaborations where universities from at least two different countries were represented; the majority of authors were affiliated with universities from the United States (n = 39). In 22 instances, this information was not available in the full text of the publication. Data collection took place in a total of 17 countries; in 20 instances the origin of data was not specified, in 6 cases data was scraped from an international database. Most inspected studies were book chapters or papers in conference proceedings (n = 49), fifteen were journal articles, one was a dissertation. The majority of studies in our review addressed topics the learning sciences, specifically regarding collaborative learning, problem-solving, and computer-supported collaborative learning (CSCL); other significant fields include healthcare and identity research.

3.2   Study Design

The majority of studies were empirical (n = 44), four were theoretical (no empirical data was collected), and 13 papers explicitly explored theoretical issues with empirical data obtained in a previous study. Empirical studies were conducted on data from human participants, but sample size did not always indicate the number of human participants, sometimes it referred to their contributions in an observational setting, posts on social media, or scientific outputs in archival research.

Although the sample was described to some degree in most studies, sampling considerations were rarely reported; in 11 instances absolutely no information was given on sampling. Sample sizes ranged from 1 to 2508; twenty-four were between 2 and 50, eleven were between 51–100, and eighteen were over 100. There were 5 case studies. In eleven instances, sample size information was not reported in the study. Twenty-three studies regarded the individual participant as the source of data; five studies collected data from groups of participants, and twenty-one publications examined data from both individuals and groups. In a total of three studies, data was collected from dyads of participants. The most frequent forms of collected metadata were: participant age, sex, education, location, and timestamps for utterances.

The most common form of data was text (n = 36), followed by audio or audio-visual data (n = 20), and numerical data (n = 4). In five cases, the type of data gathered was not reported by the authors. Data were collected with a variety of methods, such as making observations in-person or asynchronously (n = 24), using an archive (pre-existing archive or database) to retrieve data (n = 21), gathering data from synchronous chatroom interactions (n = 12), administering surveys (n = 10), conducting semi-structured or structured interviews (n = 9), and leading focus group discussions (n = 2). In eighteen studies a combination of these were employed, and in eleven instances other methods were used to collect data. In two publications authors either failed to report the method of data collection or did not explain it sufficiently for us to perform extraction. The most common data collection method and data type were text retrieved from an archive and audio-video data from observation. Figure 2 shows a heatmap of co-occurrences for data collection method and data type among the publications reported on in this study.

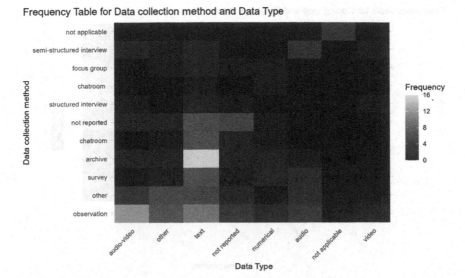

Fig. 2. Heatmap of co-occurrences in values for extracted entities Data collection method and Data type among the 66 publications reported on in this study. Colors represent the frequency of co-occurrence; yellow displays the highest, dark blue the lowest frequencies.

3.3 Coding

Most researchers employed a combination of deductive and inductive coding (n = 20) or solely deductive coding (n = 21); a small proportion of researchers used inductive coding (n = 8). In the case of seven studies, coding was not performed, and eight publications did not report what type of coding was used. Ten studies did not report any considerations in how codes were developed or where they were adopted from. The number of employed codes ranged from 2 to 52; thirty studies used 1–10 codes, fifteen used 11–20 codes, and six had more than 20. Sixteen publications did not report the number of codes they employed or the publication did not contain sufficient information for extraction. The majority of studies used both automated coding (machine performs coding autonomously based on e.g. regular expressions) and manual coding (human performs coding in some form of annotation; text coded by hand) (n = 17), or just manual coding (n = 19); five publications used automated coding only. Authors of fourteen studies failed to explicitly state how they coded their data. The most common coding type and coding process were manual deductive coding and deductive coding in a process that was not reported. Figure 3 shows a heatmap of co-occurrences for coding type and coding process among the publications reported on in this study.

Frequency Table for Coding type and Coding process

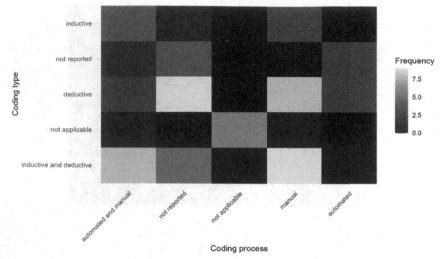

Fig. 3. Heatmap of co-occurrences in values for extracted entities Coding type and Coding process among the 66 publications reported on in this study. Colors represent the frequency of co-occurrence; yellow displays the highest, dark blue the lowest frequencies.

Coding was performed by human raters in most studies (n = 23), usually two researchers working autonomously (n = 19); in nineteen cases both humans and a computer coded data, and in one case fully automated coding was used. In fifteen studies, authors did not report whether the data was human- or machine-coded. Of the publications where this was applicable, the vast majority calculated IRR (n = 31).

3.4 Segmentation

Discourse segmentation was applicable in 54 studies, twenty-nine of those performed segmentation and reported it, twenty-five did not report this in their publication. The smallest unit of segmentation (i.e., utterance) was most frequently operationalized as "a line of data"; it was not always clear what a "line" constituted or how it became "a line". Following this, utterances were most commonly defined as a "turn-of-talk", a sentence, a response, or a second in time. Less concrete operationalizations included a "comment", a "chunk", "a line which could contain a dialogue or an event", "lines of explanation", an "interaction", and "one chat". In eleven studies where this was applicable, authors did not report their operationalization of utterance. The majority of studies conflated mid-level segmentation (stanza) with model parameterizations (stanza window, conversation), and most frequently defined stanza with a moving stanza window of 3–7 utterances (n = 14). Others defined stanza as: steps in a process, phases in a task, lesson plans, topics, questions from the interview guide and their follow-ups, or online "boards" teachers use to post material for students. Where utterances were periods of time, stanzas were a certain number of lines, e.g.: 20 lines of data representing 4.4 s during which a conversation exchange takes place, or 10 lines of data corresponding to 20 s of gameplay. In eleven instances, where it would have been applicable, authors did not explicitly state their operationalization of stanza.

3.5 Analysis

Fifty of the 66 publications generated network models with ENA. Most frequently, individual participants constituted the unit of analysis (n = 13), in a singular state or multiple states at different points in time. Units were also commonly operationalized as groups of participants (n = 12). Additionally, phases within an activity (stages, steps, or conditions; n = 8) or an entire activity (lesson plan, session; n = 3) were considered units. Less frequently, units were defined with metadata (e.g., age of participant, date of data collection), or as timestamps, interactions, outputs that individuals or groups created, or a "turn-of-talk". Sometimes authors employed a combination of these to operationalize unit, such as an individual in a phase of an activity. In instances where networks were created, and thus the designation of units was applicable, seven studies did not report their decision. Apart from ENA, other analytical methods, techniques, and tools were employed, such as Process Mining, Sequential Pattern Mining, Quantitative Multimodal Interaction Analysis, Non-negative Matrix Factorization, Agglomerative Hierarchical Clustering, Logistic Regression, Independent Samples t-Test, Two-sample Mann-Whitney U Test, Principal Component Analysis, Latent Semantic Analysis, Group Communication Analysis, Latent Dirichlet Allocation, Bartlett's Test of Sphericity, and Socio-Semantic Network Analysis.

3.6 Conceptualization

Six papers in our sample did not contain any discussion or description of ENA or QE conceptualization and reasons for it use. Those who did choose to include descriptions centered the conversation primarily around ENA, rather than QE. In fact, almost all references to QE were to home ENA as the main methodology, or to simply cite Shaffer's book, Quantitative Ethnography. Essentially, ENA was used to define QE, and QE was used to define ENA. Even in descriptions of QE independent of ENA, the definition of QE bore close similarity to that of ENA, centering the conversation around the types of data handled by QE: quantitative and qualitative, big data. Not only are ENA and QE often conflated as means for conducting research, there is also an uncertainty in whether QE is a novel field, a methodology, or a tool. Most descriptions of ENA were focused on describing the main elements involved in ENA (data, codes, units, networks) and its functionality (analysis, visualization, modelling connections). While some papers dived deeper into the complexities of ENA, describing dimensional reduction, projection spaces, temporal context, and the types of data supported, others simply defined ENA as a tool or an algorithm. Finally, some papers explicitly described how ENA was applicable to their data analysis, referencing topics like identity exploration, collaborative learning, and qualitative analysis more broadly as phenomena they aimed to investigate when using ENA on their data.

4 Discussion

Our living systematic review aims to provide an overview of choices that the QE community has made in research design and how scholars working with this methodology have conceptualized QE. Below we briefly summarize our results, place them in a greater context, and address challenges and opportunities of articulating QE-related concepts, while pinpointing areas where transparency might aid the development of QE methods.

Discourse Equals Text? QE methods are applicable to a range of discourse data, but the majority of studies in our sample involved text data, most commonly from observations, archives, chatroom discussions, or interviews. A scoping review by Kaliisa et al. [13] examining the boundaries, opportunities, and challenges of QE analyzed 60 papers, similarly noting that most QE studies worked with text-based raw data and that non-text data (e.g., videos) were always converted to text. This points to a facet of QE methodology where, albeit raw discourse data can be audio or visual in nature, in order to perform analyses, it must be transformed, most commonly transcribed, which involves a series of crucial decisions. Some discourse data may come in a more "curated" form than others, e.g., log files from a virtual collaborative game. Yet in other instances, where audio constitutes raw data, such as in the case of interviews, transcription involves making decisions, such as where to place what punctuation mark, assigning speech segments to participants, etc. When non-text data is utilized, the number of these decisions may be higher and more complex, such as in the case of recording observations. Data is hence constructed and its transformations affect coding [14]. For example, when coding interviews whether on the level of sentences of question-response, the frequency and co-occurrence of codes are potentially influenced by how the spoken utterances were transcribed. In another example, raw video data is coded based on how a series of pictures is transformed into categories describing the content of that visual data (e.g.; spoken speech, speech acts, relational location). Our results indicate that the majority of QE researchers worked with text data, only a small portion worked with raw data that was not initially text, but even those data were transformed/transcribed into text and then processed further. In QE, discourse data is most easily imagined and most commonly employed as text, visual manifestations of discourse are yet to be thoroughly explored within the QE paradigm.

Should Sampling Be an Issue? In several instances, authors did not report considerations in sampling, which may stem from the fact that many studies employed qualitative methods for data collection and part of analysis as well. Traditionally, in qualitative studies, it is not easy to calculate ideal sample size and researchers often utilize convenience sampling with no major guiding criteria regarding whom to include in the study. If QE asserts being a unified methodology, with the ability to make both qualitative and quantitative claims, should there be more emphasis on sampling in QE studies? Kaliisa et al. note that 44 out of 60 reviewed QE studies had a sample size of less than 100, and argue that this "small sample size" can lead to challenges in drawing conclusions and integrating statistical approaches, as well as affect the application of QE at scale [13]. One could also argue that this is not an issue of sample size, but of sampling: if the sample was not chosen at random from the target population, then it is the sampling procedure that prevents generalization to the wider population, not the size of the sample. Should random sampling be an expectation for QE initiatives, though? In other words, how highly does QE prioritize external validity compared to other desiderata? Also, if data collection was not systematic (e.g. it adapted flexibly to the data collection process itself or to psychosocial circumstances, as in the case of semi-structured interviews, for example), that will generally deviate from the assumptions regarding sampling distribution variance required by most quantitative methods. That inability to model error terms may prevent estimation and inference. Again, this is not a problem that can easily be solved by increasing the sample size; and it remains to be established how problematic this is for the most common QE analyses (e.g. ENA) and more widely, how highly internal validity is prioritized. Additionally, there are different types of validity and generalization as well as different criteria for power analyses and sample sizes. Beyond the mechanics of statistical methods, there are epistemic considerations of what constitutes a "fair sample" [15], which in turn depends on what it is a sample for (what analyses, conclusion and inferences) and who it is fair to.

What Constitutes the Sample? Many studies in our review report sample size, but it is unclear what or whom they consider as constituting N. In instances, authors may report a sample that consists of outputs from individuals or groups, such as drawings from children in an art class. Since each child can make several drawings, it is worth explicitly stating which of these entities constitutes the sample, e.g. the children or their drawings. Both of these can constitute the N, and as QE methods accommodate investigating both or either one, this may warrant a terminological distinction. One solution may be differentiating between a *case* (data provider, e.g. a child) and a *source* (bounded piece of discourse to be coded, e.g. a drawing); this would enable a clearer reporting of what is considered the sample and how it can be described. Additionally, being transparent about how the data is handled in e.g. the coding phase, would be useful to understand research design and generally the results. For example, data might have been collected from individual students working in dyads or teams in a classroom activity, but how that data is subsequently handled may differ: discourse from the group may be aggregated prior to coding or individual contributions may constitute autonomous units of analysis; there may be aspects of analysis that pertain to the entire group (e.g., evaluation of a collaborative exercise based on some set of criteria) and to an individual (e.g., style of collaboration based on a taxonomy).

Distinctions in Metadata? In QE studies, discourse constitutes data, and other information about data is referred to as "metadata". Metadata is used to group data providers and/or utterances in order to create various models via conditional exchangeability [2]. Authors in our review most frequently designated age, sex, time, and location as metadata. Some authors (e.g. [16]) have pointed out the interchangeability that exists between metadata (grouping variables; categorical) and discourse codes (binary representation). Perhaps making a distinction between data about data (metadata) and data about data providers (attributes) is a useful one, as aggregation and analyses may benefit from differentiating between, on the one hand, a timestamp on an utterance or the date of an interview, and on the other hand, a characteristic of a participant, such as age, sex, level of education. Another distinction might include a way of indicating what is (potentially) considered both a discourse code and a grouping variable in a particular study.

Why be Open about Coding? Coding entails a process of defining relevant and meaningful aspects of a discourse and locating them within the data. Shaffer and Ruis argue that a set of coded data should be able to make fair claims about some set of codes for each of its segments [14]. The concept of fairness they introduce is founded upon providing definitions and examples for the employed codes, i.e. a codebook. These codes can be developed inductively (grounded, emergent, bottom-up) or deductively (a priori, theoretical, top-down); reporting the process by which codes were created or from where they were adopted is a crucial aspect of validity and account-ability [5, 14]. Whereas Kaliisa et al. found that most authors were using deductive coding, our sample included studies that were using a combination of both. This may be further complicated by the fact that a coding process may include both an inductive and a deductive phase, but authors may only report on one of these, e.g. how they inductively developed the codes or in what way they deductively applied them to the corpus. In our sample, codes were often adopted from a theoretical framework, such as Technological Pedagogical Content Knowledge (TPACK) describing the kinds of knowledge necessitated by teachers, or Projective Reflection (PR), a theory of learning commonly used in QE literature on identity construction and trajectories. In such cases, using open codebooks that incorporate classifiers employed in deductive and/or automated coding would benefit all authors who subsequently wish to use this framework, as their list of classifiers would be enriched by the existing pool.

How was IRR Verified? We investigated the frequency of QE scholars employing a common measure of agreement between raters, IRR. Of the 66 studies included where IRR would have been applicable, about half calculated it, usually via Cohen's Kappa, and about half did not report whether this was performed. Kaliisa et al. coded for various types of code validation, but arrived to similar conclusions (n = 23/60), adding that many authors did not report the exact statistical procedure applied to compute IRR or did not disclose other forms of validation [13].

Does Segmentation Differ from Model Parameterization? Our results show that the operationalization of various levels of segmentation can differ greatly. For example, a turn-of-talk (e.g., a Twitter post/reply) can be one researcher's utterance and another's unit. In some cases, only the lowest level of segmentation was defined, e.g. "lines of data" with no evident operationalization of mid- or high-level segmentation. Often, how segmentation was achieved was unclear: what steps were taken to curate the data in this way and why? Some data may be generated or collected in a way that auto-matically creates some type of segmentation, such as threads in social media data or "boards" used in virtual educational environments. Are these "naturally" occurring types of segmentation the most optimal to answer the research questions authors have? How can we determine the granularity needed for our investigation? Furthermore, mid-level segmentation (stanza) was often conflated with model parameterizations, where a stanza was defined by how code co-occurrences were accumulated in ENA models (stanza window) or how utterances were grouped (conversation). Whereas often these may coincide, there is a conceptual distinction among them. Formulating justifications for these decisions and reporting on them (or creating supplementary materials) could be beneficial not only for the authors but the QE community as well.

Is QE Fully Described by ENA? As Kaliisa et al. also note, an overwhelming majority of QE scholars employ ENA to model and analyze their data. Our results indicate that other statistical and qualitative methods are also being used to complement ENA, but do those methods constitute part of QE? How can we define QE and distinguish it from other methods, methodologies? Many scholars conceptualize QE with ENA; what are the implications of defining a methodology with a (single) tool? Kaliisa et al. simultaneously call for scholars to place QE principles at the center of their research design, but also assert that the QE community is yet to define standards that delineate QE methodology [13]. This may be because if a methodology is in such close dialectic with a tool, it is difficult to separate the two. QE can be described as a unified methodology, accommodating the scrutiny of many different types of raw data, which are coded and segmented in an automated or manual process with validated codes, and aggregated in a dataset that systematically captures both qualitative and quantitative aspects of data in a human and machine-readable way. What is specific to ENA about these tenets and what other tools can be developed along these lines? As QE matures, other tools will be needed to both implement and enhance our understanding of a unified methodology.

Does Reporting Exhaust Being Transparent? The lack of reporting of various methodological decisions may have several explanations: authors might have spatial limitations, may not believe it is necessary, their decisions may not always be conscious, and so on. Yet, much can be gained from making research processes transparent, not only for the authors themselves (logging decisions, justifications, rationale for future reference), but also for a community of scholars facing similar methodological challenges or trying to interpret others' results. Transparency allows the pooling of knowledge, not only regarding best practices and clever solutions to problems, but also the conundrums themselves, and even decisions that did not work well in the end. Our results indicate that authors generally did not disclose materials generated in their initiative, although, in a few instances, authors would share a URL to a complete codebook, but it would take the viewer to an inaccessible page (e.g., Google doc needing authorization to view). This demonstrates that even if a scholar agreed with the principle of providing others with an opportunity to scrutinize processes in more detail, they may be lacking information on how to share materials generated in their research process in a FAIR (findable, accessible, interoperable, and reusable) manner.

5 Limitations

Our review had several limitations. Concerning the applied methodology, the specified entities to extract were developed by a relatively small group of researchers, albeit we conducted a pilot study to explore the developed entities, as well as other possible values and entities. Regardless, we selected relatively few entities for pragmatic reasons; although, these can be expanded upon in the coming iterations of the living review. Furthermore, categorizations within each entity were not pretested for validity. Also, our present entities need further specification, for example, we need to develop separate values for papers and posters in conference proceedings, as spatial affordances are vastly different in various forms of submissions, and this may influence reporting in manuscripts to a large extent. Also, we need to account for different forms of code validation, not only IRR, as this is a crucial tenet of QE but it is presently limited to one validity measure. Additionally, because QE hub, University of Wisconsin–Madison is over-represented in our sample, the "mirror" provided by this review is highly expressive regarding work conducted at the Epistemic Analytics Lab. Also, some regions dominated the sample, namely the US, Australia, and Europe, and at present it is not possible to draw conclusions on whether our results reflect QE in these regions or QE in general.

6 Closing Remarks

Although initially emerging from the learning sciences, QE is now situated at the nexus of multiple disciplines; and it is currently answering the challenge of establishing a lingua franca that is sufficiently specific, yet remains plastic enough for usage in vastly different research settings. Our analysis intends to spur discussions on methodological and terminological issues within the community with the aim of enhancing transparency and rigor.

Acknowledgements. This work was funded in part by the National Science Foundation (DRL-1661036, DRL-1713110), the Wisconsin Alumni Research Foundation, and the Office of the Vice Chancellor for Research and Graduate Education at the University of Wisconsin-Madison. This project also received funding from the European Union's Horizon 2020 research and innovation program under the Marie Sklodowska-Curie grant agreement No. 101028644. The opinions, findings, and conclusions do not reflect the views of the funding agencies, cooperating institutions, or other individuals.

References

1. Gee, J.: An Introduction to Discourse Analysis: Theory and Method. Routledge, London (2014)
2. Shaffer, D.: Quantitative Ethnography. Cathcart Press (2017)
3. Buckingham Shum, S., Echeverria, V., Martinez-Maldonado, R.: The multimodal matrix as a quantitative ethnography methodology. In: ICQE 2019: Advances in Quantitative Ethnography, pp. 26–40. Springer, Madison (2019)
4. Dowell, N.M.M., Nixon, T.M., Graesser, A.C.: Group communication analysis: a computational linguistics approach for detecting sociocognitive roles in multiparty interactions. Behav. Res. Methods 51(3), 1007–1041 (2018). https://doi.org/10.3758/s13428-018-1102-z

5. Cai, Z., Siebert-Evenstone, A., Eagan, B., Shaffer, D.W., Hu, X., Graesser, A.C.: nCoder+: a semantic tool for improving recall of nCoder coding. In: Eagan, B., Misfeldt, M., Siebert-Evenstone, A. (eds.) ICQE 2019. CCIS, vol. 1112, pp. 41–54. Springer, Cham (2019). https://doi.org/10.1007/978-3-030-33232-7_4

6. Zörgő, S., Peters, G.-J.Y.: Epistemic network analysis for semi-structured interviews and other continuous narratives: challenges and insights. In: Eagan, B., Misfeldt, M., Siebert-Evenstone, A. (eds.) ICQE 2019. CCIS, vol. 1112, pp. 267–277. Springer, Cham (2019). https://doi.org/10.1007/978-3-030-33232-7_23

7. Bowman, D., et al.: The mathematical foundations of epistemic network analysis. In: Ruis, A.R., Lee, S.B. (eds.) ICQE 2021. CCIS, vol. 1312, pp. 91–105. Springer, Cham (2021). https://doi.org/10.1007/978-3-030-67788-6_7

8. O'Brien, B.C., Harris, I.B., Beckman, T.J., et al.: Standards for reporting qualitative research: a synthesis of recommendations. Acad. Med. **89**, 1245–1251 (2014). https://doi.org/10.1097/ACM.0000000000000388

9. Nosek, B., Alter, G., Banks, G.: Transparency and Openness Promotion (TOP) Guidelines (2020)

10. Porter, C., Donegan, S.R., Eagan, B., et al.: A systematic review of quantitative ethnography methods. In: ICQE 2020: Conference Proceedings Supplement. ISQE, Virtual, pp. 35–38 (2021)

11. Bazeley, P.: Qualitative Data Analysis: Practical Strategies. Sage Publications, Thousand Oaks (2013)

12. Stemler, S.: An overview of content analysis. In: Practical Assessment, Research, and Evaluation, p. 7 (2000)

13. Kaliisa, R., Misiejuk, K., Irgens, G.A., Misfeldt, M.: Scoping the emerging field of quantitative ethnography: opportunities, challenges and future directions. In: Ruis, A.R., Lee, S.B. (eds.) ICQE 2021. CCIS, vol. 1312, pp. 3–17. Springer, Cham (2021). https://doi.org/10.1007/978-3-030-67788-6_1

14. Shaffer, D.W., Ruis, A.R.: How we code. In: Ruis, A.R., Lee, S.B. (eds.) ICQE 2021. CCIS, vol. 1312, pp. 62–77. Springer, Cham (2021). https://doi.org/10.1007/978-3-030-67788-6_5

15. Williamson Shaffer, D., Serlin, R.: What good are statistics that don't generalize? Educ. Res. **33**, 14–25 (2004). https://doi.org/10.3102/0013189X033009014

16. Misiejuk, K., Scianna, J., Kaliisa, R., Vachuska, K., Shaffer, D.W.: Incorporating sentiment analysis with epistemic network analysis to enhance discourse analysis of Twitter data. In: Ruis, A.R., Lee, S.B. (eds.) ICQE 2021. CCIS, vol. 1312, pp. 375–389. Springer, Cham (2021). https://doi.org/10.1007/978-3-030-67788-6_26

Case Studies

Case Studies

Peering a Generation into the Future: Assessing Workforce Outcomes in the 2020s from an Intervention in the 1990s

Eric R. Hamilton[✉], Seung B. Lee, Racquel Charles, and Joelle Molloy

Pepperdine University, Malibu, CA 90263, USA
eric.hamilton@pepperdine.edu

Abstract. This paper discusses initial results from a multiyear study of the impact of an enrichment program that the US National Science Foundation (NSF) managed in the 1990s. The Young Scholars Program (YSP) involved around 18,000 7th–12th grade students and 600 separate grants between 1989 and 1996. The purpose of YSP was to introduce high achieving middle and secondary school students to science, technology, engineering, and mathematics (STEM) fields to encourage their entry into those fields and thus increase the size and quality of the nation's STEM workforce. This paper reports on the first phase of the impact study of this program. The study relies on epistemic frame theory and quantitative ethnography to frame key issues relevant to articulating the program's impact. It involves probing the various design considerations that the funded projects pursued. It does so through in-depth interviews with the university faculty who devised the projects. These interviews are precursor to the second phase of the study, in-depth interaction with the YSP students, all of whom are now age 39–51. Epistemic frame theory provides language and metaphors to describe the shifts in expectations that the program hoped to stimulate. Quantitative ethnography provides a framework to treat the YSP program as an ecosystem with structural and cultural variables that can be quantified and visualized.

Keywords: Future of work · Epistemic frame theory · Interest-driver creator theory · Social-cognitive career theory

1 Introduction

This paper discusses the initial round of results from a multiyear study of the impact of an enrichment program that the US National Science Foundation (NSF) managed in the 1990s. The study [1] relies on epistemic frame theory and quantitative ethnography to frame key issues relevant to articulating the program's impact.

B. Wasson and S. Zörgő (Eds.): ICQE 2021, CCIS 1522, pp. 163–175, 2022.
https://doi.org/10.1007/978-3-030-93859-8_11

1.1 Young Scholars Program

The Young Scholars Program (YSP) involved around 18,000 7th–12th grade students and 600 separate grants between 1989 and 1996. The purpose of YSP was to introduce high achieving middle and secondary school students to science, technology, engineering, and mathematics (STEM) fields to encourage their entry into those fields and thus increase the size and quality of the nation's STEM workforce.

YSP Intended to Address Workforce Shortages and Underrepresentation. Workforce literature and policy documents in the late 1980s and early 1990s stressed the adverse social and economic consequences of the then-current and anticipated shortages of the STEM workforce juxtaposed with severe underrepresentation of females, African-Americans, Latinx, Native-Americans, and others in the workforce [2–4]. This study assesses and documents YSP's actual impact on the national STEM workforce by examining the relationship between YSP involvement and the academic and career trajectcories of all of the YSP participants. These participants were primarily 7th–12th grade students but also included the principal investigators (PIs) who designed and led 600 grants at the time. The initial stage of the study involves two interviews, each with a sample of twelve principal investigators.

How might such a study in 2021 about a program in the 1990s be of interest to current policy-makers in the US and elsewhere? Those reasons cut across multiple themes. The workforce context of the early 2020s differs markedly from that of the early 1990s, when global society was in much earlier stages of digital transformation and workforce preparation. Yet the challenges of building a diverse, equitable, inclusive, and more robust workforce, widely recognized at the time, are even more prominent in higher education today. Every country has a stake in fostering the success of pre-teens and teenagers in (what is now called) STEM (science, technology, engineering, and mathematics) fields and careers. The preparation of PK-12 students is a vital part of a national strategy to addressing diversity, equity, and inclusion in the STEM workforce.

Micro-Interventions for Students Versus Macro-interventions for Systems. What are the most promising ways to define and operationalize principles of effective preparation? What are the best approaches for a federal government to consider? One approach is to underwrite what could be called micro-interventions (such as the YSP) by which opportunities are provided directly to precollege students [5]. Is this approach more effective and likely transformative than larger, macro-intervention strategies that seek to alter education systems? The YSP effort began shortly before NSF embarked on a series of urban, rural, and statewide systemic initiatives [6]. The tension between micro- versus macro-intervention strategies took several years to resolve in favor, at the time, of systemic or macro-interventions [6]. The YSP program, as a micro-intervention strategy directly serving students, was phased out after eight years [7].

The Challenge of Evaluation. The distal goal of drawing more individuals into STEM careers was indeed *quite* distal in its prospects for evaluation. Evaluating the actual impact would take decades to estimate. What are the best and most cost-effective ways to do that? Few such programs have the resources for designs to carry out longitudinal evaluations. The retrospective study, funded by NSF, takes the YSP enrichment program and, as the name of the study suggests, peers a generation into the future by reaching out to a sample of the 18,000 students who participated in it (now mid-career) and the 600 or so university faculty who led the projects as principal investigators (PIs). Most of those PIs, if still living, have retired.

1.2 Assessing YSP Impact Ethnographically

So: what happened to the participants? Did the program shape their life directions? How and why? Answers to these questions are often more substantive, complicated, unexpected, and dramatic than a simple lay narrative that a school-aged experience helped lead someone into or away from a particular field later in life. Answering the question of what happened to the participants is a process that can likely be estimated depending on the number of former participants that are found and are willing to share their experience.

An ethnographic approach, though, seeking to understand the ecosystem of the individual projects and the overall program, holds promise from a government policy and investment perspective. The ecosystems blend cultural, academic, socio-economic, and demographic characteristics into structural relationships specific to both local projects and the national agenda. Observing and learning about these structural relationships fall within the definitions of traditional ethnography [8, 9]; the structural connections, in turn, are the result of design considerations about the experience and interpersonal communication that are calculated to shift students' aspirations and what can be interpreted as the students' epistemic frames.

Epistemic Frame Theory (EFT) and Quantitative Ethnography (QE). In the context of this study, epistemic frame theory [10] treats a student's full conceptualizations of self and future life paths, along with their configuration of knowledge, skills, and experience, as a single unit of analysis - called an epistemic frame [11]. Epistemic frames may be considered analogous to the construct of funds of knowledge [12] – i.e., the totality of unique personal experience and expectations, enculturation, beliefs, etc., that students brought into their respective YSP experience. Realistically, the personal epistemic frames of most adolescents relative to potential involvement in a STEM profession are ambiguous or poorly formed. The rationale for YSP included helping adolescents form realistic understandings of STEM fields and the inquiry process. EFT furnishes language for describing the transitions that individuals experience as their frames undergo a personal transformation of the kind that YSP-type programs seek to stimulate. Additionally, EFT lends itself to visual modeling that depicts construct frequency and relationships within epistemic frames involving a large number of students. It can show differences between groups of students. EFT related software (the epistemic network analysis or ENA Webtool), developed under NSF funding [13] detects or enables visual interpretation of shifts in epistemic frames that YSP alums reported as their personal growth was nurtured in the program. This approach allows sophisticated quantitative ethnographies [14] with a higher resolution than previously possible. In technical terms, ENA models connections between salient constructs that emerge from this study's data [14].

Documenting progress towards the objectives of the YSP program in a vivid and visual way for many participants is central to the design of the retrospective impact study. Doing so will take the form of a quantitatively documented ethnography developed using ENA. The analysis will draw on social-cognitive career theory (SCCT) and interest-driven creator theory (IDC), the two other theoretical frameworks on which the study relies.

Social Cognitive Career Theory (SCCT). The introduction of SCCT in the mid-1990s [15] emphasized critical variables known to affect career interests. SCCT provides important markers for this study. Its three primary variables include self-efficacy, social support from family and others, and life expectations adults or children have about future career paths. SCCT situated those variables into a single framework, though it was not until long after YSP ended for theory-testing to take place in the form of path analysis [e.g., 16, 17]. YSP projects generally treated self-efficacy and life expectations as malleable variables and social support as a semi-malleable variable.

Interest-Driven Creator Theory (IDC). A third theoretical framework is also relevant to the YSP participants and to the university faculty who designed the YSP experiences. YSP sought to capitalize on and shape participant interest in STEM professions. Interest-driven Creator Theory (IDC) is an evolving learning design framework that is relevant as a formalization of the growing realization that attending to student interest and motivation is essential to pipeline strategies. IDC was articulated explicitly to address what its internationally prominent originators identify as a counterproductive culture of high-stakes examinations in their respective countries in Asia [18].

IDC positions critical variables in a way that can improve intervention design. It partitions elusive constructs along the continuum of interest, motivation, and resilient persistence that characterizes virtually every STEM professional's career path. These partitions give a more finely grained way to think about how participants progressed towards deepening and solidifying their career choices.

1.3   Objective of the Paper

This paper reports on the first phase of the YSP impact study. It involves probing the varied design considerations that the funded projects pursued. It does so through in-depth interviews with the university faculty who devised the projects. These interviews are precursor to the second phase of the study comprised of in-depth interaction with the YSP students, all of whom are now age 39–51. Epistemic frame theory provides language and metaphors to describe the shifts in expectations that the program hoped to stimulate. Quantitative ethnography provides a framework to treat the YSP program as an ecosystem with structural and cultural variables that can be quantified and visualized. This initial analysis aims to contribute to a more in-depth understanding of the diverse set of project designs and implementation strategies utilized in the various projects over the program's 8-year duration.

2 Methodology

2.1 Data Collection

Data for this analysis was collected through semi-structured interviews with 12 former YSP PIs. Convenience sampling was used in this initial phase, as many former PIs are now retired, passed away, or otherwise difficult to reach. Nonetheless, the sample consists of scholars from a broad range of academic institutions in the US. As shown in Table 1, the YSP PIs who participated in the interviews comprise a diverse group with varying disciplinary and demographic backgrounds. Institutionally, they represent both public and private universities across different regions of the US. Some YSP projects took place in a residential format while others were commuter programs.

The interview questions revolved around the design of each YSP project, processes for recruitment and selection of participants, and the perceived impact of the project on the participants, the PIs, and the hosting institutions. The interviews took place via Zoom, with each interview recorded and then transcribed. The data segmentation that ENA requires was defined by each turn of talk, or utterance, during an interview.

Table 1. Interviewed young scholars project principal investigators (PIs).

Participant no.	Gender	Area of expertise	Institution state	Institution type	YSP project format
1	M	Chemistry	MI	Public	Residential
2	M	Physics	OR	Public	Residential
3	M	Physics	MT	Public	Residential
4	F	Science Education	MT	Public	Residential
5	M	Materials Science	WA	Public	Commuter
6	M	Chemistry	NY	Public	Residential
7	F	Mathematics Education	KY	Public	Commuter
8	F	Natural Resources	NY	Private	Residential
9	M	Mathematics and Statistics	IN	Private	Residential
10	M	Physics	OH	Private	Commuter
11	F	Engineering Education	VA	Public	Residential
12	M	Biology	NY	Public	Residential

2.2 Coding

The responses provided by the YSP PIs were coded independently by two raters using a codebook containing 9 constructs. The constructs were developed from a grounded analysis of the data. The codes were organized around the following three categories: recruitment, design, and student impact (see Table 2 for codebook). The raters participated in a process of social moderation to reach agreement on the final coding for 509 total utterances included in the dataset [19, 20].

Table 2. Codebook used for the analysis of the PI interviews.

Category	Code	Description
Recruitment	High achievement students	Selection of high-achieving students (through GPA, teacher recommendation, etc.)
	Underrepresented groups	Recruitment of students from underrepresented groups including women
Design	Multi-stakeholder collaboration	Collaboration and cooperation between different stakeholders in the development and implementation of the YSP project
	Research integration	Direct involvement of students in faculty research
	STEM field exposure	Curriculum focusing on exposing students to different topics within the STEM field
	College student mentors	Undergrad and graduate students serving as facilitators and mentors in the project
	Diverse experiences	Opportunities for students to engage in diverse experiences, such as campus visits and networking events
Student Impact	Academic motivation	Development of student interest and confidence in STEM subjects or research
	Influence on Student Path	Impact on student's academic and/or career path

2.3 Epistemic Network Analysis

Following the coding process, ENA was used to model the discourse patterns exhibited by the YSP PIs in the interviews. An utterance was specified as the unit of analysis. A conversation was defined as the set of utterances related to the same topical question posed during the interview. Connections between codes were limited to those occurring in the same conversation. Analyses were conducted in two stages, with an initial examination of the overall model followed by comparisons of individual networks located on the periphery of the ENA space. The latter was intended to explore key differences in the design, implementation, and perceived impact of YSP projects.

3 Results

3.1 Overall Network Model

Figure 1 displays the overall ENA model for the discourse patterns exhibited by all 12 YSP PIs who participated in the interviews. The STEM FIELD EXPOSURE code is central to the overall model, with moderate connections to several constructs, including DIVERSE

EXPERIENCES, MULTI-STAKEHOLDER COLLABORATION, ACADEMIC MOTIVATION, and UNDERREP-RESENTED GROUPS. This suggests that providing students with exposure to various STEM topics was a central feature of YSP projects. One PI observed that:

[The students] were always introduced to all of the engineering disciplines that [the university] had. Usually, I tried to find somebody young, somebody exciting, who was doing something that they could understand and that had relevance, you know, to talk to them about chemical, civil, etc. ...I do believe that it influenced some of them. Now am I going to say that they went into STEM? I don't know if they did or not. But I do know that it gave them information that that they could not have gotten someplace else. (Participant 11)

Attention was also given to provide diverse experiences to students, such as campus visits, field trips, cultural events, and networking activities.

We'd pile them in the car and...go to the children's museum and talk about design programs... [we] basically just wanted to get the kids involved and have fun and say: Well, this is really exciting! We did all kinds of field trips, and so we'd go to [the air force base], which is fairly close to here, there was pretty much a field trip every week. And we'd get the scientists and engineers on our field trips to explain a lot of that. (Participant 7)

In addition, the connection between STEM FIELD EXPOSURE and MULTI-STAKEHOLDER COLLABORATION suggests that interdisciplinary and interdepartmental collaboration often appears to have played a significant role in project execution. As one participant remarked, such cooperation was especially important in developing relevant curricula for younger students:

Well, I had done a lot of work with science teachers, and I found that science teachers told me that they needed to do hands-on stuff with their students and do engineering-related hands-on things to demonstrate the practicality of what they teach in science... And so, in dealing with the younger kids, what we did is we took that information that we had already developed and we tried to adapt it to younger kids. And that worked pretty well because the kids were excited. (Participant 5)

Promoting academic motivation—especially interest and efficacy in STEM areas—also appears to have been a core component of the projects, with PIs believing that student trajectories were influenced by the YSP experience. Promoting such motivation falls into the category of attempting to stimulate epistemic frame shifts. One PI noted that:

I would say, at the level of achievement that they demonstrated, they could not have done it without some program like what we did at the YSP. And, you know, at some point, we had students aspiring to be Westinghouse winners. These little kids from ordinary backgrounds, they would not have even known Westinghouse existed without their involvement in the program. (Participant 1)

For some of the PIs, providing STEM-learning opportunities for students from underrepresented groups was a major priority in the recruitment and design of their respective projects.

So we were trying to reach kids who didn't live in the more urban areas and who ... fall through the cracks. Kids that had a lot of potential, a lot of ability, but didn't have good role models or didn't have people...family resources didn't have money. All the different reasons that they sort of get fall out of the mainstream. So those were the students that we started out talking about

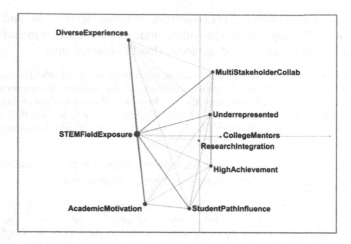

Fig. 1. Discourse pattern exhibited by all 12 former YSP Principal Investigators in sample.

that we wanted to try to find when we wrote the grant proposal...how we could recruit and find those students and then how we could best give them experiences that would open the wider world to them. And in particular in STEM areas. (Participant 4)

The lack of any particularly dominant connections between codes is noteworthy. This relatively well-balanced network in the overall model may be reflective of the variations in the emphasis placed by each PI in the design and implementation of their respective projects. In many cases, the PIs played the roles of curricular designers, program coordinators, and instructional facilitators. Because the PIs were so instrumental to the operation of the YSP, properly accounting for their aspirations, approaches and perceived outcomes becomes essential for fully developing an insightful YSP ethnography that enables assessing the YSP program impact.

3.2   Comparison of Individual Network Models

The means of each participant's interview responses are shown in Fig. 2. It can be seen that the mean points are located in close proximity to one another, without any noticeable patterns of clustering among them. Significant overlaps exist in the 95% confidence intervals between most of the means, except between those located at the outer edges of the ENA space. In order to better understand the differences in the structures of connections underlying the individual networks, comparisons focused on the networks for the participants whose means are situated at the extreme positions of the x-axis (Participants 9 and 8) and the y-axis (Participants 2 and 12).

The individual networks, as well as the means and 95% confidence intervals for Participants 9 and 8 are presented in Fig. 3. For Participant 9, the strongest connections are present in the left side of the ENA space. In addition to STEM topics, the project run by Participant 9 appears to have emphasized boosting academic interest in STEM topics as well as offering various activities for students:

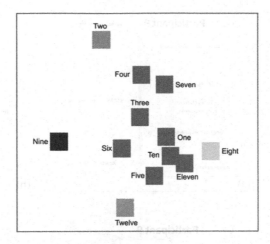

Fig. 2. The means of each participant's responses.

I think it would be highly influential in the sense that [the YSP program] convinced these students...to see what the world was like outside of their small community...to be on a college campus, to interact with a diverse group of other students from other schools...and it is an opening world to them. The fact that we toured these different places gave them a sense of jobs and careers and things that people do. (Participant 9)

For Participant 8, the most prominent association involves UNDERREPRESENTED GROUPS and STUDENT PATH INFLUENCE. The project not only actively recruited students from underrepresented racial and ethnic groups but also those with disabilities:

We drew on cooperative extension, which also had at the time a large office in [the city], which is where most of our students of color came from. And we also were successfully able to recruit a number of students with disabilities...we had another student who was deaf from birth and she had to have an interpreter all the time. She ended up getting a Ph.D. ...in neurobiology or something like that. (Participant 8)

A two sample t-test assuming unequal variance found that along the x-axis, the location of mean for Participant 9 ($M = -0.06$, $SD = 0.25$, $N = 47$) was statistically significantly different from the location of the mean for Participant 8 ($M = 0.04$, $SD = 0.05$, $N = 26$; $t(51.40) = -2.70$, $p = 0.01$, Cohen's $d = 0.50$).

Figure 4 displays the individual networks, means, and 95% confidence intervals for Participants 2 and 12. For Participant 2, the most prominent association is between DIVERSE EXPERIENCES and STEM FIELD EXPOSURE. This implies that the YSP project focused on providing both STEM learning and other experiences for the students. As noted by Participant 2, outdoor activities were a critical part of the daily schedule and allowed the young students to engage more fully in the learning tasks:

Middle schoolers are an interesting group, you know that sort of... they have a very strict set of activities they like to participate in. And this was before everybody had an iPhone and that sort of thing. So we didn't have to worry about those kinds of distractions, fortunately. But this is a group with kind of raging hormones and they like to have lots of activity. So we didn't have

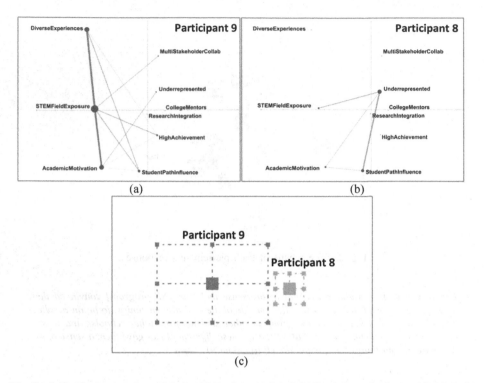

Fig. 3. Individual network models for (a) Participant 9 and (b) Participant 8, along with (c) their respective means and 95% confidence intervals.

them sitting in class for eight hours a day. There were outside activities. We go for walks and give them a chance to work out some of the kinks, but otherwise they were active all day in the science activities. And I was quite amazed at how long they were able to participate, the kind of level of concentration that we were able to achieve. (Participant 2)

The connections in the network model for Participant 12 seem to be concentrated among codes in the bottom of the ENA space, particularly around ACADEMIC MOTIVATION, HIGH ACHIEVEMENT, and STEM FIELD EXPOSURE. This suggests that the project worked with high achieving students to build their efficacy in science topics through STEM-related activities.

But there was also a sense that students were surprised, I think, at some of the joy of empirical research and just research for its own sake... there definitely were some students who seemed genuinely impressed and kind of excited by what it's like to actually do research. (Participant 12)

A two sample t-test assuming unequal variance found that along the y-axis, the mean location for Participant 2 ($M = 0.07$, $SD = 0.18$, $N = 31$) was statistically significantly different from that of Participant 12 ($M = -0.05$, $SD = 0.15$, $N = 30$; t (57.56) $= -2.62$, $p = 0.01$, Cohen's $d = 0.67$).

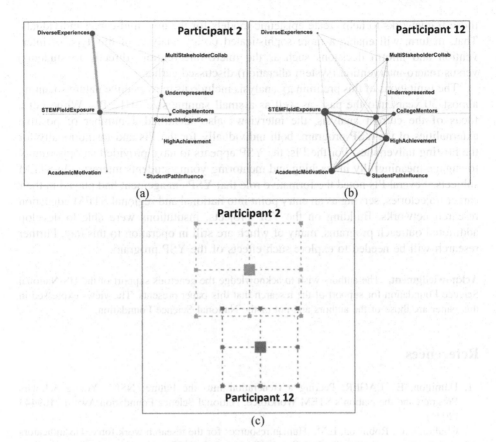

Fig. 4. Individual network models for (a) Participant 2 and (b) Participant 12, along with (c) their respective means and 95% confidence intervals.

4 Discussion

The results of this analysis affirm that exposure to the STEM field was a central feature of the YSP program and demonstrate that multidisciplinary coordination and inclusion of diverse activities were common to many projects. At the same time, the interviews also point to the diversity in the design and delivery of individual projects. Differences were observed between several projects in the recruitment approaches and implementation strategies utilized by the PIs. These findings confirm the need for a nuanced approach to studying the complex nature of their potential effects on the academic and career trajectories of students.

Through a more fully developed understanding of the project designs, this analysis contributes to building an ethnographic understanding of the YSP program's national and local ecosystems. This serves as a first step in the process of sense-making of student trajectories using the SCCT and IDT frameworks. A fuller ethnographic understanding of these findings will require consideration of the design features emerging from the first phase of the study reported here, along with the constructs from those frameworks to help create epistemic models for the now mid-career individuals. That, in turn, will enable a more sophisticated policy analysis of this type of intervention and inform decisions such as the micro-intervention (directly to students) versus macro-intervention (system alteration) discussed earlier.

The limitations of this preliminary analysis include its retrospective nature spanning almost 30 years into the past, as well as a small sample size of 12 PIs. While not a focus of the current analysis, the interviews also identified a number of positive externalities of the YSP program, both individually for the PIs and institutionally for the hosting universities. For the PIs, the YSP appears to have provided an opportunity to engage meaningfully in teaching and mentoring young students interested in STEM subjects. Several PIs noted the formative role that YSP engagement had played in their career trajectories, serving as an entry point into national and regional STEM education research networks. Building on the YSP projects, institutions were able to develop additional outreach programs, many of which are still in operation to this day. Further research will be needed to explore such effects of the YSP program.

Acknowledgment. The authors wish to acknowledge the generous support of the US National Science Foundation for support of the research that this paper presents. The views expressed in this paper are those of the authors and not of the National Science Foundation.

References

1. Hamilton, E.: EAGER: Peering a Generation into the Future: NSF's Young Scholars Program and the Nation's STEM Workforce. National Science Foundation Award 2109443 (2021)
2. Chubin, D.E., Robinson, E.M.: Human resources for the research work force: US indicators and policy choices. Sci. Publ. Policy **19**(6), 334–342 (1992)
3. Pearson, Jr., W., Fechter, A.: Who Will Do Science? Educating the Next Generation. ERIC (1994)
4. Holden, C.: Wanted: 675,000 future scientists and engineers. Science **244**(4912), 1536–1538 (1989)
5. Jackson, A.: The demise of the young scholars program. Notices AMS **45**(3) (1998
6. Williams, L.: The National Science Foundation Systemic initiatives: a retrospective assessment, in projecting forward: learning from educational systemic reform. In: Consortium for Mathematics and Its Applications (COMAP), p. 1 (2018)
7. Sharp, L.: Short-Term Impact Study of the National Science Foundation's Young Scholars Program (1994)
8. Taylor, B.C.: Ethnography. In: The International Encyclopedia of Organizational Communication, pp. 1–10 (2017)
9. Jones, J., Smith, J.: Ethnography: challenges and opportunities. Evid. Based Nurs. **20**(4), 98–100 (2017)
10. Shaffer, D.W.: Epistemic frames for epistemic games. Comput. Educ. **46**(3), 223–234 (2006)
11. Shaffer, D.W., et al.: Epistemic network analysis: a prototype for 21st century assessment of learning. Int. J. Learn. Media **1**(1), 1–21 (2009)
12. Moje, E.B., et al.: Working toward third space in content area literacy: an examination of everyday funds of knowledge and discourse. Read. Res. Q. **39**(1), 38–70 (2004)

13. Nash, P., Shaffer, D.W.: Epistemic Youth Development: Educational Games as Youth Development Activities, Vancouver, BC (2012)
14. Shaffer, D.W.: Epistemic network analysis: understanding learning by using big data for thick description. In: Fischer, F., et al. (eds.) International Handbook of the Learning Sciences, pp. 520–531. Routledge, New York (2018)
15. Fouad, N.A., Santana, M.C.: SCCT and underrepresented populations in STEM fields: moving the needle. J. Career Assess. **25**(1), 24–39 (2016)
16. Stahlke Wall, S.: Toward a moderate autoethnography. Int. J. Qual. Methods **15**(1), 1609406916674966 (2016)
17. Brown, S.D., et al.: Social cognitive career theory, conscientiousness, and work performance: a meta-analytic path analysis. J. Vocat. Behav. **79**(1), 81–90 (2011)
18. Chan, T.-W., et al.: Interest-driven creator theory: towards a theory of learning design for Asia in the twenty-first century. J. Comput. Educ. **5**(4), 435–461 (2018). https://doi.org/10.1007/s40692-018-0122-0
19. Herrenkohl, L.R., Cornelius, L.: Investigating elementary students' scientific and historical argumentation. J. Learn. Sci. **22**(3), 413–461 (2013)
20. Frederiksen, J.R., et al.: Video portfolio assessment: creating a framework for viewing the functions of teaching. Educ. Assess. **5**(4), 225–297 (1998)

How STEM Game Design Participants Discuss Their Project Goals and Their Success Differently

Denise M. Bressler[1]($\boxtimes$) , Leonard A. Annetta[1] ,
Alexis Dunekack[1], Richard L. Lamb[1] , and David B. Vallett[2]

[1] East Carolina University, Greenville, NC 27858, USA
bresslerd19@ecu.edu
[2] University of Nevada, Las Vegas, NV 89154, USA

Abstract. This study explored whether participation in a high school STEM game design enrichment program influenced students' discussions of their project goals and success. In our sample, seven students participated in the game design program, while ten received traditional instruction. Post-interviews were conducted using a semi-structured protocol in order to capture students' lived experience in a rich, meaningful way. Transcripts were qualitatively coded by two researchers. Connections between codes were analyzed using epistemic network analysis. Based on experience grouping, we investigated whether there was a difference in how students discussed 1) their projects? and 2) their success? Our findings revealed that students who received traditional instruction discussed performance goals, while game design participants discussed learning goals. Game design participants also discussed persistence in relationship to their success; the traditionally instructed students did not attribute their success to persistence. Overall, our combined results indicate that students who received traditional instruction were performance-oriented, while game design participants were mastery-oriented. Designing STEM games is one potential method for helping students develop the mastery orientation that they need for success in future STEM careers and for their future in general.

Keywords: STEM · Game design · Mastery · Performance · Goal orientation · Persistence

1 Introduction

The STEM pipeline is the educational pathway that takes students from early education through high school, college, and into science, technology, engineering, and mathematics (STEM) careers. In the United States, few students stay through the entire STEM pipeline [1, 2] which is a detriment to the caliber of the STEM workforce.

There are noticeable leaks in the pipeline along the way. Despite a natural and intrinsic interest in STEM during infancy [3], students can form negative emotional responses towards STEM early in their schooling and these responses persist [4]. As students enter adolescence, their interest in STEM drops precipitously declining dramatically between elementary school and secondary school [2]. Even if students

© Springer Nature Switzerland AG 2022
B. Wasson and S. Zörgő (Eds.): ICQE 2021, CCIS 1522, pp. 176–190, 2022.
https://doi.org/10.1007/978-3-030-93859-8_12

graduate high school with STEM career intentions, it does not guarantee they will enter the profession. Many students who start their college education as STEM majors switch to non-STEM majors before getting their degree [1].

Fortunately, we know how to help students stay in the STEM pipeline and achieve success. Research shows that there is a link between a mastery orientation and high perseverance in STEM [4]. Within the workforce, STEM professionals who have a mastery orientation are more productive and successful than those with a performance orientation [5]. Due to overemphasis on discrete facts and a lack of engaging, authentic experiences [6], interventions that promote a mastery orientation within STEM are few and far between; experts argue that we need to create and implement learning approaches within STEM that will help students develop a mastery orientation [29].

In the following sections, we will make the case that traditional instructional environments emphasize a performance orientation while designing STEM games emphasizes a mastery orientation. In other words, designing STEM games is an effective approach to STEM learning that has the potential to shift students' focus from performance goals to learning goals, and help them develop persistence. We will report on a research study exploring the experience of designing STEM games as it compares to traditional school projects. Since a significant number of students drop out of the STEM pipeline, the goal of this study was to investigate whether designing STEM games helps students develop the mastery orientation necessary for staying in the STEM pipeline.

2 Background

There are key differences between mastery-oriented students and performance-oriented students. Some of these differences can be seen through the goals that students have [7] and whether they can persist through challenging tasks [8, 9].

2.1 Orientation Differences

Project Goals. When students approach a task, they are concerned with certain reasons or purposes that define their goals [7]. Some students have learning goals and are focused on learning new skills and improving their competence. These students are mastery oriented. Other students have performance goals and are focused on seeking evidence of performing better than others [8, 10]. These students are performance oriented.

In the classroom context, research determined that a focus on learning goals was beneficial to achievement while a focus on performance goals was detrimental to achievement [9]. Students with learning goals not only have deeper cognitive engagement and higher learning performance [11], but also higher confidence in the intellectual abilities [12]. When compared to students with performance goals, students with learning goals consistently demonstrate higher achievement even when prior achievement and demographics are included as controls [13]. Essentially, student goals have a consistent and predictable relationship with classroom achievement, and students with a focus on learning goals have the most positive outcomes [11].

Persistence. Persistence is a quality that enables a person to continue doing something despite difficulties; it is shaped by the expectation of success [14]. When students have higher levels of expectancies for success, they are more likely to persist and demonstrate higher achievement [15–17]. Mastery-oriented students generally demonstrate higher persistence, while performance-oriented students show lower persistence.

In the classroom context, persistence serves as a building block for academic achievement. Research has shown that persistence is related to academic achievement, such as exam performance [18]. Persistence has also been shown to be a strong predictor of adolescent grade point average [19]. On the Third International Mathematics and Science Study (TIMSS), researchers reported that students' task persistence had a predictive relationship with national mean scores [20]. Ability to persist at a task in adolescence is even related to educational attainment during adulthood [19].

2.2 Differences in Instructional Approaches

Project Goals. In traditional school environments, performance goals are promoted over learning goals. Typically, schools use a grading structure to provide feedback on how well students perform. Experts indicate that grades tend to reflect a student's abilities rather than a student's learning [21]; therefore, grading promotes performance goals over learning goals. Those students who have performance goals are also focused on their ability in comparison to others, and grades give students a concrete way to their judge their ability in relationship to others. This social comparison can be very detrimental to students—it can hamper students' judgements of themselves [22].

Goal orientation can be shaped by the learning environment [22]. Designing games is a unique learning environment that highlights learning goals over performance goals. When students design games, there is a focus on learning because designing games exposes students to content in a whole new way. The designers need to know the content well in order to create the game. Research has shown that students will engage in extensive research in order to improve their game design [23].

Persistence. In traditional school environments, certain teaching practices can have a negative impact on student's ability to persist; students develop a learned helplessness [25]. When tasks require persistence, students with learned helplessness feel that they cannot overcome the challenge [26]. When students perceive their teachers as controlling, there is a greater chance they will feel a sense of learned helplessness [27]. Students are more likely to persist when they think their schoolwork is important and useful [28]. Sadly, for many students, school is full of drudgery and boring seatwork.

Unlike traditional teaching practices that can be too controlling, students designing games work without much support [24]; therefore, they feel a greater sense of autonomy and a lesser sense of learned helplessness. Authoring computer games can give students a sense of ownership, which may help them persist through the design process [41]. Rather than feeling as though they cannot overcome the challenge, designing a game becomes a challenge that they are motivated and enthusiastic to overcome [42]. When students design games, research has shown that they will engage with the project for long periods of time, and they are motivated to complete it [23].

2.3 Research Questions

We need to provide high school students with opportunities where they can focus on learning goals and where they can persist through challenges in order to succeed. Designing games has the potential to help students build out these skills; however, experts have confirmed that there is a lack of research comparing the experience of designing computer games to other conditions, particularly traditional instruction [30]. In project GRADUATE, high school students became STEM game creators while their teachers became the facilitators of content and pedagogy, ensuring misconceptions were not perpetuated in the games. To determine how designing STEM games differed from traditional school projects, we interviewed GRADUATE participants and non-participants about a memorable project they completed during the school year. The following questions guided our investigation. Based on experience grouping, is there a difference in how students 1) discussed their projects and 2) discussed their success?

3 Methodology

Setting and Sample. Two high schools in a rural Mid-Atlantic region of the United States participated in the study. Both high schools had high dropout rates. A small subset of students from each high school participated in an enrichment program called GRADUATE (Games Requiring Advanced Developmental Understanding Around Technological Endeavors). Approximately 80 students participated in GRADUATE where they learned to develop "serious educational games" with a focus on STEM education. Participants were tasked with storyboarding their games and then building a functional game. For the story, students were expected to create an exciting narrative, complete with interesting characters and a compelling plot line. To build the game, students used customized software. The game design software did not require sophisticated programming or animation—in fact, it simplified the process for the designer. However, basic programming was necessary.

As a foundation, the science teachers developed lesson plans about the environment and were trained to use the game design software over the summer. Then, during the school year, the teachers implemented their lesson plans and worked with the students to create games based on the environmental concepts they had learned. Under the guidance of university doctoral students and their science teachers, over 25 students were able to finish their games. Completed games tackled science topics ranging from sickle cell anemia to diabetes and medical ethics to neuroscience.

At the end of the school year, students from the same class were randomly selected to participate in detailed, semi-structured interviews about their most memorable school project from that year. A total of 17 students were interviewed. Seven of the students (3 girls, 4 boys) participated in the GRADUATE enrichment program. The remaining ten students (5 boys, 5 girls) did not participate in GRADUATE.

Data Collection. Data were collected via individual interviews based on an interview protocol. There were two separate interviewers who both abided by the same protocol. The interview started with a statement to set the context: "Think about a project that you are most proud of during your time in high school." All questions pertained to that project. For example, students were asked, "What did you learn by doing this project?" The protocol helped ensure specific and consistent topics were addressed across all students. Interviews lasted anywhere from 5 to 25 min. The average duration was approximately 10 min. All interviews were audio recorded and transcribed.

Data Analysis. To analyze the interview data, there were several readings of the transcripts. Employing the constant-comparative method [31], the lead researcher reviewed transcripts by starting with open coding. During coding, initial memos were kept in order to document possible connections between codes. Thirty-two codes were generated. During peer debriefing, the authors condensed the list of codes into six vital codes for further analysis. In relationship to the project (#1), students talked about knowledge (#2) and confidence (#3). In relationship to success (#4), students talked about learning (#5) and persistence (#6). To check for inter-rater reliability, two authors each coded 20% of the utterances. Cohen's kappa was calculated for each code: project (0.84), knowledge (0.77), confidence (0.74), success (0.71), learning (0.89), and persistence (0.84). Agreement was at least moderate for all codes and overall interrater reliability (0.80) for the study was strong [32]; therefore, one researcher coded the remaining data.

In total, over 735 utterances were coded using the six vital codes. For each research question, the coded utterances were analyzed using epistemic network analysis (ENA) [34]. ENA has two distinct advantages: it captures connections *between* codes and can statistically compare the code connections from one group to that of another group.

First, unlike simple coding and counting strategies, ENA is a method for investigating connections *between* codes in the data [35]. With ENA, each sentence uttered is not a distinct event, but rather connected to immediately previous statements. Research has shown that ENA reveals more nuanced differences than coding and counting [36, 37].

Second, ENA represents code connections as network models [35] that can be statistically compared. ENA generates the models by utilizing the moving stanza window method [34, 38]. First, ENA looks for code connections within each utterance. Then, ENA looks for code connections between the referent utterance and those inside a small window of previous statements. All of these code connections are then represented by a network model where the qualitative codes are the nodes of the model. To establish if there is a difference between two models, ENA calculates the centroid for each model and uses a t-test to determine whether there is a statistical difference between them.

To understand whether there were differences in how students discussed their project goals and their success, we compared two ENA models for each research question. The first model combined all the code connections from the GRADUATE participants, or the *treatment* group. The second model combined all the code connections from the students who received traditional instruction and did not participate in GRADUATE, or the *comparison* group. The centroid from each model was compared along the x-axis using a two-sample t-test assuming unequal variance. If differences existed, then we investigated what code connections were causing the difference.

4   Results

All 17 interviewees when asked to talk about a memorable project from their school year that made them feel proud. We used ENA to explore how the discussions differed between GRADUATE participants and non-participants. Even though what project the students chose to talk about was irrelevant to the study, it is worth noting that all of the GRADUATE participants mentioned the game design project as the project which garnered the most pride. The comparison students spoke about a variety of project types including hands-on science projects and history projects that had an emotional impact.

RQ1: Project Goals. For RQ1, we wanted to know if GRADUATE participants discussed their goals differently than non-participants. To answer this question, we created an ENA model, and connections between codes for GRADUATE participants (Treatment) were compared to connections between codes for students with traditional instruction (Comparison). Figure 1 shows the plotted points for treatment participants (red) and comparison students (blue). The plotted points of collective responses to each interview question are the dots. Statements made by GRADUATE participants are indicated by red dots; statements made by non-participants are indicated by blue dots. Each interview included multiple questions, so each group is represented by multiple dots. The average of these points, or centroid, is shown as a square with a 95% confidence interval for each dimension represented by the rectangular outline.

Fig. 1. Comparison for project goals discussion for treatment (red) and comparison (blue). (Color figure online)

ENA explained 65.6% of the variance in coding co-occurrences along the x-axis and 29.4% of the variance on the y-axis. A two-samples t-test (assuming unequal variances) was used to determine if there was a significant difference between the mean for each experience group. At the alpha = 0.05 level, the t-test (t(22.53) = −5.39; P < 0.01) revealed a significant difference between the treatment group (M = −0.97, SD = 0.80, N = 13) and the comparison group (M = 0.97, SD = 1.03, N = 13) along the x-axis. Cohen's d was equal to 2.11, which was interpreted as a large difference between the groups. A post-hoc Bayesian analysis [44] with a regularizing Cauchy prior set to 0.707 indicates a median effect size of about 1.3 with a 95% Credible Interval ranging between 0.5 and 2.2 (Fig. 2, left). The data strongly (BF$_{10}$ > 10) support the hypothesis that the mean scores are not equal across a wide range of potential prior distributions (Fig. 2, right).

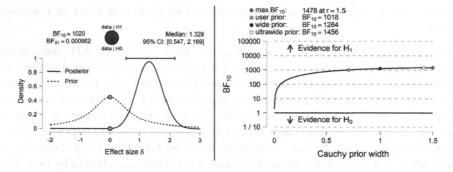

Fig. 2. Post-hoc Bayesian analysis for RQ1

Along the x-axis, there was a significant difference in the network connections. To determine why this occurred, we analyzed the individual networks. Investigating the strength of the connections between codes can reveal what codes are causing centroids to shift left or right. The individual diagrams are shown in Fig. 3. The diagram for the game designers has relatively weak connections between *knowledge* and *confidence* along with *project* and *confidence* therefore the line weights are lighter. In contrast, there is a thick, dark red line between *knowledge* and *project* indicating a very strong connection. Since the connection between *knowledge* and *project* is so strong, it shifts the centroid to the left on the x-axis. The diagram for the comparison group shows that the strongest connection is between *project* and *confidence*. Since these codes on located to the right on the x-axis, the strength of this connection shifts the centroid right.

The *project* code was used whenever students mentioned the project or details pertaining to it. The *confidence* code was used whenever students expressed confidence in their ability to do something. Therefore, the strong connection between *project* and *confidence* indicates that the comparison students expressed confidence around certain aspects of the project. One student said, "she saw that I was really good with working with computers" and another said, "so many people told me it was phenomenal." It's worth noting that these students talked about their competence in light of getting favorable feedback on their projects.

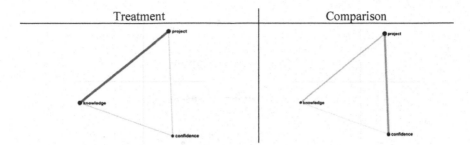

Fig. 3. Individual network diagrams highlighting connections for project discussion. (Color figure online)

While the comparison group expressed confidence around their projects, this was not true for the GRADUATE participants in the treatment group. There were no strong connections to the *confidence* code because students in the treatment group lacked confidence in the coding aspect of designing a serious educational game. For example, one GRADUATE participant said, "the coding aspect was a little hard to learn" while another one said, "I had to get with somebody to help me work the coding and stuff."

In contrast to the comparison group, the treatment group had a strong connection between the *project* code and the *knowledge* code. This indicates that those in the treatment expressed that they gained knowledge through working on the project. Some participants stated that they gained content knowledge while working on their STEM game, such as, "I learned a lot of environmental stuff." Other participants discussed gaining knowledge of coding, for example, "coding…isn't really that easy, but once you figure it out, it's an enjoyable thing to learn." When GRADUATE participants talked about their STEM game projects, they seemed excited about the fact that they learned something new and gained coding skills.

RQ2: Success. For RQ2, we wanted to know if GRADUATE participants discussed their success differently than non-participants. To answer this question, we created a second ENA model with a different set of codes, and connections between the codes were compared across groups. Figure 4 shows the plotted points and the centroid for the treatment group (red) and the comparison group (blue).

ENA explained 29.2% of the variance in coding co-occurrences along the x-axis and 43.7% of the variance on the y-axis. A two-samples t-test (assuming unequal variances) was used to determine if there was a statistically significant difference between the mean for each experience group along the x-axis. At the alpha = 0.05 level, the t-test (t $(21.51) = -4.30$; $p < 0.01$) revealed a statistically significant difference between the treatment group ($M = -0.54$, $SD = 0.74$, $N = 13$) and the comparison group ($M = 0.54$, $SD = 0.52$, $N = 13$) along the x-axis. Cohen's d was equal to 1.69, which was interpreted as a large difference between the experience groups. A post-hoc Bayesian analysis [44] with a regularizing Cauchy prior set to 0.707 indicates a median effect size of about 1.0 with a 95% Credible Interval ranging between 0.4 and 1.8 (Fig. 5, left). The data strongly ($BF_{10} > 10$) support the hypothesis that the mean scores are not equal across a wide range of potential prior distributions (Fig. 5, right).

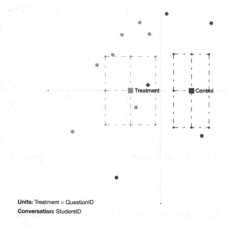

Units: Treatment > QuestionID
Conversation: StudentID

Fig. 4. Comparison for success discussion for treatment (red) and comparison (blue). (Color figure online)

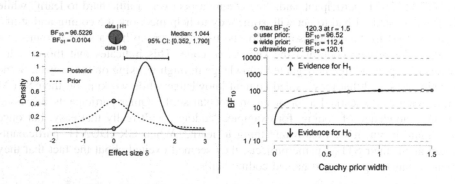

Fig. 5. Post-hoc Bayesian analysis for RQ2

Similar to the results for the first research question, there was a significant difference in the network connections present among each group along the x-axis. To examine why this difference occurred, we analyzed the individual network diagrams. The individual diagrams are shown in Fig. 6. The diagram for the treatment group shows that the strongest connection is between *persistence* and *success*. Since the *persistence* code is located to the left on the x-axis, the strength of this connection shifts the treatment group's centroid to the left. For the comparison group, the strongest connection is between *learn* and *success*. Since these codes on located to the right on the x-axis, the strength of this connection shifts the comparison group's centroid to the right.

The *learn* code was used when the student indicated that something was learned. The *success* code was used when the student indicated that something was successful or that they felt successful. Therefore, the strong connection between the *learn* code and the *success* code indicates that individuals in the comparison group learned that they could be successful. For example, when reflecting on their projects, one individual said, "It was actually good" and another individual said, "That was the first project I

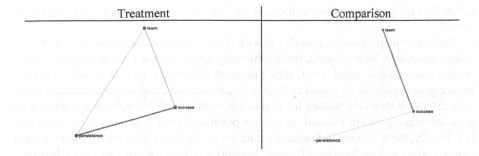

Fig. 6. Individual network diagrams highlighting connections for success discussion

have ever done that I really felt like I could be proud of it." It's worth noting that there are extremely weak, practically non-existent connections to the *persistence* code.

The *persistence* code was used when the student indicated that they had pushed themselves or worked for an extended period of time. In contrast to the comparison group, the treatment group had a strong connection between the *persistence* code and the *success* code. This indicates that those in the treatment expressed that their success —and possibly enjoyment—was due in part to their persistence. For example, one GRADUATE participant stated, "I did like the gaming project because I have never worked so hard in my entire life." Another GRADUATE participant said, "I would work until I was satisfied with what I had accomplished that day." It is also worth noting that there was some strength to the connection between the *persistence* code and the *learn* code, whereas in the comparison group, this connection was virtually non-existent. Some students in the treatment group seemed to express that they learned the value of hard work. For example, one interviewee mentioned that "I just learned that I needed to just put my effort into it."

5 Discussion

In this study, we examined interview data from students who did and did not participate in the GRADUATE program to determine whether there were differences in how STEM game design participants discussed their project goals and their success. According to our findings, GRADUATE participants discussed learning goals and success as a result of their persistence. Students who received traditional instruction discussed performance goals and they did not mention persistence in relationship to their success.

Project Goals. For RQ1, we used ENA and determined that GRADUATE participants discussed their projects differently than non-participants. Students who received traditional instruction expressed confidence around their projects especially in relationship to positive feedback. GRADUATE participants lacked confidence but talked about gaining knowledge. These patterns in the data indicated that traditionally instructed students were focused on performance goals ("I wanted to get a good grade"), while

GRADUATE participants were focused on learning goals ("I was just...trying to learn").

Students with performance goals focus on ability and seek confirmation of it [8, 22]. When discussing their projects, the traditionally instructed students seemed to have a performance goal in mind. First, they discussed confidence and those with a performance goal need to be confident in their ability before pursuing judgement [8]. Second, they discussed their competence in conjunction with favorable feedback and those with a performance goal are focused on getting positive feedback about their competence [8]. Finally, the traditionally instructed students spoke about projects that were in their comfort zone and performance-focused students can better ensure success when they chose easier tasks [8].

Students with learning goals aim to increase their competence often by learning something new [8]. When the GRADUATE participants spoke about their projects, they seemed to have a learning goal in mind. Unlike the traditionally instructed students, the GRADUATE participants did not display confidence. Since a student with a learning goal is focused on understanding new material, they do not yet display confidence; in fact, such students are actually willing to display ignorance [8] and some of the GRADUATE participants did. When the GRADUATE participants spoke about their projects, they focused on how they gained knowledge about content and coding, and students with learning goals are trying to acquire new skills and knowledge [8].

Prior research supports the idea that game design shifts the focus away from performance goals to learning goals. Experts synthesized 55 game design studies and found that making games changes students' attitudes related to project goals [39]. Schools generally orient students towards performance goals, expecting them to perform well on assessments. In turn, students seek feedback in the form of good grades. Whereas game designers seem to have a better grasp of the long-term learning benefits [39].

Success. For RQ2, we used ENA and determined that GRADUATE participants discussed success differently than non-participants. GRADUATE participants discussed persistence in relationship to their success. Traditionally instructed students discussed that they learned that they could be successful; however, they did not attribute success to persistence. These patterns indicated that non-participants took a performance approach to their achievement ("I felt really good cause you know I got a good grade for it"), while GRADUATE participants took a mastery approach ("I learned that I can do more than what I expect myself to do").

When students take a performance approach, their ego is deeply involved [22]; their satisfaction with the activity is derived from how well they performed [8]. Statements from traditionally instructed students had a strong connection between *learn* and *success*. Basically, these students felt really good because they realized that they had succeeded. Also, overcoming obstacles is not in line with those who deeply care about their performance because difficulties can negatively impact a student's view of their ability [8]; therefore, the traditionally instructed students did not mention persistence in relationship to their success.

When students take a mastery approach, they are deeply invested in the task [22]; their satisfaction with the activity is derived from how much effort they exerted [8].

Statements from GRADUATE participants had a strong connection between the *persistence* code and the *success* code. Basically, the students felt really good because they had worked really hard to succeed. Also, those who take a mastery approach are more likely to seek out challenges [8] and demonstrate persistence towards their goals [9]; therefore, the GRADUATE participants discussed persistence in relationship to their success.

Prior research in game design supports this finding that game design helps students focus on effort and persist through challenges. First, researchers compared students playing games to students creating games and determined that those in the creation condition exerted more effort than those in the play condition [40]. Second, students creating games have been observed putting a great deal of effort into their game designs [41]; the students' thinking was not only effortful, but they would persist at it. Finally, in a class of children making their own computer games, researchers noted that the students were particularly determined to persevere [42].

Orientation Differences. Our results indicate that GRADUATE participants were mastery-oriented while traditionally instructed students were performance-oriented. Mastery-oriented students are focused on learning goals [7] and more capable of persisting through challenges [9]; thus, the GRADUATE participants were mastery-oriented. Performance-oriented students are focused on performance goals [7] and less capable of persisting through challenges [8]; thus, the traditionally instructed students were performance-oriented.

Helping our students develop a mastery orientation is beneficial for several reasons. First, mastery-orientation consistently predicts achievement over performance-orientation [13]. Second, mastery-oriented students often have a healthier relationship with failure; they are more likely to associate positive emotions with failure [33] and they view challenges as problems that can be solved with effort [10]. Lastly, a mastery orientation is a good predictor of self-efficacy [11]. Students develop their self-efficacy beliefs largely through mastery experiences, such as designing games [15]. In fact, designing games as been shown to raise self-efficacy [43]. A person's self-efficacy beliefs predict subsequent behavior better than their knowledge or prior attainments [15].

6 Conclusion

Experts argue that students need more learning approaches within STEM that will help them develop a mastery orientation [29]. Our research shows that designing STEM games can offer this type of experience. Our findings demonstrate the potential for STEM game design experiences to help students focus on learning goals and persist through challenges which are important components of a mastery orientation.

This study had several limitations. First, this is largely exploratory work because it is based on a single post-assessment: we only reported on post-interviews. Second, these findings are rigorous and can be replicated; however, they need to be cross validated with other measures in the same domain to confirm the findings. Third, there are assumptions within the analysis. The assumptions are embedded in the qualitative coding and in the online software package. These assumptions play a role in the patterns observed in the data. Before the findings can be deemed robust, they will need to be replicated using alternative approaches to discourse analysis, such as a quantitative method that simplifies complex relationships.

References

1. Chen, X.: STEM attrition among high-performing college students in the United States: scope and potential causes. J. Technol. Sci. Educ. 5(1), 41–59 (2015)
2. Potvin, P., Hasni, A.: Interest, motivation and attitude towards science and technology at K-12 levels: a systematic review of 12 years of educational research. Stud. Sci. Educ. 50(1), 85–129 (2014)
3. Gopnick, A., Meltzoff, A.N., Kuhl, P.K.: The Scientist in the Crib: What Early Learning Tells us About the Mind. HarperCollins Publishers, New York (1999)
4. Murphy, S., MacDonald, A., Wang, C.A., Danaia, L.: Towards an understanding of STEM engagement: a review of the literature on motivation and academic emotions. Can. J. Sci. Math. Technol. Educ. 19(3), 304–320 (2019)
5. Hazari, Z., Potvin, G., Tai, R.H., Almarode, J.: For the love of learning science: connecting learning orientation and career productivity in physics and chemistry. Phys. Rev. Spec. Top. Phys. Educ. Res. 6(1), 1–9 (2010)
6. National Research Council: A Framework for K-12 Science Education: Practices, Cross-Cutting Concepts, and Core Ideas. The National Academies Press, Washington (2012)
7. Pintrich, P.R.: The role of goal orientation in self-regulated learning. In: Boekaerts, M., Pintrich, P.R., Zeidner, M. (eds.) Handbook of Self-Regulation, pp. 451–502. Academic Press, Cambridge (2000)
8. Dweck, C.S.: Motivational processes affecting learning. Am. Psychol. 4(10), 1040–1048 (1986)
9. Linnenbrink, E.A.: The dilemma of performance-approach goals: the use of multiple goal contexts to pro- mote students' motivation and learning. J. Educ. Psychol. 97(2), 197–213 (2005)
10. Dweck, C.S., Leggett, E.L.: A social-cognitive approach to motivation and personality. Psychol. Rev. 95(2), 256–273 (1988)
11. Wolters, C.A., Yu, S.L., Pintrich, P.R.: The relation between goal orientation and students' motivational beliefs and self-regulated learning. Learn. Individ. Differ. 8(3), 211–238 (1996)
12. Koestner, R., Zuckerman, M.: Causality orientations, failure, and achievement. J. Pers. 62(3), 321–346 (1994)
13. Keys, T.D., Conley, A.M., Duncan, G.J., Domina, T.: The role of goal orientations for adolescent mathematics achievement. Contemp. Educ. Psychol. 37(1), 47–54 (2012)
14. Eccles, J.S., Wigfield, A.: Motivational beliefs, values, and goals. Annu. Rev. Psychol. 53(1), 109–132 (2002)
15. Bandura, A.: Self-Efficacy: The Exercise of Control. W.H. Freeman and Company, New York (1997)
16. Eccles, J.S.: Expectancies, values, and academic choice: origins and changes. In: Spence, J. (ed.) Achievement and Achievement Motivation. Freeman, San Francisco (1983)
17. Wigfield, A., Eccles, J.S.: The development of achievement task values: a theoretical analysis. Dev. Rev. 12, 265–310 (1992)
18. Elliot, A.J., McGregor, H.A., Gable, S.: Achievement goals, study strategies, and exam performance. J. Educ. Psychol. 91(3), 547–563 (1999)

19. Andersson, H., Bergman, L.R.: The role of task persistence in young adolescence for successful educational and occupational attainment in middle adulthood. Dev. Psychol. **47**(4), 950–960 (2011)
20. Boe, E.E., May, H., Boruch, R.F.: Student Task Persistence in the Third International Mathematics and Science Study: A Major Source of Achievement Differences at the National, Classroom, and Student Levels. Office of Educational Research and Improvement, Washington (2002)
21. Schinske, J., Tanner, K.: Teaching more by grading less (or differently). CBE—Life Sci. Educ. **13**(2), 159–166 (2014)
22. Ames, C.: Classrooms: goals, structures, and student motivation. J. Educ. Psychol. **84**(3), 261–271 (1992)
23. Owston, R., Wideman, H., Ronda, N.S., Brown, C.: Computer game development as a literacy activity. Comput. Educ. **53**, 977–989 (2009)
24. Allsop, Y.: A reflective study into children's cognition when making computer games. Br. J. Edu. Technol. **47**(4), 665–679 (2016)
25. Diener, C.I., Dweck, C.S.: An analysis of learned helplessness: continuous changes in performance, strategy, and achievement cognitions following failure. J. Pers. Soc. Psychol. **36**(5), 451–462 (1978)
26. Abramson, L.Y., Seligman, M.E., Teasdale, J.D.: Learned helplessness in humans: critique and reformulation. J. Abnorm. Psychol. **87**, 49–74 (1978)
27. Filippello, P., Buzzai, C., Costa, S., Orecchio, S., Sorrenti, L.: Teaching style and academic achievement: the mediating role of learned helplessness and mastery orientation. Psychol. Sch. **57**(1), 5–16 (2020)
28. Pokay, P., Blumenfeld, P.C.: Predicting achievement early and late in the semester: the role of motivation and use of learning strategies. J. Educ. Psychol. **82**(1), 41–50 (1990)
29. Henry, M.A., Shorter, S., Charkoudian, L., Heemstra, J.M., Corwin, L.A.: FAIL is not a four-letter word: a theoretical framework for exploring undergraduate students' approaches to academic challenge and responses to failure in STEM learning environments. CBE Life Sci. Educ. **18**(1), ar11 (2019)
30. Denner, J., Campe, S., Werner, L.: Does computer game design and programming benefit children? A meta-synthesis of research. ACM Trans. Comput. Educ. **19**(3), 1–35 (2019)
31. Glaser, B.G., Strauss, A.L.: The Discovery of Grounded Theory: Strategies for Qualitative Research. Aldine Publishing Company, New York (1967)
32. McHugh, M.L.: Lessons in biostatistics interrater reliability: the kappa statistic. Biochemia Medica **22**(3), 276–282 (2012)
33. Tulis, M., Ainley, M.: Interest, enjoyment and pride after failure experiences? Predictors of students' state-emotions after success and failure during learning in mathematics. Educ. Psychol. **31**(7), 779–807 (2011)
34. Shaffer, D.W.: Quantitative Ethnography. Cathcart Press, Madison (2017)
35. Shaffer, D.W., Collier, W., Ruis, A.R.: A tutorial on epistemic network analysis: analyzing the structure of connections in cognitive, social, and interaction data. J. Learn. Analyt. **3**(3), 9–45 (2016)
36. Csanadi, A., Eagan, B., Kollar, I., Shaffer, D.W., Fischer, F.: When coding-and-counting is not enough: using epistemic network analysis (ENA) to analyze verbal data in CSCL research. Int. J. Comput. Support. Collab. Learn. **13**(4), 419–438 (2018). https://doi.org/10.1007/s11412-018-9292-z
37. Swiecki, Z., Ruis, A.R., Farrell, C., Shaffer, D.W.: Assessing individual contributions to collaborative problem solving: a network analysis approach. Comput. Hum. Behav. **104**, 105876 (2020)

38. Siebert-Evenstone, A.L., Irgens Arastoopour, G., Collier, W., Swiecki, Z., Ruis, A.R., Shaffer, D.W.: In search of conversational grain size: modeling semantic structure using moving stanza windows. J. Learn. Analyt. **4**(3), 123–139 (2017)
39. Kafai, Y., Burke, Q.: Constructionist gaming: understanding the benefits of making games for learning. Educ. Psychol. **50**(4), 313–334 (2015)
40. Vos, N., Van Der Meijden, H., Denessen, E.: Effects of constructing versus playing an educational game on student motivation and deep learning strategy use. Comput. Educ. **56**(1), 127–137 (2011)
41. Ke, F.: An implementation of design-based learning through creating educational computer games: a case study on mathematics learning during design and computing. Comput. Educ. **73**, 26–39 (2014)
42. Robertson, J., Howells, C.: Computer game design: opportunities for successful learning. Comput. Educ. **50**(2), 559–578 (2008)
43. Newton, K.J., Leonard, J., Buss, A., Wright, C.G., Barnes-Johnson, J.: Informal STEM: learning with robotics and game design in an urban context. J. Res. Technol. Educ. **52**(2), 129–147 (2020)
44. Shane Tutwiler, M.: Post-hoc Bayesian hypothesis tests in epistemic network analyses. In: Eagan, B., Misfeldt, M., Siebert-Evenstone, A. (eds.) Advances in Quantitative Ethnography: First International Conference, ICQE 2019, Madison, WI, USA, October 20–22, 2019, Proceedings, pp. 342–348. Springer, Cham (2019). https://doi.org/10.1007/978-3-030-33232-7_31

Teachers' Beliefs Shift Across Year-Long Professional Development: ENA Graphs Transformation of Privately Held Beliefs Over Time

Anita M. Benna[✉] and Kyle Reynolds

Indiana University Northwest, Gary, IN, USA
anitmart@iu.edu

Abstract. While classroom teachers are continuously trying to improve their instruction to increase student learning and engagement, dissatisfaction with professional development initiatives are often reported. Researchers examined the extant professional development literature and utilized the following distinct elements in this research design: a) teacher voice; b) teacher collaboration; c) critical reflection; and d) extended professional development time. In addition, the importance of alignment between teachers' beliefs and the focus of professional development initiatives should not be underestimated. These five elements frame this mixed method study that is undergirded by a qualitative, multi-tiered data analysis of eight data sources including assessments of teacher's beliefs and understanding of Problem-based Learning tenets as they navigate shifts in their classroom. This study is supported by a "beliefs of practice structure" framework [1] that includes both the teachers' professed beliefs and their enacted beliefs, or pedagogical beliefs. Epistemic Network Analysis quantified the qualitatively coded data into visual graphs depicting teacher's beliefs of practice structures before, at the midpoint, and at the end of the study. Statistically significant differences were found between the teacher's Pre study graphs and their Mid study graphs, as well as between the Pre and Post study graphs, substantiating shifts in beliefs of practice structures that more closely align with PBL tenets. Data analysis confirms that the professional development model and its emphasis on the critical reflection cycle emboldened novice kindergarten teachers to implement changes in their classrooms.

Keywords: Teacher professional development · Epistemic Network Analysis · Critical reflection

1 Introduction

A significant number of research studies examining the relationship between student achievement and teacher quality have shown a positive correlation, however, gauging the most effective ways to increase teacher quality has been more elusive [16]. While classroom teachers are continuously trying to improve their instruction to increase student learning and engagement, dissatisfaction with professional development initiatives are often reported [10]. Researchers examined the extant professional

B. Wasson and S. Zörgő (Eds.): ICQE 2021, CCIS 1522, pp. 191–206, 2022.
https://doi.org/10.1007/978-3-030-93859-8_13

development literature and found the following distinct elements to be consistently more successful in encouraging shifts in the teacher's pedagogical practices: a) teacher voice; b) teacher collaboration; c) critical reflection; and d) extended professional development time, and e) teacher's beliefs [12, 15, 16, 19, 21]. Upon review of studies concerning the impact of professional development on teacher change as it relates to pedagogical shifts in practice, teacher beliefs play a significant role, and success is related to the alignment between teachers' beliefs and the focus of the professional development initiative [5, 8, 10, 13, 14]. These five elements, then, frame this study.

2   Literature Review

2.1   Problem-Based Learning

This professional development initiative was centered on encouraging teachers to implement two problem-based learning (PBL) units over the course of one year. The basic tenets of PBL include a shift in instructional practice by teachers to allow for student-led learning, including: student choice; problem-solving opportunities; individual and group inquiry; shifts in roles of teacher and students; and teachers' beliefs about the new instructional practice.

Student choice is a fundamental component undergirding an open-ended, problem-based classroom that respects the self-directed abilities and independence of the students. This requires teachers to envision their classrooms as having a strong instructional design in what appears to be an unstructured space. These new instructional practices also require a shift in how the teacher defines student learning and how it is achieved [21], causing conflict between the effectiveness of traditional verses student-led learning environments [14]. Within a constructivists' view, students construct knowledge in situations where there are extended opportunities to problem-solve using an inquiry approach. The teacher-student role reversal is not straightforward and the teacher's beliefs about how students learn [8] and student's ability to take on a new role, appears to impact teachers' decisions regarding relinquishing control of the learning environment [15]. These enacted beliefs encourage or mitigate whether the teacher pivots to co-learner or guide, and whether the students are then given an opportunity to take on a leadership role in their own learning experience.

2.2   Teacher Beliefs

In traditional teacher beliefs research the question being studied has focused on the order of shifts of beliefs and practice. Does a shift in beliefs create a shift in practice, or does the teacher attempt a shift in practice first and then the belief system is modified? However, it has been shown that teachers hold entangled beliefs and practices that are an interwoven arrangement of a "beliefs of practice structure" [1] that includes how students learn, the teacher's views of student capabilities, and beliefs about pedagogical practices like problem-based learning. Research indicates that these beliefs are played out in the "rough and tumble" of the classroom [5]. These beliefs are thought to be held as a "floating raft", and as one belief shifts and the raft tips, other beliefs attempt to "right the raft "by aligning or dismissing beliefs that do not cohere with the newly adopted ones [20]. Disequilibrium, then, is this process by which teachers internally struggle with two conflicting beliefs simultaneously, and then resolve the incoherence over time as described as above. Teachers' beliefs of practice structures include teachers' attitudes, beliefs, and actions regarding inquiry and problem-based learning, and can be modified if they are addressed in the professional development model [15]. This study employs the term "pedagogical beliefs" to refer to a teacher's instructional practice. The notion that teachers' beliefs and practice are held in entangled ways has never been in question, however, how they are held, and their relational value has been somewhat evasive [8, 15, 16, 21]. This research builds on the literature base by examining three novice kindergarten teachers' beliefs of practice structures and the ways in which these structures were modified across the implementation of two, 6-week problem-based learning (PBL) units with engineering design components.

2.3   Effective Professional Development Elements

Teacher Voice/Choice. We find in professional development literature that an increase in the teacher's voice regarding the planning and decision-making increases teacher engagement and their desire to change their pedagogical beliefs. Teachers want to be co-designers of this professional development opportunity due to the individualized nature of each teacher's unique classroom situation, while desiring to engage in collaborative efforts with grade-level colleagues during such shifts in practice decisions. Encouraging collaboration among participants increases the desire to share both positive and negative experiences thereby creating a natural "coaching/mentoring" model between teachers that mitigate competition and builds trust [19].

Critical Reflection. In his book, *How We Think*, Dewey (1933), discusses the notion of "reflective thought" saying that it is "any active, persistent, and careful consideration of any belief or supposed form of knowledge in the light of the grounds that support it, and further conclusions to which it tends." While these ideas support our study, we borrow Liu's words (2015) regarding the notion of critical reflection, as a "reflective practice into a more sophisticated, critical practice that will in turn transform their learning – that is, learning that results in changes in understanding, attitudes, and especially behavior as a teacher" (p. 138). The addition of a transformation of behavior component here supported our professional development goals of shifts in pedagogical beliefs. Researchers, then, created a critical reflection cycle of pedagogical beliefs' challenges, by creating weekly conversations in a focus group format, that included a continuous cycle of: a) discussions of beliefs of practice structures; b) teacher's personal beliefs about PBL tenets; c) discussions about first classroom attempt; d) peer mentoring/coaching; e) teachers' decisions about second attempt; f) oral reports on second attempt; g) teacher request for classroom observations; h) additional discussions regarding progress; and i) teacher's decisions to implement additional pedagogical shifts as their beliefs of practice structures began to shift, to align and cohere to new beliefs due to disequilibrium and then reconciling conflicting beliefs.

Longevity/Classroom Presence. The last two components that are supported by the literature are similar, yet distinct aspects of effective professional development models. They include the desire by teachers for the professional development providers to maintain a strong classroom/school presence, allowing for continuous conversations centered on attempts at innovation. Opportunities for discussions about pedagogical beliefs and internal critical reflection "moments" teachers experience, increase teacher confidence. This fuels a desire to see higher levels of students' abilities, engagement, and achievement. Similar, yet distinct, are the teachers' desire for long term professional development initiatives. This element is grounded in the research that has shown that teacher's want access to providers who have shown interest or "buy-in" for an extended period of time [12, 15, 16].

The above review of the literature informed the following research design. Teacher educators and professional development providers seeking transformative teacher change, cry out for studies employing critical reflection cycles that require teachers to examine their privately held conceptions (beliefs, attitudes, behaviors) as they consider pedagogical changes [15]. The purpose of this study was to examine modifications in teachers' beliefs of practice frameworks as they negotiated PBL tenets in their classrooms. The research questions were: (a) How are beginning teachers' beliefs of practice structures altered as they navigate professional development that introduces new beliefs about instructional practices? (b) What aspects of Professional Development encourage shifts in teachers' beliefs of practice structures?

3   Methods

A mixed methods approach utilizing both qualitative and quantitative data was employed during this year-long professional development initiative. Qualitative data was utilized to catch a glimpse of teachers' privately held beliefs of practice structures: (a) before the study began (August); (b) at the midpoint-after the implementation of the first PBL unit, but before the second (November); and (c) at the end of the study (April). Data sources include: an open-ended PBL questionnaire, a Teacher Reflection and risk Assessment Form, transcripts of Pedagogical Conversations, Focus-Groups, Classroom Interviews, and Classroom Observations. Quantitative data analysis employed Epistemic Frame Theory to create epistemic network graphs of the mean of all three teachers' personal beliefs of practice structures using Epistemic Network Analysis at three distinct stages: before the study-PRE graph, midway (between the first and second 6-week PBL unit)-MID graph and on the last day of the study- POST graph.

3.1   Context

This study takes place in an urban elementary school within 50 miles of Chicago. Perkins New Tech Elementary School (pseudonym) utilized project-based learning practices in all grades, kindergarten through fifth, with a total student population of 481. It had 48% minority student status and 89% qualified for free/reduced lunch. Perkins Elementary had 24 teachers and the average class size ranged from 24–27 annually. After discussions with the school principal, it was determined that this research study would focus on three novice kindergarten classroom teachers as the primary participants, with one teacher holding one year of experience and the other two beginning their first year of teaching. The overarching goal was the implementation of a PBL environment where students determined the problem, and an engineering design component was integral.

3.2   Professional Development

Professional development for the teachers was a fundamental aspect of this study. The two researchers provided professional development for the 3 kindergarten teachers using a scaffolded reflection cycle model that included teacher voice, teacher decision-making, frequent presence in the school/classroom, a long-term commitment, and a critical reflection cycle of: pedagogical innovation conversations; classroom attempts; post conversations; peer mentoring/coaching; additional attempts; peer mentoring/coaching; and continuous classroom observations for feedback. This cycle created a perpetual immersion component for the three kindergarten teachers.

3.3   Data Sources

Data was retrieved from instruments specifically designed to ascertain teacher's privately held beliefs of practice structures that encompassed teacher attitudes, beliefs, and understandings of PBL tenets. In addition, beliefs regarding how students learn, and the roles of the teacher and learner in the classroom were queried. Each data source warranted distinct questions purposefully designed to elicit specific information about the teachers' beliefs of practice notions held at the pre, mid, and post stages of the study. The following data sources were developed and employed: three major Professional Development Sessions (Pre/Mid/Post) audio-taped and transcribed; teacher's written responses on a Problem-based Learning Questionnaire (Pre/Mid/Post); PBL classroom observation forms and notes; brief individual interviews before and/or after classroom observations (audio-taped & transcribed); infrequent student-to-student discourse audio-tapings; Teacher Reflection & Risk Assessment (mid/post); and weekly Pedagogical Conversation Focus Group Sessions (audio-taped & transcribed).

Major Professional Development Sessions. Teachers were provided with three major professional development opportunities separate from instruction, purposefully away from the act and practice of teaching. The first session (PRE) was held for 2 days prior to the study in August and the (MID) session was held one day in November, between the implementation of the two units, and a final session (POST) included a 3/4 day of professional development on the last day of the study in April, which was designed for final assessment, reflection, and discussion. The many hours of professional development at each stage were audio-taped and transcribed. During the first two-day, professional development time teachers completed written assessments and then were immersed (as the student) in a problem-based learning situation that included engineering design elements. This was followed by discussions and reflections related to problem/project-based learning tenets and their implementation in a classroom.

During both 6-week units, teachers planned the lessons and assessment using a backwards design approach while the researchers held a co-constructing role by proposing various resources and suggesting additional ideas undergirding the teacher's weekly goals/objectives. Ultimately, teachers determined the final plans and researchers supported their decisions regarding new instructional practices and content they would implement. Finally, researchers encouraged teachers to weave engineering design elements into the final student projects for each 6-week unit (Fall/Spring).

Problem-Based Learning Questionnaire. Researchers created a six-question constructed response questionnaire to which teachers individually responded in Qualtrics on the first day of the study, midway, and on the last day of the study. The questions were: *1. What are the most important ideas in problem-based learning and why do you think this? 2. What is your role as a teacher in a PBL classroom? 3. Compare your role in a PBL classroom versus other instructional practice lessons. 4. What is the role of the student in a PBL Classroom? 5. What are the most difficult aspects of implementing PBL in your classroom? 6. Please discuss your personal beliefs about the strengths and weaknesses of PBL as an instructional practice.* This data source was created to examine and compare teacher's beliefs of practice structures (professed beliefs-words, and pedagogical beliefs-instructional practice) throughout the duration of the study.

Teacher Observations/Short Interviews/Student Discourse. Each researcher observed one to two teachers over several weeks (approx. 35–40 min each) using the PBL Learning Questionnaire. The PBL tenets purposely observed were a) the roles of the teacher and students: b) the amount of ownership given to students; and c) opportunities for student-to-student discourse. Also, when the teacher had a preparation period prior to or after the teaching they agreed to a short audio-taped interview. The questions that were asked before instruction related to the teachers' intentions, and these reasons reveal attitudes/beliefs that are thought to be the precursors towards actions. Potentially these responses revealed the teachers' underlying beliefs of practice structures [1] within their entangled nature of beliefs and instructional practices frameworks. These questions were: a) What are you going to implement today? b) What do you want the students to learn? and c) What do you think students will do? Questions asked after the instruction were: a) How do you think it went? b) What was your favorite part of the lesson? and c) What do you think the students liked best about today's lesson? After-teaching interviews are thought to reveal the teacher's self-efficacy beliefs of themselves as successful teachers through their lens of how they viewed student capabilities, reactions, and overall learning in the lesson. These beliefs are thought to impact whether teachers continue to implement changes [1]. Occasionally, there were additional observations made when teachers requested assistance with a problem they were having in the classroom with the shift in teacher and student roles.

Teacher Reflection and Risk Assessment. This instrument was designed to elicit changes in their beliefs of practice structures regarding Engineering/PBL tenets. This data source was completed by the teachers in the middle and on the last day of the study. At these two critical points teachers were asked: 1) "What one thing did I learn about my teaching, and my students in Problem-based Learning?" 2) What one thing did I learn about my teaching and my students in Engineering Design practices?" This was a purposeful attempt to understand the adaptations of their beliefs of practice structures by asking teachers to articulate any shifts in beliefs. It was specifically designed to pinpoint signs of disequilibrium where teachers might be contemplating opposing beliefs or attempting reconciliation of conflicting beliefs, so that researchers could determine whether they were held simultaneously. Lastly, it was created to allow teachers to discuss and reveal their beliefs about student capabilities and how they believe students learn across time.

Pedagogical Conversations: Weekly Focus Group Sessions. This data source was the strongest source of data in the study and included a critical reflection cycle of: pedagogical conversations; peer mentoring/coaching; pedagogical beliefs decisions/ actions; and classroom observation/coaching. This cycle was continuous throughout the units lasting approximately 14 weeks. During these weeks, researchers asked questions requiring the teachers to reflect aloud on the past week's events, and to consider the next week's plans and the aspects of problem-based learning practices they would like to implement or modify. Questions were purposefully designed to elicit the following beliefs of practice structures: A) How they viewed their pedagogical decisions/actions: 1) What did they try? 2. What went well? 3) What did they struggle with? B) Beliefs about student capabilities: 1) What were the students' reactions? 2) What went well? 3) What did they struggle with? C) Beliefs about how students learn & valuing student talk: 1) Can students learn from one another? Did you have students talk to each other? Researchers questioned teachers about their pedagogical beliefs/decisions/actions during the past week's events. Next, they were asked to reflect on the upcoming week's plans to determine which aspects of problem-based learning pedagogies they would re-try or implement for the first time.

3.4   Data Analysis

Qualitative Analysis. Data was analyzed using a complex qualitative coding schema. Over the course of approximately 8 months, two researchers coded all data sources utilizing grounded theory method [9] employing a multi-phase cycle of: code, compare/record, discuss-change wording of operational definition; repeat. During this time there were 12 interrater reliability checks at various stages throughout the coding process. Inter-rater reliability (IRR) sessions were held more frequently initially, then tapered off as the researchers internalized the codes and their operational definitions. IRR sessions averaged 85–100% consistency. Researchers began this multi-faceted analysis by examining words that symbolized an idea; the idea was listed next to the words and other words were added that explained the same idea. Each teacher's responses were coded by sentence and were discussed within a given data source before researchers moved to a new data source. This was done to establish codes grounded within the teachers' beliefs of practice structures first within data sources, and then across them [9]. When wording was similar to an established code, but clearly held a nuanced shift in meaning, additional codes were added, and operational defi- nitions were reconsidered and modified. For example, researchers struggled with the similarities and differences between the codes of Teacher-directed and Keeper of the Knowledge. After multiple coding incongruencies between researchers, original data sources were re-analyzed. The nuanced differences emerged due to this intense scrutiny of the original data. It was revealed that one represented the idea from a teaching standpoint, while the other represented a student learning point of view. Since the codes were established from the teacher's responses which revealed their personally held beliefs, data analysis generated both positive and negative problem-based learning codes across data sources and time. This process culminated in the creation of a PBL Coding Chart (Table 1). The disequilibrium code was established as we sought to capture moments when a teacher held conflicting beliefs within the same response to a question or within the same conversation.

Table 1. Problem-based learning coding chart.

Code/ Opposite	Operational definition	Example(s)
Collaborate Can't collaborate	Ability/inability to work/discuss ideas with others in a group	(Collab) "My students will naturally collaborate with each other now when given a problem. They look at a friend and say, "Well, how'd you get that?" (Can't) "Collaboration abilities are difficult with children so young."
Disequilibrium	An internal struggle to align or dismiss new beliefs that do not cohere with other beliefs	They have trouble explaining what engineers do, …but they know. But, I don't think they know. They know, but they can't do it I realized now that they can, well some can, well most can't, but I had kids like tell the others we're just wasting recess time right now, so they can do it
Engaged/ Not engaged	Greatly interested, participating/ Not interested or involved	(Engaged)When we let them come up with the problem to solve, they're way more interested (Not)They used to just zone out and not really listen
Independent Not independent	Don't need direction and guidance from teacher /Need direction/guidance	(Independent) "Now they ask one another or just figure it out instead of coming to me." (Not) They would just be frustrated and come to me. They wouldn't try to do it
Motivated/ Not motivated	Desire or willingness to participate/ Lack of a desire/willingness to participate	(Motivated) "Letting kids just go! It increases motivation!" (Not) "They wouldn't have cared enough to listen." "They used to refuse to try to do it."
Problem-solve/ Can't reason	Figure out the why& how of something/ Unable to think through a problem	(Problem-solve) "They are actually willing to sit down and think!" "They can solve problems without me now." (Can't reason) "They can't think through a problem."
Process/ Product	Process-focuses on the path to get to the end Product-focuses on end result	(Process): "Their project broke 3 times, but I never saw them give up. They kept trying to figure out a different way to make it work." (Product) "I'm worried about how well their projects are executed. Projects could potentially fail, but the designs can always be altered in the end."

(continued)

Table 1. (*continued*)

Code/ Opposite	Operational definition	Example(s)
Relevant	Applicable to students' worlds; it's important to them;	"When they come up with the idea, it's more authentic to them." "It matters in their everyday life."
Relinquish Control Teacher Directed	RelCon-Give up telling students what to do; let them be in charge Teacher Directed-Step by step directions	(Relinquish Control): "They are actually taking responsibility over their own learning. They decide; we don't." "Figure it out in your own way." (Teacher Directed): We were saying, 'Okay, you want recess? Do this and this and this.' And they'd just do what we said, and not try to solve the problem at all
Student Discourse	Student/student talk social negotiation	"Now they use each other to help and ask questions." "Just watching them bounce ideas off each other." "And they talked it through in their grown-up groups."
Student Ownership/ Keeper of the Knowledge	Students' ideas drive the projects/ Teacher decides how much to tell students	(Student Ownership) "It's where they get to choose how they're going to solve the problem. It makes it their project, not ours." (KotK) "I feel like when you just lecture and give answers, you take away the whole inquiry part of it." "We were telling them every step." "We tell them what they're doing and why."
Trust	Believe in the efficacy of another	You guys are very passionate so we knew your ideas would be good. Working with you was easy We could trust you because you knew our students

Quantitative Analysis. ENA utilizes qualitative data from coded interviews and questionnaires that are then transferred to a binary coded data set, and then produces a graph that visually displays the ideas being studied. Here, the graphs represent privately held cognitive thought or beliefs. Individual graphs are constructed through the display of teachers' private ideas and interconnectedness within the knowledge domain of problem-based learning [15]. The idea flow includes specific knowledge constructs and their relationship between and among other components, as ideas are bantered about through conversation, oral or written [2]. Individual interview questions, and open-ended questionnaire responses where conceptual understanding is recorded, could be considered its own conversation, thereby demonstrating participants' understanding through the connectedness of ideas [6]. In addition, ENA has the capability to create graphs depicting knowledge/beliefs' construction or modifications over time, such as in this study.

ENA creates visual representations of privately held notions and beliefs by utilizing Epistemic Frame Theory. Epistemic Frame Hypothesis utilizes these assumptions: a) it is possible to systematically identify a set of meaningful features in the data or codes; b) the data has local structure or conversations; and c) the most significant feature of the data is the way in which the codes are connected to one another within conversations [17, 18]. This modeling creates a visual graph of connectedness of ideas termed an epistemic frame. In this study, segmentation of the data was first achieved by determining that the most basic meaningful parts of the data were sentences. This level of analysis allowed researchers to capture sentences in succession that may hold beliefs that do not cohere, seeking to push the literature forward with answers as to whether teachers hold conflicting beliefs simultaneously. Next, we defined the conversations as the grouping of items that included one teacher's response to each question on a written assessment, or one response in a structured interview or focus group. This purposeful conversation decision allowed researchers to compare responses to questions on the same assessments that were given before, midway, and at the end of the study. We used a moving stanza window of 4 where the connection structure was defined as the 3 lines preceding any given line. The Epistemic Frame Hypothesis posits that the epistemic frame, or "the structure of connections among cognitive elements", is more important than the mere presence or absence of those elements in isolation" [18]. This epistemic frame is internalized by individuals as they engage with other group members over time such as teachers. They internalize shared culture and identity by engaging in the epistemology that is reflective of that community of practice, exhibiting that community's epistemic frame [11]. Epistemic Frame Theory, then, is a reasonable way to assess the nature of understanding within a professional development initiative created for a group of kindergarten teachers. ENA created a model of the connections between conversations by quantifying the co-occurrence of codes within conversations, producing a weighted network of co-occurrences, along with associated visualizations for each unit of analysis. Most significantly, ENA analyzed the entire set of teachers' networks simultaneously, resulting in a collection of networks that could be compared both visually and statistically between and among teachers across time [2].

4   Results

The purpose of this study was to examine modifications in teachers' beliefs of practice frameworks as they negotiated PBL tenets in their classrooms. The focus centered on an examination as to how and why teachers might make shifts in their beliefs of practice structures, and which aspects of the professional development encouraged such changes in pedagogical beliefs. We sought to create a professional development model that might be more effective in encouraging teachers to make deliberate shifts in their pedagogical beliefs, or practices. Our attempts to deepen teachers' convictions for pedagogical shifts in their practice that more closely align with a student-centered, problem-based learning classroom environment was achieved by including: a) the teachers voice as co-designers and decision-maker; b) peer collaboration; c) long-term engagement/presence in classroom by researchers; and d) a critical reflection cycle of: pedagogical innovation conversations, classroom attempts, post conversations, peer mentoring/coaching; additional attempts; peer mentoring/ coaching; and continuous classroom observations for feedback. These elements created a sense of trust that was explicitly discussed across data sources. As outlined in the methods section, researchers established a disequilibrium code that was employed only when a teacher would speak about an idea or belief and an opposing idea or belief within the same conversation. The disequilibrium code represents the idea that the teacher is privately negotiating two conflicting beliefs simultaneously.

The graphs are discussed: A) Pre- before the study (August); B) Mid- midway (November); and C) Post-after the professional development ended (April). Figure 1 reveals that the overall teachers Pre, Mid, and Post means are located in different quadrants and that the pattern of shift is an arc-shaped trajectory from quadrant 3 to 2 to 1. This has been shown to be a known pattern associated with ENA's capabilities in modeling datasets across time. Quantitative analysis revealed statistically significant differences between the Pre and Mid graphs, and the Pre and Post graphs. Along the Y axis, a two-sample t-test showed Pre (mean = −1.01, SD = 0.62, N = 3 was statistically significantly different at the alpha = 0.05 level Mid (mean = 0.54, SD = 0.29, N = 3, t(2.84) = 3.93, p = 0.03, Cohen's d = 3.21). In addition, again along the Y axis, Pre (mean = −1.01, SD = 0.62, N = 3, was statistically significantly different at the alpha 0.05 level from Post (mean = 0.47, SD = 0.64, N = 3; t(4.00) = 2.86, p = 0.05. Cohen's d = 2.34). These data show that teachers changed their beliefs of practice structures in a substantial manner across time.

Figure 2 demonstrates that each quadrant is characterized by distinct codes which are stationary, allowing comparisons across teachers' and time. Importantly, these codes hold either a positive or negative view of problem-based learning (See Table 1). This allows us to characterize each quadrant as containing particularly positive or negative PBL codes.

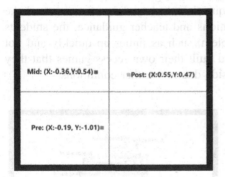

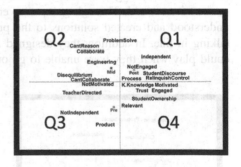

Fig. 1. Pre/Mid/Post means   **Fig. 2.** Code locations by quadrant

Quadrant 3, where teachers began this study (Pre-Mean), possesses the most negative PBL codes of all quadrants. The second most negative PBL coded quadrant is quadrant 2, and quadrant 1 houses codes that are the second most positive, with quadrant 4 representing the most positive PBL coded quadrant. This data authenticates that teachers not only changed their beliefs' structures but moved from a negative view of problem-based learning to a stronger, more positive position regarding this new instructional practice. Teachers began in quadrant 3 (Pre), which is characterized by negative notions of teachers' beliefs about student capabilities that include ideas that students are not independent and not motivated. In addition, teacher's pedagogical beliefs before the study were that learning needed to be teacher directed and that the product of the engineering design component was more important than the process such as test and retest and design and redesign. The data for the All Teachers Pre graph (Fig. 3) consisted of assessments on day 1 of the first professional development day. Teachers completed the PBL Questionnaire that asked them about their beliefs about a) the most important ideas regarding a PBL environment and why; b) the teacher's role in a PBL classroom compared to a traditional classroom; c) the student's role in a PBL classroom; d) the most difficult aspects of implementing the strengths and weaknesses regarding PBL as an instructional practice. This instrument stands without supporting pedagogical beliefs' data since this was the first day of the study. It is considered inadequate to ask participants their professed beliefs without considering their pedagogical beliefs because participants may tell researchers what they want to hear. However, in this study, this concern is mitigated by the fact that there were no conversations regarding any topics of the study prior to asking the teachers to complete the assessments the first day of professional development. Therefore, we are confident that teachers provided honest responses extracted from their beliefs of practice structures before the study began. Examining this graph by teacher, we find that 2 of the 3 teachers held the Disequilibrium code before the study began. For one teacher, the Disequilibrium code was bound to every other code except can't reason. The second teacher connected it to: not independent, student ownership, and product, prior to professional development.

The first unit taught to the kindergarteners was decided by the students as they thought about a problem in their world. To them, not being allowed to have recess after lunch was their biggest concern, but when questioned, they did not understand the reasons it occurred. Through group conversations and teacher guidance, the students understood and created solutions to the problem, such as lining up quickly and not talking in line. In addition, they designed and built their own recess games that they could play when they were unable to go outside due to weather conditions.

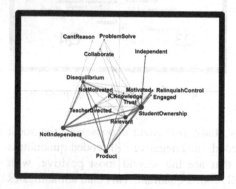

Fig. 3. All teachers' Pre

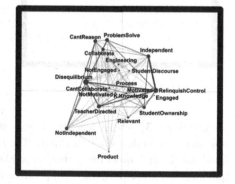

Fig. 4. All teachers Mid graph

The All Teachers Mid graph (Fig. 4) was created at the midpoint of the study, after the first unit and a 6-week critical reflection cycle, classroom observations and interviews. The graph was derived from the following data sources: teaching the first 6-

week unit, engaging in a cycle of critical reflection of pedagogical beliefs that included weekly focus group meetings, classroom observations/short interviews before or after according to time constraints, completion of the first Teacher Beliefs and Risk Assessment querying: "What did I learn about my teaching, and my students in Problem-based Learning?", and, finally, the second PBL assessment. It provides strong, detailed evidence of a shift in teacher's overall beliefs of practice structures, moving from the Pre mean graph in quadrant 3 to quadrant 2, moving from the most negative to the second most negative PBL coded quadrant. This quadrant and graph is characterized primarily by the Disequilibrium code. It is here, at the midpoint, that Disequilibrium is the largest node and holds the most connections to all other codes, with the strongest connections to Relinquish Control and Teacher Directed. These ideas are the fundamental beliefs that undergird a PBL environment and were one of the focal points of the cycle of critical reflection and focus group interactions. If teachers do not relinquish control, students can't take ownership, and do not have a voice or choice in their own investigations. When teachers direct the learning, the students are relegated to following directions and answering rote questions, instead of determining questions related to their own personal interests within the unit's objectives and standards. Clearly at this point in the study teachers were continuously "trying-on" new beliefs while contemplating their professed and pedagogical beliefs. As they enacted innovations in their classrooms, the critical reflection cycle reinforced the idea that attempting a particular pedagogical change more than once, gives students the opportunity to learn how to navigate the role reversal and ultimately lead their own investigations. A prime example regarding this construct and its outcome, chronicles one teacher who stated that the students, when sitting on the rug after recess, wouldn't listen to her. I asked her the size of the rug and the number of students sitting there. I asked her if she had ever considered spreading pairs of students out around the room to discuss a certain idea. She tried it the following week and reported back that on day 1, the students were all rolling around the classroom, but on day 2 she required them to sit with knees touching and to be face-to-face. On day 3 sometimes a student would speak to their partner, and by day 4 some groups were talking. By day 5 all groups were discussing the ideas that the teacher initiated. She could not believe how quickly they learned how to talk. She realized how capable they were when she gave them a chance to learn how to be in charge of their own learning. This one instance brought excitement and fuel for the teachers to keep trying new practices and allowing students to navigate them across time.

This Mid graph represents the shifts by the teachers to add new beliefs more closely aligned with PBL positive codes to their internal beliefs' framework. The graph also reveals less evidence of them trading-in previously held beliefs for new beliefs, but instead, at this point, clinging to both the new and the old beliefs. The graph displays beliefs related to negative student capabilities such as Can't Reason, as well as two opposing codes Can't Collaborate and Collaborate. In addition, Problem-solve is located here. Through extensive data analysis researchers determined that teachers used the positive code Problem-solve and the negative code Can't Reason as opposites. So, the evidence reveals that at the midpoint of the study, teachers did indeed hold contradictory beliefs. This notion is debated further as the Pre, Mid, and Post graphs are scrutinized.

The All Teachers Post Graph (Fig. 5) shifted to quadrant 1 which is where the second most positive PBL beliefs are situated. These codes are: Student Discourse, Relinquish Control, Independent, Process, and Not Engaged. The only negative code in quadrant 1 is Not Engaged. We see that teachers have traded in the beliefs about the Product in favor of the Process of inquiry. Also Relinquish Control appears, trading in the opposing Teacher Directed code from previous graphs. Teachers' beliefs about the value of student talk shifted from original beliefs such as "students won't stop talking" to "they are really talking about their investigations and negotiating with each other". In the weekly critical reflection, teachers revealed that when they trusted students enough to give them ownership, the students collaborated more than they originally believed possible. As one teacher said, "With PBL I realized that I was their low ceiling holding them under what I thought a 5-year-old umbrella should look like. Whereas now I'll raise it up and see how far they can go. It's not about their age, and I really thought it was at first." Another teacher described her shift in beliefs this way: "I think that once I realized that they were capable of working together to solve a problem, I gave them more problems to solve. With the window boxes, I wasn't sure how they'd handle going to the gym. I was a little bit nervous, but they surprised me. They were able to work together to figure it out. I don't think at the beginning of the year I would've even tried doing something like that with them."

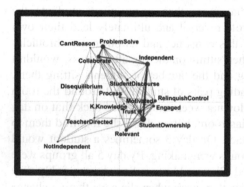

Fig. 5. All teachers' Post graph

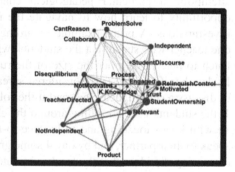

Fig. 6. Difference network graph

The Difference Network graph (Fig. 6) compares the initial (Pre) and final (Post) beliefs of practice structures, revealing teacher's new internal beliefs now more aligned to PBL tenets. This graph substantiates the impact of the professional development model's components on teacher's beliefs of and practice throughout the study.

5   Discussion

Significantly, this is one of the first studies in teacher beliefs' research that visually displays the transformation of teachers' privately held beliefs as they navigate a year-long intensive PD centered on problem-based learning tenets by employing Epistemic Network Analysis. Also, this study uses a "beliefs of practice structure" model [1] that trades in the traditional teacher beliefs research question of "Which comes first, the shift in practice or beliefs?" to graphing struggles of teachers as they wrestle with the entangled nature of beliefs that include their pedagogical beliefs. Teachers navigated a professional development model of critical reflection addressing their entire beliefs of practice structure. Pedagogical conversations, peer mentoring/coaching, pedagogical beliefs decisions/actions, and classroom observation emboldened teachers to modify their beliefs of practice structures that included new understandings of the value of a) student voice and student-choice; b) holding higher views of student capabilities; and c) relinquishing control of the classroom so students could begin to own their investigations and ultimately their learning. These findings support "Thaagard's Coherence Theory of Justification" [20] where beliefs are held as a floating raft and as teachers' contemplated beliefs (new and old), they held them simultaneously. Their disequilibrium caused the raft to tip and waver back and forth, which is discussed in the literature, but never visually displayed as in this study. By using E NA, the data pushes the literature forward by unveiling beliefs' structures visually, while in disequilibrium. Then, as beliefs are bantered about, they are ultimately rejected or accepted because of coherence or incoherence with the newly modified beliefs of practice structure.

References

1. Martin, A., Park, S., Hand, B.: What happens when a teacher's belief structure is in disequilibrium? The entangled nature of beliefs and practice. Res. Sci. Educ. **49**(3), 885–920 (2019)
2. Arastoopour, G., Swiecki, Z., Chesler, N.C., Shaffer, D.W.: Epistemic network analysis as a tool for engineering design assessment. In American Society for Engineering Education Annual Conference (2015)
3. Cherubini, L.: Reforming teacher preparation: fostering critical reflection and awareness in the context of global education. Excelsior Leadersh. Teach. Learn. **3**(2), 43–55 (2009)
4. Chesler, N., Ruis, A., Collier, W., Swiecki, Z., Arastoopour, G., Shaffer, D.W.: A novel paradigm for engineering education: virtual internships with individualized mentoring and assessment of engineering thinking. J. Biomech. Eng. **137**(2), 1–8 (2015)
5. Crawford, B.: Learning to teach science as inquiry in the rough and tumble of practice. J. Res. Sci. Teach. **44**, 613–642 (2007)
6. Csanadi, A., Eagan, B., Kollar, I., Shaffer, D.W., Fischer, F.: When coding-and-counting is not enough: using epistemic network analysis (ENA) to analyze verbal data in CSCL research. Int. J. Comput. Support. Collab. Learn. **13**(4), 419–438 (2018). https://doi.org/10.1007/s11412-018-9292-z
7. Dewey, J.: How We Think, 2eRev. edn. DC Heath, Lexington (1933)
8. Evans, R., Luft, J., Czerniak, C., Pea, C. (eds.): The Role of Science Teachers' Beliefs in International Classrooms. SensePublishers, Rotterdam (2014). https://doi.org/10.1007/978-94-6209-557-1
9. Glasser, B., Strauss, A.: The Development of Grounded Theory. Alden, Chicago (1967)
10. Jones, M.G., Leagon, M.: Teacher attitudes and beliefs: reforming practice. Handb. Res. Sci. Teach. **2**, 830–847 (2014)
11. Lave, J., Wenger., E.: Legitimate peripheral participation in communities of practice. In: Supporting Lifelong Learning, Routledge, pp. 121–136 (2001)

12. Liu, K.: Critical reflection as a framework for transformative learning in teacher education. Educ. Rev. **67**(2), 135–157 (2015). https://doi.org/10.1080/00131911.2013.839546

13. Luft, J., Roehrig, G., Patterson, N.: Contrasting landscapes: a comparison of the impact of different induction programs on beginning secondary science teachers' practices, beliefs, and experiences. J. Res. Sci. Teach. **40**(1), 77–97 (2003)

14. Lumpe, A., Haney, J., Czerniak, C.: Assessing teachers' beliefs about their science teaching context. J. Res. Sci. Teach. **37**, 275–292 (2000)

15. Marra, R.: Teacher beliefs: the impact of the design of constructivist learning environments on instructor epistemologies. Learn. Environ. Res. **8**, 135–155 (2005)

16. Posnanski, T.J.: Professional development programs for elementary teachers: an analysis of teacher self-efficacy beliefs and a professional development model. J. Sci. Teach. Educ. **13** (3), 189–220 (2002)

17. Shaffer, D.W., Collier, W., Ruis, A.R.: A tutorial on epistemic network analysis: analyzing the structure of connections in cognitive, social, and interaction data. J. Learn. Anal. **3**(3), 9–45 (2016)

18. Shaffer, D., et al.: Epistemic network analysis: a prototype for 21st century assessment of learning. Int. J. Learn. Media **1**(1), 1–21 (2009)

19. Thomas, M., Liu, K.: Patterns and perspectives: a grounded analysis of prospective teacher reflection in ePortfolios. J. Technol. Teach. Educ. **20**(3), 305–330 (2012)

20. Thagard, P.: Coherence in Thought and Action. MIT Press, Cambridge (2002)

21. Windschitl, M.: Inquiry projects in science teacher education: what can investigative experiences reveal about teacher thinking and eventual classroom practice?. Sci. Educ. **87** (1), 112–143 (2003)

An Epistemic Network Analysis of Students' Beliefs About Natural and Educational Scientists

Valentina Nachtigall[1]([⊠]), Alina Nößler[1], and Hanall Sung[2]

[1] Ruhr-University Bochum, Universitätsstr. 150, 44780 Bochum, Germany
valentina.nachtigall@rub.de
[2] University of Wisconsin–Madison, Madison, WI 53706, USA

Abstract. Ample research has demonstrated that students hold inaccurate beliefs about scientists, and that these beliefs affect different variables, such as study and career choices. However, while numerous studies have focused on investigating students' images and beliefs about natural scientists, research has not yet examined students' beliefs about scientists within the social sciences and humanities. Against this background, the present study explored secondary school students' beliefs about the work and skills of educational scientists and compared these beliefs with their views of natural scientists. For this purpose, we surveyed secondary school students and conducted an Epistemic Network Analysis of their answers to certain open-ended questions. Our findings show that students tend to view educational scientists as practitioners who work in educational or socio-pedagogical institutions and who need social skills. On the contrary, natural scientists are seen as researchers who work in laboratories and need cognitive skills. Thus, these findings suggest that educational scientists are less associated with scientific research than natural scientists. Those inaccurate beliefs could lead to wrong expectations related to studying educational science or social sciences more generally. Hence, the findings presented here point to the need to foster more adequate beliefs about scientists in students

Keywords: Beliefs about scientists · Survey · Epistemic network analysis

1 Introduction and Background

"Scientific research? Don't only biologists do that?" This statement, given by a student attending a compulsory course on statistics within an educational sciences program at the university of the first author, suggests that scientific research is more likely associated with the work of natural scientists and less with the work of social scientists. This anecdotal evidence is also supported by empirical evidence, namely by findings of a survey that regularly assesses the attitudes towards science and research in a representative sample of the German population aged 14 and over. This survey recently demonstrated that the terms *science* or *research* are mostly associated with the following fields and disciplines [1]: medicine (40%), technology (17%), and the natural sciences (i.e., biology: 15% and physics: 12%). Only 2% of the participants associated the social sciences or humanities with research or science.

© Springer Nature Switzerland AG 2022
B. Wasson and S. Zörgő (Eds.): ICQE 2021, CCIS 1522, pp. 207–220, 2022.
https://doi.org/10.1007/978-3-030-93859-8_14

These findings are in line with research on (school) students' beliefs about the work and characteristics of scientists. Since the 1950s, ample research has demonstrated that students tend to imagine scientists as male and elderly *physicists or chemists* with beards and glasses, and who wear a white lab coat while conducting experiments in a laboratory [2–4]. These natural scientists are attributed to be highly intelligent and brilliant individuals, but who – at the same time – lack social skills, meaning that they tend to have difficulties in interacting with other people, work and live isolated, and have no social life outside their work [3, 5].

While students' stereotypical and inadequate beliefs about the work and characteristics of *natural scientists* have been revealed and replicated by numerous studies, research has not yet focused on exploring students' beliefs about scientists within the social sciences and humanities. To our knowledge, only a previous study of the first author offers first insights into school students' (inadequate) beliefs about the work and characteristics of scientists within the social sciences and humanities [6]. As these findings suggest, students think that social scientists and scientists within the humanities work in schools, kindergartens, socio-pedagogical organizations, or medical institutions. Consequently, according to students' imagination, these types of scientists need strong social skills. That is, they need to empathize with people, have to interact well with people, and have to be good listeners [6].

Taken together, in addition to the fact that the terms research or science are more strongly associated with the natural sciences (or with STEM more generally) than with the social sciences [1], school students seem to see natural scientists as researchers who work in laboratories and have strong cognitive skills [3], while, on the contrary, social scientists are perceived as practitioners who work in (socio-)educational institutions and have strong social skills [6].

School students seem to not only see natural scientists and scientists within the social sciences and humanities in the aforementioned ways, but also prototypical students whose favorite school subjects are either the natural sciences or the humanities. As a study by Hannover and Kessels [7] demonstrates, 9th and 8th graders described a prototypical peer favoring the natural sciences as less socially competent but at the same time as more intelligent than a prototypical peer favoring the humanities. Their findings further showed that the students' description of the prototypical student who favors the natural sciences was less similar to their self-views than the prototypical student who favors the humanities. Hannover and Kessels concluded that their findings might explain why the majority of students does not choose to approach a career in the natural sciences.

Students' stereotypical and inadequate images and beliefs about natural scientists or scientists within the field of STEM more generally have also been demonstrated to be associated with their (*low*) interest in studying or majoring in these disciplines, their achievement in STEM, and their interest in approaching a career in STEM [2–4, 8]. For instance, students' inaccurate and restricted view of scientists as highly intelligent, talented, and brilliant people who always succeed and never fail can – due a potential mismatch with their self-images – negatively affect their achievement and interest in STEM [9, 10]. On the contrary, the results of our previous study suggest that students' inappropriate and confused views of social scientists and scientists within the humanities as very socially competent practitioners in (socio-)educational areas are related to their *high* interest in studying social sciences after graduating from school [6]. These findings support Pauly's [11] assumption that students' inadequate beliefs about the work of scientists within the social sciences and humanities are associated with their inaccurate expectations related to studying these disciplines [12] and to the fact that especially the humanities – at least in Germany – suffer from a high drop-out rate of university students [13]. While the social sciences do not suffer from a high drop-out rate in Germany, the social sciences, and in particular the educational sciences, have experienced a strong decline of students who continue their studies with a master's degree after finishing their bachelor's degree [14]. In order to face these issues, it is necessary to foster appropriate beliefs about the work and skills of scientists within the social sciences and humanities in school students' already such that these disciplines are no longer appreciated for the wrong reasons [11].

Interventions for fostering adequate beliefs about *natural scientists* have already been developed and investigated by several studies [2]. These studies are based on the ample research demonstrating that students' images and beliefs about natural scientists are "confused", "superficial", "ambiguous", "restricted", "inaccurate", "stereotypic", and "controversial" [3, p. 143]. However, as mentioned before, research has not yet focused on investigating students' beliefs about scientists within the social sciences and humanities. Addressing this research gap, is the goal of the present study. Thereby, we aim to provide empirical evidence that both adds to our previous study [6] and may serve as a basis for the development of respective interventions for fostering more appropriate beliefs about scientists within the social sciences and humanities in students.

However, in our previous study [6], we assessed students' beliefs about scientists within the broad field of social sciences and humanities. As this field comprises many (also methodologically) different disciplines, the student answers may have been imprecise and undifferentiated. Consequently, in the present study, we decided to focus on a certain discipline within the social sciences, namely educational science. Hence, we aim at conceptually replicating the findings of our previous study by exploring students' beliefs related to the work and skills of educational scientists (Research Question 1).

Furthermore, building on the argument developed above, it can be hypothesized that school students' beliefs about the work and characteristics of social scientists differ from or are even contrary to their beliefs about the work and skills of natural scientists. However, to our knowledge, students' beliefs about social and natural scientists have not yet been empirically compared. Addressing this research gap is a further goal of the present study. In this regard, we are particularly interested in whether students – when they are explicitly asked to describe the work and skills of both natural and educational scientists – indeed associate scientific research more strongly with natural scientists than with educational scientists (Research Question 2).

2 Method

For investigating our two research questions, we surveyed secondary school students and assessed their beliefs about the work and skills of educational and natural scientists by using different open questions. To compare students' beliefs about educational versus natural scientists, we conducted an Epistemic Network Analysis (ENA) [15].

2.1 Research Context

For exploring students' beliefs about the work and skills of educational scientists (Research Question 1), and for comparing them with students' beliefs about natural scientists (Research Question 2), we conducted a survey with secondary school students visiting an interdisciplinary out-of-school lab at a large German university. The students attended a project focusing on social science research methods. Out-of-school labs are non-formal learning settings, often located at universities, which are usually visited by whole classes. They try to provide students with authentic experiences of scientific ways of thinking and working, whereby they aim to foster students' interest in and their understanding about science [16]. Thus, an out-of-school lab appeared to be an ideal setting for investigating students' beliefs about the work and skills of scientists.

2.2 Participants

Participants were 24 10th graders from an educational science course of a secondary school in Germany (Age: $M = 16.54$, $SD = 0.58$, 75% girls). Due to new governmental restrictions and regulations during the COVID 19 pandemic, the data collection, which took place in December 2020, had to be stopped. Therefore, given our small sample size, the present investigation has to be considered a pilot study.

2.3 Procedure and Measures

In order to assess students' beliefs about the work and skills of scientists, we administered two identical questionnaires, one for measuring students' beliefs about educational scientists and one for assessing students' beliefs about natural scientists. Students successively worked on both questionnaires at the beginning of the out-of-school lab project. To avoid and control for sequence effects, one randomly assigned half of the participants started with the questionnaire assessing their beliefs about educational scientists, and the other half started with the questionnaire referring to natural scientists.

Both questionnaires included open-ended questions, semantic differentials and a 'Draw-a-Scientist Test'. However, for the analysis presented here, we focus on the following three open-ended questions, which are nearly similar to the questions used in our previous work [6]: (1) In which places do educational/natural scientists work? (2) Which skills should educational/natural scientists have? (3) How do educational/natural scientists proceed at work or, in other words, which methods do educational/natural scientists use?

2.4 Data Coding

Based on both our previous work [6] and grounded analysis, we developed – through this combination of top-down and bottom-up procedure [17] – seven codes to classify the student. Two raters coded 100% of the data and reached mostly satisfying agreements [18]. The two raters, however, resolved their disagreements by discussion. Table 1 shows our codebook and the inter-rater reliability statistics, which refer to the agreements of the two raters prior to discussion.

Table 1. Coding Scheme and inter-rater reliability statistics prior to discussion

	Code name & description	Educational scientists		Natural scientists	
		Examples	κ	Examples	κ
Question 1	RESEARCH LOCATIONS: Students name locations that are related to research	"university"; "research institutes"	1.00	"universities"; "laboratories", "research centers"	1.00
	LOCATIONS OF PRACTICE: Students name locations that are related to different (e.g., pedagogical, medical, or social) areas of practice	"school"; "hospital"; "kindergarten"; "psychiatric ward"; "nursing home"; "youth center"	0.65	"school"; "hospital"; "surgery";	1.00
Question 2	SOCIAL SKILLS: Students name skills that especially relate to the ability to interact with others	"empathy"; "an understanding for children"; "helpfulness"; "kindness"	0.75	"communicative"; "social competencies"	1.00
	COGNITIVE SKILLS: Students name characteristics that refer to human cognition	"method knowledge", "intelligence", "problem solving abilities"	0.86	"professional knowledge"; "abstract thinking skills"; "intelligence"	0.90
	PERSONAL SKILLS: Students name skills that relate to the motivation, engagement, self-discipline, and/or resilience of scientists	"conscientious"; "creative"; "patience"; "solution-oriented"; "interest"; "enthusiasm"	0.83	"patience"; "creativity"; "assiduity"; "interest in research"; "diligence"	0.74
Question 3	RESEARCH METHODS: Students describe ways for scientifically investigating something	"observation of individual people/ groups of people"; "surveys and evaluations"	0.83	"studies, laboratory examinations, experiments, animal experiments, pilot projects"	0.51
	PRACTICAL METHODS: Students describe methods that relate to social and/or interpersonal interactions	"conversations, group activities, social welfare"; "talking about problems"	0.83	"team meetings"	1.00

3 Results

To explore students' beliefs about the work and skills of educational scientists (Research Question 1), and to compare them with students' beliefs about natural scientists (Research Question 2), we first report the descriptive statistics of the coding and counting procedure. It should be noted that the results that we present here are based on a binary coding of the student answers, whereby multiple statements of the same category within an answer are ignored. After reporting the descriptive statistics, we then conduct an epistemic network analysis in order to investigate and compare students' patterns of beliefs about scientists. Finally, we qualitatively analyze student answers.

3.1 Descriptive Statistics

Table 2 shows the frequencies of students' answers to the three open-ended questions sorted by the seven codes.

Table 2. Frequencies of student answers

Question	Code	Frequencies	
		Educational scientists	Natural scientists
1	Research locations	10	24
	Locations of practice	23	13
2	Social skills	20	2
	Cognitive skills	5	17
	Personal skills	16	16
3	Research methods	15	23
	Practical methods	13	2

Regarding the first open-ended question (locations), the descriptive statistics show that almost all participants (except for one) associate educational scientists with locations of practice, while they all stated that natural scientists work in research locations. With respect to the second open-ended question (skills), the results show that the majority of the students attribute social as well as personal skills to educational scientists, and cognitive as well as personal skills to natural scientists. Regarding the third open-ended question (methods), the results show that students associate both research and practice methods with the work of educational scientists, while they almost exclusively name research methods with respect to natural scientists.

3.2 Epistemic Network Analysis

To compare students' beliefs about the work and skills of educational versus natural scientists, we conducted an ENA. For this purpose, we duplicated the sample, such that one sample represented the student beliefs regarding natural scientists and the other sample represented their beliefs with respect to educational scientists.

In a first step, we constructed mean epistemic networks for each sample. Figure 1 depicts the mean epistemic network for students' answers to the questions referring to locations, skills, and methods of educational scientists. As Fig. 1 shows, students make strong connections between SOCIAL SKILLS and LOCATIONS OF PRACTICE. They further link these two features to PRACTICAL METHODS, RESEARCH METHODS, and PERSONAL SKILLS. But they make only weak connections to both RESEARCH LOCATIONS and COGNITIVE SKILLS.

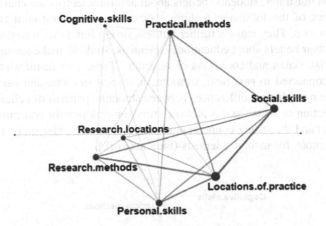

Fig. 1. Mean ENA network diagram showing the connections between the features that students attribute to the work and skills of educational scientists.

Figure 2 shows the mean epistemic network for students' answers to the questions referring to locations, skills, and methods of natural scientists. As this network shows, students especially associate RESEARCH LOCATIONS and RESEARCH METHODS with the work of natural scientists. These two features are further strongly linked to either COGNITIVE SKILLS or PERSONAL SKILLS. LOCATIONS OF PRACTICE play a less important role in students' beliefs about natural scientists, while PRACTICAL METHODS as well as SOCIAL SKILLS play almost no role.

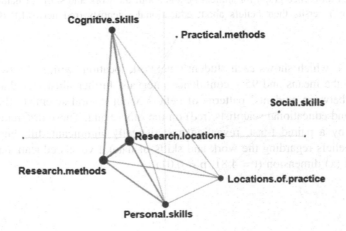

Fig. 2. Mean ENA network showing students' pattern of beliefs about natural scientists.

In a second step, after constructing the two mean epistemic networks, we created a subtracted network. Thereby, as can be seen in Fig. 3, the differences between students' beliefs about natural scientists and educational scientists become clear. As this difference graph illustrates, students' beliefs about natural scientists are characterized by a dense network of the following features: COGNITIVE SKILLS, RESEARCH LOCATIONS and RESEARCH METHODS. They make a further but less strong link to PERSONAL SKILLS. On the contrary, in their beliefs about educational scientists, students make strong connections between SOCIAL SKILLS and LOCATIONS OF PRACTICE. These two features are further but less strong connected to PRACTICAL METHODS, RESEARCH METHODS and PERSONAL SKILLS. However, the most distinct differences between students' patterns of beliefs relate to the strong connection of SOCIAL SKILLS and LOCATIONS OF PRACTICE for educational scientists (red network) and the strong connection of COGNITIVE SKILLS, RESEARCH LOCATIONS, and RESEARCH METHODS for natural scientists (blue network).

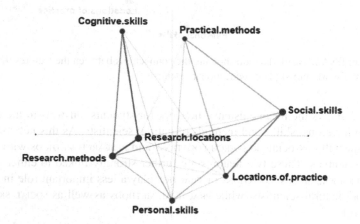

Fig. 3. ENA difference graph for student beliefs about the work and skills of natural scientists (blue network) versus their beliefs about educational scientists (red network). (Color figure online)

Figure 4, which shows each student's network location (within the two samples) along with the means and 95% confidence intervals, further illustrates that there is a difference between students' patterns of beliefs about natural scientists (blue) on the one hand and educational scientists (red) on the other hand. These differences are also supported by a paired t-test, revealing a statistically significant difference between students' beliefs regarding the work and skills of natural versus educational scientists on the first (x) dimension ($t = 4.81$, $p < 0.01$).

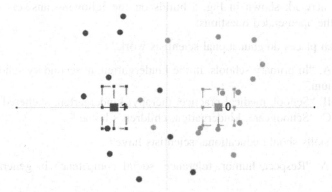

Fig. 4. ENA scatter plot showing the duplicated sample of students with regard to their beliefs about natural scientists (blue) and educational scientists (red). (Color figure online)

3.3 Qualitative Analysis

To get a better understanding of the differences between students' beliefs about natural versus educational scientists, we qualitatively analyzed the answers of students that particularly represent the two networks (blue versus red) shown in the difference graph (see Fig. 3).

Figure 5 shows the network of features that three students stated with regard to educational scientists. The black box in Fig. 5 marks these students' node position in the network. As all three students have the same location, the respective dots overlap.

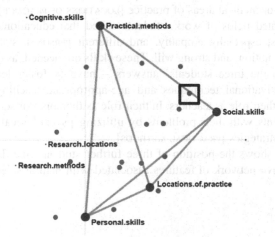

Fig. 5. Individual ENA networks with ENA scatter plot showing the connections made by student A, B, and C stated with regard to their beliefs about educational scientists. (Color figure online)

The red network shown in Fig. 5 builds on the following answers of the three students to the open-ended questions:

(1) In which places do educational scientists work?

Student A: "In primary schools, in the kindergarten, at secondary schools, such as the Gymnasium."
Student B: "School, medical practice, therapy, kindergarten, sheltered workshop."
Student C: "School/care, kindergarten, children's home."

(2) Which skills should educational scientists have?

Student A: "Respect, humor, tolerance, social competence in general, patience, fun."
Student B: "Empathy, solution-oriented, willingness to help."
Student C: "Empathy, strong will, single-minded."

(3) How do educational scientists proceed at work or, in other words, which methods do educational scientists use?

Student A: "Every educational scientist has other and own methods but, for instance in schools, some teachers try to encourage and motivate students to proceed and not to cease."
Student B: "Psychology and talking with affected people about problems (communication)."
Student C: "With theories (Freud, Piaget, etc.), adapt their work to the age of their students."

As these answers indicate, students apparently imagine educational scientists as being teachers, social workers, or therapists who work in respective pedagogical, socio-educational, or medical areas of practice [LOCATIONS OF PRACTICE]. Consequently, given these associated fields of work, students stated that educational scientists need both SOCIAL SKILLS, especially empathy, and different PERSONAL SKILLS, such as patience, solution-orientation, and strong will. These skills are needed, as educational scientists – according to the three students' answers – have to foster learning in students by utilizing motivational techniques and age-appropriate teaching methods [PRACTICAL METHODS] in their role as teachers. In their role as therapists or social workers, they have to help patients with their problems by utilizing psychological knowledge and communication strategies [PRACTICAL METHODS].

Figure 6 shows the position of three further students (the dots again overlap) and their respective network of features associated with natural scientists.

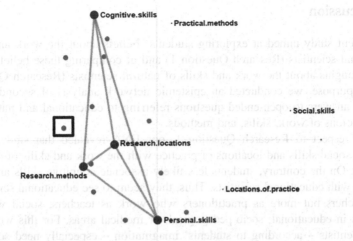

Fig. 6. Individual ENA networks with ENA scatter plot showing the connections made by student D, E, and F stated with regard to their beliefs about natural scientists. (Color figure online)

This blue network depicted in Fig. 6 is based on the following answers of the three students to the open-ended questions:

(1) In which places do natural scientists work?

Student D: "In laboratories."
Student E: "University, laboratory"
Student F: "Laboratories."

(2) Which skills should natural scientists have?

Student D: "Patience, precise working, good eyes, being smart."
Student E: "Abstract thinking, patience, creativity."
Student F: "Keep one's balance, careful working, and proper handling of, for instance, specimens."

(3) How do natural scientists proceed at work or, in other words, which methods do natural scientists use?

Student D: "They look at different specimens/bacteria and compare them."
Student E: "Research, questionnaires."
Student F: "They take specimens and analyze them."

These answers suggest that natural scientists are associated with chemists or biologists, who work in laboratories [RESEARCH LOCATIONS] and are characterized by intelligence and thinking abilities [COGNITIVE SKILLS]. For their research, which mainly consists of analyzing different specimens [RESEARCH METHODS], natural scientists also need PERSONAL SKILLS, such as patience and precision.

4 Discussion

The present study aimed at exploring students' beliefs about the work and skills of educational scientists (Research Question 1) and at comparing these beliefs with students' thoughts about the work and skills of natural scientists (Research Question 2). For this purpose, we conducted an epistemic network analysis of secondary school students' answers to open-ended questions referring to educational and natural scientists' locations of work, skills, and methods.

With respect to Research Question 1, our ENA revealed that students mainly associate social skills and locations of practice with the work and skills of educational scientists. On the contrary, students less likely associate cognitive skills and research locations with educational scientists. Thus, they seem to see educational scientists less as researchers but more as practitioners who work as teachers, social workers, or therapists in educational, socio-pedagogical, or medical areas. For this work, educational scientists – according to students' imagination – especially need social skills, such as empathy. These findings are in line with our previous study in which we explored students' beliefs about the work and characteristics of scientists within the social sciences and humanities [6]. Our previous study showed that scientists within the social sciences and humanities are especially associated with locations of practice and social skills. Thus, the findings of the present study conceptually replicate the results of our previous study, meaning that the findings with regard to students' beliefs about scientists within the broad field of social sciences and humanities (revealed by our previous study) are in line with the present study's findings regarding students' beliefs about educational scientists.

With respect to Research Question 2, our analysis revealed that students' patterns of beliefs significantly differed depending on the disciplinary affiliation of scientists. Specifically, their pattern of beliefs about natural scientists was almost diametrical to their pattern of beliefs about educational scientists. While natural scientists were associated with cognitive skills, research locations, and research methods, educational scientists were associated with social skills, locations of practice, and practical methods. Students however attributed both natural and educational scientists to need personal skills. But as the qualitative analyses of certain student answers revealed, the personal skills attributed to natural scientists differ from the personal skills associated with educational scientists. Specifically, the qualitative analysis showed that natural scientists are assumed to need patience, precision, and diligence for conducting their research (e.g. analyzing different specimens in laboratories). Educational scientists, however, are required to have an iron will and to be solution-oriented in order to teach and motivate students in school or to help patients with their problems. These findings fit to the results by Hannover and Kessels showing that school students attribute higher intelligence but lower social skills to prototypical peers who like science than to prototypical peers who like humanities [7].

Based on research demonstrating that students' views of scientists are associated with, for instance, their study and career choices [2, 3, 6, 8–10], our findings emphasize the need to foster more adequate beliefs about the work and skills of both natural and educational scientists in students. The fact that school students in the present study perceived educational scientists rather as teachers, therapists, or social workers and less as researchers may be a reason why students – at least in Germany – increasingly decide to not continue a scientifically oriented master's program after earning their bachelor's degree in educational science [14]. However, due to the small sample size of the present study, further research is needed to replicate the findings reported here.

Acknowledgements. We would like to thank Prof. Dr. Nikol Rummel for her insightful advice on and contribution to the design of the present study. Moreover, we thank Isis Tunnigkeit for her help with coding the data. We are also very thankful to Brendan Eagan and Yuanru Tan for their support in conducting certain ENA analyses.

References

1. Ziegler, R., Kremer, B., Weißkopf, M.: Medizin und neue technologien, analysen und erkenntnisse, intelligenz und ausdauer – welche vorstellung hat die bevölkerung von wissenschaft und forschenden? ergebnisse der offenen fragestellungen im wissenschafts-barometer 2017. [Medicine and new technologies, analyses and findings, intelligence and persistence – What is the public's imagination of scientific research and scientists? Findings of the open-ended questions of the science barometer 2017]. Wissenschaft im Dialog gGmbH, Berlin, Germany (2018)
2. Finson, K.D.: Drawing a scientist: what we do and do not know after fifty years of drawings. Sch. Sci. Math. **102**(7), 335–345 (2002)
3. Christidou, V.: Interest, attitudes and images related to science: combining students' voices with the voices of school science, teachers, and popular science. Int. J. Environ. Sci. Educ. **6**(2), 141–159 (2011)
4. Miller, D.I., Nolla, K.M., Eagly, A.H., Uttal, D.H.: The development of children's gender-science stereotypes: a meta-analysis of 5 decades of US draw-a-scientist studies. Child Dev. **89**(6), 1943–1955 (2018)
5. Pion, G.M., Lipsey, M.W.: Public attitudes toward science and technology: what have the surveys told us? Public Opin. Q. **45**(3), 303–316 (1981)
6. Nachtigall, V., Rummel, N.: Social scientists need to be nice and empathetic: exploring students' beliefs related to social sciences and humanities. In: Gresalfi, M., Seidel Horn, I. (eds.) The Interdisciplinarity of the Learning Sciences, 14th International Conference of the Learning Sciences (ICLS) 2020, vol. 1, pp. 641–644. International Society of the Learning Sciences, Nashville (Tennessee), USA (2020)
7. Hannover, B., Kessels, U.: Self-to-prototype matching as a strategy for making academic choices. Why high school students do not like math and science. Learn. Instruction, **14**(1), 51–67 (2004)
8. Cundiff, J.L., Vescio, T.K., Loken, E., Lo, L.: Do gender–science stereotypes predict science identification and science career aspirations among undergraduate science majors? Soc. Psychol. Educ. **16**(4), 541–554 (2013). https://doi.org/10.1007/s11218-013-9232-8
9. Lin-Siegler, X., Ahn, J.N., Chen, J., Fang, F.F.A., Luna-Lucero, M.: Even Einstein struggled: effects of learning about great scientists' struggles on high school students' motivation to learn science. J. Educ. Psychol. **108**(3), 314–328 (2016)
10. Hong, H.Y., Lin-Siegler, X.: How learning about scientists' struggles influences students' interest and learning in physics. J. Educ. Psychol. **104**(2), 469–485 (2012)

11. Pauly, Y.: Was sind und zu welchem Zweck brauchen wir geisteswissenschaftliche Schülerlabore? [What are OSLs for social sciences and humanities, and why do we need them?]. In: Dernbach, B., Kleinert, C., Münder, H. (eds.) Handbuch Wissenschaftskommunikation [Handbook of science communication], pp. 205–210. VS Verlag für Sozialwissenschaften, Wiesbaden, Germany (2012)

12. Heublein, U., et al.: Zwischen studienerwartungen und studienwirklichkeit, Ursachen des Studienabbruchs, beruflicher Verbleib der Studienabbrecherinnen und Studienabbrecher und Entwicklung der Studienabbruchquote an deutschen Hochschulen. [Between study expectations and study reality, reasons for drop-out, career of students who drop-out, and development of the drop-out rate at German universities]. DZHW, Hannover, Germany (2017)

13. Heublein, U., Schmelzer, R.: Die Entwicklung der Studienabbruchquoten an den deutschen Hochschulen. Berechnungen auf Basis des Absolventenjahrgangs 2016. [The development of student-dropout rates at German universities. Calculations based on the graduation year 2016]. DZHW, Hannover, Germany (2018)

14. Abs, H.J., Kuper, H., Martinin, R.: Datenreport Erziehungswissenschaft 2020 [Data Report Educational Science 2020]. Verlag Barbara Budrich, Opladen (2020)

15. Shaffer, D.W., Collier, W., Ruis, A.R.: A tutorial on epistemic network analysis: analyzing the structure of connections in cognitive, social, and interaction data. J. Learn. Analytics **3**(3), 9–45 (2016)

16. Scharfenberg, F.J., Bogner, F.X.: Outreach science education: evidence-based studies in a gene technology lab. Eurasia J. Math. Sci. Technol. Educ. **10**(4), 329–341 (2014)

17. Chi, M.T.: Quantifying qualitative analyses of verbal data: a practical guide. J. Learn. Sci. **6**(3), 271–315 (1997)

18. Landis, J.R., Koch, G.G.: The measurement of observer agreement for categorical data. Biometrics **33**(1), 159–174 (1977)

Mapping the Content Structure of Online Diabetes Support Group Activity on Facebook

Szilvia Zörgő[1]([⊠]) [iD], Anna Jeney[2] [iD], Krisztina Csajbók-Veres[3],
Samvel Mkhitaryan[4] [iD], and Anna Susánszky[1] [iD]

[1] Institute of Behavioral Sciences, Semmelweis University, Budapest, Hungary
s.zorgo@maastrichtuniversity.nl
[2] Department of Cultural Anthropology, Eötvös Loránd University,
Budapest, Hungary
[3] Center for Intercultural Psychology and Education, Eötvös Loránd University,
Budapest, Hungary
[4] Department of Health Promotion, CAPHRI Maastricht University,
Maastricht, The Netherlands

Abstract. Diabetes is one of the most prevalent chronic diseases and necessitates ongoing self-management to control symptoms. People with diabetes (PWD) express various needs, which are often met in online support groups. Our objectives were to examine related discourse in Hungarian Facebook groups in order to map the content and structure of information PWD are sharing. We aimed to juxtapose our findings with the functionality of eHealth tools available to Hungarian patients to understand what these tools may be lacking. We extracted a total of 200 threads from two public self-help groups. Codes were developed inductively and applied to the entire corpus with the Interface for the Reproducible Open Coding Kit. We used Epistemic Network Analysis to model our data. The mean network of the entire dataset indicates that discourse was chiefly centered on providing help regarding lifestyle-related issues, especially diet. Critical facets of discourse included the need by experienced PWD to provide guidance to the newly diagnosed, share "street-level" knowledge on diabetes, and ensure a sense of support and community. Existing eHealth tools could be supplemented with an app that automatically downloads blood glucose meter measurements, warns patients about predicted high glucose levels, enables location-based information exchange, and promotes social support in adhering to diet and exercise. Ideally, this app would connect patients with their physicians and/or dietitians.

Keywords: Reproducible Open Coding Kit (ROCK) · Epistemic Network Analysis (ENA) · Diabetes · Social media · eHealth

1 Introduction

Diabetes is currently one of the most prevalent chronic diseases; the number of people with diabetes (PWD) in the US has tripled in the past 20 years with figures also increasing in Europe [1]. Regardless of type, diabetes requires ongoing self-management to control symptoms and negative effects through careful attention to

© Springer Nature Switzerland AG 2022
B. Wasson and S. Zörgő (Eds.): ICQE 2021, CCIS 1522, pp. 221–236, 2022.
https://doi.org/10.1007/978-3-030-93859-8_15

nutrition, sleep, exercise, etc., and includes performing various daily tasks, such as checking blood glucose levels and adhering to medical regimens. PWD may spend up to 8000 hours per year managing their disease outside of the medical setting [2].

Patients report experiencing diabetes-related stigma, exclusion, rejection, blame, and negative judgement, which may lead PWD to feel isolated from others [3]. Due to these experiences, coupled with the need to navigate the intricacies of self-management, PWD express strong preferences for peer support [4], which demand is often met in online support groups, collectively referred to as the Diabetes Online Community (DOC). Via these forums, patients can interact asynchronously to acquire and share information e.g., in the domains of nutrition and treatment options.

Core activities in such online social support networks include obtaining information about the disease, sharing personal opinions and experiences, receiving emotional support for distress arising from demanding self-care regimes and medical complications resulting from the disease [5]. Ubiquitous availability, anonymity, selective disclosure, and social networking present ample opportunities for sharing information, being validated, as well as receiving advice and empathy [5].

Oser et al. direct attention to other motivations that drive participation in DOCs: patients may perceive a lack of "real-world" knowledge (e.g., travel advice for PWD) among healthcare providers or system contributors, patients may seek to educate themselves to practice health literacy and further their knowledge, and they may have unmet psychosocial needs, which they prefer to address with social support outside of the medical setting [2].

Several authors have discussed difficulties in judging the veracity of disease-related information shared in such online support groups, where information gains credibility through social validation: consensus is reached through comments and other forms of engagement [5]. For example, Weitzman et al. warn that disclosed information may frequently be aligned with diabetes science, but group discourse may have gaps in medical disclaimer use and critical moderation [5]. Albeit the extent to which DOCs influence clinical outcomes is unclear [2, 5], their effects on well-being are less disputed. Many studies report improved well-being among DOC participants: a reduction in feelings of isolation [6, 7], an increased sense of belonging [8] and empowerment [9], as well as increased self-efficacy in diabetes self-management [1, 6].

DOC discourse provides crucial insight into how patients interact with information and with each other, their psychosocial and clinical needs, as well as their disease-related behavior, especially regarding domains where conventional care is perceived to be lacking [1]. Analyzing such discourse lays the foundation for developing eHealth systems to better serve the psychosocial needs of PWD and to help them cope with daily routines involved in managing the disease.

Our objectives were to examine DOC discourse in Hungarian diabetes-related Facebook groups in order to map the content and structure of information that patients are sharing.

RQ1: What kind of content is shared in patient self-help groups and how do patients interact with these?
RQ2: How are these pieces of content related to each other?

Findings were juxtaposed to the functionality of eHealth tools available to Hungarian patients to understand what these tools may be lacking and what direction further development aimed at aiding diabetes self-management may take.

2 Previous Approaches to Mapping Shared Content

Research of diabetes-related social media groups includes studies conducted on major platforms, such as Twitter, Instagram, Facebook, and personal blogs. According to a recent review of such works [2], authors have thus far chiefly focused on post content (subject matter of posted content and related comments), message features (type of content, e.g.: text, picture, video), and engagement (number of likes, comments, shares). In some cases, additional information has also been scrutinized, such as number of group members, number of new members in past 30 days, frequency of posts, and months in operation (e.g.: [1]).

In most cases, authors were interested in what subject and type of content received the most engagement and used multivariable logistic regressions to evaluate associations among various group characteristics. For example, Gabarron et al. employed seven discourse codes (1: health education, 2: research and innovation, 3: diabetes-related technology, 4: interviews and personal stories, 5: awareness days and celebrations, 6: recipes and food-related information, and 7: miscellaneous) to deductively code posts on three social media platforms of the Norwegian Diabetes Association [6]. Comments under posts were not coded, and each post (N = 1449) could only receive one discourse code. The authors employed binomial regression analyses of the effects of content topic (discourse codes), social media channel (Twitter, Facebook, Instagram), and post features (emojis, picture/text/video) as predictors of user engagement. They concluded that "interviews and personal stories" received the most, while recipes and food-related information received the least engagement; furthermore, videos and emojis were the most engaging post features. Although these are important details concerning the relationship between post subject and engagement, these analyses do not lend deeper insight into the actual content that is being shared, with what purpose it is shared, and how participants meaningfully engage in knowledge construction and/or social validation.

Another common feature of publications regarding the content shared by DOCs is providing code frequencies or the relative frequencies of codes as percentages of total posts coded. For example, one of Greene et al.'s key findings was that "Providing information" was the most frequent code in their dataset (65.7%), followed by "Support" (28.8%) and "Advertisements" (26.7%). Yet, to what these codes relate is unclear, e.g., regarding what aspect of diabetes self-management (e.g., blood glucose measurement, nutrition, exercise, psychosocial distress) is information or support provided? Albeit code frequencies are valuable indicators of relevance regarding coded content, individual occurrences of codes tell the analyst little about how meaning is constructed within posts and threads, and how codes interact with each other to form substance.

Zhang et al. took a more detailed approach by inductively developing hierarchical codes and reporting the distribution of child codes within their parents, not merely the relative frequency of the parent codes [10]. For example, the authors state that 74% of all examined DOC messages (posts and comments, N = 1352) were related to the parent code "Information" (eliciting or providing information), and reported that 57.9% of that parent code consisted of messages tagged as "Medical info" and 20.1% as "Lifestyle" (ibid). Although it is clear from the publication that "Emotion" was the second most frequent code in the narrative corpus, the reader does not know how this code is related to "Community-building", the last of three parent codes, nor is the reader privy to how these parent and child codes relate to each other in the individual "messages" or the entire corpus. Hierarchical code structures may be a solution to some limitations of coding-and-counting analyses, but it does not address the problem of temporality in discourse data and its socio-cognitive effects [11].

Rus et al. employed multi-level negative binomial regression analyses of message features as predictors of user engagement in diabetes-related Facebook pages. The coding scheme was adopted from the National Cancer Institute's guidelines on health communication elements. Regression analyses were performed on coding categories regarding both discourse content and message features; content within the post text (e.g., causal information, control information, timeline, consequence information, negative/positive affect) was not distinguished conceptually from message features, such as the presence or absence of imagery or external links. Results show that "Imagery x Control Information" and "Imagery x Consequence Information" emerged as significant interactions predictive of user engagement. [12] This approach highlights the importance of interaction among codes to gain more insight on how message features relate to user engagement. Yet the reader is only privy to a small subset of interactions, while crucial connections could remain unearthed.

Albeit coding-and-counting methods may be useful in describing basic characteristics of the coded narrative corpus, they often disregard or attempt to control for phenomena that are essential to meaning construction. Treating discourse codes and/or message features as independent entities assumes that meaning-making by an individual (e.g., in a post) or by a group of individuals (e.g., in a thread) can be modelled and understood by inspecting frequency alone without reference to other codes. Coding-and-counting reflects code frequencies in isolation, but do not take into account how those codes are connected to other codes to convey meaning, and how participants are engaging with that meaning and with each other to co-produce knowledge. Hence, identifying message features that predict high levels of engagement tell us little about the content of the message, and reporting code frequencies within a corpus does not unveil the underlying interdependent nature of discourse elements. Rarely does a single code (similarly to a single word) carry meaning in isolation; meaning emerges from the interplay of linguistic and conceptual elements, as well as their temporality [11]. Rather than through codes and frequencies, meaning is more accurately captured via code co-occurrences and code constellations.

Epistemic Network Analysis (ENA) generates networks that model and describe code interactions within units of analysis, which can be, for instance, individual contributors, posts, threads, or entire narrative corpuses. Because text is segmented and code co-occurrences are accumulated accordingly, ENA can account for temporality within verbal data. Networks are constructed based on adjacency matrices capturing code connection counts for each unit of analysis, and a cumulative adjacency matrix aggregates matrices for each unit of analysis. These are represented as vectors, where columns in this matrix correspond to code pairs and rows to a point in high-dimensional space. Spherical normalization is performed to account for the fact that the length of the vectors is potentially affected by the length of narratives in each unit. In this process, each vector is divided by its own length, resulting in a normalized vector quantifying the relative frequencies of code co-occurrence, which is hence expressed as connection strengths falling between zero and one. ENA then performs dimensional reduction via singular value decomposition (SVD), a technique commonly applied in principle component analysis. The resulting space expresses the differences among units, whose networks receive two, coordinated representations: 1) a projected point or "ENA score" (the location of a unit's network in the low-dimensional projected space) and 2) a weighted network graph (nodes correspond to the codes, edges represent the relative frequency of connection between two codes). For a more detailed explanation of the mathematics of ENA, see [13]. In the present study, we employed ENA to simultaneously harness the explanatory power of qualitative content analysis and describe coded and quantified DOC discourse by modelling the relationship among codes, as well as their relative frequency.

3 Methods

3.1 Sampling

Facebook is one of the most commonly used social networking websites for connecting people with chronic illnesses [1]; on average, 1.59 billion active users engage with/produce content daily [5]. Of the available major social media platforms, Facebook use far outweighs any other (Twitter, Instagram, etc.) in Hungary [14]. Thus, we chose Facebook to explore user-generated content in Hungarian DOCs. The "groups" feature is designated for dedicated communication about shared interests; we used the search function to identify diabetes-related public groups.

We employed purposive, homogeneous sampling; our inclusion criteria were as follows: public Facebook self-help group founded and populated by adult patients of diabetes; language is Hungarian; minimum 100 members; post frequency is minimum once a week; and last post occurred within a week. Our exclusion criteria were: group is private; group is explicitly tied to a religion, an organization, a hospital, or a university; group was founded by and/or is maintained by a health practitioner, e.g., physician, nurse, or naturopath; group is organized around a single healthcare product or product line; group is aimed at healthy living in general. Two researchers performed the search for possible groups to be included in the sample.

The majority of such groups were private and required acceptance into the group to view shared content. As user consent should have been obtained from all members within private groups to investigate such discourse (including those no longer present in the group but contributing to examined content), we decided to analyze the content of public groups only. Two groups fit our inclusion criteria; these two public groups constituted "cases", i.e. data providers in our study. Group 1 had 2800 members at the time of preregistration, Group 2 had 1900 members. Neither researcher was an administrator or member of either group that was reviewed. Scraped data could not pre-date March 13, 2020, the beginning of the first COVID-related lockdown in Hungary; we implemented this restriction as we surmised that pre- and post-COVID discourse (and hence expressed needs) would differ greatly and should not be included into the same sample.

3.2 Data Extraction and Segmentation

We extracted 100 threads (posts and their first-level comments) from both data providers (N = 200); a thread constituted a source in our study. Data was scraped manually on March 16th, 2021 from the website and placed into individual sources (text files) containing a thread each. Only text data was collected; engagement data and message features, such as whether it contained photos/videos were not extracted because our research questions addressed text content only. We were not interested in examining what content generated the most engagement; every thread was considered a vital constituent of DOC discourse. Sometimes, a post consisted of only a picture and no comments; in this case, the source would be empty after scraping. To compensate for empty sources, we manually extracted additional threads (n = 63) in chronological order (Fig. 1).

```
1   ---
2   ROCK_attributes:
3     -
4       groupID: 1
5       tid: 5
6       year: 2021
7       month: 02
8   ---
9   [[uid=7d27c79j]] [[tid=5]]
10  [[uid=7d27c79k]] Cukorbetegek csemegéje: a lenézett majd felmagasztalt csicsóka, avagy a titokzatos
    jeruzsálemi articsóka... [[Share]] [[Lifestyle]]
11  ---<<post_delimiter>>---
12  [[uid=7d27c79m]] Olyan az íze, mint a csípős reteknek. Nem finom. [[Soc_Regul]] [[Lifestyle]]
13  [[uid=7d27c79n]] Csak 1 baj Van vele! Bazi nagy hasmenést okoz ... [[Soc_Regul]] [[Lifestyle]] [[Symptoms]]
14  [[uid=7d27c79p]] Ma csipszet belole csináltam finom volt [[Soc_Supp]] [[Lifestyle]]
15
```

Fig. 1. Example of a coded and segmented source in adherence to the Reproducible Open Coding Kit (ROCK) standard. Attributes are highlighted in yellow; the thread identifier is in green; discourse codes are in teal; and segmentation is highlighted in purple. (Color figure online)

In the extraction process, sources were formatted to delimit post from comments and both post and each subsequent comment were separated by a newline character. Thus, our lowest level of segmentation (utterance) was a turn-of-talk (post or comment), a post-delimiter constituted mid-level segmentation, and all threads were housed in separate text files. Every utterance received a unique utterance identifier (uid) and every thread received a unique thread identifier (tid). Our dataset contained a total of 1333 utterances. Uids were generated using the Reproducible Open Coding Kit (ROCK) R package and all of our coding and segmentation adheres to the ROCK standard [15]. All sources were anonymized prior to coding and analysis.

3.3 Code Development

Discourse codes were developed inductively in several stages. We began by four researchers free-coding 10 threads and developing a preliminary codebook. Subsequently, these four preliminary codebooks were triangulated to create a tentative codebook, which was employed by the same four researchers to deductively code an additional 10 threads. Following this deductive coding stage, the four researchers triangulated their coded data and refined the codebook to create the final version. We juxtaposed the final version of our codebook to discourse codes we extracted from a precursory search in DOC-related research published between 2018 and 2021. We triangulated our codes with those salient in the literature, yet, because none of these articles provided their codebooks as supplementary information (e.g., URL to a repository), we were only privy to code labels and often (but not always) to short descriptions of utilized codes. Even though we found substantial overlap and similarity among these codes and ours, because identical code labels may refer to vastly different constructs [16], we cannot assert with confidence that we are measuring the same phenomena. Our final code structure contained three parent and 16 child codes. Table 1 displays our code labels and a description for each, as well as our Inter-rater reliability (IRR) scores.

Table 1. Final code structure and code descriptions and Inter-rater reliability (IRR) computed with Cohen's kappa (κ) for the two pairs of raters

Parent code	Child code	Kappa	Description
Activity	Ask4Help	1	Eliciting the opinions or experiences of others in the group
	GiveHelp	0.733	Stating an opinion, own experience, recommendations in response to a demand
	Soc_Supp	0.733	Comforting, encouragement, congratulating, celebrating, reinforcing
	Soc_Regul	0.733	Assessing the quality and reliability of shared information; correcting, warning others about fraud or danger, negotiating validity of information
	Share	0.845	Unsolicited sharing of personal information or external content
Appraisal	Dissat	0.727	Satisfaction or dissatisfaction with a specific doctor, pharmaceutical, or the healthcare system in general
	Satisfact	0.789	

(continued)

Table 1. (*continued*)

Parent code	Child code	Kappa	Description
Content	Instruments	0.775	Tools used in diabetes care (e.g., blood glucose meter)
	Lifestyle	0.842	Recipes, healthy food, changes in body weight, exercise
	Healthcare	0.831	Specific physician or the healthcare system in general
	Pharma	0.696	Insulin and strictly diabetes-related pharma products
	COVID	0.789	Vaccine, disease, risk estimation
	TestValues	0.776	Disclosing blood glucose level, various parameters, or biomedical test result
	Products	0.697	Any prescription or over-the-counter drug, home remedy that is not part of conventional diabetes care
	Trade	0.726	Insulin-trade and barter of other diabetes-related drugs, products
	Symptoms	0.723	Side-effects of conventional or non-conventional diabetes care, symptoms of diabetes or comorbidities

3.4 Coding

Codes were split among four researchers; a pair of raters "specialized" in the parent code Content and another pair of raters focused on Activity & Appraisal. To calculate IRR, we computed Cohen's kappa (κ) on 3% of the data ($n_{utterances} = 40$) for the codes designated to the two pairs of raters. For each of the 16 codes, the rate of agreement was above a minimum kappa threshold of 0.65 [17].

Subsequently, we employed the Interface for the Reproducible Open Coding Kit (iROCK) to deductively code the entire narrative corpus. Coding was performed on the level of utterances; one utterance could receive any number of codes. Within the pairs, each individual coded 100 threads; the two coded versions of sources (threads) were then merged with the ROCK R package. Attributes (relevant characteristics of threads) were added to the merged text files; we logged the following attributes for each thread: group ID (case 1 or case 2), thread ID (tid), and date (year and month). Upon completing coding, we parsed all 200 sources with the ROCK package and exported them into a csv file constituting our qualitative data table. In this dataframe, each row contained an utterance and every column represented a variable (attributes and discourse codes). Attributes were displayed in categorical form, discourse codes in binary form.

3.5 Analysis

We uploaded our qualitative data table into the Epistemic Network Analysis webtool to generate networks. After exploring various model parameters and iterating between the networks and coded data, we decided to employ a weighted whole conversation stanza window to accumulate code co-occurrences (Table 2).

Table 2. Parameters of networks generated with Epistemic Network Analysis (ENA)

Unit	GroupID > tid
Conversation	GroupID > tid > Post_Delimiter
Stanza window size	(Weighted) Whole conversation
Codes	Activity, Appraisal, Content codes
Projection	MR1: 5.3%, SVD2: 10%

Our study was preregistered at Open Science Framework Registries. Our employed R scripts, detailed codebook, disclosed results, and extra visualizations can be openly accessed at our public repository: https://osf.io/7q65c/. This project constitutes part of a larger investigation entitled "E-patients and e-physicians in Hungary: The role and opportunities of digital health solutions in the healthcare system", a grant awarded by the National Research, Development and Innovation Office, Hungary. The ethics permit was issued by Semmelweis University Regional and Institutional Committee of Science and Research Ethics (SE RKEB: IV/10924–1/2020/EKU). Quotes from coded threads are disclosed in italics and quotation marks, and are followed by the thread identifier in parentheses; all quotes were translated from Hungarian by the authors.

4 Results

4.1 General Discourse Content and Structure

The most prominent codes in the mean network of the entire dataset were *GiveHelp* and *Lifestyle*, which exhibited strong connections to each other, denoting instances of patients discussing diet-related issues, exchanging recipes, and conversing about weight-related questions. Patients most frequently solicited help from others regarding *Lifestyle* (e.g., content and timing of meals), *Products* (e.g., herbs, OTC products, complementary medicine), and *Pharma* (pharmacological products used in conventional diabetes care). Help was provided in these domains, as well as regarding the interpretation of *Symptoms* (e.g., the normalcy or frequency of pain and various sensations, weight gain).

Shares in posts and replies were almost exclusively about *Lifestyle*, namely participants disclosing what they had for a meal; blood glucose levels were also frequently shared without any accompanying information. The marked co-occurrence of *Lifestyle* and *Social Support* indicates inter-member positive feedback and encouragement concerning diet, and comforting regarding changes in body weight. Aside from welcoming new members into the group and greeting each other on national holidays, *Social Support* also manifested in the normalization of diabetes-related *Symptoms*, and encouragement concerning blood glucose levels (*TestValues*). There was a strong connection among *GiveHelp*, *Pharma*, and *Symptoms*, indicating discourse around insulin use, types of diabetes medication, and experienced or anticipated side-effects of these. The most commonly mentioned side-effect was weight gain. *Instruments* were not commonly mentioned in the dataset, but manifested as discussion on what blood glucose monitoring devices and test strips are the best and where to buy them. There were no mentions of diabetes-related apps or websites.

Both *Social Support* and *Social Regulation* were markedly connected to *Lifestyle*, indicating instances of members discussing the validity of a lifestyle-related issue (e.g., particular food or ingredient) and coming to a consensus about it. Explicit mentions of *Satisfaction* or *Dissatisfaction* with a conventional doctor, pharmaceutical, or the healthcare system in general were uncommon and exhibited only weak connections to other codes.

Group 1's network structure closely resembles the mean network of the entire dataset, with strong connections among *GiveHelp*, *Symptoms*, and *Pharma*, as well as *Lifestyle*, *Social Support*, and *Social Regulation*. Group 2 members, on the other hand, were more focused on providing help regarding *Lifestyle* issues and also *Sharing* about those. There was a significant difference in the discourse of the two groups, mainly driven by the strong connection between *GiveHelp* and *Pharma* in group 1 (Fig. 2).

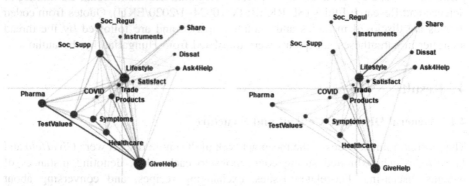

Fig. 2. Mean epistemic networks for diabetes self-help group 1 (red, left) and group 2 (green, right) showing the weighted structure of connections among Activity and Content codes. The thickness of the edges (lines) indicates the relative frequency of co-occurrence between each pair of codes; the size of the nodes (black circles) indicates the relative frequency of each code within that group. (Color figure online)

We also inspected differences according to year (2020 vs. 2021), as the COVID vaccine was introduced in early 2021, presenting a possible shift in DOC discourse. In 2020, group 1 participants were *Sharing Lifestyle* and *TestValues*-related information, but *Asking for Help* or *Giving Help* was not prominent at all. Participants were more engaged with discussing various pharmaceuticals and diabetes-related symptoms. In 2021 providing help for group 1 members became very prominent regarding *Lifestyle* and *Pharma*, as well as *Symptoms*. Manifestations of the code *COVID* (discussions on e.g., vaccines and risk) were much more frequent in 2020 than the following year. Group 2 retained the same basic network structure in both years, with most dominant co-occurrences among *GiveHelp*, *Lifestyle*, and *Share*. The 2021 mean network is slightly more connected, indicating that more threads contained a wider array of codes (e.g., *Pharma*, *Healthcare*, *Symptoms*) (Fig. 3).

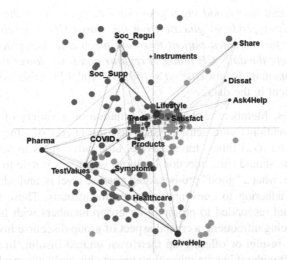

Fig. 3. Difference graph showing the subtracted mean networks for both groups. The thickness and saturation of each line indicates the relative difference between the two groups: red lines indicate connections with higher relative frequencies among group 1 members, and green lines indicate connections with higher relative frequencies among group 2 members. The points show the network locations (ENA scores) of each group 1 member (red points) and group 2 member (green points). The colored squares are the mean network locations (mean ENA scores) of each group, and the dashed lines around the means represent the 95% confidence intervals on each dimension. (Color figure online)

4.2   Critical Facets of Group Discourse

Initiation and Guidance. One key characteristic of self-help group discourse was experienced PWD guiding newly diagnosed patients regarding basic illness- and self-care related information. Such mentorship was given, for example, on how insulin works and why it is commonly associated with weight gain: "*Insulin is the most potent weight-gain hormone [...] because it lowers sugar, but if you don't use it immediately, you don't build muscle, it gets stored in fat. Insulin is a growth factor for the body*" (tid 39). Also, mentorship emerged concerning the differences between types of insulin: "*The active ingredient is the same in both, but there's a difference in absorption. XR indicates that it's absorbed over a long period, so not a big amount all at once, but gradually. It usually has less side-effects than metformin, but even those decrease over time*" (tid 70). Not only side-effects are discussed in such a configuration, but symptoms as well: a newly diagnosed patient posted that they had received insulin from the physician and was told to "*stay on a strict diet*", yet they stated they were experiencing dizziness. An "older" patient replied by telling the newcomer that this is "*totally normal*" and that her "*body is used to higher blood glucose levels and needs time to acclimatize*" (tid 64). Diet and nutrition signified another domain where inter-member guidance was frequently provided, e.g.: "*Things that are absorbed slowly, like whole-grain, rye, seeds, are recommended for diabetics. If it gets absorbed slowly, that* *obviously means that your blood sugar goes down more slowly. If the daily CH intake is low, then the liver produces glucose from the stored CH and releases it into the blood stream, so for a treated patient this may mean a higher glucose level in the morning. Make sure the daily CH intake is regular and is not lower than, but is equal to the allowed amount. In my case, it's 160 gr."* (tid 61). Discussion on diet and nutrition was salient in the data.

Illness Intricacies. Members exchanged information on a variety of issues that may not arise in conventional care settings, such as: the effects of time differences and daylight savings on meal times, travel advice, alternative spots to administer insulin and how often one should shift injection location, whether it is safe to use insulin past its expiration date, what a "good" pre-breakfast glucose level is, and why glucose levels fluctuate despite adhering to conventional recommendations. These issues were not only addressed, but responded to promptly by group members with first-hand experience. Despite it being infrequent, a crucial aspect of group discourse involved members asking others for insulin or offering up their own unused insulin. In some instances, members were left without insulin when they reportedly could not reach their provider, on other occasions, members were prescribed different medication and were left with a surplus of the previous drug. These initiatives were posted publicly but then negotiated privately among individuals involved in the trade. The onset of COVID introduced a new topic of discourse among group members that, due to many reasons, may not have been easily discussed with their provider, namely: which vaccine they were offered by their GP and which they prefer, whether or not to get a vaccine at all, how great of a risk diabetes presents in contracting COVID and complications that may arise. Finally, first-hand experience was exchanged regarding blood glucose meters (specific brands and their advantages), complimentary therapies (products and home remedies), and diabetes-friendly groceries (specific brands and locations to buy).

Social Support and Regulation. A vital feature of group discourse was ensuring a sense of support and community to those sharing problems, questions, or experiences. Social support manifested in encouraging others in continuing their diet, congratulating individuals on their adequate glucose levels, and providing positive feedback on shared experiences, test values, recipes, and external resources (links to diabetes-related information). Social support was often accompanied by social moderation, especially when more contestable statements were made; strong opinions emerged on COVID vaccines, specific foods, and determining adequate glucose levels. For example, one member posted a picture of a meal and asked *"What do you think of a yummy dinner like this?"* Some responded with positive feedback, such as *"Looks good!"* and *"Give me some!"* or *"Rather for lunch [not dinner]!"*, others were more openly opposed: *"Don't recommend this for diabetics"* and *"Sure, if you want a CH of 8 in the morning"* (tid 72). When the validity of a claim was contested, it was usually negotiated until a group consensus seemed to emerge. In some cases, this was more easily accomplished than others, such as in the case of a disputed glucose level: the comment *"Don't try to tell a new diabetic that a glucose level of 10 is normal"* was followed by *"But I was told that it shouldn't be higher than 10 and if so, I'm good."* The thread ended with *"It's not good; they can't get better if they are misinformed"* (tid 100).

5 Discussion

We aimed to map the content and structure of discourse in diabetes-related Facebook groups in Hungary, and through juxtaposing our findings with available eHealth tool functionalities, understand what is it that eHealth tools may be lacking, but online support groups are continuing to provide to patients.

In a review of 15 DOC studies, Oser et al. compile needs, which members of such patient groups exhibited and the observed outcomes of having these needs met [2]. The authors report a need to receive and to provide psychosocial, technical, informational, age-specific peer support with a strong focus on diabetes self-management. Oser et al. emphasize that more experienced PWD may feel the need to provide the same kind of support they themselves received earlier on in their illness trajectory, which is also supported by Greene et al. [2, 18]. Expressing gratitude, giving and receiving encouragement is salient across cultures and age-groups [19]; providing help and social support were very prominent in our data as well. Asking for help was less dominant in our networks, indicating that a single request for information or feedback was usually met with many responses providing support. There was a marked need to share information regarding symptoms and experiences, and for those to be normalized or validated by other members. Yet, the majority of sharing and acts of providing help were concerning lifestyle, notably, diet. In a study by Stellefson et al., 30% of all posts were recipes, which the authors argue build a greater sense of community [1].

Due to the fact that diabetes patients denote a high-risk population for contracting SARS-CoV-2 [20], we were expecting COVID to be a salient topic within our data. Despite this, the code representing this topic did not exhibit a high frequency, and its manifestations were mostly regarding the different vaccines in the time preceding their rollout in Hungary. This indicates that patients were more keen on discussing potential side-effects of various vaccines than disclosing e.g. post-immunization experiences or risk. We found a marked connection between providing help and product-related discourse; many participants were asking about and answering questions on conventional and non-conventional products employable in diabetes care. This connotes a salient topic in most DOC studies [1, 2]. Greene et al. assert that adverse event reporting occurred frequently in the DOC discourse they examined, such as adverse effects of medications and diet supplements [18]. This was not salient in our sample, but neither was satisfaction (with physicians, healthcare) explicitly stated with a high frequency. Thus, "venting" about challenges and frustrations was not as prominent in our sample as was elsewhere [2].

Apart from being a forum to give and receive peer social support, as well as exchange knowledge and experiences on various products and drugs in diabetes care, patient groups we examined exhibited what Kingod calls "biosociality" [21]. The term was coined for describing acts of peers jointly constructing and shaping self-care knowledge and behaviors based on lived experience. In our sample, code co-occurrences of Social Support and Social Regulation frequently manifested as "biosocial" negotiation regarding specific pieces of disclosed information (glucose levels, nutrition, etc.). Some studies have examined the content and outcomes of biosocial negotiation in terms of validity; for example, Greene et al. state that only 3%

of posts in their sample contained inappropriate or unsupported therapeutic information [18]. Despite studies suggesting claims in DOC discussions are by-and-large clinically sound, the potential for misinformation to spread is still present if discourse is left "unsupervised" by medical professionals [18]. Patient-driven discourse leads into domains that do not generally receive attention in conventional care, such as travel-related and other "street-level" disease-management information [18], which signifies a vital part of successful self-care. Additionally, due to the plurality of participants [18] in such support groups (e.g., patients, family members, advertisers, healthcare workers living with diabetes), the potential repository of (mis)information is vast and bears the capacity to address a wide array of issues.

About a dozen apps accessible to Hungarians have been developed for PWD, which are available in Hungarian and English. Most of these apps provide help regarding diet, nutrition, and exercise, as well as measuring and tracking blood glucose levels. Less common, albeit potentially useful functions, include the possibility to contact peers through social media platforms, and, via manually entered data, a warning function to forecast the consequences of a poorly chosen meal on glucose levels. Another useful and increasingly common function is the ability to store and transfer data from a glucose meter to a telephone application, enabling values to be downloaded and presented during medical consultation.

6 Conclusions

Building on the finding that giving and receiving peer support, normalization and validation, and "street-level" information, as well as performing biosocial negotiation on a plethora of topics were all prominent features of diabetes support group functioning in our sample, existing eHealth tool functionality could be aggregated and augmented in several ways. For example, it would be beneficial if an application could be integrated with the blood glucose meter, and would automatically record each value. That log could be supplemented with manually entered information on diet (consumed food and drinks as well as their date and time) and insulin use (time and administered dose). These jointly could warn patients when glucose levels are not adequate and provide positive feedback when they are optimal. This app could also have a function for connecting peers based on location, allowing them to share information on e.g., suitable restaurants, exercise programs, and groceries at specific stores in the area. Peer connectivity could also lead to the organization of location-based social events or illness-, symptom-specific social support. Also, open peer-to-peer invitations to exercise programs could enhance participation, as social support is a known driver of adherence to exercise regimes. Furthermore, enabling a way to continue asynchronous chat would be ideal, perhaps on a forum where information could be periodically reviewed by a practitioner. Ideally, the app could be downloaded and used not only by patients, but their physician and/or their dietitian, which, if necessary, would provide them with information on the administered treatment, glucose levels, and nutrition.

7   Limitations and Future Directions

Our study had several limitations.If individuals would have been considered cases instead of groups, additional data, namely, demographic information (e.g., age, sex, and level of education) and health literacy measures could have enriched analysis and provided extra dimensions in interpretation. This information was only partly available to us, hence we opted not to include it in the study. This research initiative could have been also been supplemented with a social network analysis to shed more light on how group participants are interacting with each other. We did not measure engagement in this study (e.g., number of likes and shares) because it did not constitute part of our research questions, but a secondary analysis could focus on which pieces of content were most popular and impactful in DOCs. Our investigation did pertain to discourse content though, and we disregarded visual and external content (i.e., pictures, gifs, and links were not included). It is common in social media discourse analyses to limit the scope of data to that displayed on the platform under investigation; we followed this protocol, although, external content could potentially be included in a secondary analysis. In social media analyses, pictures are frequently coded as a type of communication ("post feature"), alongside other general codes such as text and video. As group discourse did not exhibit much variety among types of communication (it consisted almost exclusively of text), we decided not to include these codes in our study. Our future analyses may benefit from empirically proving this observation, but it did not fall under our present aims. Finally, we encountered our greatest limitation at data collection: there were no more public diabetes groups on Facebook apart from the two presently under scrutiny. And, as Stellefson et al. also notes: private groups may exhibit vastly different behavior in terms of thread content and social activities [1]; these remained outside of our investigation due to the fact that this data was not publicly accessible.

Acknowledgements. This project constitutes part of a larger investigation entitled "E-patients and e-physicians in Hungary: The role and opportunities of digital health solutions in the healthcare system" conducted as part of a grant awarded by the National Research, Development and Innovation Office, Hungary (Grant: FK_20; Duration: 2020.09–2024.09).

References

1. Stellefson, M., Paige, S., Apperson, A., Spratt, S.: Social media content analysis of public diabetes facebook groups. J. Diabetes Sci. Technol. **13**, 428–438 (2019). https://doi.org/10.1177/1932296819839099
2. Oser, T.K., et al.: Social media in the diabetes community: a novel way to assess psychosocial needs in people with diabetes and their caregivers. Curr. Diab. Rep. **20**(3), 1 (2020). https://doi.org/10.1007/s11892-020-1294-3
3. Liu, N.F., Brown, A.S., Folias, A.E., et al.: Stigma in people with type 1 or type 2 diabetes. Clin. Diabetes **35**, 27–34 (2017). https://doi.org/10.2337/cd16-0020
4. Kwan, B., Jortberg, B., Warman, K., et al.: Stakeholder engagement in diabetes self-management: patient preference for peer support and other insights. Fam. Pract. **34**, 358–363 (2017). https://doi.org/10.1093/fampra/cmw127

5. Herrero, N., Guerrero-Solé, F., Mas-Manchón, L.: Participation of patients with type 2 diabetes in online support groups is correlated to lower levels of diabetes self-management. J. Diabetes Sci. Technol. **15**, 121–126 (2021). https://doi.org/10.1177/1932296820909830
6. Gabarron, E., Larbi, D., Dorronzoro, E., et al.: Factors engaging users of diabetes social media channels on facebook, twitter, and instagram: observational study. J. Med. Internet Res. **22**, e21204 (2020). https://doi.org/10.2196/21204
7. Mattson, M., Hall, J.: Linking health communication with social support. In: Health as Communication Nexus: A Service Learning Approach. Kendall Hunt Publishing, Dubuque (2011)
8. Wong, D., Amon, K.L., Keep, M.: Desire to belong affects instagram behavior and perceived social support. Cyberpsychol. Behav. Soc. Netw. **22**, 465–471 (2019). https://doi.org/10.1089/cyber.2018.0533
9. Tenderich, A., Tenderich, B., Barton, T., Richards, S.: What are PWDs (people with diabetes) doing online? A netnographic analysis - PubMed. J. Diab. Sci. Technol. **13**, 187–197 (2019)
10. Zhang, Y., He, D., Sang, Y.: Facebook as a platform for health information and communication: a case study of a diabetes group. J. Med. Syst. **37**, 9942 (2013). https://doi.org/10.1007/s10916-013-9942-7
11. Csanadi, A., Eagan, B., Kollar, I., Shaffer, D.W., Fischer, F.: When coding-and-counting is not enough: using epistemic network analysis (ENA) to analyze verbal data in CSCL research. Int. J. Comput.-Support. Collab. Learn. **13**(4), 419–438 (2018). https://doi.org/10.1007/s11412-018-9292-z
12. Rus, H.M., Cameron, L.D.: Health communication in social media: message features predicting user engagement on diabetes-related facebook pages. Ann. Behav. Med. **50**(5), 678–689 (2016). https://doi.org/10.1007/s12160-016-9793-9
13. Bowman, D., et al.: The mathematical foundations of epistemic network analysis. In: Ruis, A.R., Lee, S.B. (eds.) ICQE 2021. CCIS, vol. 1312, pp. 91–105. Springer, Cham (2021). https://doi.org/10.1007/978-3-030-67788-6_7
14. Statista: Social media penetration rate in Hungary in 2020, by platform (2020)
15. Zörgő, S., Peters, G.-J.: Epistemic network analysis for semi-structured interviews and other continuous narratives: challenges and insights. In: Eagan, B., Misfeldt, M., Siebert-Evenstone, A. (eds.) ICQE 2019. CCIS, vol. 1112, pp. 267–277. Springer, Cham (2019). https://doi.org/10.1007/978-3-030-33232-7_23
16. Peters, G.-J.Y., Crutzen, R.: Pragmatic nihilism: how a theory of nothing can help health psychology progress. Health Psychol. Rev. **11**, 103–121 (2017). https://doi.org/10.1080/17437199.2017.1284015
17. Eagan, B.R., Rogers, B., Serlin, R., et al.: Can We Rely on IRR? Testing the Assumptions of Inter-Rater Reliability (2017)
18. Greene, J.A., Choudhry, N.K., Kilabuk, E., Shrank, W.H.: Online social networking by patients with diabetes: a qualitative evaluation of communication with Facebook. J. Gen. Intern. Med. **26**, 287–292 (2011). https://doi.org/10.1007/s11606-010-1526-3
19. White, K., Gebremariam, A., Lewis, D., et al.: Motivations for participation in an online social media community for diabetes. J. Diabetes Sci. Technol. **12**, 712–718 (2018)
20. Singh, A.K., Gupta, R., Ghosh, A., Misra, A.: Diabetes in COVID-19: prevalence, pathophysiology, prognosis and practical considerations. Diabetes Metab. Syndr. **14**, 303–310 (2020). https://doi.org/10.1016/j.dsx.2020.04.004
21. Kingod, N.: The tinkering m-patient: co-constructing knowledge on how to live with type 1 diabetes through Facebook searching and sharing and offline tinkering with self-care. Health (London) **24**, 152–168 (2020). https://doi.org/10.1177/1363459318800140

Quality and Safety Education for Nursing (QSEN) in Virtual Reality Simulations: A Quantitative Ethnographic Examination

Mamta Shah[1(✉)], Amanda Siebert-Evenstone[2], Hollie Moots[1], and Brendan Eagan[3]

[1] Elsevier, Philadelphia, USA
{m.shah, h.moots}@elsevier.com

[2] Nelson Institute for Environmental Studies, Wisconsin Center for Educational Research, University of Wisconsin-Madison, Madison, USA
alevenstone@wisc.edu

[3] Wisconsin Center for Educational Research, University of Wisconsin-Madison, Madison, USA
beagan@wisc.edu

Abstract. In this paper, we argue that virtual reality (VR) simulations can be used to (a) scaffold nursing students' practice of cognitive-psychomotor-social skills, and (b) provide feedback on their decisions; thus, mimicking what pre-licensure students can expect to encounter in the real workplace. To demonstrate this possibility, we undertake a quantitative ethnographic (QE) examination of modeling faculty and student discourse in VR simulations and associated debriefing sessions and interpreting how quality and safety education for nurses (QSEN) competencies of patient center-care, teamwork and collaboration, and safety are practiced in the context of a fundamentals of nursing scenario. Combining the affordances of VR and QE can help transform nursing education research and practice on supporting and measuring students' emerging clinical readiness.

Keywords: Nursing education · Virtual reality simulations · Fundamentals of Nursing · QSEN competencies · Epistemic Network Analysis · Quantitative Ethnography

1 Introduction

Developing students' clinical readiness is a high priority for prelicensure nursing programs. Naturally, exposure to clinical situations is recognized as a cornerstone approach to engage undergraduate nursing students in domain-related activities. However, there are practical barriers to how frequently and deeply students can immerse themselves in these authentic situations. High-fidelity simulation experiences are advantageous alternatives in helping students prepare for clinical experiences [1].

High-fidelity simulations such as virtual reality (VR) are frequently adopted for workforce education and training purposes across multiple fields [2]. However, recent advancements in VR technology are rapidly catalyzing changes in the healthcare

© Springer Nature Switzerland AG 2022
B. Wasson and S. Zörgő (Eds.): ICQE 2021, CCIS 1522, pp. 237–252, 2022.
https://doi.org/10.1007/978-3-030-93859-8_16

education sector [3]. In the context of nursing education, VR simulations are promising because nursing students can (a) participate in a three-dimensional environment that generates images and sounds emulating a clinical scenario, (b) communicate with team members and virtual characters, (c) perform relevant actions and (d) receive haptic feedback from elements in the environment [4]. Empirical evidence is growing regarding the effectiveness of VR simulations in nursing education [5, 6]. However, investigations uncovering how nursing faculty scaffold and sequence instruction using VR simulations, and tracing how learners progress before-during-after participating in VR simulations are scarce.

In this paper, we argue that VR simulations can be used to (a) scaffold nursing students' practice of cognitive-psychomotor-social skills by situating their practice within specific content areas (e.g., fundamentals, medical-surgical, pediatrics), and (b) provide feedback on their decisions; thus, mimicking what learners will encounter in the real workplace. To demonstrate this possibility, we undertake a quantitative ethnographic (QE) examination of modeling faculty and student discourse in VR simulations and associated debriefing sessions and interpreting how quality and safety education for nurses (QSEN) competencies [7] are practiced in the context of a fundamentals of nursing scenario.

The organization of this paper is as follows: we begin by introducing fundamentals as a core course in undergraduate nursing. Research on the trends and gaps in ascertaining the effectiveness of simulations for developing students' clinical readiness is reviewed in the context of nursing fundamentals. Next, we review extant literature on VR simulations in nursing. We underscore the need for using Quantitative Ethnography (QE) to examine the effectiveness of VR simulations for supporting clinical readiness. To ground our examination, we introduce the Quality and Safety Education for Nurses (QSEN) competencies. We present a rationale for modeling discourse related to patient-centered care, teamwork and collaboration, and safety in a nursing fundamentals scenario involving SLS with Virtual Reality (SLS with VR). We then proceed to describe the study methods, including a description of participants and settings, followed by a report of findings. We conclude with directions for future research and implications for practice.

This work seeks inspiration from Shaffer and colleagues' [8] vision for 'digital medicine', which they defined as "the augmentation of human abilities through the external generation and application of medical knowledge that will make health care safer and more effective by enhancing our ability to diagnose and treat disease." We hope that our investigation provides a worked example of how the affordances of VR and QE can help transform nursing education by creating, processing, and interpreting information for researchers and educators to understand nursing students' emerging clinical readiness.

2 Theory

2.1 Fundamentals of Nursing

Fundamentals is a foundational course in undergraduate nursing education. The objective of a fundaments course may include an emphasis on developing students' competencies in "communication and collaboration; implementation of holistic, evidence-based, patient-centered care; providing safe patient care; and demonstration of professional values of caring: altruism, human dignity, and social justice [p, 23; 9]." Clinical experiences during the early stages of nursing education vary widely and are often inconsistent even within a single program [10]. Additionally, fundamentals clinical experiences often focus on routine task completion without the opportunity for higher-level thinking, problem-solving, or collaboration [11].

Typically, simulations are first implemented in a fundamentals course. They are then threaded throughout the nursing curriculum. In an integrated review, Stroup [12] concluded that fundamentals courses provide important opportunities to apply and evaluate simulation effectiveness. According to Dearmon and colleagues [13], early years in nursing students' programmatic journey are characterized by anxiety about patient interaction, budding practice with critical thinking, and psychomotor skills that need further mastery. The use of simulation at this level has proven to be beneficial in all of these areas [13]. However, much of the existing literature considers simulation as a means of assessing the competency of psychomotor clinical skills. For instance, Bornais and colleagues [14] assessed the skill competency of fundamentals students using standardized patients, while Yang and colleagues [15] provided students with single-skill-focused simulation opportunities to assess competency in skills such as vital signs, feeding, and aseptic technique. Beyond the assessment of psychomotor skills, there is a glaring need for furthering our understanding regarding how simulations help students achieve clinical objectives within a fundamentals course.

2.2 Virtual Reality Simulations in Nursing

A surge of recent papers has communicated the potentials of virtual reality (VR) simulations for nursing education. For instance, Dean and colleagues [16] argued that the value of immersive VR simulation experiences lies in their potential to nurture empathy in nursing students so that their ability to engage in patient-centered care is enhanced. They elaborated on this potential by proposing that VR simulations can be used to foster an understanding of what it feels like to communicate with and care for patients with specific characteristics. In another study, Ramakrishnan and colleagues [17] demonstrated the application of three VR simulations designed to support students' situational awareness, clinical judgment, clinical decision making, and understanding of patients' perspectives. Lastly, Bayram and Caliskan [5] reviewed research on VR simulations and their effectiveness in helping students engage in safe practices while providing quality caring for patients. Broadly, positive support was found for VR simulations and their effect on helping students identifying patients correctly, improving effective communication, improving the safety of the high-alert medication, and ensuring correct-site, correct-procedure, correct-patient surgery, reducing the risk of healthcare-associated infections, and reducing the risk of patient harm resulting from falls [5]. However, most studies included in the review focused on measuring change for an isolated nursing skill (e.g., effective drug administration) or outcome (e.g., preventing patient falls).

Studies measuring the effectiveness of VR simulations should consider accounting for the complex nature of clinical work. We believe that adopting a Quantitative Ethnographic (QE) approach can advance nursing education research and practice on VR simulations in this direction. QE unites research methodologies by quantifying the qualitative to examine large data (e.g., conversations, transcripts) from digital environments (e.g., simulations, intelligent tutoring systems) and discover meaningful patterns in human behavior and interaction [18]. QE techniques such as Epistemic Network Analysis (ENA) have been employed to assess and visualize communication patterns and teamwork dynamics in a high-performing primary care team [19]. Scholars have also analyzed multimodal data to visualize team movement in nursing simulations [20]. QE techniques such as ENA provide a valuable approach to create models of situated action [21]; that is, to generate representations of participation in simulated clinical settings. The Quality and Safety Education for Nurses (QSEN) framework provides useful indicators to model and interpret nursing students' emerging readiness for clinical work. We believe that doing so in a Fundamentals of Nursing course might be a good starting point.

2.3   Quality and Safety Education for Nurses

The Quality and Safety Education for Nurses (QSEN) framework was designed to prepare nurses with the competencies necessary to continuously improve the quality and safety of the health care systems in which they work. Cronenwett and colleagues [7] adapted the Institute of Medicine competencies for nursing; that is, patient-centered care, teamwork and collaboration, evidence-based practice, quality improvement, safety, and informatics. In doing so, they operationalized the QSEN competencies and proposed statements of the knowledge, skills, and attitudes (KSAs) for each competency that should be developed during prelicensure nursing education.

According to Preheim, Armstrong and Barton [22], nurses with a strong foundation in patient safety and quality improvement are better able to assimilate into the current complex health care environment. These researchers also emphasized specific QSEN competencies and related KSAs that are important for students to be introduced to early on, specifically in a fundamentals of nursing course. As such, we use patient-centered care (PCC), teamwork and collaboration (TCC), and safety as our primary codes in tracing how SLS with VR simulation and associated debriefing afforded faculty and students those experiences (see Table 1).

2.4   Current Study

In this study, we examine the following research question, *'What similarities and differences can be found in the connections students and faculty make between Quality and Safety Education for Nurses (QSEN) competencies through participation in virtual reality simulations and debriefing as it relates to Fundamentals of Nursing?'* We collected discourse data from a nursing fundamentals scenario in SLS with Virtual Reality and debriefing. We then conducted a qualitative analysis of the interactions to identify and understand the key elements of QSEN competencies: patient-centered care, safety, teamwork and collaboration and associated KSAs, and importantly, how these elements are connected to one another. Once key elements were identified, the structure of connections between these elements was represented as a network of relationships using epistemic network analysis (ENA). This resulted in a visual representation of the structure, a mathematical model of the structure, and a way to compare the quantified data with its underlying qualitative data. After assessing important elements of nursing using ENA, we compared these results to the qualitative findings. Finally, we describe the implications of this study. Below, we elaborate on the study methods, report findings, and discuss key takeaways.

3   Methods

This investigation is situated in a larger pilot study undertaken at Elsevier, a global health and analytics company in Fall 2020 (October-November 2020). The objective of the pilot was to identify actionable insights and feedback on the efficacy, usability, and viability of SLS with Virtual Reality, a VR simulation system for undergraduate nursing education prior to its release in early 2021. Given the uncertainty of college re-openings due to the COVID-19 pandemic, the pilot study was designed flexibly; that is, researchers could support participants and collect data synchronously and asynchronously in an online-only, hybrid, or in person. This was possible because SLS with Virtual Reality is designed for participants to collaborate in a virtual space while being present in physically remote locations.

3.1   SLS with Virtual Reality

SLS with Virtual Reality (SLS with VR) is created with a goal for faculty to facilitate immersive clinical experiences alongside current practices in nursing simulation labs (e.g., hands-on simulations). Faculty have a choice of 100 scenarios across multiple content areas in nursing (e.g., fundamentals, medical-surgical, pediatrics). From the faculty side, SLS with VR scenarios are selected, viewed, and moderated from an interactive interface (i.e., moderator tool). Meanwhile, students participate in the VR scenarios using Oculus Quest headset equipment and hand controllers. Moderating faculty have a full view of what students are experiencing in the VR space. Faculty also have access to orders and actions that help them facilitate a scenario, including opportunities to introduce multiple virtual characters (e.g. patient, nurse, doctor, dietitian, employer, and distractions (e.g. phone calls) that students must interact with and address respectively (see Fig. 1).

3.2   Participants

Tanya (pseudonym) is a faculty in a traditional nursing program (i.e., Bachelors of Science in Nursing, BSN) at a public college in the northeastern region of the United

States. She is the lead instructor for the Fundamentals of Nursing course and has 6–10 years of experience facilitating or assisting with simulations, typically engaging BSN students in their 1st semester of sophomore year.

Broadly, Tanya was motivated to engage her students in simulated clinical experiences for helping them develop communication, professionalism, and clinical judgment skills through exposure to diverse patients. Supporting students to practice patient safety, focused assessment and medical administration were additional skills Tanya focused on. Typically, Tanya's goal for pre-briefing was to ensure that students are as prepared as they can be to engage in a simulation so that they can have an opportunity to apply what they are learning in class. As such, Tanya provided her students with written objectives for the simulation at least four days in advance of a simulation. On the day of the simulation, she reminded students of the objectives by writing them on the whiteboard in the classroom and discussing them in a large group. For debriefing, Tanya deemed important the need to help students be cognizant of how they met the scenario objectives and the gaps that persisted in their knowledge, and identify takeaways from the simulation session. In terms of assessment, Tanya evaluated students' performance as satisfactory, unsatisfactory, or incomplete. Anecdotal verbal feedback and written feedback were also provided. Actual participation in the simulation was non-punitive.

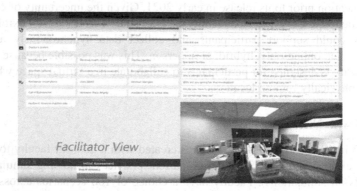

Fig. 1. Moderator tool and faculty view within SLS with virtual reality.

Tanya participated in the pilot along with 29 students who were in their second year of RN-BSN program. These students expressed several hopes from VR simulations developed for nursing education. Obtaining a deeper understanding of the patient-nurse relationship in the care process was a recurrent theme. For instance, one student expressed "[I look forward to obtaining] a better grasp on patient interaction while performing my procedures." Another reported "I hope we can learn how to manage feedback from our patients. I hope to gain a more interactive perspective and be able to accommodate my patient better than a lab simulation." Students also hoped VR simulations would more closely emulate working in a clinical environment. For instance, one student said, "[VR] will help us be able to do tasks and be able to participate more and maybe get more of a real feeling since we have not been able to go to a real clinical site." Another student looked forward to opportunities for "dealing with patient family members and speaking with other members of the healthcare team."

3.3   Procedure

Over seven weeks (October to November 2020), researchers supported Tanya asynchronously by sharing onboarding materials, VR student and instructor guides and safety tips, and instructions to set up the play space for students. She also had access to preparatory and follow-up activities for her students- readings, pre/post-sim quizzes, and pre/post exercises which were tailored to the scenarios being offered within the SLS with VR ecosystem. In addition, Tanya had access to materials for each scenario including case descriptions, pre-briefing and debriefing guides, and dialog transcripts for characters in respective scenarios within the SLS with VR ecosystem. Lastly, a sandbox scenario was made available to all participants, and Tanya was encouraged to orient her students to the VR environment and controls before they participated in scenarios directly or as observers. Researchers also supported Tanya synchronously by facilitating a remote, but hands-on 90-min SLS with VR training session prior to the start of the study. Synchronous remote support was also provided when researchers observed Tanya facilitate scheduled sessions using SLS with VR starting from pre-briefing, running the simulation, and debriefing with her students.

For the purpose of this study, we chose to examine Tanya's simulation practices using SLS with VR over two weeks (once in October and once in November 2020). Each session followed the same procedure (pre-briefing, running a scenario using a scenario in SLS with VR, and de-briefing). Each session typically had 1–2 students who role-played as nurses in the virtual reality scenario and 1–2 students that observed. For all these sessions, Tanya chose a fundamentals scenario from the SLS with VR catalogue of scenarios.

3.4   Fundamentals of Nursing Scenario in SLS with Virtual Reality

The purpose of the fundamentals scenario Tanya chose was to provide students with the opportunity to conduct a basic nursing assessment while managing and prioritizing multiple distractions. The overview of the scenario is as follows:

Kyle Miller, a 41-year-old Caucasian male, was admitted Monday morning for a low-grade fever and cellulitis of the forearm secondary to a recent puncture wound. IV antibiotics were administered, and the affected area was cleaned and covered with dry gauze. Kyle's temperature has since returned to baseline, and he is slated for a Tuesday morning discharge to home. The scenario takes place on Tuesday at 0800, at which time a basic assessment is due. The provider has requested an SBAR update to help plan for discharge, but the hospital unit has multiple distractions and Kyle's visitor asks many questions. During this scenario, students will have the opportunity to conduct a basic nursing assessment while managing and prioritizing multiple distractions.

3.5   Data Coding and Analysis

Discourse during SLS with VR was audio-recorded and transcribed so that each line designated a new *turn of talk*, where a turn is defined as starting with a statement by one individual and ending when another individual spoke [23]. Transcribed data were inductively coded for relevant nursing KSAs as well as deductively coded for QSEN competencies- patient-centered care (PCC), teamwork and collaboration (TCC), and safety. To address the reliability and validity of qualitative coding, we used social moderation, where two raters coded all 770 lines of data and then achieved agreement on each code [24]. Each utterance was coded for the occurrence (1) or nonoccurrence (0) of the skills that are essential to QSEN (see Table 1) thus, quantifying qualitative data.

3.6   Epistemic Network Analysis

To measure QSEN competencies and associated knowledge, skill, and attitudes during SLS with VR simulation and debriefing phases, we used Epistemic Network Analysis [ENA; 25] to model the connections between the three primary codes: patient centered care, teamwork and collaboration, and safety. ENA measured these connections by quantifying the co-occurrence of QSEN codes within a defined segment of data.

Table 1. Codebook of QSEN competencies and associated knowledge, skills, and attitudes.

Code and definition	Examples of Relevant Knowledge (K), Skills (S), Attitudes (A)
Patient-Centered Care (PCC): Recognize the patient or designee as the source of control and full partner in providing compassionate and coordinated care based on respect for the patient's preferences, values, and needs	K-Demonstrate a comprehensive understanding of the concepts of pain and suffering S-Assess presence and extent of pain and suffering A-Appreciate the role of the nurse in relief of pain
Teamwork and Collaboration (TCC): Function effectively within nursing and inter-professional teams, fostering open communication, mutual respect, and shared decision-making to achieve quality patient care	K-Discuss effective strategies for communicating S-Follow communication practices that minimize risks associated with handoffs among providers and across transitions in care A-Respect the centrality of the patient/family as core members of any health care team
Safety: Minimize risk of harm to patients and providers through both system effectiveness and individual performance	K-Delineate general categories of errors and hazards in care S-Demonstrate effective use of technology and standardized practices that support safety and quality A-Protect patient confidentiality

In this study, we used a moving stanza window [26] of four utterances (each line plus the three previous lines) within a given conversation. We chose this window size based on our qualitative analysis of the discourse. We also ran the model at a range of different window sizes (i.e. 3–7) and the interpretation of the result remained consistent. A conversation, in this case, included all turns of talk associated within one phase within the implementation. Codes that occurred outside of this window were not considered connected. For the dimensional reduction, we chose a technique called a *means rotation* [27] that combines (1) a hyperplane projection of the high-dimensional points to a line that maximizes the difference between the means of two units and (2) a singular value decomposition. The resulting metric space highlighted any differences between the units by constructing the dimensional reduction that placed the means of the two units as close as possible to the X-axis of the space. In this study, we rotated the space by the Simulation and Debriefing phases to highlight differences across the phases on the x-axis. Subsequently, ENA created two coordinated representations for each unit including the weighted network graph, which visualized these connections as network graphs where the nodes corresponded to the codes and edges reflected the relative frequency of the connection between two codes, and a plotted point. In this way, we quantified and visualized the structure of connections among elements of QSEN competencies and compared differences in talk across phases.

Mean networks for each phase were calculated by averaging the connection strengths across the phase and plotting the resulting network in the space. For example, the mean network for the simulation phase represented the average network for that time. Mean ENA scores were created by calculating the average ENA scores on each dimension for each phase, and then plotting the resulting value in the space. Statistical tests were performed on the mean ENA scores to test whether there were statistical differences between groups.

4   Results

Our analysis of discourse revealed rich insights into how Tanya facilitated QSEN related discussions with her students while moderating the fundamentals scenario using SLS with VR and debriefing. After reviewing the qualitative data, we found that there were important differences in how the instructor discussed safety during the simulation and debriefing phases of the implementation.

4.1   Quantitative Findings

To investigate and compare how Tanya engaged with her learners, we created mean networks of the connections between codes for the Simulation phase and the Debriefing phase. Within the ENA space, we performed a means rotation between Simulation and Debriefing, which creates a metric space where the first dimension explains the most difference between those two phases (See Fig. 2). Each of these means represents the average discourse network for that respective phase. Figure 3 shows the individual mean network plots for the simulation phase, on the left in blue, and the Debriefing phase, on the right in red.

First, both phases make strong connections between PCC and TCC. However, in the simulation phase, the instructor and students made more connections between PCC and safety. On the other hand, in the Debriefing phase, the instructor and participants made more connections between TCC and safety. To more clearly compare the similarities and differences between phases, we created a difference network (see Fig. 4).

Figure 4 shows two representations of the phases. First, it shows the mean and confidence interval for each phase which represents the average discourse network across that phase. Second, this figure shows the difference network comparing the Simulation and Debriefing mean networks. Connections represented in red lines were stronger among Debriefing discourse, while connections in blue occurred proportionally more often in Simulation discourse. Thicker lines indicate larger differences in connection strength, while thinner lines indicate smaller differences in the strength of connections.

Based on these representations, the average discourse pattern of students and the instructor in the Simulation phase focused more on connecting PCC and Safety compared to the Debriefing phase where the discourse focused more on connections between Safety and TCC. The faint and thin line connecting PCC and TCC indicates that on average both the Simulation and Debriefing phases made roughly the same number of connections between these two topics. Referring to Fig. 4, we see that both phases make many connections between these topics so that a comparison between the phases shows little difference.

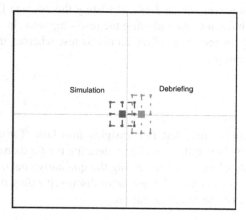

Fig. 2. Means (squares) and 95% confidence intervals (dashed lines) for Simulation (blue) and Debriefing (red) phases. (Color figure online)

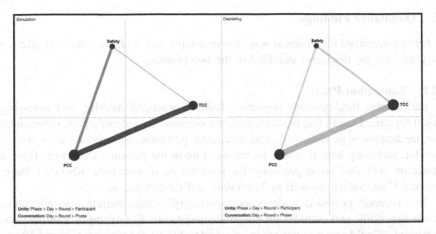

Fig. 3. Network representation of the simulation (blue) and debriefing (red) phases. Thicker lines represent more frequent connections. (Color figure online)

Despite these commonalities in connection patterns between PCC and TCC, there were systematic differences between the two phases. A two-sample t-test assuming unequal variance showed the discourse pattern in the Simulation phase (mean = −0.13, SD = 1.20, N = 51 was statistically significantly different at the alpha = 0.05 level from the Debriefing phase along the X-axis (mean = 0.40, SD = 0.48, N = 16; t (61.18) = −2.56, p = 0.01, Cohen's d = 0.49). This statistical difference in discourse patterns is mainly driven by the instructor and students making more connections between PCC and Safety in the Simulation phase and more on connections between Safety and TCC in the debriefing phase. In other words, the big difference between the two phases is how the discourse makes connections to safety.

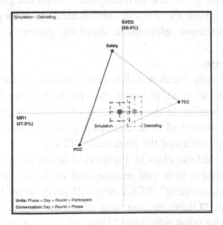

Fig. 4. Means (squares) and confidence intervals (dashed lines) for Simulation (blue) and Debriefing (red) phases. Difference network comparison between simulation phases, where thicker lines represent greater differences. (Color figure online)

4.2 Qualitative Findings

To better understand the different ways the instructor and students discussed safety, we analyzed how the discourse unfolded in the two phases.

4.2.1 Simulation Phase

As part of this fundamentals scenario, students practiced meeting and assessing a patient for care. During this practice, students assessed the patient's pain, determined if pain medication was indicated, and discussed pertinent pain-related data with the provider, including how it would be managed upon the patient's discharge. Here, the simulation provided an opportunity for students to demonstrate KSAs of Patient-Centered Care, Safety, as well as Teamwork and Collaboration.

This scenario provided students an opportunity to demonstrate key indicators of knowledge, skills, and attitudes for patient-centered care. For example, a student asked the patient, "Could you rate your pain on a scale of 0-10, 0 being no pain and 10 being the worst pain?" (PCC-K, S). After discussing pain and other symptoms with the patient, the student then summarized the assessment for the doctor (TCC). Each time the teacher facilitated this scenario, students got experience communicating patient preferences (PCC – S) to another member of the healthcare team (TCC – S).

Also, during the simulation phase, Tanya challenged students to address patient privacy concerns. In this case, the instructor posed as the patient's employer and requested medical information and updates. With this experience, students explored the ethical and legal implications of patient-centered care while providing the necessary sensitivity and respect for the patient's privacy (PCC-S). Students dealt with a belligerent employer and had to navigate communicating with the employer without releasing private health information as a potential error (Safety-K). One student responded to the employer and said, "Per the hospital policies, I am not allowed to disclose any information." In this example, the student demonstrated a strategy to prevent an error in disclosing protected information (Safety-S), value their role in preventing that error (Safety-A), and provide patient-centered care (PCC). The students needed to identify and utilize an effective communication strategy to minimize patient risk while presenting pertinent information about the patient's condition.

4.2.2 Debriefing Phase

After the simulation, Tanya facilitated debriefing sessions which provided the opportunity to draw attention to specific topics and push students to consider alternative decisions and actions. Similar to the simulation phase, Tanya made frequent connections between the importance of both centering patient needs (PCC) and communicating those needs to members of the care team (TCC).

For example, Tanya led the class in a reflection about assessing pain by discussing how it is common to assess pain and recommend medicine but "not follow through getting the rest of the assessment" (PCC). She followed up by focusing on the role of communication, asking, "Okay, so you said communication. You think your communication was good. So what was good? Give me some specifics. What did you do well with the communication?" (TCC). One student responded, "We both helped each other. And also in talking to each other. We had to discuss what was going on" (TCC).

In this instance, and across the debriefing Tanya made sure that students reflected on how they understood the situation and how they communicated these assessments to others.

Safety was also a consistent topic during debriefing. Tanya helped students identify errors as well as safety-related issues that arose during simulation. In one example, Tanya made sure students understood the appropriate identification of the patient, allergies, and prioritization of assessment & interventions (PCC, Safety – K, A). While discussing how students assessed their patients, Tanya focused on how students used standardized practices and tools to ensure patient safety (Safety-S). For example, Tanya asked students, "when you took the dressing off, did you wear gloves?" This question about basic safety practice was used to further discuss connecting what they did in the simulation with real-world practices and past experiences.

To emphasize the importance of TCC and Safety, Tanya told students, "you were using our closed loop communication with each other and open teamwork communication during the VR, which we encourage you to use." Tanya and the students discussed the importance of maintaining a closed-loop communication to protect patient rights but remaining in open communication with the providers. Navigating who needs to know what led to further discussion about the importance of effective communication between the student nurses, the patient, and other members of the healthcare team (PCC – K, S; TCC – K, S, A; Safety).

Within the scenario and emphasized in the debrief, Tanya made sure to dive into these nuances of communication. She encouraged students in the observer roles to comment on the overall communication, asking "how was their communication with the patient and the family". The student observers identified the importance of communication stating, "I'll be prepared to talk with the family members and other members of the healthcare team" and "be prepared a little better with SBAR" when asked how they would use their role as observer to guide them when they participate as students. In each of these instances, not all students had the same role in the simulation, however, Tanya used debrief to ensure all students received a similar experience. Though the simulation had objectives and expected student actions, each scenario took a slightly different course based on the students' actions. In one instance, students never contacted the provider. In another, the employer didn't call. But the educator was able to bring these issues up during debrief and facilitate meaningful discussion and learning.

In each instance, she spent time discussing closed-loop communication as an important tool for communicating information with other members of the healthcare team (TCC- S; Safety – S). Importantly, though, when Tanya taught students about safety during the debriefing, she focused her discussion on how the students communicated risk with others.

4.2.3   Comparing Simulation and Debriefing Discourse

Throughout the fundamentals scenario in SLS with VR—simulation and debriefing— the instructor and students interacted with the patient, gathered the patient's background, assessed patient needs, recommended next steps, and communicated with the patient, family, and other providers. This scenario was therefore rich in examples of and connections between all three QSEN competencies as students practiced patient-centered care (PCC), maintained patient safety (Safety), and worked in teams to address patient needs (TCC). However, there were important differences in how participants made connections between these three topics.

Both the simulation and debriefing included many and about the same relative number of instances where participants made connections between providing patient-centered care (PCC) and working and communicating in teams (TCC). At the same time, there were important differences in how Tanya and her students discussed safety in relation to these two codes. Across the phases, the simulation included more opportunities to connect PCC with Safety, while the debriefing included more instances of TCC and Safety. In the simulation, Tanya directed student practice to communicating with patients and protecting patient privacy. While in the debriefing, Tanya facilitated reflections on how students communicated risk with others.

5 Discussion

This paper demonstrates that we can meaningfully model nursing education discourse during a VR simulation and associated debriefing. It shows that, by using QE, we can find statistically significant differences between phases that also reflect the underlying qualitative stories. As such, advances in digital technologies and research methods can usher new directions in nursing education especially as it relates to shaping students' clinical readiness [8, 21].

Using the QSEN competency framework [7] to study SLS with VR simulation and debriefing activity, this paper demonstrated how undergraduate students can be supported to identify with professional nursing roles that reach far beyond tasks, skills, and procedures. They can be supported to develop a beginning awareness of safety and quality in the context of a health care system, nurse-sensitive quality indicators, and local and national safety initiatives impacting health care delivery. Nurturing a well-rounded clinical competency is important; a fundamentals course is a relevant starting point for introducing and examining the efficacy of pedagogical approaches that support this goal [9–13]. In the future, this research will be expanded to additional content areas in nursing education (e.g., medical-surgical).

Examining discourse and moment-to-moment interactions using ENA can expand nursing educators' ability to assess participation in simulation-based experiences. They can also broaden the data sources nursing education researchers rely on for measuring the effectiveness of novel simulation modalities such as VR [5, 6]. Making tools accessible and usable for nursing educators would be a relevant direction for the QE community to strive towards [28].

References

1. Hayden, J.K., Smiley, R.A., Alexander, M., Kardong-Edgren, S., Jeffries, P.R.: The NCSBN national simulation study: a longitudinal, randomized, controlled study replacing clinical hours with simulation in prelicensure nursing education. J. Nurs. Regul. 5(2), S3–S40 (2014)

2. Kamińska, D., et al.: Virtual reality and its applications in education: survey. Information **10** (10), 318 (2019)
3. Lee, M.J.W., Georgieva, M., Alexander, B., Craig, E., Richter, J.: State of XR & Immersive Learning Outlook Report 2021. Immersive Learning Research Network, Walnut (2021)
4. Jenson, C.E., Forsyth, D.M.: Virtual reality simulation: using three-dimensional technology to teach nursing students. CIN: Comput. Inform. Nurs. **30**(6), 312–318 (2012)
5. Bayram, S.B., Caliskan, N.: The use of virtual reality simulations in nursing education, and patient safety. In: Contemporary Topics in Patient Safety, vol. 1. IntechOpen (2020)
6. Chen, F.-Q., et al.: Effectiveness of virtual reality in nursing education: meta-analysis. J. Med. Internet Res. **22**(9), e18290 (2020)
7. Cronenwett, L., et al.: Quality and safety education for nurses. Nurs. Outlook **55**(3), 122–131 (2007)
8. Shaffer, D.W., Kigin, C.M., Kaput, J.J., Scott Gazelle, G.: What is digital medicine? In: Future of Health Technology, pp. 195–204. IOS Press (2002)
9. Konrad, S., Fitzgerald, A., Deckers, C.: Nursing fundamentals–supporting clinical competency online during the COVID-19 pandemic. Teach. Learn. Nurs. **16**(1), 53–56 (2021)
10. Mulcahy, A., Gruben, D., Wells-Beede, E.: Overcoming resistance: implementation of 100% simulation for first semester nursing students. Clin. Simul. Nurs. **50**, 107–111 (2021)
11. McKenna, L., Cant, R., Bogossian, F., Cooper, S., Levett-Jones, T., Seaton, P.: Clinical placements in contemporary nursing education: where is the evidence? Nurse Educ. Today **83**, 104202 (2019)
12. Stroup, C.: Simulation usage in nursing fundamentals: integrative literature review. Clin. Simul. Nurs. **10**(3), e155–e164 (2014)
13. Dearmon, V., et al.: Effectiveness of simulation-based orientation of baccalaureate nursing students preparing for their first clinical experience. J. Nurs. Educ. **52**(1), 29–38 (2013)
14. Bornais, J.A., Raiger, J.E., Krahn, R.E., El-Masri, M.M.: Evaluating undergraduate nursing students' learning using standardized patients. J. Prof. Nurs. **28**(5), 291–296 (2012)
15. Yang, J., Shen, L., Jin, X., Hou, L., Shang, S., Zhang, Y.: Evaluating the quality of simulation teaching in fundamental nursing curriculum: AHP-fuzzy comprehensive evaluation. Nurse Educ. Today **77**, 77–82 (2019)
16. Dean, S., Halpern, J., McAllister, M., Lazenby, M.: Nursing education, virtual reality and empathy? Nurs. Open **7**(6), 2056–2059 (2020)
17. Ramakrishnan, A., Lleva, A., Okupniak, C.: Virtual reality in clinical simulation: a modality for undergraduate nursing education. In: INTED2020 Proceedings, pp. 7359–7366 (2020)
18. Shaffer, D.W.: Quantitative Ethnography. Cathcart Press, Madison (2017)
19. Wooldridge, A.R., Carayon, P., Shaffer, D.W., Eagan, B.: Quantifying the qualitative with epistemic network analysis: a human factors case study of task-allocation communication in a primary care team. IISE Trans. Healthc. Syst. Eng. **8**(1), 72–82 (2018)
20. Echeverria, V., Martinez-Maldonado, R., Power, T., Hayes, C., Shum, S.B.: Where is the nurse? Towards automatically visualising meaningful team movement in healthcare education. In: Rosé, C.P., et al. (eds.) AIED 2018. LNCS (LNAI), vol. 10948, pp. 74–78. Springer, Cham (2018). https://doi.org/10.1007/978-3-319-93846-2_14
21. Shaffer, D.W.: Models of situated action: computer games and the problem of transfer. In: Games, Learning, and Society: Learning and Meaning in the Digital Age, pp. 403–431 (2012)
22. Preheim, G.J., Armstrong, G.E., Barton, A.J.: The new fundamentals in nursing: introducing beginning quality and safety education for nurses' competencies. J. Nurs. Educ. **48**(12), 694–697 (2009)

23. Sacks, H., Schegloff, E.A., Jefferson, G.: A simplest systematics for the organization of turn taking for conversation. In: Studies in the Organization of Conversational Interaction, pp. 7–55. Academic Press (1978)
24. Herrenkohl, L.R., Cornelius, L.: Investigating elementary students' scientific and historical argumentation. J. Learn. Sci. **22**(3), 413–461 (2013)
25. Shaffer, D.W., Collier, W., Ruis, A.R.: A tutorial on epistemic network analysis: analyzing the structure of connections in cognitive, social, and interaction data. J. Learn. Anal. **3**(3), 9–45 (2016)
26. Siebert-Evenstone, A.L., Irgens, G.A., Collier, W., Swiecki, Z., Ruis, A.R., Shaffer, D.W.: In search of conversational grain size: modelling semantic structure using moving stanza windows. J. Learn. Anal. **4**(3), 123–139 (2017)
27. Swiecki, Z., Ruis, A.R., Farrell, C., Shaffer, D.W.: Assessing individual contributions to collaborative problem solving: a network analysis approach. Comput. Hum. Behav. **104**, 105876 (2020)
28. Buckingham Shum, S.: Quantitative Ethnography Visualizations as Tools for Thinking (Keynote Address). In: 2nd International Conference on Quantitative Ethnography (2020). https://simon.buckinghamshum.net/2021/02/icqe2020-keynote-qe-viz-as-tools-for-thinking

Reflections of Health Care Workers on Their In-Hospital Experiences During the Onset of COVID-19

Danielle P. Espino[1(✉)], Yutong Tan[1], Orit Zigman Lador[1],
Stephanie Alvarez Pham[1], Megan Hokama[2], Luiz Oliveira[1],
Seung B. Lee[1], and Zachariah Mbasu[3]

[1] Pepperdine University, Malibu, CA 90263, USA
danielle.espino@pepperdine.edu
[2] University of Arizona, Tucson, AZ 85721, USA
[3] Africa Maths Initiative, Kisumu 40100, Kenya

Abstract. The early stages of the COVID-19 pandemic intensified the role of healthcare workers in hospitals. This study examines how healthcare workers reflected on their in-hospital experiences in the early stages of the pandemic in North America. Audio diary entries from The Nocturnist podcast recorded from March – June 2020 were analyzed using epistemic network analysis (ENA) and heat map models. Overall, there was a shift from responding to immediate needs in March 2020 (such as Anger with Policies and Fear with Resource Availability) to deeper reflections in May-June 2020, more focused on Psychosocial Support and Purpose and more complex emotions involving Sadness and Compassion. Uncertainty was a prominent emotion throughout the May – June 2020 period. These results help document the complexity of reflections early in the pandemic, while informing ways to better support health care workers in future crisis.

Keywords: COVID-19 · Health care workers · Reflections · Pandemic · Crisis · Hospital experience · Emotions · Mental health · Frontline workers

1 Introduction

The strenuous physical and intellectual labor of healthcare workers in hospitals was unexpectedly intensified due to the rising cases of the COVID-19 pandemic in early 2020. Long shift hours and stressful working conditions were no longer the only characteristics attached to hospital burnout. The overcrowding of emergency rooms, lack of medical supplies, large death tolls, and continuous emotional undertakings compounded the role of a healthcare worker during this time of international crisis [7]. As people applauded healthcare workers for their dedication to caring for patients, most people were unaware of the severity of the pandemic as they sought refuge in their own homes [4, 5]. Inevitably, healthcare workers were forced into questioning their own morals and judgment within a healthcare system that was unprepared for a global pandemic.

© Springer Nature Switzerland AG 2022
B. Wasson and S. Zörgő (Eds.): ICQE 2021, CCIS 1522, pp. 253–267, 2022.
https://doi.org/10.1007/978-3-030-93859-8_17

Throughout 2020, the selfless sacrifice of healthcare workers dominated public discourse during the spread of COVID-19. However, this story of sacrifice has not fully conveyed the emotions and reflections healthcare workers have experienced, as these emotions and reflections can be complex and distressing [5]. Researchers have questioned how emotions can drive healthcare workers to work during crises and how they can cause emotional distress [12]. Despite the rewards of helping others that healthcare workers achieve, it does not minimize the fact that sacrifices are not met without risks or losses. Due to the scarceness of empirical research on the lived experiences of healthcare workers during crises, specifically in the United States, the following sections explore the emotions and reflections of healthcare workers who worked during the COVID-19 pandemic from March 2020 - June 2020.

1.1 Reflections of Healthcare Workers in Times of Crisis

The COVID-19 pandemic has posed several challenges and consequences on individuals [3]. Some studies have analyzed the experiences of healthcare workers during worldwide, national, or regional pandemics, including Ebola, Swine Flu Pandemic (H1N1), Middle East respiratory syndrome-coronavirus (MERS-CoV), and now COVID-19 [9, 19]. Such studies have examined the experiences of emergency room workers during outbreaks and various issues such as hospital readiness, resource availability, and patient safety [14, 18]. Specifically, during the COVID-19 pandemic, researchers have analyzed the emotional toll on healthcare workers that emerge from such outbreaks [17, 19, 21].

During health epidemics, medical staff strictly follow control procedures and wear personal protective equipment to work. However, healthcare workers are still at risk of contracting a virus. When healthcare workers have close contact with patients of the outbreak, it adds to the intense experience and emotions related to their safety and their colleagues and families [8]. A survey of 32,174 nurses working during the COVID-19 pandemic found that 58% of employees feared for their safety, 64% of employees were highly concerned about the safety of their family and friends, and 74% of employees were concerned about the lack of personal protective equipment [2]. Additionally, emotions around distress were more apparent when healthcare workers witnessed colleagues contracting the infection, becoming sicker, and intubated for respiratory failure [19]. In consequence, healthcare workers are more likely to experience fear, fatigue and uncertainty. This response contributed to overall emotional distress during an outbreak.

Observations in studies show that healthcare workers use coping strategies. Employee coping strategies were observed in reflections on anticipated aid in personal protective equipment, increased family support, financial incentives, and a possible vaccination for the disease infection. In situations involving the COVID-19 pandemic, medical staff participated in support measures independently or with their families, while minimizing outside contact [19]. Strategies such as a positive attitude at work, infected staff getting healthier after infection, adequate protective equipment, and a decline in disease transmission after strict infection control practices significantly reduced stress and staff anxiety [21]. Through a process of reflection, healthcare professionals described their inherent professional and ethical obligations, which prompted them to continue working through the difficult circumstances [8]. During times of crisis, it is important to understand the complexities of employees' emotions and reflections.

1.2 Examining Emotions in Reflections

Healthcare professional's voices are vital to understanding the emotional importance of certain topics or constructs within emergency medical spaces. Analyzing the way an individual strings words together can provide insight into the psychological thought processes behind an emotional or contextual reaction [11]. The process of sentiment analysis examines an individual's voiced attitudes, reflections, and emotions towards entities such as topics, infrastructures, and products [11]. One's attitudes towards a specific topic can be unraveled in the lexical word choice as it is often implicit in nature [11]. Furthermore, word choice not only identifies reflection of personal attitudes and emotions, but can also potentially influence how we transform cognitive thought processes over space and time [1, 11].

In this study, positive and negative valence emotions were loosely identified according to Plutchik's wheel of emotions, a widely known psychological model [13]. Text emotion classification studies frequently employ Plutchik's wheel of emotions to effectively differentiate information about emotions by identifying affective word choice [10, 20]. At the center of this model are eight primary emotions: joy, trust, fear, surprise, sadness, distrust, anger, and anticipation [13]. Although fatigue, uncertainty, perseverance, and compassion are not traditionally classified on Plutchik's wheel of emotions, previous research literature indicates that these emotions are prevalent in COVID-19 medical worker's experiences – e.g., compassion fatigue transferred from patient care [15]; uncertainty linked to inaccessibility to medical equipment [8]; perseverance connected to positive attitudes in the workplace [9].

1.3 Examining Reflections During COVID-19

COVID-19 exemplified the challenges of providing optimal care during a crisis, impacting healthcare workers and patients, their families, and communities. By examining reflections of healthcare professionals in times of crises, the research can influence public policy change within the healthcare system and determine appropriate measures in assisting healthcare workers during states of emergencies. Sentiment analysis studies have informed legislation reform to better benefit healthcare providers through the funding of educational programs, the preparation of medical equipment assistance, and the utilization of mental health support [11]. Although an immense number of studies have identified the negative stressors surrounding healthcare workload during the COVID-19 pandemic, limited research has examined how these experiences were mentally processed at the time. Contributing to this area can potentially highlight how healthcare professionals process emotion over time and eventually develop synchronous or asynchronous programs that assist healthcare workers navigate stressors of extreme crises. This study seeks to examine how health care workers reflected on their in-hospital experiences during the March - June 2020 period of the COVID-19 pandemic, primarily in the United States.

2 Methods

The data analyzed in this study consists of audio diaries recorded by healthcare workers identified by The Nocturnists podcast as part of a series named "Stories from a Pandemic." These audio diaries were recorded between March 2020 and June 2020 from healthcare workers from 13 states across the U.S and one from Canada. The healthcare workers served in various roles such as doctors, nurses, medical interns, and other hospital-based roles. While there were over 50 audio diary entries in total, only audio entries from healthcare workers who reflected on their in-hospital work experience from the pandemic were examined. This ensured a more cohesive analysis of a shared context of health care workers early on in the pandemic. Excluded from examination were any entries that referenced non-hospital experiences, such as being at home sick with COVID-19 and sharing experience on their disease, or those who were working remotely. This resulted in the examination of 40 entries.

The audio diaries reflect on the day-to-day hospital experiences of healthcare workers during the first three months of the COVID-19 outbreak. The healthcare workers were anonymous. The only details shared was a first name (though some were listed as anonymous), position, city, and diary entry date, which can be found on a map list on The Nocturnist podcast website (http://coviddiaries.thenocturnists.com). A separate web page contained transcripts of each audio diary entry (https://thenocturnists.com/stories-from-a-pandemic-full-transcript). To verify the accuracy of the transcriptions, each researcher listened to the original audio diary entry to ensure accuracy of the transcript, and made minor adjustments accordingly.

The transcribed audio diary entries were coded based on the healthcare workers' experiences and were categorized by professional, personal, and emotional constructs as seen in Table 1 and 2. Through a grounded analysis of the data, professional constructs examined included Resource Availability, Situational Assessment, Medical Intervention, Psychosocial Support, Preventive Measures, Purpose and Policies. Personal constructs examined included Routine and Relationships. The emotional constructs identified included five negative emotions (Uncertainty, Fatigue, Sadness, Fear, Anger) and four positive emotional constructs (Compassion, Anticipation, Perseverance, Grateful). Several emotional constructs were informed by Plutchik's Wheel of Emotion [13].

The coding process involved annotating when an emotional construct was identified in connection to a professional or personal construct (e.g. Fear related to Resource Availability), and when a professional, personal or emotion construct was singularly mentioned. Occurrences of different emotions related to the same professional or personal construct were annotated with multiple codes. Each audio diary entry was coded independently by two raters, followed by a process of social moderation to reach agreement on the final coding of the data [7].

Analysis of the data was carried out in two stages. The first stage examined constructs using epistemic network analysis (ENA), a tool in quantitative ethnography for modeling the connections between constructs in data [16]. Models were generated to look at connections between professional and personal constructs, and then among emotion constructs. Professional/personal constructs were examined separate from

Table 1. Codebook of professional and personal constructs used in analysis.

Construct	Definition	Examples
Resource Availability (Professional)	Referring to shortages or obtaining staff or any equipment such as PPE, ventilators, beds, etc.	... I couldn't go in the room because there's not enough PPE They're adjusting staffing... adjusting beds
Situational Assessment (Professional)	Describing number of cases, number of patients, etc. or observing/referencing death or people dying	ER volumes across the board are down, ER deaths are down I have had three patients of mine die suddenly
Medical Intervention (Professional)	Referencing medical procedures or treatment of patients or alleviating symptoms, including intubation, oxygen flow, etc.	...One of our junior residents performing a relatively urgent placement of a large IV in the neck, a central line to a patient that was unstable after getting intubated...
Psychosocial Support (Professional)	Referring to or providing psychological (mental health), emotional, or social support or help to patients & families / colleagues (e.g. managing FaceTime between patient and family member; being de facto family member for patient, etc.)	I am preparing the family to see their [family member]...critically ill in our ICU. And the words, whatever I use to describe it, it does nothing to prepare them for when I turn the phone around and they see them there for the first time
Preventative Measures (Professional)	Referencing availability of testing or getting tested or vaccine trials	He was also tested for, uh, the coronavirus and his rapid test was positive...
Purpose (Professional)	Finding purpose in their roles as health care professionals in the pandemic, being fulfilled by work, contributing/helping problem; referencing time; referencing ethics of health care work	It was both insane and exhilarating because my training had taught me how to do this... I felt like residency had taught me the tools to take care of this, which was kind of incredible
Policies (Professional)	Referencing changes to employer or government policies/protocols such as contact/social distancing, temperature, CDC guidelines or comments related to health care system (e.g. brokenness, lack of leadership)	My hospital has a strict visitor policy that was enacted in the beginning of March, which has meant a lot of births and deaths unwitnessed by loved ones
Relationships (Personal)	Mentioning relationships with spouses/partners, kids, other family, friends, pets, etc.	...I was walking back to then go talk with my parents. Now, my own parents have been sick, and I suspect it is COVID, they never get sick and they're on the older side...

(continued)

Table 1. (*continued*)

Construct	Definition	Examples
Routine (Personal)	Referencing routines or return to "regular" or "normal" life, and what it will mean (e.g. risk involved; new normal, work/life balance)	*Now we're starting to have a little bit of our regular business again/You know, everyone talks a lot about, like wanting to get back to normal and I'm like, "What is normal anymore?"*

Table 2. Codebook of emotion constructs used in analysis.

Construct	Definition	Example
Anger	Emotion related to frustration, rage or annoyance	*We are day whatever of Corona Land. And at this point, I'm just angry*
Fatigue	Emotion related to tiredness, exhaustion, lacking energy or sleep; crushed, overwhelmed, defeated, burdened	*I mean, the level of trauma, death, acuity, volume and just being overwhelmed*
Fear	Emotion related to fear (i.e. apprehension, scared, worried, anxious, afraid)	*Constantly changing ventilator requirements, some really scary compliance physiology, increasing pressors...*
Sadness	Emotion related to sadness, grief, hopelessness, disappointment, longing, missing, or nostalgia	*It's really been one of the most tragic moments I have witnessed. Um, I'm sorry to share a sad story, but I think these stories are important*
Uncertainty	Experiencing uncertainty, doubt, questioning, state of confusion, unclear/mixed emotions or direction	*These things aren't feasible, aren't sustainable. Everything feels like we don't have any control over it*
Anticipation	Emotions related to anticipation, interest, vigilance, hope, and wonder how things will be	*When I go in to consent another person in another room, while we're waiting on it to thaw, I feel hope, we feel energized*
Compassion	Relating to or feeling for someone else's struggles or the situation; seeing perspectives of others	*And rather than be defensive, it's up to us to be understanding, to understand where they're coming from and to try to rebuild that trust*
Grateful	Emotions related to appreciation, gratitude, joy, serenity, ecstasy, excitement	*I thankfully have a day off today to recover after working five out of seven days in the first week of this crisis*
Perseverance	Emotions related to acceptance, trust, admiration, positivity	*We're, we're doing our best to get as ready as we can, but, but today was okay*

emotion constructs to first understand these respective trends of reflection. A single audio diary entry was defined as both the unit of analysis and the conversational unit, within which all connections were contained. A minimum edge weight of 0.03 was applied in the network model to enhance the visibility of the most salient connections.

The second stage of analysis used heat maps, a data visualization method usually used primarily in quantitative research to show data networks wholly and concisely at the same time, using different colors to represent the extent of a specific monitoring value [6]. This approach was utilized in order to better visualize emotion constructs that were conveyed in relation to professional and personal constructs, which would otherwise be too cluttered in a joint ENA space. One axis of the heat map represented the professional and personal constructs, and the other axis expressed the emotions. Darker colors indicated an increased frequency in the related constructs.

3 Results

3.1 Epistemic Network Analysis (ENA)

ENA was utilized to model how the professional and personal constructs and then emotion constructs were reflected in the audio diary entries in relation to one another. Figure 1 shows the overall network model for the nine professional and personal constructs from March – June 2020. The nodes represent each respective construct that was coded and the edges between the nodes represent the strength of the connection between each construct using an infinite stanza window size. A thicker line represents a stronger connection while a thinner line represents a weaker connection. The x axis is defined by Resource Availability on the left and Preventative Measures on the right. The y axis of the model is defined by Policies on the bottom and Psychosocial Support at the top. The strongest connection is seen between Resource Availability and Medical Treatment, indicating an overall emphasis on professional constructs related to equipment/resources and medical intervention for patients.

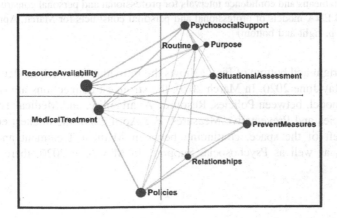

Fig. 1. ENA model of professional and personal constructs from March – June 2020

The top left of Fig. 2 displays the means and confidence intervals of audio diary entries by month. As the months go from March to May-June 2020, the means move up and to the right, indicating a shift from connections between Policies, Resource Availability, and Medical Treatment to Routine, Purpose, and Psychosocial Support. Along the Y axis (SVD2), a Mann-Whitney test showed that March 2020 (Mdn = −0.40, N = 10) was statistically significantly different at the alpha = 0.05 level from April 2020 (Mdn = 0.06, N = 18 U = 137.00, p = 0.03, r = −0.52).

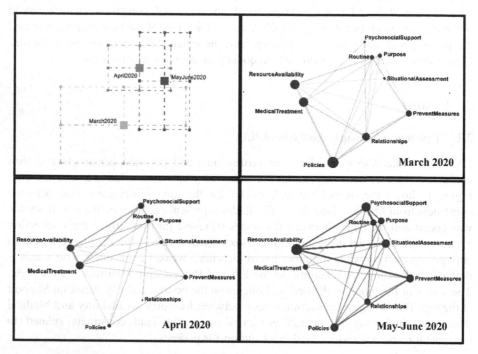

Fig. 2. Group means and confidence intervals for professional and personal constructs by month (top, left) and ENA models of professional and personal constructs for March, April, and May-June 2020 (top, right and bottom)

The top right and bottom of Fig. 2 shows the individual network models for March, April and May-June 2020. In March 2020, the strongest connections are on the lower half of the model, between Policies, Resource Availability, and Medical Treatment, as well as Policies and Preventative Measures. For April 2020, the thickest edges are on the upper left of the space, continuing between Medical Treatment and Resource Availability, as well as Psychosocial Support. In May-June 2020, there are several more connections that are more focused on the upper half of the model, with strong connections between Resource Availability and several constructs, including Preventative Measures, Situational Assessment, and Psychosocial Support. There is also a thick connection between Purpose and Psychosocial Support. Overall, there is a shift to a more balanced network and varied reflection towards May-June 2020.

Figure 3 shows the overall network model for the nine emotion constructs from March – June 2020. Along the x axis, the space is distinguished by Grateful on the left and Sadness on the right. The y axis is defined by Grateful on the bottom and Fear at the top. The overall strongest connection is seen between Fear and Uncertainty, indicating the reflection of strong negative emotions.

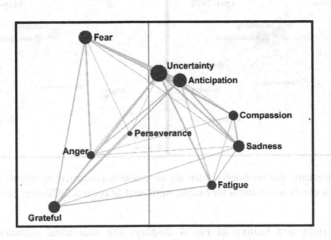

Fig. 3. ENA model of emotion constructs from March – June 2020

The top left of Fig. 4 displays the means and confidence intervals emotion constructs reflected in audio entries by month. From March to May-June 2020, the means move left to right, indicating a shift from Grateful to Sadness. Along the X axis (SVD1), a Mann-Whitney test showed that March 2020 (Mdn = −0.25, N = 10) was statistically significantly different at the alpha = 0.05 level from May-June 2020 (Mdn = 0.23, N = 12 U = 94.00, p = 0.03, r = −0.57).

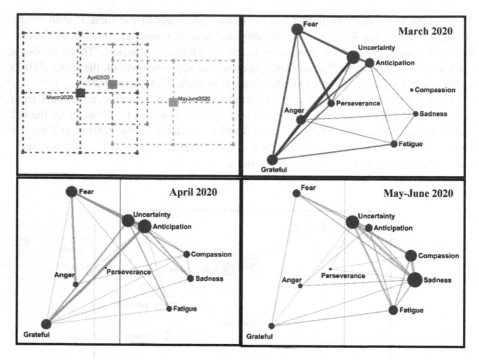

Fig. 4. Group means and confidence intervals for emotion constructs by month (top, left) and ENA models of emotion constructs for March, April, and May-June 2020 (top, right and bottom)

The top right and bottom of Fig. 4 displays the individual network models of emotion constructs for March, April and May-June 2020. In March 2020, the strongest connections are on the left half of the model, among Uncertainty and Fear, Anger, Grateful and Anticipation, and Fear and Grateful. For April 2020, the thickest edges are between Grateful and Anticipation, Uncertainty and Fear, and Uncertainty and Anticipation. In May-June 2020, the network model displays prominent connections on the right side between Uncertainty and Compassion, Sadness, and Fatigue, as well as between Compassion and Sadness. Overall, there is a shift from left (Grateful, Fear, Uncertainty) to right (Compassion, Sadness, Uncertainty) from March to May-June 2020.

3.2   Heat Maps

Including both emotion and professional/personal constructs in the same ENA model became challenging to identify connections between emotion and professional/personal constructs, since both emotion to emotion and professional/personal to professional/personal connections seen in Figs. 1, 2, 3 and 4 would be in the same model. To focus on the relationships between emotion and professional/personal constructs and complement the ENA models of emotion to emotion and professional/personal to professional/personal constructs examined above, heat maps were used to visualize the frequency of emotions reflected in conjunction to professional/personal constructs in any given utterance. Using a gradient, lighter shades of blue indicate lower frequencies of the emotion in relation to the construct and darker shades of blue indicate higher frequencies. Figure 5 depicts a heat map of emotions connected to professional/personal constructs from March – June 2020. Overall, the highest co-occurrences are Uncertainty with Medical Treatment, Anger and Fear with Policies, and Fear with Resource Availability.

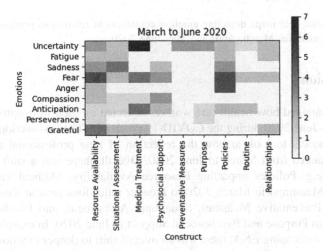

Fig. 5. Heat map depicting emotion constructs in relation to professional/personal constructs from March – June 2020.

Figure 6 shows individual heat maps of emotion constructs related to professional and personal constructs by month. For March 2020, the highest frequency is Anger with Policies, followed by Fear with Resource Availability. In April 2020, this shifts to Uncertainty with Medical Treatment, followed by Anticipation with Medical Treatment and Grateful with Resource Availability, though the overarching emotion across several constructs was Fear. In May-June 2020, the highest occurrence is Uncertainty with Purpose, followed by growing Sadness across various constructs including Policies, Resource Availability, and Situational Assessment, Fatigue with Resource Availability, and Compassion with Psychosocial Support.

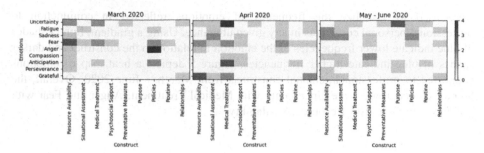

Fig. 6. Individual heat maps depicting emotion constructs in relation to professional/personal constructs by month for March, April and May-June 2020.

4 Discussion

This study examined how health care workers reflected on their in-hospital experience from March – June 2020 during the COVID-19 pandemic. The first section of the study used ENA models to look at how the reflection of nine professional and personal constructs changed from March to June 2020. Overall, there was a shift from immediate needs (e.g. Policies impacting Resource Availability, Medical Treatment and Preventative Measures) in March 2020 to broader reflections around Resource Availability (with Preventative Measures, Situational Assessment, and Psychosocial Support), as well as Purpose and Psychosocial Support in June 2020. In examining the nine emotion constructs using ENA, there was an overall shift to deeper emotional reflection from March to June as Fear, Uncertainty, Anger and Grateful shifted to more complex emotions involving Sadness and Compassion. Combining both emotion and professional/personal constructs in the same ENA model made identifying the relationship between them difficult, since connections of both emotion to emotion and professional/personal to professional/personal constructs were also present. To address this challenge, the use of heat maps helped to visualize the connections between the professional/personal constructs and emotion constructs. In March, most prevalent was Anger with Policies and Fear with Resource Availability, which shifted in May-June 2020 to Uncertainty with Purpose, growing Sadness with the overall situation (with Policies, Resource Availability, Situational Assessment), and Fatigue with Resource Availability, and Compassion with Psychosocial Support. Such trends reinforced and complemented what was seen in the ENA models of professional/personal and emotion constructs.

As the pandemic became an abrupt concern in March 2020, health care workers focused on the impact of policies, indicative of the initial shock the pandemic had on many workers and created an unexpected impact in hospitals around the country. Shortages in supplies and equipment such as PPE, masks, ventilators, and hospital beds were sudden. Policies such as who could get tested and when to wear protective gear affected health care workers' daily life and became a prime concern, as such decisions had possible consequences on the safety of both healthcare workers and their patients.

With this sudden impact of the pandemic in hospital settings, direct emotions such as fear, anger and uncertainty were evident, notably in connection to such policies:

We have very limited testing. I've already seen a couple of positive cases, but we're only allowed to test patients who will definitely be admitted, which is a nightmare because people should know when they're going home, and we're sending people home on the subway who probably have COVID and we can't confirm whether or not they do.

Moving into April 2020, reflections on professional/personal constructs were less related to policies and shifted more to Psychosocial Support, along with Medical Treatment and Resource Availability. As the number of people hospitalized with COVID-19 increased, health care workers found themselves becoming the stand-in for family members who were not allowed to physically be present with their loved ones in the hospital while undergoing medical treatment. As prominently noted in the April ENA model but less visible in the April heat map, descriptions of Psychosocial Support were usually conveyed with professional instead of emotion constructs, and was a noticeable part of the health care worker experience:

I just found a screenshot on my phone…it's from a moment when I was in a FaceTime conversation with the daughter of a patient whose father was intubated in our makeshift COVID ICU this past week. This image of this young daughter in her 20s and father in his, maybe, 50s, who seemed like a friendly guy, despite being critically ill with a breathing tube and feeding tube and all the bands to secure those things wrapped around the middle of his face. Well, I just needed to capture this in words because I know I need to delete this image…it's this moment that I have seen so many times in the last week.

While emotions during this time continued to include Uncertainty with some positive feelings including Anticipation and Grateful, Fear continued to be a prevalent emotion during this time period, especially across many constructs, such as Medical Treatment:

They do not behave the way patients in acute respiratory failure behave, they are so labile and so unpredictable and so different than any other patient I have ever seen in my almost 20 years of ICU experience. And I can't even begin to wrap my mind around it. Medicine, as I know it right now, is not working for these patients and that terrifies me, because I just feel like we're treading water and I don't know how to get them out of it. And I feel like we're still not gaining any ground. I'm in a loss and I'm scared and I don't know what the next six weeks are going to look like.

In May – June 2020, there is a shift to professional/personal constructs related to Situational Assessment, Purpose, and Preventative Measures. In these months, the professionals had more time to internalize and process the gravity of the COVID-19 impact in the healthcare field. For example, healthcare professionals made more Situational Assessment utterances, as the reflecting on surges in case counts earlier in the pandemic and considering their purpose as healthcare workers:

I was there during the surge of COVID in New York City when we totally overflowed not just our medical ICU, but the entire ICU floor, and had to set up satellite ICUs in other parts of the hospital that weren't meant to be ICUs. And that was its own kind of chaos and intensity… when COVID began, I was all in there. It felt kind of exciting and I felt purposeful.

This deeper internalization was also indicated in emotion constructs to reflect more connections to Compassion and Sadness in May-June 2020, a shift away from the emotions of the Anger and Grateful from March. Health care professionals were relating more to the ongoing circumstances, expressing more compassion and grief for others as losing loved ones continued.

> *Now that feels like it's all over and I honestly feel very alone. And it's hard for me to say exactly why that is. What we saw and experienced was just so unlike anything I'd ever seen and just the horror and tragedy of it. I'm feeling an intense need for mourning and memorial...over one hundred thousand people died in this country alone. This isn't the ending at all. We need space for mourning and memorial to honor those we have lost and the pain of bearing witness.*

This paper provided insights around the complex reflections conveyed by health care workers in audio diaries regarding their in-hospital experiences during the onset of COVID-19. While examining the transcripts of the diary entries provided tangible results about the health care worker experience, it does not fully account for the richness of expression captured in the audio itself. A future analysis could benefit in examining more than what was said, but how it was said, and accounting for the vocal inflections in the audio. As diary entries were recorded at the time of intense in-hospital experiences, such raw emotion could not be adequately accounted for in a text-based analysis.

The decision to examine trends among the professional/personal constructs separate from the emotion constructs was important to analyzing all aspects conveying the story of how health care workers reflected, as emotions were not always conveyed with professional and personal constructs. Separating the analysis helped to uncover what were the topics and then emotions reflected by health care workers during this time period. Combining both emotion and professional/personal constructs in the same ENA space became crowded and difficult to identify the relationship between emotions and professional/personal constructs. Heat maps were used further helped to illustrate how emotions were conveyed in relation to professional and personal constructs, capturing whenever they were expressed as such. While the heat maps would benefit from more data points, it serves as an initial example of how heat maps could potentially compliment ENA model visualizations. Overall, these study results both document the unique vantage point of health care workers during a historic global pandemic and bring awareness and insights to better support the mental well-being of health care workers in the future.

References

1. dos Santos Alencar, M.A., de Magalhães Netto, J.F., de Morais, F.: A sentiment analysis framework for virtual learning environment. Appl. Artif. Intell. **35**(7), 520–536 (2021)
2. Silver Spring: Survey: Nurses Fear Going to Work Due to Lack of Protection from Virus More than 32k Nurses Share Experience from the Front Lines. American Nurses Association (2020). https://www.nursingworld.org/news/news-releases/2020/survey-nurses-fear-going-to-work-due-to-lack-of-protection-from-virus-more-than-32k-nurses-share-experience-from-the-front-lines
3. Bavel, J.J.V., et al.: Using social and behavioural science to support COVID-19 pandemic response. Nat. Hum. Behav. **4**, 460–471 (2020). https://doi.org/10.1038/s41562-020-0884-z

4. El-Masri, M., Roux, G.: Can COVID-19 mark the rediscovery of nursing. Can. J. Nurs. Res. **52**(3), 174–175 (2020)
5. Freer, J.: Selfless sacrifice or failed by the state? Remembering nurses who have died from covid-19. Int. J. Nurs. Stud. **113**, 103736 (2021). https://doi.org/10.1016/j.ijnurstu.2020.103736
6. Guo, H., Zhang, W., Ni, C., Cai, Z., Chen, S., Huang, X.: Heat map visualization for electrocardiogram data analysis. BMC Cardiovasc. Disord. **20**(277) (2020). https://doi.org/10.1186/s12872-020-01560-8
7. Herrenkohl, L.R., Cornelius, L.: Investigating elementary students' scientific and historical argumentation. J. Learn. Sci. **22**(3), 413–461 (2013). https://doi.org/10.1080/10508406.2013.799475
8. Juvet, T.M., et al.: Adapting to the unexpected: Problematic work situations and resilience strategies in healthcare institutions during the COVID-19 pandemic's first wave. Safety Sci. **139**, 105277 (2021). https://doi.org/10.1016/j.ssci.2021.105277
9. Khalid, I., Khalid, T.J., Qabajah, M.R., Barnard, A.G., Qushmaq, I.A.: Healthcare workers emotions, perceived stressors and coping strategies during a MERS-Cov outbreak. Clin. Med. Res. **14**(1), 7–14 (2016). https://doi.org/10.3121/cmr.2016.1303
10. Kulahcioglu, T., de Melo, G.: Semantics-aware typographical choices via affective associations. Lang. Resour. Eval. **55**(1), 105–126 (2020). https://doi.org/10.1007/s10579-020-09499-0
11. Miller-Lewis, L.R., Lewis, T.W., Tieman, J., Rawlings, D., Parker, D., Sanderson, C.R.: Words describing feelings about death: a comparison of sentiment for self and others and changes over time. PLoS ONE **16**(1), e0242848 (2021). https://doi.org/10.1371/journal.pone.0242848
12. Pask, E.J.: Self-sacrifice, self-transcendence and nurses' professional self. Nurs. Philos. **6**(4), 247–254 (2005). https://doi.org/10.1111/j.1466-769x.2005.00215.x
13. Plutchik, R.: A general psychoevolutionary theory of emotion. In: Theories of Emotion, pp. 3–33 (1980). https://doi.org/10.1016/b978-0-12-558701-3.50007-7
14. Ruchlewska, A., et al.: Effect of crisis plans on admissions and emergency visits: a randomized controlled trial. PLoS ONE **9**(3), e91882 (2014). https://doi.org/10.1371/journal.pone.0091882
15. Sacco, T.L., Ciurzynski, S.M., Harvey, M.E., Ingersoll, G.L.: Compassion satisfaction and compassion fatigue among critical care nurses. Crit. Care Nurse **35**(4), 32–42 (2015). https://doi.org/10.4037/ccn2015392
16. Shaffer, D.W.: Quantitative Ethnography. Cathcart Press, Madison (2017)
17. Sun, K., et al.: Transmission heterogeneities, kinetics, and controllability of SARS-Cov-2. Science **371**(6526) (2020). https://doi.org/10.1126/science.abe2424
18. Vasli, P., Dehghan-Nayeri, N.: Emergency nurses' experience of crisis: a qualitative study. Jpn. J. Nurs. Sci. **13**(1), 55–64 (2016). https://doi.org/10.1111/jjns.12086
19. Yin, X., Zeng, L.: A study on the psychological needs of nurses caring for patients with coronavirus disease 2019 from the perspective of the existence, relatedness, and growth theory. Int. J. Nurs. Sci. **7**(2), 157–160 (2020). https://doi.org/10.1016/j.ijnss.2020.04.002
20. Zeng, X., Chen, Q., Chen, S., Zuo, J.: Emotion label enhancement via emotion wheel and lexicon. Math. Probl. Eng. **2021**, 1–11 (2021). https://doi.org/10.1155/2021/6695913
21. Zhang, Y., et al.: The psychological change process of frontline nurses caring for patients with COVID-19 during its outbreak. Issues Ment. Health Nurs. **41**(6), 525–530 (2020). https://doi.org/10.1080/01612840.2020.1752865

How Anxiety Affects Affect: A Quantitative Ethnographic Investigation Using Affect Detectors and Data-Targeted Interviews

J. M. Alexandra L. Andres[✉], Stephen Hutt, Jaclyn Ocumpaugh, Ryan S. Baker, Nidhi Nasiar, and Chelsea Porter

University of Pennsylvania, Philadelphia, PA 19104, USA
aandres@upenn.edu

Abstract. This study integrates the analysis of student interaction data with classroom interviews in order to better understand how students' trait-level anxiety relates to in-the-moment measures of students' affective experiences (i.e., boredom, confusion, delight, engaged concentration, and frustration). We first use quantitative data to drive the data collection, with the interviews being triggered by previously-developed models of student emotions, allowing us to focus interviews during times where specific emotional experiences of interest have just occurred. We then analyze the log data, finding differences in how students with high and low science anxiety manage their emotions (and subsequent behaviors). Finally, we connect these behaviors back to the strategies students articulate in the interviews, finding that many students with higher anxiety scores have an external locus of control, are less likely to seek evidence that they are wrong, and are more likely to make major changes to their solutions in response to their frustration.

1 Introduction

As technology advances, it is becoming possible to scale up the collection of rich, ethnographic data that was typically only available in small-scale studies. In education, qualitative methods such as student interviews can provide critical information about how students learn [1] and in turn, improve learning theory. However, interview methods are resource-intensive and suffer from the "one-shot" problem [2]. Out of context, students may not be able to provide accurate insight on their cognition in a specific key situation hours earlier [3]. Even if interviews are conducted during class, in real-time, in a class of 25 students working quietly, it can be challenging to identify relatively rare events of interest, especially if such events are short-lived. By taking a quantitative approach to directing student interviews we can collect qualitative data from fleeting, yet educationally relevant, experiences.

One such fleeting experience known to impact student education is in-the-moment affect. Educationally relevant affective states (e.g., boredom, confusion, delight, engaged concentration, and frustration [4]) have been shown to have both short and long-term impacts on student outcomes. Short-term impacts include effects on learning gains [5, 6], analytical reasoning [7], motivation [8], and self-efficacy [9] with

© Springer Nature Switzerland AG 2022
B. Wasson and S. Zörgő (Eds.): ICQE 2021, CCIS 1522, pp. 268–283, 2022.
https://doi.org/10.1007/978-3-030-93859-8_18

long-term impacts including college enrollment [10] and career trajectories [11–13]. However, less work has explored whether the learning outcomes predicted by these momentary affective experiences might also be modulated by more enduring affective experiences such as trait-level anxiety.

On their own, both state (in-the-moment) and trait-level anxiety have been shown to impact learning [14] as well as other types of affective experiences and emotion regulation [15]. There has been considerable attention to test anxiety in educational research [16], but work has also considered anxiety surrounding specific subjects or fields [17, 18], including science anxiety – the focus of this paper. Science anxiety is distinct from general anxiety [18]. It can be caused by an array of sources, including lack of role models, gender and racial stereotyping, and the stereotyping of scientists in the popular media. Students suffering from science anxiety are often calm and productive in their nonscience courses, including their mathematics courses, but experience anxiety symptoms in a science setting [19].

Given the context-specific and highly internal nature of anxiety and student regulation (both emotion and learning), these constructs lend themselves to study via interviews. Indeed, students (especially younger students) may find it challenging to articulate metacognitive strategies using traditional self-report instruments such as surveys [20]. This study employs a quantitative ethnography methodology that uses real-time affect detection [4, 5] to direct *in situ*, open-ended interviews where students were encouraged to talk about their learning experiences, strategies, and interests. These interviews are then analyzed to examine the interplay between student affect and anxiety. By leveraging real-time affect detection, we target interviews at key moments in the learning process, such as theoretically-aligned affect patterns (e.g., the inhibitory or facilitative cycles identified in [4]). Through this approach, we scale up qualitative data collection to whole classrooms at a time, generating a rich dataset of qualitative (interview) and quantitative (interaction and affect) data. We leverage this combination to explore how anxiety alters student motivation, self-efficacy, and interaction.

1.1 Quantitative Ethnography Research on Emotion

Quantitative Ethnography (QE) is a methodology that blends quantitative and qualitative methods to enable scalable qualitative analysis, using an integrated representation across qualitative and quantitative methods [22].Within education research, the combination of ethnographic and statistical tools supports a deeper examination of what learners do and why [22].

Although Epistemic Network Analysis is the most common method used for QE [23], the key quality of QE research is a "focus on validity and the linkages and consistency between quantitative models and qualitative analysis, both of which are sound on their own, and both of which are attending to the same mechanisms at work in the same set of data." [23, p.2]. Much of the existing work in QE has taken complex data, encoded it (by a human or automated system [24], and then analyzed it using a combination of qualitative and quantitative methods attending to the same themes (e. g. [25]). In this paper, we instead use quantitative analysis to drive the collection of complex, rich data. We then use further quantitative analysis both to understand the phenomena of interest and drive the selection of cases to study qualitatively. By doing so, we analyze our themes around anxiety and – as will be discussed below – frustration using a blend of quantitative and qualitative methods.

Our work studying emotion using QE joins an increasing scientific discourse demonstrating that QE can contribute to theoretical understanding of emotion in context. Martin et al. [26] present one of the first analyses of emotion within a QE framework. Their research used qualitative information (interviews and conversations) in tandem with codified changes in facial expression and body motion to identify moments in which students demonstrated changes in understanding. Their findings demonstrated how instances of joy coincided with periods of increased interaction with the learning platform and knowledge elaboration among participants. The framework adopted within the study displayed potential for the interlacing of human coders and computational techniques towards the development of whole-body analysis that would be capable of identifying proxies of learning in informal learning environments.

Espino et al. [27] also used QE to explore the range of emotions, their valence, and their antecedents during a transition to online learning. Student emotions were analyzed in relation to specific areas of change affected by a switch to online learning (e.g., workload, schedule, teacher interaction). Their findings revealed that in response to factors of focus, instructional format, and workload, anxiety was the most commonly experienced negative emotion. The quantitative results of their study are supplemented by excerpts of student responses that reflect upon their experiences with a new instructional format. This work indicates the key importance of anxiety within online learning and the potential of QE methods for research in this area.

1.2   Other Relevant Past Research on Anxiety

Characterized as a loosely coupled ensemble of cognitive, affective, somatic arousal, and behavioral components, anxiety is evoked in response to mental representations of future threats or danger [28, 29]. Anxiety remains an insufficiently studied emotion in education, primarily studied in terms of test anxiety [30] or anxiety about subject domains [31–33], rather than in terms of its immediate manifestations or impacts.

Recent research has shown that anxiety inhibits working memory [34] and can manifest as avoidance behaviors [35] and increased apprehension around learning [36]. These impacts can, in turn, impede optimum performance [37] and potentially limit future college and career choices [38]. In academic settings, the effects of subject anxiety are perhaps most studied in mathematics (see review in [39]) but have also been examined in other areas, including learning English as a foreign language [40] and science [9, 32, 41].

Prior research has demonstrated the value of quantitative data for understanding anxiety in educational settings. Studies have shown changes in learner experiences in response to anxiety in terms of physiological [42], motivational [41], self-regulated learning [43], and performance [29] components. However, quantitative analysis alone may not be enough to study a state as internal as student anxiety. In addition, quantitative analysis by itself cannot fully capture the experiences and personal justifications that influence student actions, calling for a more blended approach.

2 Methods

2.1 Betty's Brain and Affect Detection

Betty's Brain is an open-ended, computer-based learning environment that uses a learning-by-teaching paradigm to teach complex scientific processes [44]. Betty's Brain, shown in Fig. 1, asks students to teach a simulated virtual agent (Betty) about scientific phenomena (e.g., climate change, ecosystems, thermoregulation) by constructing concept maps that demonstrate the causal relationships involved. As students construct their concept map, they must navigate through multiple hypermedia information sources where they can read about a variety of concepts and their relations. They choose how often to test Betty's knowledge, and they may elect to interact with a virtual mentor agent (a simulated experienced teacher named Mr. Davis) if they are having trouble teaching Betty.

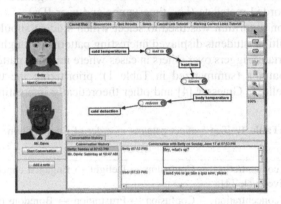

Fig. 1. Screenshot showing a partial concept map (right) being used to teach the student agent (Betty, top left), with help from the mentor-agent (Mr. Davis, bottom left).

Real-time affect detection was implemented using models that had been previously integrated into Betty's Brain [21]. Detectors had been trained on ground truth incidences of boredom (BOR), confusion (CON), engaged concentration (ENG), delight (DEL), and frustration (FRU) collected using the BROMP method for conducting quantitative field observations [45]. Each detector generated an affect prediction (a probability between 0 and 1) every 20 s based upon previous student interactions.

2.2 Dataset

The dataset was collected at an urban Tennessee middle school, from 99 sixth-graders who used Betty's Brain in their regular science class. This school's population is 60% White, 25% Black, 9% Asian, and 5% Hispanic, with 8% enrolled in the free/reduced lunch program. Individual demographics were not collected. The same students used Betty's Brain to complete two science inquiry scenarios conducted in December 2018 (study 1) and February 2019 (study 2). In study 1, students spent four daily sessions (approx. 50 min/day) using Betty's Brain to complete a causal map about climate change. In study 2, students spent three daily sessions modeling thermoregulation. During both studies, qualitative interviews were used to explore how students were working with the system during specific affective experiences. At the end of study 2, science anxiety surveys were administered alongside questions about students' perceptions of difficulty and familiarity with the topic and questions about Mr. Davis. Between the two studies, minor changes were made to Betty's Brain, including small changes to make Mr. Davis seem more polite. All other procedures were identical.

2.3   Student Interviews

A total of 594 interviews (358 from study 1 and 236 from study 2) were recorded during classroom observations. These interviews were triggered by an app called the Quick Red Fox (QRF; [43]), which used the automated detectors of student affect (see 2.1) to prompt individual interviews. Interviewers were signaled via QRF, which automatically recorded metadata (i.e., timestamps and user IDs).

A prioritization algorithm was used to select which student should be interviewed in cases when multiple students displayed interesting patterns at roughly the same time. We prioritized certain triggers over others in cases where multiple patterns were present in the detector outputs (summarized in Table 1), prioritizing the two affect cycles outlined by D'Mello & Graesser [4] and other theoretically interesting transitions.

Table 1. Top 5 affect patterns in order of prioritization.

Rank	Pattern
1	Engaged concentration → Confusion → Delight → Engaged concentration (Facilitative cycle [4])
2	Engaged concentration → Confusion → Frustration → Boredom (Inhibitory cycle [4])
3	Confusion → Delight
4	Confusion → Frustration
5	Frustration → Engaged concentration

This prioritization algorithm also helped to ensure that students were not repeatedly chosen for interviews in a short period of time. If interviewers were not comfortable interrupting a student for an interview, they could skip the prompt, and the system would suggest another student.

Interviewers sought a helpful but non-authoritative approach when speaking with students. They often asked students what their strategies were (if any) for getting through the system. As new patterns and information emerged, questions designed to elicit information about intrinsic interest (e.g., "What kinds of books do you like to read and why?" or "What do you want to be when you grow up?") were sometimes added to see whether or not students would mention science interest outside of their current environment. Overall, however, students were encouraged to speak about what they wanted and to provide feedback about their experience with the software.

Interviews were transcribed, preserving critical metadata such as timestamps and filenames (that contained additional date and time information) as well as information on the interviewer and student being interviewed. These transcriptions were then synchronized with other data streams (e.g., affect predictions and interactions logs) to provide additional context for analysis.

2.4 Anxiety Measure

A revised version of the Math Anxiety Scale (MAS; [46]) was used to collect students' science anxiety scores at the end of study 2. MAS was chosen as it is suitable for younger learners [47] and has been shown to have good test-retest reliability [48]. Recent research with this scale has shown good internal consistency, with Cronbach's α 0.87, calculated from the responses of 250 secondary school students [49].

Questions were adapted to ask students to reflect upon science topics instead of mathematics. The scale collects responses involving learners' general disposition about science beyond their interaction with the current learning environment. This scale contains ten items (five of which are reverse coded) that inquire about students' experiences and opinions on studying science. Items are rated on a 5-point Likert scale where higher scores indicate higher anxiety [46, 47]. Student anxiety scores are calculated by adding the values from each of these ten items. In this study, 95 students completed this survey, leading to the exclusion of four students. Anxiety scores ranged from 10 to 44 with a mean score of 22.35 (SD = 8.24), where 46 students had above-average anxiety (48.42%) and 49 below-average anxiety (51.58%).

3   Results

This study integrates quantitative and qualitative methods to understand how anxiety manifests when students interact with Betty's Brain. Specifically, we quantitatively examined how affect differs over time for anxious students, and how anxious students interacted with the system differently than other students. Then, a qualitative analysis of students' metacognitive awareness (as seen in student interviews) provided a richer, thicker description of the factors leading to quantitative differences between students with different anxiety levels.

3.1   Changes in Affect Over Time

We first consider the impact anxiety might have on affect over time, looking at how far into a learning session (class period) a student was. For each affect inference, we calculated how long it occurred after the student's first interaction that day. We then examined the affective changes and patterns that emerge in the students over the course of each session in relation to their anxiety scores.

Linear mixed-effect models (LMEM) were used to assess how student affect changes over time. These models consider fixed effects, random effects, and noise as linearly contributing to the dependent variable (e.g., affective states; [50]). In these models, anxiety scores and the amount of time since the start of each session were both treated as fixed effects and student IDs as random effects.

Table 2 summarizes the LMEM results across the two studies. In study 1, we observed a significant interaction between anxiety and time into the session when predicting frustration. Student anxiety had no effect on frustration levels early in the session, but later in the session, those levels diverged, and students with above-average levels of anxiety are significantly more likely to get frustrated than their lower-anxiety peers. This result was replicated in study 2, where students with higher anxiety were also significantly less likely to experience boredom, engaged concentration, and delight later in the session.

Table 2. Beta coefficients for LMEM predicting affect (N = 95, p < .05) in study 1 (S1) and study 2 (S2) (Boredom, Confusion, Frustration, Engagement, Delight). Significant (p < 0.05) coefficients shown in bold.

Predictors	Dependent variables (S1)					Dependent variables (S2)				
	BOR	CON	FRU	ENG	DEL	BOR	CON	FRU	ENG	DEL
(Intercept)	**−0.05**	**−0.05**	**0.01**	**−0.02**	**0.1**	**0.03**	0	**0.01**	**0.06**	**0.08**
Anxiety score	−0.01	−0.03	0.1	0.01	−0.04	0.01	0.04	0.1	0	0
Time Into session	**−0.28**	**0.35**	**0.43**	**0.02**	0.04	**−0.25**	**0.38**	**0.35**	**0.05**	**0.13**
Interaction (Anxiety* time Into session)	0	0	**0.03**	0	0.01	**−0.04**	0	**0.01**	**−0.05**	**−0.01**

MANOVA was conducted to examine the effects of anxiety on frustration across both studies. The results from this analysis revealed that anxiety was associated with differences in the range (F (1, 93) = 4.88, p < 0.01) and SD (F (1, 93) = 3.16, p = 0.01) of frustration predictions but not the means (F (1, 93) = 1.57, p = 0.21), suggesting that students with higher anxiety experience a greater variance of frustration feelings.

We also examined whether anxiety was associated with different patterns of affect across days (i.e., were high anxiety students more likely to feel frustrated on Day 3 of the study than Day 1?). Within this analysis, we averaged each student's affect predictions within each day, and used mixed-effect models to predict the proportion of an affective state by the interaction of anxiety (high/low) and day of the study, with student ID as a random effect, creating one model per affective state per study. For engaged concentration, anxiety showed a significant interaction with day of study (p = .04). A simple slopes analysis indicated that higher anxiety students were less likely to experience engaged concentration in later stages of the study. However, no effect of day of study was observed for frustration (p = .51) or any of the other momentary affective states investigated in this study.

3.2   Behavioral Differences Based on Affect

In order to further explore the relationship between frustration and anxiety, a second thread of analysis was conducted examining student actions following instances of frustration. We focused on what the students did immediately following an instance of frustration, and then further explored the correctness of those actions (where that analysis was appropriate).

We examined actions in the 20 s following an instance of frustration (defined as when frustration had the highest probability among the five affective states). This time interval was chosen to align with both the initial BROMP field observations [45] and the detectors, which generate new affect predictions every 20 s [21]. Some students never had a frustration prediction; thus, the filtered data set includes 69 students for study 1 (33 above-average anxiety and 36 below-average anxiety students) and 41 students for the second study (21 above-average anxiety and 20 below-average anxiety students).

We calculated the frequency of 38 types of student interactions (examples in Table 3) within Betty's Brain in each 20-s window, averaged this across students, and then mapped data to each student's pre-test score and anxiety score, including their label as an above-average or below-average anxiety learner. T-tests were performed in order to determine if there were differences in actions between the anxiety groups.

Table 3. Examples of types of student actions (S1 = Study 1; S2 = Study 2).

Action	Definition
Causal map Elements moved	The student moved (rearranged, but did not delete) a set of map elements (i.e., concepts and/or links) in the causal map; N = 2049 (S1), 1080 (S2)
Delete causal link	The student deleted a causal link between two labels on the causal map; N = 49 (S1), 73 (S2)
Delete entity	The student deleted a concept (and any links connected to it) from the causal map; N = 252 (S1), 76 (S2)
Quiz taken	The student gave the teachable agent a quiz, which tests the accuracy of the causal map; N = 94 (S1), 84 (S2)

Only study 2 showed significant differences between above-average and below-average anxiety learners. Students with higher anxiety had a higher tendency to move causal map elements ($t(20) = -2.18$, $p = .04$) and delete entities ($t(20) = -2.42$, $p = .02$) following predictions of frustration while students with below-average anxiety were more likely to delete causal links ($t(19) = 3.37$, $p < .001$) and take quizzes ($t(19) = 2.17$, $p = .04$) after frustration predictions. However, given the substantial number of potential behaviors examined here, after a Benjamini & Hochberg correction [51], only the finding around deletion of causal links remained statistically significant – the other findings must be treated as suggestive but inconclusive.

Further analysis was conducted to determine whether students who were deleting parts of their causal map were doing so in an effective or ineffective manner. Specifically, Mann-Whitney tests were used to determine whether there were meaningful differences in the proportion of effective and ineffective deletion actions between high versus low anxiety students. Deleting correct answers was treated as ineffective, and deleting incorrect answers was treated as effective.

These results reveal a marginally significant difference for the deletion of concept map entities (Delete Entity actions). High-anxiety students made fewer effective deletions of entities (the labels on the map) than low anxiety students (U = 12, z = −1.78, p = 0.07). However, no difference between groups was found for deletion behavior involving causal links (U = 17, z = −0.47, p = 0.63). The presence of a marginal difference between some deletion actions between groups suggests that less-anxious students may be making more systematic changes to their concept map than more-anxious students.

3.3   Interview Findings

We next turned to interview transcripts to consider any potential differences between high and low anxiety students. We analyzed all the interviews that were conducted within 80 s of a frustration prediction (a sub-sample of 28 interviews out of the original 594 conducted). The analysis focused on exploring the relationship between frustration and different anxiety levels from the experiences of students. The difference in behaviors between frustrated/more anxious students and frustrated/less anxious students also corresponded to differences in the interview data. This data for this analysis was drawn from 93 of the students in the original sample, as six students above did not have any interviews. Below, we discuss in detail several representative responses, drawn from 7 of these students. These responses provided particularly illustrative evidence around anxiety and frustration.

Within the analyses below, pseudonyms were assigned using http://random-name-generator.info/, which generates names based on the frequencies within all U.S. census data, ignoring local community or subgroup variation, and ignoring the actual gender or age of the student. Three students with higher anxiety are referred to pseudonymously as Rebecca, Elmer, and Mandy while four students with lower anxiety are given the pseudonyms of Stephanie, Dwight, Marty, and Nancy.

One core difference in behavior noted above was the difference in what more anxious and less anxious students delete when they become frustrated. Less anxious students deleted individual causal links when they were frustrated – focusing on the specific errors in their understanding. By contrast, more anxious students deleted concepts, clearing away significant parts of their map, a less productive behavior. Rebecca articulates this strategy in her interview, stating that

> I'm just getting really frustrated, I had to delete most of my web because I was getting really confused at it... When I did the quiz, I got 3 of them wrong and 3 of them that he didn't –they didn't know... And so, when I did that I was like, which one did I get wrong, even though I pressed on it, I tried changing the answer but I still got it wrong, so I'm just like, I need to start back over, because then that'll be the easiest for me.

Rebecca's comments indicate that she felt she could not iterate on her map when some incorrect answers were present and therefore thought it would be easiest to start from scratch. It is possible that her anxiety caused her to feel that she could not productively iterate her solution.

Another core difference in the quantitative results above was the tendency of less anxious students to take quizzes after becoming frustrated. For example, Stephanie, a less-anxious student, reports, "Like, I'm tryin' to – just tryna figure out what mistakes I could improve. So I can get a better grade on the other test," showing the interviewer her quiz result. Similarly, Dwight, another less-anxious student, notes:

> Um, so, I've given him a lot of tests, and the ones that he gets wrong, I'm just trying to go through and like...see where I can add something, or like, if it's wrong... And then that helps me, and I just did that and he got a higher grade, so it's been working.

Like the behavioral findings, these interviews reflect a greater willingness among lower-anxiety students to collect evidence on where and how they are wrong.

By contrast, students with higher science anxiety are apprehensive about quizzes. Not only do they not take as many quizzes (as documented in the behavioral findings); even when they do, they do not use them very productively. For example, Elmer, a more anxious student, focuses on taking quizzes where he will get a better score:

> Um, so, I realized that I hadn't taken an everything quiz, and I was like, well, of course I haven't, because I'm not getting anything good on the other quizzes, and then I took one, and I got one right, and the other ones are just getting everything wrong... So I've just been taking everything quizzes [about the whole concept map] instead of the separate quizzes [about individual parts of the map] because I've been getting better scores.

Jon, another more anxious student, reports a similar strategy: "Um, what I'm doing is just quizzing my guy. And...I'm quizzing him on the...bodily responses to cold. Because I think I'll do better than that one." Instead of using the quizzes to target improvements to their causal map, these students appear to be using the quizzes in areas they are confident in to calm the distress they are feeling about not having all of the answers.

More generally, the more anxious students seemed to interpret struggles with the material as communicating something more general about their competence. For example, during various interviews over the course of both studies, Mandy made general statements about science (e.g., "It's hard," or "science is hard...") or the specific topic she was studying in Betty's Brain (e.g., "I don't really get thermoregulation...").

Another difference that emerged within the interview data was differences in responses to the pedagogical agent, Mr. Davis. For example, when the interviewer asked Rebecca (a more anxious student) if Mr. Davis gave her anything useful, she responded,

> He said to just remember that we're goin – that when we're...doing this, we're learning and are going to get more smart...It made me feel even more frustrated. Because, like, I want, like, really useful information, not really motivation because I don't need the motivation, I get frustrated because I don't have the information.

Upon further prompting, Rebecca noted that Mr. Davis had given her information but that she had not found it useful:

> He told me to go to the [virtual textbook] if I'm having any trouble... I went there but I don't really understand it... it says, "plants increase oxygen." It doesn't really tell how it increases the oxygen. It doesn't really tell how you use it or anything. It's not really being specific.

Elmer, another more anxious student, commented that "He's had one thing that he said that was useful, but everything else has just been like, 'Hm, let's take a look at your progress.'" In other words, high-anxiety students seemed to be unable to process the help they were being given.

By contrast, several less anxious students seemed better able to work with the advice being provided by Mr. Davis. For example, Marty reported, "Well, I know, like, what to do if I don't understand, like, how to do something. Like I can ask Mr. Davis if I don't understand how." Similarly, Nancy told an interviewer,

> Um, he's been helpful, he's, um. What I really like is that he's not just recommending pages in the teacher's book, he's telling us where our stuff is wrong, more exact... What I really like is that he's not just recommending pages in the teacher's book, he's telling us where our stuff is wrong, more exact.

Dwight, another less anxious student, also stated "he told me where I should look for something and then that helped. It was pretty helpful."

In general, the findings in these interviews demonstrate a pattern where students with higher anxiety appear to be less able to regulate their learning process, perhaps because they see it as something they are unable to fully control. This may cause them to either overlook or deliberately skip activities that might be essential for their learning, possibly because they do not recognize the opportunities provided to them.

4 Discussion

This study employs a quantitative ethnographic approach, including the analysis of students' metacognitive strategies (articulated in ethnographic interviews) to better understand how student anxiety influences behaviors in computer-based learning. We do this by examining multiple aspects of learner experiences involving both state-level and trait-level anxiety. By using real-time affect detection to identify critical points in the learning process, we guided qualitative data collection to explore how anxiety alters student motivation, self-efficacy, and interaction. In this work, we analyze two studies where students used Betty's Brain to construct causal maps of complex scientific phenomena in middle school science classes, comparing students who score above and below the cohort's average on a science anxiety scale.

Across both studies, the findings show that trait-level anxiety measures help quantitatively differentiate state-level affective experiences, which influences both students' behaviors and their metacognitive descriptions of their strategies. Specifically, students with higher trait-level science anxiety are more likely to experience frustration, but only in the second half of a daily one-hour session. At the beginning of the day, both more- and less-anxious students are equally likely to be frustrated; as the day goes on, frustration is more likely for high anxiety students than low-anxiety students.

Interestingly, while only frustration showed temporal divergence in the first study, two other states showed divergence in the second study. Specifically, higher-anxiety students were less likely to experience engaged concentration and delight in the second half of each learning session. This complements the finding that they also experienced higher levels of frustration during this time period. These changes are potentially driven by anxious fixation on challenges where students' engagement is impeded by increased focus on the source of frustration [52]; anxiety may also impede experiences of delight when students are unable to achieve their own standards of success [53].

Analysis of student interviews that followed instances of frustration provided additional insights into students' experiences. Excerpts from student interviews ground the quantitative data by providing in-depth information pertaining to participants' experiences and viewpoints on their use of Betty's Brain. From this we are better able to contextualize codified affect and behavior in elaborated narratives [54].

Previous research has demonstrated that anxiety may manifest in a variety of ways during learning, such as speeding through problems [35] and disengagement from activities [55]. We found that higher anxiety learners were more likely to make inefficient changes as a result of their deletions and edits, indicative of uncertainty that can lead to concern with unimportant details and inability to understand knowledge content [56]. We posit that the behavioral differences may only emerge within the second study due to the effect of the novelty of the interactive platform in study 1, which wore off in study 2, resulting in more pronounced engagement effects [57].

4.1 Limitations and Future Work

One potential limitation of this work is the different timescales of crucial measurements. While we measured trait-level anxiety via a survey, we considered state-level affect with predictions being generated every 20 s. Future work should examine anxiety at a similar time scale to affect, though this would require a state-level anxiety measure. Anxiety is generally not included in classroom observation affect protocols [45], as it is harder to measure in this fashion, so additional effort will be needed to collect the training data needed to develop an automated detector of anxiety.

If state-level anxiety could be automatically measured, this would also open up possibilities for future qualitative work. Using the same targeted interview approach used in this paper, interviewers could be directed to students at moments of peak anxiety. Such an approach could yield a rich qualitative dataset that could be used to better understand the interaction between anxiety, affect, and student learning, at a finer grain size, contributing both to affect and learning theory [58].

4.2 Conclusion

This study used interaction data, affect measurements, and qualitative data from targeted student interviews, to study how trait-level anxiety relates to affect and behavior during a complex learning activity. Our results provide insight into the relationship between anxiety and emotion, most notably frustration, during learning experiences.

More-anxious students were more likely to be frustrated and less likely to be engaged and delighted later in the sessions. Students with higher levels of anxiety had a higher tendency to delete entire sections of their work when frustrated, while frustrated students with lower anxiety were more likely to delete individual elements and take quizzes to better understand the quality of their solutions. This work takes a step towards better understanding anxiety in an ecologically valid setting, and brings us closer to better supporting high anxiety students using learning technology in the classroom.

References

1. Schofield, J.W.: Computers and Classroom Culture. Cambridge University Press (1995)
2. Wessel, D.: The potential of computer-assisted direct observation apps. Int. J. Interact. Mob. Technol. (iJIM) **9**(1), 31 (2015)
3. Stetler, C.B., Caramanica, L.: Evaluation of an evidence-based practice initia-tive: outcomes, strengths and limitations of a retrospec-tive, conceptually-based approach. Worldviews Evid.-Based Nurs. **4**, 187–199 (2007)
4. D'Mello, S.K., Graesser, A.: Dynamics of affective states during complex learning. Learn. Instr. **22**, 145–157 (2012). https://doi.org/10.1016/j.learninstruc.2011.10.001
5. DeFalco, J.A., et al.: Detecting and addressing frustration in a serious game for military training. Int. J. Artif. Intell. Educ. **28**(2), 152–193 (2017). https://doi.org/10.1007/s40593-017-0152-1
6. D'Mello, S.K., Olney, A., Person, N.: Mining collaborative patterns in tutorial dialogues. J. Educ. Data Min. **2**(1), 1–37 (2010)
7. D'Mello, S.K., Person, N.K., Lehman, B.: Antecedent-Consequent Relationships and Cyclical Patterns between Affective States and Problem Solving Outcomes. In: Artificial Intelligence in Education, pp. 57–64 (2009)
8. Rodrigo, M.M.T., Anglo, E.A., Sugay, J.O., Baker, Rsj.: Use of unsupervised clustering to characterize learner behaviors and affective states while using an intelligent tutoring system. In: International Conference on Computers in Education, pp. 57–64 (2008)
9. McQuiggan, S.W., Robison, J.L., Lester, J.C.: Affective transitions in narrative-centered learning environments. J. Educ. Technol. Soc. **13**, 40–53 (2010)
10. Maria Ofelia, Z., Pedro, S., Baker, R.S., Heffernan, N.T.: An integrated look at middle school engagement and learning in digital environments as precursors to college attendance. Technol. Knowl. Learn. **22**(3), 243–270 (2017)
11. San Pedro, M.O., Ocumpaugh, J., Baker, R.S., Heffernan, N.T.: Predicting STEM and non-STEM College major enrollment from middle school interaction with mathematics educational software. In: Educational Data Mining, pp. 276–279 (2014)
12. San Pedro, M.O.Z., Baker, R.S., Heffernan, N.T., Ocumpaugh, J.L.: Exploring college major choice and middle school student behavior, affect and learning: what happens to students who game the system? In: Proceedings of the Fifth International Conference on Learning Analytics And Knowledge, pp. 36–40 (2015)
13. Almeda, M.V., Baker, R.S.: Predicting student participation in STEM careers: the role of affect and engagement during middle school. J. Educ. Data Min. **12**, 33–47 (2020)
14. Byron, K., Khazanchi, S.: A meta-analytic investigation of the relationship of state and trait anxiety to performance on figural and verbal creative tasks. Personal. Soc. Psychol. Bull. **37**, 269–283 (2011)

15. Cisler, J.M., Olatunji, B.O., Feldner, M.T., Forsyth, J.P.: Emotion regulation and the anxiety disorders: an integrative review. J. Psychopathol. Behav. Assess. **32**, 68–82 (2010)
16. Zeidner, M.: Test anxiety in educational contexts. concepts, findings, and future directions. In: Emotion in Education (2007)
17. Tobias, S.: Math anxiety: an update. NACADA J. **10**(1), 47–50 (1990). https://doi.org/10. 12930/0271-9517-10.1.47
18. Mallow, J.V., McDermott, L.C.: Science anxiety: fear of science and how to overcome it. Am. J. Phys. (1988). https://doi.org/10.1119/1.15495
19. Udo, M.K., Ramsey, G.P., Mallow, J.V.: Science anxiety and gender in students taking general education science courses. J. Sci. Educ. Technol. (2004). https://doi.org/10.1007/ s10956-004-1465-z
20. Schooler, J.W., Ohlsson, S., Brooks, K.: Thoughts beyond words: when language overshadows insight. J. Exp. Psychol. Gen. **122**, 166 (1993)
21. Jiang, Y., et al.: Expert feature-engineering vs. deep neural networks: which is better for sensor-free affect detection? In: Artificial Intelligence in Education, pp. 198–211 (2018)
22. Shaffer, D.W.: Quantitative Ethnography. Cathcart Press, Madison (2017)
23. Kaliisa, R., Misiejuk, K., Irgens, G.A., Misfeldt, M.: Scoping the emerging field of quantitative ethnography: opportunities, challenges and future directions. In: Ruis, A.R., Lee, S.B. (eds.) ICQE 2021. CCIS, vol. 1312, pp. 3–17. Springer, Cham (2021). https://doi. org/10.1007/978-3-030-67788-6_1
24. Cai, Z., Siebert-Evenstone, A., Eagan, B., Shaffer, D.W., Hu, X., Graesser, A.C.: nCoder+: a semantic tool for improving recall of nCoder coding. In: International Conference on Quantitative Ethnography, pp. 41–54 (2019)
25. Nguyen, H., et al.: Establishing trustworthiness through algorithmic approaches to qualitative research. In: Ruis, A.R., Lee, S.B. (eds.) ICQE 2021. CCIS, vol. 1312, pp. 47–61. Springer, Cham (2021). https://doi.org/10.1007/978-3-030-67788-6_4
26. Martin, K., Wang, E.Q., Bain, C., Worsley, M.: Computationally augmented ethnography: emotion tracking and learning in museum games. In: Eagan, B., Misfeldt, M., Siebert-Evenstone, A. (eds.) ICQE 2019. CCIS, vol. 1112, pp. 141–153. Springer, Cham (2019). https://doi.org/10.1007/978-3-030-33232-7_12
27. Espino, D.P., Wright, T., Brown, V.M., Mbasu, Z., Sweeney, M., Lee, S.B.: Student emotions in the shift to online learning during the COVID-19 pandemic. In: Ruis, A.R., Lee, S.B. (eds.) ICQE 2021. CCIS, vol. 1312, pp. 334–347. Springer, Cham (2021). https://doi. org/10.1007/978-3-030-67788-6_23
28. American Psychological Association (APA): Diagnostic and Statistical Manual of Mental Disorders: Depressive Disorders (2013)
29. Zeidner, M.: Anxiety in education. In: Pekrun, R., Linnenbrink-Garcia, L. (eds.), International Handbook of Emotions in Education, pp. 265–288. Routledge, Milton Park (2014)
30. von der Embse, N., Jester, D., Roy, D., Post, J.: Test anxiety effects, predictors, and correlates: a 30-year meta-analytic review. J. Affect. Disord. **227**, 483–493 (2018)
31. Horwitz, E.K.: Language anxiety and achievement. Annu. Rev. Appl. Linguist. **21**, 112–126 (2001)
32. Mallow, J.V: Science anxiety: research and action. Handb. Coll. Sci. Teach. 3–14 (2006)
33. Foley, A.E., Herts, J.B., Borgonovi, F., Guerriero, S., Levine, S.C., Beilock, S.L.: The math anxiety-performance link: a global phenomenon. Curr. Dir. Psychol. Sci. **26**, 52–58 (2017)
34. Ashcraft, M.H., Kirk, E.P.: The relationships among working memory, math anxiety, and performance. J. Exp. Psychol. Gen. (2001). https://doi.org/10.1037//0096-3445.130.2.224
35. Ashcraft, M.H.: Math anxiety: personal, educational, and cognitive consequences. Curr. Dir. Psychol. Sci. **11**, 181–185 (2002)

36. Plake, B.S., Parker, C.S.: The development and validation of a revised version of the mathematics anxiety rating scale. Educ. Psychol. Meas. **42**, 551–557 (1982)
37. Hong, Z.-R.: Effects of a collaborative science intervention on high achieving students' learning anxiety and attitudes toward science. Int. J. Sci. Educ. **32**, 1971–1988 (2010)
38. Ashcraft, M.H., Krause, J.A.: Working memory, math performance, and math anxiety. Psychon. Bull. Rev. **14**, 243–248 (2007)
39. Suárez-Pellicioni, M., Núñez-Peña, M.I., Colomé, À.: Math anxiety: a review of its cognitive consequences, psychophysiological correlates, and brain bases. Cogn. Affect. Behav. Neurosci. **16**(1), 3–22 (2015). https://doi.org/10.3758/s13415-015-0370-7
40. Na, Z.: A study of high school students' english learning anxiety. Asian EFL J. **9**, 22–34 (2007)
41. González, A., Fernández, M.V.C., Paoloni, P.V.: Hope and anxiety in physics class: exploring their motivational antecedents and influence on metacognition and performance. J. Res. Sci. Teach. (2017). https://doi.org/10.1002/tea.21377
42. Clarke, S., Horeczko, T., Cotton, D., Bair, A.: Heart rate, anxiety and performance of residents during a simulated critical clinical encounter: a pilot study. BMC Med. Educ. **14**, 1–8 (2014)
43. Hutt, S., et al.: Who's stopping you? – Using microanalysis to explore the impact of science anxiety on self-regulated learning operations. In: Proceedings of the 43rd Annual Conference of the Cognitive Science Society (2021)
44. Biswas, G., Leelawong, K., Belynne, K., Schwartz, D., Davis, J.: Incorporating self regulated learning techniques into learning by teaching environments. In: The Twenty Sixth Annual Meeting of the Cognitive Science Society (2004)
45. Ocumpaugh, J., Baker, R.S., Rodrigo, M.M.T.: Baker Rodrigo Ocumpaugh monitoring protocol (BROMP) 2.0 technical and training manual (2015)
46. Betz, N.E.: Prevalence, distribution, and correlates of math anxiety in college students. J. Couns. Psychol. (1978). https://doi.org/10.1037/0022-0167.25.5.441
47. Johnston-Wilder, S., Brindley, J., Dent, P.: A survey of Mathematics Anxiety and Mathematical Resilience among existing apprentices (2014)
48. Pajares, F., Urdan, T.: Exploratory factor analysis of the mathematics anxiety scale. Meas. Eval. Couns. Dev. **29**(1), 35–47 (1996)
49. Mahmood, S., Khatoon, T.: Development and validation of the mathematics anxiety scale for secondary and senior secondary school students. Br. J. Arts Soc. Sci. **2**, 169–179 (2011)
50. Barr, D.J., Levy, R., Scheepers, C., Tily, H.J.: Random effects structure for confirmatory hypothesis testing: keep it maximal. J. Mem. Lang. **68**, 255–278 (2013)
51. Benjamini, Y., Hochberg, Y.: Controlling the false discovery rate: a practical and powerful approach to multiple controlling the false discovery rate: a practical and powerful approach to multiple testing. J. R. Stat. Soc. **57**, 289–300 (1995). https://doi.org/10.2307/2346101
52. McQuiggan, S.W., Lee, S., Lester, J.C.: Early prediction of student frustration. In: International Conference on Affective Computing and Intelligent Interaction pp. 698–709 (2007)
53. Pekrun, R.: The control-value theory of achievement emotions: assumptions, corollaries, and implications for educational research and practice. Educ. Psychol. Rev. **18**, 315–341 (2006). https://doi.org/10.1007/s10648-006-9029-9
54. Turner, D.W., III.: Qualitative interview design: a practical guide for novice investigators. Qual. Rep. **15**, 754 (2010)
55. Kirsch, M., Windmann, S.: The role of anxiety in decision-making. Rev. Psychol. **16**, 19–28 (2009)
56. Rosenfeld, R.A.: Anxiety and learning. Teach. Soc. **5**(2), 151–166 (1978)

57. Tsay, C.H.-H., Kofinas, A.K., Trivedi, S.K., Yang, Y.: Overcoming the novelty effect in online gamified learning systems: an empirical evaluation of student engagement and performance. J. Comput. Assist. Learn. **36**, 128–146 (2020)
58. Willis, M., Cromby, J.: Bodies, representations, situations, practices: qualitative research on affect, emotion and feeling (2020)

Comparing Parent and Physician Perspectives on the Transition to Palliative Care in Pediatric Oncology

Judit Nyirő[1]([✉]) [iD], Enikő Földesi[1] [iD], Péter Hauser[2] [iD],
Katalin Hegedűs[1] [iD], and Szilvia Zörgő[1] [iD]

[1] Institute of Behavioral Sciences, Semmelweis University, Budapest, Hungary
judith.nyiroe@med.uni-muenchen.de
[2] Velkey László Child's Health Center, Borsod-Abaúj-Zemplén County Central
Hospital and University Teaching Hospital HU, Miskolc, Hungary

Abstract. One of the emerging challenges in pediatric oncology is how to make the transition to palliative care more effective and meet the needs of the affected families. To do so, what "good communication" signifies for the different stakeholders needs to be explored. The aim of our project was to compare the perspectives of pediatric oncologists and bereaved parents regarding the transition to palliative care and identify key differences in their communication preferences. Our data consisted of semi-structured interviews; after coding and segmentation, the data was modeled using Epistemic Network Analysis (ENA). Our results indicate that while parents in our cohort favored communication that is primary oncologist-led and preferred the physician's active involvement in pediatric palliative care (PPC), physicians prioritized multidisciplinary teamwork and did not see themselves as essential participants of PPC. Based on our findings, communication approaches contributing to a more efficient transition to palliative care include the distribution of communication tasks within the care team and the production of information material. These approaches may be relevant for both healthcare providers and families in countries with an oncologist-centered communication model and scarce availability of specialized PPC services.

Keywords: Epistemic Network Analysis · Pediatric oncology · Palliative care · Communication

1 Introduction

1.1 Theory

In pediatric oncology, difficult conversations occur throughout the treatment trajectory, from diagnostic disclosure to end-of-life care. Despite rapidly evolving treatment options and significant improvement in clinical outcomes, there are still cases where the disease cannot be cured, and the goals of care primarily shift to palliation. Pediatric palliative care (PPC) is defined as complex care provided by a multidisciplinary team, which aims to relieve the suffering of pediatric patients and their families living with life-limiting diseases [1]. There is no one-size-fits-all practice for integrating palliation

© Springer Nature Switzerland AG 2022
B. Wasson and S. Zörgő (Eds.): ICQE 2021, CCIS 1522, pp. 284–297, 2022.
https://doi.org/10.1007/978-3-030-93859-8_19

into oncology care, instead multiple models exist depending on location, availability of palliative subspecialty professional and disease prognosis [2]. Accordingly, the transition between curative and palliative care may be intermittent or abrupt and requires the effective cooperation of oncology providers and PPC specialists. Moreover, in both teams, the close cohesion of the given team's multidisciplinary professionals (e.g., physicians, nurses, pharmacists, psychologists, social workers) is needed to provide high-quality care in accordance with the principles of PPC guidelines [3].

This transition between the two forms of care also needs to be highlighted from a communication point of view, as many issues arise, and effective communication is a powerful tool a physician can utilize to advocate for the child's interests. Parents, as central stakeholders, have to make very difficult decisions in their children's place or together with them during this period. To alleviate this burden, discussions about PPC should be about more than just the physician giving information; it should be a continuous bidirectional conversation with the family, shared decision-making, and care-planning. Research shows that parents understanding and prioritizing PPC lead to less use of cancer-directed therapy and less suffering at the end of life [4]. Clinicians are often worried about causing additional distress by introducing PPC, however, it has been shown that good communication can also benefit the parents, relieve distress and uncertainty, even when delivering bad news [5].

To gain a better understanding of the parents' decision-making processes, more research has to be conducted about their needs, conceptions of PPC and communicational preferences. Literature comparing their attitudes with the physicians' perspective is scarce, thus it is still unclear what elements of verbal and non-verbal communication influence parental perceptions of PPC.

1.2 Background and Aims of Research

In Hungary pediatric oncology services are provided by the Hungarian Pediatric Oncology Network, which consists of seven centers across the country. Of the 250 children diagnosed yearly, 25% will require palliative care later on. Most PPC services are realized in the outpatient setting, in the form of home care. As Hungarian inpatient pediatric oncology centers are still lacking a sufficient amount of palliative care professionals, the implementation of PC in a hospital setting is solely under the discretion of the primary oncologist and the oncology team, which also involves psychologists and social workers at all centers.

Our research group investigated the timing and circumstances of the transition to PPC in Hungary first from the physicians', then from the bereaved parents' view [6, 7]. We explored the verbal and non-verbal communication aspects of this discussion in detail, including its participants and language use. Our qualitative preliminary analysis showed that in Hungary there is a very clearly distinguished border between active oncological care and the introduction of PPC. In our cohort, both parties equated PPC with end-of-life care and agreed on its introduction only after all curative treatment options were exhausted. This shift to palliation is in most cases marked by one single conversation which we dubbed the "palliative care discussion". Regarding this discussion, both parents and physicians require the attendance of multiple people in a so-called team setting, although preferences on whom this team should consist of differ.

Physicians mainly equated the multidisciplinary team with the presence of a psychologist, while parents articulated their need for family members' presence.

Our current project is a continuation of this previous research. There were some questions within our data that remained ambiguous, and we wanted to approach these from a different angle through a secondary analysis. Our aim is to gain a deeper understanding of the participants and the content of the palliative care discussion, its verbal and non-verbal properties, and specific word use in order to compare and contrast physician and parental opinions on this discussion and develop recommendations for medical communication strategies. Our research questions were as follows:

RQ1: What are the most essential components of the palliative care discussion from a physician and parental perspective, and what are the differences between the two groups?

RQ2: What advantages and disadvantages can physicians and parents identify regarding the psychologist's presence at the palliative care discussion and what are the differences between the two groups?

2 Data and Methods

2.1 Sampling and Data Collection

For our present initiative we utilized data from two of our previous projects involving active physicians (n = 20) of the Hungarian Pediatric Oncology Network and parents (n = 27) who had lost their child to a malignancy within the past 1–5 years and was previously treated at one of the centers of the Hungarian Pediatric Oncology Network.

We contacted all actively working physicians of the Hungarian Pediatric Oncology Network by e-mail and a subsequent telephone call and conducted interviews with every physician willing to participate. Parents were recruited via telephone by the child's lead oncologist and then contacted by a clinical psychologist, who later also conducted the interview. Based on the available statistics, we expected ca. 50 eligible families; we defined our stopping criteria as when all potential interviewees have been contacted at least once. All parents who accepted and fit our inclusion criteria were included into the study.

All physicians were interviewed individually; the structured interviews comprised of 13 questions and lasted 45 min on average, with a range of 15 and 110 min. In the case of parents, in 18 instances, one parent was present for the interview, in 3 instances, both parents were present; we conducted 23 semi-structured interviews in the parental group overall. Interviews were sound-recorded, transcribed verbatim, and anonymized. At the end of the interview, we administered a short questionnaire to record relevant demographic and clinical variables (these constituted attributes in our study).

Participants in both studies provided informed consent to participate anonymously. Approval was obtained from the Semmelweis University Regional and Institutional Committee of Science and Research Ethics, Reference Number: SE-TUKEB 96-1/2016.

2.2 Coding and Segmentation

We developed the code structure based on our previous study; each research question had a different set of codes. We used relevant codes from the previous study, which we wanted to examine with a secondary analysis, renamed them in some cases, but retained their definition. We employed several rounds of coding and triangulation before finalizing the code structure. Our final code structure has 3 clusters, 2 levels of abstraction, and a total of 37 codes at the lowest level. Table 1 shows a schematic version of the codebook containing the codes used for our present research questions.

Table 1. Codes used in RQ1 and RQ2 and their descriptions.

	PARENT CODE	CHILD CODE	DESCRIPTION
RQ1	CONTENT	Hope	Sustainment of parental hope; spirituality, eternity, miracle
		Did everything	Team decision; tried all curative treatments available incl. abroad; based on a protocol
		Support	Openly stating support to organize palliative care; parents will not be left alone, can call or visit the department anytime
		Child's interest	Value this period as a family, gain memories, quality time; the child won't suffer and will be pain-free
		Information	Information about the practical aspects of palliative care; physical symptoms at the end of life
		Trying	Not preventing the parents from trying out complementary or alternative cures or treatments abroad
	SENTIMENT	Positive	Essential/important/relevant
		Negative	Should be avoided
RQ2	FUNCTION	Consultation	Conversation with parents after the palliative care discussion
		Insight	Gains insight by being at the discussion
		Qualified	Sees things from a different perspective; more competent in handling mental health issues
		Witness	Serves as witness
		Plus one	Extra participant at the discussion
		Knows family	Knows the family well, followed their story
		Lead	Guide the family psychologically during palliation
		No role	Doesn't make a difference; focus is on the family and physician
	OPINION	Advantage	The function is advantageous for the family/physician/both
		Disadvantage	The function is disadvantageous for the family/physician/both

Coding and segmentation were carried out manually by one rater using the Interface for the Reproducible Open Coding Kit (iROCK). This interface allows researchers to upload their data in text files, upload their codes and segmentation, and code discourse by dragging and dropping codes and section breaks into the text. We considered the interview transcript as our highest unit of segmentation (source), but had mid-level segmentation as well, delimited by the data collection instrument (question and response, plus follow-ups). The smallest unit of segmentation (utterance) was one sentence, every utterance received a unique identifier; coding and segmentation were performed on this level. This process was iterative: the lead author employed each code cluster separately, thus creating three coded versions of every source.

2.3   Data Curation and Analysis

Subsequent to coding and segmentation, we used the Reproducible Open Coding Kit (ROCK) R package to merge the three versions of each source and aggregate information. We created a qualitative data table where every line consisted of an utterance, the collected demographic and clinical characteristics in categorical form (attributes), the segmentation, and the discourse coding in binary form. The unique utterance identifiers served as the foundation upon which all related data was aggregated.

Hermeneutic analysis was performed with de- and re-contextualization: we employed the ROCK to inspect coded fragments based on code. Codes in isolation were insufficient to interpret narratives, thus we used Epistemic Network Analysis (ENA) to model the structure of code co-occurrences within interviews. This process is described in more detail elsewhere [8, 9], but briefly: ENA constructs networks based on adjacency matrices that capture code connection counts for every unit of analysis. Within this matrix, columns correspond to code pairs, and rows to a point in high-dimensional space. ENA calculates this for each unit separately and represents it as a vector. Then, to account for varying narrative lengths, spherical normalization is performed, where each vector is divided by its own length. This results in a normalized vector capturing the relative frequencies of code co-occurrence and this also transforms connection strengths to fall between zero and one. ENA then performs dimensional reduction via singular value decomposition (SVD), resulting in networks with two, coordinated representations: 1) a projected point or "ENA score" (the location of a unit's network in the low-dimensional projected space) and 2) a weighted network graph (nodes correspond to the codes, edges represent the relative frequency of connection between two codes).

In our present study, we considered interview transcripts (sources) as our units, and grouped those units based on subsample: physicians and parents. We also performed exploratory analyses with cohorts based on participant attributes. Conversation, an ENA model parameter designating which utterances are grouped together, was operationalized as narrative segments within a source delimited by our mid-level segmentation. Code co-occurrences were accumulated with a weighted whole conversation stanza window, that is, codes occurring anywhere within the same conversation were considered to be connected, and the weights of the connections were determined by the number of times each code occurred within the conversation. Network model parameterization is described in Table 2.

Table 2. Parameters of network configurations generated with epistemic network analysis.

UNIT	Group > Source
CONVERSATION	Group > Source > Mid-level segmentation
STANZA WINDOW SIZE	(weighted) Whole conversation
CODES	RQ1: Content cluster, Sentiment cluster
	RQ2: Function cluster, Opinion cluster
PROJECTION	RQ1: MR1: 21.5%, SVD2: 21.9%
	RQ2: MR1: 16.6%, SVD2: 15.4%

Our operationalization, data collection instruments, final codebook and other materials are available in our open repository: https://osf.io/ubwxa/. This study was preregistered at Open Science Framework Registries. Code labels are marked in italics; quotes from interviews are disclosed in italics and quotation marks and followed by the interview identifier in parentheses; all quotes were translated from Hungarian by the authors.

3   Results

3.1   Demographic Characteristics

Our sample consisted of 20 physicians from all treatment centers of the Hungarian Pediatric Oncology Group. Interviews were conducted with a total of 27 parents who spoke about a total of 21 children in 23 interviews. In three cases, both parents attended the interview; in two cases, both parents were interviewed, but separately. Treatment centers of the children consisted of three hospitals (two in Budapest, one in the countryside). All children were diagnosed with a solid tumor, most commonly Medulloblastoma (n = 4), Glioblastoma (n = 3), Neuroblastoma (n = 3) and Rhab-domyosarcoma (n = 3). Table 3 contains demographic and clinical details of the interviewed physicians and families.

3.2   Content of Communication

Based on our previous research, we identified six content elements in communication during the palliative care discussion, and we were interested in how strongly these elements interact with codes *Positive* (good, important, essential, relevant) and *Negative* (inappropriate, irrelevant, to be avoided). Figure 1 shows the mean networks for both doctors and parents concerning the interaction of these elements.

Physician Mean Network: The most prominent codes interacting with positive appraisal were *Information* and *Child's interest*. *Information* encompassed instances about the practical aspects of palliative care and physical symptoms in children that their parents might notice at the end of life. *Child's interest* manifested as medical

Table 3. Demographic characteristics.

Physician demographics	n = 20
Sex	Females n = 12; Males n = 8
Age	Median: 39.5 years; Range: 31–62 years
Work experience	Median: 14 years; Range: 5–36 years
Location of workplace	Budapest n = 8; Countryside n = 12
Parent demographics	**n = 27**
Sex	Females n = 21; Males n = 6
Age	Median: 38 years; Range: 28–55 years
Marital status (during child's illness)	Married/relationship: n = 22; Single: n = 5
Education	University degree: n = 19; High school diploma: n = 6
Children demographics	**n = 21**
Diagnosis	CNS tumor: n = 14; Other solid tumor: n = 7
Location of treatment center	Budapest n = 15; Countryside: n = 6
Age at the time of death	Median: 7.5 years; Range: 9 months–19 years
Time between diagnosis and death	Median: 23 months; Range: 3 months–8 years

advice to parents regarding how to behave around the child, reassurance that the child will not suffer physically and will receive adequate analgesia. This code also included advice such as: *"Try to continue life as normal and gain as many new experiences together as possible"* (ID:20). The code *Trying* denoted that physicians were not attempting to prevent the parents from trying out treatments abroad or alternative treatments. These gestures made by physicians were regarded as mainly positive and the only other code it co-occurred with was *Hope* (sustaining hope in the parents). Utterances of *Hope* and *Did everything* (e.g. child could not be cured elsewhere either, team decision, based on protocol) were negligible and displayed weak connections to other codes. *Support* displayed weak connection with almost all other content codes. Although physicians primarily perceived *Information* to be positive, a subgroup of participants deemed it negative, citing that parents were unprepared to hear details on palliation: *"At the moment it is enough that palliative care exists, but the what and how will be decided later, if the parents want to"* (ID:17); *"...they are in such a shock, they would not remember what was said anyway"* (ID: 6). The large scatter of opinions on *Information* reflects the complexity of the question.

Parent Mean Network: Parental discourse was dominated by *Support*, which was regarded overwhelmingly positive and implied utterances in which the physician openly stated their support in practical matters regarding palliative care: *"[The doctor] emphasized and wanted to know how we will manage this situation"* (ID: 32). Support also included parental reassurance that PPC does not equal leaving them to their own devices, but that they can still go back to the oncology department or call the physician with questions at any time: *"If there would be written material, a flyer, I don't know...that would also be good.... Or a phone number to call him if I have questions, something like this, anything..."* (ID:25). Each code was associated with *Support* and there was no difference in the frequency of their co-occurrence. *Child's interest* and *Information* were the other two codes regarded relatively positive by parents, denoting their preference for receiving adequate information. Similar to the physician network, instances of *Hope* and *Did everything* were trivial, but in contrast to it, no code was found to be notably negative.

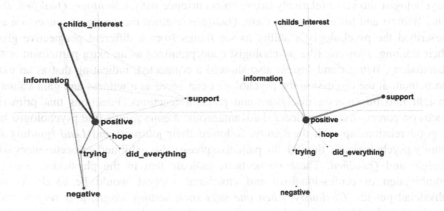

Fig. 1. Mean epistemic networks for the physician group (blue, left) and parental group (lilac, right) showing the weighted structure of connections among Communication and Sentiment codes. The thickness of the edges (lines) indicates the relative frequency of co-occurrence between each pair of codes; the size of the nodes (black circles) indicates the relative frequency of each code within that group.

Key Finding: Positive appraisal was dominant in both groups' mean network, but there was a significant difference in which content elements it connected to within the narratives. Physicians' discourse featured three preeminent codes (*Information, Child's Interest* and *Trying*), denoting instances about the practical questions of palliative care. At the same time, *Support* (the physician's active help during PPC) had a weak connection to these codes, suggesting that physicians in our cohort did not see themselves as a major driver of palliative care. Communication elements that dominated the physician network were scarcely represented in the parental narratives; instead, *Support* was highly regarded as positive. In summary, parents were less focused on the content physicians engaged with and there was a gap between the two groups' communication preferences. Despite physicians not considering their active participation in PPC a priority, parents have voiced a strong need for their involvement.

3.3 Role of the Psychologist

In a previous study, we identified various functions of the psychologist during the palliative care discussion and our aim was to see whether certain functions are outlined by doctors and parents as being particularly important or unfavorable. Figure 2 shows physician and parent mean networks displaying the connection of these functions to codes *Advantage* (a function is particularly beneficial or helpful) and *Disadvantage* (a function is of no great importance; it is irrelevant or harmful).

Physician Mean Network: Multiple codes containing the professional qualities of the psychologist showed a relatively strong co-occurrence with *Advantage*; *Qualified, Plus one, Witness* and *Insight*. Among them, *Qualified* retained the strongest connection and described the psychologist's ability to see things from a different perspective given their training. *Plus one* (the psychologist conceptualized as an extra participant at the discussion), *Witness* and *Insight* also showed a connected, indicating that as an extra participant at the discussion the psychologist can serve as a witness and gain valuable insight into information disclosure and parental reactions. Functions that primarily focus on parents were also deemed advantageous: *Knows family* (the psychologist had a good relationship with the family, followed their journey) and *Lead* (guiding the family psychologically through the palliative phase) also exhibited co-occurrences with *Insight* and *Qualified*. These connections indicate that in the physicians' view, a combination of professionalism and emotional support would be ideal. As one physician put it: *"Obviously, when one says such serious words, it is very useful – don't misunderstand me – to have a witness…On the other hand, obviously spiritual care will be much more important than medical care after that"* (ID:7). The only functions physicians thought disadvantageous were *Plus one* and *Witness*: *"It's important to create an intimate setting… too many is too many…"* (ID: 9).

Parent Mean Network: A key characteristic of the parental network was the strong connection between *Advantage* and *Consultation*. The code *Consultation* did not require the psychologist to be present at the palliative care discussion itself, but that they sit down with the parents immediately afterwards to help them process what was said and answer any remaining questions. Correspondingly, *No role* (psychologist has no function at the discussion) was regarded considerably disadvantageous: *"The presence of the psychologist or lack of it was all the same for me… this is a situation where all attention is focused on the doctor and the parent"* (ID:38). *Knows family* was also discussed as somewhat beneficial in parent narratives, but unlike the physicians, mentions of *Qualified, Insight, Lead* and *Witness* were uncommon.

Key Finding: Physicians were engaged with functions connected to the professional qualities of a psychologist (*Qualified, Insight, Witness, Plus one*); at the same time, functions focusing on emotional support (*Lead, Knows family*) also emerged as advantageous. In the parental network, *Consultation* was the most beneficial, while *No role* was the most disadvantageous function, suggesting that in parents' perspective, the psychologist's key role comes only after the discussion, in the form of a separate conversation that allows them to discuss the received information with another

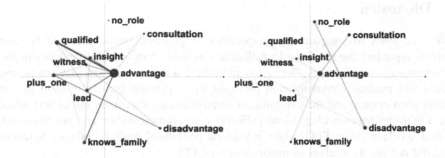

Fig. 2. Mean epistemic networks for the physician group (blue, left) and parental group (lilac, right) showing the weighted structure of connections among Role of psychologist and Opinion codes. The thickness of the edges (lines) indicates the relative frequency of co-occurrence between each pair of codes; the size of the nodes (black circles) indicates the relative frequency of each code within that group.

professional. The markedly different two mean networks illustrate the complexity of the psychologist's role at the palliative care discussion and the distinctive views these stakeholders have on the psychologist's crucial functions. Figure 3 shows the differences between the physician and parent mean networks concerning both research questions modelled as difference graphs. The mean networks, represented as solid squares, show a significant difference between the two groups in both RQs. The results of the networks introduced in this paper did not show significant change when grouping by further attributes, for instance location, gender or age.

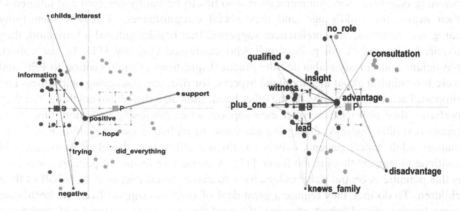

Fig. 3. Difference graph showing the subtracted mean networks for both groups regarding both communication content and physician's role. The thickness and saturation of each line indicates the relative difference between the two groups: blue lines indicate connections with higher relative frequencies among Physicians, and lilac lines indicate connections with higher relative frequencies among Parents. The points show the network locations (ENA scores) of each Physician (blue points) and Parents (lilac points). The colored squares are the mean network locations (mean ENA scores) of each group, and the dashed lines around the means represent the 95% confidence intervals on each dimension.

4 Discussion

We used ENA to compare the perspectives of pediatric oncologists and bereaved parents regarding the transition to palliative care and identify key differences in their communication preferences. Our results indicate that there was a gap between parental needs and medical communication preferred by physicians both in relation to communication content and the psychologist's involvement. Parents in our cohort wished for a more primary oncologist-lead palliative care communication and the physician's active involvement in PPC, while physicians prioritized multidisciplinary teamwork and did not see themselves as major drivers of PPC.

In our previous study, instances that conveyed defensiveness (transitioning to PPC was a team decision, it is based on protocol) were physicians' second most frequently referenced topic. Through secondary analysis, however, network models of our data did not display the primacy of this code. This suggests that there was a subgroup of physicians who, when talking to the parents, felt they needed to defend their decision to transition to palliative care. These doctors built their discourse around these codes, while other elements of communication were less prominent. Concerning the preferences of the parents, our secondary analysis revealed that emphasis on the physician's support interwove their discourse and strongly interacted with all other codes.

Communication is an integral part of everyday medical care, especially in advanced disease, yet literature is lacking in frameworks focusing on the communication of serious illness in pediatrics. DeCourcey et al. describe the development of such an intervention, called the Pediatric Serious Illness Communication Program (PediSICP), which aims to improve care alignment with patient and family goals [10]. This alignment of healthcare providers' perspectives and families' needs is essential when planning palliative care; communication also has to be family-centered and tailored to their needs, the child's age, and their social circumstances. A review identifying caregiver communication preferences suggested that besides tailored information, they required a trusted health professional who expressed empathy [11]. In our cohort, physicians consciously elaborated the practical questions of the transition to PPC and were less mindful about the emotional aspects, for instance, conveying helpfulness and support. Parents in our study, on the other hand, indicated that above anything else they preferred their physicians to offer their support when discussing palliation. One study reported similar findings: during the transition to palliative care, in addition to information, adult cancer patients mostly sought the affirmation that their physician will continue to support them in the future [12]. A distinctive feature of pediatric oncology is that parents, as central stakeholders, have to make critical decisions on behalf of their children. To do that, they require a great deal of help and support from the healthcare team. In our parental cohort, accounts of a need for support co-occurred with each topic in communication, yet physicians did not emphasize its importance to the same extent. This might suggest that physicians saw this discussion as a sort of closure of their leading role in the child's care and considered PPC primarily as the responsibility of the palliative subspecialty professionals. One explanation might be physicians' lack of complete understanding of palliative care and of their own relevance in providing it; there is a need for a larger number of in-depth, comprehensive palliative care trainings for physicians to eliminate preconceptions about palliation being solely a competence of nurses and psychologists. Correspondingly, in our cohort parents overwhelmingly voiced their wish that the treating physician would not let their hand go and even if they are transferred to palliative services, the physician stay actively involved in and collaborate with the PPC unit.

Compared to our previous fully qualitative study, data modelling with ENA confirmed that the parental demand for a consultation with the psychologist is very marked in their discourse, while it is negligible in the case of doctors. A separate conversation with the psychologist allows parents to process the information they received from the physician and ask any remaining questions. A similar communication model was described by Sisk et al., who proposed that distributing responsibility by role assignment is an effective team-based approach [13]. This involves the physician appointing a team member (nurse, psychologist, another oncologist) who will consult with the family at given times. Thus, the intimacy of the discussions is ensured (a need parents also expressed in our cohort), and the burden of information disclosure would be shared concurrently among the care team. Multidisciplinary teamwork is essential in oncological care, still, when it comes to provision of information and prognostic disclosure, many stakeholders view it as the chief responsibility of the primary oncologist. However, the exclusion of other team members from the information flow either inadvertently or intentionally, might lead to mixed signals and misinformation, which confuses families. Therefore, even though a one-on-one conversation with the lead oncologist might be preferred by the parents, as seen in our cohort as well, it is also the physician's responsibility to adequately inform other team members about the topics of discussion. Accordingly, when it comes to separate conversations (e.g., consultation after the palliative care discussion), they can effectively communicate with the family as well and preserve the integrity of disclosed information.

When visually inspecting our network models, a clear picture of parents' preference for a one person, lead oncologist-centered communication model emerged. This model corresponds with the so-called "solo practice model" described by Bruera et al., where the oncologist attempts to take care of all patient-related issues during the palliative phase alone [14]. One explanation for this preference might be the low number of available palliative professionals in the country, and therefore the lack of cooperation between oncology centers and specialized PPC services: an ineffective cooperation means that parents will not have a chance to get to know the PPC team ahead of time, which can lead to mistrust towards them and a stronger attachment to their oncologist. In case of a well-established collaboration, the oncologist would have the opportunity to introduce the family to the PPC team earlier in the treatment trajectory, which would allow the parents to get to know them and form a relationship, thus becoming less dependent on the primary oncologist. Physicians can also utilize screening tools, which help them assess the palliative care needs of children and their families to facilitate timely referrals [15]. If specialized PPC services are not accessible and palliative care has to be provided by the oncology team, the primary physician needs to find a way to make this model sustainable. One solution presented in related literature, and also mentioned by parents in our cohort, is the creation of summarized information leaflets or a website where they could be reliably informed about what the transition to palliative care entails, what palliative and mental health support services are available, and who they can turn to with their questions [10].

5 Limitations

Several limitations of our study warrant discussion. Firstly, physicians and parents were not paired in our investigation, hence while physicians disclosed their general opinions on interview questions, parents elaborated on one particular conversation with one physician. This means that physician interviews not necessarily reflected how they would communicate in all situations. Structured interviews also did not necessarily provide an opportunity for physicians to digress into adjoining topics. Secondly, the original palliative care discussions were not recorded; participants' memories were subject to time and other sources of bias. The physician subsample can be regarded as representative, since interviews were conducted with physicians from all seven Hungarian pediatric oncology centers, all positions and age groups. On the other hand, parent participants were recruited from three locations and were not selected systematically; they were included into the study based on the treating physicians' discretion, who might have been more likely to reach out to parents with whom they fostered a good relationship. Also, our sample lends insight into the attitudes of parents in our cohort, but the level of transferability to Hungarian parents in general is unclear, much less so for other geographical areas and cultures.

6 Conclusions

While the availability of PPC services depend largely on financial matters and governance, and therefore is not necessarily under the physician's influence, certain communication approaches could provide solutions for them to impact the palliative care of affected families in a positive way regardless of external circumstances. These communication approaches include the creation of websites and leaflets that specifically target the transition to PPC and role assignment in the multidisciplinary team regarding information disclosure. With our initiative, we aimed to facilitate communication between physicians and families during the transition to palliative care and increase the effectiveness of PPC; we believe our results and conclusions may be applicable in countries with a similar PPC infrastructure and teamwork setting.

Acknowledgements. This study received funding from the Hungarian Pediatric Oncology Network and was supported by the ÚNKP-20-2 New National Excellence Program of the Ministry for Innovation and Technology from the National Research, Development and Innovation Fund. The authors wish to thank Gjalt-Jorn Peters for his assistance in data curation. We also wish to thank all our interviewees, doctors and parents alike, for trusting us with their experiences concerning an incredibly difficult situation.

References

1. Craig, F., Abu-Saad Huijer, H., Benini, F., et al.: IMPaCCT: standards of paediatric palliative care. Schmerz **22**, 401–408 (2008). https://doi.org/10.1007/s00482-008-0690-4
2. Kaasa, S., Loge, J.H., Aapro, M., et al.: Integration of oncology and palliative care: a lancet oncology Commission. Lancet Oncol. (2018). https://doi.org/10.1016/s1470-2045(18)30415-7
3. Hill, D.L., Walter, J.K., Casas, J.A., et al.: The codesign of an interdisciplinary team-based intervention regarding initiating palliative care in pediatric oncology. Support. Care Cancer **26**, 3249–3256 (2018). https://doi.org/10.1007/s00520-018-4190-5
4. Wolfe, J., Klar, N., Grier, H.E., et al.: Understanding of prognosis among parents of children who died of cancer. JAMA **284**, 2469 (2000). https://doi.org/10.1001/jama.284.19.2469
5. Levine, D.R., Mandrell, B.N., Sykes, A., et al.: Patients' and parents' needs, attitudes, and perceptions about early palliative care integration in pediatric oncology. JAMA Oncol. **3**, 1214 (2017). https://doi.org/10.1001/jamaoncol.2017.0368
6. Nyirő, J., Zörgő, S., Enikő, F., Hegedűs, K., Hauser, P.: The timing and circumstances of the implementation of pediatric palliative care in Hungarian pediatric oncology. Eur. J. Pediatr. **177**(8), 1173–1179 (2018). https://doi.org/10.1007/s00431-018-3170-6
7. Földesi et al (2021) Bereaved parents' perspective on medical communication during the transition to palliative care in pediatric oncology in Hungary. Manuscript submitted for publication
8. Shaffer, D.W., Collier, W., Ruis, A.R.: A tutorial on epistemic network analysis: analyzing the structure of connections in cognitive, social, and interaction data. J. Learn. Anal. **3**, 9–45 (2016). https://doi.org/10.18608/jla.2016.33.3
9. Swiecki, Z., Marquart, C., Sachar, A., Hinojosa, C., Ruis, A.R., Shaffer, D.W.: Designing an interface for sharing quantitative ethnographic research data. In: Eagan, B., Misfeldt, M., Siebert-Evenstone, A. (eds.) ICQE 2019. CCIS, vol. 1112, pp. 334–341. Springer, Cham (2019). https://doi.org/10.1007/978-3-030-33232-7_30
10. DeCourcey, D.D., Partin, L., Revette, A., et al.: Development of a stakeholder driven serious illness communication program for advance care planning in children, adolescents, and young adults with serious illness. J. Pediatr. (2021). https://doi.org/10.1016/j.jpeds.2020.09.030
11. Hrdlickova, L., Polakova, K., Loucka, M.: Important aspects influencing delivery of serious news in pediatric oncology: a scoping review. Children **8**, 166 (2021). https://doi.org/10.3390/children8020166
12. Umezawa, S., Fujimori, M., Matsushima, E., et al.: Preferences of advanced cancer patients for communication on anticancer treatment cessation and the transition to palliative care. Cancer **121**, 4240–4249 (2015). https://doi.org/10.1002/cncr.29635
13. Sisk, B.A., Dobrozsi, S., Mack, J.W.: Teamwork in prognostic communication: addressing bottlenecks and barriers. Pediatr. Blood Cancer (2020). https://doi.org/10.1002/pbc.28192
14. Bruera, E., Hui, D.: Integrating supportive and palliative care in the trajectory of cancer: Establishing goals and models of care. J. Clin. Oncol. **28**, 4013–4017 (2010). https://doi.org/10.1200/jco.2010.29.5618
15. Chong PH, Soo J, Yeo ZZ, et al (2020) Who needs and continues to need paediatric palliative CARE? an evaluation of utility and feasibility of the paediatric palliative screening scale (PaPaS). BMC Palliative Care. https://doi.org/10.1186/s12904-020-0524-4

Democracy and Social Inequalities in the Organization of Education During the COVID-19 Pandemic: The Case of Brazil and Sweden

Karoline Schnaider[1]([⊠]), Stefano Schiavetto[2], and Daniel Spikol[3]

[1] Umeå University, Umeå, Sweden
karoline.schnaider@umu.se
[2] State University of Campinas, Campinas, Brazil
s072392@dac.unicamp.br
[3] University of Copenhagen, Copenhagen, Denmark
ds@di.ku.dk

Abstract. Challenges that arise during a time of crisis, as the current COVID-19 pandemic, are a basis for recognizing how different governments handle the governance of units such as schools and issues related to democracy and social inequality. By paying attention to similar or contrasting issues in the political welfare states' characteristics and organization, the crisis's impact on different countries can be identified and can provide learning examples beyond the study's phenomena. Although Brazil and Sweden are historically and culturally diverse countries, they also share similarities in being politicized by global trends such as neoliberalism. The paper examines the two governments' discourses and how centralization, decentralization, and neoliberalism and the resulting shift to privatized public services can form a basis for understanding declines in democracy and social inequality in education in both countries. The following research question guides the work, *how are democracy and social inequality expounded in Brazil's and Sweden's way of organizing education during the COVID-19 pandemic?* To investigate how democracy and social inequality were expounded in Brazil's and Sweden's way of organizing education during the COVID-19 pandemic, we used a quantitative ethnographic approach to analyze the governments' discourses. With quantitative ethnographic techniques we identified how the states organized discussions and actions to investigate and solve socio-educational issues related to democracy and how access to resources for education related to inequalities. The governmental intensity of keeping the economy functioning was observed to be influenced by the advance of neoliberalism in both countries. In organizing the education during the COVID-19 pandemic, neoliberalism is pertaining to authoritarianism in Brazil and more culturally contingent actions related to the ethos - "openness" - in Sweden.

Keywords: Education · Democracy · Social inequality · Organization · Quantitative ethnography

© Springer Nature Switzerland AG 2022
B. Wasson and S. Zörgő (Eds.): ICQE 2021, CCIS 1522, pp. 298–317, 2022.
https://doi.org/10.1007/978-3-030-93859-8_20

1 Introduction

A crisis' impact can be identified by paying attention to similar or contrasting issues in different countries' political welfare states' characteristics and organization. With various consequences, it provides learning examples beyond the study's phenomena. Although Brazil and Sweden are historically and culturally diverse countries, they also share similarities in being politicized by global trends such as neoliberalism. One topic playing a significant role worldwide has been the rise of neoliberalism by leaders such as Pinochet in Chile, Thatcher in the United Kingdom, and Guedes and Bolsonaro in Brazil, but also transpiring more unarticulated in welfare states such as Sweden [1]. A core of neoliberalism is privatization, although it is not excluding the state from co-financing or responsibility in reducing social inequalities through, for instance, inclusive laws [1].

A neoliberalist authority accommodates fewer assistance policies [1, 2] and has less interference even in fundamental areas such as education. It is occupied by private and for-profit entrepreneurship that can affect democracy and equality. Individual economic growth becomes the basic principle to a collective reduction of inequalities - an economization of politics and a depoliticization of the economy - in which citizens sacrifice politicized citizenship in the belief that economic growth is sufficient for individual and collective well-being [2].

In this paper we look deeper into Brazil's and Sweden's way of organizing education during the COVID-19 pandemic crisis. We examine the governments' discourses and how centralization, decentralization, and neoliberalism, and the resulting shift to privatized public services, can form a basis for understanding the decline in democracy and social inequality in education in both countries. The following research question guides the work, *how are democracy and social inequality expounded in Brazil's and Sweden's way of organizing education during the COVID-19 pandemic?*

2 Background

The organization of the society in Brazil and Sweden is briefly sketched in this section. It is the footing for understanding how education got affected differently in the countries during the pandemic times. Brazil and Sweden share a similar governance structure where the state or federation is responsible for higher education institutions. In contrast, decentralized entities such as states (Brazil) and municipalities (Sweden) have responsibilities for secondary education and municipalities for the primary in Brazil. Through the ministry and Departments of Education, the governments coordinate incentives and policies between decentralized and other state institutions and the civil society.

2.1 Democracy and Inequality in Education

The states' centralized and decentralized coordination of schools in Brazil and Sweden is one of the pillars for democratic governance to overcome inequalities. According to Dahl [3], democracy can be attributed to the political regimes of the 20th century that institutionalized political equality as a fundamental requirement – the so-called pol-yarchies – permeating laws, policies, and the governance of schools. For the effec-tiveness of democracy, especially after the Second World War, public funding of primary and secondary education was observed. For instance, since the promulgation of the new Federal Constitution in 1988 in Brazil, which ended in a military dictatorship between 1964–1985, several governmental sectors and civil society representatives created democratic regulations to put the new Federal Constitution into effect. The last policy document related to education was completed in 2018 [4]. The Swedish Department of Education is basing its governance on laws and practices, continuously reviewed by the state and society and applied mainly since the second half of the 20th century, which has been effective in enhancing democracy and reducing inequalities. Thus, the recent effort made by the Brazilian government to improve social inequalities is a more modern democratic and creative historical moment, which was current in Sweden for more than half a century. Since the second half of the twentieth century, Sweden is a world reference for low social inequalities and high-quality education. At the same time, Brazil has figured worldwide between 2002 and 2015 to overcome social disparities, with programs focused on amending the effects on education.

2.2 Privatization and Neoliberalism

Since democracy has not proven to be a stable accomplishment, rather it is an ongoing dynamic process between government and society and institutionalized laws do not always have guaranteed outcome for the benefit of citizens [3]. At the same time, one of the main threats to democracy is social inequality, which is likely to generate segregation in access to essential resources and the population's spaces of power. Moreover, cultural discrimination, life reduced to material survival, political apathy, and less representation of social groups in government can favor the rise of authori-tarian and populistic political figures. According to Brown [2], such changes in social inequality ideologically relates to a strive for individual economic development as the primary driver of equality that simultaneously reduces political citizenship to econo-mization. Resulting in political apathy, sacrificial citizenship means that the "citizen is bound to the sole and supervening value of economic growth, and thus, may be sacrificed to capital's needs, vicissitudes, and inequalities at their job, in their nation or post-national constellation." [2, p.9].

Neoliberalism has been observed in the scientific literature for four decades now as a growing privatization, deregulation, with states' diminished role in the economy, and programs for equality, raising questions about its possible impacts on democracy and inequalities [2]. Political equality is maintained through, e.g., education, but under new meta-stabilities between government and society, which provide the students with mainly juridical equality in the world of work under sacrificial citizenship. Neoliberal changes have been observed in education in Brazil, accelerated by the privatization and for-profit trends [5–9].

Since the election of a neoliberal president in 2018, Brazil underwent profound changes. Privatization of public services and strict measures to cut welfare investments were in progress and even accentuated during the COVID-19 pandemic [10]. For instance, a budget reduction of 25% for academic research was a change in the educational system due to this. Subsequently, a reduction of all the universities' budgets was made [11, 12] to analyze the quality of the programs to prepare professionals for the job market [13] and to generate "economic growth" by producing more doctors, nurses, dentists, and engineers while limiting "sociologists, anthropologists, and philosophers" [14].

Burström [15] addressed the accelerated privatization and the effects on democracy and inequality in Sweden. For instance, the Swedish public service increasingly occupied for-profit companies between the early 1990s and 2016 (from 2% to 19%, [16]). According to Diderichsen [17], the changes have made Sweden more comparable with the United Kingdom than with the other Nordic countries. Recently, the same trends were seen in elderly care, where 25% of the maintenance got dominated by two large companies [18]. Dahlgren [19] showed that market-oriented health care reforms in Sweden reduced efficiency, priority for patients, fewer opportunities for quality control of services, resulting in an expansion of social inequalities that seemed to undermine the power of the democratic institutions. A recent study confirmed that during the COVID-19 pandemic, privatization appeared to be one problem alongside intensive work by professionals and the absence of supportive leadership, resulting in high mortality [20].

In summary, the paper takes the stance that democracy is under threat in both Brazil and Sweden by the advance of neoliberalism. The stance is based on an observation of how each government dealt with education during the COVID-19 pandemic and its impacts on inequalities. In Brazil and Sweden, the threat is a relationship between the minimization of citizen participation in the public power, which is fundamental for defining a state as democratic [3], and the advance in the privatization of public services, in a neoliberal ethics [1, 2]. Despite sharing this neoliberal minimization of citizen participation in democracy, Brazil and Sweden exemplify two trends of contemporary neoliberal heterogeneity. While the South American country expresses an authoritarianism in the conduct of neoliberal reforms, by an elected party that centralizes the decision-making, the Nordic country expresses a broad decentralization of the decision-making process, in a culture more tolerant of a "sacrificial citizenship" [1, 2]. The paper explores the impact these shifts had on education during the COVID-19 pandemic.

3   Data Processing

To investigate what effects the two governments' measures had on democracy and social inequality in education, methods of quantitative ethnography was used to analyze the governments' official communication. The quantitative ethnographic techniques allowed us to process and analyze a large amount of data [21]. We discuss the data collection, the initial segmentation, the code generation, the second data segmentation, and the data analysis in this section.

3.1 Data Retrieval and First Segmentation

Data communicated by the Brazilian and Swedish governments were observed during the years 2020–2021 when the COVID-19 pandemic had advanced worldwide. The content of the governments' discourses was relevant to explore because it was considered to convey information about the changes in the organization of education related to democracy and social inequality. Manual searches were performed on the respective countries' web pages, www.mec.gov.br (Brazil), and the website www.regeringen.se (Sweden).

Several selection criteria were operated to obtain a valid collection of data for the paper (Table 1). Consensus among the researchers was reached by discussing the categories available in the filer function on the respective governments' webpages. After testing different search options, similar settings were made to match the information from the Brazilian and the Swedish website and make it comparable. General inclusion and exclusion criteria were defined as connected to the purpose of the study. *Coronavirus* and *Corona* were deemed to be the aptest search terms to get results of each government's actions related to the COVID-19 pandemic. The *Content* was not activated and excluded searches of specific media types such as articles, information material, reports, etc., as different data sources were essential to get a broad representation of information. *Basic education* and *Child- and youth education* were used respectively to get search results related to the specific area under study – the governments' measures and incentives associated with the organization of education. Similarly, the *Ministers* (Brazil) and the *Department* (Sweden) were used to filer the information communicated by the governmental institutions related to education in each country. Because the phase when the COVID-19 pandemic began to bear on the organization of schools was similar in both countries, the *Period* delimiting the searches was set between March 1, 2020, to the present time, April 22, 2021. The information contained the statements of the Ministers of Education, memoranda, amendments to the law, etcetera.

Table 1. Search settings.

Search settings:	Brazil	Sweden
Search term:	Coronavirus	Corona
Content:	–	–
Area:	Basic education	Child- and youth education
Ministers:	Ministry of Education	–
Department:		Education
Period:	March 1, 2020–April 22, 2021	March 1, 2020–April 22, 2021

Text data from the two web pages were manually downloaded and imported into separate documents. Respective native languages were converted into English with online translation tools, followed by a manual screening of the texts to correct translation errors and clean the files by removing irrelevant data. The first round of segmentation included separating the texts into lines or clusters of lines depending on how the content addressed or framed different social inequality and democracy aspects. All text data was transferred to a spreadsheet before the second segmentation and code generation and resulted in 3766 rows for the entire dataset.

3.2   Code Generation, Second Segmentation, and Coding

The initial stage of code generation included hypothesis modeling. A hypothesis is a proposed explanation of the studied phenomena, a conceptual statement yet untested, formulated into a prediction that quantifies defined variables [22]. The hypothesis that guided the data processing was based on social inequality and democracy in education and predicted that some of their components would occur more often in the Brazilian and Swedish discourse.

Repeated procedures of top-down and bottom-up moderation were undertaken to define the variables (the codes) by identifying values (codewords) to determine the codes [23]. Social inequality and democracy formed overarching classes and were deductively guiding the top-down processes when understanding the data. It included social moderation [24] and manual screening of the first 200-word frequency counts made in NVivo 12, ranging in occurrence from 1600 ("education") to 50 ("way"). A manual search of the dataset followed this step to define the potential codewords. Data was additionally screened numerous times in the bottom-up moderation to refine the categories by sorting additional codewords under each category and grouping them under a suitable label. Eight codes were defined during these processes (Table 2).

Table 2. Codebook.

Category:	Final codes:	Codewords:	Definition:	Example:	HC1/AC[a]:	HI1/HC[b]:	HC2/AC[c]:
Inequality:	*Support and opportunities*	School, Transport, Food, Meal, Nutrition, Principal, Premise, Higher education, Support, Opportunity, Opportunities, Condition	Discourses around how to support the teaching organization to maintain school attendance, mandate to principals, providing transportation, food, technologies, postponing exams to access higher education	"This shall also apply to study start support for certain unemployed people who need to enroll in a basic or upper secondary education. High school students' student aid will continue to be paid out"	.99**	.99**	.99**
	Organization and methods	Face-to-face, Online, Distance, Remot, Teach, Adapt, Technolog, Technique, Special school, Special education, Special need, Subject	Discourse around the teaching organization, closing of schools, reopening of schools, distance, face-to-face and hybrid education, technologies, and techniques	"Distance learning means that teaching is interactive and takes place in real time by using information and communication technology"	.99**	.91*	.91*

(continued)

Table 2. (*continued*)

Category:	Final codes:	Codewords:	Definition:	Example:	HC1/AC[a]:	HI1/HC[b]:	HC2/AC[c]:
	Learning	Learn, Study, Studies, Development, Activit, Knowledge, Qualit, Course	Discourses on how to prevent the decline in quality of learning for students involving study methods, learning strategies and guidelines	"The purpose is to increase the state subsidy that principals can apply for to offer law school to students who have not reached or risk not reaching the knowledge requirements for the grade E"	.97**	.96*	.99**
Democracy:	*Investments*	Million, Fund, Resource, Aid, Investment	Discourses around the reallocation of ordinary resources and how to apply extraordinary resources, related to the reorganization of education during the pandemic	"In terms of resources, SEK 944 million will be added in 2020 and SEK 1,174 million in 2021, including study funds for these investments"	.97**	.91*	.94*
	School system management	Compulsory, Preschool, Right, University, Universities, Primary, Secondary, Basic education, Assess	Discourses around the explorations of the impacts of the pandemic on the teaching units (schools and universities) and how to solve them	"Basic education - The MEC, the National Council of Education Secretaries (Consed) and the National Union of Municipal Education Directors (Undime) are analyzing the possibility of making the fulfillment of the 200 school days more flexible, as provided for in the Law of Guidelines and Bases (LDB) and study the maximum workload that can be offered in distance mode"	.99**	.99**	.99*
	COVID-19 spread control	Spread, Infection, Recommendation, Measure, Consequence	Discourses on how to contain the spread of the new corona virus in educational environments	"The spread of infection needs to be reduced to limit the effects on human health and economic consequences"	.99**	.99**	.99*

(*continued*)

Table 2. (*continued*)

Category:	Final codes:	Codewords:	Definition:	Example:	HC1/AC[a]:	HI1/HC[b]:	HC2/AC[c]:
	Gover-nance and society	Ministry, Minister, Inep, National agency, Decide, Necessary, Program, Close, Reopen, State, Municipal, Federal, Return, Participat, Extraordinary, Strength	Discourses around the involvement of the society in the investigation and solution of the pandemic's impact in primary and secondary education	"For the representative of Unicef, this process of reopening schools will be the biggest challenge that new municipal leaders will face in 2021"	.99**	.99**	.99**
	Laws application and new regulations	Enem, Education act, Regulation, Provision, pnae, section, fnde, ordinance, adjustment, amendment, law	Discourses on laws regarding the reorganization of education	"Through an amendment to the ordinance, upper secondary schools can now, under certain conditions, combine local education with certain distance or distance education"	.99**	.97*	.97*

* rho ≤ .05, ** rho < .01

[a] Kappa (K > .9) – level of agreement between the first human rater and the automated classifier in nCoder
[b] Kappa (K > .9) – level of agreement between the first and second human raters in nCoder
[c] Kappa (K > .9) – level of agreement between the second human rater and the automated classifier in nCoder

Before coding, a second source- and delimiter-based segmentation was carried out to prepare the data for analysis with ENA[1] [25]. Source-based segmentation included grouping the lines in the text data by adding columns in the spreadsheet with meaningful contextual information that could help determine the social inequality and democracy categories and from which ENA was operating (used as conversations). Metadata was added as a significant source for segmentation, in which the lines were used as "utterances". Time was an essential factor as the different time periods during the COVID-19 rendered different kinds of information. Two columns for month and year were therefore added as a delimiter-based segmentation [26].

Coding was performed with the software nCoder[2] [27] to assess inter-rater reliability (IRR) and agreement between raters and validity to the conceptualization of the codes. nCoder was used by two human raters (H1/H2) and an automated classifier (AC) that examined approximately 10 percent of the total number of coded expressions through the eight codes (Table 3). The agreement level between the raters on all the codes resulted in a Cohen's kappa of > .90 (see codebook, Table 2).

---

[1] https://www.epistemicnetwork.org/.

[2] https://www.n-coder.org/.

Table 3. Descriptive statistics of datasets.

Country (units):	# unique datasets	# hits	# coded lines ($N = 3766$)
Brazil	1	67	1553
Sweden	1	99	2212

3.3 Data Analysis

The coded data was used with the Epistemic Network Analysis (ENA) Web Tool v1.7.0 (Marquart et al., 2018) to visualize networks modeling the occurrence of social inequality and democracy in the two governments' discourses related to the organization of education during the pandemic year. ENA uses stanzas to connect items in the data and is modeled with stanza windows based on the chosen conversation for each unit of analysis (Brazil and Sweden). A moving stanza window of size 10 was set in ENA after testing different alternatives with similar results due to the uncertainty in codewords between the rows. ENA visualizes centroids (boxes with plotted points) that indicate the units' means. Each unit connection is also modeled in ENA weighted networks enabling interpretation of the x and y-axes dimensions and the frequency of co-occurrence between codes [28].

4   Result and Analysis

The ENA network connections were initially analyzed visually - the units' (centroids) position in the x-y projection space to obtain a general perspective on the differences between the Brazilian and Swedish discourses on social inequality and democracy in the organization of education during the COVID-19 pandemic. The next step included an exposition of the ties between the nodes (codes). The thickness of the lines and the size of the codes were associated and addressed and linked to their definitions and codewords. By integrating stanzas from the text data to exemplify the meaning of the connections, the interpretative loop was closed [21].

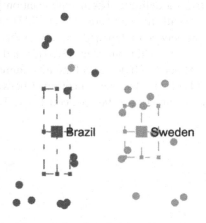

Fig. 1. Mean of the plotted points for each country.

The centroids (boxes) with plotted points (Fig. 1) visually indicate that the Brazilian discourse is statistically significantly different from the Swedish discourse. A Mann-Whitney test reinforced that observation on the X-axis (Table 4). The model had co-registration correlations of .95 (Pearson) and .94 (Spearman) for the first dimension and co-registration correlations of .98 (Pearson) and .98 (Spearman) for the second. These measures indicate that there is strong goodness of fit between the visualization and the original model.

Table 4. Mann-Whitney test statistics on differences between Brazil and Sweden.

Countries	Axis	Median (N)	P-value*	R (effect size)
Brazil vs. Sweden	X	Mdn = .79	p = .001	r = .97

* alpha level < .05

The subtraction network (Fig. 2) suggests that Brazil's position in the left dimension on the x-axis relates it more firmly to democracy in the democracy-inequality continuum. In contrast, Sweden's situation on the right side relates it more firmly to the discourse around inequality. In the y-axis dimension, Brazil's communication is oriented relatively evenly towards the state-organized discussions and actions to investigate and solve socio-educational issues to strengthen learning (Learning) by governing (Governance and society) with laws and regulations (Laws application and new regulations), and investments (Investments). Sweden's position on the y-axis hints at measures differentiating the access to resources to support (Support and opportunities) and organize (Organization and methods) the education to benefit different groups. The following quotes can illustrate these observations: Brazil – "The National Education Development Fund (FNDE), linked to the Ministry of Education (MEC), anticipated the transfer of R $ 67.9 million, the amount of the fourth instalment of the National School Transport Support Program (PNATE), scheduled for the end of the month." (ID: 2559) Sweden - "As long as teaching is provided, for example through distance learning, student support in the form of study aid, study grants, and study start support will continue to be provided as usual." (ID: 6).

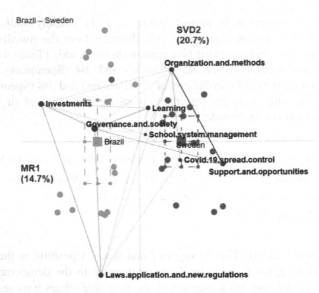

Fig. 2. Subtraction network modeling comparison between Brazil and Sweden.

4.1 Analysis of the Countries

This section describes the close-up perspective on Brazil's and Sweden's discourses around democracy and social inequality in education identified in the previous paragraph.

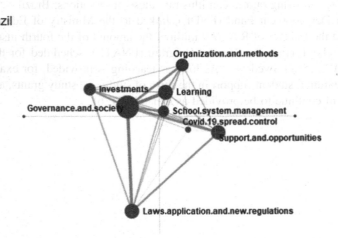

Fig. 3. Network modeling democracy and inequality in education related to Brazil.

Brazil. The network in Fig. 3 signals a complex engagement by the Brazilian government to maintain democracy in the organization of education during the corona crisis. There are some strong relationships between the codes in the network. For instance, the Ministry of Education increased its efforts to establish programs to monitor the impacts of the pandemic and to forecast the forthcoming steps on a federal and municipal level (Governance and Society). This lead to adjustments of regulations and amendment of educational laws (Laws Application and New Regulations). These actions were taken to prevent the decline in the quality of learning in primary and secondary schools (Learning). In addition, governmental efforts (Governance and Society) directly impacted the organization of teaching and learning in schools, such as closing schools and transitioning to online modes, adopting new methods, technologies, and techniques (Organization and Methods). How the readjustments could be catered for and support the continuation of teaching and school attendance by allocating and differentiate the resources food, hygiene, and distribution of teaching managed on a local level by principals (Support and opportunities) were also observed. The following quote can exemplify these observations: The course is aimed at teachers, pedagogical coordinators, school principals, and assistants, all from the last year of pre-school and the first two years of elementary school and is also useful for managers of educational networks and all interested civil society, that is, parents and guardians, for example, who are interested in collaborating with their children's literacy, can also access content available entirely online and free of charge, and practice with the little ones" (ID: 2855).

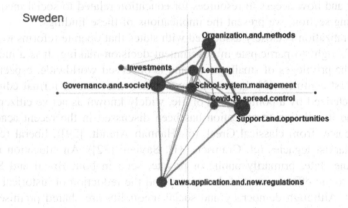

Fig. 4. Network modeling democracy and inequality in education related to Sweden.

Sweden. The connections in Fig. 4 suggest that the Swedish government was managing the corona crisis' effects on education that is different from how the Brazilian government acted. There are some strong relationships between the codes in the network related to the Swedish government's discourse. First, the network connections propose that governmental agencies and societal entities investigated issues and suggested solutions (*Governance and Society*) and necessary measures, e.g., curriculum changes and access to resources, while handling the extraordinary events in the time of crisis to maintain education (*Support and Opportunities*). The first decision to close secondary schools while still having primary schools open, required remote and distance education (*Organization and Methods*) and adaptation of the school organization to comply with rules of social distance while sustaining the rights for education (*School System Management*). These measures were anchored in the educational legislation already in force, emphasizing the Education Act (2010: 800) (*Law Application and New Regulations*). The concern with avoiding a drop in the quality of teaching (*Learning*) is related to all these investigations and actions. However, the funds for dealing with them are not salient in the discourses (*Investments*). The quote illustrates these observations: "Throughout the pandemic, the Ministry of Education has consulted with experts, educational actors, responsible authorities and organizations, representatives of school principals, employee organizations and student and student organizations to gain knowledge about how the virus has affected the activities and identify what needs exist" (ID: 686).

5   Discussion

This study addresses how democracy and social inequality are salient in Brazil's and Sweden's ways of organizing education during the COVID-19 pandemic. By quantitative ethnographic techniques [21], we focused on how the two states organized discussions and actions to investigate and solve socio-educational issues related to democracy and how access to resources for education related to social inequalities. In the following section, we present the implications of these findings.

Democratization is closely associated with states that operate reforms to extend the population's right to participate in government decision-making. It is a movement to minimize the privileges of small groups and is observed worldwide, especially in the 20th and 21st centuries [3]. In the democratization movement, formal education has been characterized by a politicization of life, widely known as active citizenship. This concept and its relation to education has been discussed in the recent academic and political debate, from classical Greek (cf. Hannah Arendt, [29]), liberal (cf. Bobbio, [30]), to Marxist legacies (cf. Gramsci, [31]; Saviani [32]). An education institutionalized by the state, primarily public or private, seen in both Brazil and Sweden, is committed to the effectiveness of democracy and the reduction of historical and social inequalities. Although democracy and social inequality are shared premises between the countries, there are significant differences in how Brazil and Sweden framed their discourses around education during the last year. Brazil's Ministry of Education (MEC) engaged in discussions and actions more related to democracy. At the same time, the Swedish Department of Education's (SDE) debates related more to social inequality in the democracy-inequality continuum. While the Brazilian MEC centralized its decision-making, the Swedish SDE mediated between health authorities and schools to optimize decisions on a decentralized level. These observations are the pillars for further analysis of Brazil's and Sweden's actions and engagement in supporting education. Both countries focused on supporting the educational system, which can be related to the countries' ethos in observing human rights.

5.1 Wielding Democracy Through Centralization and Decentralization

The Brazilian government's centralization can be observed in the country since the Social Liberal Party's victory in 2018 [34]. During the COVID-19 pandemic, the centralization showed traces of authoritarianism when the Ministry of Education avoided complying with democratic prerogatives. The discourses emphasize school governance by laws and regulations and is one effect of authoritarianism. The discourses reveal a top-down model that reduced a decision-making according to local needs and had a direct impact on education. For instance, the MEC's Minister Abraham Weintraub publicly minimized the pandemic's seriousness and protested mayors' and governors' decisions to close schools [35]. National universities wanted to close schools and continue with remote education to contain social inequalities in education [36–39]. Instead of bringing together governors, mayors, health authorities, and education-related institutions for decision-making on joint actions to minimize the impacts of the pandemic on education, MEC insisted on taking its own path and asked the population to pressure governors and mayors to regain what the Minister of Education called "common sense" and reopen schools [40]. For example, MEC provided hygiene kits to schools throughout the year even when they were closed to provide good sanitary conditions and reactivate face-to-face education. Hence, Brazilian centralization is expressed through the MEC's decision-making taken in isolation from other educational institutions, states, and municipal governments. It contradicts the inclusive character given to local institutions for investigating local needs and participating in decision-making, which is a hallmark of the country's re-democratization [41, 42]. The centralized governance affected democracy because it ended up in authoritarian instead of more inclusive and decentralized practices to solve various issues. The authoritarianism also resulted in social inequalities because social actors were silenced and imprecise federal funding to support local needs was delivered. Conclusively, the year 2020 ended with a decline in the local entities' participation in the decision-making with a rise in social inequalities in education [43].

Contrary to the Brazilian centralization, the Swedish discourse related to a decentralized democratic structure. During the COVID-19 pandemic, the Swedish people's historic high trust in the state made newly adopted decisions approved quickly on a local level. According to Nygren and Olofsson [44], the Swedish culture shows specific ethopolitics, understood as governing of conduct and individual responsibilization where the state is a mediator between specialists to provide recommendations for personal choices. For instance, the Swedish government acted between the SDE, The Swedish Public Health Agency, municipalities, and school principals. These actions were observed in the government's discourses that dealt with maintaining equal education with resources and re-organization of local entities. The authorities' executive power made the National Health Agency's recommendations to, e.g., keep schools open, principals occupied with organizing hybrid teaching in face-to-face, distance, and remote modes. At the same time, local entities were complying with the "[p]ersonal responsibility rather than legislation [...] to take measures so that employees could keep social distancing" [17].

5.2   Neoliberalism

Over the past 40 years, most democratic countries around the world have operated neoliberal policies. From a neo-Marxist perspective, neoliberal rationality is based on a redefinition of the state as a regulator of social life by reducing welfare state policies. For instance, deregulation of capital and organized labor, public services' privatization, for-profit, and favorable financial environments for foreign investors to expand multinational companies are a few examples. According to a Foucaultian perspective, a neo-liberal rationality is re-signifying the government, the subjectivities and subjects. Subjectivities and subjects are active in capital entrepreneurship and competitive environments that demand the state to be a guarantor (and not a regulator) of the new subjects' and subjectivities' demands. Inspired by these theoretical perspectives, Wendy Brown [1, 2] investigated the neoliberal rationality and how the reduction and resignification of the primary democratization agent [3], the state, has impact on democracy and social inequalities. Drawing on these perspectives, some aspects are fascinating to illuminate. First, Brown [1] observes that resignification moves the states' actions towards conservative morality. It is a reduction and a cultural revision of the classical liberal concept of freedom (i.e., the satisfaction of personal needs) diminished to "unregulated personal license", which has been present in historically privileged groups' discourses and actions and increased their role in social movements and political parties worldwide. Connections between neoliberalism and increased conservative morality, associated with political right-populist and extreme parties expanding their presence on the political scene, are salient in Brazil's and Sweden's governance. Second, Brown also notes that the reduction and resignification impact citizens' review of their citizenship resulting in them sacrificing political participation in the pursuit of individual economic growth because it is the primary condition for empowerment and social development. Both principles are setbacks in democratization [3]. Although these two tenets can be observed in Brazil and Sweden, the first principle around conservative morality is emphasized in Brazil's discourse around education. In contrast, sacrificial citizenship is used to understand the Swedish government's actions.

The presidential election in 2018 explicitly advanced the neoliberal ideology, and privatizations of public services took off along with strict measures to cut investments on welfare policies, which got even more accentuated in Brazil during this time [45]. The discourses conveyed by the Brazilian government and actors such as Weintraub (MEC), Paulo Guedes (Minister of Economy), Damares Alves (Minister of Culture), and Jair Bolsonaro (President of the Republic) indicate a strong interest in restructuring national education to eliminate what they call "cultural marxism." [46] This tendency is considered an ideology that dominated the Brazilian discourse and foreign schools and universities and international organizations such as the UN, depriving them from traditional moral values. For instance, sex education, LGBTQIA +, feminism, human rights, and the politicization of life are examples of what they call distortions of traditional values during the last decades.

The Brazilian government's restructuring of national education is also a privatization project. It reduced the state's interference in the economy and society. One privatization measure advocated during this time was home-schooling - seen as a freedom for the family to offer education [46]. Another measure was the implementation of voucher policies – as a freedom for low-income families to enroll students in private for-profit or confessional schools [47]. However, these neoliberal projects suffered widespread common and congressional resistance. Later, MEC protested against mayors' and governors' decision to close schools while allowing for the Ministry of Economy to implement activities that promoted individual economic growth to avoid social inequalities [40]. In summary, there is a centralization of political power by the federal government in Brazil, which conflicts with the country's recent democratization [3] and leads to authoritarianism. Privatization of education associated with a conservative morality, a depolitization of citizenship, and a conception of personal economic growth became means for reducing social inequalities [2] and can be observed in the federal government's actions during the pandemic to change education.

Brown's perspective is helpful to identify how the decentralized governance in Sweden relates to the Swedish ethos, salient in the government's discourse around education during the COVID-19 pandemic. In the early 1980s, Sweden began adopting neoliberal policies promoted by center-right parties. Deregulation and decentralization and slowly privatized education were some of the outcomes. The reforms resulted in transferred responsibilities from the government to municipalities and principals for the governance and financing of education [7]. These measures were necessary to improve education and social justice in schools since deregulated and decentralized projects and financial resources could better meet local demands [8]. The other Nordic countries also adopted these changes, but while they authorized privatization and for-profit entrepreneurship to a limited extent, Sweden "has been eager to incorporate neoliberal ideas" [7, p. 128]. According to Nygren and Olofsson [44], the Swedish culture shows a specific ethopolitics in this way, where governing of conduct and individual responsibilization is strong. The state is a mediator between specialists and authorities and provides recommendations for personal choice, which signifies Swedes' high trust in the state and its distinction to other countries. According to Strang, ethopolitics is also marked by financial values being salient in the public debate and "that a functioning economy is a prerequisite for people's well-being and health." [48] Thus, individual economic growth is viewed as a key to a collective reduction of inequalities, which made the governments decide not to lockdown during the COVID-19 to keep the economy running and generate social advances. Alongside the absence of supervision and supportive leadership, neoliberalist tendencies are factors that influenced the government's discourse around social inequality during the pandemic, mainly focused on local measures to support schooling. The decentralized governance reduced equal schooling for all by providing fewer opportunities for quality control of services, which undermined the democratic institutions' power to secure social equality in areas such as education, instead occupied by private and for-profit entrepreneurship. Consequently, the neoliberalized ethos with high trust in the state resulted in a transfer of responsibility for the well-being from the critical and politically active citizen to the successful individual citizen focused on economic growth. In summary, Sweden's culture is more tolerant to neoliberal advances, sacrificial citizenship, and decision-making distributed under a functioning economy, which weaken citizens' abilities to be critical to the government's decisions [48].

6 Conclusions

Understanding the Brazilian and Swedish organizations of education during the pandemic is essential since both countries can influence other parts of the world. The crisis' impact on the countries was identified by paying attention to similar or contrasting issues in the political welfare states' characteristics and organization. This article specifically observed the entities responsible for the democratic and citizen formation: the Ministry of Education in Brazil and the Department of Education in Sweden. The following research question guided the explorations of the governments' discourses: *how are democracy and social inequality expounded in Brazil's and Sweden's way of organizing education during the COVID-19 pandemic?*

Two underlying causes affected democracy and social inequalities in Brazil and Sweden's way of organizing education during the COVID-19 pandemic. First, Brazil's centralized government instituted programs for teaching and learning. In contrast, the Swedish decentralized government offered support to principals to adopt local measures. Accelerated privatization of education was identified as a similarity in both countries. The advance of neoliberalism influences the governments' actions to keep the economy functioning during the COVID-19 pandemic, where individual economic growth is the main driver to overcome social inequalities and affected education during this period. Neoliberalism was observed in the authoritarian actions taken by the current Brazilian government and more culturally contingent actions related to the openness of the Swedish ethos. For instance, the new government in Brazil was reducing welfare policies on a central level, where education was an essential entity for changes. Conservative political parties and social groups embraced neoliberalism, which marked the redefinition of the classical liberal freedom into conservative morality - a satisfaction of personal needs for neoliberal freedom and unregulated personal license - which in many cases justified oppression [1]. The Swedish ethos - governing of conduct and individual responsibilization – resulted in an increased shift towards an economization of citizens' life. High trust in the state characterized by a decentralized and delegated political responsibility to authorities undermined citizens' critical vigilance of political decision-making. An economization of citizenship and depolitization of the economy [2] increasingly forms the Swedish culture into sacrificial citizenship.

The COVID-19 pandemic led to an increased economization of political life associated with neoliberalism and reduced citizen participation in collective decision-making, which affect the organization of education. A relevant issue is the democratization [3] expanding popular participation in the collective decision-making under intense social movements. It is interesting to reflect on recent and further changes in democracy and its impacts on policies to reduce social inequalities. For this reason, questions of interest are raised based on the observations of the governments' discourses and consecrated literature without any pretensions of solving them. This study is limited why more investigations are required to enable more precise and profound conclusions.

References

1. Brown, W.: In the Ruins of Neoliberalism: The Rise of Antidemocratic Politics in the West. Columbia University Press, New York (2019)
2. Brown, W.: Sacrificial citizenship: neoliberalism, human capital, and austerity politics. Constellations **23**(1), 3–14 (2016)
3. Dahl, R.A.: Polyarchy: Participation and Opposition. Yale University Press, London (1973)
4. Brasil.: Base Nacional Comum Curricular. Ministério da Educação, Brasília (2018)
5. Peroni, V.M.V. (eds.): Redefinições das fronteiras entre o público e o privado: implicações para a democratização da educação. Liber Livro, Brasília (2013)
6. Adrião, T.: Dimensões e formas da privatização da educação no Brasil: caracterização a partir de mapeamento de produções nacionais e internacionais. Currículo sem Fronteiras **18** (1), 8–28 (2018)
7. Dovemark, M., Kosunen, S., Kauko, J., Magnúsdóttir, B., Hansen, P., Rasmussen, P.: Deregulation, privatisation and marketisation of Nordic comprehensive education: social changes reflected in schooling. Educ. Inq. **9**(1), 122–141 (2018)
8. Johannesson, I.A., Lindblad, S., Simola, H.: An inevitable progress? Educational restructuring in Finland, Iceland, and Sweden at the turn of the millennium. Scand. J. Educ. Res. **46**(1), 325–339 (2002)
9. Wiborg, S.: Privatizing education: free school policy in Sweden and England. Comp. Educ. Rev. **59**(3), 473–497 (2015)
10. Matos, C.C., Reis, M.E., Silva, S.P.: As Reverberações do Pensamento Liberal na Educação e sua Atualidade em Tempos de Pandemia. In: Uchoa, A.M., Sena, C., de Gonçalves, I.P.F. (eds.) Diálogos Críticos, volume 3: EAD, Atividades remotas e o ensino doméstico: cadê a escola? Editora Fi, Porto Alegre (2020)
11. Luna: 1 ano do corte de Weintraub: balbúrdia é o governo Bolsonaro (2020). https://www.cartacapital.com.br/opiniao/1-ano-do-corte-de-weintraub-balburdia-e-o-governo-bolsonaro/
12. Raic, D.F.F., Cardoso, M.C., Pereira, S.A.C.: A universidade pública em cenários neoliberais e fascistas: barbúrdias de resistência em tempos de Covid-19. Revista Eletrônica de Educação **14**(1), 1–19 (2020)
13. Mariz, R.: Ministro da Educação vai cortar 30% das verbas de todas as universidades federais (2019). https://oglobo.globo.com/sociedade/educacao/ministro-da-educacao-vai-cortar-30-das-verbas-de-todas-as-universidades-federais-23634159
14. Rezende, C.: Weintraub: 'Não quero sociólogo, antropólogo e filósofo com meu dinheiro' (2020). https://noticias.uol.com.br/colunas/constanca-rezende/2020/06/14/weintraub-nao-quero-sociologo-antropologo-e-filosofo-com-meu-dinheiro.htm?utm_source=twitter&utm_medium=social-media&utm_content=geral&utm_campaign=uol
15. Burström, B.: What is happening in Sweden? Int. J. Health Serv. **49**(2), 204–211 (2019)
16. Sivesind, K.H.: The changing roles of for-profit and nonprofit welfare provision in Norway, Sweden, and Denmark. In: Sivesind, K., Saglie, J. (eds.) Promoting Active Citizenship, pp. 33–74. Palgrave Macmillan, London (2017).
17. Diderichsen, F.: How did Sweden Fail the Pandemic? Int. J. Health Serv. **51**(4), 417–422 (2021)
18. Meagher, G., Szebehely, M.: The politics of profit in Swedish welfare services: four decades of Social Democratic ambivalence. Crit. Soc. Policy **39**(3), 455–476 (2019)
19. Dahlgren, G.: Why public health services? Experiences from profit-driven health care reforms in Sweden. Int. J. Health Serv. **44**(1), 507–524 (2014)
20. Szebehely, M.: Internationella erfarenheter AV covid-19 i äldreboenden. Underlagsrapport till SOU, 80 (2020)

21. Ruis, A.R., Lee, S.B.: Advances in quantitative ethnography. Springer, Cham (2021). https://doi.org/10.1007/978-3-030-33232-7
22. Field, A.: Discovering statistics using IBM SPSS statistics. Sage, London (2013)
23. Shaffer, D.W., Ruis, A.R.: How We Code. In: Ruis, A.R., Lee, S.B. (eds.) ICQE 2021. CCIS, vol. 1312, pp. 62–77. Springer, Cham (2021). https://doi.org/10.1007/978-3-030-67788-6_5
24. Shaffer, D.W.: Quantitative Ethnography. Cathcart Press, Madison (2017)
25. Marquart, C.L., Hinojosa, C., Swiecki, Z., Eagan, B., Shaffer, D.W.: Epistemic Network Analysis (Version 1.7.0) [Software] (2018). https://app.epistemicnetwork.org
26. Zörgő, S., Swiecki, Z., Ruis, A.R.: Exploring the Effects of Segmentation on Semi-structured Interview Data with Epistemic Network Analysis. In: Ruis, A.R., Lee, S.B. (eds.) ICQE 2021. CCIS, vol. 1312, pp. 78–90. Springer, Cham (2021). https://doi.org/10.1007/978-3-030-67788-6_6
27. Hinojosa, C., Siebert-Evenstone, A.L., Eagan, B.R., Swiecki, Z., Gleicher, M., Marquart, C.: nCoder [Software] (2019). https://app.n-coder.org/
28. Shaffer, D.W., Collier, W., Ruis, A.R.: A tutorial on epistemic network analysis: analyzing the structure of connections in cognitive, social, and interaction data. J. Learn Anal. 3(3), 9–45 (2016)
29. Arendt, H.: The Promise of Politics. Knopf Doubleday Publishing Group, New York (2009)
30. Bobbio, N.: O futuro da democracia: uma defesa das regras do jogo. Paz e Terra, Rio de Janeiro (1986)
31. Gramsci, A.: Os Intelectuais e a Organização da Cultura. Civilização Brasileira, Rio de Janeiro (1991)
32. Saviani, D.: Escola e democracia: teorias da educação, curvatura da vara, onze teses sobre educação e política. Autores Associados, Campinas (1999)
33. Marshall, T.H.: Part I: Citizenship and Social Class. In: Marshall, T., Bottomore, T. (eds.) Citizenship and Social Class. Pluto Press, London (1992)
34. da Silva, M.G., Rodrigues, T.C.M.: O Populismo de Direita no Brasil: Neoliberalismo e Autoritarismo no Governo Bolsonaro. Mediações 26(1), 86–107 (2021)
35. Martins, I.: Weintraub pede volta às aulas em cidades com poucos casos de coronavírus. (2020). www.correiobraziliense.com.br/app/noticia/eu-estudante/ensino_educacaobasica/2020/04/16/interna-educacaobasica-2019,845316/weintraub-pede-volta-as-aulas-em-cidades-com-poucos-casos-de-coronavir.shtml
36. Hartmann, M., Boff, T.: Aulas a distância aumentam fosso entre escolas públicas e particulares (2020). https://gauchazh.clicrbs.com.br/educacao-e-emprego/noticia/2020/05/aulas-a-distancia-aumentam-fosso-entre-escolas-publicas-e-particulares-ckabhvddv006l015nlc5sjrpe.html
37. Roubicek, M.: O que diz o primeiro dado de desemprego na pandemia (2020). https://nexojornal.com.br/expresso/2020/04/30/O-que-diz-o-primeiro-dado-de-desemprego-na-pandemia
38. Pasti, A., Bandeirs, O.: Como o ensino a distância pode agravar as desigualdades agora. Nexo Jornal (2020). https://www.nexojornal.com.br/ensaio/debate/2020/Como-o-ensino-a-distância-pode-agravar-as-desigualdades-agora
39. UFJF: Pesquisa da Andifes demonstra papel das universidades no combate à Covid-19. (2020). https://www2.ufjf.br/noticias/2020/05/11/pesquisa-da-andifes-demonstra-papel-as-universidades-no-combate-a-covid-19/
40. Ministério da Educação do Brasil: Nota Oficial de 16 de Março de 2020 (2020). http://portal.mec.gov.br/index.php?option=com_content&view=article&id=86341:comite-de-emergencia-do-mec-define-primeiras-acoes-contra-o-coronavirus&catid=33381&Itemid=86

41. Brasil: Artigo 211 da Constituição da República Federativa do Brasil (1988). http://www.senado.leg.br/atividade/const/con1988/con1988_04.02.2010/art_211_.asp
42. Brasil: Artigo 8 da Lei de Diretrizes e Bases da Educação Nacional (1996). http://www.planalto.gov.br/ccivil_03/leis/l9394.htm
43. Todos pela Educação: 2º relatório anual de acompanhamento do Educação Já. (2021), https://todospelaeducacao.org.br/wordpress/wp-content/uploads/2021/02/2o-Relatorio-Anual-de-Acompanhamento-do-Educacao-Ja_final.pdf
44. Nygren, K.G., Olofsson, A.: Managing the covid-19 pandemic through individual responsibility: the consequences of a world risk society and enhanced ethopolitics. J. Risk Res. **23**, 1031–1035 (2020)
45. Beltrão, J.A., Teixeira, R.D., Taffarel, C.N.Z. Melo, F.D.A., Tranzilo, P.J.R.: A Ofensiva dos Reformadores Empresariais da Educação em Tempos de Pandemia: o desastre social como oportunidade para avançar na privatização da Educação Básica. In: Uchoa, A.M., da Sena, C., de Gonçalves, I.P.F. (eds.) Diálogos Críticos, volume 3: EAD, Atividades remotas e o ensino doméstico: cadê a escola? Editora Fi, Porto Alegre (2020)
46. Taffarel, C.N.Z., Nevez, M.L.C.: Tendências da educação frente à correlação de forças na luta de classes: uma análise do governo Bolsonaro na perspectiva educacional. Estudos IAT **4**(2), 310–329 (2019)
47. Franco, C., Maranhão Filho, E.M., A.: A teocratização, privatização e militarização no governo Bolsonaro: perspectivas antidemocráticas e contrárias à educação. Mandrágoras **26**(1), 203–224 (2020)
48. Strang, J.: Why do the Nordic countries react differently to the covid-19 crisis? (2020). https://nordics.info/show/artikel/the-nordic-countries-react-differently-to-the-covid-19-crisis/

Changes, Longings, and Potentials for Future Pedagogical Practices: Investigating University Teachers' Experiences During the Spring 2020 Lockdown

Liv Nøhr[✉], Emil Bøgh Løkkegaard, Ruth Horak,
Maria Hvid Stenalt[iD], and Morten Misfeldt[iD]

University of Copenhagen, Copenhagen, Denmark
lnsl@ind.ku.dk

Abstract. This paper takes a quantitative ethnographic approach to understand how the lockdown in the spring of 2020 affected the teachers' work situation at a large university in Denmark. Based on free-text responses from survey data, we create epistemic networks to explore how teachers articulate changes, longings, and potentials for their own future digital teaching practices based on their experiences of the first lockdown. The findings illustrate that interaction and human contact, which play a pivotal role in teachers' didactical skillsets and efforts to create good learning environments, were missing during the lockdown. The study also highlights that teachers' perceptions of the inability of digital, technological solutions appear to relate to on-campus teaching ideals. As such, this paper argues that future crisis-handling, as well as developments and refinements of digital teaching formats, at the university, should be attentive to support and foster better areas of contact and interaction between students and teachers.

Keywords: COVID-19 · nCoder · University Teachers · Epistemic Network Analysis · Digital Teaching

1 Introduction

As COVID-19 stepped onto the world stage, universities worldwide found themselves in the precarious situation of attempting to maintain their day-to-day workflows and activity levels in an abruptly digitalized context. Though most universities have undergone some level of digitalization, few teachers on campus-grounded universities had ever facilitated all their teaching online before. This amounted to several difficulties for the teachers, as they had to reconfigure their teaching to fit a digital classroom.

As teachers had to navigate in this extraordinary scenario, they had several concerns that interrelated across different aspects of teaching. These concerns include the difficulties they faced, aspects of online formats they questioned, and/or possibilities they found promising. Though the case is unique, the way teachers connect concerns regarding digital teaching can illustrate how they understand digital teaching (compared to their prior teaching experience) and indicate how to better support teachers generally as well as in the case of another crisis.

© Springer Nature Switzerland AG 2022
B. Wasson and S. Zörgő (Eds.): ICQE 2021, CCIS 1522, pp. 318–333, 2022.
https://doi.org/10.1007/978-3-030-93859-8_21

The paper is set in the context of the University of Copenhagen (UCPH) in Denmark, where a cross-organizational working group was established with the purpose of monitoring the effect of the lockdown on teaching and learning within the university. In Denmark, the use of IT has been part of a political agenda since 2007, but the use of technology in teaching various greatly within the country [1]. Like most other universities, UCPH has units that are responsible for managing instructional technology and facilitating teachers, both concerning pedagogics and technological skills (ibid.). Though teachers are supported by the units, teachers are themselves responsible for planning and organizing the individual courses.

The working group chose to investigate the lockdown using several combined approaches (see 1.2), including a teacher survey, where teachers were asked (1) how they changed their way of teaching during the lockdown period, (2) what they were missing from teaching on campus, and (3) if they had any positive experiences with online teaching they would consider bringing into their on-campus teaching. Using teachers' replies to these questions, this paper is based on the following research question:

What concerns about transitioning to digital teaching did teachers at UCPH describe during a spring 2020 survey, how did these concerns interrelate, and what perception of digital teaching does this indicate?

To begin with, we summarize the international existing knowledge of online teaching during COVID19-related lockdowns at various tertiary educational institutions, and outline what we know about the UCPH teachers' work situation during the lockdown. Then, we investigate the teachers' concerns and how they interrelate. This is done by a combination of qualitative and quantitative methods, focusing primarily on the way teachers express their concerns in their free-text responses in the teacher survey.

We use nCoder [2] to code the teachers' 1445 qualitative replies to the three aforementioned questions into themes related to analogue and digital elements, flexibility, interaction with students, teaching formats and questions related to time and work conditions. The coding of replies into broader themes allows us to address the question of which main changes the teachers experienced during the lockdown, their longings, the problems and pedagogical potentials they point out, as well as the relationship between them.

In the analysis, we explore the most prominent concerns in a descriptive manner. Furthermore, we run an Epistemic Network Analysis (ENA) [3–5] to map the interrelation between different themes, both within the same questions, and the interrelation of themes across questions and teachers. Finally, we will discuss our findings and their significance in the broader context of the digitalization of university teaching.

1.1   Teachers' Experiences During COVID-19 Internationally

Teachers' experiences of online teaching in times of emergency have been brought into focus through ongoing discussions of what and how to learn from COVID-19. Despite little experience with online teaching, existing research illustrates how teachers quickly embraced digital technologies for online teaching [6], experienced it to work better than expected [7], and were positive about the innovations of teaching methods [6]. However, the literature also points out that the crisis-response migration method adopted by many universities in the Spring of 2020 was limited to delivery format [8] without paying sufficient attention to the disrupture of teachers' normal work conditions and teaching practices. According to the study by Watermeyer et al. [9], the abrupt move towards online delivery of content was a vulnerable and professionally disempowering experience on the teachers' part. It is suggested that teachers overcame the transition despite workload and time organization issues [10], technical issues [11], and at the expense of quality educational interactions [12].

1.2   The University of Copenhagen and the Lockdown in Spring 2020

UCPH is a public campus-based university with a limited portfolio in digital/online teaching. The university has a unit-based support structure helping teachers with technology use. Digitalizing education has been part of government policies since 2007, and the general level of digitalization in Denmark is slightly higher than similar countries (e.g., Norway) [1]. The level of digitalization varies greatly however within Denmark (ibid.).

The first lockdown period lasted from mid-semester (March 12th, 2020) until the end of the semester [13]. In this period, UCPH implemented new technological solutions to enable the transition to online teaching formats. The technological landscape thus changed during this period, i.e., the Zoom platform which became fully accessible in the end of March.

Early in the process, UCPH decided to establish a cross-organizational working group that should monitor the transition closely. The purpose of the initiative was to leverage the lockdown experience to achieve long-term improvements by applying the insights from the lockdown to enhance the general quality of digital and on-campus teaching and learning. The working group applied a combined approach consisting of 1) a meta-study of the already existing knowledge in the organization, 2) qualitative interviews with teachers and students, 3) a student survey, and 4) a teacher survey.

The general conclusion across the different research elements was that the transition was challenging [13], both due to the lack of technological solutions available, and the lack of experience with online teaching for the teachers' part. Teachers reported that the forced digitalization could only be regarded as an emergency solution that they would not choose to repeat under normal circumstances. Furthermore, teachers and students both reported that the learning outcome decreased during the lockdown [13, 14]. They highlighted a limited number of interactive elements in teaching and decreased contact between teachers and students as the key problem in establishing an effective online learning environment. From the meta-study, it is evident that teachers evaluate online teaching along the same parameters as campus teaching, despite a broad agreement that the two are fundamentally different. Finally, the teacher survey shows that teachers generally found one-way communication, such as recorded lectures or presentations of core concepts, the easiest to translate into an online setting [13].

2   Methods

2.1   The Survey

The meta-study revealed a lack of knowledge of teachers' experiences during the lockdown. To make up for this lack, a teacher survey was developed. The survey focused on teachers' general thoughts on the transition, the type of teaching they had adopted, the resources they used to help them transition, and teachers' experiences with digital teaching before the lockdown [13]. Thus, the survey design consisted of six different modules covering the themes 1) experiences during the lockdown, 2) future use of digital tools, 3) educational tools, 4) online oral exams, 5) practical challenges, and 6) demographic information about the teacher. The modules entailed a combination of Likert scale-, multiple-choice-, and free-text questions.

The survey was distributed to 3105 teachers across UCPH who were teaching during the lockdown. 837 replied, which amounts to a response rate of 26.9%. Questions of teachers' prior experience with digital teaching and their assessment of students' learning were then investigated by comparing along parameters such as faculty, experience, teacher demographics, and work conditions [13].

The three free-text questions that we will investigate to gain a better understanding of the interrelation of concerns that teachers had during the transition are:

- Q1: "what have you changed in your remote teaching practice?"
- Q2: "what do you miss the most from teaching on campus?"
- Q3: "are there any positive aspects of remote teaching that you hope will continue when on-campus teaching starts again? Which, and why?"

Not all teachers responded to the free-text questions. 269 responded to Q1, 525 to Q2, and 571 to Q3. Teachers were only asked to reply to Q1 if they had altered their remote teaching during the lockdown, which naturally results in a smaller number of replies.

Table 1. Distribution of free-text responses compared to faculties.

Faculty	Frequency	Percentage
Health and Medical Sciences	489	35.8
Humanities	313	22.9
Science	284	20.8
Social Sciences	181	13.3
Law	70	5.13
Theology	28	2.05

The free-text replies stem from across UCPH, with the majority coming from the Faculty of Health and Medical Sciences (35.8%), Faculty of Humanities (22.9%) and Faculty of Science (20.8%) (Table 1). To a certain extent, this corresponds to the general size difference among the faculties at UCPH, with the Faculty of Health and Medical Sciences being the largest, followed by the Faculty of Science, and then the Faculty of Humanities.

2.2 Semi-automated Coding of Free-Text Responses Using nCODER

Due to the large number of free-text responses, manual coding became impractical. Therefore, we used the semi-automated coding tool, nCoder, to code the free-text responses [2]. We chose the initial signifiers in close engagement with the data, developing codes based on exploratory readings of the answers and comparisons of the words most frequently used in the responses.

An automated coder, such as nCoder, identifies whether a piece of data belongs to a certain category. By using nCoder we constructed sets of 'rules' consisting of specific words or phrases that imply specific themes. These 'rules' were then applied to the dataset and used to assign corresponding values to the free texts replies [2]. nCoder helped us validate our sets of rules by drawing a random subset, which we hand-coded individually and then compared with the coding from our initial signifiers. This back-and-forth movement allowed a deeper exploration of the data and the discovery of relevant signifiers. After the individual hand-coding, we would update signifiers in the classifier if deemed relevant. Then, we passed it on to a second-rater, who would also individually hand-code it. When faced with irregularities in the code, we worked collaboratively towards consistent intercoder reliability, through elaborating on our signifiers. Finally, nCoder provides a kappa value that measures the precision in the machine coding compared to human coding. It also provides a rho-value that approximates the share of codes that would differ if both humans and machines coded the whole dataset (ibid.). We used these as indicators to assure stable codes across the material, aiming for a rho-value less than 0.3 on a subset of a minimum of 80 replies.

2.3 Epistemic Network Analysis

To understand the relations between teachers' concerns and compare them across the three different questions, we conducted an Epistemic Network Analysis (ENA). ENA is a quantitative ethnographic technique for quantifying, visualizing, and interpreting network data [3–5]. Theoretically, the general assumption of ENA is that the structure of connections *among* elements is more important than those elements in isolation [3]. Thus, ENA allows us to identify and measure connections in the coded free-text replies and represent them in network models. With these models, we can compare how teachers' concerns are connected across the different questions.

We applied ENA to our data using the ENA Web Tool (Version 1.7.0). We defined the *units* of analysis as the three questions divided by individual teacher and were interested in the relation of themes between them. As such, the individual teacher and question were also our *conversation*, that is, the lines (relationship) which the ENA establishes between the themes and the units.

Furthermore, the ENA algorithm uses a moving window to construct network models for each of the lines in the data, showing how codes in the current line are connected to codes that occur within the recent temporal context [15]. Here, we opted for the Conversation Method which models connections within an entire activity (all free-text answers are related to one another).[1] The resulting networks are then aggregated for all lines for each unit of analysis. In our case, this aggregation is achieved through binary summation in which networks for a given line reflect either presence or absence of co-occurrence of codes.

The ENA model normalized the networks for all units of analysis before they were subjected to dimensional reduction, which accounts for the fact that different units of analysis may have different amounts of coded lines in the data. For the dimensional reduction, we used a singular value decomposition, which produces orthogonal dimensions that maximize the variance explained by each dimension [4].

Networks were visualized using network graphs where nodes correspond to the codes, and edges reflect the relative frequency of co-occurrence, or connection, between two codes. This results in two coordinated representations for each unit of analysis: (1) a plotted point, which represents the location of that unit's network in the low-dimensional projected space, and (2) a weighted network graph. The positions of the network graph nodes are fixed, and those positions are determined by an optimization routine that minimizes the difference between the plotted points and their corresponding network centroids. Because of this co-registration of network graphs and projected space, the positions of the network graph modes can be used to interpret the dimensions of the projected space and explain the positions of the plotted points in the space.

As ENA is a mixed method, our analysis consists of both quantitative and qualitative elements. The quantitative part of the analysis involves creating the network and investigating quantitative connections between codes; that is, comparing different connections both within and across the three questions in terms of their 'strength' (how many free-text responses make up given connections). As such, we can visualize connections between codes and get quantitative measurements of what connections are more present than others. The qualitative part consists of 1) interpreting the projected space the connections are made within, as well as 2) drawing on and describing the free-text responses which the connections consist of. This allows us to close the interpretive loop: we start with a coded dataset which we use to create and visualize a network; we use quantitative measurements as indicative of 'strong' or relevant connections in the data. Finally, we use the free-text responses to understand the connections qualitatively.

3 Results

3.1 The Teacher Survey

Several findings emerged from the teacher survey. First, while teachers managed to transition to online education, they generally assessed the students' learning outcome in 2020 to have decreased compared to 2019. With 58% assessing the learning outcome to

---

[1] Another choice could have been the Moving Stanza Window, which models connections only when utterances are in close temporal proximity within an activity. However, as the free-text responses relate to the same overall questions, and each response is not temporally related as such, this method did not seem relevant.

be either lower or significantly lower, the general assertion of the quality of the digital education was that it did not reach the same level as its pre-pandemic, on-campus counterpart.

Second, the survey shows that teachers lacked experience with online teaching. Only 24% of the teachers had some or extensive experience in digital teaching methods before the lockdown, and an overwhelming 44% did not have any experience in digital teaching methods whatsoever.

Third, teachers were asked if they had changed their remote teaching practice during the corona lockdown. The 591 teachers responding 'yes' to this question were asked what had motivated them to change their remote teaching. Learning technology was the most prominent reason for changing the remote teaching approach, either due to discovering new technologies (70%) or by becoming more familiar with the technologies (48%). Some also changed their approach due to specific requests from students (33%) or because they lacked the pedagogical options they needed in their initial choices (32%). For a minor part of the teachers, the change was due to the realization that the time consumption was disproportional to the students learning outcome (14%).

Given that so many teachers were inexperienced and assessed the students' learning outcomes to have decreased significantly, our Epistemic Network Analysis thus seeks to add some qualitative layer of complexity to the teacher survey's quantitative assessment of the teachers' struggles during the lockdown.

3.2   Coding and nCoder

To examine the teachers' concerns during the lockdown, we coded the free-text responses. We started by developing codes related to each question individually but ended up recoding the data into broader themes that applied to all three questions. The themes built on the initial codes, which consisted of dictionaries developed through close reading of the free-text responses, grouping words together that seemed to signify specific attitudes, difficulties, solutions etc., and combining them with words and phrases indicative of findings from the previous work of the working group (i.e. the teacher survey etc.). Thus, recoding occurred due to similarities in the codes across the questions, but also due to similarities when relating them more broadly to the findings of the cross-organizational working group at UCPH. An overview of the six themes can be seen below, including definitions and qualitative examples.

Table 2. The six codes, definitions, examples, and the IRR.

Name	Definition	Example	IRR
Analogue elements	When chalk, blackboards, rooms, body language, and/or other physical elements are mentioned	*"Practically, I have missed black/whiteboard."* *"Ultra-difficult to do clinical teaching with demonstrations on patients when neither patients nor students are physically present, and the speciality is visually focused."*	$k = 0.80$ $rho = 0.26$ $n = 80$

(continued)

Table 2. (*continued*)

Name	Definition	Example	IRR
Digital elements	References to cameras, microphones, chats, Zoom, Padlet and other digital platforms and/or technologies	*"Video lectures are good but if the students lack knowledge on a central element, it is only caught in the Q&A-session and that is too late."*	$k = 0.89$ $rho = 0.08$ $n = 80$
Flexibility	References made to flexibility or flexible solutions in different areas such as location, scheduling, sickness etc	*"I am thinking that one could teach remotely for brief periods of time, it is very nice sometimes to not have to travel to the actual teaching site, but everybody can stay home."*	$k = 0.81$ $rho = 0.20$ $n = 80$
Interaction with students	Social and pedagogical, formal, and informal aspects of interaction and communication with students	*"To be present in the same room and teach vividly, that is, where one can sense the atmosphere in the room and continuously interact face-to-face with the students."* *"I miss getting to know the students better in the breaks [...]"*	$k = 0.80$ $rho = 0.22$ $n = 80$
Teaching formats	When referencing concrete ways of teaching i.e., discussions, practical exercises, lectures etc	*"To do discussion exercises with larger teams where I do not have to control the dialogue as much as on Zoom."*	$k = 0.78$ $rho = 0.22$ $n = 80$
Time and salary	Mentions of work conditions in relation to either time consumption, salary, or both	*"Time-saving. You can freely draw on teachers in other countries for courses. Maybe some hotshots that would not have attended a physical course. That is probably most relevant for PhD-courses and PhD-defenses."*	$k = 0.83$ $rho = 0.18$ $n = 101$

The themes are coded to have a rho-value smaller than 0.3 and a kappa-value of ~0.80. Each of them touches upon different aspects of digital teaching, from pedagogical (teaching formats, interaction with students) to technical (digital/analogue elements) to aspects related to work conditions (flexibility, time, and salary). Using nCoder, the six codes were distributed to a total number of 1445 free-text answers, resulting in 1837 codes. It is expected that the amount codes are higher than the number of responses, since some of the responses have multiple codes attached to them while others only have one or even none. The themes, definitions, examples, and the IRRs can be seen in Table 2.

Table 3. Frequency of themes.

Teaching formats	509	35.23%	Interaction with students	664	45.95%
Digital elements	414	28.65%	Flexibility		70	4.84%
Analogue elements	127	8.80%	Time and salary		53	3.67%

As is evident from Table 3, the applicability of the themes onto the data differs. Interaction with students is the most pronounced theme, which 45.95% of the answers relate to. Teaching formats (35.23%) and digital elements (28.65%) are also highly relevant, applying to approximately a third of the replies. Less apparent are analogue elements (8.80%), and the themes relating to the work situation, flexibility (4.84%), and time and salary (3.67%).

3.3 The Epistemic Network Analysis Model

We estimated the models by grouping the units by question. This enabled us to compare which concerns the teachers interrelated when answering the three questions. To investigate the difference between the three estimated models, we compared their mean values (two at a time), using a t-test assuming unequal variance at a significance-level of 5%. All tests were significant, indicating that the three types of questions resulted in different connections and networks.

As the ENA is projecting a multidimensional space into a comprehensible 2-dimensional space, one needs to check the goodness of fit of the nodes into the two axes. Using a Pearson correlation, we find that the X-axis has a 0.92 correlation, and the Y-axis has a 0.91 correlation.

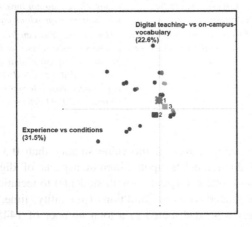

Fig. 1. Plotting of the model including means.

The networks and the corresponding projected dimensional space can be seen in Fig. 1. The x-axis explains 31.5% of the variance, and thus has the largest explanatory power of the two dimensions. We named it "Experiences vs conditions" as it is fluctuating between teaching formats and interaction with students, placed in the left-side quadrants, and analogue elements, as well as flexibility, time, and salary, placed in the right-side quadrants (see Fig. 2, 3 and 4 for node labels). Digital elements are also placed on the right side, but positioned more towards the middle than the other three themes. Thus, on the x-axis, the pedagogical experiences (left side) are projected against the limitations, possibilities and constraints the teachers experienced (right side) during the lockdown. These include the reliance on digital elements in teaching, the lack of analogue elements, the possibilities of flexibility, savings and increases in time, and questions of lacking salary compensation.

The y-axis explains 22.6% of the variance in data. We named it "Digital teaching vocabulary vs on-campus vocabulary" as it has digital elements in the upper quadrants, and interactions with students at lower quadrants, close to time and salary, flexibility and analogue elements. Teaching formats are positioned somewhat closer to the middle, yet still in the upper half, although it is placed closer to interactions with students than digital elements. This axis thus represents the overall frame of the questions; that is, the sudden shift to online teaching during the lockdown. As all free-text responses are rooted in experiences with digital teaching, it makes sense that the upper side of the axis almost solely consists of digital elements, while the remaining codes are positioned in opposition to it, in the lower side of the axis. This indicates a general dynamic: whether it is teaching formats, interactions with students, or flexibility, they relate to experiences with digital teaching, consisting of digital elements.

Question 1: "What have you changed in your remote teaching practice"
Q1 deals with what teachers' report has changed during the lockdown. Thus, the responses naturally reflect changes in their teaching practice.

Table 4. Frequency of themes in Q1.

Teaching formats	101	36.46%	Interaction with students	79	28.52%
Digital elements	176	63.54%	Flexibility	6	2.17%
Analogue elements	16	5.78%	Time and salary	15	5.43%

Table 4 shows that digital elements, teaching formats, and interaction with students are the most important themes in Q1, while flexibility, analogue elements, and time and salary are less apparent. Given the context of the question, this distribution is not surprising as it deals with changes teachers made in their digital teaching practices. Such changes are reflected in the themes with the highest frequency.

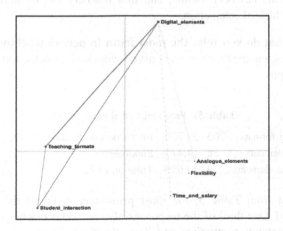

Fig. 2. Model of network for Q1.

The strongest connection in the network of Q1 is between digital elements and teaching formats (Fig. 2). It has a connection strength of 0.18, which implies the share of free-text responses that are coded as both digital elements and teaching formats. Its 'strength' should thus be understood in relation to the other connections both within Q1 and within Q2/3: It is the strongest connection in Q1 because it reflects that a larger number of free-text responses are coded both as digital elements and teaching formats than any of the other codes, but it is also generally strong when compared to the connections within the other questions.

When looking at the replies, this includes examples such as *"I went from lectures on zoom to recording it and putting it online on YouTube"* [ID171]. Here, we see how a teaching format ("lectures") is related to various forms of digital elements (Zoom, YouTube, online) in an answer on how the teacher changed teaching practice. Another example is: *"Cut review into multiple small videos. Supplemented recorded lectures with videos with assignments"* [ID331]. These two examples highlight the specific ways teachers changed their teaching by rethinking on-campus teaching formats through engaging with digital elements.

Digital elements and interaction with students is another interesting connection in the model (Fig. 2). With a connection strength of 0.14, it is the second strongest connection in Q1. It indicates how digital elements have affected the interaction while teaching or how the possibilities of interaction within one (or more) digital element(s) made teachers choose one or the other. An example is: *"We started doing teacher presentations in Adobe Connect but changed to Zoom as the lockdown continued and we thought that the contact with the students was important"* [ID314]. One digital element can thus hinder the interaction with students, while another supports it. This is an example of the iterative learning process many teachers underwent.

Finally, there is a connection between student interaction and teaching formats with a connection strength of 0.11 (Fig. 2). One example of this could be: *"Increased use of group work and student involvement, more dialogue – but this is very challenging online"* [ID587]. Responses within these themes highlight how challenging the interaction with students has been online, and that teachers had to adjust their teaching formats due to a lack of interaction.

Question 2: "What do you miss the most from in-person teaching on campus?"
In the second question, the teachers were asked what they miss the most from in-person teaching on campus.

Table 5. Frequency of themes in Q2.

Teaching formats	205	33.72%	Interaction with students	496	81.58%
Digital elements	88	14.47%	Flexibility	8	1.32%
Analogue elements	83	13.65%	Time and salary	6	1%

As is evident from Table 5, the most prominent theme is the interaction with students (81.58%). One third of the responses also mentions teaching formats, such as *"(...) Better opportunity to monitor and 'feel' the dynamic between the students particularly related to group work"* [ID70]. Digital elements are less often mentioned than in the other questions (14.47%), while analogue elements are more often mentioned (13.65%). Flexibility and time and salary are rarely mentioned (>2%).

The strongest connection in the network of Q2 is found between teaching formats and student interaction (connection strength of 0.21) (Fig. 3). As such, it is also the strongest connection when compared across the three different questions. This covers responses such as: *"The students' interaction during lectures"* [ID147]. The short response highlights simply that the teacher misses the interaction among students during the lectures. In relation to this, the connection between teaching formats, interactions with students, and analogue elements are also interesting. For example:

"The clinical teaching, where the students themselves have their fingers on the patients and talk to them themselves, is impossible to replace with digital teaching. Class-teaching in clinical courses is nicer for me as a teacher, as I can have a dialogue with the students that makes the course more interesting. (...)" [ID166].

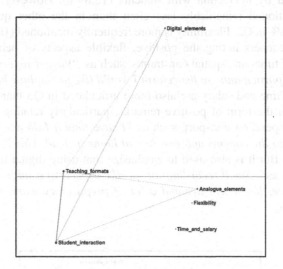

Fig. 3. Model of the network in Q2.

In this citation, the teacher establishes a relation between an analogue element (the patients) and the teaching format (clinical teaching) which contributes positively to their dialogue (interaction) and thus the learning outcome. In most responses to Q2, the relation to analogue elements is positive; that is, analogue elements have a positive effect on the general interaction with and between students and the learning outcome.

We also identify a connection between digital elements, teaching formats and student interaction (Fig. 3). These can be exemplified through: *"The feeling of where the students are. To have discussions with big classes, where I do not have to control the dialogue as much as I do on Zoom"* [ID119]. Here, there is a connection between the teaching format (discussions in big classes), the student interaction and the digital element. As opposed to the analogue elements which are positively connotated, the teachers report that digital elements can make it more difficult to conduct teaching and uphold the interaction with and between students.

Question 3: "Are there any positive aspects of remote teaching that you hope will continue when on-campus teaching starts again? Which, and why?"

When replying to whether there were any positive aspects of remote teaching that teachers hope will continue, the frequency of the codes is highly different from the earlier distributions (Table 6).

Table 6. Frequency of themes in Q3.

Teaching formats	203	35.25%	Interaction with students	89	15.89%
Digital elements	150	26.79%	Flexibility	56	10%
Analogue elements	28	5%	Time and salary	32	5.71%

Teaching formats (35.25%) and digital elements (26.79%) are the most frequent themes, followed by interaction with students (15.89%). However, interaction with students is mentioned remarkably less often than in the other questions, e.g., as opposed to 81.58% in Q2. Flexibility is more frequently mentioned (10%) in Q3, which is reflected in teachers noting the positive, flexible aspects of being able to teach independently of time- and spatial constraints, such as: *"Virtual supervision gives more flexibility for all participants, so henceforth I would like to continue having that option (...)"* [ID154]. Time and salary are also more articulated in Q3 than in general. This theme appears in the form of positive remarks, particularly relating to the decreased amount of time spend on transport, such as *"I save time if I do not have to commute every day to go to the campus and can stay at home instead. This is the only positive aspect."* [ID18]. But it is also used to emphasize that using digital tools is more time consuming, such as: *"Small recordings of specific aspects of a subject can possibly be used in the future, but it will demand a lot of preparatory work, to create a good product"* [ID209].

Fig. 4. Model of the network in Q3.

As found in Q1, the strongest connection in Q3 is between teaching formats and digital elements (Fig. 2 & Fig. 4). The connection strength, however, is 0.12, which is lower than the connection in Q1. In fact, we generally see weaker connections between themes in Q3 than in Q1 and Q2. The relative weakness of connections in Q3 implies a quantitative difference between the strength of connections between themes across the different questions. Thus, connections between the themes is more pronounced in Q1/2 than in Q3. Despite this quantitative difference, however, an example of the connection between teaching formats and digital elements in Q3 could be: *"The students benefitted greatly of video-recorded lectures (asynchronous) supplemented with a question-hour. I could possibly substitute a few of the ordinary lectures with videos and question-hours"* [ID24].

Here, a regular teaching format ("lecture") is broken down into an element of listening and an element of questioning. This is then seen as a positive change the teacher wishes to continue post-lockdown.

Another example is: *"Use of chat-function in one-way teaching (e.g., lectures). Small recordings of one-way teaching. Supervision by Zoom"* [ID210]. Here, individual digital elements are identified as supplements to on-campus teaching (Chat, recordings, Zoom), but primarily through integration into a traditional classroom teaching format, and not as part of altering the teaching formats to better fit the digital elements.

The perception of digital elements as supplements to pre-established teaching formats constitutes an important part of what the teachers report as being positive aspects of digital teaching. It is not a continuation of 'digital teaching' per se that teachers picture as the ideal future scenario, but rather an egregious assimilation of certain digital elements into on-campus teaching formats. This is in part due to teachers finding digital teaching inadequate or insufficient in terms of supporting interaction with students. This can be illustrated through the relation between teaching formats and interactions with students (0.07), the latter also being connected to digital elements (0.04):

> *"As I said before, remote teaching can only function as a supplement to on-campus teaching. Remote teaching should work in a way where teachers get the opportunity to look at (have eye contact with) the students and have a dialogue with them."* [ID19].

The teachers are thus outspoken about the limitations (i.e., in terms of interaction) of digital teaching, seen as somewhat independent of or in opposition to on-campus teaching.

3.4   Looking Across the Survey

By large, the responses to the questions connect the three themes: teaching formats, digital elements, and interaction with students. However, the connections occur with varying connection strength. As such, the 'strongest' connections occur in Q1 and Q2, while the connections between the themes generally are weaker in Q3.

In the responses to Q1, we saw how teaching formats were altered as the teachers' digital toolbox expanded, or as a way of establishing better interaction with students. Responses to Q2 cemented the importance of interaction with students, while showing how this was positively related to (missing) analogue elements, whereas experiences with digital elements held a more ambiguous position. Finally, Q3 showed that, from the teachers' perspective, the perceived potentials of digital elements consisted primarily in supplementing traditional, on-campus teaching. This was in large part due to the perceived inadequacy of digital solutions in terms of supporting interaction with students.

The findings from the free-text replies are supported by the general findings in the survey: 1) That technological competencies brought about changes in lockdown teaching, partly motivated by lacking interaction with the students and 2) that the teachers' experience with digital teaching was limited before the lockdown. Thus, it appears that limited technological and didactical experience with digital teaching led teachers to translate what they knew worked well on campus into a new (digital) format. This also points back to one of the major observations in the qualitative interviews and meta-study: teachers' evaluation of quality digital teaching depends on its capacity to imitate or mimic on-campus teaching.

4   Learning from a Crisis

One must be cautious when drawing general conclusions about future digital teaching based on data from a disruptive crisis. Certainly, many teachers acquired new (technological) skills, which enabled them to use software earlier unknown to them. However, it is difficult to say whether this development is only directed at managing new technological tools, or if it also pertains to new digital didactics. Keeping in mind that the connections between themes is weakest in Q3, this question however points towards the opposite: that the assimilation of certain digital elements into on-campus teaching formats, such as video-recorded lectures, is what the teachers view as possibilities for the future – not a side-by-side integration of digital and on-campus teaching formats. Given the context of the transition to digital teaching, the teachers' experiences did not lead to radical changes in teaching approaches. Rather, it demonstrated that it is a challenge to cultivate fruitful, digital learning environments without having sufficient time, knowledge, and experience. Therefore, the teachers' experiences of digital teaching during the lockdown seem inconclusive and not suited to support broad statements on the possibilities and limitations of digital teaching per se. In many ways, the situation was (and still is) an "extreme case", a crisis, and should be treated as such [16].

Despite this, the teachers' experiences highlight the overall importance of interaction and basic human contact at universities. Both on a level of social welfare and learning outcomes, immediate interaction and contact with other people play a pivotal role in creating good learning environments. Hence, in case of another crisis, and in a future context of developing and refining digital learning formats at the university, efforts should be undertaken to support and foster contact between students and teachers.

References

1. Tømte, C.E., Fossland, T., Aamodt, P.O., Degn, L.: Digitalisation in higher education: mapping institutional approaches for teaching and learning. Q. High. Educ. **25**, 98–114 (2019)
2. Cai, Z., Siebert-Evenstone, A., Eagan, B., Shaffer, D.W., Hu, X., Graesser, A.C.: nCoder+: a semantic tool for improving recall of nCoder coding. In: Eagan, B., Misfeldt, M., Siebert-Evenstone, A. (eds.) ICQE 2019. CCIS, vol. 1112, pp. 41–54. Springer, Cham (2019). https://doi.org/10.1007/978-3-030-33232-7_4
3. Shaffer, D.W.: Quantitative Ethnography. Cathcart Press, Madison (2017)
4. Shaffer, D.W., Collier, W., Ruis, A.R.: A tutorial on epistemic network analysis: analyzing the structure of connections in cognitive, social, and interaction data. J. Learn. Anal. **3**(3), 9–45 (2016)
5. Shaffer, D., Ruis., A.: Epistemic network analysis: a worked example of theory-based learning analytics. In: Handbook of Learning Analytics (2017)
6. Langford, M., Damsa, C.: Online teaching in the time of COVID-19: academic teachers' experiences in Norway. Centre for Experiential Legal Learning (CELL), University of Oslo (2020)
7. Hjelsvold, R., Nykvist, S.S., Lorås, M., Bahmani, A., Krokan, A.: Educators' experiences online: How COVID-19 encouraged pedagogical change in CS education. In: Norsk IKT-Konferanse for Forskning OG utdanning (No. 4), Chicago (2020)
8. Adedoyin, O.B., Soykan, E.: Covid-19 pandemic and online learning: the challenges and opportunities. Interactive Learning Environments (2020)
9. Watermeyer, R., Crick, T., Knight, C., Goodall, J.: COVID-19 and digital disruption in UK universities: afflictions and affordances of emergency online migration. High. Educ. **81**, 623–641 (2021)
10. Giovannella, C., Marcello, P.: The effects of the Covid-19 pandemic seen through the lens of the Italian university teachers and the comparison with school teachers' perspective (2020)
11. Nambiar, D.: The impact of online learning during COVID-19: students' and teachers' perspective. Int. J. Indian Psychol. **8**(2), 783–793 (2020)
12. Tartavulea, C.V., Albu, C.N., Albu, N., Dieaconescu, R.I., Petre, S.: Online teaching practices and the effectiveness of the educational process in the wake of the COVID-19 pandemic. Amfiteatru Econ. **22**(55), 920–936 (2020)
13. Misfeldt, M., et al.: Evaluering af online-nødundervisning forår 2020. Københavns Universitet, København (2020)
14. Jensen, L.X., Karstad, O.M., Mosbech, A., Vermund, M.C., Konradsen, F.: Experiences and challenges of students during the 2020 campus lockdown. Results from student surveys at the University of Copenhagen, pp. 1–73, Rep. University of Copenhagen (2020)
15. Siebert-Evenstone, A.L., et al.: In search of conversational grain size: modelling semantic structure using moving stanza windows. J. Learn. Anal. **4**(3), 123–139 (2017)
16. Flyvbjerg, B.: Five misunderstandings about the case-study research. Qual. Inq. **12**(2), 219–245 (2006)

Getting There Together: Examining Patterns of a Long-Term Collaboration in a Virtual STEM Makerspace

Tiffany Wright[✉], Luiz Oliveira, Danielle P. Espino, Seung B. Lee, and Eric Hamilton

Pepperdine University, Malibu, CA 90263, USA
tiffany.wright2@pepperdine.edu

Abstract. This study examines the patterns of group discourse among adolescent students from Brazil and the United States collaborating virtually on a long term robotics project. Data comes from transcripts of four video conference call "meet-ups" that took place between November 2018–May 2019. Epistemic network analysis was used to examine the patterns of utterances over time which indicated a shift from facilitator guided discussions to collaborative idea generation among students. The results identify a shift towards a consolidation of ideas consistent with convergent thinking expressed in Online Collaborative Learning Theory.

Keywords: Collaboration · Learning · Global · Virtual · Online · STEM · Makerspace · Discourse

1 Introduction

Innovation is critical in collaborative learning environments. A collaborative learning environment can encourage student curiosity and participation, leading to a more diverse and open learning environment and ultimately increased knowledge contribution. While cognitive age influences a student's independence in the learning environment, learning outcomes should reflect student's ability to formulate their unique learning goals [1]. Through this exploratory process, they can reshape and amalgamate concepts for enriched learning. This process aligns with a constructivist approach to learning in which teachers guide students in constructing their realities based on how they perceive the world [1].

Learning activities that support embodied cognition, such as robotics in the current study, provide students with a deeper comprehension of learning exploration. In "… having students embody their understanding in surrogates then observe the surrogate behavior through activities like programming video-game-like virtual environments with avatar surrogates and programming robot surrogates…increases student learning, understanding, and motivation" [9, p. 219]. In collaborative settings, students can construct knowledge by synergizing ideas to develop new concepts and advanced outputs. While an instructor may initially drive this process, significant social and cognitive factors assist students in achieving their learning goals.

© Springer Nature Switzerland AG 2022
B. Wasson and S. Zörgő (Eds.): ICQE 2021, CCIS 1522, pp. 334–345, 2022.
https://doi.org/10.1007/978-3-030-93859-8_22

1.1   Examining the Learning Environment

One framework that supports an understanding of the learning environment in collaborative, virtual settings is the Community of Inquiry. The Community of Inquiry (CoI) framework accounts for three learning development elements: teaching presence, social presence, and cognitive presence [5]. While Garrison et al. [5] frame teaching presence in terms of the instructor's leadership, this study considers the presence of peer teaching as well. Instead, the instructor acts as a facilitator, encouraging students to take ownership of their projects. The elements of teacher and social presence overlap to create an advanced intellectual opportunity in which students can promote peer-to-peer learning.

Diaz et al. [3] conducted a study in which students ranked the value of each of the three elements of CoI and found that students ranked teaching presence as higher value than social presence. Diaz and fellow researchers reasoned that students might have "correctly view[ed] teaching presence as a necessary condition for the development of social presence" [3, p. 27]. This idea emphasizes the significance of the instructor's role in supporting a foundation for learners to build relationships with peers and encourage solid connections for collaboration. Social presence can support individual growth in students' learning experiences through dialogue and partnership, promoting autonomy via self-directed learning [2]. Furthermore, social presence can evolve to foster cohesion through intellectually focused learning, moving from inquiry to achieved learning goals [4]. Learners can collaboratively develop an environment that promotes new knowledge and formulates ideas beyond the guidance of an instructor.

Cognitive presence is central to the evolving nature of student learning. This is best described by examining the formulation of students' thoughts through individual and collaborative exercises that generate new ideas. Instructors' facilitation of discourse has been shown to have a significant influence on fostering and maintaining a cognitive presence in student learning [6]. Thus, discourse can connect the instructor's prompting of collaborative learning and the student's ability to progress in independent thinking. The latter encourages thoughtful contributions during collaboration sessions. Shea and Bidjerano [12] propose that learning presence further supports cognitive presence in that socio-emotional factors such as self-efficacy and self-regulation play vital roles in learning development. Researchers examined core elements from the CoI framework to support the knowledge creation process detailed in the Online Collaborative Learning Theory.

1.2   Online Collaborative Learning Theory

This study examines the Online Collaborative Learning (OCL) theory within the context of CoI to detail processes of student knowledge creation [7]. The overarching concepts of idea generation, idea organizing, and intellectual convergence intersect to promote knowledge building and social application [7]. Idea generation fosters the sharing of ideas, sparking the curiosity of learners. Through developed brainstorming of the previous stage, idea organizing encourages learners to shape concepts and merge ideas. Intellectual convergence creates the foundation for advanced knowledge, driven through the thought development and collaboration of previous OCL stages.

OCL promotes discovery amongst learners, encouraging their reliance on each other as peers rather than on a teacher as prompted by the traditional learning environment. Pedagogy in the OCL context provides that the teacher "plays a key and essential role, a role that is neither as 'guide on the side' nor 'sage on the stage." Instead, it connects students with "the language and activities associated with building the discipline, inducting the learners into the language and processes of the knowledge community" [7, p. 94]. As a result, collaboration in the online space encourages innovation and allows learners to pool resources from their various locations. OCL in the practice of social media collaboration has been shown to provide a collaborative environment that encourages discourse and interaction within a safe space [10].

Harasim [7] describes discourse as a critical element of knowledge creation leading to the solidification of knowledge building in peer collaboration. They describe the shift from discourse to the final product of new knowledge as moving from divergent to convergent thinking:

> The OCL process includes discourse, collaborative learning, and knowledge building. Innovation and creativity are essential to building knowledge and are key aspects of divergent thinking. Divergent thinking refers to a process that generates many questions, ideas, responses, or solutions. It is associated with brainstorming and creative thought, developing questions, and drawing on ideas from different perspectives and many sources (including personal observations and experiences). While divergent thinking involves generating many ideas, the process associated with identifying the best ideas and discarding the weak ones is called convergent thinking. Convergent thinking refers to narrowing down the options based on existing information and analysis and selecting the best. [7, p. 92]

The OCL theory provides a linear model for learner's journeys from idea generation to knowledge building and social application. However, the trajectory can also be presented as an iterative process as ideas continue to evolve and knowledge acquisition is continuously refined. For instance, Mnkandla & Minnaar [10] provide the following regarding the idea organizing stage:

> [I]deas must be organized and refined by the students through the processes of problem-solving and making sense of academic content. Students start organizing, analyzing and filtering ideas through agreement or disagreement with others in the group. Input from the facilitator might be needed as a form of moderation and analysis to cluster ideas into meaningful units and knowledge building. Analytical skills are needed in the process. [10, p. 242]

The progression from organizing to analysis to open discussion regarding ideas may not be realized in one sitting. A rich collaborative process involves revisiting ideas and coming to unified conclusions on concepts that may have once been disagreed upon or previously left unresolved. The iterative nature of this process may involve additional support from the instructor/facilitator to guide students to comprehensive conclusions as a team. Students are also positioned to develop their cognitive skills beyond the subject matter and their socio-emotional efforts to work productively with others.

1.3   A Global, Virtual STEM-Focused Collaborative Makerspace

The context for this study involves a learning community that provides a forum for students to collaborate across continents on STEM (Science, Technology, Engineering, and Mathematics) projects. Learners at the middle and high school grade levels communicate asynchronously using a cloud-based team messaging platform (Slack) and connect synchronously through video conference calls known as global meet-ups. These meet-ups are a key component to the collaborative experience in project-based efforts. In these meet-ups, learners share projects, provide feedback to peers, and contribute to advancing STEM knowledge within the learning community. Cross-cultural collaboration encourages varied perspectives and opportunities for participants to learn about the impact of project topics on the demographics of their peers from other countries. Sample project topics have included sharing of research on climate change, technological innovation, and mathematical challenges to artifacts such as apps, Scratch games, and robotics.

Participants collaborate in two main ways. One way is through soliciting feedback on individual projects to make improvements, which usually spans over two to three weeks. The second way involves students investing in knowledge building and developing relationships with peers to advance and deepen project development throughout an extended period of time, usually lasting several weeks. Collaborations are sometimes led by an adult facilitator who meets with students weekly to help support the project to completion. Other adult experts also join project meetings as observers to share their expertise and feedback to support student's ideas.

This paper will examine overall discourse patterns of long-term collaboration in a STEM-focused, global digital makerspace community, with support from facilitators. Specifically, the research presented in this study will explore how a facilitator's presence influences students' discourse patterns over time and how social and cognitive patterns shift for learners throughout a long-term collaboration.

2   Methods

The data for this analysis consisted of discourse collected from the transcripts of four online global meet-ups that took place in November 2018, January 2019, March 2019 and May 2019. The meet-ups involved three students from Brazil, three students from the United States, and adult facilitators/observers to support their effort. The transcriptions were coded using the codebook developed from a grounded analysis of the data, seen in Table 1, which included Content Focus, Cooperation, Coordination, Curiosity, Feedback, Idea Introduction, Information Sharing, Participatory Teaching, and Social Disposition. Coding was done independently by two raters who then came together in a process of social moderation to reach agreement on the coding [8].

Table 1. Codebook of constructs used in analysis.

Construct	Definition	Example
Content-focus	Dialogue focused on the meet-up's STEM-related educational content	*And then I used a light sensor to uh to sense the light from an LED that was attached to a small 3D printed car*
Cooperation	Related to the defining of roles in carrying out the project (determining tasks and responsibilities of members) as well as utterances that refer to how the collaboration will move forward	*In case of doubt, I am available through e-mail to help with the codes*
Coordination	Related to scheduling and identifying methods of communication and time/date (logistical issues) for future interactions	*I'll send out an email. And then, if you can start responding and communicating using that email thread that would be great*
Curiosity	Seeking clarification, elaboration, or further information for better understanding of content-related issues	*Oh wow. So the robot would have an arm that draws?*
Feedback	Communicating one's feedback, suggestions or opinions on subject-related or technical topics/ideas and projects (responding to, adding on, or expanding upon current discussion)	*So. Yes, so maybe we could use the subtitles system on the on the YouTube platform itself, which can you can change languages, you can deactivate if you want*
Idea Introduction	Introduction of new ideas/perspectives related to projects and technical topics	*We could do…we could do it like a natural problem, such as like ocean pollution or helping animals or a big problem*
Information Sharing	Sharing of information on subject-related or technical topics, including project updates (The individual's personal take/understanding on the subject/not necessarily fact-based, or based on personal experience)	*I was going to say is that I started the coding on the robot and it probably will not take long for me to finish and I might finish. So I remember I did say like a few weekends ago that I was going to finish on the weekend…*
Participatory Teaching	Helping others to learn subject matter by providing factual knowledge	*Exactly its the same motor. So you're going to connect the red one where he showed red and then the black one where he showed red. That's the part that's interchangeable*
Social Disposition	Demonstrating pro-social tendencies (to other people), especially in expressing appreciation, acknowledgement, or validation	*Okay. So hello everyone. I'm glad that we are here. So I thought we might start by introducing ourselves and who's in the room*

The coded data was then examined using epistemic network analysis (ENA), a technique in quantitative ethnography to visualize data through statistical methods, to identify meaningful patterns in discourse. ENA models the connections among relevant constructs in the data by quantifying the frequency of their co-occurrences within conversations [11]. For this study, an individual participant was used as the unit of analysis, and each meet-up constituted a conversation to which the connections were limited. A moving stanza window of 7 lines (each line plus 6 previous lines) was used to model the connections made between constructs occurring within the recent temporal context [13].

Table 2. Frequency and percentage of total utterances by role in each meetup.

	November 2018	January 2019	March 2019	May 2019
Student	107 (18%)	207 (40%)	228 (61%)	280 (57%)
Facilitator	144 (24%)	208 (40%)	96 (25%)	119 (24%)
Observer	345 (58%)	111 (20%)	54 (14%)	91 (19%)
TOTAL LINES	596	526	378	490

3 Results

Table 2 shows the total number of utterances and percentage of total utterances made by each participating role throughout the four meetups. Student utterances increased from 107 (18% of total utterances) in Nov. 2018 to 280 (57% of total utterances) in May 2019. Observer utterances decreased from 345 (58% of total utterances) in Nov. 2018 to 91 (19% of total utterances) in May 2019. Overall, facilitator and observer utterances decrease while student utterances increase, showing an increased amount of student participation from Nov. 2018 to May 2019.

The ENA models for each meet-up can be seen in Fig. 1. The nodes represent each coded construct and lines between the nodes represent the strength of the connection between each construct as defined by the window size. A thicker line represents a stronger connection while a thinner line represents a weaker connection. The X axis of the model is defined by Social Disposition on the left and Participatory Teaching on the right. The Y axis of the model is defined by Information Sharing on the bottom and Cooperation/Curiosity at the top.

The November 2018 model shows thick connections between Content Focus and Social Disposition, and between Content Focus and Info Sharing. In January 2019, the strong connections include Content Focus and Curiosity, and Content Focus and Social Disposition. For March 2019, thicker lines are again seen between the Content Focus and Curiosity, as well as Content Focus and Participatory Teaching. In May 2019, the model shows strong connections again between Content Focus and Participatory Teaching, and also Content Focus and Cooperation.

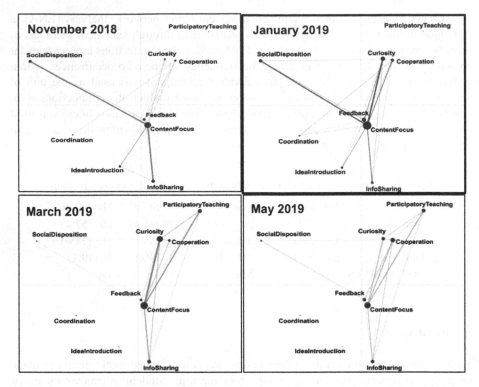

Fig. 1. ENA models for meet-ups in November 2018, January 2019, March 2019 and May 2019.

Figure 2 displays the group mean location (squares) of all the participants in each respective meetup. The boxes around the mean location represent a confidence interval of 95%. A wider box in a certain direction signifies that more constructs were captured in the mean, while a smaller box signifies that less constructs were captured in the mean. From the means and confidence intervals, there is a movement up and to the right over time. For Fig. 2, along the X axis (SVD1), a Mann-Whitney test showed that January 2019 (Mdn = −0.14, N = 8) was statistically significantly different at the alpha = 0.05 level from March 2019 (Mdn = 1.03, N = 8 U = 61.00, p = 0.00, r = −0.91). Along the Y axis (SVD2), a Mann-Whitney test showed that January 2019 (Mdn = −0.18, N = 8) was also statistically significantly different at the alpha = 0.05 level from May 2019 (Mdn = 0.52, N = 7 U = 46.00, p = 0.04, r = −0.64).

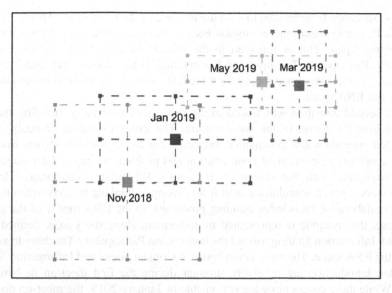

Fig. 2. Group means and confidence intervals for meet-ups in November 2018, January 2019, March 2019 and May 2019.

4 Discussion

A key component of the long-term collaboration that was noted during the analysis was the change in the participation level of the students in the meet-ups. This transition was reflected in the increasing proportion of utterances spoken by students during the course of the project collaboration. Accordingly, the frequency of participation by adults, both as the facilitator and as observers, decreased over time. This was representative of the evolving role that the adults played in the collaboration. At the early stages, students required more guidance and support in becoming familiar with one another and the project context. However, as the collaboration continued, the students were able to take a more active role in the discussions, accounting for about 60% of the utterances by the March and May 2019 meet-ups.

In addition to the quantitative rise in student participation, the analysis was able to identify a qualitative shift in the content of the group discourse over the course of the collaboration, which occurred along two main dimensions.

First, there was a shift from socially-oriented discussion in the earlier meet-ups toward a more task-driven engagement in later meet-ups. This transition is captured in the ENA model along the x-axis. During the early stages of the collaboration, a greater portion of the discourse was focused on becoming familiar with one another and building relationships. For this reason, the meet-ups in November 2018 and January 2019 exhibit stronger connections to Social Disposition, resulting in the group means for these meet-ups to be located toward the left side of the ENA space. However, as the collaboration progressed, the discussion became more centered around project-related, task-driven topics. This is reflected in the thicker edges linking Content Focus to Curiosity, Participatory Teaching and Cooperation in the March 2019 and May 2019 meet-ups. As such, the group means for these later sessions are situated toward the right side of the ENA space.

The second transition was linked to the process of knowledge building that progressed over the course of the collaboration. The group discourse gradually moved from idea generation and information exchange during the initial meet-ups towards a greater emphasis on conceptual consolidation and problem solving at later stages. This is in alignment with the stages of Harasim's [7] online collaborative learning (OCL) theory, which articulates a shift from divergent thinking to convergent thinking during collaborative knowledge building processes. In the ENA model of the group's discourse, this dynamic is represented by movement along the y-axis, defined at the edges by Information Sharing toward the bottom and Participatory Teaching toward the top of the ENA space. The association between Content Focus and Information Sharing and Idea Introduction are relatively stronger during the first meet-up in November 2018. While these connections are still visible in January 2019, the meet-up discourse placed greater emphasis on Curiosity and Cooperation. After the group decided to move forward with the idea to create a drawing robot, the discourse patterns in March and May 2019 no longer display connections to Idea Introduction. Rather, linkages to Participatory Teaching and Cooperation became more prominent, as the group focused on identifying technical solutions and sharing knowledge and support in their effort to successfully complete their project. Reflective of this process from November 2018 to May 2019 is the gradual upward movement of the group mean representing each meet-up.

Based on these two key transitional dimensions identified in the group discourse, it may be possible to interpret the ENA space for this collaboration in the following manner: (1) social versus task orientation of the discourse along the x-axis; and (2) emphasis of the collaborative discourse on divergent versus convergent thinking processes along the y-axis. Figure 3 displays an overlay of this interpretative framework with graphs resulting from ENA, namely the network model for the May 2019 meet-up and the group means for the individual meet-ups. As shown in the latter diagram, the meet-up discourse demonstrated an upward-right movement during the seven-month period of collaboration. This represents a gradual transition from an interactive dynamic characterized by social orientation and divergent thinking processes toward one that was more driven by task orientation and convergent thinking processes.

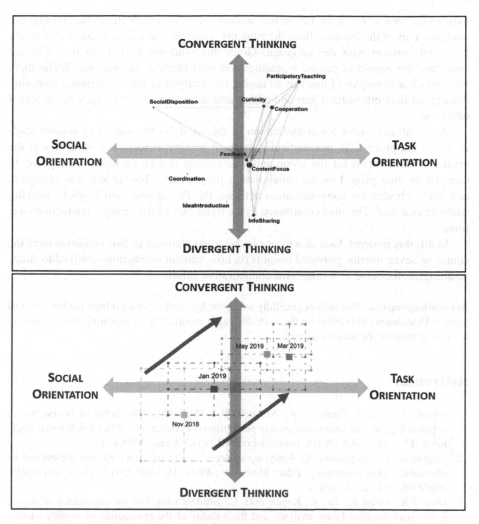

Fig. 3. Interpretative framework of the collaborative discourse overlaid with network model for the May 2019 meet-up (above) and group means for individual meet-ups (below).

4.1 Considerations and Future Study

This study examines the group discourse patterns of students engaged in a long term collaboration. The increased proportion of student utterances with each meet-up indicated how students became more involved in their collaborative effort. The discourse patterns indicated a shift from a socially oriented, divergent thinking pattern towards a more task oriented, convergent thinking pattern as they continued to work together. Two key aspects not accounted for in this study include the consideration for culture and language differences. Two students from Brazil were only fluent in Portuguese, and relied on translation for communication. While the ENA helps to account for this in the transcript, the comfort level in communicating in a more English oriented environment may have been a factor in the initial amount of engagement from the Portuguese students. Part of the increase from the students' engagement might be attributed to the increased comfort with the language. Given the students were from two different countries, the impact of culture is another potential element for analysis. While there were no clear examples of this impact during the analysis of the transcripts, examining through an in-depth cultural lens and taking into account non-verbal cues might reveal otherwise.

An additional factor for consideration in this study is the impact of student leadership in the process. In this particular study, it became evident one student was the greater content expert for the group and was willing to take on leading the group to completing their project as the collaboration progressed. This student was bilingual, and able to bridge the communication between the Portuguese- and English-speaking students as a peer. This also contributed to the dynamics of the group's interaction over time.

In all, this in-depth look at a meet-ups between students in two countries over the course of seven months provided insights on how student interactions evolved to shape meaningful discourse in a long-term collaborative effort.

Acknowledgements. The authors gratefully acknowledge funding support from the US National Science Foundation (#1612824) for the work this paper reports. Views appearing in this paper do not reflect those of the funding agency.

References

1. Akyol, Z., Ice, P., Garrison, R., Mitchell, R.: The relationship between course socio-epistemological orientations and student perceptions of community of inquiry. Internet High. Educ. **13**(1–2), 66–68 (2010). https://doi.org/10.1016/j.iheduc.2009.12.002
2. Angelaina, S., Jimoyiannis, A.: Analysing students' engagement and learning presence in an educational blog community. Educ. Media Int. **49**(3), 183–200 (2012). https://doi.org/10.1080/09523987.2012.738012
3. Díaz, S.R., Swan, K., Ice, P., Kupczynski, L.: Student ratings of the importance of survey items, multiplicative factor analysis, and the validity of the community of inquiry survey. Internet High. Educ. **13**(1–2), 22–30 (2010). https://doi.org/10.1016/j.iheduc.2009.11.004
4. Garrison, D.R.: Online community of inquiry review: Social, cognitive, and teaching presence issues. J. Asynchronous Learn. Netw. **11**(1), 61–72 (2007)
5. Garrison, D.R., Anderson, T., Archer, W.: Critical inquiry in a text-based environment: computer conferencing in higher education. Internet High. Educ. **2**(2), 87–105 (1999). https://doi.org/10.1016/S1096-7516(00)00016-6
6. Gorsky, P., Blau, I.: Online teaching effectiveness: a tale of two instructors. Int. Rev. Res. Open Distrib. Learn. **10**(3) (2009). https://doi.org/10.19173/irrodl.v10i3.712
7. Harasim, L.M.: Learning Theory and Online Technology. Routledge (2012)
8. Herrenkohl, L.R., Cornelius, L.: Investigating elementary students' scientific and historical argumentation. J. Learn. Sci. **22**(3), 413–461 (2013). https://doi.org/10.1080/10508406.2013.799475
9. Jonassen, D.H., Land, S.: Theoretical Foundations of Learning Environments. Routledge (2012)

10. Mnkandla, E., Minnaar, A.: The use of social media in e-learning: a metasynthesis. Int. Rev. Res. Open Distrib. Learn. **18**(5). https://doi.org/10.19173/irrodl.v18i5.3014
11. Shaffer, D.W.: Quantitative ethnography. Cathcart Press, Madison (2017)
12. Shea, P., Bidjerano, T.: Learning presence: towards a theory of self-efficacy, self-regulation, and the development of a communities of inquiry in online and blended learning environments. Comput. Educ. **55**(4), 1721–1731 (2010). https://doi.org/10.1016/j.compedu.2010.07.017
13. Siebert-Evenstone, A., Arastoopour Irgens, G., Collier, W., Swiecki, Z., Ruis, A.R., Williamson Shaffer, D.: In search of conversational grain size: modelling semantic structure using moving stanza windows. J. Learn. Anal. **4**(3), 123–139 (2017)

Exploring Interactions Between Computational and Critical Thinking in Model-Eliciting Activities Through Epistemic Network Analysis

Guadalupe Carmona[(⊠)] [iD], Beatriz Galarza-Tohen,
and Gonzalo Martinez-Medina

The University of Texas at San Antonio, San Antonio, TX 78248, USA
Guadalupe.carmona@utsa.edu

Abstract. In this exploratory study, we used Epistemic Network Analysis (ENA) as an analytic tool to help us better understand the possible interactions and structural connections between computational thinking and critical thinking as elicited in an open-ended authentic problem-solving task that was solved collaboratively. We found that, although students' final solutions and solving processes were qualitatively different, the structural connections found in ENA are quite similar among all teams. We interpret this as a direct reflection of the nature of the task, which is complex and open-ended, and therefore, allows for multiple possible solutions. However, the underlying structure appears to be stable, which contributes to validating the purposeful design of the activity to elicit the construct of computational thinking. Moreover, we observed that during the collaborative solution process, all teams made strong connections between elements of critical thinking and computational thinking that evolved over time. Graphs that were generated by ENA display the diversity in student thinking, as well as a similar epistemic structure in the solution of the model-eliciting activities. The interactions between critical thinking and computational thinking are evident, although components of these constructs were elicited in different ways in each team's solution.

Keywords: Models and modeling · Model-eliciting activities · Computational thinking · Critical thinking · Epistemic network analysis · STEM education · 21st century competencies

1 Introduction

Important dimensions of human competence have been identified as valuable for many centuries to achieve local and global prosperity for the common good in areas that include: education, work, health, and other life contexts. However, what distinguishes the recently called "21st century competencies" is the goal of *deeper learning* [1], to prepare next generation of students attaining strong levels of mastery across multiple areas of skill and knowledge. The role of education is even more critical in supporting the preparation in these competencies, which include: *problem solving, critical*

B. Wasson and S. Zörgő (Eds.): ICQE 2021, CCIS 1522, pp. 346–361, 2022.
https://doi.org/10.1007/978-3-030-93859-8_23

thinking, communication, collaboration, and *self-management.* Recently, business leaders and researchers have joined educators in their efforts and commitment for a broader and more diverse population to develop these competencies in ways that can be extended and transferred to other situations beyond school to solve new problems in multiple settings [2].

However, little is known about the epistemic nature of these 21st century competencies, how they develop, and the interactions and structural connections that exist among them. Moreover, more needs to be learned about rich problem-solving contexts in which these competencies emerge and develop to prepare the next generation so that *all* students have the opportunity to succeed beyond school in a technology-based age of information [3, 4].

2   Theoretical Framework: Models and Modeling Perspective, Computational Thinking and Critical Thinking

2.1   Models and Modeling Perspective

A *Models & Modeling Perspective* is centered on the nature of students learning mathematics when they interpret real-life situations and have the need to "mathematize" in order to predict, describe, explain, or construct mathematically significant systems [5]. This perspective proposes *model-eliciting activities* (MEAs) as authentic open-ended collaborative tasks to be solved by groups of 3–4 students. In the way MEAs are designed, the solution calls for a mathematical model to be used by an identified client, or a given person who needs to solve a real-life problem [6]. In order for the client to implement the model adequately, the students must clearly elicit their thinking process and justify their solution. Thus, they need to describe, explain, manipulate, or predict the behavior of the real-world system to support their solution as the best option for the client. As in real life, there is not a single solution, but there are optimal ways to solve the problem [6, 7].

From a *Models & Modeling Perspective,* models are conceptual systems embedded in representational media and developed for a particular purpose [5]. MEAs are designed to focus on richer, deeper and higher-order understandings of relevant constructs that provide the foundation for mathematical reasoning. In addition, MEAs make learners' thinking visible through the multiple representations students use in the solution process as they continuously interpret and re-interpret the goals and givens in authentic problems [7]. Thus, students' models involve dynamic representational fluency among written, spoken, constructed, and drawn media as they revise and refine their thinking [5].

As students engage in the modeling process, they elicit their understanding of relevant mathematical constructs, while also developing competencies that are needed for success in solving real-life problems. Relevant competencies include *critical thinking, communication, collaboration, and self-management* [4, 8, 9].

2.2 Computational Thinking

Computational thinking (CT) is a construct that has gained much relevance especially in the past decade as a form of literacy and a powerful skill that is needed for success beyond school in a technology-based age of information, and which extends beyond programming [e.g. 15, 16]. More recent conversations focus on the need to provide access to computational thinking to all students in K-12 classroom settings, promoting effective learning environments for students to develop and learn these foundational conceptual tools, and extend this knowledge to other contexts in which new problems can be solved [2, 4, 16].

Computational thinking is defined as the processes in formulating problems and their solutions so that these can be effectively carried out by anyone, and not only by computer scientists [17]. Computational thinking has been considered "the highest order of problem-solving" [18] and a necessary skill that all individuals should develop in order to thrive and become active citizens in our technology-driven world [19].

Computational thinking builds on power and limits of computing processes, allowing students to solve problems, design systems and understand human behavior by thinking recursively, parallel processing and recognizing virtues and dangers of any activity [20].

In this study we use a characterization of computational thinking as a collection of cognitive problem-solving skills that include the ability to: (a) decompose: or break a problem down into smaller, more manageable parts; (b) recognize patterns: or finding similarities between items; (c) abstract: or remove details to simplify a solution so that it can be generalized; and (d) create algorithms: or automate processes by designing a sequence of logical instructions to facilitate a solution [24]. Consistent with this approach, computational thinking has also been associated with modeling, especially when the focus is on abstraction as a process and a product, as when a problem calls for the need to solutions that are reusable and generalizable to different contexts [5, 9, 21, 22].

2.3 Critical Thinking

Critical thinking (CritT) is considered an essential aspect of higher order understanding highly regarded by different stakeholders in education, research, and industry [1, 3]. Over the past years, several frameworks have been developed to identify and analyze critical thinking emerging from collaborative group problem solving [8, 27, 30]. Studies show that MEAs successfully supports the full process of critical thinking as described by Dewey [31] and Ennis [28–30]. For this study, we use a framework that has been used in previous studies to characterize critical thinking in the context of MEAs [8], using five descriptors of the process, including:

1. Initiation: Identification of a common question or problem and discussion to ensure that question or problem is understood by the group.
2. Exploration: All discussion which expands upon the problem or question to support formation of a solution.
3. Solution: Positing an answer to the question or problem and the initial explanation of that answer or solution.

4. Judgment: All discussion where the answer or solution is debated, modified, or tested.
5. Resolution: When the participants agree upon a final solution or answer.

2.4 Studying the Relationship Between Computational Thinking and Critical Thinking

There are only a few studies exploring the connections between computational thinking and critical thinking (e.g., [17, 32]). While some approaches identify similarities and differences in the operationalization of these constructs, there is agreement that they both emerge within problem-solving situations. However, as a field we're still developing our understanding on an epistemic structure for computational thinking, critical thinking, and the possible connections between these two; and more specifically, when students engage in open-ended collaborative problem-solving activities that are designed for *all* students to participate and learn.

A better understanding of the characteristics of learning environments in which computational thinking emerges, the nature of computational thinking, and how it relates to other foundational 21st Century conceptual tools such as critical thinking are of utmost importance to articulate an educational plan that fosters "computational thinking for all" [3, 18].

In this exploratory study, we propose utilizing a model-eliciting activity called the Tic-Tac-Toe Problem that was purposefully designed to elicit computational thinking [33] and identify whether critical thinking also emerges in students' solution processes. Then, we use Epistemic Network Analysis (ENA) to explore the structural relationship between computational thinking and critical thinking as these emerge while students solve the Tic-Tac-Toe Problem.

3 Research Questions and Rationale

We report an exploratory study guided by two research questions:

- What is the structural relationship between computational thinking and critical thinking as both constructs emerge in the context of a genre of open-ended authentic collaborative group tasks called model-eliciting activities (MEAs)?
- How do computational thinking and critical thinking dynamically interact and evolve during the collaborative process, and how is this interaction characterized as students solve the model-eliciting activity?

Although some authors have identified connections between computational thinking and critical thinking (e.g., [17]), there is a lack of theoretical frameworks that explicitly describe how both constructs are connected [32]. In this study, we use ENA [14] to identify and quantify connections between critical thinking and computational thinking emerging while students solve a genre of open-ended collaborative group tasks called MEAs [5]. Explicitly articulating these connections will increase our understanding of the epistemic connections between critical thinking and computational thinking as students engage in model-eliciting activities that are purposefully designed for *all students* to participate and elicit their understanding of these relevant constructs. Therefore, this study is an important step to provide broader access for *all* students to develop these highly sought skills.

4 Modes of Inquiry

Quantitative Ethnography is a methodological approach that uses qualitative and quantitative approaches to understand data-rich evidence about the discourse of cultures [34]. It respects the insights gained by ethnography and applies the power of statistical techniques. An ethnographer makes observations and collects rich data to understand patterns of discourse of the culture being studied. Quantitative Ethnography uses inferential statistical techniques to facilitate systematic interpretations to find meaning in shared and learned patterns of values and systems of symbols (e.g., language) [34–36].

Discourse analysis is the study of language at use in the world, where language is viewed as socially constructed and related to situated contexts. It deals with the interpretive processes that individuals use to give meaning in social, cultural, and political terms [10, 11, 34]. ENA is a theory-driven technique that allows for a more comprehensive discourse analysis of large datasets related to how learning occurs by takings advantage of combining powerful qualitative and quantitative analytical tools [12].

According to Shaffer & Ruis [12], an epistemic frame involves "the actions and interactions of an individual engaged in authentic tasks" (p. 176). ENA is a method for the analysis of cognitive networks by modeling the association between elements of complex thinking. The connections among cognitive elements are more important than studying those elements in isolation. ENA is used to examine the connections and uses visualization and statistical techniques to identify patterns. It quantifies the co-occurrence of concepts within a conversation [12, 13, 34, 36].

ENA analyzes data segmented, based on the principles of discourse analysis, starting with lines and grouping the conversations in stanzas. Relationships are calculated and depicted graphically and to look at the co-occurrence of concepts in the conversations that students have while learning a concept.

Several studies based on *Models & Modeling Perspectives* have relied on discourse analysis to study underlying meaning from students' solutions in MEAs [10, 11]. These studies have helped us better understand the nature of the modeling process and the constructs students develop in their solution models, as their thinking is elicited through multiple representations [5]. In this study, we propose that a *Models & Modeling* perspective is consistent with the approach to learning proposed by *epistemic frame theory* [12]. Moreover, we argue that students' modeling processes can be analyzed as an epistemic frame, considered as "the actions and interactions of an individual engaged in authentic tasks" such as MEAs. Therefore, we explore ENA as a novel theory-based approach to better understand the nature of the constructs that students elicit, develop, and co-develop within a problem-solving episode of a MEA. In this way, ENA can help shed some light in better understanding the possible interactions and structural connections among relevant competencies previously mentioned, such as computational thinking and critical thinking.

5 Methods

We designed the Tic-Tac-Toe model-eliciting activity for high school students to elicit computational thinking. In the context of the Turing Test and artificial intelligence [37], we asked students to work in teams and create an algorithm for a computer game that would allow the machine to never lose in the game of tic-tac-toe when playing with a human [33]. Clear objectives in the MEA allow the students to continuously judge the quality of their solution by fostering multiple opportunities for reflection and explanation [6, 7]. These aspects facilitate application and communication of critical thinking skills and other foundational conceptual tools as learners "select, filter, organize, and transform information" [8].

Our participants were a group of 11 students at a Career and Technical Education high school program in South Texas. Most students were male Hispanics and African Americans. Students were divided into three teams (3-3-4 students, respectively) and were given one hour to collaborative solve the Tic-Tac-Toe MEA. Each of the three teams produced a different solution or algorithm. The three solution algorithms were qualitatively different, and they all elicited students' ideas related to computational thinking and critical thinking. In this MEA, the algorithm produced is what we identify as a model or solution (i.e., a conceptual system that is expressed using representational systems to construct, describe, and explain behaviors of other systems).

The primary sources of data were the videorecordings of the conversations from each team while collaboratively solving the MEA. These contain multiple sets of data sources. During the recorded episodes, students were engaged in generating the solution for the MEA. The focus was on the participant interactions as they elicited and co-constructed a solution that involved computational thinking and critical thinking. The video recordings for the three teams were transcribed and time stamped.

Analytic coding methods were used for each of the three transcripts [37]. Based on the theoretical characterization we used for each construct, two coding schemes were used: one for critical thinking (CritT), consisting of five categories: initiation, exploration, solution, judgment, and resolution; and one for computational thinking (CT), consisting of four categories: decomposition, abstract, patterns, and algorithms. Table 1 provides the code book we used including the name of the code (construct/category), definition of the code, and examples of the code or excerpts of the transcripts illustrating each category.

Table 1. Code book containing code names, definitions, and examples.

Name	Definition	Examples
Initiation (CritT)	Identification of a common question or problem	*"We have to win every time? I kind of want to do that"*
Exploration (CritT)	All discussion which expands upon the problem or question to support formation of a solution	*"are you talking about the corners?"*
Solution (CritT)	Positing an answer to the question or problem	*"Yeah, yeah. Like you put, like what I'd do is the one in the middle... I always start in the middle, and then, wherever they make a move, that's what corner... this side"*
Judgment (CritT)	All discussion where the answer or solution is debated, modified, or tested	*"... you are looking at a tie... cause if he just put it like this... no one is going to win... so... it just ah... see... no one wins."*
Resolution (CritT)	When participants agree upon a final solution	*"You start off (inaudible)... start off here... so I think... any time, yeah... (inaudible) doesn't matter cause you'd win anyways... so I guess...(inaudible) strategy we start in the corners... to be the winner..."*
Decomposition (CT)	Break a problem down into smaller parts	*"see... I just went (inaudible). You can start in the corner... it's not... perfect but it wins, sometimes, like if someone knows what you're doing, they'll take the corners too... here... there you go..."*
Patterns (CT)	Finding similarities between items	*"I'd start at the corner here, these corners"*
Abstract (CT)	Remove details for generalization	*"Well, these are all the rules... all these rules are (inaudible) to follow us. So this is... there's a circle starting in every single spot... like that's the first rule, telling the human where to go first."*
Algorithm (CT)	Automate processes by designing a sequence of logical instructions	*"Right here. So I guess that is the way to beat it, if they start in any kind of corner, I guess, you could just put it on the opposite side, that just ruins your rhythm."*

Two separate raters coded each transcribed line of the discourse by participant, identifying each corresponding characteristic for computational thinking and critical thinking and coded using a 1 if a specific characteristic in our code book was evident and a 0 otherwise. When raters identified different codes for the same line, social moderation was used to find an agreed-upon code.

A database was produced and configured for ENA. Lines in the transcript were organized into stanzas, and binary coding was produced for each line of dialogue. We defined the units of analysis as all lines of data associated with a single value of team subsetted by participant (i.e., student).

Once coding was finalized and verified, ENA [12, 14, 34] was applied to this data using the ENA Web Tool (version 1.7.0) [31, 39]. The ENA algorithm uses a moving window to construct a network model for each line in the data, showing how codes in the current line are connected to codes that occur within the recent temporal context [40], defined as 20 lines (each line plus the 19 previous lines) within a given conversation. The resulting networks are aggregated for all lines for each unit of analysis in the model. In this model, we aggregated networks using a weighted summation in which the networks for a given line reflect square root of the product of each pair of codes.

Our ENA model included the identified codes for critical thinking and computational thinking: Initiation, Exploration, Solution, Judgment, Resolution, Decomposition, Pattern, Abstract and Algorithm. We defined conversations as all lines of data associated with a single value of Activity. For example, one conversation consisted of all the lines associated with the Tic-Tac-Toe activity.

The ENA model normalized the networks for all units of analysis before they were subjected to a dimensional reduction, which accounts for the fact that different units of analysis may have different amounts of coded lines in the data. For the dimensional reduction, ENA performed a singular value decomposition (SVD), projecting and centering the data without rescaling it. This projection maximized the variance accounted for the data in a two-dimensional orthogonal space: SVD1 and SVD2, that we then interpreted in relation to the research questions and our analytical framework.

ENA generated mean network graphs that show the two-dimensional orthogonal space generated by SVD1 and SVD2. We analyzed the graphs based on the strength of the connections between nodes representing our operational definition for computational thinking (abstract, decompose, recognize patterns and create algorithms) and critical thinking (initiation, exploration, solution, judgment, and resolution) for each of the teams: 1, 2, and 3. We verified these interpretations by going back to the transcripts and validating with the discourse.

6 Results and Interpretations

Figures 1, 2 and 3 provide visual representations of the ENA which show connections among cognitive elements of computational thinking and critical thinking, respectively for each participating Team 1, Team 2, or Team 3. In the mean network graph showing the representation of the shared space for the three teams simultaneously, we see that the amount of variance explained by the variables represented in axes SVD 1 and SVD 2 is almost 55% of the total variance: 32.5% for SVD 1 and 22.4% for SVD 2. In this section, we provide our interpretations of the ENA Models. First, we report our interpretations of the space generated by SVD 1 and SVD 2. Then, we interpret the ENA Models generated for Teams 1, 2, and 3 in terms of the co-occurrences of the different characteristics of Critical Thinking and Computational Thinking.

We propose an interpretation of the structural connections between computational thinking and critical thinking elicited during the Tic-Tac-Toe problem-solving episode by focusing on the structure of the connections in the data as displayed in each graph. Then, we extended our interpretation to analyze the orthogonal space of SVD 1 and SVD 2, based on the position of each pair of coordinates or nodes corresponding to each characteristic of computational thinking and critical thinking in this two-dimensional space.

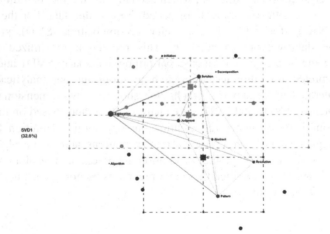

Fig. 1. Network graph for Team 1, showing centroids and confidence intervals.

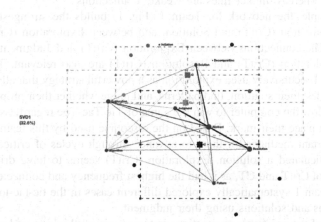

Fig. 2. Network graph for Team 2, showing centroids and confidence intervals.

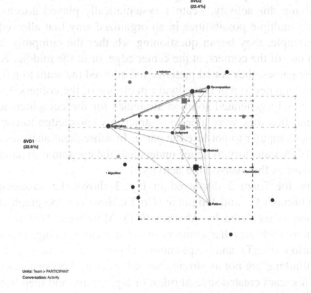

Fig. 3. Network graph for Team 3, showing centroids and confidence intervals.

6.1   Comparing Graphs for Teams 1, 2 and 3

ENA was performed on the co-occurrences of each pair of components and the network formed provides a model of the structure of these connections. Based on this ENA, we interpret the network models as the structure of connections among the elements of computational thinking and critical thinking elicited by the students' discourse as they solved the Tic-Tac-Toe MEA. Thicker lines within the network represent stronger connections, whereas thinker lines are weaker connections.

For example, the network for Team 1 (Fig. 1) builds the strongest connections between Exploration (CritT) and Solution, and between Exploration (CritT) and Patterns (CT). The connections between Exploration (CritT) and Judgment (CritT), and between Exploration (CritT) and Resolution (CritT) are also relevant. This indicates that as Team 1 recursively used exploration as a powerful strategy that allowed them to concurrently test their solution, find patterns, and judge whether their proposed solution did indeed allow the computer to win the game of Tic-Tac-Toe regardless of where the human might place their mark. Based on the discourse used by this team, Exploration was an important mediator for them to advance through cycles of critical thinking as the Team articulated a solution. Exploration (CritT) seems to have driven all other components of CritT and CT, as it had the highest frequency and connected to all other codes. As Team 1 systematically explored different cases in the tic-tac-toe game, they found patterns and solutions using their judgment.

In terms of the epistemic connections between critical thinking and computational thinking for Team 1, ENA indicates that the strongest connection was between Exploration (CritT) and Patterns (CT). This is consistent with the description in the qualitative descriptive analysis revealing that the team used a systematic trial-and-error approach to solving this activity. Team 1 systematically played dozens of tic-tac-toe games, assessing multiple possibilities in an organized way that allowed them to find patterns. For example, they began questioning whether the computer first needed to place a mark in one of the corners, at the center edge, or in the middle. After exploring multiple possible games, they found patterns that allowed the team to judge that a good strategy for the computer to win is to always mark one of the corners. Exploration and finding patters slowly generated solution strategies for the computer, and it was not until the very end that they were able to abstract this knowledge to come up with an algorithm for the computer to not lose the game. In subsequent analyses, we anticipate developing an ENA trajectory to better understand the epistemic dynamic cycles over time for each team as they solved the activity.

The network for Team 2 displayed in Fig. 2 shows the strongest connections between Resolution (CritT) and Judgment (CritT). However, the graph shows that this strong connection is mediated by Abstract (CT). Moreover, Abstract (CT) also has strong connections with all other components of critical thinking, including Solution (CritT), Resolution (CritT) and Exploration. Co-ocurrences among components of computational thinking are not as strong, but still evident, between Abstract (CT) and Pattern (CT). This team created several rules, or algorithms, and then tested these rules with concrete possible scenarios in the tic-tac-toe game. In contrast with Team 1 who had an approach from particular case-by-case to generalizing, Team 2 created more general rules and then tested to see if they would hold under particular cases they identified. Thus, Team 2 went from more general to particular cases, and this is illustrated in their network model showing more connections between Abstraction (CT) with other characteristics of critical thinking and with Patterns (CT). Moreover, the graph also shows some weaker connections with Algorithms (CT) and other characteristics.

The network model for Team 3 displayed in Fig. 3 indicates that the strongest connection was between Exploration (CritT) and Solution (CritT). However, Exploration (CritT) was also connected with Abstract (CT), Decomposition (CT) and Patterns (CT), which are all elements of computational thinking. Another interesting set of connections Team 3 made, although weaker, was between Abstract (CT) and Solution (CritT), between Abstract (CT) and Judgment (CritT), and between Abstract (CT) and Decomposition (CT). From the network model, it appears that judgment and abstraction mediate the many co-occurrences this team made among components of critical thinking and computational thinking.

The strategies used by Team 3 appear similar to the ones from Team 1 in that they also went from playing many instances of the tic-tac-toe game, and using particular cases to generalize to a solution. Early in their team activity, one of the members proposed a winning strategy from the beginning (i.e., having the computer go first and take a corner). However, other team members did not appear to understand that this was a more abstract solution and they continued playing instances of the tic-tac-toe game until they found enough patterns to arrive to the same conclusion as their peer had suggested earlier. In this process, the students try different strategies and come up with partial solutions which they verify and integrate to a more generalized solution at the end of the episode.

Looking at the centroids for Teams 1, 2, and 3 in these graphs, as well as the respective confidence intervals, we observe that the confidence intervals all overlap. Considering each centroid as a summary of the ENA network for the three teams, we see that all the centroids are relatively close to each other and aligned. Both, the closeness of the centroids and the overlap of the confidence intervals indicate that the epistemic frames between teams is similar in the variables described by SVD 1 and SVD 2. Although this is visually evident, we also conducted a Mann-Whitney U Test for a pairwise mean comparison for all teams (Team 1 vs Team 2, Team 1 vs. Team 3, and Team 2 vs. Team 3). We found no significant difference between teams.

Although it is clear from the ENA for each Team, and their respective network models, that the three teams used different strategies in their solutions, we interpret this statistical result as content validity of the task, that the MEA did indeed elicit students' computational thinking and critical thinking for all teams; and that, although qualitatively different, there is a strong interaction between these two constructs as students generate their solutions to the task. We also noticed that, although each team did show evidence of eliciting computational thinking and critical thinking during the Tic-Tac-Toe problem-solving episode, each of the three teams generated distinct concept spaces which characterize their cognitive processes related to these two constructs.

6.2   Interpretation of SVD 1 and SVD 2

Observing the positions of the network graph nodes—and the connections they define, we interpreted the dimensions of the projected space and describe the positions of plotted points in the space. Therefore, in making interpretations of the underlying constructs for SVD 1 and SVD 2, we notice the following:

- SVD 1 shows two sets of characteristics for computational thinking and critical thinking that are grouped and organized based on what appears to be describing a continuum for *problem solving,* defined as a continuum from givens to goals [5]. For example, we observe that on one end (positive side of the axis, from greatest to least magnitude) are: resolution (CritT); decomposition (CT), pattern (CT), and abstract (CT) almost at the same level, solution (CritT), and judgment (CritT). These are all characteristics that correspond to processes that students engage in with data or other cognitive tools and resources that are generated by their own team during the problem-solving episode as they develop their solution. On the opposite end (negative side of the axis) are: initiation (CritT), algorithm (CT), and exploration (CritT). Descriptors on this second group seem to be characteristics that correspond to processes that students follow based on information provided directly in the problem statement.
- SVD 2 shows two sets of characteristics for computational thinking and critical thinking that are grouped and organized based on what appears to be a continuum for *deeper learning.* [1] On the one end (negative side of the axis, from greater to least magnitude) are: pattern (CT), algorithm (CT) at the same level as resolution (CritT), and abstract (CT). These all seem to be characteristics that are more abstract and transferable to different problem-solving situations beyond the context in which the Tic-Tac-Toe MEA is embedded. On the opposite end (positive side of the axis) are: judgment (CritT) almost at the same level as exploration (CritT), solution (CritT), decomposition (CT), and initiation (CritT). Descriptors on this second group seem to be characteristics that are more problem-specific and situated within the Tic-Tac-Toe MEA and which have a more interpretive aspect from the team members.

7 Conclusions and Next Steps

In this exploratory study, we used ENA as an analytic tool to help us better understand the possible structural connections between computational thinking and critical thinking as elicited in a collaborative authentic problem-solving task called the Tic-Tac-Toe model-eliciting activity (MEA). We found that while solving this MEA, the structural connections elicited by the three teams of students were very similar. We interpret this as a direct reflection of the nature of the task, which is complex and open-ended, and therefore, allows for multiple possible solutions. We found that all teams made strong connections between critical thinking and computational thinking, although the solution processes were qualitatively different. Nevertheless, we found that Exploration (CritT) and Abstraction (CT) appear to be key mediating components that facilitate connections with other characteristics of critical thinking and computational thinking as students elicit their solution models.

Graphs that were generated by ENA display the diversity in student thinking, as well as a similar epistemic structure in the solution of the MEA. The interactions between critical thinking and computational thinking are evident, although components of these constructs were elicited in different ways in each team's solution.

This study warrants further exploration on the design of model-eliciting activities as an efficient learning environment that elicits computational thinking and critical thinking, and be able to better understand the nature of these two constructs, as well as the structural connections that are generated. Moreover, this study opens future studies to use ENA to better understand the dynamic epistemic nature of modeling cycles that students engage in with MEAs, in which they express, test, revise, and refine a progression of preliminary solutions of possible tic-tac-toe game strategies.

Acknowledgments. This material is based upon work supported by the National Science Foundation under Award #1736209 and the Institute of Education Sciences, U.S. Department of Education (grant R305B160008). Any opinions, findings, and conclusions or recommendations expressed in this material are those of the authors and do not necessarily reflect the views of the funding agencies.

References

1. National Research Council. Education for Life and Work: Developing Transferable Knowledge and Skills in the 21st Century. Committee on Defining Deeper Learning and 21st Century Skills, J.W. Pellegrino and M.L. Hilton, Editors. Board on Testing and Assessment and Board on Science Education, Division of Behavioral and Social Sciences and Education. The National Academies Press, Washington, DC (2012)
2. National Research Council. A Framework for K-12 Science Education: Practices, Crosscutting Concepts, and Core Ideas. Committee on a Conceptual Framework for New K-12 Science Education Standards. Board on Science Education, Division of Behavioral and Social Sciences and Education. The National Academies Press, Washington, DC (2012)
3. Lesh, R., Zawojewski, J., Carmona, G.: What mathematical abilities are needed for success beyond school in a technology-based age of information? In: Lesh, R., Doerr, H.M. (eds.) Beyond Constructivism: Models and Modeling Perspectives on Mathematics Problem Solving, Learning, and Teaching, pp. 205–222. Lawrence Erlbaum Associates, Mahwah (2003)
4. Lesh, R., Hamilton, E., Kaput, J. (eds.): Foundations for the Future in Mathematics Education. Lawrence Erlbaum Associates, Mahwah (2007)
5. Lesh, R., Doerr, H.M.: Beyond Constructivism: Models and Modeling Perspectives on Mathematics Problem Solving, Learning, and Teaching. Lawrence Erlbaum, Mahwah (2003)
6. Lesh, R., Hoover, M., Hole, B., Kelly, E., Post, T.: Principles for developing thought-revealing activities for students and teachers. In: Kelly, A.E., Lesh, R.A. (eds.) Handbook of Research Design in Mathematics and Science Education, pp. 591–645. Lawrence Erlbaum Associates, Mahwah (2000)
7. Carmona, G., Greenstein, S.: Investigating the relationship between the problem and the solver: who decides what math gets used? In: Lesh, R., Galbraith, P.L., Haines, C.R., Kaiser, G. (eds.) Modeling students' mathematical modeling competencies, pp. 245–254. Springer, New York (2009)
8. Weltzer-Ward, L.M., Carmona, G.: Support of the critical thinking process in synchronous online collaborative discussion through model-eliciting activities. Int. J. Emerg. Technol. Learn. **3**, 86–88 (2008)
9. Hjalmarson, M., Holincheck, N., Baker, C.K., Galanti, T*.: Learning models and modeling across the STEM disciplines. In: Johnson, C.C., Mohr-Schroeder, M., Moore, T., English, L. (eds.) Handbook of Research on STEM education. Routledge, New York (2020)

10. Gee, J.P.: Introduction to Discourse Analysis: Theory and Method. Routledge, London (1999)
11. Jang, H.: Identifying 21st century STEM competencies using workplace data. J. Sci. Educ. Technol. **25**(2), 284–301 (2016)
12. Shaffer, D.W., Ruis, A.R.: Epistemic network analysis: a worked example of theory-based learning analytics. In: Lang, C., Siemens, G., Wise, A.F., Gasevic, D. (eds.) Handbook of Learning Analytics, pp. 175–187. Society for Learning Analytics Research (2017)
13. Siebert-Evenstone, A., Shaffer, D.W.: Cause and because: using epistemic network analysis to model causality in the next generation science standards. In: Eagan, B., Misfeldt, M., Siebert-Evenstone, A. (eds.) ICQE 2019. CCIS, vol. 1112, pp. 223–233. Springer, Cham (2019). https://doi.org/10.1007/978-3-030-33232-7_19
14. Shaffer, D., Collier, W., Ruis, A.R.: A tutorial on epistemic network analysis: analyzing the structure of connections in cognitive, social, and interaction data. J. Learn. Anal. **3**(3), 9–45 (2016). https://doi.org/10.18608/jla.2016.33.3
15. Papert, S.: Mindstorms: Children, computers, and Powerful Ideas. Basic Books, New York (1980)
16. Wing, J.M.: Computational thinking. Commun. ACM **49**(3), 33–35 (2006)
17. Kules, B.: Computational thinking is critical thinking: connecting to university discourse, goals, and learning outcomes. In: Proceedings of the Association for Information Science and Technology. American Society for Information Science, Silver Springs (2016)
18. National Research Council. Report of a workshop on the scope and nature of computational thinking. The National Academies Press, Washington, DC (2010)
19. International Society for Technology in Education (ISTE). Computational thinking competencies (2018). https://www.iste.org/standards/iste-standards-for-computational-thinking
20. Computer Science Teacher Association (CSTA). Computational thinking standards (2017). https://www.csteachers.org/page/standards
21. Kale, U., et al.: Computational what? relating computational thinking to teaching. TechTrends **62**(6), 574–584 (2018). https://doi.org/10.1007/s11528-018-0290-9
22. Arastoopour Irgens, G., et al.: Modeling and measuring high school students' computational thinking practices in science. J. Sci. Educ. Technol. **29**(1), 137–161 (2020). https://doi.org/10.1007/s10956-020-09811-1
23. Yin, Y., Hadad, R., Tang, X., Lin, Q.: Improving and assessing computational thinking in maker activities: the integration with physics and engineering learning. J. Sci. Educ. Technol. **29**(2), 189–214 (2020)
24. Krauss, J., Prottsman, K.: Computational Thinking {and Coding} for Every Student. Corwin, Thousand Oaks (2016)
25. Caeli, E.N., Yadav, A.: Unplugged approaches to computational thinking: a historical perspective. TechTrends **64**(1), 29–36 (2019). https://doi.org/10.1007/s11528-019-00410-5
26. Ching, Y.-H., Hsu, Y.-C., Baldwin, S.: Developing computational thinking with educational technologies for young learners. TechTrends **62**(6), 563–573 (2018). https://doi.org/10.1007/s11528-018-0292-7
27. Chowdhury, B., Bart, A.C., Kafura, D.: Analysis of collaborative learning in a computational thinking class. In: Proceedings of the 49th ACM Technical Symposium on Computer Science Education, pp. 143–148 (2018). https://doi.org/10.1145/3159450.3159470
28. Ennis, R.H.: A concept of critical thinking. Harv. Educ. Rev. **29**, 128–136 (1962)
29. Ennis, R.H.: Critical thinking: a streamlined conception. Teach. Philos. **14**(1), 5–25 (1991)
30. Ennis, R.: Critical thinking assessment. Theory Pract. **32**(3), 179–186 (1993)
31. Dewey, J.: How We Think. Prometheus Books, Buffalo (1910)

32. Voskoglou, M.G., Buckley, S.: Problem solving and computers in a learning environment. Egypt. Comput. Sci. J. ECS **36**(4), 28–46 (2012)
33. Carmona, G., Pate, E., Galarza, B.: Can Machines Think? In: C-SPECC High School Curriculum: Model-eliciting activities. CC BY-NC-SA 4.0 (2019)
34. Shaffer, D.W.: Quantitative Ethnography. CathCart Press, Madison (2017)
35. Bian, W., Yiling, H., Ruis, A.R., Wang, M.: Analysing computational thinking in collaborative programming: a quantitative ethnography approach. J. Comput. Assist. Learn. **35**(3), 421–434 (2019). https://doi.org/10.1111/jcal.12348
36. Buckingham Shum, S., Echeverria, V., Martinez-Maldonado, R.: The multimodal matrix as a quantitative ethnography methodology. In: Eagan, B., Misfeldt, M., Siebert-Evenstone, A. (eds.) ICQE 2019. CCIS, vol. 1112, pp. 26–40. Springer, Cham (2019). https://doi.org/10.1007/978-3-030-33232-7_3
37. Turing, A.: Computing Machinery and intelligence. Mind **59**(236), 433–460 (1950)
38. Miles, M.B., Huberman, A.M.: Qualitative data analysis. Sage Publications, Thousand Oaks (1994)
39. Marquart, C.L., Hinojosa, C., Swiecki, Z., Eagan, B., Shaffer, D.W.: Epistemic Network Analysis (Version 1.7.0) [Software] (2018). http://app.epistemicnetwork.org
40. Siebert-Evenstone, A., et al.: In search of conversational grain size: modeling semantic structure using moving stanza windows. J. Learn. Anal. **4**(3), 123–139 (2017). https://doi.org/10.18608/jla.2017.43.7

Discovering Differences in Learning Behaviours During Active Video Watching Using Epistemic Network Analysis

Negar Mohammadhassan[✉][iD] and Antonija Mitrovic[iD]

University of Canterbury, Christchurch, New Zealand
negar.mohammadhassan@pg.canterbury.ac.nz,
tanja.mitrovic@canterbury.ac.nz

Abstract. AVW-Space is an online video-based learning platform that aims to improve engagement by providing a note-taking environment, personalised support and peer-reviewing. The effectiveness of AVW-Space in supporting active video watching has been evaluated in several studies, using quantitative analyses of learning outcomes and engagement based on student logs. However, there have been no qualitative analyses on the longitudinal data of student interactions. This paper uses Epistemic Network Analysis (ENA) to identify behavioural differences in video-based learning. We first investigate how students interact with the platform and then compare the interactions and performance of students who started late with the early starters. The work presented in this paper demonstrates the potentials of applying ENA in understanding learning behaviours and evaluating the effectiveness of educational support in computer-based learning environments more comprehensively.

Keywords: Video-based learning · Epistemic network analysis · Personalised nudges · Learning analytics

1 Introduction

Video-based learning (VBL) has been widely used in formal and informal education [1, 2]. The rapid growth of Massive Open Online Courses (MOOCs), and informal VBL platforms such as YouTube, has accelerated the use of videos in higher education. However, the lack of interaction between teachers and students makes maintaining and monitoring engagement challenging in VBL [1, 3]. AVW-Space [4] is an online VBL platform that supports engagement by providing note-taking, micro-scaffolds for reflection, reviewing environment, visual learning analytics and personalised nudges [5, 6]. Several studies have proved the effectiveness of AVW-Space in increasing engagement during VBL, using quantitative analyses of interaction data. However, there has been no ethnographic research on the longitudinal data of student interactions. This paper investigates learning behaviours in AVW-Space and its effectiveness in enhancing engagement more deeply using quantitative ethnography.

In AVW-Space, the teacher first selects videos from YouTube. Then, students watch videos and write comments. An early study with AVW-Space [7] showed that

© Springer Nature Switzerland AG 2022
B. Wasson and S. Zörgő (Eds.): ICQE 2021, CCIS 1522, pp. 362–377, 2022.
https://doi.org/10.1007/978-3-030-93859-8_24

students who commented on videos learnt more than students who watched videos passively. Thus, personalised Reminder nudges were added to AVW-Space to encourage students to write comments [5]. Later on, we added personalised Quality nudges to encourage students to write high-quality comments [6]. AVW-Space also supports social learning by allowing the teacher to make comments available for peer-reviewing. Previous studies revealed that rating comments led to increased conceptual understanding [7].

In previous studies, we invited students to use AVW-Space for learning oral presentation skills before presenting their final project. We classified students post-hoc into different categories based on ICAP framework [8]. The ICAP framework classifies learners' overt behaviour into four categories: Interactive, Constructive, Active and Passive. Studies showed the more engaged students become, the more effectively they learn [8]. Passive learners receive information by only watching videos. Active students make comments which merely repeat the received information. Constructive learners add new information that was not explicitly taught, by reflecting on their knowledge. The Interactive category is not applicable in our case, since AVW-Space does not support direct interaction between students. We labelled Constructive Students (CS) as those who had at least three comments showing critical thinking, reflection or self-regulation [6] (based on the median number of such comments). Students who had less than three such comments were classified as Active (AS), while those who only watched videos without making comments were labelled as Passive (PS). Our previous studies showed significant differences in the number of videos watched, comments, nudges received and ratings made (PS < AC < CS) [5, 6]. However, all previous analyses were based on student logs. Thus, the first research question (**RQ1**) addressed in this paper is how different categories of students interacted with AVW-Space.

Studies have shown a striking increase in watching videos closer to assignment/exam deadlines [9, 10]. However, watching videos on a regular basis results in more learning compared to watching videos in a short time and closer to deadlines [9, 11]. We are interested in learning behaviours of early starters (ES), i.e. students who start watching videos early, in contrast to late starters (LS). Thus, the second research question (**RQ2**) is how ES and LS interact and perform differently in AVW-Space.

Section 2 provides an overview of related work and introduces AVW-Space. After describing the datasets, we present the codebook of interactions in Sect. 3. Next, we address RQ1 and RQ2 in Sects. 4 and 5, respectively. Lastly, we provide a summary of findings and discuss future work.

2 Related Work

The analyses of log data are common in learning analytics research since logs capture behaviour patterns over time [12]. There are methods for extracting temporal learning strategies from log data, such as clustering [13], sequence mining [14] and process mining [15]. However, sequence mining only highlights local patterns, and process mining does not allow statistical testing. ENA [16] is a popular approach for extracting patterns from log data which provides visualisations for qualitative interpretation along with statistical tests.

Gamage and colleagues [17] used ENA to compare first-time MOOC learners with learners who had previous experience with MOOCs. ENA was applied to identify behavioural differences during video watching and social tasks, such as posting in discussion forums. Saint et al. [18] combined ENA and process mining to provide richer insights on the self-regulated learning behaviours of low/high performing students in a learning management system. ENA was also used in an educational game for teaching complex systems in science to investigate how learners responded to the game events such as feedback and new phenomena differently and how their strategies evolved [19]. Karumbaiah et al. [20] applied ENA on event logs from Physics Playground, an educational game for teaching Physics, to discover why some students quit the game.

AVW-Space supports engagement in two spaces: 1) Personal space (Fig. 1), where students watch videos and make comments, and 2) Social space (Fig. 2), where students review and rate comments made by their peers. Personal Space is always available for students, while Social Space becomes available after the teacher selects comments to be displayed for reviewing. AVW-Space provides interactive visualisations of comments written by previous students in Personal Space, which show the distribution of comments over various video parts [5]. When commenting, students have to select an aspect that the comment relates to. The aspects are micro-scaffolds defined by the teacher, to direct students to reflect on the key points of the video [7].

Fig. 1. Personal Space in AVW-Space.

There are types of nudges in Personal Space: Reminder and Quality nudges (Table 1). Nudges are personalised interventions aiming to enhance constructive behaviour. The nudges were designed based on the results of initial studies with AVW-Space [5] to encourage students to write more comments, use various aspects and improve the quality of comments. AVW-Space automatically assesses the quality of comments as students write them [22], and generates nudges that guide students toward critical thinking and reflection. Previous studies showed that Reminder nudges increased the number of comments [5] and that Quality nudges significant improvement in the quality of comments [8]. However, there has been no temporal analysis on how students respond to the nudges, which is the focus of this paper.

In Social Space, students can rate comments by choosing the rating options defined by the teacher. The rating options are defined to trigger reflection [7]. Although the

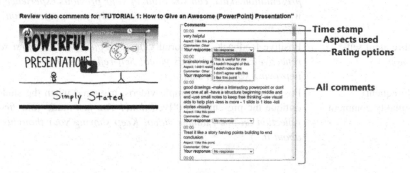

Fig. 2. Social Space in AVW-Space.

Table 1. Reminder and Quality nudges integrated into AVW-Space.

Reminder nudges	Description
No comment	Triggered if the student made no comments (*"Don't forget to make a comment on the techniques for presentation skills mentioned in the video"*)
No comment with reference point	Given with an example comment to the student who made no comments after receiving the No Comment nudge
Aspect under-utilised	Triggered if the student has not used a specific aspect, to encourage using that aspect. (*"Have you seen this before? Share your thoughts with the class by making a comment using the 'I did/saw this before' aspect"*)
Diverse aspect	Positive feedback, when the student used all aspects
Quality nudges	Description
Elaborate more	Triggered if the student made a short/off-topic comment, to encourage more elaboration on the video (*"Try to elaborate more on the video in your next comment"*)
Vague comment	Triggered only in tutorial videos, if the student made a vague comment, using e.g. "that", "thing", to discourage ambiguity (*"This comment sounds a bit vague, can you clarify more in your next comments?"*)
Repeating comment	Triggered only in tutorial videos if the student made a comment that merely repeats the video content, to encourage critical thinking
Critical thinking	Triggered if the student made a comment showing critical thinking, to encourage students to write self-reflections and plan for future improvement

(continued)

Table 1. (*continued*)

Quality nudges	Description
Final reflection	Triggered if the student watched the whole tutorial video but made no reflective comments (*"Now that you've learned more about presentation skills, can you think of your previous experience and write a comment on how you can improve your presentation skills "*)
First/Frequent self-reflection	Positive feedback, for tutorial videos (*"You made your first self-reflective comment for this video! Self-reflections help in improving your soft skills."*)
First/Frequent high-quality comment	Positive feedback in example videos, triggered when the student critique the presentation (*"Well done! You just made your first reflection on this example video! Keep sharing your thoughts about it."*)

effectiveness of rating has been evaluated via quantitative analysis, there has been no analysis on the transitions between Personal Space and Social Space. This paper investigates the transitions between these spaces via ethnographic analysis to provide insights into potential enhancements in AVW-Space.

3   Methods

We conducted a study in a first-year engineering course at the University of Canterbury in the context of giving oral presentations. The participants first completed Survey 1, and were instructed to watch four tutorial videos on giving presentations, and later to critique four example videos of real presentations. Nudges were provided during this phase. In the second phase, students were instructed to review and rate comments made by their peers. Finally, Survey 2 was released to students.

Survey 1 contained demographic questions, questions about the participant's knowledge on giving presentations, experience and training in giving presentations, how often they used YouTube generally or for learning. The last part of Survey 1 included the Motivated Strategies for Learning Questionnaire (MSLQ) [23]. Survey 2 included the same questions about giving presentations to investigate whether students have increased their knowledge. For knowledge questions in both surveys, the participants were asked to write everything they knew about visual aids, structure and delivery (one minute per question). The students' answers were marked automatically, using the ontology of presentation skills [21]. The marks for conceptual knowledge questions are used as the pre/post-test scores (CK1/CK2).

294 students completed Survey 1 and watched videos. The logs contain a total of 61,483 entries, which were coded as described in Table 2. The video pause and video play events do not include auto-pause and auto-play before/after commenting, since we are interested in manual playing/pausing students do intentionally. The *Comment* code

is a generic one, but we also defined the codes for comments of specific quality assessed by AVW-Space (*CommentQ1/2/3*). Similarly, we generated a generic code *Nudge*, and more specific codes *Quality Nudge, Reminder Nudge* and nudges presenting positive feedback (*NPositiveFeedback*). We require the specific codes for detailed analysis of interactions in Personal Space, but generic codes suffice in the analysis of the transitions between Personal and Social Space. Each code is defined for a single action type except the *Revisit* code, which aggregates a sequence of three log entries: 1) an action on the rating page (review page load or rating), 2) loading the list of videos, and 3) loading the video page in Personal Space. This sequence of actions is interesting from an educational perspective since it could indicate that the student is writing/revising her/his comments after reviewing the comments made by classmates. However, some students might copy others' comments from reviewing pages, which is a form of cheating. On the other hand, *Revisit* could also indicate that the student did not know what to write about, and peer-reviewing inspires them to make a new comment. We used the ENA1.7.0 Web tool [24] for investigating the interactions.

Table 2. Description of codes derived from event logs in AVW-Space.

Personal space	Description	Example
VLoad	Loading a video page	Pageload: video watch
VPlay	Playing a video	Video state changed: playing
VPause	Pausing a video	Video state changed: paused
VEnd	Reaching the end	Video state changed: page = Watch, state = ended
Nudge	Receiving a nudge	Nudge
NReminder	Reminder nudge	Nudge: no_comment_reminder_nudge
NQuality	Quality nudge	Nudge: final_self-reflection_nudge
NPositiveFeedback	Positive Feedback nudge	Nudge: first_self-reflection_nudge
Comment	Making a comment	Comment created
CommentQ1	A short/off-topic comment	Comment = "smart", quality = 1
CommentQ2	Comment that elaborates or criticises the video	Comment = "Follow a structure and build to conclusion as to make story clear", quality = 2
CommentQ3	Reflective or self-regulative comment	Comment = "I try to leave a slide for each key idea", quality = 3
Social space	Description	Example
RLoad	Loading the rating page	Video review
Rate	Rating a comment	Rating_id = 6, comment_id = 1190
Revisit	The transition from rating page to personal space for the same video	1) Rating_id = 7, comment_id = 955 2) Pageload: Space Instance 3) Pageload: Video Watch

4 Learning Behaviour Differences in ICAP Categories

We analysed the actions performed by different ICAP categories on tutorial videos since most students (96.5%) started by watching tutorial videos. As reported in Table 3, *VPlay*, *VPause* and *NReminder* are the most frequent events in all three categories. PS had the highest frequency of *NReminder* and *Vplay,* as expected, since they only watched the videos. CS received *NPositiveFeedback* more frequently than AS since CS wrote more high-quality comments (*CommentQ3*). However, the co-occurrence of these actions should be investigated. Thus, we generated the epistemic networks, with the units of analysis defined as the ICAP category, subsetted by student_id, and stanza = 3. The reason for this window size is that triggering each nudge involves changes in video status, making a comment and getting the nudge, and we wanted to capture the co-occurrence of these actions. We aggregated networks using a binary summation of the co-occurrence of the event codes. The conversation was defined as a single video, subsetted by student_id. Our model had co-registration correlations of 0.97 (Pearson) and 0.97 (Spearman) for the first dimension, and co-registration correlations of 0.97 (Pearson) and 0.97 (Spearman) for the second. These measures indicate that there is a good fit between the visualisation and the original model. Figure 3 shows the networks generated for each student category. As can be seen, networks generated for AS and PS have a strong co-occurrence between *NReminder* and *VPlay* compared to CS. The network generated for PS does not have connections to *CommentQ1/2/3* and *NPositiveFeedback* since PS did not make any comments.

Table 3. Frequency of events in tutorial videos for different ICAP categories.

Events (14,633)	CS (105)		AS (114)		PS (75)	
	Freq.	Count	Freq.	Count	Freq.	Count
VPlay	32%	2492	36%	1,732	39%	769
VPause	25%	1991	25%	1,218	25%	499
VEnd	4%	278	5%	231	5%	91
NPositiveFeedback	5%	372	2%	101	0	0
NReminder	12%	960	15%	723	21%	410
NQuality	6%	473	8%	380	10%	201
CommentQ1	0	4	0	10	0	0
CommentQ2	11%	884	7%	326	0	0
CommentQ3	5%	407	2%	81	0	0
Total		7,861		4,802		1,970

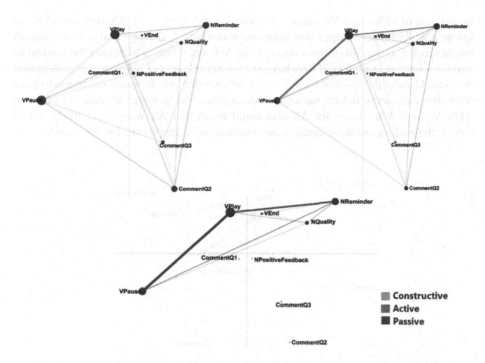

Fig. 3. Epistemic Networks for responses to nudges for the three student categories.

To test the differences between CS and AS (Fig. 4), we applied a two-sample t-test on the location of points in the projected ENA space. There was no significant difference along the X-axis (p = .1) between AS (mean = .13, SD = 1.25) and CS (mean = −.13, SD = 1.02). However, there was a significant difference along the Y-axis (t = -9.98, p < .001, Cohen's d = 1.36) between AS (mean = .07, SD = .60) and CS (mean = −.77, SD = .65). The mean for AS is positioned in the top half of the ENA space, which is more focused on nudges and video watching, while the mean of CS is located in the bottom half, which includes comment making and video pause. Also, the network reveals that the co-occurrences of *CommentQ2/3* with *VPause* are stronger for CS than AS. Furthermore, the co-occurrences of *VPause* and *CommentsQ2/3* are stronger than nudge-comment co-occurrences for CS. That means that CS were more likely to make comments intuitively without being nudged. As expected, co-occurrences of *NPositiveFeedback* and *CommentQ2/3* were more frequent for CS, as they were more likely to continue making good-quality comments. The connection between the NReminder-CommentQ3 are stronger than the co-occurrence of *NQuality and CommentQ3* for CS, meaning that CS make self-reflective comments more than AS when receiving Reminder nudges. In other words, CS are more likely to make high-quality comments without directly being nudged. However, the difference network does not have any connection between *NQuality* and *CommentQ3*, meaning there was no difference in this co-occurrence between CS and AS. Thus, Quality nudges were equally helpful for CS and AS to improve the quality of their comments. The co-occurrence of *VPlay* and *NReminder* is stronger for AS, meaning AS are more likely to ignore the Reminder nudges and continue watching. A Quality nudge that students might receive at the end of the video is Final Self-reflection, which asks the student to make a reflective comment, if they have not submitted one yet. The stronger connection between *VEnd* and *NQuality* for AS could indicate that AS are more likely not to have reflective comments before the end of the video. The stronger connection between *NQuality and NReminder* for AS also could mean that AS were more likely not to satisfy the nudges, so these nudges are repeated more frequently for AS than CS.

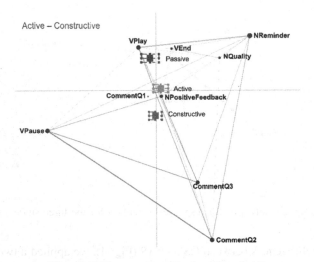

Fig. 4. Difference networks for CS and AS.

We found no significant difference between AS (mean = 013, SD = 1.25) and PS (mean = −.01, SD = 1.14) on the X-axis (p = .43). However, there was a significant difference along the Y-axis (t = 12.29, p < .001, Cohen's d = 1.71) between AS (mean = .07, SD = .60) and PS (mean = .98, SD = .42). The comparison network for AS-PS (Fig. 5) emphasises mostly the differences in commenting since PS did not make any comment. The strong co-occurrence of *NReminder* and *VPlay* is more frequent for PS than the co-occurrence of *NReminder-VPause*, indicating that PS were more likely to ignore nudges and continue watching the video rather than pausing the video and taking time to read the nudges and comment. Co-occurrence of *NQuality* and *NReminder* is more frequent for PS, meaning PS did not satisfy the nudges, and they kept getting nudges. The co-occurrences with *VEnd* for AS indicates that AS were more likely to watch the video to the end compared to PS. There is a strong connection between *CommentQ2* and *NReminder* for AS in comparison to *NQuality and CommentQ2* and *VPlay/VPause and CommentQ2*. That means AS were more likely to make comments with quality 2 when receiving Reminder nudges and to trigger Reminder nudges again (Aspect Under-utilised nudge). The co-occurrence of *CommentQ3 and VEnd* indicates that the AS were likely to make reflective comments at the end of videos.

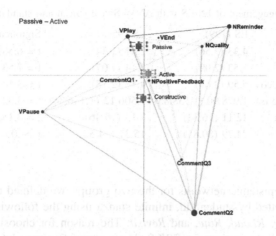

Fig. 5. Difference network for AS and PS.

When comparing CS to PS (Fig. 6), we found no significant difference along the X-axis (p = 0.49), but there was a significant difference along the Y-axis (t = 21.95, p < .001, Cohen's d = 3.10) between CS (mean = −.77, SD = .65) and PS (mean = .98, SD = .42). As expected, the strong connection of *VPlay* and *NReminder*, and the connections from *VEnd* to nudges, indicate that PS ignored nudges. In contrast, there are many co-occurrences of *VPause* with comment making and nudges for CS.

5 Learning Behaviour Differences Early and Late Starters

We labelled all students post-hoc as Early Starters (ES), i.e. students who started soon after AVW-Space was made available, and Late Starters (LS), i.e. students who only started interacting with AVW-Space after comments were made open for rating. We found no statistically significant differences in the self-reported MSLQ scores of ES/LS. Thus, the LS reported being as self-regulated as the ES. We found no significant differences in the experience and training on presentation skills of ES/LS and how often they used YouTube generally or for learning. We compared the number of students in different ICAP categories in ES/LS (Table 4). A chi-square test of homogeneity between ES/LS and ICAP categories revealed no significant differences (Chi-square = 4.297, p = .11). Table 5 shows how many sessions and days ES/LS interacted with the system, their video-watching time, number of comments they made and rated. There was a significant difference between the two groups on all measures except for ratings.

Table 4. Distribution of ICAP categories in ES/LS.

	Constructive	Active	Passive
Early (199)	79 (39.69%)	73 (36.68%)	47 (23.61%)
Late (95)	26 (27.36%)	41 (43.15%)	28 (29.47%)

Table 5. Engagement of ES/LS with AVW-Space (mean and standard deviation).

	ES (199)	LS (95)	Significant
Sessions	4.33 (3.56)	2.41 (1.44)	t = 6.58, p < .001
Days	3.53 (2.09)	2.14 (1.07)	t = 7.53, p < .001
Unique videos	5.59 (2.67)	4.57 (2.78)	t = 3.14, p <. 01
Video time (s)	1,978.90 (1,138.85)	1,506.12 (1,146.36)	t = 3.32, p <. 001
Comments	12.11 (16.33)	7.13 (10.46)	t = 3.15, p < .01
Ratings	24.79 (80.81)	15.37 (54.52)	p > .05

To generate epistemic networks for the two groups, we defined units as the group (ES or LS) subsetted by student_id, infinite stanza using the following codes: *VLoad, Comment, Nudge, RLoad, Rate*, and *Revisit*. The reason for choosing infinite stanza was to consider all interactions for ES/LS. The conversation was defined as session_id subsetted by video_id and student_id. The frequencies of the selected codes are very similar (Table 6), except that *Rate* and *Comment* have lower frequencies for LS. The model had co-registration correlations of 0.9 (Pearson) and 0.9 (Spearman) for the first dimension and co-registration correlations of 0.97 (Pearson) and 0.95 (Spearman) for the second. There was a significant difference along the X-axis (t = 3.42, p < .001, Cohen's d = .43) between LS (mean = .21, SD = .72) and ES (mean = −.10, SD = .71), but there was no significant difference along the Y-axis. Figure 6 shows the comparison network for ES/LS. There were more frequent co-occurrences of coherent events within each space for ES (e.g. *Nudge* and *Comment* or *VLoad and Comment* in Personal Space, and *RLoad* and *Rate* in Social Space). However, there were more frequent co-occurrences between Personal Space events and Social Space events (e.g. *RLoad and Nudge/Comment/VLoad*, and *Rate* and *Comment*) for LS. That reveals LS had more transitions between Personal and Social Space, while ES were focused on the activities in a single space at a time. Also, connections to *Revisit* were more frequent for LS. Revisiting videos immediately after rating comments of the same videos happened only 26 times. The difference network shows that LS made comments when revisiting. We expected that some LS leveraged from comments they rated, and when they revisited the Personal Space, they made similar comments to what they had rated. This behaviour could increase learning for students who have already made some comments before reviewing, since peer-reviewing could inspire new ideas. However, reviewing others' comments before making any comments could interfere with learning.

Table 6. Frequency of events for ES/LS.

Events (17,946)	ES (199)		LS (95)	
	Frequency	Count	Frequency	Count
VLoad	11%	1,496	12%	531
Comment	18%	2,412	16%	678
Nudge	30%	4,086	32%	1,403
RLoad	3%	430	4%	152
Rate	38%	5,176	36%	1,556
Revisit	0	13	0.3%	13
Total		13,613		4,333

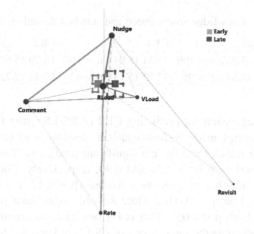

Fig. 6. Comparison networks for ES/LS in personal and social space.

We investigated the event logs of students who re-watched the video immediately after rating some comments on that video. We were interested in seeing whether there are any similarities between the comments students rated and the comments they made afterwards. We compared the comments they rated with comments they made after revisiting. The 26 cases of immediate revisiting happened for 21 students (10 LS and 11 ES). Only in 12 cases, revisiting resulted in new comments. In 6 of these cases, the students made a comment with very similar content to what they just rated. For instance, a student first rated these comments: *"The passion is really important "*and *"Show your ideas actively and clearly. Make them love your ideas and be enthusiastic about your topic "*, and then revisited the same video and made this comment: *"Body language is important, and showing enthusiasm to the audience can increase audience participation. The presentation framework is clear. Use statistics with simple visual effects. "* Commenting after revisiting was observed mostly in Constructive students

(66.66%). Only 7 students started reviewing before making a comment, and only 1 student made a comment similar to the comments he/she rated first.

Since there were significant differences in the interactions of ES/LS, we investigated the learning outcomes of the two groups. ES had more time to absorb information and be focused on one activity at a time, while LS might have benefitted from social learning in the rating phase. Table 6 presents the conceptual knowledge scores from Surveys 1 and 2. CK1-all is the average CK1 score for all students who completed Survey 1. CK1 and CK2 are the scores for those who completed both surveys. We found no significant difference in CK1-all scores (t = .99, p = .33) and CK1 scores (t = 1.44, p = .16) between ES/LS. ANCOVA on CK2 with CK1 as the covariate revealed no significant difference. No difference on CK2 could be because LS started watching videos closer to the post-study survey and had the domain-specific vocabularies active in their short-term memory (Table 7).

Table 7. Knowledge scores (mean and standard deviation) for ES/LS

	CK1-all	CK1	CK2
ES	14.19 (5.33), n = 199	13.51 (5.04), n = 104	13.99 (5.67), n = 104
LS	13.51 (5.84), n = 95	12.23 (5.13), n = 43	12.48 (5.72), n = 43

We ran linear regression for predicting CK2 of ES/LS using CK1, the number of comments made, ratings made, videos watched, sessions and days spent on AVW-Space to investigate which variables are significant predictors. The models trained for ES and LS performed with R^2 = 0.35 and 0.40, respectively. For ES, the significant predictors were the number of comments written (β = 0.47, t = 4.91, p < .001) and CK1 (β = 0.31, t = 3.66, p < 0.001), while the only significant predictor for LS was CK1 (β = 0.3, t = 2.09, p < 0.05). That is ES benefit from commenting more which motivated us to investigate the interactions of ES/LS in Personal Space in more detail.

We applied ENA for tutorial videos, with the units of analysis defined as the ES/LS, subsetted by video_id, student_id, and stanza = 3. The conversation was defined as a single video, subsetted by student_id. Our ENA model included the following codes: *VPlay, VPause, VEnd, PositiveFeedback, NReminder, NQuality, CommentQ1, CommentQ2* and *CommentQ3*. The model had co-registration correlations of 0.96 (Pearson) and 0.96 (Spearman) for the first dimension and co-registration correlations of 0.95 (Pearson) and 0.94 (Spearman) for the second. Figure 7 shows the networks generated for ES/LS. Along the X-axis, there was a significant difference between LS (mean = .12, SD = .75) and ES (mean = −.05, SD = .76); (t = −3.05, p < .001, Cohen's d = .22), but there was no significant difference along the y axis. As can be seen, ES had more co-occurrences of *NReminder* or *NQuality* with *CommentQ2* and between *VPlay* and *CommentQ2*, while LS had more co-occurrences of *VPlay* and *VPause*. Also, the mean of ES is positioned on the left side of the ENA space, which includes nudges and commenting. In contrast, LS is on the left side of the network where video watching codes are situated. This means that ES were more likely to make comments after receiving nudges, whereas LS were more likely to watch videos. This is consistent with our earlier t-test result, which showed ES had significantly more comments than LS.

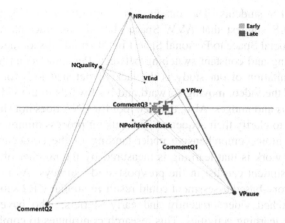

Fig. 7. Comparison network of ES/LS in personal space

6 Conclusions

We used ENA to identify the co-occurrences of actions in video-watching to capture learning behaviours. We compared the interactions of students in various ICAP categories during video watching and commenting in Personal Space. ENA generated for the student categories provided insights aligned with our previous analyses, showing that CS wrote more reflective comments than AS, and PS did not make any comments. However, ENA revealed additional insights which highlight the need for providing more support for engagement. ENA showed that PS ignored nudges and continued watching videos rather than commenting. ENA also showed that CS are likely to make reflective comments without directly being nudged. On the other hand, AS were likely to make no reflective comments before the end of the video, and are likely to respond to the final self-reflection nudge. AS are also more likely to watch the video to the end compared to PS. Thus, providing a progress report could remind the student of the importance of each activity in AVW-Space, such as commenting or fully watching videos. Also, allowing students to review the nudges they have received for a video could direct them to realise better what is expected in the commenting task.

We investigated the actions of early and late starters to compare their learning behaviours. Quantitative analyses on the number of days and sessions spent on the system, and the summary of activities (video watching, commenting and rating) showed that early starters spent more time watching videos and wrote more comments. ENA showed that early starters focus on a single space at a time, while late starters are more likely to switch between Personal and Social Space. We also found that late starters are more likely to revisit Personal Space after reviewing comments written by their peers. This could be a constructive learning behaviour if the student made some comments by her/himself first, then reviewed the classmates' comments and finally revisited Personal Space to revise previous comments and create a new comment. We found no significant difference in pre/post-study conceptual knowledge of ES/LS. However, linear regression on CK2 identified commenting as an important behaviour in learning for ES students. The insights from combining ENA and quantitative analysis on ES/LS suggest that AVW-Space should continue allowing students to transition from Social Space to Personal Space, but it should discourage peer-reviewing before commenting and constant switching between Personal/Social Space tasks.

The main limitation of our study is the lack of detailed logs for actions such as skipping parts of the video, moving forward and backwards in the video and hovering over visualisations and nudges. Also, the web tool for ENA does not show the direction of co-occurrence to clarify their sequence. Thus, using process mining along with ENA could provide a more comprehensive understanding of the co-occurrences. Another limitation of our work is that learning is measured by the number of domain-specific phrases that the student can list in the pre-/post-study surveys. As mentioned earlier, this type of memory-based assessment could result in similar CK2 scores between late starters who watched videos recently and early starters, who have been regularly engaged with the learning activities. This research contributes to combining ENA and quantitative analysis to better understand student behaviour in computer-assisted educational systems to discover new ways of supporting students' needs.

References

1. Yousef, A.M.F., Chatti, M.A., Schroeder, U.: The state of video-based learning: a review and future perspectives. Int. J. Adv. Life Sci. **6**, 122–135 (2014)
2. Gilboy, M.B., Heinerichs, S., Pazzaglia, G.: Enhancing student engagement using the flipped classroom. J. Nutr. Educ. Behav. **47**, 109–114 (2015)
3. Zhang, H., Miller, K.F., Sun, X., Cortina, K.S.: Wandering eyes: eye movements during mind wandering in video lectures. Appl. Cogn. Psychol. **34**, 449–464 (2020)
4. Mitrovic, A., Dimitrova, V., Weerasinghe, A., Lau, L.: Reflective experiential learning: using active video watching for soft skills training. In: Proceedings of 24th International Conference Computers in Education, pp. 192–201. Asia-Pacific Society for Computers in Education (2016)
5. Mitrovic, A., Gordon, M., Piotrkowicz, A., Dimitrova, V.: Investigating the effect of adding nudges to increase engagement in active video watching. In: Isotani, S., Millán, E., Ogan, A., Hastings, P., McLaren, B., Luckin, R. (eds.) AIED 2019. LNCS (LNAI), vol. 11625, pp. 320–332. Springer, Cham (2019). https://doi.org/10.1007/978-3-030-23204-7_27
6. Mohammadhassan, N., Mitrovic, A., Neshatian, K., Dunn, J.: Investigating the effect of nudges for improving comment quality in active video watching. Comput. Educ. **176**, 104340 (2022). https://doi.org/10.1016/j.compedu.2021.104340
7. Mitrovic, A., Dimitrova, V., Lau, L., Weerasinghe, A., Mathews, M.: Supporting constructive video-based learning: requirements elicitation from exploratory studies. In: André, E., Baker, R., Hu, X., Rodrigo, M.M.T., du Boulay, B. (eds.) AIED 2017. LNCS (LNAI), vol. 10331, pp. 224–237. Springer, Cham (2017). https://doi.org/10.1007/978-3-319-61425-0_19
8. Chi, M.T.H., Wylie, R.: The ICAP framework: linking cognitive engagement to active learning outcomes. Educ. Psychol. **49**, 219–243 (2014)
9. Caglayan, E., Ustunluoglu, E.: A Study exploring students' usage patterns and adoption of lecture capture. Technol. Knowl. Learn. **26**(1), 13–30 (2020). https://doi.org/10.1007/s10758-020-09435-9

10. Giannakos, M., Jaccheri, L., Krogstie, J.: Exploring the relationship between video lecture usage patterns and students' attitudes. Brit. J. Educ. Technol. **47**, 1259–1275 (2015)
11. Lallé, S., Conati, C.: A Data-Driven Student Model to Provide Adaptive Support During Video Watching Across MOOCs. In: Bittencourt, I.I., Cukurova, M., Muldner, K., Luckin, R., Millán, E. (eds.) AIED 2020. LNCS (LNAI), vol. 12163, pp. 282–295. Springer, Cham (2020). https://doi.org/10.1007/978-3-030-52237-7_23
12. Paquette, L., Grant, T., Zhang, Y., Biswas, G., Baker, R.: Using epistemic networks to analyze self-regulated learning in an open-ended problem-solving environment. In: Ruis, A. R., Lee, S.B. (eds.) ICQE 2021. CCIS, vol. 1312, pp. 185–201. Springer, Cham (2021). https://doi.org/10.1007/978-3-030-67788-6_13
13. Gasevic, D., Jovanovic, J., Pardo, A., Dawson, S.: Detecting learning strategies with analytics: links with self-reported measures and academic performance. Learn. Anal. **4**, 113–128 (2017)
14. Zhou, J., Bhat, S.: Modeling consistency using engagement patterns in online courses. In: LAK21: 11th International Learning Analytics and Knowledge Conference, pp. 226–236. Association for Computing Machinery, New York (2021)
15. Shabaninejad, S., Khosravi, H., Leemans, S.J.J., Sadiq, S., Indulska, M.: Recommending insightful drill-downs based on learning processes for learning analytics dashboards. In: Bittencourt, I.I., Cukurova, M., Muldner, K., Luckin, R., Millán, E. (eds.) AIED 2020. LNCS (LNAI), vol. 12163, pp. 486–499. Springer, Cham (2020). https://doi.org/10.1007/978-3-030-52237-7_39
16. Shaffer, D.W., Collier, W., Ruis, A.R.: A tutorial on epistemic network analysis: analyzing the structure of connections in cognitive, social, and interaction data. Learn. Anal. **3**, 9–45 (2016)
17. Gamage, D., Perera, I., Fernando, S.: Exploring MOOC user behaviors beyond platforms. Int. J. Emerg. Technol. Learn. **15**, 161–179 (2020)
18. Saint, J., Gašević, D., Matcha, W., Uzir, N.A., Pardo, A.: Combining analytic methods to unlock sequential and temporal patterns of self-regulated learning. In: Proceedings of 10th International Conference Learning Analytics & Knowledge, pp. 402–411. ACM, New York (2020)
19. Scianna, J., Gagnon, D., Knowles, B.: Counting the game: visualizing changes in play by incorporating game events. In: Ruis, A.R., Lee, S.B. (eds.) ICQE 2021. CCIS, vol. 1312, pp. 218–231. Springer, Cham (2021). https://doi.org/10.1007/978-3-030-67788-6_15
20. Karumbaiah, S., Baker, R.S., Barany, A., Shute, V.: Using epistemic networks with automated codes to understand why players quit levels in a learning game. In: Eagan, B., Misfeldt, M., Siebert-Evenstone, A. (eds.) ICQE 2019. CCIS, vol. 1112, pp. 106–116. Springer, Cham (2019). https://doi.org/10.1007/978-3-030-33232-7_9
21. Dimitrova, V., Mitrovic, A., Piotrkowicz, A., Lau, L., Weerasinghe, A.: Using learning analytics to devise interactive personalised nudges for active video watching. In: Proceedings of 25th Conference User Modeling, Adaptation and Personalization, pp. 22–31. ACM (2017)
22. Mohammadhassan, N., Mitrovic, A., Neshatian, K., Dunn, J.: Automatic assessment of comment quality in active video watching. In: Proceedings of 28th International Conference Computers in Education, pp. 1–10. Asia-Pacific Society for Computers in Education. (2020)
23. Pintrich, P.R., de Groot, E.V.: Motivational and self-regulated learning components of classroom academic performance. J. Educ. Psychol. **82**, 33–40 (1990)
24. Marquart, C.L., Hinojosa, C., Swiecki, Z., Eagan, B., Shaffer, D.W.: Epistemic Network Analysis (Version 1.7.0) [Software] (2018)

Exploring Group Discussion
with Conversational Agents Using Epistemic
Network Analysis

Ha Nguyen^(⊠)

University of California-Irvine, Irvine, CA, USA
thicn@uci.edu

Abstract. Conversational agents—dialogue systems that provide learning support to students in real time—have shown promise in facilitating science discussion. To enact conversation norms, the appearances, personalities, or tones of the agents often resemble personas that students are familiar with, such as peers or mentors. This study uses epistemic network analysis (ENA) to explore how students interacted with two personas agent (a peer and an expert) in collaborative settings. Data came from chat logs of three student groups with low, mixed, and high ability. The groups interacted with both prototypes. The chat logs received qualitative codes for discussion types, including claim-making, reasoning, building on prior ideas, and responsiveness to the agents. ENA visualized the differences in discussion between groups and between the agent conditions. Overall, the higher-ability groups engaged in more claim-making in tandem with building on prior ideas when interacting with the peer agent, compared to the expert agent. Meanwhile, the low-ability group showed more syntheses of previous ideas when responding to the expert agent. Findings illuminate the design space for adapting agent personas to group settings to facilitate productive exchange.

Keywords: Collaboration · Conversational agent · Epistemic network analysis · Case study

1 Introduction

A fundamental challenge in science education in the United States is promoting students' sustained interest and participation in scientific practices [1]. Engaging in collaborative discussion offers ways for students to build on the knowledge of others, gain agency, and develop interest in science [2–4]. Conversational agents, or chatbots in this study, have shown particular promise in facilitating discussion [5–7]. These agents use natural language understanding of text and speech to provide suggestions that enrich students' idea generation, argumentation, and conceptual knowledge [5, 6].

A key goal in designing conversational agents is to make them more conducive to discussion and subsequent learning [8–10]. The agent's appearances, tones, and gestures may enact human characteristics such as friendliness, competence, or sociability, to prime users to demonstrate conversational norms as if they were interacting with human partners [11, 12]. Agents can adopt the appearance and lingo of a mentor,

© Springer Nature Switzerland AG 2022
B. Wasson and S. Zörgő (Eds.): ICQE 2021, CCIS 1522, pp. 378–394, 2022.
https://doi.org/10.1007/978-3-030-93859-8_25

teacher, or peer in educational contexts to simulate classroom norms [8, 13–15]. Learners with limited understanding may seek help from a mentor agent, whereas more capable learners may deepen their knowledge through giving help to a peer agent [13].

However, considerations of agent design have mostly been applied to individual interactions between a student and an agent and not to collaborative contexts. In the latter case, students' interactions with the agents may vary with group dynamics [16]. This is because the hints and questions from the agent may get ignored in groups where elaboration is not the norm [6]. A factor that may influence such group dynamics is ability composition [17, 18]. For example, students with low or average knowledge may not participate as much when the conversation is dominated by high-ability peers.

The current research explores how students' interactions with conversational agents vary in three student groups of low, mixed, and high abilities within a high school science curriculum. The author draws from prior agent designs in individual tutoring settings to test two prototypes: a peer and an expert agent [8, 13–15]. In a within-subject design, student groups (each consisting of two to three 9th graders) interacted with both prototypes in randomized orders, as they built a concept map of the marine ecosystems. The following questions guide the research:

RQ1. How do students' collaborative discussion patterns vary with different group composition?

RQ2. Within student groups, how do discussion patterns differ when interacting with the peer versus the expert agents?

Overall, students in the mixed and high-ability groups showed more connection between making claims, providing reasoning, and building on prior ideas, compared to the low-ability group. The groups also showed distinct patterns when interacting with the peer versus expert agents. Students in groups with higher levels of prior knowledge appeared to engage in more reasoning and claim-making when interacting with the peer version. Meanwhile, individuals in the group with lower knowledge levels showed more reasoning and reflection on prior ideas when responding to the expert agent.

These findings illuminate how responses to agent designs vary with group composition. This understanding has important design and learning implications. From a design perspective, findings contribute to research on developing agent personas that can be perceived as natural social partners and encourage productive conversational norms. From a learning perspective, learning systems and facilitators may examine the diverse patterns that student groups display. Such consideration helps to identify patterns that are conducive to knowledge construction. It also assists the development of adaptive learning scaffolds for different student groups.

2 Background

2.1 Collaborative Conversational Agents

Engaging in knowledge building efforts, where students collaboratively share ideas and build on one another's knowledge, is an important process to enrich students' science understanding [2–4]. Through exchange, individuals outline their personal and sociocultural experiences, discuss, negotiate, and develop a shared understanding of learning phenomena [4, 19].

Students engage in a range of knowledge building discussion moves, from stating claims to elaborating on and expanding shared knowledge [20]. This wide array of discussion moves presents opportunities for teachers to support different participation structures [20]. For example, teachers can decide on which students may initiate questions or propose actions, ask questions to redirect student attention, or propose tasks for students to build on one another's ideas and artifacts [3, 21, 22]. These participation structures shift knowledge building from teachers as the sole transmitter of knowledge to students and the tools or systems that they engage with [3, 22].

Conversational agents can play an analogous role to teachers in fostering knowledge building communities. These agents use natural language understanding to process students' talks and provide in-time support for conceptual understanding and participation [5–7]. More than tools to enrich student discourse, agents are active participants in the group conversations. Agents can propose prompts for the groups to explain, contrast, and support their ideas, thus fostering different discussion moves.

2.2 Peer and Expert Agent Designs

Agent designs that replicate human behaviors or social norms can influence users' perceptions. In turn, users subconsciously display social behaviors when interacting with the computer agents [11, 12]. Users may enact social norms such as gender stereotyping or reciprocating help with the machines, even with minimal interface cues or when they acknowledge that machines may not have motivation or feelings [11].

Researchers have thus underscored the importance of designing agents to foster more natural human-computer interactions. Two distinct agent profiles have emerged in learning contexts: peer and expert agent. The peer agent profile is based on the similarity-attraction effect [23], which suggests that learners would be attracted to agents that parallel them in appearance, knowledge, or interest [14, 15]. In a study where researchers assigned students to work with computers whose characteristics either aligned with or mismatched students' personalities, students conformed more to the personality that was similar to their own and found it more attractive and intelligent [24].

The similarity-attraction effect gives rise to the peer agent design: human-like characters that appear close to the target groups in age and knowledge level [14]. A related design is the learning-by-teaching model [26], where student users are responsible for explaining target concepts to the agent, who presumably has limited prior knowledge.

Meanwhile, learners may attribute more trust to agents whom they perceive to possess higher knowledge levels [27], in ways that are similar to how they would interact with a teacher or domain expert. This conjecture has led to the designs of expert-like agents—characters that are more knowledgeable, with talk moves that simulate the human instructors [14, 15, 28].

User perceptions and responses to agent designs can be leveraged in designing agents to produce optimal learning and domain interests. For example, choices of agent designs could adapt to learners' domain knowledge [13]. Learners with limited understanding and skills may benefit from interacting with the expert-like agent. Meanwhile, more capable learners can attempt to teach the peer agent. Such interactions provide opportunities for learners to acquire alternative viewpoints and deepen knowledge.

2.3   Agent Designs Influence Human-Agent Interactions

The content of user replies also varies with how users perceive the agent [14, 28–31]. For example, users rated a casual tone agent as friendlier and provided more elaborate survey responses to the agent than one that relied on a formal questionnaire style [30]. In exchange with learning robots, learners who interacted with a robot that behaved as a peer showed more affective displays, compared to a robot that resembled a tutor [31].

Research from human-human tutoring interaction lends further insights into potential differences in the content of students' responses to the different agent profiles. In inquiry-driven classrooms, teachers tended to use questions to elicit students' thinking, and students replied to teachers' elicitations, elaborated on their thinking, or offered argumentation [32]. In peer tutoring, rather than only focusing on providing explanations, students may also express emotions such as triumph, anger, and confusion around the learning problems [33]. They also pose provoking questions to their partners [34]. Thus, we may expect different discussion patterns with the agent profiles. Students may engage in more explanation and argumentation with the expert agent, while being open to brainstorming ideas when it comes to discussing with the peer agent.

In addition, embedding the agents in group discussion introduces an interesting dynamic, since students with different levels of prior domain knowledge may interact with each other and with the agents in varied ways. In mixed-ability groups, students with a higher level of domain knowledge tend to become the "mentors" who provide help and explanations to lower-ability students. In turn, the lower-ability peers can benefit from spontaneous help-seeking [17, 18]. We can thus explore whether high-ability students will dominate the conversations in interactions with the peer agent, or if other students will also see the agent as lower-ability and may engage in elaborative talk.

How can we analyze the content of student discussion to reveal differences in interactions between the agent profiles? Education researchers have focused on the types of argumentative discourse students make, vocabulary, conversational topics, and contributions to the group's discussion [35–37]. Researchers have also examined how several discussion moves can co-occur within the same conversational window to formulate the epistemic structure of the discussion [35]. Analyses of co-occurring moves can reveal key insights to compare the discussion structures between student groups and agent prototypes. Such analyses can explore questions such as: In which agent condition do students brainstorm ideas while responding to the agent more frequently?

3   Methodologies

This study presents a qualitative discourse analysis of students' discussion moves with one another and the conversational agents. The analyses focus on three purposefully sampled student groups of low, mixed, and high prior knowledge in science. The study applies ENA [38] to examine the differences between group compositions and agent conditions. The choice of ENA builds on understanding of collaboration and learning not as isolated cognitive elements, but the associations of those elements to form systemic understanding [38].

3.1   Study Setting

This research is situated in a high school environmental science programs called Marine Science Exploration (MSE). The program represents a multi-year partnership between a local state park, education and biology researchers, and local school districts in southwestern United States. The state park has been working for several years on a marine protected area to study how habitats respond to reduced human impacts.

Early in the curriculum (lesson 3 out of 8), students receive an introduction to the marine protected areas and are asked to brainstorm the elements and processes that may affect the marine habitats. In classroom observations of those lessons, the park educators and teachers noticed that not all students participated in the group discussion. Furthermore, students tended to get fixated on certain ideas and linear relationships, instead of thinking about more complex processes. The idea of a collaborative conversational agent came as a potential solution to improve students' conceptual understanding and participation.

3.2   Agent Design

Conceptual Nudges. The agent, nicknamed Kibot, can embed itself in student text-based discussion and provide nudges. Figure 1 presents examples of Kibot's dialogues. The nudges build on key aspects of scientific reasoning when learning about systems, namely Elements, Evidence, and Causal Coherence [39].

Element captures the components and processes in the ecosystem. The agent thus monitors and gives hints for students to consider key terms from organisms (e.g., fish, plankton), human activities (e.g., plastic pollution, fishing regulation), and processes (e.g., salinity). Evidence describes how students use data or observations to warrant their claims. Causal coherence, meanwhile, refers to whether students can use a coherent and logical chain of reasoning to connect observable concepts to scientific ideas.

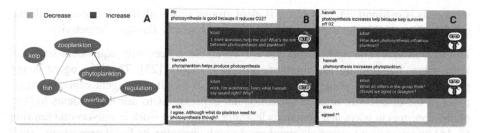

Fig. 1. Examples of co-constructed concept map (Panel A); the peer agent (B); and the expert agent (C). The agents send similar types of nudges, but their wording and expressions differ.

The pipeline for Kibot's causal coherence hints is as follows. The agent first applies the dependency parser from the Python's package "spaCy" [40] to segment students' chat into subjects and objects. For example, a sentence such as "fish are dangerous because it eats other fish" would yield a link between "fish" (the subject) and "other fish" (the object). As the students' conversation unfolds, the overlapping connections form a concept map of connected terms. Next, Kibot compares the students' concept map with an "expert" concept map. The expert map is created in three feedback sessions with four state park educators and six marine biology researchers. Kibot uses two algorithms to compare the student answers and the expert map: (1) Levenshtein-based string similarity to capture instances where students' answers closely resemble expert concepts, and (2) word embedding [40], where shorter distance between the respective word vectors for students and experts' answers serves as a proxy for higher similarity.

If there exists a missing link between a term that the students already mention and a term in the expert map, Kibot provides a hint, for example, "I see. **Does plankton [term students have mentioned] play any other roles in this system**?" After seven chat turns, if the students still have not mentioned the target missing term, Kibot provides more explicit prompts, for example, "I am wondering if **plankton [term students have mentioned] and photosynthesis [missing term]** can be linked in any ways?".

Finally, Evidence describes the extent to which students apply reasoning from scientific data or their own observations to back up their claims. The agent asks students to elaborate on their reasoning by explaining their ideas or whether they agree with statements from their peers. These nudges draw from research on transactive exchange where students build on prior ideas with reasoning and elaboration [5, 10]. To encourage equal participation, Kibot alternates between asking students to elaborate on a claim they just make and nudging those who have participated the least in the discussion.

Agent Design. The activity with the conversational agent takes place when students just watch an overview video of the marine protected areas (MPA) at the state park. In groups of two to three, students engage in a chat with each other and with the two Kibot prototypes. The goal of the chat is to build a concept map of the marine ecosystem and to reason through the connections in the map. The interaction order with the agents is randomized: Half of the student groups start with the peer agent, while the other half start with the expert agent, and switch halfway through the activity.

The Peer Agent. The agent is designed to resemble a peer with equivalent levels of knowledge, building on the similarity-attraction theory [23]. The peer agent is not presented as knowledgeable, but is learning from the chat. The agent eagerly participates in the discussion, often using colloquial expressions to ask the students to "explain" concepts in ways that benefit its learning. Similar to work in one-on-one tutoring [8, 14], the peer agent expresses emotions through changing its facial expressions, such as showing a frown when confused or a lightbulb when asking questions.

The Expert Agent. The expert agent, who showcases mastery of the content knowledge, generally speaks in a formal tone and does not use colloquial phrases [8]. Contrary to the peer agent that changes its expression, the expert agent keeps the same expression throughout its interactions with the students.

In sum, the agent prototypes (peer and expert agent) send the same conceptual nudges to students at similar frequencies. However, their design and vocabulary vary to give impressions of different levels of competence.

3.3 Participants

Participants were ninth grade students in two classes (51 students) taught by the same science teachers in a public high school in southwestern U.S. The school served a diverse student population that was majorly White and Hispanic/Latino in the 2019–20 school year. The students were participating in the MSE program during their science class time. The school had one-to-one laptop policy, and students were familiar with using chat windows to converse with one another. Because of social-distancing measures due to COVID-19, students were sitting far apart from each other and mostly used the chat interface to communicate with one another. Students had experiences with collaborative groupwork in their science class, but reported limited experiences with learning chatbots prior to the lessons.

Prior to seeing the agent interface or interacting with the agents in groups, all participants individually answered a pretest. The pretest aimed to capture students' science domain knowledge of the MPA. In the pretest, students answered three open-ended questions about the marine ecosystem and the role of regulation, e.g., "How do marine protected areas affect fish populations and other things in the ocean". Consistent with the curriculum's focus, student responses were scored as the sum of number of correct elements, correct causal relationships, and evidence. The scores were then rank ordered, and student groups were categorized as low-ability (all three students scored below average), mixed (at least one above average), and above-average (all above average). Using purposeful random sampling [41], the author randomly selected one group from each ability category. Group *Plankton* (low-ability) consisted of a female and two male students. Group *Fish* (mixed-ability) had three female students, and group *Whale* (high-ability) had one female and two male students.

3.4 Data Sources

The main data source came from the three groups' chat logs with the agents. Each chat per prototype (peer or expert) lasted 12.5 min on average, SD = 1.2 min (Group Plankton: 12 min with peer; 11 min with expert; Fish: 14 min with expert; 12 min with peer; Whale: 14 min with peer; 12 min with expert).

The unit of code was a single chat message (total N = 407 utterances; each group had 136 messages on average, SD = 23.5 messages). The messages went through two coding iterations. In the first iteration, the author used a priori codes for the types of contribution to group's knowledge building [19, 42]. Although there were other codes included in prior frameworks [19], such as emotion or making hypotheses, these codes had fewer than three occurrences each and were thus excluded from the final analyses. In the second iteration, the author conducted close reading of the group chats to devise emergent codes. An additional code (*Respond to Kibot*) emerged in this stage to note whether student's utterance was self-initiated or in response to the agent's nudges. Table 1 provides examples of the codes.

Table 1. Coding scheme for student discussion.

Code	Definition	Example
Claim	Statement links systems elements	Kelp provides habitat
Reasoning	Statement draws from pre-existing knowledge, scientific facts and data, or evidence in the lesson	Plastic pollution reduces fish population **because it contaminates their habitat**
Build on self	Statement draws on previous ideas a student has stated	A: Sea urchins increase kelp A: Sea urchins decrease kelp because they eat a lot of kelp
Build on friend	Statement draws on previous ideas that peers have stated	A: Plastic pollution should be banned B: Yes, because it harms the animals
Respond to Kibot	Statement in response to the agent's nudges	Kibot: What do you think, A? Do you agree or disagree? A: I agree because a ban should let fewer people into that area and there will be less overfishing

To establish reliability, the author and a research assistant separately coded 20% of the chat and showed substantial agreement with the original codes, Cohen's κ = .96. The author coded the rest of the data. Each chat message received a dichotomous code for whether the code was present (coded as 1) or not (coded as 0). This means that a message can receive more than one code if multiple discussion moves existed, for example, if the student built on friends' ideas while making claims.

3.5 Procedures

This study applied Epistemic Network Analysis (ENA) in the rENA package [43] to examine the co-occurrences of codes within a moving chat-window of three.

Discussion types were considered associated if they appeared in the same sliding text window (e.g., a window of size three measures co-occurrences within three consecutive texts).

In ENA, co-occurrences of discourse types formed a binary matrix (1: occur; 0: not occur). Then, the matrix was normalized and singular value decomposition (SVD) was applied to reduce the dimension of vectors to two dimensions that explained the most variance in the data. ENA allowed for visualizations of the discussion network for each group. Each code (e.g., claim, reasoning, respond to Kibot) became a node in the diagram, with lines indicating that the two nodes co-occurred within the chat windows. ENA also allowed for visualizing subtraction networks, that is, the differences between the epistemic networks for each condition per group. The visualization subtracted the connection weight of each node in the networks, and indicated larger connection between discourse types by showing thicker, darker lines.

To answer RQ1 about potential differences in students' interactions with the conversational agents between the low, mixed, and high ability groups, this study first ran ENA with students in groups as the unit of analyses over all utterances (i.e., both agent prototypes). Analyses plotted the subtraction networks for group pairs (e.g., low-mixed, mixed-high, high-low) to highlight differences between their discussion networks.

To answer RQ2 about how student's discussion may differ when interacting with the bot prototypes, the author conducted ENA within each group. Individual students' chat occurrences within group within conditions constituted the unit of analyses.

4   Results

4.1   Between-Group Differences in Discussion Networks

The first research question examines the extent to which group discussion networks varied with ability compositions. The author created subtraction networks (Fig. 2) and compared the connections between discussion types between groups. Each dot in the figure represents an individual student, and the colors denote the groups they belong to (i.e., black for Plankton, purple for Fish, and blue for Whale).

Overall, students in the higher-ability groups appeared to show more complex discussion moves. For example, when comparing groups Fish and Plankton (left panel, Fig. 2), the purple line in Fig. 2 suggests a link between *Reasoning* and *Building on friends' ideas*. This indicates that individuals in group Fish (the relatively higher ability group) showed more connections in these discussion moves. Similarly, the blue lines in the central and right panel (Fig. 2) shows that group Whale, the high-ability group, showed more connections between *Claims* and *Building on prior ideas* in comparison to the other two groups. To illustrate, consider the following excerpt from group Plankton (low).

Kibot: What would happen if kelp increases?
S1: Fish increase/zooplankton increase/phytoplankton increase.
S2. Pollution increases/fish increases.
S1: Global warming increases/water temperature increases.

Kibot: Why do you think so?

S3: When the temperature rises it affects the fish.

In this exchange, students were mostly making claims without providing reasoning for their answers. They also did not explicitly mention previous ideas to build on. In contrast, the following excerpt from group Whale illustrates how S5 built on his friend's idea ("regulation increases fish") to give explanations and inquired about a related relationship (breeding-fish).

Kibot: What would happen if regulation increases?

S4: Regulation increases fish.

S5: Regulation increases fish because it protects the fish from overfishing.

S5: Does breeding increase fish?

In sum, group comparisons reveal that students in higher-ability groups appeared to show more connection between making statements, reasoning, and engaging in transactive exchange, compared to the low-ability group.

4.2 Within-Group Differences in Interactions with Peer Versus Expert Agents

The observed differences in interactions between groups suggest that there may exist variation with group composition. The second research question explores these differences using another grain size: within-group shifts in interactions between the peer and expert agents. To answer this question, this study used ENA to compare the discussion networks between the two agent conditions for each group (Figs. 3, 4 and 5; red lines = more connections for expert agent; blue = peer agents).

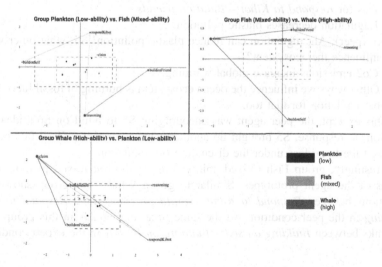

Fig. 2. Between-group comparisons (ENA subtraction networks) of the overall discussion in groups Plankton (low-ability; black), Fish (mixed ability; purple), and Whale (high-ability; blue). (Color figure online)

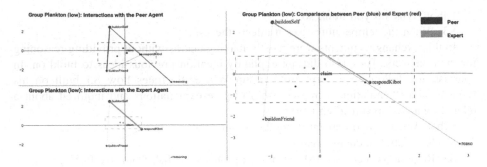

Fig. 3. Comparisons of group Plankton (low ability) between expert (red) and peer (blue) agents. (Color figure online)

Overall, the most noticeable difference between the peer and expert discussion networks for group Plankton (low ability) is the connection between *Build on self* and *Respond to Kibot* in the expert condition, compared to the peer condition (Fig. 3). While this group mostly stated simple claims, the students more frequently built on prior claims when responding to nudges from the expert agent than those from the peer agent.

Meanwhile, group Whale (high ability; Fig. 4) demonstrated more discussion connections in the peer condition, compared to the expert agent. Individuals in this group made more links between *Claim – Respond to Kibot; Claim – Build on self;* and *Respond to Kibot – Build on friends*, as highlighted by the blue lines for the peer condition. Take the following excerpt from group Whale as an example of code co-occurrences for *Respond to Kibot – Build on friends*:

S6: Regulation decreases plastic pollution.

Kibot (peer): Ah, regulation can reduce plastic pollution! S5, what other ways do human influence the ecosystem?

S4: Co2 emissions increase global warming.

S5: Other ways we influence the ocean ecosystem is burning of fossil fuels, so there should be regulation for that too.

In this excerpt, the peer agent was encouraging S5 to build on S6's idea around regulation. In response, S5 brought up another related concept ("fossil fuel burning") and linked the two ideas under the discussion on regulation.

Interestingly, group Fish (mixed ability; Fig. 5) showed mixed patterns in comparisons of the agent prototypes. Similar to group Whale, this group showed more connections between *Respond to Kibot – Build on friends* and *Respond to Kibot – Reasoning* in the peer condition. At the same time, individuals in this group showed more links between *Building on self – Building on friends* in the expert condition.

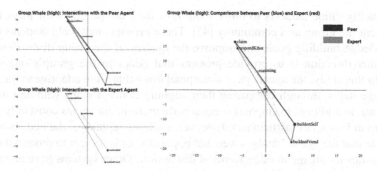

Fig. 4. Comparisons of group Whale (high ability) between expert (red) and peer (blue) agents. (Color figure online)

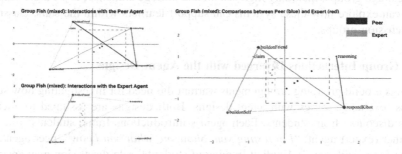

Fig. 5. Comparisons of group Fish (mixed ability) between expert (red) and peer (blue) agents. (Color figure online)

Notably, the coordinates of individual students within each condition (e.g., red dots for expert agent; blue for pee) were close to one another. This suggests that between-agent differences might have been driven by the group as a whole, instead of by an individual.

5 Discussion

5.1 Grouping Arrangements Show Different Discussion Patterns

This research examines ability grouping as one factor that may be associated with group interactions. Overall, students in the higher-ability groups showed more reasoning and claim-making, in combination with elaboration on prior ideas from the group. Transactive exchange, where students build on each other's knowledge to co-construct ideas, is a key principle in knowledge building [22]. Such exchange allows students to discuss the concepts at hand in depth to advance individual learning [22, 44, 45].

Finding of the different interactive patterns between the groups suggests the design need to provide further scaffolds on knowledge building for certain groups, instead of providing nudges at similar intervals across groups. Scaffolds can be reflective prompts that explicitly guide students to think about how they are putting their ideas together and present the group as a community [45]. These prompts may help students to focus on knowledge building goals and improve the quality of the group discussion [45].

Another direction is to provide prompts that adapt to the group's ongoing discourse. In this study, the agents gave conceptual hints that were adaptive to the groups' knowledge states, through comparing their ongoing concept maps with an underlying expert map. In addition, to emphasize equal participation, the agents constantly directed its nudges at less active participants. However, students' uptake of the nudges varied. It is possible that the agents' nudges were not opportune or sufficient to prompt the lower-ability groups to engage in other forms of discussion. Other systems have attempted to address this issue through using natural language processing to categorize students' chats and dynamically select the agents' messages from candidate talk moves [46, 47]. Prior work has compared the impact of such dynamic conversational systems among different age groups, including high school and college students [47]. Future empirical work can explore how these systems can support learners within the same classrooms or discussion groups.

5.2   Group Interactions Diverged with the Agent Designs

Findings around grouping arrangements warrant the need for investigating how student groups' exchange varies with agent designs. Both designs are assumed to elicit scientific discourse from students. Each agent's introductions frame students' role as an explainer (expert agent: "*I'm testing you. Show me what you know*"; peer agent: "*I'm here to learn with you.*"). Explicit framing of students' role discussion may encourage engagement and improved outcomes across ability groups [17].

Interestingly, the current study reveals that interactions with the two agent designs were not similar across groups with different ability compositions. Students in the low-ability group more frequently provided reasoning when responding to the expert version. Meanwhile, those in the high-ability groups engaged in more transactive exchange with the peer agent. These findings overlap with hypotheses around student-agent interactions in one-on-one tutoring systems [13]. Students with higher levels of understanding may engage in deeper elaboration of ideas when they are trying to provide help for a peer agent, and those with emergent domain knowledge may more frequently respond to the nudges from the expert agent.

Analyses of data from the mixed-ability group suggest that these patterns were likely taken up by the group. This means that the lower-ability students in this group also became explainers to the peer agent. Thus, combining the peer and expert agents may result in a richer set of discussion patterns in the mixed ability group. A follow-up analysis can follow a larger sample of heterogeneous ability groups, to explore which types of social dynamics may support shared interaction norms.

6   Conclusions

Prior work has explored design paradigms in learning exchange between individual students and conversational agents [8, 14, 15]. Interactions likely diverge in group settings, where individuals are influenced by the participation norms from others in the group. The current study illustrates how interactions are embedded within social structures such as ability composition. Analyses suggest the affordances of ENA in comparing group interactions across dimensions of group compositions and agent designs.

A limitation to the current research is that it only presents a small sample of cases. Future research can examine whether these patterns exist in a larger sample, particularly in groups with mixed ability. Iterations of this work will apply other research designs, such as between-subject designs, to examine the pathway between varied group interactions and student learning. These analyses can also account for variables such as students' gender, social status, and participation tendency.

In addition, student interactions with the conversational agents were brief because they were constrained within one class period. A direction for future exploration is to track how the observed interactive patterns evolve over time, as students gain more exposure to the agents' nudges. Another direction is to examine whether students transfer the discussion moves to another task without the appearance of the agents.

Finally, the current research focuses on students' ability (as indicated by prior understanding of element, evidence, and causal links within systems). Future work can explore other dimensions that may influence student learning, such as different preferences for engagement in collaborative work.

Overall, this study reveals interaction dynamics when collaborative agents are embedded in group discussion. The patterns that this research uncovers broaden the design space for learning systems. They also suggest the learning moments that facilitators (whether teachers or conversational agents) may consider to develop appropriate support for productive discourse and subsequent learning.

References

1. Zacharia, Z., Barton, A.C.: Urban middle-school students' attitudes toward a defined science. Sci. Educ. **88**(2), 197–222 (2004)
2. Hoadley, C.M., Kilner, P.G.: Using technology to transform communities of practice into knowledge-building communities. ACM SIGGROUP Bull. **25**(1), 31–40 (2005)
3. Scardamalia, M., Bereiter, C.: Technologies for knowledge-building discourse. Commun. ACM **36**(5), 37–41 (1993)
4. Stahl, G., Cress, U., Law, N., Ludvigsen, S.: Analyzing the multidimensional construction of knowledge in diverse contexts. Int. J. Comput. Support. Collaborative Learn. **9**(1), 1–6. Springer, New York (2014). https://doi.org/10.1007/s11412-014-9189-4
5. Dyke, G., Howley, I., Adamson, D., Kumar, R., Rosé, C. P.: Towards Academically Productive Talk Supported by Conversational Agents. In Productive Multivocality in the Analysis of Group Interactions, pp. 459–476. Springer, US (2013). https://doi.org/10.1007/978-3-642-30950-2_69

6. Kumar, R., Beuth, J., Rose, C.: Conversational strategies that support idea generation productivity in groups. In: Spada, H., Stahl, G., Miyake, N., Law, N. (eds.), Connecting Computer-Supported Collaborative Learning to Policy and Practice: CSCL2011 Conference Proceedings, pp. 398–405. International Society of the Learning Sciences (2011)

7. Tegos, S., Demetriadis, S.: Conversational agents improve peer learning through building on prior knowledge. Educ. Technol. Soc. 20(1), 99–111 (2017)

8. Kim, Y., Baylor, A.L.: Research-based design of pedagogical agent roles: a review, progress, and recommendations. Int. J. Artif. Intell. Educ. 26(1), 160–169 (2016)

9. Seering, J., Luria, M., Kaufman, G., Hammer, J..: Beyond dyadic interactions: considering chatbots as community members. In: Proceedings of the 2019 CHI Conference on Human Factors in Computing Systems, pp. 1–13 (2019)

10. Walker, E., Rummel, N., Koedinger, K.R.: Adaptive intelligent support to improve peer tutoring in algebra. Int. J. Artif. Intell. Educ. 24(1), 33–61 (2014)

11. Moon, Y., Nass, C.I.: Adaptive agents and personality change. In: Conference Companion on Human Factors in Computing Systems Common Ground - CHI 1996, pp. 287–288 (1996)

12. Nass, C., Steuer, J., Tauber, E.R.: Computers are social actors. In: Proceedings of the SIGCHI Conference on Human Factors in Computing Systems, pp. 72–78 (1994)

13. Graesser, A.C.: Conversations with AutoTutor help students learn. Int. J. Artif. Intell. Educ. 26(1), 124–132 (2016). https://doi.org/10.1007/s40593-015-0086-4

14. Kim, Y., Baylor, A.L.: A social-cognitive framework for pedagogical agents as learning companions. Educ. Tech. Res. Dev. 54(6), 569–596 (2006)

15. Liew, T.W., Tan, S.-M., Jayothisa, C.: The effects of peer-like and expert-like pedagogical agents on learners' agent perceptions, task-related attitudes, and learning achievement. Educ. Technol. Soc. 16(4), 275–286 (2013)

16. Oliveira, A.W., Sadler, T.D.: Interactive patterns and conceptual convergence during student collaborations in science. J. Res. Sci. Teach. 45(5), 634–658 (2008)

17. Saleh, M., Lazonder, A.W., De Jong, T.: Effects of within-class ability grouping on social interaction, achievement, and motivation. Instr. Sci. 33(2), 105–119 (2005)

18. Webb, N.M., Farivar, S.: Promoting helping behavior in cooperative small groups in middle school mathematics. Am. Educ. Res. J. 31(2), 369–395 (1994)

19. Muhonen, H., Rasku-Puttonen, H., Pakarinen, E., Poikkeus, A.M., Lerkkanen, M.K.: Knowledge-building patterns in educational dialogue. Int. J. Educ. Res. 81, 25–37 (2017)

20. Gillies, R.M., Nichols, K., Burgh, G., Haynes, M.: Primary students' scientific reasoning and discourse during cooperative inquiry-based science activities. Int. J. Educ. Res. 63, 127–140 (2014)

21. Chi, M.T.H., Siler, S.A., Jeong, H., Yamauchi, T., Hausmann, R.G.: Learning from human tutoring. Cogn. Sci. 25(4), 471–533 (2001)

22. Hewitt, J., Scardamalia, M.: Design principles for distributed knowledge building processes. Educ. Psychol. Rev. 10(1), 75–96 (1998)

23. Byrne, D., Nelson, D.: Attraction as a linear function of proportion of positive reinforcements. J. Pers. Soc. Psychol. 1(6), 659–663 (1965)

24. Nass, C., Moon, Y., Fogg, B.J., Reeves, B., Dryer, D.C.: Can computer personalities be human personalities? Int. J. Hum. – Comput. Stud. 43(2), 223–239 (1995)

25. Kim, Y.: Desirable characteristics of learning companions. Int. J. Artif. Intell. Educ. 17(4), 371–388 (2007)

26. Biswas, G., Segedy, J.R., Bunchongchit, K.: From design to implementation to practice a learning by teaching system: Betty's brain. Int. J. Artif. Intell. Educ. 26(1), 350–364 (2015). https://doi.org/10.1007/s40593-015-0057-9

27. Chaiken, S., Maheswaran, D.: Heuristic processing can bias systematic processing: effects of source credibility, argument ambiguity, and task importance on attitude judgment. J. Pers. Soc. Psychol. **66**(3), 460–473 (1994)
28. Heidig, S., Clarebout, G.: Do pedagogical agents make a difference to student motivation and learning? Educ. Res. Rev. **6**(1), 27–54. Elsevier (2011)
29. Rosenberg-Kima, R.B., Baylor, A.L., Plant, E.A., Doerr, C.E.: Interface agents as social models for female students: the effects of agent visual presence and appearance on female students' attitudes and beliefs. Comput. Hum. Behav. **24**(6), 2741–2756 (2008)
30. Kim, S., Lee, J., Gweon, G.: Comparing data from chatbot and web surveys effects of platform and conversational style on survey response quality. In: Proceedings of Conference on Human Factors in Computing Systems, pp. 1–12 (2019)
31. Chen, H., Park, H.W., Breazeal, C.: Teaching and learning with children: impact of reciprocal peer learning with a social robot on children's learning and emotive engagement. Comput. Educ. **150**, 103836 (2020)
32. Chin, C.: Classroom interaction in science: teacher questioning and feedback to students' responses. Int. J. Sci. Educ. **28**(11), 1315–1346 (2006)
33. Agne, R.R., Muller, H.L.: Discourse strategies that co-construct relational identities in STEM peer tutoring. Commun. Educ. **68**(3), 265–286 (2019)
34. King, A., Staffieri, A., Adelgais, A.: Mutual peer tutoring: effects of structuring tutorial interaction to scaffold peer learning. J. Educ. Psychol. **90**(1), 134–152 (1998)
35. Gašević, D., Joksimović, S., Eagan, B.R., Shaffer, D.W.: SENS: network analytics to combine social and cognitive perspectives of collaborative learning. Comput. Hum. Behav. **92**, 562–577 (2019)
36. Howley, I., Kumar, R., Mayfield, E., Dyke, G., Rosé, C.P.: Gaining insights from sociolinguistic style analysis for redesign of conversational agent based support for collaborative learning. In: Suthers, D.D., Lund, K., Rosé, C.P., Teplovs, C., Law, N. (eds.) Productive Multivocality in the Analysis of Group Interactions. CCLS, vol. 15, pp. 477–494. Springer, Boston, MA (2013). https://doi.org/10.1007/978-1-4614-8960-3_26
37. Rosé, C.P., et al.: Analyzing collaborative learning processes automatically: exploiting the advances of computational linguistics in computer-supported collaborative learning. Int. J. Comput. Support. Collaborative Learn. **3**(3), 237–271 (2008)
38. Shaffer, D.W., Collier, W., Ruis, A.R.: A tutorial on epistemic network analysis: analyzing the structure of connections in cognitive, social, and interaction data. J. Learn. Anal. **3**(3), 9–45 (2016)
39. Nguyen, H., Santagata, R.: Impact of computer modeling on learning and teaching systems thinking. J. Res. Sci. Teach. **58**(5), 661–688 (2020)
40. Honnibal, M.: Spacy: industrial-strength natural language processing (NLP) with python and cython (2015)
41. Patton, M.Q.: Qualitative Research & Evaluation Methods: Integrating Theory and Practice. Sage, Thousand Oaks, CA (2014)
42. Kumpulainen, K., Wray, D.: Classroom Interaction and Social Learning: From Theory to Practice. Psychology Press, Hove (2002)
43. Marquart, C.L., Zachar, S., Collier, W., Eagan, B., Woodward, R., Shaffer, D.W.: rENA: Epistemic Network Analysis (2018). https://cran.r-project.org/web/packages/rENA/index.html
44. Van Boxtel, C., Van der Linden, J., Kanselaar, G.: Collaborative learning tasks and the elaboration of conceptual knowledge. Learn. Instr. **10**(4), 311–330 (2000)
45. Yang, Y., van Aalst, J., Chan, C.K.K., Tian, W.: Reflective assessment in knowledge building by students with low academic achievement. Int. J. Comput. Support. Collaborative Learn. **11**(3), 281–311 (2016). https://doi.org/10.1007/s11412-016-9239-1

46. Adamson, D., Rosé, C.P.: Coordinating multi-dimensional support in collaborative conversational agents. In: International Conference on Intelligent Tutoring Systems, pp. 346–351. Springer, Berlin, Heidelberg (2012). https://doi.org/10.1007/978-3-642-30950-2_45

47. Adamson, D., Dyke, G., Jang, H., Rosé, C.P.: Towards an agile approach to adapting dynamic collaboration support to student needs. Int. J. Artif. Intell. Educ. **24**(1), 92–124 (2014)

Success-Enablers of Learning Analytics Adoption in Higher Education: A Quantitative Ethnographic Study

Asma Alzahrani[1]([✉]), Yi-Shan Tsai[1], Vitomir Kovanović[2],
Pedro Manuel Moreno-Marcos[3], Ioana Jivet[4], Naif Aljohani[5],
and Dragan Gašević[1,5]

[1] Centre for Learning Analytics at Monash, Faculty of Information Technology,
Monash University, Clayton, VIC, Australia
asma.alzahrani@monash.edu
[2] UniSA Education Futures, University of South Australia,
Adelaide, SA, Australia
[3] Department of Telematics Engineering, Universidad Carlos III de Madrid,
Getafe, Spain
[4] Open Universiteit, Heerlen, The Netherlands
[5] Faculty of Computing and Information Technology, King Abdulaziz
University, Kingdom of Saudi Arabia, Jeddah, Saudi Arabia

Abstract. This paper focuses on the area of success-enablers in learning analytics (LA) adoption from the perspective of senior managers in higher education institutions (HEIs). A significant body of academic literature exists about challenges in LA. However, to date, the success-enablers from the perspectives of institutional senior managers have received limited attention. This research aims to address this gap reporting on the findings of a study that conducted a series of semi-structure interviews with senior managers at 44 European HEIs. A detailed thematic analysis was conducted on the interviews to tease out the main success-enablers. Then, connections of different success-enablers were analyzed using epistemic network analysis (ENA). The analysis showed that the success-enablers in HEIs that had fully adopted LA depended on the involvement of high-level stakeholders, setting an embedded strategy, getting a technology support from the external partnership, or having a strategic analytical culture. The HEIs that were preparing or only partly adopted LA depended on success-enablers such as having a developing analytical culture or a delegation of expertise in LA-related activity. The findings of this study can help HEIs create strategies that can support successful adoption of LA.

Keywords: Epistemic network analysis · Higher education · Learning analytics · Success-enablers · Adoption scope

1 Introduction

Learning analytics (LA) is widely considered a promising approach to enhancing learning and teaching by harnessing vast amounts of data collected by contemporary learning technology. Examples of popular uses of LA include but are not limited to

© Springer Nature Switzerland AG 2022
B. Wasson and S. Zörgő (Eds.): ICQE 2021, CCIS 1522, pp. 395–409, 2022.
https://doi.org/10.1007/978-3-030-93859-8_26

prediction and description of learning outcomes, measurement of 21st-century skills, penalization of learning experience and feedback at scale [5]. While the interest in LA has been high for more than a decade now, the current pandemic situation with COVID-19 has forced many higher education institutions (HEIs) to accelerate the use of online learning at a large scale [1, 10]. This in turn increased a demand for improving learning experience where LA can play a significant role.

In spite of high interest, many studies show that systematic adoption of learning analytics in HEIs is still in the early stages [9, 28]. A European project – SHEILA – investigated LA adoption in 46 European HEIs and found that only a third of HEIs had implemented LA [28]. A similar situation was identified in the UK HEIs, where there were high desires toward LA but low LA adoption rate [21]. Saint & Gutierrez [24] found that the main drivers of LA adoption in the UK were organisational factors because of possible advantages of student retention and tracking of progression. Sclater [25] investigated the state of LA in UK universities by conducting a series of interviews with staff in the UK universities and found that the UK universities had different objectives for using LA, whether to enhance students experience, provide better feedback, or improve student retention. Although many HEIs plan to adopt LA, a wide adoption of these tools might be a challenge. The results of the survey and interviews with institutional senior managers at European HEIs in a study reported in [28] show that over two thirds of institutions had implemented LA or were preparing to adopt LA. However, when asked if they had accomplished the objectives set out for LA, only few participants who had implemented LA were able to prove their success. A similar situation was observed in the UK HEIs, where most respondents hesitated to report any significant results from their LA activities [25]. The respondents in those studies [25, 28] were senior managers in HEIs, who are some of the main stakeholders in LA adoption [12] and who are mostly interested in using LA to enhance institutional performance in European HEIs [32]. Previous studies that discussed LA adoption have focused more on challenges rather than on success enablers [19, 20, 32]. Gašević, Tsai, Dawson, and Pardo [14] discussed the success factors, such as cultural change and infrastructural upgrade. However, there is less discussion regarding success enablers and their related factors for LA adoption to answer why learning analytics adoption fails or succeeds. This is a critical perspective to be considered in order to drive a strategic adoption in LA at HEIs.

To analyze the success-enablers factors that affect LA adoption and implementation process, there is a need to understand how success factors might vary among HEIs that were with different scope of adoption including those who are preparing, partially adopted, or fully adopted LA. In order to address these gaps, the study reported in this paper was set out to address this research question:

What factors are associated with the success-enablers within different LA adoption scope?

2 Literature Review

2.1 Learning Analytics Adoption

Previous studies in learning analytics (LA) have led to the development of conceptual models and frameworks to understand main elements and dimensions in LA adoption or readiness. For instance, Greller and Drachsler [15] proposed a framework that aims to guide the development of LA services. The framework included six different dimensions: (1) stakeholders, (2) objectives, (3) instrument, (4) data, (5) internal limitations, and (6) external constraints. Within this framework, ethics and privacy are the most important external constraints. Drachsler and Greller [13] also developed the "DELICATE" checklist that covers the most important ethics and privacy criteria that are relevant to establish 'trusted LA' and to help "overcome the fears connected to data aggregation and processing, policies" [p. 96]. Arnold, Lonn, and Pistilli [2] found five factors that are important for LA readiness including: (1) ability, (2) data, (3) culture and process, (4) governance and infrastructure, and (5) readiness perception. Colvin, Dawson, Wade, and Gašević [8] identified three models of LA implementation (i.e., input, output, and process) and conclude that the factors that have been discussed broadly in most models include technological readiness, leadership, organizational culture, staff and institutional capacity, and strategy. These factors could potentially be barriers or enablers of LA success. However, success-enablers are factors which could be interesting to investigate in order to better understand the LA adoption with respect to the scope of LA adoption.

2.2 Success Factors in Learning Analytics

Researchers differ in their perspectives about key factors of success that are associated with learning analytics (LA) adoption. Tsai, Gašević, WhitelockWainwright [28] argued that expertise in data analytics, data culture, staff buy-in, and technological infrastructure are four key dimensions of institutional capacity to enable successful adoption of LA. Clark and Tuffley [7] conducted a study that aimed to find specific areas on which HEIs can concentrate to ensure a LA system is successfully implemented. The authors used Delone and McLean's (D&M) information system success model to measure LA success in three demographically different Australian universities. The model focuses on three main elements: (1) functionality, (2) usability, and (3) activity system or utility. The study findings show that LA has much potential in terms of improving teaching and learning. Another study by Clark et al. [6] proposed a framework that seeks to define and explore the Critical Success Factors (CSFs) for the implementation of LA within the higher education sector. They explore the perspectives of higher education practitioners using mixed-methods that included factor analysis, profile analysis, and thematic analysis. In that study, the authors demonstrate five CSFs of LA implementation: (1) strategy and policy at organisational level, (2) information technological readiness, (3) performance and impact evaluation, (4) people's skills and expertise, and (5) data quality. Even so, the study did not prioritize the factors based on their importance to the LA adoption that may help to focus more on these factors in setting the strategy for LA adoption.

Recently, Tsai, Kovanović, and Gašević [29] conducted a study that looked at associations among factors that influence adoption processes or the change in priorities when institutional experience with LA increases. They identified connections between certain areas of success from less experienced institutions; that are, connection between the success in improving the data culture and gaining experience of LA. However, the authors have not explored factors that could contribute to success, and whether the phenomenon differs when adoption scopes vary. In this study, we address this gap by looking at three different adoption scopes: (1) preparation – the HEI took some preparation steps such as the development of a data warehouse, setting strategies, or developing a partnership with external stakeholders, but LA was not yet implemented; (2) partial implementation – LA was implemented in some parts of an HEI; and (3) full implementation – the implementation and strategies of LA cover the whole HEI. The objective of the study reported in this paper was to achieve a better understanding of the success-enablers of learning analytics by following the quantitative ethnographic methods through the use of semi-structured interviews and epistemic network analysis.

Based on the literature reviewed above, we may conclude that the common success factors are: analytical culture, analytical capabilities, stakeholders' involvement, strategy, technological infrastructure, policies, and impact evaluation. However, five of these factors will be included in this study as they appeared to be the most prominent success factors (see Sect. 3), and the details of theses success factors have been discussed below.

Analytical Culture. Culture is defined in [16] as "the collective programming of the mind that distinguishes the members of one group or category of people from others." [p. 6]. Culture in LA looks at whether or not stakeholders are aware of and accept data-informed decision making [2]. It has been discussed as an important element in LA adoption [32], and in LA readiness [2, 11, 23], where Dawson et al. [11] identified staff culture in LA as "sharing and encouraging conversations around LA" [p. 241]. In addition, analytical culture has been considered a key facilitator of LA implementation [2, 15]. Overall, LA should be adopted when institutions are ready to invest and commit based on supportive LA culture. In this paper, we consider 'analytical culture' as the culture of LA at HEIs.

Analytic Capabilities. Higher education found it difficult to take advantage of data due to the lack of data analytic expertise [31]. The expertise required for data analytics involves the ability to extract valuable information out of educational data and determine which data is more beneficial to achieve organizations goals within a time frame [34]. Clark et al. [6] identified people's skills and expertise, as a success factors in LA. The authors included three items under 'people skills' dimensions including team competence and expertise. In this paper, we focus on evaluating the institution's analytical capabilities and actions taken to improve them.

Stakeholders Involvement. Stakeholders involvement has important implications for LA adoption. Adopting new computer systems requires reorganizing business processes and organisational environment to ensure that the stakeholders welcome and cooperate with the change. Thus, stakeholder involvement has been considered a challenge [15, 19, 27, 31, 32] and at the same time it can be crucial to the success of LA deployment [29]. Stakeholders involvement can improve the process of LA and having a system that provides educational benefits that reflect stakeholders' expectations and needs [17]. Thus, stakeholders should be allowed to take a part in decision-making that affects them. In this paper, we consider the extent to which the planning and or implementation of LA have involved consultations with stakeholders at various levels (e.g., high-level, student, teachers).

Strategy. In organizational settings, IT tools are often used strategically to achieve a defined business goal. According to Nguyen [22], many organizations adopt new IT to keep up with emerging technology trends that other organizations have already implemented. However, the lack of definition or strategy for the purpose of adopting IT tools can lead to the failure of the business. In HEI settings, LA adoption needs a strategy to achieve educational goals. The result of the interviews with the participants from three Australian universities shows that having clear strategies can be a success-enabler in LA adoption [7]. Dawson et al. [11] categorized the strategy in LA adoption as iterative and preceding based on the empirical research of over 20 HEIs in Australia. In this paper, we focus on the broad meaning of strategies on the institutional level whether they involve initial piloting, extensions of existing learning and teaching strategies, or specially dedicated strategies for LA.

Technology. Technology features have been considered as "foundation elements" in the LA implementation [3, p. 258]. Technology infrastructure supports collecting, storing, processing, managing and visualizing educational data [20]. Clark et al. [6] argue that the adoption of LA requires a technology infrastructure upgrade to enable adoption and enhance scalability. They identified five items that can be used to measure the success in technology: (1) technologies used for implementation readiness, (2) condition of equipment, (3) system complexity issues, (4) type of hardware and software chosen, and (5) usability of the software. In this paper, we focus on the actions that have been taken to prepare a technological infrastructure for LA.

3 Methods

The research was carried out through a series of semi-structured interviews with senior managers at 46 European HEIs between August 2016 and February 2017.

We excluded two institutions in this study because they expressed no engagement with LA at the time of the interview. This resulted in 44 interviews used for epistemic network analysis (ENA). The participants were senior managers including Deans of Learning and Teaching to Heads of IT, Directors of E-learning Centres, and positions established especially for LA research and development.

The current study focuses on success enabler and how this code was used alongside previous study on LA adoption in European HEIs. Thus, the main factor in this study is the 'success-enablers', which is one of the sub-codes of success and it was identified as 'enablers for the success in learning analytics. It was used alongside other codes to understand what factors were identified as success-enablers by senior manager in European HEIs. Using ENA, we identified association of the 'success-enabler' code with five thematic groups codes (which are success factors that are identified by interviewees as enablers) including analytical culture, analytical capabilities, stake-holders involvement, strategy, and technology (for further information about the themes, see https://bit.ly/La_std_codes).

The final coding scheme ends up with 21 thematic categories, which comprise 99 codes in total based on relevant literature review [27] (for further information about the thematic groups, see https://bit.ly/LA_Thematic_group). The coding process was carried out by four researchers in total. The leading researcher proposed and explained the initial coding scheme to the other three researchers. After practicing coding independently, all researchers compared their results to resolve disagreement. A coding comparison query was run twice (with two different interviews) until each code had an agreement of over 85%.

The institutions varied in terms of location, size, subject coverage, ranking, and nature of their LA adoption scope. In this study, we focused on comparing success enablers by the scope of LA adoption. Almost 50% of institutions (n = 20) had not adopted LA or had plans for this (scope = none). Eleven institutions had implemented LA throughout the institution (scope = full), followed by 10 institutions that had adopted LA in only part of the institution (scope = partial), and four institutions had taken certain action in preparation for LA implementations (scope = prep). For further information about the sample see https://bit.ly/LA_STD_Samples). In this study, we excluded the institutions from our analysis that reported no LA adoption (scope = none) because ENA did not show any connections between success enablers and the factors studied in this paper. The reason for this result is that it might be early for those institutions to report any success or there was no existing project to be considered successful at the time data was collected from those institutions.

We analyzed the data by using epistemic network analysis (ENA), which is "a collection of techniques for identifying and measuring the connections between elements in coded data and representing them in dynamic network models" [26, p. 9]. ENA works by revealing the co-occurrence of codes within chunks of text excerpts called 'stanzas' and within each of the units of analysis [18, 29]. The units of analysis in this paper correspond to the different interviewed HEIs grouped by scope of LA adoption, full(n = 11) and prep-partial (n = 14). We grouped prep-partial because the four preparation institutions do not have particularly unique characteristics compared to other partially adopted institutions. The stanzas correspond to conversation utterances during an interview, which are two consecutive conversation utterances in our case. To answer the research question, we used ENA to analyze the strength of the connection between success-enablers and other codes, and in turn, examine the most important success-enablers related subcategories that should be taken into consideration in the strategy for LA adoption.

4   Results

4.1   Pairwise Analysis of Thematic Groups

Success-Enablers and Analytical Culture. The 'Analytics culture' code identifies the culture for learning analytics at the institution. It includes the following sub-codes: *Immature* – HEI in general has limited knowledge of LA, *Strategic* – there are initiatives to strategically improve institutional culture by offering workshops or addressing existing related to cultural challenges to the implementation of LA, *Developing* – HEI in general shows interest in applying LA to improve teaching practice and promote students' learning, *Resistant* – the culture in which some stakeholders have clear resistance to LA because of various concerns (e.g., ethical concerns), and *Developed* – HEI in general has a fairly good understanding of LA and acknowledge the potential of LA. As shown in Fig. 1, HEIs that fully adopted LA demonstrated strong connection between success-enablers and strategic culture (Fig. 1b). This indicates that the level of success can be improved in LA adoption by addressing cultural considerations and offering workshops and seminars related to LA. Moreover, the results show that the success-enablers had a strong connection with the developing culture in the prep-partial LA adopters institutions (Fig. 1a). This shows that interest in applying LA to enhance teaching and support students' learning plays an important role in the success of the LA implementation. The U08 interviewee explained this point as:

> I guess the willingness from the director to try to improve our learning capabilities and student learning capabilities, looking at data and working on data, on facts and not on impressions. - U08

Success-Enablers and Analytical Capabilities. The analytical capabilities can be described as the institution's analytical capabilities of LA and the actions taken to improve them. It contains four sub-codes of analytical capabilities: *AnaCap.Teacher* – training for teaching/support staff has been provided or is acknowledged as necessary to use and interpret data or LA tools, *AnaCap.Student* – training for students has been provided or is acknowledged as necessary to use and interpret data or LA tools, *AnaCap.Experts* – there are delegated experts to facilitate data analysis, take relevant activities related to LA, or mediate between the university and primary users), and *AnaCap.Gaps* – there is recognition of gaps existing in the understanding of LA and skills for it among stakeholders at various levels.

The result of the ENA models of fully LA adopted HEIs in (Fig. 2b) shows a connection between success-enablers and the gap of the analytical capabilities. This suggests that the full adoption group has involved more stakeholders and could see the needs to address the gaps in understanding of LA among different stakeholders. The

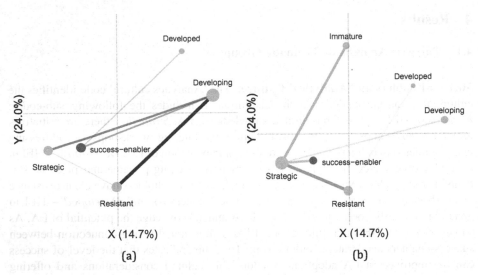

Fig. 1. Associations of success-enabler and analytical culture sub-codes. (a) prep-partial (b) full adoption institution.

HEIs that were preparing or had partial LA adoption emphasized the connection between success-enablers and experts (Fig. 2a). This indicates that the institutions with a narrow scope of adoption relied on experts when implementing LA. For example, the interviewee from U25, one of the institutions that had a partial LA adoption, claimed that having experts in LA contributed to the success of LA:

> One of the things that I'm most pleased about is the education developer. Not, and no harm to them but not a computer scientist. Not an engineer but someone for whom education's at the heart of what happens. And we need, so if we keep that focus that's a real plus. -U25

Success-Enablers and Stakeholder Involvement. The stakeholder involvement theme identified the process by which HEIs communicated and consulted different stakeholders in the planning or implementation of LA. This code had six sub-codes: *High.Level* – i.e., senior managers, *Support.Level* - e.g., IT units and student services, *Primary.Teachers* – primary stakeholders teachers, *Primary.Students* – primary stakeholders students, *External.Stakeholders* – i.e., LA service providers, and Limited, where there was little evidence of consultation with or involvement of any stakeholders.

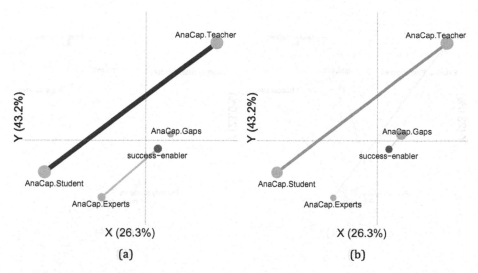

Fig. 2. Associations of success-enabler and analytical capability sub-codes. (a) prep-partial (b) full adoption institution.

The prep-partial LA adopters institutions did not show a strong connection between the success-enablers and any stakeholders types (Fig. 3a). HEIs that fully adopted LA demonstrated a strong connection between success-enablers and high-level stakeholders (Fig. 3b). This shows that the institutions with full adoption has a significant engagement with senior managers and potentially support from them. For example, one of the interviewees from U39 (LA fully adopted institutions) pointed out the importance of a supportive decisions and acceptance by the highlevel stakeholders and how they might enable the success in LA adoption:

> We've had very, very strong and positive support from university senior managers, and that makes a difference because we have not, I think from the very outset the, the relevant pro-vice chancellor has seen the potential benefits to this and has been interested in this as a resource for staff, so I think there's a really strong kind of interest there. *-U39*

Success-Enablers and Strategy. The Strategy code had three sub-codes: *embedded* – the implementation of LA is part of extant teaching, learning and business processes *independent* – HEIs had a complete and independent strategy for LA adoption, and *nascent* – a pilot study in LA is part of the LA adoption. The networks of prepared or partial adopters (Fig. 4a) did not display strong connections between success-enablers and any types of strategy. The results (Fig. 4b) showed that LA fully-adopted institutions tended to associate success-enablers with the embedded strategy. This shows that with high-level stakeholders involved in the LA activities, these institutions were more likely to be able to embed LA into their existing strategy thus increasing the priority of LA in the institutions and potentially being able to dedicate more resources to LA too. For example, one interview U40 (from LA fully-adopted institutions) explained that analytics was always a part of their strategic objectives both in relation to learning and teaching which enable the success of LA adoption.

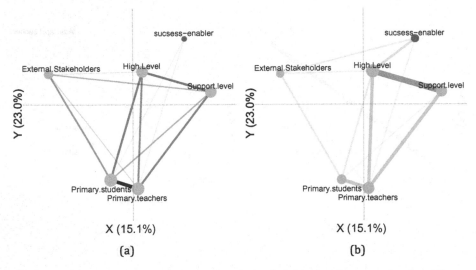

Fig. 3. Associations between success-enabler and stakeholder involvement subcodes. (a) prep-partial (b) full adoption institution.

Success-Enablers and Technology. The Technology code identified actions that the HEIs took to prepare themselves for LA technological infrastructure. Technology code had four sub-codes: *External.partnership* – e.g., making a partnership with LA service providers, Enhancement – install and develop IT systems, *Evaluation* – the HEIs carried out an evaluation of the existing IT system necessary for LA implementation, and *no technology evaluation* – there were no evaluations yet on the capacities of existing IT systems and software needed to implement LA, or evaluations on the potential of different types of data. The results showed that the institutions that were prepared or had partial LA adoption (Fig. 5a), had no obvious connections between success-enablers with any sub-codes of technology. The LA fully-adopted institutions (Fig. 5b) had a strong connection between success-enablers and external partnership. Such connection indicates that the external partnerships may help scale up the LA adoption scope. For example, one of the interviewees from U37 (LA fully-adopted institutions) indicated:

> I think having the investment in, having the Blackboard analytics product has been very helpful because that's allowed us to implement something and start working with that data. we do need to bring other data sets in from the business intelligence data sets. But it's allowed something solid to be taking place and to allow that engagement with stakeholders as well where we can be in front of them during the last twelve months. -*U37*

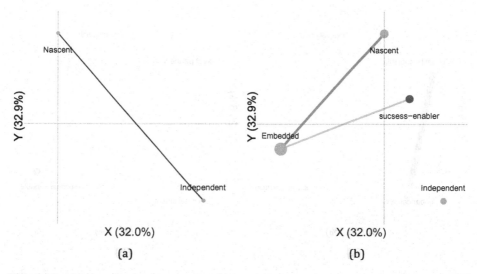

Fig. 4. Associations between success-enabler and strategy sub-codes. (a) prep-partial (b) full adoption institution.

5 Discussion

From the existing literature, several factors affecting the success of LA adoption and can be viewed as enablers including analytical capabilities, analytical culture, stakeholders involvement, strategy, technology, policies, and evaluations [6, 28]. However, this paper excluded policies and evaluation because the findings from the ENA models did not show connections between success-enablers and the sub-codes of policies and evaluations.

To answer the research question "What factors are associated with the success-enablers within different learning analytics (LA) adoption scope", the success-enablers have been discussed based on the results of epistemic network analysis (ENA) and as supported by quotes retrieved from the semi-structure interviews according to the relevant themes. Specifically, ENA revealed intriguing connections between the success-enablers and other factors among institutions that had different scope of LA adoption at the time of the interviews (LA fully-adopted institutions vs prep-partial LA adopters institutions).

Analytical culture encompasses data culture, staff culture, or institutional culture. Oster et al. [23] showed that institutions that are more focused on teaching could have a perceived culture to implement learning analytics for the practice of learning and teaching rather than for research. However, based on our ENA results, the success-enablers of the institutions that were prepared or partially adopted LA focused on the developing culture, which demonstrate that recognizing the potential of LA could scale up the success of LA adoption. Thus, cultural acceptance is necessary in a way that the institutions can achieve the potential benefits of LA [2]. In terms of analytical capabilities, the result of the ENA reported in the current paper showed a strong connection between success-enablers and expertise in LA. This means that a successful LA project required experts' teams that have various expertise and having skills in LA [4].

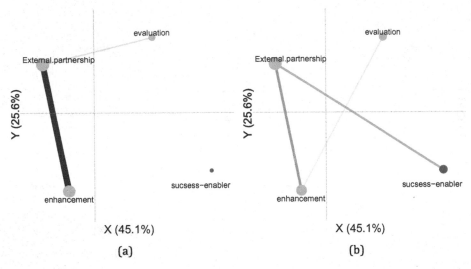

Fig. 5. Associations between success-enabler and technology sub-codes. (a) prep-partial (b) full adoption institution.

Stakeholder engagement has previously been identified in the literature as a significant element for LA adoption. A study conducted a survey with 45 senior managers, as reported in [33], found that the 'senior managers buy-in' ranked as the most important element that might affect achieving the potential of LA. In this study, the results of the ENA reported in the current paper showed that the connections between success-enablers and stakeholders involvement revealed that success-enablers were related to the involvement of high-level stakeholders. This finding suggests that the institutions with full LA adoption tended to emphasize the engagement of high-level stakeholders to deliver LA project successfully.

On the organizational level, there is a need for strategic support for LA adoption. The results of ENA reported in the current paper showed that the fully adopted LA institutions depended on the embedded strategy as a success enabler of LA adoption, which has also been considered as an antecedent for use of LA in learning and teaching practice [11]. This means that the HEIs with full LA adoption showed interest in developing an LA strategy that is derived from existing teaching or learning strategies. Clark et al. [6] also emphasize this point as a critical success factor in LA adoption.

Several studies described the important role of technology infrastructure in LA adoption. LA adoption requires upgrading existing technology infrastructure and system processes [30]. The literature refers to software and hardware [6] as key elements of technology infrastructure. However, the findings from ENA used in the current study showed a connection between success-enablers and external partnership, which means that obtaining LA support services from third-parties was strongly associated with the success of LA, especially among institutions that have university-wide adoption of LA. A possible reason for this is the HEIs did not have sufficient technology infrastructure to support LA adoption and thus they turned to relevant service providers for partnerships.

6 Conclusion

This study contributes to the field of learning analytics (LA) by examining the potential success enabler of LA adoption practices. Based on the interviews with senior managers from European HEIs, we identified, analysed, and prioritised the most dominant success-enablers of LA adoption among different success factors. We found that high-level stakeholders' engagement, embedded strategy, partnership with technology third-party, strategic analytical culture, as key success enablers of the HEIs who fully adopted LA. We further found that developing analytical culture as well as a delegation of expertise in LA, to play a role in enabling a success to adopt LA in the HEIs that were preparing or partly adopted LA. This research lays the foundations for HEIs who are thinking to lunch LA at a wide-scale or HEIs that have implemented LA to consider these success-enablers that could help them to adopt LA successfully.

The current study had limitations. This study is based on the European HEIs; as such, further research is needed to understand the success-enablers in HEIs in different regions or within different experience in LA. Future research should also explore other factors that can enable success, as the current study focused on five success factors only.

References

1. Adedoyin, O.B., Soykan, E.: Covid-19 pandemic and online learning: the challenges and opportunities. Interact. Learn. Environ. 1–13 (2020)
2. Arnold, K.E., Lonn, S., Pistilli, M.D.: An exercise in institutional reflection: the learning analytics readiness instrument (LARI). In: 4th International Conference on Learning Analytics and Knowledge, pp. 163–167 (2014)
3. Arnold, K.E., Lynch, G., Huston, D., Wong, L., Jorn, L., Olsen, C.W.: Building institutional capacities and competencies for systemic learning analytics initiatives. In: 14th International Conference on Learning Analytics and Knowledge, pp. 257–260 (2014)
4. Bichsel, J.: Analytics in Higher Education: Benefits, Barriers, Progress, and Recommendations. Technical report, EDUCAUSE Center for Applied Research, Louisville, CO (2012)
5. Buckingham Shum, S., Deakin Crick, R.: Learning analytics for 21st century competencies. J. Learn. Analytics 3(2), 6–21 (2016)
6. Clark, J.A., Liu, Y., Isaias, P.: Critical success factors for implementing learning analytics in higher education: A mixed-method inquiry. Australas. J. Educ. Technol. 36(6), 89–106 (2020)
7. Clark, J.A., Tuffley, D.: Learning Analytics implementations in universities: towards a model of success, using multiple case studies. In: ASCILITE 2019 - Conference Proceedings - 36th International Conference of Innovation, Practice and Research in the Use of Educational Technologies in Tertiary Education: Personalised Learning. Diverse Goals. One Heart, pp. 82–92 (2019)
8. Colvin, C., Dawson, S., Wade, A., Gasevic, D.: Addressing the Challenges of Institutional Adoption. Handbook of Learning Analytics, pp. 281–289 (2017)
9. Colvin, C., et al.: Edinburgh research explorer student retention and learning analytics: a snapshot of Australian practices and a framework for advancement Student retention and learning analytics: a snapshot of Australian practices and a framework for advancement. Australian Government - Office for Learning and Teaching (2015)

10. Conde, M., Rodríguez-Sedano, F.J., Fernández, C., Gutiérrez-Fernández, A., Fernández-Robles, L., Limas, M.C.: A Learning Analytics tool for the analysis of students' Telegram messages in the context of teamwork virtual activities. In: Eighth International Conference on Technological Ecosystems for Enhancing Multiculturality (TEEM 2020), pp. 719–724 (2020)
11. Dawson, S., Poquet, O., Colvin, C., Rogers, T., Pardo, A., Gasevic, D.: Rethinking learning analytics adoption through complexity leadership theory. In: 18th International Conference on Learning Analytics and Knowledge, pp. 236–244 (2018)
12. Drachsler, H., Greller, W.: The pulse of learning analytics understandings and expectations from the stakeholders. In: 12th International Conference on Learning Analytics and Knowledge, pp. 120–129 (2012)
13. Drachsler, H., Greller, W.: Privacy and analytics - it's a DELICATE issue a checklist for trusted learning analytics. In: ACM International Conference Proceeding Series, pp. 89–98 (2016)
14. Gasevic, D., Tsai, Y.S., Dawson, S., Pardo, A.: How do we start? An approach to learning analytics adoption in higher education. Int. J. Inf. Learn. Technol. **36**(4), 342–353 (2019)
15. Greller, W., Drachsler, H.: Translating learning into numbers: a generic framework for learning analytics. Educ. Technol. Soc. **15**(3), 42–57 (2012)
16. Hofstede, G.: Culture and Organizations, vol. 10 (1980)
17. Knight, S., Dawson, S., Gašević, D., Jovanovi´c, J., Hershkovitz, A.: Learning analytics: richer perspectives across stakeholders. J. Learn. Anal. **3**(3), 1–4 (2016)
18. Kovanovic, V., Tsai, Y.S., Gasevic, D.: Learning analytics adoption – approaches and maturity. In: 9th International Conference on Learning Analytics and Knowledge (LAK'19) pp. 153–154 (2019)
19. Lester, J., Klein, C., Rangwala, H., Johri, A.: Learning analytics in higher education. ASHE Higher Educ. Rep. **43**(5), 9–135 (2017)
20. Macfadyen, L.P., Dawson, S., Pardo, A., Gašević, D.: Embracing big data in complex educational systems: the learning analytics imperative and the policy challenge. Res. Pract. Assessment **9**, 17–28 (2014)
21. Newland, B., Trueman, P.: Learning analytics in UK HE 2017. Technical report (2017)
22. Nguyen, T.H.: Information technology adoption in SMEs: an integrated framework. Int. J. Entrepreneurial Behav. Res. **15**, 25–35 (2009)
23. Oster, M., Lonn, S., Pistilli, M.D., Brown, M.G.: The learning analytics readiness instrument. In: 16th International Conference of Learning Analytics and Knowledge, pp. 173–182 (2016)
24. Saint, J., Gutierrez, A.: Adoption of learning analytics in the UK: Identification of key factors using the TOE framework. In: International Conference on Information Systems Education and Research, pp. 1–14 (2017)
25. Sclater, N.: Learning analytics the current state of play in UK higher and further education. JISC, pp. 1–65 (2014)
26. Shaffer, D., Collier, W., Ruis, A.: A tutorial on epistemic network analysis: analyzing the structure of connections in cognitive, soical, and interaction data. J. Learn. Analytics **3**(3), 9–45 (2016)
27. Tsai, Y.S., Gasevic, D.: Learning analytics in higher education—challenges and policies. In: Proceedings of the Seventh International Learning Analytics & Knowledge Conference on - LAK 2017, pp. 233–242 (2017)
28. Tsai, Y.S., et al.: SHEILA: Support Higher Education to Integrate Learning Analytics. Technical report (2018)
29. Tsai, Y.S., Kovanović, V., Gašević, D.: Connecting the dots: an exploratory study on learning analytics adoption factors, experience, and priorities. Internet High. Educ. **50** (2021)

30. Tsai, Y.S., Moreno-Marcos, P.M., Tammets, K., Kollom, K., Gašević, D.: SHEILA policy framework: informing institutional strategies and policy processes of learning analytics. J. Learn. Analytics **5**(3), 320–329 (2018)
31. Tsai, Y.S., Poquet, O., Gašević, D., Dawson, S., Pardo, A.: Complexity leadership in learning analytics: drivers, challenges and opportunities. Br. J. Educ. Technol. **50**(6), 2839–2854 (2019)
32. Tsai, Y.S., et al.: Learning analytics in European higher education—trends and barriers. Comput. Educ. **155**, 103933 (2020)
33. Tsai, Y.S., Whitelock-Wainwright, A., Gasevic, D.: More than figures on your laptop: (Dis) trustful implementation of learning analytics. J. Learn. Anal. **1**(1), 1–24 (2021)
34. Tulasi, B.: Significance of big data and analytics in higher education. Int. J. Comput. Appl. **68**(14), 21–23 (2013)

Author Index

Printed in the United States
by Baker & Taylor Publisher Services